Sourcebook
for Modern Catechetics

Sourcebook
for Modern Catechetics

Edited by
Michael Warren

Saint Mary's Press
Christian Brothers Publications
Winona, Minnesota

This long-promised, long-awaited book is
for Connie Loos, who deserves so much of the credit.

Cover design by Roderick Robertson, FSC

ISBN: 0-88489-152-6
Library of Congress Catalog Card Number: 83-50246

Contents

SECTION C: The Modern Catechetical Movement

PART TWO—ISSUES

SECTION A: Experience

SECTION B: Experience of the Word

SECTION C: Evangelization

SECTION D: Catechesis

SECTION E: Bible in Catechesis

SECTION F: Theology and Catechesis

SECTION G: Catechesis and Religious Education

SECTION H: Moral Catechesis

Foreword

The *Sourcebook for Modern Catechetics* is the result of several years of effort on my part, motivated by both pastoral and academic interests. From a pastoral viewpoint, I began to notice that many persons doing catechesis and/or Christian education had little understanding of the catechetical tradition and consequently lacked adequate perspective on where current catechetical developments, especially within the Roman Catholic Church, were coming from. Thus, in chairing a graduate seminar for students completing master's degrees in religious education at a midwest university, I was stunned at their inability to use catechetical language, at their lack of theoretical orientations by which to connect Christian education to pastoral ministry, and at their ignorance of catechetical history.

I realize that *stunned* is a word that could have attached to it a nuance of the raised eyebrow of academic snobbery. However, my surprise was rooted less in knowledge elitism than in the fear that, though persons were being given credentials for a catechetical mission as pastoral leaders, they were unable to view their role from a catechetical frame of reference. Their university professors of religious education apparently had not introduced them to catechetical literature, possibly because these teachers themselves were unfamiliar with that literature. At the end of our seminar, these students sent me off with a request to mail back to them a good basic bibliography.

My experience with these students helped me understand why the United States abounds in parish religious education directors who are lacking in catechetical background. Some of these educators are caught up in the structural-developmental studies of moral and faith development, but they seem unaware that such studies – especially the hypotheses of someone like James Fowler – verify assertions by theorists of the modern catechetical movement, which is influenced not so much by developmental psychology as by pastoral experience. Not to know these catechetical sources is to be ignorant of the history into which one's own efforts fit and of the connectedness among many recent developments. Ignorance of that history opens one to serious misunderstandings of such basic Roman Catholic position papers as the *General Catechetical Directory* (GCD), the *National Catechetical Directory* (NCD), and the revised *Rite of Christian Initiation of Adults* (RCIA).

From an academic point of view, in my own teaching of religious education theory at the graduate level, I have found that much of the important material on catechesis that originally appeared in periodicals is not always accessible, even when single, bound copies appear on library shelves. Other material was originally published in handbooks that are now out of print. Discussions with other professors assured me that they, too, had difficulty making key source material available to students. They encouraged me to pursue my idea of gathering this material in a single collection of background sources.

Particularly encouraging to me in compiling this sourcebook was the interest of several Protestant professors of religious education who are now looking to the catechetical movement as a place where they could reclaim their own tradition as it stretches back before the sixteenth century. They pointed out that this source material is especially needed at a time when Protestants are showing more and more interest in the language of the catechetical tradition.

This overview of the origins of the sourcebook helps define the diverse audiences which I expect will find it valuable. They include undergraduate and graduate students studying religious education or catechetical theory and practice; directors of religious education or catechesis in local churches; and pastoral leaders, at both diocesan and local levels, who are concerned with the further evolution of catechesis. Local catechetical directors particularly need to have access to background information enabling them to make decisions out of the kind of wisdom that is grounded in broad understanding.

Organization of the Sourcebook

Needless to say, the organization and selection of material for a work like this sourcebook betray many personal preferences. These preferences became obvious to me in the course of at least five revisions from an original outline. Almost everyone I consulted about this project suggested favorite topics and readings not included in the first outline. Many of these suggestions account for changes made during the several revisions.

Part I, entitled "Historical Studies," brings together key historical materials. Section A, "International Catechetical Study Weeks," presents the summaries or conclusions of the study weeks, starting with Eichstätt and concluding with the 1971 Roman Catechetical Congress. The Congress—unlike the previous study weeks—was summoned by an official Vatican body, the Congregation for the Clergy, which has been charged since Trent with the pastoral effort we call catechesis. In their own ways, each of these international gatherings represents a giant step forward in catechetical theorizing, formulating the main operating principles of the catechetical movement. Because of the international character of these study weeks, important ideas and developments moved across national barriers and sparked worldwide reflection. Not to know these weeks is to be ignorant of a seminal development in the modern catechetical movement.

Heading Section B, "Origins," are two fine studies, until recently out of print, one by Gerard Sloyan, a chief architect of catechetical renewal in the United States, the second by Mary Charles Bryce, who contributes a popular summary of her thorough study of the Baltimore Catechism. And Joseph Collins' trilogy from the defunct *American Ecclesiastical Review* is the most recent historical study of the Confraternity of Christian Doctrine, the Catholic equivalent of the Protestant Sunday school. Scholars wishing to initiate studies similar to these will find the footnote references given here invaluable.

The matter of origins is carried further in Section C, "The Modern Catechetical Movement." It presents material important for the correct understanding of the most recent developments in catechetics, including the three position papers mentioned above: the GCD, the NCD, and the RCIA.

Part II, "Issues," presents what are for the most part classic statements on matters of special significance in the theory of Christian education or catechesis. My expectation is that readers will find themselves regularly referring to one or another of these pieces.

Finally, Part III presents the apostolic exhortation which emerged from the 1974 Roman Synod on Evangelization.

As a final word, I wish to summarize my hopes for this compilation of sources. I have believed for some years that movements need a literature in order to develop and progress. A literature is a sort of roadway along which the vehicle of the movement goes forward. In the pastoral area called youth ministry, for example, I myself have set out to develop a literature so that the field could evolve to the next stage. I see this sourcebook as an important addition to the literature of the catechetical movement, significant especially for the way it will make key material in the literature of catechesis more accessible. Of course, not every reader will find every article helpful. The sourcebook's contents, however, are rich enough to provide quality fare for varied tastes.

Readers will notice minor changes from original texts made to ensure uniform American spelling and nonsexist language.

Acknowledgments

This book would never have been published without the encouragement and assistance of many persons. Chief among these is Berard Marthaler, who from the first assured me that a sourcebook was needed and who suggested important changes in the book's organizational structure. Others to whom I owe special thanks are: Mary Charles Bryce of Catholic University, who offered, out of her keen respect for matters historical, more important encouragement than perhaps she is aware; Wilfrid H. Paradis, director of the NCD project and later director of the Department of Education at the United States Catholic Conference, who wrote several important letters attesting to the value of the sourcebook idea; Edward Brown, who as a graduate assistant in the Theology Department at St. John's University, patiently duplicated, arranged, and rearranged the sourcebook material; and fellow faculty members and administrators at St. John's who supported my petition for a research grant during the semester the sourcebook was compiled.

Finally, special thanks are due to Thomas Zanzig and Stephan Nagel, editors at Saint Mary's Press. They saw the need for this book and were instrumental in adding it to the long list of titles the Press has brought out in the past thirty years in the service of religious education.

To all and for all, I give deep thanks.

Introduction

BERARD L. MARTHALER

IT HAS BEEN twenty-five years since Gerard L. Sloyan compiled *Shaping the Christian Message.* The publication of that work marked the coming of age of the catechetical movement in the United States. There had been individuals – bishops like Flaget of Bardstown, Kentucky, and Edwin O'Hara of Kansas City; laypersons like Dorothy Sadlier; clerics and religious women like Anthony Fuerst, Rudolph Bandas, Rosalia Walsh, and Maria de la Cruz Aymes – who worked to upgrade the level of religious instruction by adapting teaching stratagems and catechisms to particular situations. Each in his or her own way recognized that catechesis could be judged successful only if it had lasting effects beyond childhood and adolescence. As gifted as these pioneers were, however, they worked largely in isolation, unaware of what others were doing and had done.

Sometime in the 1930s the catechetical movement came to be. To call it a movement implies an orchestration of activities, events, and cooperation to heighten the awareness of the Church at large as to the nature and aims of catechesis. The plan was to involve the faithful. They were to be not simply beneficiaries of improved catechesis but its agents. In the United States the catechetical movement qua movement might be dated in 1935 when Bishop Edwin O'Hara, then of Great Falls, Montana, and later of Kansas City, Missouri, took the lead in establishing the National Center of Religious Education–CCD in Washington. The center became a clearinghouse and a catalyst for bringing together and focusing the efforts that individuals had been making. The national center was the point at which the liturgical movement, the biblical movement, and religious education converged. After World War II, itinerant scholars from Europe infused new life and ideas into the movement, though often they showed little awareness of or appreciation for how much was being done and had already been done at the grassroots level. The main contribution of the European catechists was to popularize the "new theology" at a time when American theologians were largely content to explicate the work of Vatican Council I.

It was in this period that Sloyan published *Shaping the Christian Message.* The work consisted of a series of essays. Sloyan's own survey (reprinted here as Reading 9) of religious education from ancient through early medieval times aside, the principal contributions were by Europeans—J. D. Crichton, Joseph Colomb, F. H. Drinkwater, Francois Coudreau, George Delcuve, et al. Taken together, the essays represented an attempt by the editor to root the catechetical movement in tradition. Some of the studies addressed practical questions, but it was the historical studies which gave the book its character and lasting importance. Insofar as Sloyan selected the essays in a conscious attempt to describe the nature, objectives, and tasks of catechesis, the date of publication marks the time when the catechetical movement came of age. It coincided with the renaissance of the graduate programs in religious education in American Catholic universities and was followed a few years later by the appearance of *The Living Light*, the first publication under Catholic auspices in the United States devoted exclusively to religious education.

Gerard S. Sloyan played an important role in both developments; he reorganized the entire religious education curriculum at the Catholic University, providing a forum in the summer sessions for the new wave of Catholic biblical scholars, ecclesiologists, liturgical specialists, and moral theologians. Early on, he spotted the need for a journal to do in the United States what *Lumen Vitae* was doing in the French-speaking world. He collaborated with the staff at the National Center for Religious Education–CCD in bringing about *The Living Light*, a quarterly devoted to the interests of professionals in Catholic religious education.

Michael Warren has drawn on *The Living Light*, *Lumen Vitae*, and many other sources to piece together a record of the catechetical movement. The writings he has assembled include reports of meetings, historical studies based on research and personal experience, interpretative essays, and official documents. They deal with theoretical issues and practical problems.

While the sourcebook presents a record of people, events, and issues, it is not a history in the usual sense. The essays tell us something about the times when they were written, but they only hint at the circumstances which brought them forth. The catechetical movement was not a self-contained development, isolated from the rest of life. Many activities, programs, and other movements in the Church and society had an impact on catechesis, and catechesis, on them. These influences came together in the early sixties at the time of the Second Vatican Council.

Vatican II provides a convenient benchmark for dating the selections in the sourcebook: Some predate it, some are contemporaneous with it, and some come later. The studies which predate the council, while calling for more effective teaching of the catechism, tend to be reactionary in the sense that they are critical of particular programs and practices. They conceive the catechetical task in narrow categories and are tentative in proposing remedies. Statements and studies produced while the council was in session are bolder and more visionary. They see the catechetical task as central to the Church's mission, intimately linked to evangelization, and an essential part of pastoral ministry. More recent documents echo the council's call for reform and renewal.

Less than a decade after Vatican II the *General Catechetical Directory (GCD)*, which had been mandated by the council, warned that renewal was entering "a period of crisis." It singled out a number of dangers including the inability "to understand the depth of renewal as though the issue were merely one of eliminating ignorance of the doctrine that must be taught" (no. 9). The *GCD* adds that, when the matter is conceived so narrowly, the remedy is unequal to the real needs. Stated in other words, goodwill, better materials, and more time spent on catechesis are not enough. The issue is a better understanding of catechetics.

Catechetics backs away from catechetical activity in order to put it in proper perspective. Catechetics is concerned with the nature of the catechetical task, how it relates to the Church's overall mission, its place in the pastoral ministry. Tactics are important, but they can be appreciated and evaluated only in the context of a grand strategy. Catechetics studies practice in order to formulate and test theory. Catechetics and catechesis are related like ethics and ethos, statistics and raw data.

The modern catechetical movement breathed new life into an old word. Catechesis becomes the focal point for a number of strategies aimed at revitalizing the Church and making its members more self-conscious of their identity as Christians. Like most words with a history, the etymology of *catechesis* is not adequate to the rich meaning it has acquired over the centuries. Catechesis suggests an echo. Literally it means "re-sounding," as in, the earth resounded with his praise! Although it was – and is – used by secular authors, catechesis and its cognates – catechism, catechist, catechumen, etc. – are very much "churchy" words.

Given the range of church activity which is labeled catechetical, no definition of catechesis has won universal acceptance. *Sharing the Light of Faith*, the catechetical directory for Catholics in the United States, associates it with endeavors which range from community building to prayer, from initiation into the Christian community to fostering attitudes, behaviors, and knowledge contributing to spiritual and moral maturity. Almost every pastoral ministry has its catechetical dimension.

In celebrating the paschal mystery, the liturgy, whether in baptism, eucharist, or one of the other sacraments, makes a statement about life in general and Christian life in particular. Sacramental catechesis prepares one for worship; mystagogy reflects on the experience of the celebration to uncover the reality beneath the symbols – the transcendence and presence of God, awe and familiarity.

The Church's efforts to build the kingdom of God witness to what it means to be Christian and provide an experiential catechesis for those who struggle to bring about peace and social justice. Peacemakers and prophets listen to the word even while proclaiming the message to others. Programs and materials prepared to raise the consciousness of the Christian community on such issues as racial discrimination, the right to life, aging, ecology, and nuclear armaments are in many cases avowedly catechetical.

Catechesis supplies a religious dimension to moral development and decision-making. It is concerned about behavior, individual and communal, and even more about commitment, values, and attitudes. The mature Christian, by definition, is inner-directed – one who takes responsibility for his or her action and inaction. Catechesis affirms the need for Christians to be inner-directed, but it also reminds them that they are not a law unto themselves. The Christian community emphasizes a certain outer-directedness based on responsibility to God the creator.

Nothing has done more to force a new look at the nature of catechesis than the renewed missionary activity of the Church. Catechesis and evangelization are all but indistinguishable in practice. In the so-called post-Christian culture of Europe and North America, catechesis fails because evangelization, the initial call to conversion of life and values, has been presumed. In fact, however, family customs, national identity, schools, the calendar of holidays and holy days, and the arts, which at one time could be depended on to inculcate some knowledge of Christian and Catholic culture, have been eroded by secularism, individualism, and hedonism. These same "isms" (compounded by colonialism) have affected other cultures. In Africa and elsewhere, where Christianity was never a part of the traditional way of life, catechesis is often seen as undoing tribal customs and values. Catechists are being called upon to develop strategies so that Christianity can become a truly indigenous religion, preserving the best of tribal ideals and values without compromising the gospel message. Missionaries know that catechesis, to have any lasting effect, requires more than simply translating the Bible and the penny catechism into African tongues.

In the last decade and a half Gabriel Moran has been alerting religious educators in general and Catholics in particular to the way that the language one uses defines one's role and the aims and means of the task. The theme runs through a number of his writings, including the selection included in this sourcebook as Reading 21. Moran distinguishes two languages of religious education. One he calls ecclesiastical; the other, educational. He prefers the latter, but he does not advocate abandoning the former, which he says is the language of catechetics. It speaks of salvation, Church, covenant, messianic kingdom, sacraments—terms which have meaning only in a faith context. Moran's chief complaints about catechetical language seem to be two: (1) It is too parochial, and (2) it is unduly influenced by theology. The criticisms must be taken seriously.

In the past, catechesis of the Catholic community was indeed "parochial" if by that it is meant that catechesis was limited in its scope and purview. Catechetical programs were designed for children and adolescents. For many years, even before the Third Plenary Council of Baltimore, formal catechesis consisted largely of mastery of the questions and answers in the catechism text. Catechesis was parochial in that it focused more on the hierarchical Church than it did on the kingdom preached by Jesus. The emphasis was on the salvation of souls—my own, my fellow Catholics', and potential Catholics'—with little attention to salvation of the world and all that it implies. There was little in the catechism that raised broader issues about religious questing, about ritual and moral judgment outside a religious context.

Moran's second complaint is more complex, but in brief it is, "Theology stands outside the discussion of religious education and merely dictates the content to be used."[1] The corollary of this, though Moran does not spell it out, is that "orthodoxy" becomes the primary measure of success in catechesis. The tension between theology and catechesis has existed for some time. In the 1930s, Josef Jungmann argued for a "kerygmatic" theology, a broader, more inclusive understanding of theology which would address the life situation of the day. After Vatican II, as theologians began to give greater weight to experience as a theological locus, catechists had less cause to be defensive. There are still those U.S. Catholics who would make chapter 5 of the *National Catechetical Directory* ("Principal Elements of the Christian Message for Catechesis") serve as a checklist to evaluate catechetical programs. It is, however, a misuse of the directory, which makes it clear that the worshipping community, social ministry, and the individual's maturation in faith (chaps. 6, 7, and 8) are part and parcel of the source and aim of catechesis.

There is much that is positive (as Moran admits) to be said for catechesis. Focused on Christian life in a specific tradition, catechesis socializes believers into a concrete community. Whatever is to be said of the degree to which it has shed parochialism, no one charges catechesis as it is understood today with being narrow in scope. Nothing Christian (to paraphrase Terence) is alien to it. To say that it relies on ecclesiastical language (as long as that is not understood in a narrow institutional sense) also has its advantages. One advantage is to situate the catechetical endeavor squarely within the pastoral ministry of the Church.

Pastoral ministry suggests the idea of service. It takes inspiration from the person and preaching of Jesus. The Church's threefold mission in the world, which corresponds to Jesus' work as prophet, priest, and servant, shapes pastoral ministry: (1) preaching and teaching the gospel, (2) celebrating the paschal mystery in word and sacrament, and (3) serving the world, especially its most disadvantaged people. Thus, pastoral ministry is concerned with the whole person – economic, social, educational, physical, psychological, and emotional as well as spiritual needs. It takes into consideration and at times works to change the environment in which people live. Although particular tasks are apportioned by reason of ordination and office, pastoral ministry is a responsibility of the Christian community as a whole. Thus, catechesis is a communal responsibility even though some members are designated as catechists and directors of catechetical programs. Catechesis implies a commitment and a vision of church that transcends contracts and job descriptions.

As pastoral ministry brings the Church into contact with the world in a general way, catechesis brings the Church into the particularized world of education. Education is understood here, in the words of Lawrence Cremin of Columbia University, as ". . . deliberate, systematic, and sustained effort to transmit or evoke knowledge, attitudes, values, skills and sensibilities, a process that is more limited than what anthropologists would term enculturation or the sociologist socialization, though obviously inclusive of some of the same elements."[2] (Is it necessary for an academician, while saying that schooling and education describe very different realities, to reaffirm his or her commitment to schooling as a most effective means of education?) According to Cremin's definition education is more limited than catechesis, at least as it is described here and understood in many of the documents in this sourcebook. On the other hand, Moran argues that catechesis is parochial (as enculturation and socialization in concrete communities must be) and more limited than education. The positions are not mutually exclusive.

A good deal of catechesis, like a good deal of education, is not deliberate, systematic, or sustained. Formal catechesis, however, has or should have these characteristics. It plans experiences for growth in faith as in the *Rite of Christian Initiation of Adults*. Formal catechesis makes conscious use of group processes to develop relationships which bond members to the community and to one another. It uses teaching stratagems to inform and instruct, as in the many packaged programs available through commercial publishers. And as every experienced practitioner knows, catechesis is a matter of bringing everyday experiences into dialogue with the gospel message in such a way that the one throws light on the other.

The rather inclusive understanding of catechesis described here is made possible by the fact that the catechetical movement over the past fifty years or so has had a symbiotic relationship with biblical scholarship, the liturgical movement, and the "new theology." It has been able to assimilate and use the practical insights of learning theory based on experience and the findings of developmental psychology. Borrowing from anthropology, sociology, and psychology, it has come to have a better understanding of how individuals and groups appropriate symbols to establish a sense of identity and a world of meanings and values. Despite these gains to catechesis that have resulted from advances in the religious and social sciences, there is also a danger. From time to time both theoreticians and practitioners have shown a tendency to latch on to certain approaches as if they provided a panacea for all the ills that beset catechesis. Fortunately, as is evident in many of the writings selected for this sourcebook, there were always some leaders in the catechetical movement who cautioned against running after fads whether they had their roots in some novel theological insight or came from the social sciences.

Ultimately, the most dependable safeguard of genuine catechesis is the Christian community itself. In the context of faith the community has shown an uncanny ability to sift the wheat from the chaff. It has over the long run resisted the blandishments of ideologies – cloaked sometimes in the dress of theology, sometimes in the attractive garb of the social sciences – to reduce catechesis to religious instruction. The intensity of experience, the depth of understanding, and the breadth of vision one receives in catechesis depend on the quality of the community's liturgical celebration, its commitment to adult catechesis, and the extent of its social ministry.

One comes away from studying the *Sourcebook for Modern Catechetics* with a number of reasoned conclusions, fresh insights, and lasting impressions. In one way it chronicles the Americanization of the catechetical movement. In the quarter century since Sloyan's *Shaping the Christian Message* appeared, American writers have come into their own. They continue to read the works of their European colleagues and follow the proceedings of the international meetings with interest and profit. Now, however, Americans are also being read and studied. Their background in learning theory, adult development, and the social sciences in general, while not unique to the United States, seems to have greater impact here than elsewhere. Their work is nicely complementary to the more theological approach coming in via liberation theology and foreign scholars. The modern catechetical movement was built on dialogue: Americans and Europeans, theologians and educators, first and third worlds. Quite simply, the sourcebook shows that catechesis reflects the state of health and well-being of the Christian community.

The *Sourcebook for Modern Catechetics* is a worthy sequel to *Shaping the Christian Message*. Michael Warren is to be commended for his efforts.

NOTES

1. Gabriel Moran, "Two Languages of Religious Education," *The Living Light* 14 (Spring 1977): 10.

2. Lawrence Cremin, *American Education: The Colonial Experience, 1607-1783* (New York: Harper & Row, 1970), p. xiii.

PART ONE
Historical Studies

READING 1

Introductory Overview

MICHAEL WARREN

I HAVE CHOSEN to begin Part I of the sourcebook with documentation from the International Catechetical Study Weeks,[1] which, with one exception,[2] occurred during the 1960s. Some readers will certainly ask why, especially when Section B, "Origins," contains historical studies chronologically far more inclusive than these study weeks, which did not begin until 1960. My reason is that I see the study weeks as important focal moments of the modern catechetical movement. Taken together, they form a backdrop for more recent developments. Without proper attention to the study weeks, one tends to distort and in other ways to misunderstand what has happened and continues to evolve in the movement. Although my presentation of the resolutions and conclusions of the six international gatherings gives only the faintest flavor of their full significance, my hope is that some readers will take the trouble to go back to the complete proceedings of the study weeks in order to see the continuities and progression that have marked catechetics since 1960.

Some readers will also ask why I have omitted the 1956 Antwerp International Study Week[3] as well as the better-known 1959 Nijmegen week, whose proceedings appeared in English as *Liturgy and the Missions.*[4] I omitted the Antwerp week because it lacked the international and missionary character of the later study weeks. Even with thirty-two nations represented by the four hundred participants, the vast majority were from The Netherlands, France, or Germany. On the other hand, the Nijmegen week was more international and had more of a missionary flavor than the one in Antwerp. Still, it was an outcome of a congress on pastoral liturgy held in Assisi in 1956 and thus did not have the direct catechetical focus of the later study weeks. Eichstätt, however, was directly catechetical and also fully international, since 75 of its 175 participants were from mission territories and since the sessions were simultaneously available in an additional language, Spanish.[5]

In order to present the study weeks systematically, I will first note some special features that need highlighting if their significance is to be properly appreciated and then explain some ways in which the study weeks have been misunderstood.

The above introductory comments hint at the first of three special features of these study weeks which must be highlighted in a proper appreciation, namely, their international character. At a time when religious education thinking in the United States tends to be focused on the North American continent and carried out in one language, English, the modern catechetical movement has consistently held on to its international character.[6] Leaders have convened from throughout the world, thereby effecting a significant cross-cultural exchange of ideas. In the proceedings of these various study weeks, one finds serious attempts on the part of Western – and mostly white – leaders to cross over to other cultural frames of reference. This exchange reached a high point at Medellín, Colombia, where cultural specificity emerged as a central catechetical theme and where the kind of catechesis done in the Third World began to influence the First World rather than vice versa. Ironically, this international focus runs counter to the caricature of catechesis as provincial, with its scope narrowed to the drilling of children in "church," in-house concerns.

The second feature of the study weeks is their missionary character. The missionary context – that is, the context in which the little flock or community invites non-Christians to hear the Good News that has been whispered in Jesus – dominates the study weeks. This missionary character explains the consistent concern in these gatherings for authenticity of communal life,[7] as well as for adapting the message to the mentalities of different groups of people. It further explains why the theme of conversion continually appears in the study weeks.[8] Eventually, of course, catechetical leaders in so-called Christianized countries came to see that the missionary emphasis appropriate to mission countries was the very effort also needed back home. Missionary concern had come full circle.

There is an additional aspect to the missionary concern of modern catechetics. At a time when religious pluralism is seen as an enriching factor in the religious experience of human persons, Christians have had to undertake a serious reevaluation of missionary theory, some of which had elitist, intolerant, or even colonial overtones. It is important to recognize that catechetical leaders took an important role in this reevaluation.[9] Very early, especially among French theorists, stress was put on the quiet proclamation that comes from authenticity of life lived in accord with the Gospel. In fact, as Nebreda points out in Reading 3, the catechetical community had a decisive role in the reformulation of mission theory. The documents that emerged from the Bangkok and Katigondo weeks were, at the Vatican council, "substantially incorporated into the radically new draft elaborated by the mixed committee in charge of preparing the final text for *Ad Gentes* ("Decree on the Missionary Activity of the Church"), especially in Chapters I and II."[10]

The influence of Bangkok and Katigondo on *Ad Gentes* brings me to the third feature of the study weeks that must be highlighted – their influence on events in the wider church. In general, the catechetical movement has tended to underestimate its impact on certain developments within the Roman Catholic Church. For example, more study should be done to explore the way catechetical insights helped shape developments at Vatican II, beyond what we already know of their effects on *Ad Gentes* and on *Christus Dominus* ("Decree on the Pastoral Office of Bishops").[11] At least one important influence, albeit a postconciliar one, has been overlooked – the role of the 1968 Medellin Catechetical Week in setting for the Latin American churches the pastoral agenda that was affirmed by a meeting of the Latin American bishops a week later in the same Colombian city.[12] That agenda, set by catechists and taken up by the bishops, highlighted the need for the church to struggle for liberation in the face of oppression. Eventually, this line of thinking emerged in the theology of liberation, which continues, at least to some extent, to revise theological method.

The catechetical concern for social justice found in the two catechetical synods, the 1974 Synod on Evangelization and the 1977 Synod on Catechesis, carries on the main theme of Medellin.[13] Despite certain inadequacies,[14] these synods stand as further evidence of the influence of the catechetical movement on the Roman Catholic Church worldwide. They are best seen against the backdrop of the five study weeks and the one Roman congress presented here.

Correcting Some Misunderstandings

If one is to appreciate these International Catechetical Study Weeks for what they are – key moments in the evolution of catechetics –

without either overstating or overlooking their significance, it is best to view them as a series of attempts to deal with sharply defined problems or sharply defined facets of catechesis.[15]   They represent an evolving series of focuses, each building on the insights of those preceding. While schematizing study weeks into periods – as Erdozain has done in Reading 8 – is valuable for heuristic purposes,[16] it can lead to some distortions if it fails to accent the continuity and progression of the weeks.

For example, to put Eichstätt into the framework of a "kerygmatic catechetics,"[17]   as if its chief concern were the message, would be to misjudge its true import. The catechetical movement certainly did not move from a focus in 1960 on kerygma to a new focus in 1962 on anthropological concerns. The modern catechetical movement has never neglected anthropological matters. In the mid-1950s in France, for instance, a messy controversy erupted over Joseph Colomb's *Catéchèse Progressive* methodology.[18] This approach brought young people gradually to religious and Christian insights in ways suited to their ages.[19]   So fully anthropocentric was Colomb's focus that it frightened certain functionaries in Rome. Eventually, Rome ordered written corrections of Colomb's "errors" inserted into his catechetical works for the young.

To carry the matter further back in time, an examination of Jungmann's own work as historian, liturgiologist, and catechetical theorist and a careful reading of his seminal essay, *The Good News Yesterday and Today,* show that he consistently worked from a conviction that the word of God is meant as a word finding its response in human experience. Jungmann, in all his writings, shows an anthropological focus—certainly not as evolved as the later concern for human experience in the catechetical movement—but still, for all that, central to his thought.

To add to the need for care in making schematic generalizations, Alfonso Nebreda, writing in *Teaching All Nations,* has warned of the danger of taking the Eichstätt conclusions too much at their face value.[20]   Nebreda claims that a team of German catechetical experts came to Eichstätt with a ready-made set of conclusions mirroring the specifically German context and concerns linked to the recently developed German catechism. Their propositions were vigorously opposed by the French group, representing Lumen Vitae and the Institute for Pastoral Catechetics in Paris. In the end, conclusions of the Eichstätt week were a compromise masking quite different points of view rather than a consensus based on dialogue. Nebreda insists that Eichstätt found the "kerygmatic formula" wanting.[21] Thus, to distinguish a kerygmatic phase from an anthropological phase and to identify Eichstätt with the former seems to misinterpret the catechetical movement as it was in the early 1960s.

Further, to say, as Erdozain does, that the Bangkok week put a special emphasis on adaptation in the sense that "for the first time" there is talk of providing for stages and of using a language with which persons being catechized are familiar[22] is to set up artificial junctures in the concerns shown by modern catechesis. If there has been any quantum leap in modern catechetics, it has not been one from content to person but rather one to a recognition of the relation of catechesis to political realities and to a realization that the beloved community has to attend to systemic evil found in social and political structures. I take pains to point out these matters because Erdozain's article is a generally good summary of the catechetical movement and is often cited as authoritative.[23] Erdozain has, however, missed important nuances, which must be noted if we are to understand accurately our recent history. The modern catechetical movement is a person-centered movement from Jungmann on, and it has not, to my knowledge, split meanings from experience.

No treatment of these international gatherings would be complete without acknowledging the key role of Johannes Hofinger, SJ, who organized them and developed the funding that made them possible. Future scholarship might come to judge that these study weeks and the global consciousness they fostered were a contribution even more significant than Hofinger's important writings. As a student and admirer of Jungmann,[24] Hofinger showed farsightedness in organizing the study weeks, which gave the catechetical revolution a rich, cross-cultural fertilization.

As a final note, however, I wish to point out the lack of an international gathering of catechetical leaders over the past ten years and the undesirable consequences of this dearth of face-to-face collaboration. I myself doubt that the catechetical movement could have progressed as far as it has in twenty years were it not for the sort of intense sharing that came about in the study weeks. What exactly will be the long-term outcome of another ten-year period without a major international gathering, I cannot say. However, the evidence of the six international conferences dealt with here suggests it would be a loss for catechetics and for the entire church.

NOTES

1. Actually, catechetical congresses across national boundaries were held in Europe early in the twentieth century, and later in 1928 and 1950. Sloyan

sketches some brief background for these in Gerard Sloyan, "Developments in Religious Education Since 1800," *The Living Light* 2, no. 4 (1965): 82–97, see esp. pp. 86–89; another source is Francis J. Buckley, "Catechetical Congresses," *New Catholic Encyclopedia* 16:52–53.

2. The 1971 Roman Catechetical Congress is an exception in more than a chronological sense. This assembly was not summoned, as were the others, through the collaboration of catechetical leaders themselves; rather, it was "officially" summoned by the Sacred Congregation for the Clergy, the Vatican body charged since Trent with catechetical matters. National hierarchies appointed and, in many cases, funded the travel of their official delegates. At this congress the *General Catechetical Directory* was presented to the international catechetical community. I include the Roman congress here because its proceedings are in such continuity with the previous five study weeks.

3. The proceedings of the Antwerp congress, organized by Lumen Vitae, can be found in that catechetical center's journal, *Lumen Vitae* 11, no. 4 (1956); and ibid. 12, no. 1 (1957). See also, P. Birch "Congress at Antwerp," *The Sower* 198 (1956): 108–110.

4. Johannes Hofinger, ed., *Liturgy and the Missions* (New York: P. J. Kenedy & Sons, 1959).

5. A thorough report on Eichstätt is found in Gerard Sloyan, "The International Study Week on Mission Catechetics," *Worship* 35 (1960–61): 43–46, 48–57. For the English-language edition of the proceedings, see Johannes Hofinger, ed., *Teaching All Nations: A Symposium on Modern Catechetics* (New York: Herder and Herder, 1961).

6. A survey of *Religious Education,* the journal of the Religious Education Association of the United States and Canada (R.E.A.), over the past forty years shows this lack of international focus. A comparison of the contents of *The Living Light* with *Religious Education* for the sixteen years that *The Living Light* has been in print discloses a more international focus for *The Living Light,* the catechetical journal. I realize that such a comparison is of unequal elements since *The Living Light,* as a Roman Catholic publication, shows concern for worldwide Roman matters, whereas the R.E.A. is an interdenominational association. Weak as my illustration may be, it still points in the direction of my claim.

7. This concern appears everywhere in the literature of the modern catechetical movement. Some fine statements of it can be found in the papers of Nagpur Theological Conference on Evangelization, held in 1973. See J. Pathrapankal, ed., *Service and Salvation* (Bangalore: Theological Publications in India, 1973).

8. Conversion has been a category in catechetical literature back to its beginnings. However, it tended to be omitted in systematics and relegated to moral theology's treatment of penance. Bernard Lonergan's theological work moved the matter to a much more central place in theology. Unfortunately, some theologians seem quite unaware of conversion's centrality in catechetical theory and choose to ignore catechetical literature as a significant source. For an example of a thorough overlooking of catechetical sources in an otherwise well-researched article, see Charles Curran, "Christian Conversion in the Writings of Bernard Lonergan," in *Foundations of Theology* , ed. Philip McShane (Notre Dame, IN: University of Notre Dame Press, 1972), pp. 41–59.

9. For a good statement, see D. S. Amalorpavadass, "Theology of Evangelization in the Indian Context," in *Service and Salvation,* pp. 19–39. Other

fine statements on this question also appear in that volume.

10. Alfonso Nebreda, "Some Reflections . . . on History and Present Scene in Religious Education," *Teaching All Nations* 11, no. 2 (1974): 88. I consider this entire article (pp. 85–98) of special importance for the way Nebreda clarifies certain misunderstandings about various aspects of the catechetical movement. It deserves considerable attention.

11. This influence is explained by Berard Marthaler in "The Genesis and Genius of the *General Catechetical Directory*," reprinted in this sourcebook as Reading 18.

12. The best statement to date of this relationship may be the following: Joseph A. Komonchak, "Christ's Church in Today's World: Medellín, Puebla, and the United States," *The Living Light* 17, no. 2 (1980): 108–120. Nebreda alludes to the connection between the two meetings in "Some Reflections," p. 91.

13. See Michael Warren, "A Third World Focus," *Religious Education* 74, no. 5 (1979): 496–502.

14. Some of the interventions at both synods were painfully naive and even inane. The quality of reflection was quite uneven. The bishops in some cases were trying to catch up to the catechetical movement; some did not succeed.

15. Nebreda carefully outlines the specific focus of Bangkok in "Some Reflections," pp. 86–88.

16. See Luis Erdozain's article, "The Evolution of Catechetics," in this sourcebook, Reading 8.

17. The term *kerygmatic catechetics* is not a good one. It has caused problems, as we shall see below, right back to Jungmann. Somehow in the early 1960s, when the catechetical renewal was finally taking hold in the United States, this particular term "stuck" as the term to describe what catechetics was all about. Again, see Nebreda on this matter, in "Some Reflections," p. 89.

18. For reports on the controversy, see Georges Delcuve, "The Catechetical Movement in France: The Recent Statement by the Episcopal Commission on Religious Teaching," *Lumen Vitae* 12 (1957): 671–702; and Gerard Sloyan, "Books on Religious Education: 1955–1965," *Worship* 40 (1966): 209–217, esp. p. 210.

19. Colomb's theory of catechesis is set forth in his monumental work, *Le Service de l'evangile*, 2 vols. (Paris: Desclée, 1968).

20. See Nebreda, "Some Reflections," pp. 85–86.

21. Ibid., p. 89.

22. See Erdozain, "The Evolution of Catechetics," in this sourcebook, Reading 8.

23. See, for example, reliance on Erdozain in Mary Boys, " 'Heilgeschichte' as a Hermeneutical Principle in Religious Education" (Ph.D. diss., Columbia Teachers College, 1978), pp. 101, 107–108.

24. See Hofinger's tribute to Jungmann: "J. A. Jungmann: In Memoriam," *The Living Light* 13, no. 3 (1976): 350–359.

General Conclusions
of the Eichstätt Week: 1960

I. Catechetical Revival

At present, we are faced in our mission apostolate with an extremely urgent and responsible task Complete success in this task will never be achieved by any mere increase in catechetical activity. What we need is something more: a reform that takes account of the findings of modern psychology and the conclusions reached by the recent kerygmatic renewal.

The chief aim of this kerygmatic renewal is to present the truth of our faith as an organic whole. Its core is the Good News of our redemption in Christ. Its fruit should be the grateful response of our love.

It is in the light of this central message of Christian catechesis that all other truths of the faith must be viewed, presented, and made fruitful for Christian life.

II. Need for a Clearly Outlined Program

We need a general but clearly outlined program for the catechetical apostolate. Such a program should meet the special catechetical needs in the mission lands today but in no way neglect such needs in every country. To draw up this program, ten specialists in catechetics have been chosen. These experts shall work under the guidance of an episcopal commission consisting of Archbishop Hurley, Archbishop Mark Gopu, Archbishop Young, and Bishop Yougberé.

III. Liturgy

There is latent in the liturgy a colossal wealth of meaning and a tremen-

Reprinted from Appendix I of *Teaching All Nations: A Symposium on Modern Catechetics*, eds. Johannes Hofinger and Clifford Howell (New York: Herder and Herder, 1961), pp. 387–391, by permission of The Crossroad Publishing Company.

dous instructive power. These lie in its prayers, songs, and readings; in the actions of the priest and people, the frequency of its celebration and the assembly for it of all the faithful. Therefore, the liturgy should be celebrated in a manner which will bring out to the full its catechetical content and enable the people to take an active part in it devoutly and intelligently. Hence, in order that the liturgy may produce its due catechetical effect, it should display its intrinsic excellences by means of its intelligibility, beauty, and clarity. Only thus can its full catechetical value be exploited. But this cannot be done unless certain reforms are introduced. Some proposals will be found set forth in a separate document.

IV. Bible

The Bible must be given a very prominent place in catechetical teaching because it is the inspired Word of God and the most important of all the Church's didactic books. It sets forth the divine actions whereby God has revealed himself; its method of presentation is so vivid and lively that it is suited to human capacities, and it is explicitly ordered towards humanity's salvation.

Hence, catechetics must be solidly built up on a biblical foundation; every age group should be taught biblical texts and made familiar with events in biblical history.

V. Textbooks

Good textbooks are an absolute necessity for catechetical work. The suggestions which are most important for their compilation have been set forth in a special section.

Those who teach religion in the missions need a teacher's aid book even more than do those similarly engaged in countries where Christianity has already been established. These aid books should not only provide the necessary material but also give guidance for its use.

The mere revision or modification of textbooks or catechisms which are not drawn up according to the principles of the catechetical renewal cannot produce a work which fulfills the basic demands of catechetics.

Good new textbooks can be composed only by authors who are thoroughly acquainted with the findings of modern catechetics.

VI. Postulata on the Catechetical Centers

To ensure the practical cooperation of all in the catechetical apostolate, the participants in this study week support the following measures:

1) A catechetical office should function in each diocese, according to the decree *Provido sane concilio*. Besides the appointment of a diocesan commission, this implies the formation of a catechetical center, from which teachers of religion can get both advice and catechetical material.

2) The director of this diocesan center must be prepared for the task by special studies and be given time and opportunity to promote the catechetical renewal in an efficient manner.

3) In each country, a national center shall serve as a link between the various diocesan centers and the catechetical movement abroad. Such a center may organize efforts toward a better adapted catechesis by means of enquiries, study sessions, publication of books and magazines, and the like.

4) Wherever necessary the national centers should work in close cooperation with regional centers fulfilling the same task on a linguistic basis.

5) The various national centers, especially those in the mission countries, should help one another by pooling their documentation and the fruits of their experiments in the catechetical apostolate.

6) In particular, the help already given by several institutes for the formation of specialists in catechetics should be increased so that future directors of religious instruction in the missions would be able to obtain the special preparation they need.

VII. Catechists (Lay Teachers)

All catechists should have at least one year of solid training. This must impart to them above all a complete grasp of the fundamentals of Christian doctrine concerning human salvation, together with an adequate competence in catechetical methods.

At the same time, great stress must be laid on the spiritual training and character formation given to catechists as well as on their social behavior so that they may become not only good teachers but also "witnesses to Christ."

In this religious training, the Bible and the liturgy must be given the prominent place also due them in the catechetical apostolate later on.

VIII. Catechetical Training in Seminaries

The catechetical renewal has not as yet brought forth its due fruit in the missions. The chief reason for this is the inadequate training in catechetics of future missionaries. This applies not merely to indigenous priests but also to those from the home countries.

It is absolutely essential that future missionaries be given a training in catechetics suited to the needs of our own day. This would involve a series of lectures and also sufficient training in practice. The course would have to familiarize the future missionary with the aims, viewpoint, and technique of the modern catechetical movement; would be designed expressly in the light of the missionary apostolate; and would impart to him or her a degree of competence in teaching catechism.

It is just as important that the major subjects of theology (dogma, morality, exegesis) should be presented to the future missionary from the same angle, so that he or she may grasp vividly and clearly the organic unity of the Christian message of salvation, the religious content of each doctrine, and its application to Christian life.

IX. Cooperation

Catechetical cooperation of Christian countries with mission countries will assume various forms, notably developing intercommunication between catechetical centers and experts in missionary countries and also with centers and experts in Christian countries. These countries will help one another in catechetical and pastoral training of seminarians and priests, in the study of the psychology of the peoples to be evangelized, in studies of missiology and ethnology, in the progress of catechetical institutions, in the foundation of catechetical centers, and in the improvement of books and periodicals.

Basic Principles of Modern Catechetics: A Summary Report from Eichstätt

Our Aim

I. **Catechesis carries out the command of Christ to proclaim God's message of salvation to all people.** Christ carried out the will of his Father by giving his Church the commission "to preach the gospel to every creature," "to make disciples" for him, and to provide him with "witnesses throughout the world" (Mark 16:15; Matt. 28:19; Acts 1:8). The catechist does what Christ did and commissioned the Church to do: He or she proclaims the Good News of salvation and helps people to accept it and to become disciples who will give witness to it. Catechesis then does more than teach the doctrines of the Church; it wins men, women, and children for Christ and after baptism unites them further to him. All principles and methods of catechizing flow from the missionary command of Christ.

Our Message

II. **Catechesis proclaims the merciful love of the Father for us and proclaims the Good News of God's Kingdom.** Carrying out the commission of Christ, the Church brings a message from God which surpasses by far what the hearts of people can conceive or hope for (1 Cor. 2:10; Eph. 3:20).

The Church proclaims to all people that the eternal and grace-giving Kingdom of God is at hand, a Kingdom prefigured in the Old Testament, begun by Christ in the New, and growing toward the fullness of glory at the end of time (Mark 1:15; Matt. 24:14, 25:34). All men are invited to the wedding feast prepared by the King of Kings from all eternity (Matt. 22:2ff.).

This message proclaims that God is not merely an idea or a remote

Reprinted from Appendix III of *Teaching All Nations: A Symposium on Modern Catechetics,* eds. Johannes Hofinger and Clifford Howell (New York: Herder and Herder, 1961), pp. 394–400, by permission of The Crossroad Publishing Company.

and silent being but a living personal God, the almighty Creator and eternal Father. It tells of a world not drifting into chaos but being transformed into "a new heaven and a new earth" (Apoc. 21:1). It speaks not of the dissolution of all things but of a "new creature" and of an eternal and living union with our Father in heaven.

III. **Catechesis is Christ-centered, reflecting the fulfillment in and through Christ of the Father's loving design.** God the Father carried out his plan through Christ, his Son, born of the Virgin Mary, our Savior and Lord. Salvation is found only in him (Acts 4:12). Through Christ we know about the Father and receive the Good News of the Father's Kingdom. By his death, resurrection, and ascension, Christ saves us from our sins. He works in us through the Holy Spirit and leads us toward that day when he will judge all men and bring the world to its perfection. He is the Word (John 1:1), the Mediator (1 Tim. 2:5), the Way and the Life (John 14:16).

Catechesis gives due importance to the historical treatment of God's design: how God prepared for Christ's coming in the Old Testament, how his coming brought about our salvation, and how Christ continues to communicate himself through the Holy Spirit till he returns as the Lord of glory.

IV. **Catechesis proclaims that Christ continues to live and work in his Church through the Holy Spirit and the ministry of his shepherds.** By the action of the Holy Spirit in the Church and particularly in the hierarchy, Christ gathers people together through his word; sanctifies and gives them life through the mystery of his passion, resurrection, and ascension communicated in the sacraments; and gives them power to be witnesses before the world.

The Church is truly Christ's Body. He unites the members to himself and to one another and assigns to each member a specific function. The Church is the chosen race, a people God means to have for himself, a holy people called to priestly service in the world (1 Pet. 2:9). The Church is the city built on the mountain top, lighted by Christ's light and shining brightly for all nations to see (Matt. 5:14; Isa. 2). She is the family of God on earth, the home which the Father offers to all wanderers, the community of people advancing to its eternal destiny.

V. **Catechesis emphasizes that worship is the heart of Christian community life.** Whenever the Church celebrates liturgy, she assembles as a holy people. Christ is in her midst, and she is vivified by the Holy Spirit. In the service of the word (Mass of the Catechumens), Christ nourishes his Church by the word of life and carries her prayer up to the Father. In the celebration of the Eucharist (Mass of the Faithful), Christ engulfs her in the sacrifice of the redemption and saturates her anew with his life. By the one eucharistic bread, the many are made one Body (1 Cor. 10:17). By the Good News, the prayer, and the sacramental celebration, the people are filled with inner strength, spiritual knowledge, and understanding enabling them to proclaim the word of God without fear (Acts 4:31).

Worship is primarily directed to the praise of God. At the same time it is the supreme expression of catechesis. Catechesis leads to worship and draws its life from worship. Worship is the inexhaustible source of faith, grace, and the apostolate.

Our Response

VI. Catechesis teaches us to respond to God's call by an inner change of heart manifested in a life of faith and hope and of loving obedience to his commands. Humankind's first response to the message of salvation is that inner change of heart described in the Gospel as absolutely necessary to enter the Kingdom. Turning to God, people begin to realize all that God has done, is doing, and will do for them. In this acceptance of Christ, which must be made by catechumen and Christian alike, people recognize the God of love who will save them from their sins. Repenting of their sins and filled with joy at the recognition of their Savior, they are moved to obey the commandment of love. "The man who loves God is the man who keeps the commandments he has from me" (John 14:21).

VII. Catechesis makes Christians aware of their responsibility for the world and the betterment of its condition. The Christian sees the world as the work and possession of the Father in heaven and feels responsible for it as "son and heir." What is called the "profane" or "natural" order is no less from the hand of God. The Christian must value it in itself if he or she is to contribute to its sanctification in Christ. This is particularly true of the social order. If the Christian does not endeavor to restore it to its proper condition in regard to family, professional, economic, civic, and cultural life, he or she is betraying the trust of the heavenly Father.

VIII. Catechesis leads the Christian to share the faith with others. Catechesis makes Christians keenly aware that the growth and welfare of God's Kingdom depend on them. It stimulates the missionary spirit so that the followers of Christ strive for sanctity, not only for the sake of their own salvation and greater happiness but also that their community may see their good example and praise the Father who is in heaven (Matt. 5:16). It is the Holy Spirit who makes them witnesses of his word and life and enables them, according to the measure of their faith and the gifts they have received from God, to communicate the message of salvation with its spiritual values to all with whom they come in contact. Sanctity of life, the praise, the joy of Christians, their contentment and assurance, their willingness and ability to share the message, and especially their love, which embraces even enemies, are the signs by which others are led to experience the realities and values of God's Kingdom.

Our Method

IX. **Catechesis, following God's method, proclaims "the wonderful works of God," which show forth the truth and especially the love contained in them, moving the heart and inspiring the whole of life.** Catechesis follows God's method of proclaiming the glad tidings of salvation. The wonderful works of God as narrated in the Old Testament and the miracles, discourses, and events in the New Testament lead us to an understanding of the divine message and of its impact in our lives (Heb. 1:1). In these events God has come close to us, has revealed and united himself to us, and has shown us the way to live through him and in him. Catechesis is at the service of this divine revelation and adapts itself to God's own way of winning men and women.

X. **Catechesis embraces a fourfold presentation of the faith: through liturgy, Bible, systematic teaching, and the testimony of Christian living.** Each of these forms of presentation has its specific function in the winning of the non-Christian and the development of the Christian. Catechesis strives to combine liturgy, Bible, doctrine, and the testimony of Christian living so that the organic unity of the Christian message is more clearly presented.

The *liturgy* does more than communicate the Christian mystery to the mind of the participant. It uses sound pedagogical principles, namely, the intuitive process, activity, teaching by experience, the imparting of values. It appeals to the entire person, the sensibilities, the intellect, and the will. It is the means of impregnating the whole life with the spirit of Christ. For, in the liturgy, the mystery of redemption not only is proclaimed through the words of holy Scripture but also is expressed in prayers and hymns, presented in sacred signs, and rendered sacramentally present and efficacious.

Catechesis is as inseparable from the *Bible,* the inspired word of God, as a plant from its roots. The Bible is the basis of the Church's proclamation and, thus, also of her catechesis. We use the Bible to follow the history of salvation in the way God himself made it known. These sacred books take us from the creation of the world to its end and show us how Christ is the fulfillment of all.

The *systematic presentation* of the faith has its roots in the creeds and preaching of the early Christian proclamation and has derived its organic development from the authoritative teaching of the Church throughout the ages. The catechism gives the learner spiritual insight into the relationship between the faith and Christian life and enables him or her to cope with the questions of the day as an articulate Christian and express his or her faith to those who inquire about it.

The Christian message and teaching is borne out through the *witness of a Christian life.* The life of the Church and her saints shows us repeatedly that Christ lives and works in the Church. The witness of a Christian life by individuals and by the community of the faithful not only nourishes the faith of Catholics but also is the way that ordinarily leads the non-Christian to Christ and to the Church.

XI. Catechesis adapts itself to the life and thought of peoples, shows due appreciation of their laudable views and customs, and integrates them harmoniously into a Christian way of life. The message of the living God should contact living humans, move their innermost hearts, and convert them from within. Before catechists begin their task, God has already worked in the individuals and nations of his creation through his truth and grace, moving them to seek and attain their salvation in Christ (Acts 17:26-27). In the love of the Good Shepherd, catechists seek to recognize the special character, manner of thought, outlook, customs, and culture of their catechumens. Beginning at the point from which the catechumen can follow, catechists instruct according to the psychology of age-group, sex, and special circumstances. Guided by the Holy Spirit, they enter into a catechumen's hidden problems and lead him or her to adopt Christ's way of thinking as the best solution. They seek in patience to correct whatever is false and erroneous but humbly endeavor to mold into the Christian way of life "whatever things are true, whatever honorable, whatever just, whatever holy, whatever lovable, whatever of good repute, if there be any virtue, if anything worthy of praise" (Phil. 4:8).

XII. Catechesis introduces the catechumen into a living community and helps him or her to strike root in it. The life of faith is a life in the community of believers. The apostles received their formation in the community which Christ gathered around himself as the family of God (Matt. 12:19). Those who were converted at the sermon of St. Peter were "taken into the community of the faithful which was inspired by the Holy Spirit" (Acts 2:41ff.). They found a home in the communal life of the primitive Church. Likewise, believers today should welcome and embrace the newly baptized. Special groups may be needed, apart from the family and the parish, to sustain and stimulate new Catholics in their faith. For only in the community can a Christian recognize the full meaning of the Lord's message and experience the bonds of charity which unite all people in Christ.

East Asian Study Week
on Mission Catechetics: 1962

ALFONSO NEBREDA

IN THE SAME SIMPLICITY with which it opened on October 31, the East Asian Study Week on Mission Catechetics closed on November 3. Outwardly, there was nothing in it comparable to the study weeks in Nijmegen on liturgy and missions (1959) and Eichstätt on catechetics and missions (1960), where the number and importance of the participants made the meetings a tempting center of interest for the news media. Apart from the natural attention and interest of the Catholic communities in Thailand and especially in Bangkok, the East Asian Study Week on Mission Catechetics could perform its work wrapped up in the gratifying anonymity of a true study meeting. Nonetheless, in view of the results, I do not think it an exaggeration to affirm that the Bangkok study week is to be considered as an important event for both the missions and the catechetical renewal.

Prepared by the discussions in and around the Eichstätt study week, the Bangkok conference succeeded in setting out the main problems of missionary catechetics, clearly stating the correct approach to them.

The main feature of this meeting, and undoubtedly the most refreshing experience for all the participants, was the unanimous and fraternal spirit in which delegates of twelve East Asian mission countries worked together with three members of the East Asian Pastoral Institute of Manila (Fathers Hofinger, Brunner, and Chao) and representatives of Paris (Canons Brien and Bournique), Rome (Father Nebreda), and the United States (Father Stone of Chicago).

Aim and Method of the Study Week

On the evening of October 31, Father Hofinger, organizer of the

Reprinted from *Lumen Vitae* 17 (1962), pp. 717–730. Reproduced by courtesy of *Lumen Vitae*. Copyright *Lumen Vitae* 1962.

meeting, in a brief opening speech clearly stated the aims and way of proceeding for the East Asian Study Week on Mission Catechetics. The original plan of the Eichstätt study week, he said, was to deal with the problem of missionary catechetics. But the unique opportunity of bringing together such an imposing number of leading authorities on catechetics from the whole world made it advantageous to stress the characteristic points of the catechetical renewal and to suggest their fundamental applicability and usefulness to missionary situations. This was the main fruit of Eichstätt. It could not reach into the delicate and complicated problem of studying the ways in which the principles of modern catechetics were to be applied to the missions. It should be, Father Hofinger went on, the main objective of the Bangkok study week to tackle that problem, thus complementing the work achieved in Eichstätt.

The program of the discussions was to follow the general outline sketched in the short summary sent previously to the participants: (1) the main difficulties of the catechetical apostolate in the missions, (2) the missionary value of modern catechetics, (3) how to adapt modern catechetics to the special missionary conditions prevailing in East Asia, (4) catechetical problems of the catechumenate, (5) the necessary training for the catechetical apostolate, and (6) how to pro- mote mutual collaboration in the field of mission catechetics.

Of these points, it is not difficult to see where the most stress needs to be placed. Father Hofinger explained: One of the main reasons why some excellent missionaries often consider modern catechetics as in- sufficient for the missions is that the catechetical literature of the Western countries obviously concerns itself with the instruction of bap- tized children or adults who already have faith. But mission catechetics in its strictest meaning concentrates its attention on people who do not yet believe, on those who are supposed to be guided in their first approach to faith and Christian life. It seems to be, therefore, the par- ticular task of this study week to discuss and present the leading catechetical principles from the point of view of their power to attract and form catechumens before baptism.

As for the way of proceeding, Father Hofinger stressed again the original plan: Since this was a meeting of experts, there would not be any paper, just a summary introduction of the problem to be discuss- ed (five or ten minutes) preparing the way for the actual discussion. There would be two sessions every day, three hours each, with fifteen- minute interruptions for refreshments.

In the present article, which has been written by request and as the official record of the study week, we shall limit ourselves to following the main lines of the discussions in their chronological sequence and presenting the various documents elaborated by the meeting. The mere reading of these records will display the exceptional transcendence of the Bangkok study week.

Catechetical Situation in East Asia

The morning session on November 1, which was to serve as background for the following sessions, was devoted to presenting an overall picture of the catechetical situation in the East Asian missions. There were delegates from the following countries: Ceylon, Hong Kong, India, Indonesia, Japan, Korea, Malaya, Pakistan, Philippines, Taiwan, Thailand, Vietnam. One delegate from each of the twelve countries presented a short summary of the catechetical situation in his respective country centered around the following three points: (1) characteristics of the catechetical situation, (2) principal difficulties of the catechetical apostolate, and (3) practical suggestions concerning main needs.

Rather than following the different lines of the individual reports, we prefer to offer here the résumé made by the conference of the main convergent lines stressed in the information presented.

1) Characteristics of the mission scene
   a. General awakening of catechetical interest.
   b. Growing realization that something must be done now.
   c. Almost everywhere in the missions, we are at the beginning.
   d. Those who thoroughly know modern catechetics in the missions are a small minority.
   e. Lack of information on the true meaning of the renewal.

2) Main difficulties
   a. Lack of professional formation.
   b. Until we get trained specialists, we cannot expect competent literature on the lines of modern catechetics.
   c. In almost every mission country, there is a lack of adequate organization for forming and informing the priests.

3) Suggestions
   a. How to train priests:
      • Use the days of recollection for priests to give several catechetical conferences because the catechetical renewal has a very deep spiritual and apostolic character.
      • Schedule catechetical seminars given by trained specialists.
      • Priests who do their theological studies in Europe should be

encouraged to complete their training at the catechetical centers of Paris or Brussels.
* Seminary studies should be given a kerygmatic orientation.
b. How to approach the bishops:
* Keep the bishop informed.
* Give him written reports on catechetical developments at home and abroad so that he can keep himself informed at his leisure.
* Where convenient, present a report of this missionary study week to the apostolic delegates so that they may, if they wish, consider it with their bishops.
c. The ideal organization: It is hoped there will be an episcopal catechetical commission headed by one or more bishops according to circumstances. This commission should have the services of one or more thoroughly trained specialists in modern catechetics. This commission should receive suggestions from its specialists and may pass them on to the other bishops.
d. Use of papal documents: It is suggested that papal documents concerning the revival of catechetics be brought to the attention of catechists: priests, religious, and laity.

Catechetical Renewal and Its Missionary Value

The rest of this day was taken up by a thorough discussion of the basic aims of modern catechetics. In view of the fact that the main concern of the Eichstätt study week had been precisely this, it would seem that it was just an unnecessary overlapping to do it again at Bangkok. Yet the participants in the East Asian study week thought it helpful to reopen the matter and elaborate upon it for the sake of a better understanding in the missions. Anyone who compares the formulation of Eichstätt with the following seven points in which the Bangkok conference summarized the main features of modern catechetics will readily detect the improvement.

1) **Basic idea.** Modern catechetics considers the catechetical apostolate as a mission imparted by the Church to participate in Christ's proclamation of the Good News of salvation. The whole of catechetics is to be inspired and regulated by this basic idea.

2) **Aim.** The aim of the catechetical apostolate is not knowledge as such, but living faith – a faith which responds to God's call (message).

3) **Message.** The emphasis is on content more than on method. With regard to content, modern catechetics emphasizes *concentration* on the central theme of God's love accomplished in Jesus Christ (dead,

risen, and living in his Church), presented as a Gospel (Good News) and oriented to life.

4) **Method.** The main lines of method are to follow the dynamics of faith: to present the religious facts, to unfold their religious meaning, and to stimulate a personal response to this call of God in Christian living.

As such, method is a servant but an indispensable one. In all its phases, it needs thorough adaptation to those who are catechized.

5) **Fourfold presentation of the faith.** Genuine catechetics requires the sound equilibrium of a fourfold presentation of the faith: through liturgy, Bible, systematic teaching, and the testimony of Christian living. Systematic teaching is not to be begun before the age of ten or twelve and, even then, needs to be completed by, and thoroughly informed with, biblical and liturgical catechesis.

6) **The catechist.** Because the teacher of religion is Christ's spokesperson and witness, the teacher is more important than the textbook. Teachers must first assimilate the message personally. They must build up their religious lives from the message in harmony with professional training.

7) **Textbooks.** Textbooks are in the service of the teacher and the pupils. Good texts are required, taking into account the development of present-day theology. Outdated texts cannot be modernized by mere modifications and revisions.

Modern catechetics, therefore, is basically a spiritual, theological, and pastoral renewal, not just a methodical and psychological improvement.

Having thus described the main characteristics of the catechetical apostolate, the way was paved to consider its applicability to and usefulness for missionary situations. The mind of the study week was vigorously expressed in the following statement:

A Corollary to the Principles of Modern Catechetics

After thoroughly analyzing the basic characteristics of modern catechetics, the participants of the study week unanimously acknowledged that these principles are fully applicable to the missions. Their missionary value results from modern catechetics' being based firmly on universally valid theological principles and on the analysis of human nature common to all men and women.

Modern catechetics, therefore, is not to be limited in its application only to the West for it is not confined merely to the ways of thinking of the Western mind. Consequently, there is no reason to search for a specifically different missionary catechesis.

Modern catechetics originated in fact from a quasi-missionary situation. Christianity was no longer commonly practiced in the home or in the community. This growing de-Christianization of formerly Christian regions made it necessary to set up as the target of catechetics to win men and women to Christ and form them into convinced Christians. The new situation forced the teacher of religion to concentrate on the very essentials of the Christian message, to present religion as a value, and to stress its importance for life.

Moreover, experience in the missions proves that modern catechetics is especially suited to missionary catechesis because of its concentration on Christ and its emphasis on biblical and liturgical catechesis.

However, although the basic principles of modern catechetics are equally valid for mission lands and Christian countries, missionary catechesis has its specific problems, particularly insofar as it constitutes a first evangelization and leads to conversion:

1) It has to prepare the ground by purifying judgments, sentiments, and even subconscious impressions to lead them to a fuller response to the doctrine of Christ.

2) It has further to lay special emphasis on adaptation, by developing the doctrine according to analogies, images, or forms of expression familiar to people of a given region or culture. It has also to suggest a committed (pledged) action which truly corresponds to the needs, both spiritual and temporal, of this given milieu.

3) Finally, even more than in Christian countries, it has to build up a community of faith, which is able to sustain in its commitment to Christ, men and women who, by their conversion, have been more or less cut off from their familial or local community.

The Three Stages[1]
of the Kerygmatic Approach for the Missions

	STAGE I Pre-evangelization[2]	STAGE II Evangelization[6]	STAGE III Catechesis Proper
Addresses	unbelievers	prepared unbelievers	catechumens
Aim[3]	to arouse interest; prepare the ground for dialogue; bridge the gap for the kerygma . . . arousing hope and awakening the sense of God	to challenge, win, convert	to form, instruct, initiate into Christian life and Christian personality . . . building up the faith
Guiding Principle	anthropocentrical[4] —take people as they are and where they are	theocentrical— christocentrical— what God revealed, the way God revealed	theocentrical— christocentrical— what God revealed, the way God revealed . . . ecclesial emphasis
Virtues of Catechist	patience, love, understanding, respect	faithfulness to God and his message	faithfulness to God and his message
Content	dialogue: anything is all right, e.g., positive apologetics[5]; motives of credibility	a dynamic heralding of the core of God's message	a detailed development of God's message, always focused on the core
Procedure	personal contact, witness	challenge, shock,[7] concentration	personal, active, adaptive, use of godparents
Result	a spiritual readiness to accept God's message	conversion	formed Christian

PRECATECHUMENATE   CATECHUMENATE

Notes on the above chart of the three stages follow at the end of this reading (see pp. 52-53).

Sketching the Process of Missionary Preaching

The second day was wholly devoted to discussing the crucial problem which Father Hofinger in his opening speech had qualified as the particular task of the study week: to discuss and present the leading catechetical principles from the point of view of their power to attract and form catechumens before baptism, carefully distinguishing the main stages of the process of missionary preaching.

A committee had previously prepared a schema of this process. In a lively discussion, which was perhaps the best example of that fraternal collaboration which characterized the meeting, the participants analyzed thoroughly the schema, corrected and elaborated it, and appended a series of explanatory notes to make the whole easier to grasp. Since the document is now sufficiently self-explanatory, it is enough to have recorded it in full on the opposite page.

Precatechumenate and Catechumenate, Catechism for Catechumens

For the practical implications of these problems, the study week considered it convenient to add a summary of the discussion held on them, thus giving fuller explanation to the three stages of the kerygmatic approach for the missions (three stages in the catechesis of the nonbeliever).

Precatechumenate and Catechumenate

1) Although very important, the question of when the catechesis proper is to begin should be determined by the factor of conversion, which clearly separates the precatechumenate from the catechumenate. Without this conversion the catechist would be defending and proving, thus making the catechumenate mere intellectual instruction and destroying its essential character, which is to build religious knowledge based on faith. Therefore, it should be the careful concern of the catechist to detect the signs of conversion (cf. "Critères pour l'admission au catéchuménat," par P.-A. Liégé, OP, in *Problèmes de Catéchuménat*, pp. 221–228).

2) The recent permission of Rome to use the separate stages for the administration of baptism should help in both stressing the sacred character of the catechumenate itself and eliciting from the catechumen

manifestations of his or her commitment. To secure this sacred character beyond and above the catechetical instruction, special emphasis should be laid on participation in the liturgy and in community life. Hence the importance of choosing and training godparents, whose task it is to initiate and guide the catechumen into the new life.

3) Since conversion is an essential prerequisite for an effective catechumenate, special caution should be exercised with those asking for baptism on the occasion of marriage.

The Catechism for Catechumens

1) A clear distinction should be made between the catechism to be used by the catechumen and the guide for the catechist. Both are needed. The guide for the catechist will contain suggestions, principles, and directives relating to all three stages of the kerygmatic approach: pre-evangelization, evangelization, catechesis proper.

2) During the precatechumenate (the pre-evangelization and evangelization), the catechism is *not* to be given to the inquirer. It is reserved for those who have been converted and who, as a consequence, are ready to enter into the catechumenate.

Nevertheless, books other than the catechism and of particular interest to an inquirer, can be of great help, e.g., accounts by converts of their experiences.

3) Since the process of pre-evangelization depends essentially on persons and circumstances – taking the individuals as they are – a catechism cannot have the content of a pre-evangelization; however, the guide should direct catechists regarding the spirit and procedure with which they must approach the non-Christian.

4) At the stage of evangelization, the guide should underline the personal and dynamic character of the message to be proclaimed. The following is a sample of *possible* points to be presented:

    a. God's call
    b. proximity of God's love in Jesus Christ
    c. need of repentance
    d. need to accept Christ as the Risen Lord

5) The catechism which is given to the catechumen should begin with a recapitulation of the kerygma, as a link between the previous stage and the catechesis proper. It is a written echo of the kerygma already accepted.

Then follows a more detailed development of the message, always oriented to the core and including whatever truths and ways of Christian life the catechumens will solemnly embrace on the day of their baptism. The basic structure is to stress clearly the personal relationship between God and humans, in either of the following two ways: (a) God's love for us (God's salvation plan, sacraments) – our answer (prayer, Christian living). (b) Or – what God has done for us – what God does now for us (the Church and the sacraments) – our answer to his call – our final union with God.

The text of the catechism is to follow, as far as possible, the historical order as presented in Scripture and help the catechumen discover the spirit and riches of the liturgical life. It is to initiate the catechumen, right from the beginning, into personal and community prayer. Additional notes may propose to the catechumens subjects of conversation with the catechist and comparisons with their former outlooks on life; in short, it should help them to think and discuss.

The Necessary Training for the Catechetical Apostolate

Having stated its views on the central problem which it had proposed to tackle, the study week then centered its discussion on the last two points of the program: training of catechetical apostles and mutual cooperation in the field of catechetics.

The first issue took the better part of the morning session of the last day. The delegates formulated the following summary of the highlights of the discussion:

The progress of catechetical renewal in the missions will depend primarily on the training of future generations of Christ's messengers: priests, brothers, sisters, and lay catechists.

1) **The training of seminarians.** Although the members of the study week fully recognize that good training in modern catechetics is now given in a growing number of major seminaries, nevertheless, they think that much more could be done:

    a. by stressing the apostolic character of priestly spirituality;

    b. by a keener kerygmatic emphasis in the teaching of theology, i.e., dogma, morality, and sacred Scripture;

    c. by a sufficient number of lectures on modern catechetics (a minimum of forty hours); and

    d. by properly supervised, catechetical practice teaching by the seminarians during the course of their training.

2) **The training of priests.** The participants in this study week recognize the absolute necessity of bringing a correct understanding and a full appreciation of modern catechetics to priests.

An initial understanding of modern catechetics could be brought to the attention of priests already in the ministry by means of a well-written series of articles in such magazines as *The Clergy Monthly* and by well-prepared conferences on the occasion of monthly recollections and retreats for priests.

Those priests who are studying in Europe and are destined for the missions should be given the opportunity to become well-acquainted with the latest catechetical developments there. Missionaries who revisit their own countries should avail themselves of the same opportunity.

In this regard, the Institut de Pastorale Catéchétique de Paris has offered to arrange special courses in its center for priests, provided such courses are requested by Asian bishops. The Paris center has already organized similar sessions for missionaries on leave from Africa.

3) **Brothers, sisters, and lay catechists.** Catechetical seminars are very important for both the apostolic formation and the spiritual life of religious and lay catechists. But lasting benefit comes only from seminars of at least eight full days with lectures and periods of discussion on prepared questions.

However, for a more complete catechetical formation, it is suggested that successive and coordinated seminars of two weeks or thirty days (twenty-five or fifty hours) of intensive work be held over a period of three or more years. It is necessary to give the same persons these interrelated seminars over a period of several years to equip them with the progressive formation their catechetical apostolate requires. Such seminars are being conducted with success in India and Ceylon.

This formal training should be intensified by the personal study of books on modern catechetics. When persons cannot buy their own books, these might be made available through a central lending library.

Mutual Cooperation in the Field of Catechetics

The rest of the day was devoted to discussion of ways and means to promote a closer collaboration in the field of mission catechetics. Very practical was this exchange of views. The main lines have been summarized below.

In order to promote closer cooperation in the field of catechetics, the following points have been proposed:

1) **Publications.** The English or French publications prepared in the various centers could be exchanged.

2) **Files.** References, summaries, and quotations could be pooled and a selection published periodically as a help to all.

3) **Newsletter.** Reports of catechetical experiences and achievements in the Far East could be presented by means of a periodical newsletter.

4) **Scientific review.** In addition to *Good Tidings,* which chiefly addresses ordinary catechists, the need is being felt for a magazine of a higher standard, destined for leaders of the Catholic movement. This magazine would deal specifically with missionary catechetical problems and review essential books.

5) **French-language publications.** For the benefit of French-speaking missionary clergy of the Far East to whom the English language is less familiar, a series of missionary studies will appear in the collection published by the Institut de Pastorale Catéchétique, Paris. Some plans have been made during this session to start implementing this project.

6) **Catechetical training center.** The participants expressed the desire to set up a Catechetical Training Center for East Asia to prepare leaders of the catechetical movement in the different countries. While providing a greater number of students the advantage of an advanced course in catechetics, this center would in no way prevent sending selected leaders to Paris, Brussels, and similar centers.

7) **Future meetings.** Meetings such as this one will do much to foster further progress. On difficult basic points, discussion should be preceded by a short exposé by a specialist on the question.

The Bombay Eucharistic International Congress (December 1964) seems to provide a fine opportunity to hold, just before it convenes, such a meeting or a more important congress for India and the adjoining countries.

Conclusion

One of the outstanding points of the study week has been the excellent mutual collaboration of the delegates. Only this close collaboration could have made it possible to work out in three days so many important problems.

The delegates concluded by making constructive suggestions for future meetings of this type: First, three days is too short a time; four days would seem to be the minimum duration for similar study weeks. Second, it would be convenient to concentrate on a narrower range of problems. Third, on specific, important points, a specialist should be commissioned in advance to study the issue and present a short report before discussion is launched.

But even as it went, the East Asian Study Week on Mission Catechetics must be considered a success, and it should pave the way to a better understanding and a more adapted solution of the problems confronting the transmission of the Christian message.

In the name of all participants in the study week, thanks are due to the Catholic communities at Bangkok, especially to the Jesuit fathers of the Xavier House and the brothers of St. Gabriel School, who spared no effort to offer us a hospitable and quiet facility for the meeting.

NOTES

1. *The three stages:* Although these three stages are the normal chronological procedure, the evangelization may precede or coincide with the pre-evangelization due to varying circumstances and people. Some authors even hold that a certain form of evangelization normally comes first—in order to shake the subject from the world, where he or she is enclosed, and open that person to the religious problem; but, even then, a minimum preparation should have preceded if the evangelization itself is to be understood.

2. *Pre-evangelization:* In this stage, we consider the *persons as individuals,* not the community. It is obvious, however, that we should take into account the influence of the environment on the individual. The apostle has to work not only on the individual but on the structure and on the mentality of the milieu which influences him or her.

3. *The aim of pre-evangelization:* A more complete explanation of the aim of pre-evangelization is as follows:

   a) To shake off the apparent security of a life entirely "insured" by the familiar life surroundings, by the possession of material riches or of techniques which transform the world. People must experience a "break" within themselves if they are to be "reawakened" to the invisible and thus be ready to welcome the gift of God. The pre-evangelization prepares such a "break" by making men and women consider the mystery of death, of life, of human thought and love, of spiritual responsibility, and so on.

   b) To show how the various ways in which humans confront themselves with the realities of this world are integrated into a higher unity. (These "various ways" include practical judgments, technical activity, science, social and economic development, spiritual aspirations. "A higher unity" refers to the one brought about by the redemptive love of God.) This unity cannot be reached through the various non-Christian practices, magic, or ritual.

   c) To purify the "sense of the sacred." Pre-evangelization must lead to the sense of God, the personal Creator who is both transcendent and immanent to humanity. If this is not secured, the whole catechesis runs the risk of being ambiguous, even if its exposition is exact and complete. Pre-evangelization, on this point, must influence the spontaneous and subconscious representations of the Godhead, as well as bring out clear ideas about it.

4. *Anthropocentrical:* The guiding principle of pre-evangelization is anthropocentrical because we must start with the individual as he or she is. The

way must be prepared in order that a person be able to understand the message not as a mere presentation of words which make sense to us but as *a challenge* by words which make sense *to him or her.* This follows from the very essence of message, which demands that we speak *to* and not *at* a person (cf. "Distinguishing the Different Stages in Missionary Preaching," by Alfonso Nebreda, SJ, [Roma, 1962], pp. 23–26).

5. *Positive apologetics:* Positive apologetics proceeds from a true understanding and appreciation of whatever is good and acceptable in a person's culture. It consists in taking due consideration of the individual with whom we speak and in removing the personal, concrete obstacles which prevent his or her ready acceptance of the kerygma.

6. *Evangelization:* Once the unbeliever has acquired a sense of God and appears spiritually ready to accept God's message, a short résumé of salvation history is to be presented in such a way that the compelling fact of Christ as the Lord comes out with striking clarity. In a technical world where individuals feel themselves lost "in a lonely crowd," stressing facts such as God coming to us in Christ and Christ living among us as our friend and personally loving each of us helps to awaken men and women to hope and helps to evoke conversion.

7. *Shock:* Shock is the internal spiritual change in a person whereby he or she accepts Christ as the Lord. The catechist, by close observation, can recognize this conversion by such signs as repentance, prayer, a new eagerness to meet Christ, living according to the Christian pattern, and so on.

Final Resolutions: Pan-African Catechetical Study Week: Katigondo, 1964

I. Having in view the common love for Holy Scripture which unites all Christians, the needs of the ecumenical movement, and the absolute need for Scripture in the vernacular, the Pan-African Catechetical Conference earnestly requests the hierarchies in all African territories, where deemed advisable, to contact the Protestant authorities in order to work together for the early publication of both the Old and the New Testaments in versions adequate both exegetically and linguistically.

We recommend that, where hierarchies judge it advisable, permission be sought for Catholics to make use of Protestant editions in the meantime.

II. In view of the importance of symbols in the liturgy and of the necessity for future liturgical adaptation in the spirit of the "Constitution on the Sacred Liturgy," the Pan-African Catechetical Study Week recommends:

1) that hierarchies be requested to make strong submissions to the Post-Conciliar Liturgical Commission in favor of emphasizing in the revised ritual of the Mass and sacraments the principal symbolic values contained in them as, for instance, the symbolism of the Word, the sacred meal, and the covenant sealed in blood;

2) that machinery be set up by the participants in the study week for the promotion of scientific research, experimentation, and exchange of information concerning the employment of symbols in: (a) liturgical celebrations as provided for in article 40 of the constitution; (b) the catechumenate; (c) priestless services; (d) seasonal, festival, social, domestic, and other rites; biblical services; and catechetical celebrations.

Furthermore, it is urged that African priests be selected and scientifically trained so that they may take the initiative in such research and experimentation.

Reprinted from *Teaching All Nations* 1 (1964), pp. 521–523, by permission of the East Asian Pastoral Institute.

III. The Pan-African Catechetical Study Week earnestly recommends that confirmation be administered to newly baptized adults within the framework of baptismal initiation and that, where the bishop is not available, a priest be delegated by him to administer this sacrament.

IV. In the spirit of the "Constitution on the Sacred Liturgy" which presents Lent as the time of preparation for baptism, the Pan-African Catechetical Study Week earnestly desires that paschal time become the time for completing the sacramental initiation of the newly baptized adults according to the tradition of the Fathers (mystagogy) and that for the other Christians it be a time for deepening their sacramental life and their Christian commitment.

Furthermore, it desires that, with this in view, the ordinary may be able to give permission for the celebration of the Easter-week liturgy on the Sundays of paschal tide.

V. Realizing the lack of preparation of seminarists and future missionaries for their primordial task as catechists and pastors, the Pan-African Catechetical Study Week earnestly recommends that seminaries and scholasticate houses grasp still better the supreme importance of catechetical training and take the necessary steps to make it more efficacious.

The whole training of future priests should tend to make them true messengers of the Word and genuine pastors after the example of Jesus Christ.

1) Let ecclesiastical studies, therefore, begin with a general introduction to the mystery of Christ, a mystery which throws light on the whole history of the human race, is unceasingly at work in the Church, and is carried on through the priestly ministry; let the teaching of all subjects converge upon a better understanding of this central mystery (cf. "Constitution on the Sacred Liturgy," no. 16).

2) The participants in the study week warn against the wrong use of scholastic method, but its qualities of clarity and precision are to be retained. Let there be greater concern to teach theology in such a way as to prepare future priests to proclaim the Good News of Christ in a living and concrete manner and in harmony with the thinking and feeling of the peoples of Africa. For this purpose all Christian dogma should be presented in the living way in which God has given us his message through the Bible and the universal tradition of the Church.

3) Let the spiritual training of future priests be centered on the liturgical life. It is by living and understanding this life that they will best prepare themselves for their function as catechists (cf. "Constitution on the Sacred Liturgy," no. 17).

4) Let them be made well aware of the problems of our day, be brought up-to-date on the progress made in pedagogy and psychology, and learn how to draw profit from this for their ministry.

5) Greater importance should be given to catechetical practice so that they can hand on, in a way both concrete and adapted to their hearers, the message they have deeply studied in their course of theology. In order to develop in them a strong apostolic personality modeled on that of the Good Shepherd, let them be initiated into human, personal, and community contacts both with the faithful and with those outside the fold.

VI. The Pan-African Catechetical Study Week:

1) favors the development of projects under the auspices of the Pontifical Works for the Propagation of the Faith to provide finances for the training and maintenance of catechists, for bursaries to help with the formation of specialists in catechetics, particularly Africans, and for the development of suitable textbooks;

2) recommends that a *missio canonica* be conferred by the bishop on all properly trained catechists; and

3) recommends that this *missio canonica* be conferred during an appropriate liturgical ceremony.

VII. In view of the constitution of the Council on Mass Media, the influence of radio programs in African society, the fact that in Addis Ababa there exists a Lutheran radio station, "Voice of the Gospel," and in other countries both government and independent stations, we request the hierarchies to consider the possibility of Catholic collaboration in these religious programs.

The Implications of Vatican II for the Mission in Asia: Manila, 1967

M OST ASIAN COUNTRIES have gained political independence recently. Some remain friendly to the West; some, not; and the half of Asia under communist rule is closed to all foreign contacts. The Asian countries, generally poor, are besieged by a host of problems, the steady increase in population being one of the most significant. Rapid social changes have followed the spread of education, modern means of communication, and the new technology. Asia is becoming secular in many aspects of its life.

There is a blossoming of *local cultures*, a renaissance of old *religions*, and the rise of *new religions* alongside a process to secularize society under the influence of Marxism in its different forms. A new materialism is spreading fast among the educated and the wealthier classes. These trends also include a greater concern for such values as justice and freedom, which are crucial to human spiritual development.

Asia has awakened like a giant that has long slumbered. It is eager and impatient to find its identity in the world of today. Asia – with its population of about two-thirds of the human race – presents a most complex situation.

Any missionary work in Asia must begin with a deep understanding of the forces at work there and of the aspirations, thought patterns, and even sentiments of the Asian people as they emerge from a long period of relative insignificance.

Public Image of the Church

In order to bring the Word of God to the peoples of Asia, we should

This reading is a report of discussion groups led by: Fr. Tissa Balasuriya, OMI; Fr. D. S. Amalorpavadass; Fr. Hans Staffner, SJ; and Fr. Engelbert Zeitler, SVD. Reprinted from *Teaching All Nations* 4 (1967), pp. 319–326, by permission of the East Asian Pastoral Institute.

reflect on how the Church today appears to them and compare it with
the ideals traced in the Second Vatican Council. The Church is admired
for her great contribution to education and social services, especially
during the past century. Many, however, felt that the Church is still
by and large on the fringe of society; conversions were merely among
culturally disintegrated or backward groups. She appeared glaringly
foreign in her way of life, her liturgy, architecture, and even her mentality. Conversion meant a rupture with the cultural life of the country.

The churches often presented the image of a ghetto group that
seemed more concerned with the defense of its privileges than the
building up of the human community. In spite of their great services,
the church institutions with their dominating network of educational
and social services have developed into symbols of countersigns instead
of signs of incarnated and redemptive love. Far from creating healthy,
interpersonal relations, the churches have in some cases tended to promote antagonism, jealousy, and even bitterness.

Since the social teachings of the Church are almost unknown in
Asia, the institutional Church is often identified with the rich.

The Church is seen as a source of material security, a distributor
of services; this tends to encourage paternalism. The priestly and
religious life does not seem to impress others as a sign of Christian
poverty and detachment, a point of special importance, since Asian
religions value these aspects very highly.

Vatican II Directives

In this context the fundamental directives of the Second Vatican Council come as a salutary reminder of the nature and mission of the Church.
The Church is recalled by the council to her pristine awareness of being a people of God formed by the Word of God nourished by his bread
and life. Christians are to live in personal communion with each other
and to give unselfish service to all. Thus, their lives are a sign and
manifestation of salvation offered to all mankind by God in Jesus Christ
and the Holy Spirit.

The Church has to rediscover the dimensions of community
dialogue, collegiality, freedom, and disinterested service. She is called
to become incarnate in the local cultures, and to dialogue sincerely with
all Christians, all believers, and also with those who do not profess any
religion. From being a ghetto, the Church is called to give herself to
the modern world, to share in its hopes and anxieties, and to collaborate
with all people of good will for the building of human communities of
fraternity, equality, justice, and peace. In so doing, the Church would

witness to the values of Christ in a manner intelligible and acceptable to people in our times.

Trends within Asia and the guidelines given by Vatican II indicate the manner in which the mission to Asia must be conceived today. It is particularly necessary to have a theology of the *plurality of religions* and of the mission of the Church in this context.

The resurgence of the Asian religions should not be considered only as an obstacle to the spread of Christianity; it could be, in the plan of God, a source of purification of Christians or a providential indication of the need for new approaches or a call for a different form of the Church's presence and activity in this part of the world.

Our attitude toward religions like Buddhism in many cases does not seem justifiable. In the past, conversion to Christianity meant often a total denial of one's religious and cultural tradition and a rejection of all that was Buddhist. It is now suggested that all the elements in Buddhism that are good should be maintained even when someone is converted to Jesus Christ.

Similarly, it was said that missionaries generally took it for granted that a follower of Confucius had to give up his loyalty to Confucius in order to be loyal to Jesus Christ. However, the well-known convert Dom Lou points out that this is a totally mistaken idea. He professes to be a Confucianist and a Christian. Brahmabhanduev Upadhyaya, a famous Bengali convert, stated: "I am Hindu by birth, I am Catholic by rebirth, I am a Catholic Hindu." And the Buddhist monk Vajrapanna quite recently expressed his conviction that his loyalty to the Buddha did not prevent him from following the teaching of Jesus Christ.

Attitude Toward Other Religions

Our attitude toward other religions should be one of deep respect motivated by love, the essence of Christianity. In the past we may have been sometimes wanting in this respect, especially in the manner in which Christianity was first introduced to several Asian countries. These religions are sensitive to our want of respect, and our approach should be one of delicate charity and disinterested service.

As a basis for a Christian approach to the religions of Asia, we may examine the various phases of the realization of the Christian mystery, Incarnation, Redemption, and Fulfillment. Just as Christ was incarnated, Christianity too should incarnate itself in these religions in everything except sin. Then, just as Christ purified and transformed humanity by his death and resurrection, the religions of Asia must undergo a mystical death and resurrection in Christ and find their fulfillment in the Church. The followers of all religions have to relive the paschal mystery. Here it is good to remark that in the past, in spite of Roman documents, we in our actual practice stressed too much the aspects of rupture, judgment, and condemnation. Today, we should stress Christianity as continuity and fulfillment.

First Approach to Persons of Other Faiths and Unbelievers

We must endeavor to work in solidarity with the people of our time unreservedly in all that is good. We must make common cause with all men and women of goodwill in the task of building the human community as recommended by the "Pastoral Constitution on the Church in the Modern World." While doing so we love others in their otherness.

Through commitment to human values, especially the struggle for social reform, Christians must bear witness to their spirit of loving service. They should, through such common work, endeavor to reveal to others the deepest nature of the Christian mystery which motivates them. Christ could, where opportunity presents itself, be presented as the fulfillment of human aspirations.

If this is at the level of human values, we have another approach at the level of religious values. To discover the religious values it is not enough to study Asian religions in the books. We must study them as practiced by people, by living with the followers of their religions, by closely observing them, and by sympathetically understanding their religious practices and life. Then our approach will sometimes take quite another turn. Theoretically, for example, we may have the impression that we should condemn Buddhism as atheistic, but at the practical level a good number of Buddhists have a devotion to a personal God.

In our approach toward Buddhism, Hinduism, or other oriental religions, we feel that Christianity would do well to meet them not vertically but horizontally, for in the former approach there could be only confrontation and not dialogue. We could therefore start by discovering common values and living them in practice. Opportunities will offer themselves to us, at a certain stage, to lead others to discover and to recognize what is unique and specific in Christianity, and this is needed for the fulfillment of these religions. In other words, it is through immanence that we lead them to transcendence. This can be better understood and further clarified through the stages of mystical experience. Thus, an encounter of religions at the level of experience of God can be recommended as an approach.

However, our problem is to know how the followers of other religions may come to recognize Christ as the only Incarnation and the culmination of revelation and intervention of God in human history. It was felt by the participants in the workshop that it was not so much by verbal assertions as by deeds and Christian witnessing that the uniqueness of Christianity would be understood and recognized. Kerygma as the verbal proclamation of the Good News has to be accompanied by signs; these signs could be physical or moral miracles. The universal, unequivocal, and infallible sign of Christ as the only Incarnation and final intervention of God in history is still fraternal love: "By this will all men know that you are my disciples if you love one another." This love or this witnessing can take various forms, e.g., disinterested social service, etc.

Religion and Culture

A question was raised as to the type of culture which should be taken into consideration in the adaptation of the Church to the local cultures of Asia. Local cultures are continually changing. Consequently, adaptation to local culture nowadays means adaptation to the present culture of a nation which has roots in the past and is open to the assimilation of what is best in the technological and scientific culture of the West.

It was strongly urged that an *institute* be set up for the study of religion, culture, sociology, and anthropology. The bishops and religious superiors should plan the initiation of the new missionaries into the language, history, culture, customs, and traditions of the country they will work in. The Congregation of the *Propaganda* should be requested to grant subsidies to such a project.

It was suggested that those Asians who are sent for studies abroad be sent preferably after their ordination and, if possible, after two or three years of ministry. If they are sent out as seminarians, it may happen that, during the formative ages of eighteen to twenty-five, they may lose contact with or even interest in their own culture.

It was proposed to request *Asian bishops* to *foster* and *accelerate* the means of cultural adaptation as part of their missionary activity and, thus, to promote the love of their own cultures.

Priests should be helped to renew themselves, according to the Vatican council, by seminars of about two weeks' duration. Priests should be trained to become sensitive toward others, to be capable of loving the men and women of our time, and to render disinterested service.

Renewal of Content of Catechesis

The theological orientations given by Vatican II, and further elaborated since then, call for a development of the content of *catechesis* especially with reference to the mission in Asia. The Asian churches have been built and inspired by a theology which has severe limitations, a theology which the Second Vatican Council has ordered us to remedy and elaborate.

Theology determines the content of catechesis; catechesis builds the thought patterns, relationships, and structures within any Christian grouping. We can evaluate the catechesis and the theology in terms of the type of Church they generate. Our missionaries in Asia have in the past done wonderful work; this is never in question. They were, however, inspired by an earlier theology, the limitations of which were not due to a want of generosity on the part of the missionaries. Vatican II has indicated the guidelines of renewal . . . and we must courageously apply these to Asia.

Theology and catechesis must be reoriented to give the *universal dimension* of the reality of God revealed in Jesus Christ. The deepest truths of Christianity have the whole of mankind as their participants and beneficiaries whether these be aware of it or not. God is the Creator and Father of all; Christ is the Lord of history and Redeemer of mankind; and the Holy Spirit works in every human heart from the first moment of creation. These truths can make Christians aware of the spiritual riches of all humankind and at the same time make others see in Christianity the fulfillment of their own highest aspirations. These truths must be put in the *forefront* of our theology and also in our catechesis.

This requires a renewal of theology and catechesis, which had tended to present God in Christ almost unconsciously, as a particularist God conceived of according to the philosophies and religious traditions of a Hebraic and a Greco-Roman civilization. The Christian worship of God in liturgy thus came to Asia as a set of unintelligible signs—be they language, rite, ritual, or even dress. The liturgy, still very Roman, needs a divesting of what are only religious rites of a particular culture; only then will it be able to become incarnate in Asia.

The Practical Renewal of Catechesis

These considerations indicate the need for a wide change in the ways of thinking among all levels in Asia and among those who train priests and religious in Asia. Textbooks need to be better adapted; the method of the catechumenate should be reconsidered in order to seriously take account of the environment from which neophytes come. Catechumens should be required to give up only what is positively and clearly wrong or superstitious.

The previous methods of the catechumenate were rather pitifully lacking in cultural or religious sensitivity, so much so that the extent of the conversion to Christianity tended to be also the measure of the success of cultural and religious segregation. We must not demand of catechumens what Christ does not demand.

The content of catechesis should be gradually presented in such a manner as to be expessed in the terminology and cultural context of the Asian countries.

Social Dimension of Catechesis in Asia

The discussions revealed that the Church all over Asia is a most important agency of education and social service. However, there is *little commitment to social reform* and to the struggle for social justice. Indeed, social justice seems to be neglected generally, even in adult catechesis, in preaching, and in the media of mass communication. Hardly anywhere does the Church appear as the champion of social justice even though it helps with assistance of the poor. Social dynamism is more evident among the Marxists, liberal communists, and socialists than among the believers in Jesus Christ.

Our social service approach tends to perpetuate the mentality of paternalism-infantilism with reference to rich and poor and even clergy and laity.

The liturgy which has the possibility of instructing the Christian community does not seem to inspire a consciousness of the needs of social justice. In many countries we do not find any planned communication of the social teaching of the Church on a fairly wide scale. The sacramental catechesis of children seems to engage most of the energies of personnel and funds in almost all the countries.

Reevaluation of Apostolic Methods

The changed circumstances demand changes in apostolic methods. It was often mentioned that the Church in its institutional aspects sometimes presented itself as a countersign to the Christian profession of poverty and respect for human personality. Dialogue within the Church should go side by side with dialogue with those outside the Church.

It was suggested that smaller groups might be a better method of witnessing to the Gospel than big institutions.

The ecclesial dimension of the apostolate should manifest itself by rallying all the pastoral activities around the bishops, the heads of the local Church. The religious should keep themselves at the disposal of the bishop and look to him for guidance in all their undertakings while the bishops should primarily regard themselves as servants of their people and as members of that college of bishops which is responsible for the whole Church and her mission.

Religious poverty and obedience should take new forms, and the relations between clergy and laity should be more fraternal.

Recommendations

1) That an All-Asian Bishops' Conference be established for Asia. This conference could hold regular meetings or general plenary sessions in order to give detailed and concerted guidelines for the apostolate in Asia.

2) That institutes for the study of culture and religions in Asia be established in mutual collaboration between bishops and religious orders.

3) That regional institutes be set up to initiate new missionaries in the language, culture, and religious customs of each place.

General Conclusions of the
Medellin International Study Week: 1968

1) In the past few years there has been a considerable renewal of catechetical activity in Latin America and in the whole Catholic world. This renewal shows the will of the Church to carry on its mission in a world of change. To educate in the faith the younger Christian generation (the adults of tomorrow) and the adults of today – the task of catechesis – is a fundamental aspect of the mission of the Church. To fail in this task would be tantamount to treason, both to the human race, to which the Church must bring salvation, and to the Gospel which the Church has received.

2) In a continent like Latin America, such a task has particular importance. Historically, this continent lives to a great extent within a Christian tradition which impregnates both the lives of individuals and the social-cultural context.

The Church retains in these countries vast possibilities for influence. This puts her in a position of great responsibility. The problem she faces consists in accepting the past, inserting herself into the present, and looking toward the future. It is impossible for the Church to ignore the richness of four centuries of Christian tradition. On the other hand, she cannot stagnate in the forms of the past, some of which, besides being ambiguous, have become increasingly inadequate or even harmful because of historical changes.

3) The Latin American continent is subjected today to acute and rapid changes:

Economic: Vast changes in systems of production demand today that all have a greater share in whatever is produced and in the whole economic process. The concentration of wealth and power in the hands

Reprinted from *The Medellin Papers,* eds. Johannes Hofinger and Terence J. Sheridan, 1969, pp. 213–219, by permission of the East Asian Pastoral Institute.

of a few, backed by the international economic system, is a serious obstacle to integral development today.

Demographic: In the next forty years, an increase in population of 400 million can be foreseen. Young people already represent more than half the population. The values of these young people are frequently at variance with those of the adult minority.

Social: All social types can be found – from the rural to the urban. The passive masses are sunk in a kind of fatalism without creativity or hope, while certain minorities seek even violent revolution as the only road toward a radical and necessary change of structures.

Cultural: The awareness of political and economic independence increases the desire for freedom and the search for a new type of man and woman in a society that becomes more and more pluralistic and secularized.

4) As a consequence, those responsible for catechesis face a series of tasks which are complicated and difficult to combine. They must:

• promote the evolution of traditional forms of faith characteristic of a great part of the Christian people and bring about new forms.

• evangelize and catechize masses of simple people, frequently illiterate, and at the same time meet the needs of students and intellectuals who are the most alive and dynamic sectors of society.

• purify traditional forms of influence and at the same time discover a new way of influencing contemporary forms of expression and communication in a society that becomes increasingly secularized.

• put to use all the resources of the Church in accomplishing these tasks and at the same time renounce forms of power and prestige that are not evangelical.

5) The International Catechetical Study Week of Medellin has made it possible to face these questions with the help of experts from Latin America and the whole world. It was impossible to find immediate and definite solutions. For this reason the catechetical study week, aware of the immense effort being made throughout the Church for a renewal of catechesis, has avoided putting together a document of a general character and prefers to underline certain points basic to carrying out the task of catechetical research in Latin America and the rest of the world.

6) We want to stress the demands of pluralism in the joint pastoral effort. The situations in which catechesis evolves are diverse – from those of the patriarchal type, where traditional forms are still accepted, to those of the most advanced contemporary urban civilizations. One

of the aims of the study week has been to stress the richness existing in the diversity of viewpoints and of forms which exist in catechesis. It is impossible, in view of this, to think in terms of a universal catechesis of the monolithic type. Increasing pluralism, while a sign of life and energy, demands a new type of unity which must be expressed in a new form of words. The study week desires that collaboration at all levels be intensified and that national and international exchanges be multiplied so as to promote this unity of faith in diversity.

7) The pluralism of situations and of the corresponding catechesis requires that we remember, in any situation, the pastoral activity of the Church must be eminently evangelizing so that a reality of faith is not presupposed until after the necessary verifications. The same pluralistic situation obliges us to recall constantly that the Christian message, as well as the existential language spoken by the world of today, demands that we do not reduce the Gospel to words or mere modifications of language but announce it by visible signs acceptable to modern people. This announcement will consist largely in the testimony of a life committed to the service of humankind and the promotion of love and unity.

8) A joint pastoral effort also demands the frank and definitive acceptance of the process of social change. Whatever the situation, those responsible must strive to meet it, knowing that the situation is in evolution and that one of the tasks of catechesis is helping that evolution and giving it some meaning. The forms of evolution can be very different, from gradual to violently revolutionary. In every case it is imperative that we make not only a diagnosis but also an effort of imagination to foresee and promote new forms of existence animated by the Gospel.

9) Today we are confronted with a phenomenon which is deeply influencing the values, attitudes, and type of existence of humankind — the mass media, or media of social communication. This phenomenon is now an irreversible historical fact. It is leading, even in Latin America, to a kind of universal culture — the culture of the image. This is a sign of the times that the Church cannot ignore: She must ponder on it "immediately and most energetically" (*Inter Mirifica*, no. 13) in order to use it wisely for the global promotion of humanity on its way to Christ.

Catechesis must start from the situation created by this media phenomenon in order to obtain an incarnate presentation of the Christian message. It is urgent, therefore, that catechetical institutes conduct a serious investigation into the effects of the media and find out exactly what is the best means of using them in the work of evangelization.

This investigation could lead to the discovery of new forms which would better express the presence of the words of salvation in a changing, strongly socialized world.

10) Among the different forms of existence, community life has particular importance. Catechesis, therefore, cannot limit itself to the individual dimensions of life. The prophetic mission of the Church, within which catechesis has its place, today encounters serious obstacles which stem from some of her institutions and distort her image in the world. In view of our task as catechists, we perceive with keen awareness the need for a thorough evangelical revision, following the line already begun by Vatican II, for instance: revising certain forms of authority as exercised at times by the Roman congregations and by this or that nunciature; revising the relationship of bishops to priests and laity who would like to see their responsibility better acknowledged; revising relations with the civil authorities; and reconsidering what concerns the present property of the Church at all levels.

11) Contemporary catechesis, in agreement with a more adequate theology of revelation, recognizes in historical situations and in authentic human aspirations the first sign to which we must be attentive in order to discover the plan of God for the men and women of today. Such situations, therefore, are an indispensable part of the content of catechesis. The progressive discovery of the total sense and definitive orientation of such aspirations and tensions, verified at each moment of the historical process, is an essential task of the prophetic mission of the Church.

To grasp the total significance of these human realities, it will be necessary to live fully with the people of our time. Thus, these human realities will be progressively and seriously interpreted in our own time within their present context in the light of the living experiences of the people of Israel, of the man Jesus, and of the sacramental, ecclesial community where the Spirit of the risen Christ is alive and continues to operate. Thus, a clearer understanding of humanity will help toward a deepening of the Christian message, and this deepening will, in its turn, promote a better understanding of humankind.

12) In each case, catechesis has its fundamental message which consists in uniting two aspects of reality. This unity is complex, differentiated, and dynamic. It exists:

- between human values and their relationship to God.
- between the projects of men and women and the salvific project of God, realized in Christ.
- between human history and the history of salvation;
- between the experience of humankind and the revealing action of God.
- between the progressive realization of Christianity within time and its eschatological fulfillment.

This is why catechesis lives in permanent tension between continuity and rupture.

13) The awareness of the Christian message has an evolutionary character. Already within biblical tradition we find various reinterpretations of certain basic elements of revelation. Through them the authentic understanding of the revealed truth goes ever deeper.

Also, in the Church, tradition is a living thing. The progressive awareness of the integral sense of revelation moves always to the rhythm of newly emerging individual and collective human experiences. That is why the fidelity of the Church to revelation is dynamic. The most important reason for modern reinterpretation is that the old interpretation reflects a pretechnical and patriarchal mentality, whereas thinking today is technical and democratic.

14) The language which the Church speaks has a peculiar importance. It will affect not only the simpler forms of teaching – catechisms, homilies – in the local communities but also the more universal forms of the magisterium. A constant effort is required so that it may become possible to perceive how this message of salvation expressed in Scripture, liturgy, the magisterium, and witness may become for modern people the words of life. It is not enough, therefore, to repeat or explain the message. It is necessary to express it always in new forms.

15) A catechesis open to the action of God demands that catechists walk to the same rhythms and at the same pace as the catechized, sharing as much as possible their lives. The catechetical process implies the need to meet human situations, to understand them in themselves, and to interpret them in the light of Christ dead and risen in order to induce a personal answer of faith.

16) The practical way of introducing the necessary changes demands audacity and reflection. The change has to be realized through specialized and ordinary groups. The specialized groups, working in close contact with catechetical institutes, take on the function of

laboratories and testing grounds for any investigation, whose results will then be adopted progressively by the ordinary groups. This demands a permanent "inventiveness" that some call "experimentation." The International Catechetical Study Week of Medellin expresses its desire that everywhere working teams be multiplied, with pastors, catechists, theologians, and specialists in human sciences coming together and pooling their experiences. It is necessary that these teams be given adequate tools for work and the indispensable freedom of action. The creation of a new type of Christian, so necessary for the Church of today, depends to a large extent on the work of these teams.

17) *Conclusion:* In the great opportunities emerging today in Latin America, we recognize a call of God who, through the action of the Holy Spirit, works in the world actualizing the living and operative presence of Christ in the human community. That presence urges everyone to be coresponsible through reflection, interpretation, expression, and action according to his or her proper role in the Church and the gifts of the Spirit.

Conclusions of the Roman International Catechetical Congress: 1971

Preamble

The International Catechetical Congress, convened in Rome by the Sacred Congregation for the Clergy from September 20 to 25, 1971, has been not only a gathering of pastors and experts from the whole world but also a significant act in the life of the Church. The fact that bishops, priests, laypeople, and religious have prayed and reflected together and the fact that participants from numerous countries have shown the same concern are signs of the importance placed on catechetical work in the world by the entire contemporary ecclesial community.

At the end of this meeting and in relation to the fundamental themes of the congress, the following conclusions are released.

Necessities, Difficulties, and Possibilities of the Ministry of the Word in Catechetical Matters of Our Present Day

1) Christian catechesis is a fundamental modality of the ministry of the word in the Church. It should participate in the preeminent, permanent, and prior character of the ministry of preaching at the heart of the pastoral service that the Church offers to men and women.

2) Catechetical activity has developed in the world during the

Excerpted from *International Catechetical Congress,* ed. William J. Tobin, 20–25 September 1971, pp. 121–128; © 1972 Publications Office, United States Catholic Conference, Washington, D.C., used with permission. These conclusions, drawn from the recommendations of various language and special interest groups, were grouped around the four themes treated by the daily main addresses. This unofficial translation is drawn from the French original.

course of this century according to a long journey of renewal. It is a very positive and providential phenomenon in the life of the Church.

The attention to the age and interests of the recipients; the search for an active pedagogy in the education of the faith, especially in the light of biblical, liturgical, and ecclesiological renewal; the progressive insertion into the catechetical responsibilities of different sectors of believers (religious, lay, etc.) in local communities – all these are significant aspects of a deep desire to adapt catechesis to human reality, in fidelity to the demands of the message of salvation.

3) Nevertheless, this ecclesial activity today presents very serious questions to those involved in the catechetical ministry. The efforts made in so many areas, even if they have enriched these sectors of activity in the Church, disclose some new horizons. Some immense needs appear to which it is necessary to respond without delay. These necessities, with their context of difficulties and possibilities, originate from the profound changes in the people, society, and Church of our day.

4) Catechesis is for humankind. The point of departure for catechetical activity is humanity's situation. One of the riches of catechetical work these last decades is the discovery of the multiple aspects of human situations: the individual dimension, the family situation, the cultural and social situations. Men and women cannot be considered apart from these multiple aspects in which they exist.

To announce the word of God to people means, therefore, to transmit to them a living word in the total context in which they live. In this sense, attention given to the situation is not only a pedagogical technique but also a fundamental demand of the word itself, because the Incarnation concerns the real person, to communicate to him or her the life of the Son of God.

5) The human situations that the Gospel message should transform and preserve are multiple and changing. To indicate only a few of them, the congress has been especially attentive to the situation of the young churches which work in new countries and in the midst of rapid social change. Development and the proclamation of the message should become a word of liberation for all persons. Consequently, catechesis will show that true salvation can only come from the Incarnate Word and that the salvation brought by Jesus has the power to transform the world even in its social and political aspects.

6) One of the major transformations in contemporary society takes

place in the area of education and in the manner of acquiring and transmitting culture. The formation of men and women also occurs outside school and extends to the whole of life under the form of ongoing education. On the other hand, the media of mass communication transform profoundly the procedures of study and education.

As a consequence, to correspond to such new situations, great attention is given to adult catechesis. There is the recognition that the catechesis of children is more than ever dependent on the faith of adults. Adults and families claim a catechetical priority.

7) Humanity's situation is equally religious. The isolation of religious groups has been succeeded by broad information and multiple contacts between religious groups. Christian catechesis should not ignore such an ecumenical dimension. In the context of pluralism, it will educate at times to a profound sense of particular identity while at the same time maintaining an openness without reticence or sectarianism. With regard to non-Christian religions the missionary spirit will show itself from the beginning by its openness and comprehension, without which there is no point of valid witness.

8) In such a context, where the social, familial, and religious situations of people are changing rapidly, the forms of catechesis themselves cannot remain where they are, under penalty of rapidly hardening and becoming unfaithful to the task entrusted by the Savior to his disciples.

If there was a time when catechetical endeavors could be accomplished essentially by a pedagogy of assimilation, today it seems that our catechetical activity would be impossible without a pedagogy of creativity.

This means that we should permit Christians (children, adolescents, or adults) to discover the manner in which their Christian life, the testimony of their faith, and their word can offer meaning to the human situation and by it make the Church arise.

9) Such creativity of the faith sees a particular need in the regions of the world where there exists a strong tradition of popular Christianity. This ordinarily has allowed generations of men and women to live the Gospel and to participate in Church life in a simple and, at the same time, vibrant way.

We cannot respond to the multiple forces of contemporary culture and of development by promoting the old popular models of Christian formation without a serious risk of degradation of the faith and ecclesial life. This implies an unrestricted effort.

Nature, Goals, and Process of Catechesis in the Church's Pastoral Activity

1) Revelation, viewed in its dynamic and comprehensive nature, involves the self-communication of God as Person to persons. It is in the context of this interpersonal relationship that the designs of God for humankind in Christ must be understood. Revelation is more than the communication of truths in formulas adapted to cultural situations.

Human experience not only is the milieu and medium of God's revealing action but also contributes to the content of this communication. Thus, a catechesis that is situational and environmental is called for.

2) God's revealing activity is not limited to Christian communities. In fact, all humanity falls under the universality of the action of the Spirit. There is a need to discern God's presence and interpret his activity expressed in all legitimate movements.

3) Besides the necessity for mass education to provide the proper opportunities for human development with dignity – which must be ongoing in time and space and in intensity and depth – people must be inserted continually into the life of faith. The language of catechesis varies not only with age levels but also with subgroups within cultures.

4) Hence, the need for adult catechesis is to be regarded as the main form of catechesis to which all others are ordered. A faith response proportioned to one's level of development within community is needed. People should be led to reflect upon experience, interpret it within community, and develop reformulations and reassimilations that express a truly adult life of faith. The witness of the adult community is the source and goal of youth catechesis. Above all, parents should receive assistance in their indispensable role of mediating the faith to their children. Recognition should be made of the plurality of theological understandings and insights. Though these are a factual reality and legitimate, polarity should be avoided through careful explanations and support for sound catechetical programs.

5) This adult religious education best takes place within small groups. Such groups can really become the faith community by their very witnessing and style of life. In this faith, ambient children and young people can be initiated into Christian life.

6) This is what it means to baptize children in the faith of parents

and the faith of the community. An extended period of preparation of parents before infant Baptism is desirable. Concerning the first reception of Communion and Penance, each child should be treated as an individual, exercising his or her own free choice. The right of parents to determine their child's readiness should be respected. Further study is required concerning the theology of Confirmation.

7) The relationship between catechesis and theology and between revelation and experience requires great study and clarification. A more dynamic interrelationship should be explored. The mass media of social communication should be considered in their revelational context. Men and women ought to acquire expertise in their use and interpretation, especially through the establishment of media centers. These should be established for language groups and cultures. In this way the various bishops' conferences can share expenses and resources.

8) The ongoing education of the clergy, beginning with pastoral catechesis in the seminary and continuing thereafter, should be the prime concern of local bishops and episcopal conferences.

The Object or Content of Catechesis and the Mutual Relationship that Exists Between the Sources of Catechesis

1) The Evangelists announced the one Gospel of Jesus Christ in different ways, according to the groups of people to which they addressed themselves. Following their example, the Church today feels itself impelled by the Holy Spirit to open to men and women of different cultural milieus and various levels of education the Christian message of salvation. This is done in their language in a way proportionate to their understanding. Thus, the vital force of the light of Christ develops its universal richness.

2) Scripture is the source and object of catechesis. It establishes contact with the message and facts which permit humankind to come to the faith and become witnesses.

Catechists should consider the fundamental expressions of the Gospel, in which immediately there are expressed and discovered the experiences, the anguish, and the expectations of humanity. Thus, the ministry of the word becomes capable of clarifying for people of different ages their proper situation in the light of Christ and according to a method suited to them. Thus, the written word of God makes possible the unexpected and important experiences of their lives. Catechists who consider themselves at the service of humankind, especially of those who belong to the lowest social categories, will pay attention to their ways of thought and expression and will use the means of communication that have a relation to their real lives.

3) All this should be done under the direction of the Church's shepherds, to whom the care of the faithful has been entrusted by the authority of Christ. Hence, the teaching of the Apostles, by the action of the Holy Spirit, can be witnessed in an ever new manner in all tongues and languages, and the unity of the faith in Jesus Christ will be preserved. In this way, the magisterium of the Church guarantees to all the faithful and all local churches their participation in the faith of the one Church of Christ.

4) The faith founded on Jesus Christ expresses itself in a common confession of faith and the eucharistic memorial. The confession of faith is much more than a formula. It is a doxology; it is the sign of the communion in the one faith and in the one eucharistic table. It signifies in the same way as the eucharistic prayer that the believer lives in communion with the Father through Jesus Christ in the love of the Holy Spirit.

5) In the light of these affirmations, we can place in relief the criteria that should inspire the identification and presentation of content, which can be expressed with the global formula – fidelity to God, fidelity to humankind.

Fidelity to God. Catechesis should safeguard in its contents: (a) the organicity of the Christian message with respect to the hierarchy of truths it contains; (b) the originality of the Christian message in expressing its triple tension – christocentric, theo- and trinitariancentric, and anthropocentric – and (c) the historical nature of the economy of salvation, which is actualized in the present but refers to a past of which it is the successor and development and announces a future in which it will be accomplished.

Fidelity to humankind. Catechesis should: (a) emphasize in its contents the vitality of the Christian message, that is, its capacity to set people in motion and push them toward an ever greater maturing of their global option of faith; (b) make the content of the Christian message accessible to people of all ages, times, and cultures by interpreting it and adapting it without changes or alterations; (c) make explicit the integrity of the Christian message as a goal, not a point of departure for catechesis; and (d) in identifying its contents, refer to a plurality of sources – for example, revelation: written or

Church, the first and formal source of the divine message—or all the experiences that manifest human existence and its problems—the source of interpretations of human existence.

Present-day Pastoral Exigencies of Catechesis

The catechized. Without minimizing what is done for children and young people, and even better to serve their belief in the faith, it is desirable that personnel, means of ongoing formation, and international research be dedicated to the catechesis of adults.

Confronted by their social duties, adults have to discover the meaning of the mystery of Christ in relation to the projects in which they are engaged.

Thus, catechesis should arouse a sense of responsibility for and involvement in the different tasks of social renewal. It also should endeavor to establish a dialogue with all who work for liberation and human development in a spirit of solidarity and universality (cf. motu proprio, *Octogesimo Anno*).

For those who are marginal or unadapted, the congress has tried to treat or affirm the evangelical and pastoral importance of the catechesis destined for them.

The catechists. Renewal of the catechetical ministry supposes: a diversity of catechetical ministries, effective and recognized responsibilities given to religious and laypeople, and the awakening of all Christians to the catechetical mission which takes place in proportion to their activity (parents' example is already significant).

This demands that financial priority be given to formation, before buildings and salaries, allowing for: (a) the formation of both staffs and diverse local catechists (more than has already been allowed), (b) a better understanding of the process of adult self-education, (c) a concerted and planned research effort to identify the needs of adults, (d) education to confront change and to deal with family and social relationships, (e) education in the ability to share in collaborative projects, and (f) the ability to free the power of meaning in the content of revelation.

It also demands that permanent or semipermanent staffs, restricted in number but highly qualified, be maintained to animate the work accomplished by those in the field. This underlines the importance of university institutes and the different services they can offer.

For such staffs—for permanent catechists presently involved—the release of resources for a decent salary is necessary. The duty to assist the catechists of the Third World is equally urgent.

The institutions. National centers are vitally needed for high-quality work at the regional, diocesan, and local levels. Catechetical reviews are an effective instrument for research and diffusion of knowledge. But the institutions cannot be content with carrying on that which exists today. From them is demanded an effort of prevision, of anticipation about what the situation could be twenty years from now. This effort of prevision goes side by side with the task of programming and evaluating what catechesis is achieving today. At all levels catechetical activity should be understood as a task subject to periodic revision—concerning both its institutions and its directives and guidelines—in such a way as not to be surpassed by the transformation of society and the Church.

The catholicity of collaboration. Collaboration is needed between episcopal conferences on the level of research and action, especially concerning the mass media, which go beyond the possibilities of a national conference.

Collaboration between the Holy See and episcopal conferences should be encouraged. This collaboration, evidenced by the *General Catechetical Directory* and the present congress, should be continued by regular meetings for work and study.

It is desirable that international meetings be organized regularly.

It is hoped that the Sacred Congregation for the Clergy will establish under its authority a special body of authorized and competent catechetical representatives, designated by the bishops' conferences, and that it will undertake a study of the goals, composition, and pace of work of such a commission.

Conclusions Presented by the Third World Delegates to the International Catechetical Congress

THE EVANGELIZATION of the Third World, which represents about three-fourths of the world's population, is confronted with specific problems that fall within the framework of this congress. As a matter of fact, the acute and rapid changes in the economic, demographic, social, political, and cultural spheres have placed the Third World in a critical situation of dependence and exploitation. Keenly conscious of this situation, the bishops' conferences of Latin America, Africa, and Asia have during the past few years given Christians of these continents the urgent mandate to involve themselves fully in the development and liberation of our people, especially young people and the poor.

In view of this situation and as a response to the call of our bishops, the following conditions are postulated for an effective catechetical apostolate:

a) In looking for an immediate solution to these problems, there is a danger that we may become absorbed in purely material development, such as could be provided by any aid program whether Christian or non-Christian.

To avoid this danger, we must reveal through our catechesis, beyond the economic and cultural aspects, the full dimensions of true liberation and development which can only be offered by the Risen Christ.

b) Our catechesis should lead those we are catechizing to become aware of their real situation and to become personally responsible for the purposeful development of their lives in their concrete situations.

Excerpted from *International Catechetical Congress,* ed. William J. Tobin, 20–25 September 1971, pp. 132–133; © 1972 Publications Office, United States Catholic Conference, Washington, D.C., used with permission.

c) Given the emphasis placed in our cultures on the role of the family and community, we realize that our catechesis should focus on initiation through an experience of living with a truly Christian group.

d) These problems, while pertaining to the Third World, involve the universal Church in its prophetic and salvific mission. This calls for a profound conversion of mentality and attitude of all Christians toward our areas. Together we must build up a true human solidarity in Christ without which the world cannot liberate itself from all the dominating forces that prevent humankind from realizing its full capacity in the plan of God.

e) In view of realizing this task of evangelization, special institutes and centers for formation and research are urgently needed. In these, there will be an unceasing search for a catechesis adapted to our particular situations. Only such a catechesis, starting from the elements of divine revelation latent in our indigenous cultures and traditional religions, will ensure a full flowering of the riches planted by God in the heart of every man and woman and in the authentic human aspirations of every people.

f) Such centers, which are to awaken creativity in the countries where they are situated, should be given all the support and trust needed for the accomplishment of their indispensable task.

g) In the light of the above, national directories may be prepared and issued only after the proper research has been effected. These should be geared toward a realistic solution of the present problems while affording momentum to further initiatives.

Final and Approved Resolutions of the English-speaking Language Group

THESE RESOLUTIONS are divided according to the six main areas of group discussion.

The *General Catechetical Directory:* Points for a Commentary

The *General Catechetical Directory* is to be commended for its concern to promote a variety of catecheses for local needs and cultural differences. In order to achieve the aims and goals intended for the directory, the congress should request that national hierarchies respect the latitude left by the directory both with regard to cultural differences and the legitimate hierarchy of truths. The congress should request also that the bishops' conferences declare to all that the directory is a service document promulgating guidelines and is not legislation. "The basic purpose of the directory," declared Cardinal Wright at the press conference on June 17 presenting the directory, "is to provide an orientation for religious formation, rather than to establish binding rules."

In the *General Catechetical Directory,* two concepts of revelation are found, especially in parts 2 and 3. The first views revelation as a communication of truths couched in conceptual terms and accomplished in structured situations such as classrooms. The other perceives revelation as the self-communication of God, proceeding from an incarnational point of view. What pertains to revelation and faith in the directory should be read in the context of the second, richer view, developed in this congress in the paper of Father Amalorpavadass. Such a reading will both clarify and systematize the presentation of revelation in the directory. The revelatory value of human experience is to be noted.

Excerpted from *International Catechetical Congress,* ed. William J. Tobin, 20–25 September 1971, pp. 137–141; © 1972 Publications Office, United States Catholic Conference, Washington, D.C., used with permission.

Finally the lack of a consistent ecclesiology in the directory is worthy of note.

Adult Religious Education and the Education of Parents

One of the central statements in the *General Catechetical Directory* affirms that "adult religious education deals with men who are capable of a fully responsible acceptance and hence it must be considered the chief form of catechesis. To it, all others necessarily are in some way oriented" (no. 20). Religious education is an ongoing process which cannot be terminated at any given point along the lifeline. We are continually believers in search of understanding. Every effort must be made, in response to people's needs and concerns, to help this growth process.

The education of children in religion begins long before their first day in school. Parents, as first educators, communicate to the child his or her earliest attitudes, sense of values, and Christian beliefs. Every effort should be made by episcopal conferences, ordinaries, and pastors to ascertain by practical steps the needs of their people in light of the serious parental responsibility for communicating Christian faith-life.

Some parent groups and adults are concerned that much of what is being taught in modern religious education programs and through modern religious textbooks is different from what they learned as children. Many even accuse religion teachers and textbook writers of doctrinal error, omissions, or misplaced emphasis. Recognizing the existence of this situation, which in many ways is polarizing the Christian community, this congress should want to reassure these groups about the great and valuable progress made in religious education during the past quarter of a century.

We should encourage mutual charity, honest dialogue, and a sincere search for understanding and reconciliation among the varying views within the Catholic community. It must be made clear that, in any age, the truths of the faith always remain the same and the congress would disassociate itself from any deviation from this doctrinal norm. However, the manner in which they are expressed necessarily varies according to cultural, social, and linguistic conditions. In addition, Catholic adults must be helped to realize that Catholic doctrine grows and develops.

Formation of Catechists

In developed nations. While recognizing the need for the training of catechists on all levels in the sacred sciences, the behavioral sciences, and methodology, this congress should urge that priority be given in any program of formation to the personal growth in the faith of catechists and in their roles as responsible members of the Christian community. For what catechists are speaks louder than what they say. Therefore, both during the formal training period and especially afterward in some ongoing and regular fashion, opportunities should be given for catechists to gather to share their insights and understanding of the Gospel in their life experiences, to worship together, and to foster their sense of witness and mission.

Generally, the congress should urge greater collaboration and shared research between departments of religious education at the university and institute level and, in particular, with reference to the following:

a) the adult learning process and educational strategies for determining the real interests and needs of particular groups.

b) the effective use of media, including the matching of media to meet the learning situation, and an understanding of the choice of media for particular situations and age groups.

c) the changing structures of family life, the challenges it faces, and its appropriate role in the transmission of a living faith.

The congress should urge that special attention be given to those catechists working with the physically and mentally handicapped. Such catechists require special training. If faith indeed is a personal response to the love of God in Christ, as manifested in the love of committed Christians, the mentally handicapped are capable of coming to and growing in the faith.

In keeping with the Church's social teaching, compensation for those engaged in full-time religious education should be appropriate to their preparation, competency, and responsibilities.

In mission areas. In view of the special role of the catechist in mission areas, as evidenced by the Commission for Catechists set up by the Sacred Congregation for the Evangelization of the Peoples, this function should be recognized and fully supported.

Because catechists in the missions have the great responsibility of being leaders in a community without priests or of being evangelizers, animators, or pioneers in a non-Christian area, their training should be encouraged and supported by suitable training personnel and funds. Furthermore, they should be accorded official ecclesiastical status.

In view of the vital role catechists play at the stage of young churches where priests are few, suitable Christian leaders scarce, and local support practically nonexistent, just salaries should be provided for catechists from the funds of Mission Aid societies.

The congress should recognize and fully endorse the efforts and plans made by the Commission for Catechists and urge that it continue.

Sacraments of Initiation

Baptism. The problem of preparing parents and godparents emphasizes the need to clarify Baptism as a sacrament of initiation into a believing community.

A conflict often arises between the responsibilty of the community to demand faith before Baptism and its responsibility to prepare people for Baptism.

In infant Baptism, the desirability of extending the period of preparation for parents and godparents might well be clarified by a study of Baptism in stages, as practiced, for example, in mission countries.

First Communion and Penance. Children should celebrate the sacrament of Penance for the first time when they personally are ready.

This readiness, out of respect for the sacrament, implies and requires their own free choice. Parents have the right to determine when the child is ready. Pastors have the obligation to assist the parents to exercise their right, especially by complementing the work of preparation by the parents.

Each child should be treated as an individual in the matter of the first reception of the sacraments of Holy Eucharist and Penance, and no law should seek to determine the order in which they are celebrated.

Confirmation. Since the central problem concerning Confirmation is one of theology, an urgent plea should be made for further study of the theology of Confirmation. We urge that further study be made regarding the appropriate age for the reception of the sacrament.

Relationship Between Revelation and Experience and Between Catechesis and Theology

Further study on these key problems is urged, in an effort to clarify these relationships.

Education of the Clergy

The communication of the word of God to men and women is one of the principal tasks of the priest. In other words, the priest is to be the catalyst for the development of an effective catechesis in and with his own community.

The theory and practice of catechetics should be an integral part of the seminary course.

It is strongly recommended that every priest avail himself of continuing education in the various aspects of priestly ministry. Since the bishop is the chief catechist of the diocese, it is his responsibility to see to it that such opportunities be available. In consequence, this congress should urge the national conferences of bishops to give high priority to continuing clergy education.

Final Resolution: The English-language group fully endorses the proposal made in the paper "Catechetics in Mass Media."

The Evolution of Catechetics: A Survey of Six International Study Weeks on Catechetics

LUIS ERDOZAIN

NIJMEGEN 1959, Eichstätt 1960, Bangkok 1962, Katigondo 1964, Manila 1967, Medellin 1968. Six international study weeks on catechetics within scarcely ten years – an expression of the vitality which has imbued catechetics in these recent years.[1] In all six cases, the same participants – more than two hundred bishops, missionaries, and specialists in catechetics – assembled from every corner of the earth. In each case, the same concern – the presentation of the Christian message in today's world – and on each occasion, too, that very same protagonist, the indefatigable Father Hofinger who was the initiator.

Nijmegen 1959 must be regarded as an experiment, the first step in this process which was to gather momentum during the following years. This was the first meeting dealing with the pastoral aspect of the missionary to be held at an international level. Nobody could foresee the outcome. Even the theme – "Liturgy and the Missions" – set clear limits to its terms of reference and compelled it to confine itself to just one aspect of pastoral work, namely, the liturgical renewal.

One was concerned with the return to first principles; religious and spiritual problems took pride of place; attention was given to promoting an active participation in the liturgy so as to form the basis for a participation in the work of the apostolate itself.[2] And, moreover, this was the current preoccupation of the times. There was no thought yet of the council; and, so, aspirations for any translation, any adjustment of the language used in the sacramental liturgy remained modest indeed. Yet a first step had now been taken, and there was just the breath of a hope. Despite the narrow bounds of such a restricted theme, it was by the pressure of the public at large that one has been able to

Reprinted from *Lumen Vitae* 25 (1970), pp. 7–13. Reproduced by courtesy of *Lumen Vitae*. Copyright *Lumen Vitae* 1970. Translated by Peter Jones from the French original.

assess the strength of a current which has been gathering impetus for years and years.

Eichstätt 1960 saw the overflowing, the explosion of a movement still trying to define itself. One paused for a moment, long enough to place it in its historical context. The theme of this week, "Catechetics and the Missions," permitted viewing catechetics in the wider context of the mission of the Church. Great trouble was taken to come to grips with the basic problems: the fundamental rules for all missionary preaching; the objects, the principles, and the methods of the renewal in catechetics. Finally, there was produced a sort of synthetized program for the training of future catechists. The work of this meeting has been gathered into one volume, *Renouvellement de la Catéchèse* (*Renewal in Catechetics*), which was rapidly translated into every major language.[3] A trend particularly marked in this work is that of the kerygma. Eichstätt may be seen, then, as mirroring the contemporary situation, and so I shall consider this congress as the important landmark and signpost of a preliminary stage, amply defined by referring to it as the kerygmatic phase.

The Kerygmatic Phase

Kerygmatic renewal is what has most influenced catechetics in our century. Quite clearly, like any movement, and particularly when the life of the Church is involved, this kerygmatic renewal did not simply drop out of a clear blue sky. It has had its own case history and a new climate of belief which have favored its growth.

1) **The origins of the kerygmatic movement.** It is not easy to trace the origins and development of a movement which has acquired a surprising universality by such diverse routes. Doubtless the Holy Spirit was at work. Looking just at the German setting, where the movement started, we can discern three early arenas for this kerygmatic renewal: (a) the ancient School of Tübingen, (b) the Munich method, and (c) the failure brought about by the excess of methodology.

a) *The School of Tübingen* held sway for a century due to its biblical, patristic and ecclesiological studies. The writings of Sailer, Moehler, and Hirscher, among others, remain as witnesses to an attempt to supersede a composite scholasticism. In opposition to a pragmatic pastorate befitting this enlightened century, these men made the case for one which is centered on Revelation, in the service of "the one and only Word of God, uttered through the Person of Christ."[4]

"We live in troubled times; but it is the Gospel, not the works of scholasticism, which has been promised unerring validity from on high. It is by clinging to the Gospel that we shall triumph."[5] Hirscher wrote this in 1823. But his ideas were not accepted then; still, he left behind him the seed which was to flower and yield fruit a century later. Meanwhile, it was the neoscholastic approach which held sway more and more among the philosophical and theological schools. Catechetics, however, remained the poor relation of this rational theology.

b) *The Munich method.* All this notwithstanding, there was continuing progress in methodology. It went through different stages. In 1912, the Congress of Vienna adopted the new, and now famous, process termed "Méthode de Munich." In its three component parts, *Presentation, Exposition,* and *Application,* it offered a simple and effective manner of working. This method was still further amplified by the "École active" popularized in Italy by Maria Montessori, in France by Quinet, and in Spain by Manjón. Following the principle that a child learns not simply by listening but even more by doing, this school stressed the value of *action.* And so the above schema was rounded off by a fourth function, that of the child's *activities.*

These innovations in method were approved by the Catechetical Congress of Munich (1928), which may be regarded as the climax of a constant endeavour in the field of pedagogy.

c) *The failure of methodology.* Despite all efforts, Christianity continued to beat a retreat among the greater part of the people.[6] Father Jungmann, in his analysis of this period, recognizes that it is not teaching which is at fault:

> Most people know all the sacraments; they know about the Person of Christ as well as about Our Lady, Peter and Paul, Adam and Eve, and a good many others. They know enough about the commandments of God and of the Church. But what is lacking among the faithful is a sense of unity, seeing it all as a whole, an understanding of the wonderful message of divine grace. All they retain of Christian doctrine is a string of dogmas and moral precepts, threats and promises, customs and rites, tasks and duties imposed on unfortunate Catholics, whilst the non-Catholic gets off free of them.[7]

The above paragraph gives a clear idea of the situation as it then was. There was the impression that catechetics had no positive result, was sterile, divorced from real life. In short, the methodological movement was passing through a profoundly critical period. Professor Arnold described it in these terms:

> The disproportion between the methodological efforts of a century and a half, and the results obtained, shake one's confidence in a movement exclusively methodological. One becomes more and more aware that it is

not only in starting from the nature and the needs of the audience, but also, and above all in the character peculiar to the doctrine, in the *subject matter* of the Gospel, that the catechetical and homiletic problem will be solved. The methodological requirements in themselves cannot be adequately satisfied unless the problem be approached from the theological standpoint.[8]

d) *A new turning point.* It is evident that the problem is not one of pure form but also of content. There was a climax reached at this point, a shift of perspective—emphasis was now to be transferred from method to content. The ground had been prepared for this, as we have pointed out, a century before, by the biblical-patristic studies of the School at Tübingen. And it was as a champion of this tradition that Father Jungmann, in 1936, produced his book *The Good News, and Our Own Preaching of the Faith,*[9] which is rightly considered to be the foundation stone of the kerygmatic renewal. Though criticized at the time, his ideas have gradually gained ground, to the extent that a quarter of a century later they had become sufficiently developed to be accepted in entirety by the International Study Week at Eichstätt. In fact, right from the start, the key issue was to be "the kerygmatic renewal in catechetics."

Quite remarkable was the convergence on this topic of both preoccupations and interests of the representatives from such far-flung countries.

All I can do here is pick out the general trends visible in the work, the context, and the broad conclusions of this session at Eichstätt.

2) Trends in kerygmatic catechetics.

a) *The basic concept, the message.* Today's world requires a new look at the faith we are proclaiming. For preaching and catechetics to get back to their original forms, one must return to first principles, to what constitutes the true kernel of the Christian message, the kerygma. This is why the movement is termed *kerygmatic.*

• One begins by placing catechetics within the mission of the Church. Catechetics fulfills our Lord's command: In the name of the omnipotence which he has received from the Father, the Lord Jesus Christ has entrusted his Church with the mission of proclaiming the Gospel to all men (Mark 16:15). It is to this work, which was at first that of Christ and then his Apostles, that the Church assigns its catechists.[10]

• The principle is then established by which the catechetical renewal is not to be brought about by a methodological adaptation but by an examination of the essence of the Faith. To succeed here, catechetics must be divested of all the peripheral elements which weigh down our catechisms. The important thing is not "how" but "what." Thus "content" comes to occupy the first place in this kerygmatic reform. Moreover, it is with content as a starting point that questions concerning form or method itself will be answered.[11]

• There is the realization that Christianity is not a system of truths, or a code of rules, but above all a *message*, the Good News. Catechetics, then, cannot be seen as the retailing of a doctrine by *teachers*, themselves more or less involved in it all, but rather the utterance of witnesses who communicate and pass on the message which is their very breath of life.

• At the center of this message is a *person* — Jesus Christ, the salvation of mankind. So catechetics must be *personalized*, following the behavior of human intercourse, and *christocentric*, that is, molding all its elements around the central figure of Christ.[12]

• With Christ, there are two events of capital importance — his death and resurrection. By his death and resurrection he has redeemed all people from sin and offers them eternal life. Catechetics is to root its message in the *paschal mystery*.

• Christ is not merely an historical figure but the synthesis of the whole history of salvation. Catechetics, then, must demonstrate how the *history of salvation* leads up to Christ and finds fulfillment in him alone. It must proclaim the Christ prophesied in the Old Testament, come among us in the fullness of time, giving his grace to all people through the Holy Spirit, and finally achieving his glorious task when he comes again at the end of time.[13]

This, then, in general, is the basic standpoint and the message that the kerygmatic movement promoted at the Eichstätt congress.

b) *The method.* The catechetical renewal remains not only faithful to content but also mindful of the manner by which God chose to be revealed. It perceives the four languages or ways in which catechetics can bring its influence to bear, as follows:

• Since the history of salvation is recounted in the Bible, catechetics must use a *biblical language*.

• Since the salvation portrayed in the Bible finds its active outlet in the liturgy, catechetics must use *liturgical language*.

• Since this redeeming work of God is seen day after day in the life of the Church and of each of its members, the "testimony" must shine through catechetics as an *existential language*.

• Since this history of salvation, narrated in the Bible, celebrated in the liturgy, and experienced in everyday life, takes progressively a concrete form in the shape of the Church, catechetics must use as well the *doctrinal language*.

Much could be said about these four languages, and we shall look at them again further on. At this juncture, I am merely drawing your attention to them. Their drafting was greeted enthusiastically by catechists, as the triumph of a coherent and well-balanced view of catechetics. The Bangkok study week testifies to this by devoting an important section of its conclusion to it.[14]

c) *The kerygma and the pastorate as a whole.* It is at this point that catechetics, faithful to the content of the message and to the paths chosen for it by God, finds itself straightway at the center of the whole pastoral work of the Church. It comes into contact with other movements which had been developing over a long period: the liturgical movement, led by Dom Lambert Beauduin in Belgium, by Pius Parsch in Austria, by the Abbey of Maria Laach in Germany; the biblical movement, prompted by the encyclical *Divino afflante spiritu* of Pius XII; the apostolic movements of Catholic Action; and family and social action.

It is clear that the kerygmatic renewal owes much to all these movements. Kerygmatic renewal has been helpful in reorganizing them, completing them, and harmonizing them around the figure of Christ.

Father Jungmann describes this historic conjuncture as follows:

> Soon there was a growing conviction: the renewal of religious life within the Church cannot spread its efforts over a variety of movements which would seem like specialized forms of apostolate to revivify methods and support pastoral action; the latter requires first and foremost a widespread but single program. The ideal image of the supernatural world, which shines through the Roman liturgy, a heritage of early Christianity, must be presented, with still greater clarity, in the explicit proclamation of the message of faith. Preaching and catechetics, religious art and ceremonial worship must join forces to provide the believer with a logical comprehension of his faith, in which will figure his sacramental and liturgical life and which will testify to a flourishing Christianity, radiating happiness. And this is possible, as long as the kerygma of the early Church rings out once again in all its fullness. To achieve this, let us put Christ back again at the center of our message. This kerygmatic restoration, in all its strength and clarity, is clearly the basic task of pastoral work in today's world.[15]

To bring this catechetical renewal down into one word, it is "concentration" of effort that must be the key—concentration of every constituent part around the kerygma. The tools were ready to hand, waiting to be assembled. It was the kerygmatic movement which, by giving pride of place to content, was able to put the stamp of form and consistency on this catechetical renewal.

d) *Assessment and conclusion.* It needed time for this movement to spread from its point of origin to the farthest limit of the missions. And yet it triumphed in all quarters. From the specialized review to lessons on the catechism at the most popular level, everywhere people were speaking the same language: *Kerygma*, the *paschal mystery*, the *history of salvation* had become the common currency. One author summed up the situation by saying: "The kerygma is in fashion."[16]

The results of this kerygmatic phase are positive ones, especially when compared with the previous stages. Catechetics shatters the childish bounds of little catechisms and springs to the forefront in the life of the Church. As the Vatican Council II will tell us, catechetics is the first of all the means used by the Church to fulfill its teaching role.[17]

I have just mentioned the council. That speeded up many things.

Ideologies, centers of interest, key words follow each other ceaselessly. Since then, the *kerygma* is on the decline. A new star rises in the catechetical sky during the 1960s—*anthropology*.

The Anthropological Phase

The word *anthropology* is very much in fashion these days. Originating in the scientific world, it carries overtones far beyond the limits of catechetics and further still from the narrow path we have chosen to follow throughout the six international sessions on catechetics.

Yet we choose this word to denote one particular phase in catechetics because it was adopted after Eichstätt and became more and more commonly used during following sessions.

1) **From the kerygma to pre-evangelization.** The Eichstätt study week, completely immersed as it was in the kerygma, had quite properly laid emphasis on the Word of God. But in stressing the theological aspect, it had perhaps lost sight of the fact that the Word of God is, too, the Word of God given to humanity and that the Revelation of God is also humanity's revelation—that the history of salvation is as well a history intended for humanity's good.

In saying this, I know full well that I am defining things too rigidly. Nevertheless, one thing is certain: Since then, a strange disquiet, even something of distrust, has become noticeable, particularly in missionary countries, with regard to the kerygmatic renewal. Despite all the emphasis in Europe on the kerygma, missionaries clung to the old methods of apologetics.

That became evident at Bangkok during the Third International Study Week on Catechetics. Separated by only two years from Eichstätt, the session in Bangkok accepted in general terms the fundamental principles of the kerygmatic renewal laid down at Eichstätt. But it put a special emphasis on *adaptation*; it insisted on the human approach, on the problems posed by catechetics, particularly during the first stage of evangelization and conversion.

For the first time, there is talk now of providing for *stages*, of preparing "the ground," of using "a language with which people are familiar":

> The catechesis has to prepare the ground by purifying judgments, sentiments and even subconscious impressions to lead them to a fuller response to the doctrine of Christ. It has further to lay special emphasis on adaptation, by developing the doctrine according to analogies, images or forms of expression familiar to men of a given region or culture. It has also to suggest a committed action which truly corresponds to the needs, both spiritual and temporal, of this given milieu.[18]

But one particular word above all was in ascendancy at Bangkok, one which had not even been mentioned at Eichstätt, *pre-evangelization*.[19] A new stage had begun in the total process of catechizing; a new wind was blowing, one of distinctly anthropological tendencies.

2) The pioneers of the expression. This movement had already started in France in the throes of full kerygmatic renewal. France, as opposed to Germanic countries – the cradle of the kerygma – had undergone the painful experience of a de-Christianization, even a total lack of belief, among large sections of its population. Suffice it to recall the book by Father Godin *France, a Missionary Land?*[20] together with the experiment of worker priests and the foundation of the French mission. These difficult conditions have always kept the pastorate on its toes and particularly attentive to the first stage in the process of conversion: how to approach the obstacle and then get over it.

Father Liégé had seen this clearly when he spoke of the psychological and sociological conditioning for faith: "It seems that many men of good will do not attain to belief in Christ, by reason of certain dehumanizing conditions of life, and that on a vaster scale than ever in our times of technical development."[21] It was then that he introduced, for the very first time, the expression *pre-evangelization*. "It is the work of pre-evangelization – not necessarily chronologically distinct from evangelization – to work at men's own milieu in order to make them accessible to the evangelical message."[22]

In this way, he is recognizing the necessity for an initial stage of purification, of acclimatization, of human contact.

What has become of the kerygmatic movement at this point? It is beginning to undergo a testing period. The word *crisis* is mentioned. Some even go to the extent of saying so explicitly.[23] Others are seriously questioning the efficacy and validity of the *kerygma*: "Are we to go on reiterating Christ's message in the very kerygmatic form which was used by the Apostles? Surely times have changed?"[24]

It was quite something even to have posed the problem so explicitly. In years gone by, there had been so much emphasis laid on the Word of God falling vertically down upon humanity below (Barth) that no one dared to talk of a meeting point for fear of being accused of psychologizing; no one dared to utter the word *apologetics* for this was a term apparently banished forever from one's vocabulary.

And yet pre-evangelization was proving more than ever necessary and suitable. A kerygmatic presentation of Christ could never remove the need for an initial preparatory stage.

It was in this way that, at the Bangkok study week (1962), the assembled catechists, with missionaries forming a large proportion of their number, set about giving an important place to pre-evangelization by specifying its nature, its aim, and the necessity for it: "The guiding principle of pre-evangelization is anthropocentric, because we must start with man as he is."[25]

The balance now is tilting quite decidedly in favor of humankind. The anthropocentric movement takes over from the kerygmatic.

3) Foundations of pre-evangelization. What is one to think of this new orientation? Is it fear brought on by failure? Or is it a concession to the psychological taste of this period? One is certainly not witnessing some pastoral strategy designed to attract approbation from one's contemporaries. The reasons go much deeper. It is an admonition to remain faithful: (a) to the very manner in which the Master and the first Apostles presented the Christian message, (b) to the Church's tradition as evidenced in the history of catechetics, and (c) to the very nature of the Christian message.

a) It is far from certain that the Apostles presented Christianity in a purely kerygmatic manner, as one would be given to think simply by reading the writings in the New Testament. Recent studies show that the opposite is the case. The four Gospels are, rather, regarded as four interpretations and theological elaborations of the message with an eye to the public for which they are intended. Moreover, we know that St. Paul, time and again, was concerned with non-Jewish communities, ones completely foreign to Israel's faith, and that on these occasions he appears in a completely different light; there is more condescension, a more human approach than a direct proclamation of Christ the Savior. One notes particularly, here, the address before the Areopagus in Athens (Acts 17:22–31).

b) This attempt to meet halfway is not peculiar to the Apostles. One can say that the whole patristic process shows a continued effort at adaptation, a conscious effort to translate the message of the Gospels into Greco-Roman language and culture. The Middle Ages was to do the same to express it yet again in terms suited to the times; and the new sciences of the modern period constitute an appeal, a critical reappraisal of the apostolic kerygma so that it may remain valid in our times. This regard for humanity's historical setting has always been there to a greater or lesser degree. One can even say that this continual hesitation between content and method, between the Word of God and the word of humanity, is a fixed pattern in history.

c) Fidelity, then, to Revelation and to the manner of Revelation chosen by God himself. We can perceive a basic example of instruction and dialogue in the very act of Revelation. Revelation – so insisted the kerygmatic movement – is not the unveiling of a doctrine or a code of morals; first and foremost it is an event, a person – Christ, who immediately opts for dialogue, for confrontation, for a relationship with humanity based on love. "The Revelation may be imagined as a dialogue in which the Word of God is expressed firstly by the Incarnation, and then by the Gospel."[26]

Firstly by the Incarnation and then by the Good News. Much could be said about the Incarnation as principal foundation for all pastoral activity and therefore for catechetics.[27] Its practical applications in this field are in the process of being realized with unparalleled success, witness the proliferation of school books, index cards, and other handy literature. A new vocabulary is coming to light. In opposition to expressions such as "kerygma," "proclamation," and "testimony," a new batch of words is produced: "Overture," "values," "experience," and "exploration" are characteristic of the period we are examining.[28]

Even by the time of the catechetical session at Katigondo in 1964, which was so firmly based on the kerygmatic line, one could perceive more than a few tendencies toward the anthropological. First, by way of contrast with the earlier sessions, it was decided to call the study week at Katigondo a *Pan-African Seminar,* just as later Manila would be called *Asiatic* and Medellín, *Latin American.*

Moreover, particular attention was paid to the culture, the outlook, the religious attitude of the African, for it is onto these that the Christian message is to be grafted. In this connection, the report presented by Father Seumois provides us with a whole spread of religious characteristics of the Africans, together with some psychological and cultural traits which are so much a part of God's call through Christ.[29]

And this will have to be allowed for in the different languages used —
biblical, liturgical, and doctrinal.[30]

The Manila study week represents a climax in this new anthropocentric orientation, just as Eichstätt had been for the kerygmatic
renewal. Vatican Council II having occurred during this time, the
thoughts of the delegates were particularly centered on the motivating
forces involved in the missionary apostolate and on the consequences
attendant on the recognition of values inherent in non-Christian
religions. The word *pre-evangelization* (together with its companion,
precatechesis) comes up time and again in the reports.[31] But one expression above all others reaches sloganlike proportions during the
discussions — *anthropological approach* (*sic*). Two reports were devoted
entirely to elucidating this anthropological viewpoint.[32]

One could examine in detail the anthropological dominance over
large sectors of the work done during the session. But we feel what
has already been referred to suffices. What is more interesting is to
follow the conductor wire leading from one pole to the other of this
double circuit.

4) Kerygma and anthropology, opposite or complementary?
Kerygmatic movement — anthropological movement: two currents
which have followed each other with astonishing rapidity. Two completely different attitudes of mind. The kerygmatic attitude refers back
constantly to the Bible and the liturgy. Very much tied to a rich
theological inheritance, it is there that it finds its coherence and is most
at home. The anthropological attitude, in contrast, opts for the
psychological approach; renouncing the already acquired treasures, it
seeks its ends choosing insecurity and hardship. These are the main
patterns in outline.

Are they in conflict? Some publications produced amid loud fan-
fares such as *Kerygma in Crisis?*[33] may give the impression that there
is a new stage being entered upon contrasting, even violently, with the
preceding one which is now already obsolete. Yet, in our opinion, there
is no opposition at all; rather, a progression, the same line of thought
taken to greater depth. The anthropological orientation appears, then,
more as the unexpected fruit of the seed sown by the kerygmatic
renewal.

The kerygmatic movement, by insisting on the importance of content, permitted a deeper understanding of the Word of God, which is
never to be found in its pure state but centered in the heart of humanity.
It is precisely because one has taken note of the implications in "God
speaks to humanity" that one has come to seek out humankind.

It must be recognized that one of the richest acquisitions of present-day catechetics is precisely the discovery of this vital, organic unity between the *subject* and *object:* two poles which had always been themes for catechetical investigation but which had never attained to that organic unity which they exhibit today in the very process of catechesis.

Word of God, word of humanity. God and humankind. Theology and anthropology merge into catechetical action. We cannot speak of God without speaking of humanity; nor, of humanity without catching sight of God. Revelation is a theology for humankind; it reveals God to his human creatures. At the same time it constitutes an anthropology; it reveals how humanity appears in the sight of God.

In principle one must agree with this theological vision of things. Yet, despite this speculative synthesis, despite this complementary nature attributed to kerygma and anthropology, the fact remains that *anthropocentric* catechesis is difficult to put into practice.

First of all, it requires from the catechist not only a constant concern for everything which makes up the mental horizons and the areas of interest of the pupil but also an all-important participation. Secondly, such a catechesis must be able to take in a whole range of proffered openings which at first sight have no hope of leading toward the divine. Lastly, and this is the most tricky of all, catechesis must, often without any choice in the matter, run the risk either of remaining in this impasse or of giving the impression of a Gospel parachuted in from outside to the astonishment and shock of those present.

Similar difficulties had already been voiced during the Manila study week.[34] Yet the crucial point is the *terminus ad quem* or, in other words, the ultimate development of catechesis. It nevertheless remains a fact that to have rooted Revelation in the concrete setting of normal life, and to have thus regarded this very setting as the starting point for evangelization, is in itself a considerable advance in anthropocentric catechetics.

But must every catechesis tend to put Christ in the foreground? Or can it not rather see its aim as a complete involvement in life without any preconceived horizons but rather cherishing the hope which is riveted in every believer's heart that salvation comes about in mysterious ways, when and how it pleases God?

All we are doing here is to pose the question, but it may be that we can provide some elements of an answer in our third section.

The Political Phase

We have set about taking stock of the anthropological bias in modern catechetics. This orientation must be accepted as *symbolizing* that point in history where we ourselves are living. However, hardly has this new tendency appeared than one can forsee the limits and the dangers of an "anthropological inflation."

1) Individualistic anthropology leaning too much on the present. One of the greatest fears provoked by this movement is that of seeing humanity on the one hand regard itself as the norm, the criterion for the Word of God, and, on the other, relapse into an individualistic subjectivity which cheapens objective reality.[35]

Regarding the danger of losing the whole meaning of the Revelation by suppressing the transcendental and gratuitous, this is the most serious accusation leveled against the anthropocentric concept. It is basically the problematical "transcendence–immanence" which is at the root of the problem. We shall deal with this later, since the second reproach may provide us with a few elements capable of casting light on the first. In fact anthropocentricism is charged not only with "reducing" the Word of God but also with reducing humanity's horizons by sealing us within subjective, individual dimensions which are confined to the present and have no historical or social extension.

There is no doubt that existentialist philosophy, by setting about the interpretation of the Revelation, has given the latter a new dimension, one overneglected until now, that is, the personal dimension. Moreover, modern biblical studies, too, have discovered the personal dimension of the Word of God in the concept of an ever-present Word which is calling humankind to the very heart of its existence.[36]

The kerygmatic renewal profited by this injection of *personalism*, to show catechetics as being no longer an indoctrination of concepts but a transmission of the Word of the living God, aimed at arousing and nourishing faith.[37]

If the aims were sweeping, their realization remained restricted. Often faith has been reduced to an option of a strictly individual nature.[38]

Since then, a whole wave of events has broken over the Church: an approach to the world, a recognition of religious pluralism, a reappraisal of its social structure, an attack on superstition, secular undercurrents such as the "death of God," etc.

Neither Eichstätt nor Bangkok felt, at least explicitly, the impact of secularization or of a changing world. A few indications were seen at Katigondo, faced with African independence, and particularly at Manila, in view of the pluralistic problem brought about by the non-Christian religions.[39]

But above all at Medellin, in 1968, the realization of a world on the road to secularization exploded most forcefully, requiring as a result a secularized catechesis.

2) **Medellin, 1968.** The vast continent of South America—where one can find, more sharply defined than anywhere else, exploitation, injustice, and at the same time the struggle to render man autonomous and free—has been vocal in its appeal (and the seminars at Medellin demonstrated this most effectively) for an autochthonous catechesis satisfying the continent's demands.

Paradoxically, perhaps a contributing factor has been the very fact that Latin America is a basically Christian land. Used as one was to turning religion into a collection of ideas and rites mechanically learnt and performed, one felt here that all these religious impedimenta, which have been inherited from the past, are without practical application in everyday life and have no connection with the main problems posed by it.

One must begin to consider, then, both social and political implications of Christian faith.

Faced with a rapidly developing world, and confronted with the present rise to maturity of the Church in Latin America, the catechetical movement recognizes the need for a full-scale renewal. This was the aim at Medellin in 1968. The acts of the congress have been mostly published in the new review *Catequesis Latinoamericana.*[40] The basic ideas, condensed into three points, are: (a) a description of the realities of the situation, humanity in its setting; (b) a theological option, the unity of God's plan; and (c) application to catechetics, a change of perspective in content and method.

Before starting in on these three points, one should point to the option made in advance by the congress, one very characteristic of its attitude: the primacy of *action.* According to this, problems will be attacked, not in a more or less lucid, speculative perspective but on the basis of a will to act and to become involved.[41]

a) *Humanity in its setting.* Since the aim is to go forward, one must first take stock of the realities of the present situation.

Two particular aspects were spotlighted: the religious heritage of the past and present-day developments.

Because of its historical background, Latin America is heir to an immense Christian tradition, which affects individual existence, as well as the socio-cultural context.

The Church enjoys many possibilities of influence in these countries, and therefore has a large amount of responsibility. The problem is to take up the past, to integrate it with the present, and to seek orientations toward the future. It is by no means possible to ignore the riches brought about by four centuries of Christian tradition. Yet, on the other hand, it would be a mistake to become fixated on past forms, some of which seem not only ambiguous, but even inadequate and harmful in the light of historical evolution. Indeed the Latin American continent today is undergoing profound and rapid changes: economic, demographic, social and cultural.[42]

That said, whatever the form of catechesis or evangelization, the first job is to identify oneself completely with the human state and to take on humanity's anguish and hopes by avoiding whatever might seem the easy way out. And why, precisely? To reveal to people the possibility of total freedom, to offer them the treasures of salvation in and with the person of Christ.

But it is wildly unrealistic and senseless to present a message of salvation if that very salvation does not start here and now, and particularly here, in this world, by freeing from injustice and oppression a good many groups of humans on the fringe of society. A good question, this: What price faith, if it remains purely spiritual with no grounding in the realities of life here on earth with its social and political aspects?

b) *The history of salvation and the history of humanity seen as one.* In every situation, catechetics has a fundamental message, which consists of a unifying principle between two poles of total reality. This unifying principle is complex, differentiated, and dynamic. It excludes dichotomy, separation, and dualism, as well as monism, confusion, and simplistic identification. This unifying principle exists: between human values and relations with God; between man's planning and God's salvific plan as manifested in Christ; between the human community and the Church; between human history and the history of salvation; between human experience and God's revelation; between the progressive growth of Christianity in our time and its eschatological consummation.[43]

This is the first time that any official document concerning catechetics has been so direct on this point of the unity of God's plan.

One might well say that the kerygmatic movement, too, though in a specialized way, insisted on this overall plan laid down by God, on this history of salvation which, culminating in the appearance of Christ, is still developing as it reaches us here and now. And this is true, but it emphasized the history of salvation as revealed in the Bible, without giving sufficient emphasis to the unique, individual history of salvation in which we ourselves are engaged.

I should like to think I am wrong in stating that a good many catechists are quite happy with the biblical renewal and do no more than use the Bible in their catechetics as a "means" or an "instrument," rather than showing it to be a particular "dimension" of catechesis itself. In fact, there was much talk, at this time, of *biblical catechesis;* but what this expression meant for the majority was virtually the unraveling of a collection of stories set in ages past. A series of *ideas* had been replaced by a series of *facts*, with no realization that a "boring historical narrative can be as meaningless as a profusion of formulas."[44] Historical–biblical systems can be as dangerous as doctrinal systems. In short, the gulf between past and present history was still there despite appearances. There was a gap to be bridged between the history of salvation and modern history, between the content and the subject, between theology and life. It was therefore necessary to build this bridge to join the so-called "sacred" world to the "profane" world. The problem was, how? Certainly not by an artificial contrivance or by a veneer, and an interior one at that, as was formerly the case,[45] but by a sincere admission of that effectiveness of Revelation which comprehends the so-called profane reality. Henceforth this will no longer be regarded merely as a presupposition, as the place where God is revealed, but as an *integral part* of the Revelation itself. In other words, what was in catechetical terminology the *subject* of catechetics becomes at the same time the *content.*

c) *The catechetical applications.* The repercussions of this theological option in catechesis are numerous. We shall analyze them from the double point of view of *content* and *method:*

• Modification in the perspective of the content: The sentiments of the Medellin study week on this point are both clear and bold. One considers the historical situations not only as the *initial indications* worthy of attention in the search for God's plan for humanity in our time but also as a vital aspect of catechetics.

> Catechetics today, in accordance with a more adequate theology of Revelation, realizes that the first place to look when seeking God's design for contemporary man is the area of history and authentically human aspirations. These are an *indispensable part* of the contents of catechetics.[46]

So it will not be necessary to locate the source of Revelation elsewhere, remote from daily life, in some far off world removed from our own, but rather in the living reality of life, in revolution and in war, in the struggles of youth, in the emancipation of men and women, in the common work of building the city. The shift of emphasis in the content springs from a new appreciation of the meaning of Christianity. Not merely a "religion," but the historical movement, started by God, toward the liberation of humankind.[47]

• A change of attitude in the method: This results from a similar change with regard to content. The starting point, the vehicle, and the content of catechesis will now be humanity in its present historical setting. The catechist is to develop, *in* humanity and *with* it, the most crucial of life's experiences in order to find the mystery of salvation and to express it in light of the Gospel.

Summing up the work and discussions, one commentator on the Medellin study week provides us with the following definition: "Evangelization (catechesis) is the means by which any section of our human society interprets its own situation, sees it, and expresses it in the light of the Gospel."[48]

> To understand the broad meaning of these human realities, it is necessary to live fully with the men of our time; thus, we shall be able to intepret these realities with progress and seriousness, in the actual historical context, in the light of experiences lived by Israel, by Christ, and by the Church's sacramental community in which the spirit of Christ risen lives and works continually. Understanding man in this way results in a deepening of the Christian message, and this deepening in turn helps us to understand man still better.[49]

One might see in this attitude a danger of subjectivity and anthropocentricism remaining enclosed within human experience, without any transcendental outlet. This is our own opinion. And that is why we should like to point to a few possible guidelines for such a study.

3) Ways of overcoming the dilemma: transcendence–immanence. First, one should take very seriously the currently accepted attitude that history, at its simplest, is none other than the history of salvation. One must accept the radical nondissociation of the love of God and love for one's neighbor. It is precisely in this double historical and social dimension that we can just perceive a hope of best resolving the famous antinomy: immanence–transcendence.[50]

Formerly, perhaps, when speaking of God, the spatial–temporal coordinates have been overworked. Now, this excessively spatial approach has come under criticism from John Robinson and Harvey Cox[51] – not to mention other authors less well-known.

I think that we can retain these two coordinates as long as they both involve *humanity*. For in the first place, it is men and women who create *space* and make *history*.

As recent exegetists have shown, it is the Bible itself which starts the process of desacralization of nature or space seen from the material point of view.[52] From the very beginning, the revelation of God's name was acted out, throughout history. Yahweh said to Moses: "You will know who I am when you have seen what I shall do for you." God's covenant with his people has its setting in their political history rather than simply nature itself. It is a history which unravels along with humanity's development. In fact, all the essential categories of the Bible relate to change and to the impetus of history, ever looking forward: *exodus, vocation, promise, messianism, the leaving of one's native land.* "To set in motion," this was the mission of Abraham, Moses, and the prophets. Yahweh is the God who *leads* his people. His transcendence consists in his being the "first," the God who goes *before us,* opening doors to the historical future. He demands a continual relinquishing. of our position in time present, to look toward the future.[53]

And there is still more. The word *history* implies a "continual action," that is, a dialogue with our neighbors. This is the other coordinate, that of the *community.* We find, too, in the Word of God this very social dimension which is essential to it. Yahweh begins by choosing a people, and it is through this people—*the Church*—that he is to bring about salvation and reconciliation. "He who from two peoples made one alone, breaking down the barriers which separated them . . . to bring about peace, and their reconciliation with God" (Eph. 2:14-15).

It is within this tension, between the *already* and the *not yet,* that is to occur the communion of love which Christ promised (John 17:11). The dimensions of space and time, of history and community life, which at first sight might appear different, simply cannot be studies in isolation.

It is strange to see that the Medellin congress comes back to this point seemingly spontaneously—a comment, surely, on the current attitude: "Among the different forms of existence, existence in community takes on a particular importance. Catechetics cannot be confined to individual dimensions of life."[54]

And a few lines further on, when discussing "our understanding of the Christian message which is continually evolving," the congress adds: "It is not enough merely to repeat or explain the message exactly. Rather, we must unceasingly reinterpret the Good News in ways that will complement man's present existence and knowledge."[55]

And so our catechesis will be immanent if "the Christian Gospel is not reduced to simple words or simple modifications in language. Rather, we must announce our message in the same way that the world today speaks its existential language: by words and signs which manifest a life of concrete commitment in love and unity."[56]

And at the same time, catechetics will safeguard transcendence on the one hand by the progressive discovery "of the total meaning and orientation of these aspirations and tensions, as they occur at each moment of the historical process,"[57] and on the other, by this dialogue with one's fellows which remains ever a challenge to our individualistic attitude.

It is in this way, following both social and historical dimensions in catechetics and in the whole of the Church's activity, that the *Kingdom* of God will grow: that very word representing so well the double polarity of the social and the eschatological.

If the Kingdom of God is not to be identified purely and simply with the evolution of this world, one still must not place it beyond this world and outside the realm of history. This kingdom has an intimate relationship with the present world. It is not indifferent as to whether men and women have made a politically sound go of things. It is with the materials of this world that the Kingdom of God is built.

Catechetics simply cannot do without this political dimension which is so close to the heart of modern man and which is bound to broaden traditional catechetics.

We always come back to the same fact: that Scripture and Tradition, the life of Christ and the life of the Church, Revelation and history are not aspects of reality which can remain apart. It is within this vital stream that discernment and a proper "reading" of the situation must be applied, in a dialectical give-and-take between concrete experience and experience so perfectly characterized in Christ.

This last development goes, perhaps, beyond the limits of a report which set out primarily to be historically based. However, it seemed apposite to touch upon this tension, which is never far away from catechetics these days, and even to regard it as the nub, the crucial question, of the historical phase through which catechetics is now passing. One might charge it with anthropocentrism. But would not that be too precipitate?

Vatican Council II itself has been accused of anthropocentric deviation. And it is Pope Paul VI who loses no time in countering:

> It is not our belief that this Council can be taxed with such a deviation with regard to its really basic aims . . . The guiding rule of our Council has been charity. And who could censure the Council for having adopted this basic guideline, when one recalls that it is Christ himself who taught us to regard love for our brothers as the distinctive sign of his disciples (John 13:31).
>
> The religion of the God-made-man comes up against the religion of man aping God. What happens? A shock, a struggle, an anathema? That could easily have been the case, but it has not happened. The old story of the Samaritan has formed the pattern for the Council's spirituality.[58]

And the pope concludes with this paragraph reflecting the spirit of catechetics and of the whole range of contemporary pastoral action:

> If we remember that behind the face of every man—and particularly when tears and suffering have made it more transparent—we can and must recognize the face of Christ, and that in the face of Christ we can and must

recognize the face of the Heavenly Father, then our humanism becomes Christianity, and our Christianity becomes theocentric, so that we too can proclaim that to know God, one must know man.[59]

Conclusion

We have tried to give a bird's-eye view of catechetics during the last twenty years. If we were allowed further to define the shape of this movement, we should liken it to a parabola which, beginning on the earth and rooted in humanity, rises almost vertically to the Word of God, then drops back again to humankind.

It is in this way that—by a detour, listening at first to the Word of God (the kerygmatic phase) in the Bible, in the liturgy, and in the lives of men and women—catechetics comes back today to a situation similar to that in force at the beginning of the century. But it is similar only on the surface and embodies quite a different spirit. Catechetics and all human sciences meet again in research and in its application—after having seen how the Word of God expresses itself unceasingly in a language at once historical and concrete—at the very heart of humanity.

Behind the words *anthropology* and *politics* used in contemporary catechetics, there is, then, more than a means of presenting the Word of God to today's world. There is a development of Revelation and Faith, along an existential coordinate, which formerly has been far too neglected. There is above all a new spirit, and a new face for humankind, which is defined first and foremost in the responsibility it assumes toward itself, toward its fellows, and before history.[60]

It is hardly astonishing that Paul VI, desirous of characterizing this new spirit which is pervading the Church, proclaims fervently: "We too are involved with mankind."

NOTES

1. One might mention in this connection the meetings of these European catechetical groups, held yearly in different European cities; the Congress on Religious Education, the catechetical assemblies which are increasing in number at both national and international levels; the institutes and catechetical and pastoral centers, formed in recent years, as well as a copious supply of literature, made up of books and relevant periodicals. It is clear that we are taking stock of a sign of the times.

2. See Georges Delcuve, "International Session at Nijmegen," *Lumen Vitae* 15 (1960): 153–158.

3. Johannes Hofinger, ed., *Teaching All Nations: A Symposium on Modern Catechetics* (Freiburg: Herder; New York: Herder and Herder, 1961).

4. It is Professor Arnold who has set about examining this exceedingly interesting period and who has brought to light the work of these pioneers in pastoral and catechetical renewal. F. X. Arnold, *Serviteurs de la foi* (Tournai: Desclée, 1957) and *Pour une théologie de l'apostolat* (Tournai: Desclée, 1961). We mention these studies as basic in the appreciation of this period.

5. Quoted by Arnold, *Serviteurs de la foi*, p. 77.

6. This is an interesting observation. Ignorance of religious matters is often quoted as a cause of lapse from the faith. That is of course true. But it is essential to see that, from the human point of view, religious instruction had never reached such a level; and, moreover, each pupil received a sound, broadly based education throughout his seven or more years.

7. Josef A. Jungmann, "Theology and Kerygmatic Teaching," *Lumen Vitae* 5 (1950): 258–263.

8. F. X. Arnold, "Revival in Dogmatic Preaching and Catechetics," *Lumen Vitae* 3 (1948): 514.

9. Josef A. Jungmann, *Die Frohbotschaft und unsere Glaubensverkündigung* (Regensburg: Pustet, 1936). The ideas contained in this book have been assembled, extended, and brought up to date in another later publication by the author: *Glaubensverkündigung im Lichte der Frohbotschaft* (Innsbruck: Tyrolia–Verlag, 1963); *The Good News Yesterday and Today* (New York: Sadlier, 1962).

10. See the "Conclusions" of the "Reports on the Eichstätt Session," in *Teaching All Nations*, ed. Hofinger, p. 394.

11. See the report presented to the congress of Eichstätt by Josef Goldbrunner, "Catechetical Method as Handmaid of Kerygma," in *Teaching All Nations*, ed. Hofinger, pp. 108–121.

12. The report of Monsignor Larrain, "Characteristics of Missionary Catechesis," as also that of Father D. Grasso, "The Core of Missionary Preaching," in *Teaching All Nations*, ed. Hofinger – amply illustrate the trend of these ideas. Moreover, the Eichstätt study week adopted them by including them in the "General Conclusions," which it put out at the end of the session. [See *Teaching All Nations*, ed. Hofinger, pp. 387–391; also reprinted in this sourcebook as Reading 2 (Part 1).].

13. Ibid.

14. "Authentic catechesis requires a sound balance between *the four languages of faith:* Bible, liturgy, systematic instruction, the testimony afforded by the life of the Christian community"; see A. M. Nebreda, "East Asian Study Week on Mission Catechetics, Bangkok (31 October – 3 November 1962)," *Lumen Vitae* 17 (1962): 721.

15. Josef A. Jungmann, "The Kerygma in the History of the Pastoral Activity of the Church," in his *Handing on the Faith: A Manual of Catechetics* (New York: Herder and Herder, 1959), pp. 396–397.

16. A. Rétie, *Foi au Christ* (Paris: Editions du Cerf, 1953), p. 7.

17. See Vatican Council II, "Declaration on Christian Education," no. 4.

18. See Nebreda, "East Asian Study Week on Mission Catechetics," p. 722.

19. I shall not enter here into the debate provoked by this expression from the moment it appeared. Without denying the importance of the reality it contains, some would wish to term it quite simply, *evangelization.* By humanizing, the argument runs, one evangelizes at the same time. The question remains open. On the one hand, the use of this word opens the way to a dichotomic

conception of the unique Christian reality; on the other, it must be recognized that this distinction in terminology aids understanding of the novelty introduced by the Good News. At least for those who do not know this Good News, there is room to make a distinction. Similarly, out of respect for those who do not believe, we cannot christen with the name of *evangelization,* an action shared with those who explicitly repudiate that word. Moreover, Vatican II, which repeatedly analyzed this stage in development, speaks of it as a "preparation for the Gospel," not as an "evangelization."

20. Henri Godin and Yvan Daniel, *La France, pays de mission?* (Lyon, 1943).

21. P.-A. Liégé, "Faith," in *Theology Library,* ed. A. M. Henry (Chicago: Fides, 1957), 4:18.

22. P.-A. Liégé, "Evangélisation," in *Catholicisme* (encyclopedia directed by G. Jacquemet), vol. 4 (Paris, 1954), col. 761.

23. A. M. Nebreda, *Kerygma in Crisis?* (Chicago: Loyola University Press, 1965).

24. D. Grasso, "Il Kerygma e la Predicatione," *Gregorianum* 41 (1960): 427; and reproduced in *Parole et Mission* 4 (1961): 173.

25. See Nebreda, "East Asian Study Week on Mission Catechetics," p. 724.

26. Paul VI, Encyclical Letter, *Ecclesiam suam* (6 August 1964), no. 72.

27. See F. X. Arnold, *Pastorale et principe d'incarnation* (Brussels-Paris: Editions du Cep, 1964). It is on this principle of the Incarnation that Arnold, just as so many others, bases all the pastoral work of the Church.

28. It is above all the work of Babin, Le Du, and Audinet, among others, which has greatly contributed to this new attitude and vocabulary.

29. X. Seumois, "Adaptation de la Catéchèse moderne à l'Afrique d'aujourd'hui," *Revue du Clergé Africain* 19 (1964): 532–548. The work of the session has been collated in the *Revue du Clergé Africain* of November 1964.

30. See the two reports given over to this topic, *Revue du Clergé Africain* 19 (1964): 549–584.

31. See *inter alia,* pp. 346–350 in *Teaching All Nations,* July 1967, which sums up the work presented to this study week at Manila.

32. J. Bournique, "The Word of God and Anthropology," and D. S. Amalorpavadass, "Workshop on Recent Developments in Catechetics," *Teaching All Nations* 4 (1967): 371–376 and 377–379.

33. Nebreda, *Kerygma in Crisis?*

34. The importance of the topic being clearly understood, a study group was set up around the subject "Catechesis and Anthropology" in which, time and time again, there was raised the problem of the relationship between anthropology and the Revelation. See J. Bournique, "Le Congrès de Manille," *Catéchèse* 29 (1967): 512–515.

35. The work of Urs von Balthasar represents a cautionary line, here, against the dangers of anthropocentricism in theology. H. Urs von Balthasar, "Apparition," in *La Gloire et la Croix* (Paris, 1965), 1:142; quoted by L. Malevez, "Présence de la théologie à Dieu et à l'homme," *Nouvelle Revue Theologique* 90 (1968): 694.

36. One need but quote the name of R. Bultmann as instigator of fixing the Word of God in its modern setting.

37. Definition of catechetics given in the *Directoire de pastorale catéchétique à l'usage des diocèses de France* (Paris, 1964), no. 4.

38. See Johannes B. Metz, "The Church's Social Function in the Light of

a 'Political Theology,' " in *Faith and the World of Politics*, Concilium: Theology in the Age of Renewal, vol. 36 (New York: Paulist Press, 1968): 3–4, in which the author criticizes the tendency which he calls "privatization" of a good many contemporary theological trends.

39. In the opening address of the Katigondo study week, Cardinal Rugambwa made reference to "the political independence which requires a new type of Christian training"; see *Revue du Clergé Africain* 19 (1964): 506. Similarly, at the Manila congress, faithful to Vatican II, there appeared time and again the concern to accept the positive values of non-Christian religions. See the issue of *Teaching All Nations*, 4 (July 1967), devoted to this congress.

40. *Catequesis Latinoamericana*, a review published by the Latin American committee of la Fe (CLAF–Department of CELAM), Asunción, Paraguay.

41. This was one of the greatest characteristics of the Medellin conference. Far from stopping at purely catechetical considerations, it stressed repeatedly the necessity for a radical change in social structures, and the need for catechetics to take part in this liberation of humanity by progressive or revolutionary means. See the General Conclusions of Medellin: "Attitudes Adopted by the Latin-American Episcopal Council" (CELAM), no. 8; reproduced *inter alia* in *Lumen Vitae* 24 (1969): 343–347, and in *Catéchèse* 34 (1968): 108–113.

42. The General Conclusions of Medellin, nos. 2–3.

43. Ibid., no. 12.

44. Gerard S. Sloyan, "What Should Children's Catechisms Be Like?" in *Pastoral Catechetics*, ed. J. Hofinger and Theodore Stone (New York: Herder and Herder, 1964), p. 44; quoted in Gabriel Moran, *Catechesis of Revelation* (New York: Herder and Herder, 1966), p. 80.

45. Some expressions still current today, such as "the application in our own life of a biblical story," "to carry the Mass into everyday life," "to hand on to others what we ourselves have contemplated," . . . bear the mark of a dualist mentality.

46. The General Conclusions of Medellin, no. 11.

47. The conclusions of the study group of the Medellin session on "The Present Course of Catechetics," *Catequesis Latinoamericana* 1 (1969): 83.

48. J. Audinet, "Le renouveau catéchétique dans la situation contemporaine," *Catéchèse* 34 (1969): 42.

49. The General Conclusions of Medellin, no. 11.

50. This is the most acute problem posed today by catechetics, and one which comes up time and again, allowing for the fact that it underlies all theology.

51. John A. T. Robinson, *Honest to God* (London: SCM Press; Philadelphia: Westminster Press, 1963); Harvey Cox, *The Secular City* (London: SCM Press; New York: Macmillan, 1965).

52. Paul M. van Buren, *The Secular Meaning of the Gospel* (New York: Macmillan, 1963); and the first few pages of Cox, *The Secular City*.

53. The entire work of Teilhard de Chardin points in this direction. Might we just transcribe this following paragraph which sums up this line of thought: "Up till then, for the spiritual, one point was in no doubt at all: if, for Man, there was any path open toward a greater life, then it could only be conceived of as a sort of 'vertical' motion, beyond the material spheres of the world. Then suddenly a completely different line of escape was discovered. The Superlife, unification, the way out so long dreamt of, so long sought after heretofore in a realm 'beyond,' in the direction of some Transcendence – perhaps, rather, it

is to be perceived as a 'forward' movement, that is, an extension of the imma-nent forces of Evolution, and it is here that it is to be found, that it awaits us?" See Pierre Teilhard de Chardin, *L'Avenir de l'homme* (Paris: Editions du Seuil, 1959), p. 342. [Trans. into English as *The Future of Man* (New York: Harper & Row, 1964).]

54. The General Conclusions of Medellin, no. 10.

55. Ibid., no. 14.

56. Ibid., no. 7.

57. Ibid., no. 11.

58. Paul VI, "Address to the Council," 7 December 1965, in *La Doc. Cath.*, 2 January 1966, cols. 62–63.

59. Ibid., cols. 65–66.

60. Vatican Council II, "Pastoral Constitution on the Church in the Modern World," no. 55.

READING 9

Religious Education: From Early Christianity to Medieval Times

GERARD S. SLOYAN

The wide-ranging contribution of Gerard Sloyan to the Roman Catholic Church in the United States in liturgical, biblical, and catechetical studies is yet to be chronicled, possibly because his work continues unabated. Especially from the time of his appointment to the chair of the Department of Religious Education at Catholic University, Sloyan was a major facilitator of catechetical renewal throughout the United States. He played leading roles in the early international catechetical weeks, in the influential Catechetical Forum, and in the Liturgical Conference. His influence was particularly effective in his scholarly research and writing.

The lengthy historical study which follows has been, for many seeking to understand the history of catechesis, an important, seminal piece of work that continues to deserve careful study. Out of print almost fifteen years, it deserves a special place in this sourcebook.

IN READING the conciliar legislation of pre-Tridentine Europe, one has the feeling that life was a good deal simpler in days when bishops could insist on enough Latinity in their clerics to have them recite pater, ave, credo, and read the text of Mass and the other

Reprinted with permission of Macmillan Publishing Co., Inc., from *Shaping the Christian Message*, ed. Gerard S. Sloyan, pp. 11–45, © Macmillan Publishing Co., Inc. 1958.

sacraments. The faithful had only to know the Lord's Prayer and creed in their own tongues; these their priests were required to be able to expound in the vernacular of the place.[1] This public instruction delivered to adults and children indiscriminately on the occasion of the celebration of the eucharistic liturgy is the oldest form of catechetical presentation. Nothing can be expected to supplant it in importance, though a myriad of devices can and should be worked out to meet the special needs of the young.

One such device is the catechism. In concept, the catechism is a doctrinal handbook prescribed by bishops as a guide to their clergy in providing a pulpit catechesis. It has inevitably made its way into the hands of children as both the first outline of faith presented to them (in abridged form) and the last summary many of them see of religious knowledge. This is a development no more than four centuries old: that each child should have a summary of doctrine in the form of a handbook for his or her own use. Yet when Martin Luther brought out his *kleine Katechismus* in 1529, following late-medieval practice already well established, he set a pattern that is with us still and gives promise of being so for many years to come.

The earliest noncanonical handbook of instruction we have and our "sole ancient source on the matter of the catechesis"[2] is the *Didaché* or *Teaching of the Twelve Apostles,* sixteen brief chapters, possibly of multiple authorship, stemming from Egypt, Syria, or Palestine sometime between the years 60 and 90. A few put it as late as 130, and fewer still place it in the third century as a Montanist document.[3] Very likely it is a compilation of materials from various periods. It echoes the decrees of the Apostolic Council (Acts 15:28 ff.) in its prescription to abstain from meat offered to idols (6:3). In general, its primitive status is not seriously questioned by scholars. Leclercq reviews the arguments concerning its Hebraic character which incline some to think that large parts of it are pre-Christian in origin, the Christian elements being interpolated.[4] There is no professedly dogmatic instruction in the *Didaché* but only Christian morality, an outline of liturgical conduct (baptism, Eucharist, public confession, fasting), and some indications as to authority and the various ministries in the early Church. There is every reason to consider it a faithful mirror of apostolic teaching methods. An interesting matter is the simple, catechism-like division at the outset between the two ways leading to life and death, basically an Old Testament pattern. Further on, Christ's command to love God and neighbor is coupled with the Golden Rule in negative form as the one means to blessedness. The Lord's precepts from the Sermon on the Mount are woven in beautifully with the Ten Commandments and with St. Paul's spirit of clear admonition to the churches. There are warnings against infanticide and killing a fetus by abortion (2:2) and some stirring phrases about open-handed generosity. Preachers must be honored as the Lord (4:1). The trinitarian formula of baptism (by triple pouring if immersion in running or other water is impracticable) is followed by the Lord's Prayer (7 and 8). The latter is to become a constant in all catechetical instruction. In the *Didaché* it is commanded to be said with its concluding doxology ("for Thine is the glory and the power for evermore") three times a day (8:2–3). "As regards your prayers and alms and your whole conduct, do exactly as you have it in the gospel of Our Lord" (15:4) is a phrase which seems to presuppose a written Gospel. There is no use made of Bible incidents in the *Didaché*, but phrases from both testaments are used with all naturalness throughout: "In every place and time offer only a pure sacrifice; for I am a mighty king, says the Lord" (Mal. 1:11–14). "You do not know the hour in which Our Lord is coming" (see Matt. 24:42).

When the Alexandrian Jew, Apollos, arrived at Ephesus, speaking with fervor of whatever had to do with Jesus, he was described (Acts 18:25) as *katēchēménos* – "instructed" in the way of the Lord from the fact of his having learned from a living voice. The sound specified the act.[5] *Katēchéthēs* meant for St. Luke the fact of having been taught about Christ (Luke 1:4); to give the instruction, *katēchēsō*, that led to understanding was Paul's ambition much more than "ten thousand words in a tongue" (1 Cor. 14:19). A man instructed, *katēchoúmenos*, should share all good things with his teacher, *katēchoûnti*, according to Gal. 6:6. The fact that oral instruction was the normal means of knowledge about Christ made the term "catechesis" come to mean either the act of teaching or the message taught. Private instruction was the primitive form, of course. Subsequently, groups were prepared for reception into the Church, and by the late third century "catechesis" commonly described what was transmitted in the "catechumenate" or sessions preparatory to baptism.[6]

Origen speaks of the books of Esther, Judith, Tobias, and Wisdom and other biblical extracts effective in inculcating moral conduct as suitable for the preparation of those "beginning the study of divine things."[7] From him and Tertullian we learn of the practice of infant baptism and therefore conclude that instruction was somehow in the parents' hands. The "church order" of Hippolytus of Rome known as the *Apostolic Tradition* describes, around the year 215, the moral stringency with which prospective candidates were screened and the form if not the subject matter of the primitive catechumenate.[8]

Origen's homilies are our first clear indication of the presence of the catechumen at Mass. Inducted into the catechumenate, after lengthy proof of goodwill, by the sign of the cross on his forehead and salt on his tongue, an imposition of hands, and a breathing on his brow, the candidate did his subsequent learning from Old and New Testament readings and sermons during the forepart of the Mass.

In the late second century, Clement of Alexandria (died circa 215) paints a charming picture of Christ as the educator of little ones (all who follow him) in his *Pedagogue.* Clement's career as an instructor in doctrine is marked by the transition within his lifetime from an earlier, simpler, catechetical pattern to a more complex, theological one. His students in the Alexandrian school of Pantaenus, whom he succeeded as head, were mostly well-to-do Greeks—therefore neither children nor the unlettered nor catechumens in the pre-baptismal sense. The presentation in *Paidagōgós* is philosophic and apologetic. "The all-loving Word," he writes, "anxious to perfect us in a way that leads progressively to salvation, makes effective use of an order well adapted to our development; first He persuades, then He forms, and after that He instructs."[9] Clement's *Protreptikós,* the first volume of his trilogy, is usually translated as *Exhortation to the Greeks;* then comes his *Paidagōgós* (in the sense of molder of character rather than intellectual instructor); finally, the doctrinal course known as the *Strōmata* or *Tapestries.* The Word himself sings a new song that charms with its beauty the ears that have been given over to paganism. All the philosophic inconsistency and moral crudity of pagan ways are to be dislodged by the knowledge of the justice and goodness of God, by the utter transcendency of Christianity.[10] Christ lays in the soul the foundation stone of noble persuasion. He has one proper title:

> Educator of the little ones, an Educator who does not simply follow behind, but who leads the way, for his aim is to improve the soul, not just to instruct it; to guide to a life of virtue, not merely one of knowledge. Yet that same Word does teach. It is simply that in this work we are not considering Him in that light.[11]

It is evident from this that the early Church grasped the twofold role of Christ as revealer and ruler of hearts. The distinction is important for all religious education: It must proclaim (*kerýssein*) a rule of divine love, or salvation accomplished, and elucidate (*didáskein*) the terms of life in the kingdom.[12]

Clement's style is rambling, but his mind is beautifully furnished. It has been said that he never came to write his treatise on Christ the teacher because of the order it would have held him to. In philosophy he is a stoic, in theology, an allegorist of Scripture. Chapters 5 and 6 of *Paidagōgós* wring all the sap from the concept of childlikeness before the loving instructor God as it is developed in the two testaments. The puffed-up mentality of the gnostics is the great enemy. Quoted above is his catechetical principle on spiritual formation as a legitimate end in teaching. Here is the way Clement states his commitment to simplicity of approach. It was Christ's way of teaching, and presumably it should be ours:

> In war there is need for much equipment, just as self-indulgence claims an abundance. But peace and love, simple and plain blood sisters, do not need arms nor abundant supplies. Their nourishment is the Word whose leadership enlightens and educates, from whom we learn poverty and humility and all that goes with love of freedom and mankind and the good.[13]

The third-century Syriac treatise called *Didaskalia* or *The Teaching of the Twelve Apostles* indulges in the fiction of having the several apostles speak up as the authors. It is a moral and disciplinary document from Syria or Palestine, not extant in its Greek original. The sole catechetical directive in the section on the states in life is a charge to the bishop to nourish the people with the word as with milk, dispensing to each according to need:

> You then (O bishops) are to your people . . . receivers of the word, and preachers and proclaimers thereof, and knowers of the Scripture and of the utterances of God, and witnesses of his will. . . . you are they who have heard how the word strongly threatens you if you neglect and preach not God's will.[14]

There is very little in this absorbing treatise that is directly doctrinal, but the Old Testament is extensively used to illustrate the virtues proper to various states.[15] When the author claims to be St. Matthew, he is somewhat embarrassingly handicapped in quoting from the Gospel according to St. John, which presumably had not been written yet.[16]

Irenaeus, bishop of Lyons in the late second and early third centuries (died 202?), met his obligation to teach with the treatise *Proof of the Apostolic Preaching.*[17] It is more apologetic than catechetical in intent, being a statement of the case against gnosticism and for the acceptance of the divine mission of the Church. Yet its net effect is instruction for Christians rather than a polemic against their enemies. In orientation the work is biblical. Its proof of the truth of the Gospel lies in establishing that the Gospel is the fulfillment of Old Testament prophecy.[18] Irenaeus contributes two important ideas to the catechetical question, one concerned with content and the other with method. He provides a basic creed, in three articles (chap. 6), which foreshadows all the creeds that are to follow:

> God, the Father, uncreated, beyond grasp, invisible, one God, the maker

of all; . . . the Word of God, the Son of God, Christ Jesus, Our Lord
. . . at the conclusion of ages, for the recapitulation of all things, is become
man . . . in order to abolish death and bring to light life (2 Tim. 1:10)
and bring about the communion of God and man; . . . the Holy Spirit,
through whom the prophets prophesied . . . who . . . has been poured
forth in a new manner upon humanity over all the earth, renewing man
to God.[19]

The baptism of our rebirth comes through belief in Irenaeus' three
articles on the three Persons, since the Father confers incorruptibility
on those, presented to him by the Son, who in turn were led to that
Word by the Spirit. As to method of presentation, Irenaeus' treatise
is not far advanced (chap. 11, eight modern pages), before he begins
with the creation narrative and retells the bulk of the Old Testament
very succinctly. His recapitulation figure of Adam and Christ (virgin
earth; virginal disobedience and virginal obedience; cross and tree) is
the beginning of a restrained search for types of our Lord through the
patriarchal period and the periods of Moses and the prophets. He
employs the narrative method with considerable effect and sets the
stage for all subsequent attempts to see in Christ the summing up of
humanity, typified by the Jews who awaited God's revelation. In
general his technique is the simple quotation of Old Testament prophecy and its fulfillment by Christ, literal wherever possible. Because
of its distinct typology, a brief "chapter" – one of one hundred such (all
are short, but this one is exceptionally brief) – may be worth quoting:

77. Again, He says in the twelve prophets (Osee 10:6) [according to the
Septuagint text]: *and they brought Him bound as a present to the king.*
For Pontius Pilate was Procurator of Judaea, and was at that time on
bad terms with Herod, king of the Jews. Now, therefore, Pilate sent Christ
. . . bound, to Herod . . . having found in Christ an apt occasion for
reconciliation with the king.[20]

Coming down to religious instruction more professedly, the magnificent course given by Cyril, bishop of Jerusalem, to the catechumens
of his flock in Lent and Easter Week of 348(?) is outstanding of its
kind. It is known as *Katēchēseis phōtizoménōn, Instruction for Those
about to be Illumined.*[21] The chief thing to bear in mind about St.
Cyril's lessons in Christian belief is that such homilies woven into the
fabric of liturgy were for centuries the sole mode of religion teaching
for young and old alike. Forty days of catechetical training were
evidently given in eighteen lectures to those inscribed for holy baptism (already called "the faithful," as if more a part of the Church than
the simple inquirers in the catechumenate).[22] These talks to the *competentes* or *electi*, as they were known in Rome, went concurrently with
prescribed ascetical practices. After baptism on Holy Saturday night,

five instructions to the *neophyti* followed. These dealt with the sacraments of baptism, confirmation, and the Eucharist and the new obligations of Christian life as outlined in 1 Pet. 2:1–23.

St. Cyril is a simple and clear teacher who does not multiply theological terms. His method is in part apologetic in that he includes the teachings of heretics, Jews, Samaritans, and pagans and coaches his hearers on how to respond. The first three catechetical talks are by way of (1) introduction, (2) a consideration of sin, the devil, repentance, remission, and (3) holy baptism. A dogmatic summary follows in the fourth catechesis: belief about God, Christ, the virgin birth, Christ's crucifixion and burial, resurrection, his return as judge, and the Holy Spirit; then about man, his soul and body, corporeal resurrection, and man's final end as known from the Scriptures. This done, Cyril has a fifth instruction on faith and, with his sixth, begins thirteen distinct catecheses on the creed as mid-fourth century Jerusalem recited it. The rule of secrecy (*disciplina arcani*) forbade its presentation in any one place before baptism, but it can be pieced together from the fact that the numbered catecheses are essentially a paraphrase and exposition of a "symbol" composed of these articles: belief in (6) one God who is a (7) Father, (8) all-powerful, (9) Creator of the heavens and earth and of all things visible and invisible, and in (10) Jesus Christ, (11) the only Son of God, begotten by the Father before all ages, through whom everything was made, (12) Incarnate, that is, made man of the Virgin and the Holy Spirit, (13) crucified and buried, (14) he rose on the third day, ascended into heaven to sit on the Father's right hand, (15) will come in glory to judge the living and the dead, with no end to his reign, and in (16–17) one Holy Spirit who has spoken through the prophets, (18) in one only Church, holy and catholic, in the resurrection of the body and life without end. A penultimate phrase in this Palestinian creed concerns belief in one baptism of repentance for the remission of sins, but St. Cyril has discussed this article in his first three catecheses.[23]

He is not accounted theologically rich or complex in the manner of his contemporaries Athanasius, Hilary, or Basil, but there is in him an echo of Christian doctrine as presented in the fourth century at its best and clearest.[24] Cyril resembles Christ in his fusion of dogmatic and moral elements when he presents the Gospel. His sermons are parochial preaching of a high order. He is as fond of paradoxes as Augustine is, and when he hits his stride they come tumbling at the hearer:

> Christ came to be baptized and to sanctify baptism, to work miracles such as walking on the water. Before His coming in the flesh, the sea saw and fled and the Jordan was turned back. Because of this the Lord assumed

a body so that the water might see Him and receive Him, the Jordan embrace Him unafraid. . . .

When men deserted God, they made likenesses of the human form and this lying likeness they worshipped as a god; but God became man to dispel the lie. . . . The Lord assumed our likeness so as to grant salvation to our nature. He took it with the purpose of conferring on it a greater grace than the defect it had suffered, of making a sinful human nature participant in God.[25]

Gregory of Nyssa's *Katēchēseos lógos* or *Great Catechetical Discourse* is another treatise of the same period (usually dated somewhat prior to 385) but a controversial manual much more philosophical than its name would imply.[26] The great dogmas are expounded—Trinity, Incarnation, Redemption—and the sacraments of baptism and the Eucharist. This, however, is done in a way suited more to masters of the catechumenate than to the catechumens themselves, and the subtitle, "against pagans, Jews, and heretics," is indicative of this fact. St. Gregory attended to individual differences in his recommendation of various approaches to persons who had believed either in many gods, or in one God but not in Jesus as the Christ, or in God but not as one in three persons (the Arians, for example). He advises instructors in religion to profit by intermediate concessions to listeners so that they may be brought to the possibility of belief in the Church. Thus:

But it may happen that the Greek, with the help of his general ideas, and the Jew, with his Scriptures, will not dispute the existence of a Word of God and a Spirit. But the design of God the Word exhibited in His becoming man will be rejected by both of them equally as being incredible and unfit to be attributed to God. We shall adopt, therefore, a different starting point in order to induce our opponents to believe in this.[27]

The proper "starting point" is surely basic to all catechetical discussion.

St. Gregory is speculative throughout. He relies on biblical data for his argument on a limited number of occasions. There is one instance, for example, where he reviews the evil perpetuated by Cain, the Sodomites, Assyrians, and Herod the Great to prove that God the healer waited until every form of human evil had been explored before he applied a cure to the disease.[28]

The lectures of St. Cyril to his catechumens described above, because of their wide diffusion, resulted in a whole series of interpretations of the creed over the next five or six decades.[29] Noteworthy among these is the *Commentarius in Symbolum Apostolorum* of Rufinus of Aquileia, usually dated around the year 404. In it there are numerous borrowings from the treatises on baptismal creeds which are common in his day and from St. Gregory of Nyssa's *Catechetical Discourse*, but Cyril's influence is preponderant. The main body of Rufinus' work has even been described as a "rather free, drastically abbreviated presentation in Latin of St. Cyril's teaching in the Catechetical Lectures, notably Catecheses 13–18."[30] Rufinus' chief service is that he enlightens us as to the composition of Western creeds, of which until his time only fragments were known from the writings of Tertullian, Cyprian, and the threefold questioning at immersion quoted in Hippolytus' *Apostolic Tradition* (see note 8 above). Rufinus is not precisely a pioneer in Latin, for the Illyrian Bishop Niceta of Remesiana (335?–415?) had produced an admirable short treatise on the creed entitled simply *De Symbolo* which gives us substantially the same articles as those of the Apostles' Creed.

Niceta has a laudable succinctness of style but a certain polemical air as he warns his flock against the "meshes" of heretics, pagans, and Jews. He devotes the last three pages of what comprise eleven in a modern book to a defense of the possibility of bodily resurrection.[31] A brief example of his style should suffice:

> Our faith, therefore, is that He who was born of the Virgin is God with us, God from the Father before all ages, a man born of the Virgin for the sake of men. He was truly born in the flesh, not in mere seeming. Certain heretics, erroneously ashamed of the Mystery of God, say that the Incarnation of the Lord was effected in a phantom . . . . This is far indeed from God's truth. For if the Incarnation is unreal, the salvation of men will be an illusion.[32]

To return to Rufinus, the point should be made that his catechetical teaching is directed to extremely thoughtful adults, despite his protestations about a "brief word" directed to "little ones in Christ and mere novices" (chap. 1). He passes along the already deep-rooted tradition that the Apostles' Creed was composed by the contribution of one article by each of the Twelve before they dispersed finally to preach to the ends of the earth.[33] There is in his pages a modicum of allegorical interpretation of the Old Testament. In the main, however, Rufinus provided his contemporaries with a most enlightening handbook of apologetics and doctrine. It is closer in spirit to the dogmatic explanations which the modern adult Catholic is used to than most of the patristic writings that went before it. Thus, in his commentary on the article "the forgiveness of sins," he writes:

> Pagans habitually make fun of us, saying that we deceive ourselves if we imagine that mere words can wipe out offences which have actually been committed. "Is it possible," they say, "for one who has committed murder to be no murderer, or for the perpetrator of adultery to be represented as no adulterer? How then is someone who is guilty of misdeeds like these going to be suddenly made holy?"[34]

Rufinus is far from devoid of the gift of biblical usage to make his points. When he writes of the article on the holy Church,[35] for example, he describes it as "without spot or wrinkle" (Eph. 5:27). The prophet's comment (Ps. 25:5) on Marcion, Valentinus, Ebion, Mani, and Arius is said to be, "I have hated the assembly of the malignant, and with the wicked I will not sit." But the Spirit says of our Church (Cant. 6:8), "One is my dove; one is she; and perfect unto her mother." The "council of vanity" and "doers of unjust things" (Ps. 25:4) denote Marcion's assembly, Ebion's Judaizing, and the teaching of Mani in those places where he proclaims himself the Paraclete.[36] Rufinus employs the Old Latin version of the Scriptures so frequently that he becomes a substantial witness to its text. Taken all together, we begin to have in his credal catechesis (it covers some eighty-seven printed pages in English) a core instruction basic to the theology and preaching of the West. He devotes a lengthy section to the mode of generation in divine Persons as contrasted with human and says in connection with the Passion:

> No doubt, inspired as you are by loving devotion to the Sacred Scriptures, you will protest to me that these facts ought to be corroborated by convincing Scriptural evidence. . . . On the assumption, however, that my argument is addressed to people familiar with the Law, I am deliberately passing over a whole forest of evidence for the sake of brevity.[37]

His "passing over" can be called an omission only by some elusive standard for he immediately begins to multiply biblical references despite the assumption he has just made. Rufinus employs the New Testament in what we would call a strict theological sense, though for the Old he indulges in every shade of typology and accommodation.

St. Ambrose's *De Mysteriis* (almost certainly authentic) is a colorful exposition in nine brief chapters which conveys to the newly baptized (*neophyti*) the idea of the change the Spirit has wrought in them through the bath of rebirth, the seal in chrism as they emerge from the waters, and the spiritual food of Christ's Body. In a sense doctrine is not so much taught as assumed. The credal explanation of the catechumenate days just before Easter is totally available to them, and the writer does no more than reword its elements with the illustrative aid of both testaments. He goes from Pentateuch to prophets, Epistles to Gospels indiscriminately. Here in classic form is the oldest catechetical assumption: that the Bible or the oral teaching based upon it is the source of all doctrine for Christians.

For Ambrose, the baptizing bishop who preaches the Kingdom of Christ and life eternal is none other than the priest of the old Law, God's visible messenger (Mal. 2:7).[38] Naaman the leprous Syrian is the soul in need of baptism, and the slave girl of Israel who knows that healing power is from her God and not from rushing rivers stands for the unredeemed Gentile nations who yet will be a grace-enlivened

Church;[39] Christ nourishes his Church with sacraments which are like the breasts of the spouse in the Canticle of Canticles, the honey on her lips, the fragrance of her garments; like a garden enclosed the Christian mysteries must be kept inviolate by the faithful, unadulterated by evil speech or deeds.[40] Baptismal regeneration is described in terms of the flood and its signs of abatement (Gen., chaps. 7 and 8), the branch brought back by the dove being the wood of Christ's cross and the raven a figure of sin which departs never to return.[41] In another place, Christ's cross is the staff of Moses turning bitter waters sweet by its regenerating effect on the natural water of a stream and so on. Ambrose's catechesis is a pedagogic marvel, but it leaves some doubt about the way in which the earlier learnings had been conveyed. In the language of modern pedagogy, it is a "culminating lesson" so successful that it makes the onlooker wonder about the many hours of "drill." This question suggests itself about all the early centuries of catechesis: What were the nonlenten and nonfestal Sundays of instruction like? Did the general level of instruction approach that of the great patristic landmarks summarized by Daniélou at the close of his introduction to *The Bible and the Liturgy*?

All the evidence available (or better, the lack of it) indicates that it was left to Christian parents and godparents to instruct their offspring in the truths of faith. No treatise directed to parents or children exists. There is, in fact, but one piece of early Christian writing addressed to adult heretics and pagans while they still had the status of inquirers (*accedentes*). This is St. Augustine's famous *De Catechizandis Rudibus* written about 405.[42] A *rudis* for him was a person untaught in Christianity, not by any means a rough fellow. Deogratias, a deacon of Carthage, had asked Hippo's famous bishop for some hints on the task of catechizing and received as a response a full-scale *enarratio* (exposition of sacred history) along with a second, briefer one. The first of these model catecheses runs to ten chapters; the latter, a masterpiece of effective compression, is one and one-half. Before he gives these two instructions, which have as their purpose leading the *rudes* toward the catechumenate, Augustine has devoted fifteen chapters to a discussion of the proper subject matter, the motivations of candidates, and various techniques of address. The treatise is pedagogical in a classic sense. It does not often descend to the particulars of doctrinal presentation, which are saved for the two catecheses themselves. Augustine suggests how best to deal with the supercilious, the half-educated, the weary, the bored. A serialized discourse is contemplated (or under the pressure of time, a single one); questions are to be used as a periodic check on the learner's grasp of things rather than as a teaching device. The catechist must labor to keep his enthusiasm alive despite the repetitive nature of his task and the elementary knowledge conveyed. The picture of the incomparable Augustine methodically laying siege to the mind of some heavy-lidded Punic laborer is sheer balm for the theologians and catechists of the ages who have put in endless hours with the very simple or the very young.

No one, actually, who teaches religion can afford to be unfamiliar with Augustine's uncanny analysis of this apostolate. His insights into the characters of teacher and taught are beyond price and yet his specifications for the content of the preliminary catechesis need careful evaluation. The Augustinian method is usable today only if catechists are determined to restore to their pupils a full-scale familiarity with the Bible. There is no question of where Augustine's emphasis lies. He is an apostle of divine love whose success lies in his having put emphasis on the Decalogue as perfectly summarized in the command to love God and neighbor. Augustine observes (chap. 4, par. 7) that in all human experience, nothing invites love more than a lover who takes the lead in loving:

> If . . . Christ came chiefly for this reason, that man might learn how much God loves him, and might . . . love his neighbor at the bidding and after the example of Him who made Himself man's neighbor by loving him . . . then it is evident that on these two commandments of the love of God and the love of our neighbor depend . . . the whole law and the Prophets.[43]

Augustine maintains that all divine Scripture written before Christ was written to foretell his coming and that the whole purpose of any subsequent writing is to tell of Christ and to counsel love. "Therefore, in the Old Testament the New is concealed, and in the New the Old is revealed."[44] No understanding of Augustine is possible without a grasp of this simple exegetical and pedagogic principle. He attacks all portions of both testaments in search of Christ and, because they contain him, Augustine is not disappointed.

His longer catechesis has as its preliminary a discussion of the contrast between the peace assured by a good Christian conscience and the mad pleasures of life which any little fever could carry off. The "void and wounded conscience . . . shall find in Him a severe Lord whom it scorned to seek and love as a gentle Father" (par. 25). Augustine describes the lover of God, on the other hand, as one who shudders at offending by sin, not so much because he or she deserves punishment thereby, but because such a person forfeits the chance to be forever with him whom he loves. After thus dividing the whole race into men and women of these two states of heart, the Augustinian catechesis proceeds to examine the opening pages of Genesis. The Lord's rest on the Sabbath after creation is no sooner told than it is used to illustrate the world's seventh age – that of repose in the peace of Christ. The Fall in Paradise becomes immediately the vehicle for a justification of that good-out-of-evil which God is always able to achieve, whether the disruption of order be angelic or human.

The good and the wicked on the earth, the wheat and the chaff, are Augustine's great preoccupation. His treatment of the deluge and of Abraham reveal what a transcendent spiritual sense the least scriptural detail can bear in his handling. All the patriarchs and prophets were like limbs emerging from a womb before the infant's head, for example (par. 33), Christ being head of the universal body. The Easter vigil liturgy of baptism, as we know it, is contained in Augustine's exposition of the Red Sea escape, the rock struck by Moses' rod, and the account of the exodus. The catechesis touches on the levitical precepts and King David's earthly Jerusalem and Jeremiah's prophecy of release after seventy years of captivity. Nowhere does Augustine satisfy himself with the mere Old Testament telling; with him, all is type and foretelling: "In that land of promise many things were done for a type of the Christ to come and of the Church; and these you will be able to learn gradually in the holy books (chap. 20, par. 36).[45]

An important cue for modern catechetics lies here. St. Augustine is making Christianity attractive by means of an interpretation of a Bible which the *rudes* will spend a whole subsequent lifetime growing familiar with in liturgical worship. His plan is effective only because there is a full-scale exposition of the sacred books in prospect. Otherwise, the Bible becomes a tantalizing conundrum without historical context or literal sense of its own. He uses the Scripture narratives in his initial instruction to whet spiritual appetites, but the technique is valid only so long as the appetite has a chance of being later satisfied. Otherwise the candidate will receive nothing but an incomplete and garbled ladling out of biblical information.

Augustine names the five ages of humanity from creation to Christ (marked off by Adam, Noe, Abraham, David, and the Babylonian migration). The sixth age is our Lord's earthly life, which he tells of in a sustained paradox which must qualify as one of the great passages in all the history of rhetoric: "Christ the Lord, made man, despised all the good things of earth that He might show us that these things are not to be despised; and endured all earthly ills . . . so that neither might happiness be taught in the former nor unhappiness be feared in the latter. . . . He hungered who feeds all, He thirsted by whom all drink is created. . . . He was bound who has freed men from the bonds of their infirmities. . . . He was crucified who put an end to our torments" (chap. 22, par. 40).

Augustine's conclusion in this longer of the two proposed catecheses is much of a piece with the whole product: incredibly fine writing which never scruples to reach the heart and which always starts from some observed phenomenon of daily life. The terrible silence of the dead, or the untrustworthiness of man, or human longing for a surfeit of power, wealth, prestige—these are the starting points of Augustine's defense of God and his love. Although it is perhaps not fair to let this simple, short treatise preparatory to the salt and sign of a catechumen's status stand for his entire catechesis, there is enough of it here to bear the weight. Augustine stands for beauty of language in religion teaching, emotional appeal based on the most intellectual considerations, and a "spiritual" reading of the data of revelation. This sentence from chapter 49 should be a death blow (of course it has been nothing of the sort) to the idea that catechisms must be written dully: "But it is one thing to love man, another to put your trust in man; and so great is the difference that God commands the former but forbids the latter." The new German catechism which concludes each lesson, "For my life" or "From the teachings of the saints," attempts to convey the sap of great teachers like Augustine in brief and memorable phrases like the above.

Tracing the decline of the catechumenate as an institution is not an easy matter, though it is sure that this decline set in toward the end of the fifth century. The assumption is that the infant baptism of the offspring of Christians was much on the increase during the period and the practice of deferring the regenerating sacrament until high maturity or until one's deathbed was much in decline. The catechumenate became the training ground for reduced numbers of converts; primarily it became an institution for parents and godparents in their children's interest. In other words, the instructional situation went from prebaptismal to postbaptismal.[46] There are scattered sixth-century references to the continuance of the catechumenate in Africa, Gaul, and Spain. St. Isidore of Seville (died 636) required instruction of the *competentes* in the creed and rule of faith at baptism, chrismation, and the imposition of hands.[47] His six brief chapters are a valuable compendium. Yet, with all his speed and compression of treatment, anointing must begin with Moses and Aaron (chap. 26, 2).

An extant poem of St. Avitus (died 526) is entitled *De mosaicae historiae gestis libri quinque.* In it, Satan is "callidus Draco" and "lethi magister." The poem recalls St. Augustine's historical approach to catechetics in that the topics treated are creation, original sin, the expulsion from paradise, the deluge, the crossing of the Red Sea.[48] The sermons attributed to St. Caesarius of Arles (died 542) show us that the distribution of catechetical material was proceeding as customarily.[49]

It was the apostolic activity of men like Saints Patrick, Columban, Augustine of Canterbury, Eligius (Eloi), Gall, Willibrod, and Boniface that required in the fifth through the eighth centuries a recasting of the whole concept of religious instruction. The challenge of apostolic times was back upon the Church in this period of expansion; and, although nothing essential was sacrificed, a simplicity of approach succeeded the highly organized catechumenate days. None of the catechetical sermons of these men has survived, busied as they were with a round of exposition in vernacular tongues foreign to them. We must assume that they achieved products modeled on the Latin discourses (with Cyril and Methodius it would be Greek) they were accustomed to from youth, rough-hewn to meet the challenge of idolatrous paganism. Pope Boniface V's letter to Edwin of Northumberland before the king became a Christian (624) outlines this catechetical program: the futility of idol worship; the need to believe in God who is the Creator, in his Son sent for our salvation; the need to accept the Gospel, signified by baptism.[50]

The recital of sacred history as given by St. Augustine in his *enarratio* continues to be normative for most Christian teachers.[51] Among the Germans and Anglo-Saxons especially, there seems to have been carried over the catechumenate practice of requiring the creed and pater to be memorized by the candidates and expounded by the bishop or priest during the lenten season preceding their baptism.[52]

With what amounts to a monotony of solicitude, the conciliar legislation of the Carolingian period tries to see to it that the clergy explain the Lord's Prayer and the Apostles' or Nicene Creed both regularly and adequately.[53]

Alcuin of York (died 804), the teacher of Charlemagne, is credited with having introduced the question-and-answer method of catechetical instruction, but the attribution seems to be faulty. What he actually did was compose 281 separate queries for his biblical commentary *Interrogationes et responsiones in Genesin.*[54] Perhaps as a result, the authorship of a manuscript dating to the year 900 is likewise ascribed to him. Entitled *Disputatio puerorum per interrogationes et responsiones,* it runs to a dozen chapters of the most amazing information, philological and otherwise.[55] Large sections are compiled directly from the writings of Origen and Isidore of Seville. Usually the questions are short and to the point, less frequently the answers. But we do find this brevity: "Can the soul have any other likeness to the Trinity?" "Yes, it can." "How, then?" "Well, in the first place, just as God exists, lives and knows, so too does the soul exist, live and know, after its own fashion."[56] The soul's three faculties of intellect, will, and memory are alleged as a further human similarity to the Trinity (since memory depends on the former two somewhat as the Spirit proceeds from Father and Son). Occasionally, a "question" will serve more as a Socratic means to retain the inquiry form, and little else. Thus:

> *Inter.* I should like to hear more on this same topic from you.
> *Resp.* And I shall continue explaining in proportion as I know.

The respondent then returns to his briefly interrupted argument, using phrases much like the soul-body analogy employed by the Athanasian Creed to teach the Incarnation, though in this case it is the Trinity which is being illustrated.

An early chapter describes the days of creation, though it turns out to be chiefly a defense of six as a perfect number. Then comes a lesson in human nature: corporeal, spiritual, and etymological (the temples beneath the cranium are called such because they move at intervals — *tempora . . . tempora*). A third chapter describes the three kinds of spirits: pure, mixed (that is, human), and brutish. Some highly questionable Hebrew philology follows on the ten Old Testament names of God, but the discussion of the divine attributes is the traditional one. His impassibility, simplicity, and immensity as described in the *Disputatio* are in much the same form as they have come to us through the medieval *summae*. Ever since Christ's coming, we are in the sixth and last age of the world (chap. 5), while chapter 6 discusses the concept and divisions of time.

Once this preliminary work has been done, sacred history proper begins. Chapters 7 and 8 describe the contents of each of the books of the two testaments. The authorship of Esther is attributed to Esther, but this spirit scarcely characterizes the work as a whole; for example, the possibility of the non-Pauline authorship of Hebrews for vocabulary and stylistic reasons is referred to, Barnabas and Clement being cited as likely composers. It is, in all, a surprisingly good summary of factual information and is almost without exhortatory material. A ninth chapter discusses sacred orders in the Church (a fifth minor order, psalmist, is included), and under "deacon" there is a digression to establish why Matthew is correctly understood to be symbolized by the man of Isaiah, Mark by the lion, Luke by the heifer, and John by the eagle. It is typical of the *Disputatio* that the etymology of *presbyter* and *sacerdos* should suffice to define the priesthood at the conclusion of the chapter, while surprisingly the episcopate is not discussed.

Chapter 10 is on the Mass (explained as a word taken from the dismissal of the catechumens as the offertory came on). *Dona et munera* refer respectively to gifts which are God's and obligations proper to humanity; a *donum* is bought with money, a *sacrificium* effected in blood. In somewhat unsettling fashion we are told the meaning (frequently a supposed derivation and no more) of *immolatio, libatio, victima, hostia.* There are listed seven chief prayers of the Mass, an early echo of the number seven in the whole catechetical process. They are: (1) *Dominus vobiscum* and *Oremus;* (2) Collect; (3) prayer for the living offerers or the faithful departed in the interest of whose pardon the sacrifice is being offered; (4) *Sursum corda* to *per Christum Dominum nostrum* of the Preface, described as a prayer for peace and reconciliation; (5) *Per quem majestatem tuam* to *Osanna in excelsis,* an invitation to all the creatures of heaven and earth to worship; (6) *Te igitur,* a plea for the conformity of the visible species to the body and blood through the action of the Spirit; and (7) the *Pater noster.* The seven petitions of the Our Father are then analyzed, three describing God's attributes and four the needs of humankind.

Chapter 11 is on faith. It employs a careful scrutiny of the phrases of the Apostles' Creed and is much in the manner of the modern catechism — though there is time to pause and explain that the "judge in Judaea at that time" was called Pontius because of his birthplace. "What does Catholic mean?" "Universal, that is, spread over the whole earth. I believe that there is for me a communion of saints, that is to say holiness and fellowship with them if I hold fast to the faith and serve by works." The password used by Jepte and his Galaadites, "shibboleth" (Judg. chap. 12), is described at length to illustrate why the twelve apostles thought it important to compose a symbol or sign of the faith Christians held before they departed on their separate evangelical missions. Then the anonymous author gives the first article as composed by Peter, the second as by Andrew, after them James, John, Philip, and so on. Matthias, although a latecomer, contributes the double article, "the resurrection of the body and life everlasting." The twelfth and concluding chapter has the questioner checking back to see whether the petitions of the Lord's Prayer were committed to memory. He is always gentle; until now it had been "my dear brother," but now we find, "Tell me, I beg you." This the cooperative *puer* does, even to pointing out that we do not ask to be freed of temptations, since we all need trial, but only those we cannot endure.

The spirit and influence of the *Disputatio puerorum* are such that the space devoted to it here seems justified. It was analytical to the point of pedantry, a theologian's work or even an encyclopedist's, but endowed with the specious cast of a student's handbook. In it the Bible is taught about rather than taught from. Philosophical terms are given full credit in this exposition of religion; and the makings of textbook catechetics are already on the horizon: orderly, exhaustive, removed from the spirit of Christ's preaching, slightly repellent to the youthful mind.

A truncated manuscript is in existence dated 841–843, twelve brief chapters of the seventy-two originally written by a good mother named Dodena (Duodena, Dhuoda), wife of Bernard of Septimania, to her son William (a page to Charles the Bald) and his little brother. This *Liber manualis* is a very warm document which disappoints only by its abbreviated condition. We have her thoughts and admonitions on loving God but not her chapters "On the Holy Trinity" or "On Faith, Hope, and Charity." Other attractive but missing titles concern the respect due to priests, the fleeing of pride, and a proposed list of trials and means to their avoidance, for example, persecution, need, illness. The mother's stated purpose is that her sons will have a mirror-image of her near when she is separated from them. Dodena's manual happens to be addressed to youth, but it is of a literary type with Alcuin's *De virtutibus et vitiis* (addressed to Wido of Marca Britanniae around 800, on Christian perfection for the solider)[57] and Paulinus of Aquileia's *Libellus exhortatorius*.[58]

It must be remembered that the function of the episcopal schools was largely to prepare a clergy rather than Christian youth generally. A canon (7) of the Council of Béziers in 1246 is more to the point in connection with religious ignorance with its requirement that:

> parish priests see to it that they explain to the people on Sundays the articles of faith in simple and clear fashion so that no one may claim a veil of ignorance. . . . Children too from seven upwards, brought to Church by their parents on Sundays and feasts, shall be instructed in the Catholic faith, and parents shall teach them *Mary's Salutation, Our Father* and *Creed.*[59]

At Albi in 1254 the same wording is repeated, with the suggestion that what the bishop cannot accomplish in his own person he should enlist "other reliable and prudent persons" to aid him in doing.[60]

The eleventh century treatises of Fulbert of Chartres[61] and Bonizon of Plaissance[62] on the sacraments are catechetical in the remote sense. The same is true of Abelard's short expositions of the Lord's Prayer, Apostles', and Athanasian creeds.[63] They are more for the information of the clergy or the pious reading of the learned – though all three are simple and direct. With the twelfth century comes the *Elucidarium* attributed to Honorius, head of the school of Autun, a prolific writer of whose life nothing is known.[64] More likely an unknown disciple of St. Anselm was its author. Again, it is a theological summary, not a child's handbook; but the question-answer form places it in the catechetical stream. A distinguishing feature which should recommend it to modern youth is that *discipulus* asks the questions while *magister* answers them. The influence of this work on medieval piety is incalculable. It was translated into many languages, including the Welsh, and flourished for several centuries.

The *Elucidarium* has a distressingly modern ring to it in dozens of places. Surely it marks the death and burial of the patristic tradition in catechetics, just as it brings to the fore the theological answer-machine which, while claiming to deal in mysteries, does not seem to be aware of any. There is a certain censorious tone to this work with its author's calm settlement of who shall likely be damned. Tradesmen have little hope, being cheats; soldiers will almost surely be lost, as will craftsmen and public penitents – evidently a bad lot in those days. (On who shall be saved he does not seem to possess as exact information, though farmers will in large part make it because they live simply.) And yet there are many ways in which it is attractive, notably the brevity of its responses and its directness. The dialogue is in three books, the first of which is dogmatic (progressing from the nature of God to the efficacy of the sacraments, with a lengthy concluding section on evil priests and prelates); the second is concerned with sin, concupiscence, the number of the elect, and the influence of angels and demons; the third has to do with the last things, especially the respective statuses of the blessed and the damned. This "summary of all Christian theology," as its subtitle describes it, uses quotations from Scripture for purposes of proof and hole-stopping rather than by way of any attempt to elucidate the sacred text. An extended quotation should convey the technique best:

> *Discipulus.* What was the cause of the world's creation?
> *Magister.* The goodness of God, so that there might be those on whom to confer His grace.
> *D.* How was it done? – *M.* "He spoke and all things were made" (Ps. 22:9).
> *D.* And did He use words? – *M.* For God, to speak is to create all things by His Word, that is, in the Son; which is why we read, "In wisdom have you done all things" (Ps. 103:24).
> *D.* Was there any delay in the act of creating? – *M.* In the twinkling of an eye, which is to say as quickly as one could open his eye, or rather as the surface of the opened eye could perceive light.
> *D.* Did He create successively? – *M.* He made everything but once and at the one time: "He who endures forever created all things simultaneously" (Eccles. 18:1).

All this sounds extremely familiar to the modern ear. It could get past most theological censors. There are, however, nine choirs of angels for the Trinity's sake (being thrice three). Satan, who did not forsee his downfall, wanted to improve his lot and tyrannize over others. And for his pride? (*"Quid tunc?"*) "M. Ejected from the palace and thrust into prison, he who had been brightest in splendor was pitched in deepest darkness; once the foremost in fame, he is now the most hateful in horror." Such is the pattern of the treatise: an alternation of sound doctrine with poetic theology and occasionally barely defensible surmise or even legend.

Its author is especially hard on the evil lives of clerics and religious, with a certain boldness and balance one does not come upon in most anticlerical tirades. "Should the sons of priests be ordained?" he asks. By no means, for a poisoned strain flows in their veins, father to son. He is sound on their ability to "confect" true sacraments but weak in declaring that they do not receive the Body of Christ but only eat and drink judgment to themselves. The section on the predestination of the elect and the reprobate is helpful toward understanding why St. Augustine was claimed by the reformers. ("Whatever the predestined do they cannot perish because all works together unto good for them, even their very sins.") One encounters in this handbook "the mystical body of Christ, that is the Church," but enthusiasm is tempered by the discovery that Christ is the head, the eyes are the prophets and apostles, the ears the obedient, the mouth teachers in the Church, and the feet the farmers who feed it. The agricultural origins of this earnest schoolmaster are not hard to trace.

The *Elucidarium* is not a child's book (children could take little comfort from learning that all three-year-olds are saved whereas at five some are saved and some not). Nonetheless, it must have informed thousands of adults who in turn formed many children theologically. One has to admire the writer in the sweep of his knowledge – easy to lampoon but almost impossible to imitate. He knows no doubts; his is the ancient view that the last judgment will come in the middle of the night and the bear who ate the wolf who ate the man will pose no problem for God at the resurrection. But through all these pyrotechnics there runs the salvation theme in undisputed clarity. "The Father delivered up the Son and the Son delivered himself out of charity, but Judas delivered him over out of avarice." He has an eye to beauty and to tradition. "Why did Christ die on a cross?" "To save all at the four corners of the earth." "What does it mean to say that Christ sits at the right hand of the Father?" "That his human nature is at rest in the glory of divinity." He grows lyrical at the lot of the blessed and what it is *discipulus* may expect ("the handsomeness of Absalom, the strength of Samson, the prestige of Joseph in Egypt, the love of friends like David's for Jonathan"). And yet the net effect of the *Elucidarium* is slightly depressing, for religious encyclopedism is well in the saddle and a cloud no big-

ger than a man's hand is on the horizon. It will burst when 483 distinct
questions and answers have been assembled in one book. (In one national catechism the number is seven hundred.) The technique is deadly
because it lends itself to memorization so readily.

Another catechetical development followed when the question-and-
answer method was already well rooted. This was the practice of
teaching sacred truth by sevens. St. Augustine's *Sermon on the Mount*
had given the lead to this technique, with its harmonization of the seven
petitions of the Lord's Prayer and the beatitudes.[65] Bishop Joscelin of
Soissons (died circa 1099) remarks that he is familiar with the usage
and does not particularly favor it.[66] It is to Hugh of St. Victor (died
circa 1119) that we owe it chiefly, in his four-page work *De quinque
septenis seu septenariis.*[67] Hugh lists as his "five sevens" catalogues
of the capital sins (pride, envy, anger, weariness of spirit, greed, glut-
tony, and lust), the petitions of the Lord's Prayer, the gifts of the Holy
Ghost (in reverse order from the Vulgate's translation of Isa. 11:2f),
the virtues (humility, meekness, compunction, desire for the good, mercy, cleanness of heart, peace), and beatitudes (that is, states of
blessedness: the Kingdom of Heaven, the land of the living, consolation, one's fill of goodness, mercy, the sight of God, and the sonship
of God). Having elaborated on the ways the chief vices destroy a person, he finds a parallel between each vice and one of the seven things
Christ taught us to pray for. His treatment of the gifts of the Spirit
is less choppily mathematical, yet taken all together the little work is
abstract and even dull, except for one who has all the information
beforehand and can marvel at the cleverness of the harmonization.

St. Thomas Aquinas follows the pattern of Hugh of St. Victor with
regard to the numbering of petitions in his *opusculum* (7, *ed. Rom.*)
on the Lord's Prayer. For example:

FOURTH PETITION

Give us this day our daily bread. It frequently happens that a person will
become timorous as a result of great learning or wisdom. Then it is that
he needs fortitude of spirit lest he grow weak at critical times. *It is he
who gives the weary fresh spirit, who fosters strength and vigor where
there is none.* (Ezech. 2:2). . . . We must realize that in the first three
petitions spiritual things are asked for which begin here in this world but
are not made perfect except in life eternal. . . . For when we ask that
the name of God be hallowed, we ask that the holiness of God be made
known. Again, when we ask God's kingdom to come, we petition to be
made sharers in eternal life. And when we pray that God's will be done,
we ask that it be done in us. All of these things, even if they be begun
in this world, cannot be had perfectly except in life eternal; therefore it
is necessary to ask for some necessities which can be possessed perfectly
in the present life. . . .[68]

This is taken from one of the fifty-seven reports of sermons which St. Thomas preached in the Church of St. Dominic in Lent of 1273, the last Lent of his lifetime.[69] He preached in Italian each evening to students and townsfolk, probably in three successive series: on the Apostles' Creed (fifteen short *collationes*), the Lord's Prayer (ten), and the Law (charity and the Decalogue—thirty-two).[70] His sermons never took longer than half an hour, some of them only fifteen minutes. Peter d'Andrea was his probable reporter.

The sermons are free of scientific language and argumentation, but they are extremely methodical. Kraus calls them "brisk and authoritative" and attributes to them the defects of a *reportatum*. One marvels at the perfection of order in St. Thomas while being slightly worn down by it. Thus he will say, "Our debt to Him (as Father) is fourfold. Firstly we owe Him honor: *If I am Father, where is my honor?* (Mal. 1:6). This honor consists in three things: (a) In reference to God, by giving Him praise. . . ."[71] The other three things owed to God besides honor are imitation, obedience, and patience under chastening; under honor, purity of body and just judgment of our neighbor are required as well as formal praise, and so on. The Thomistic catechesis is largely nonspeculative. He shows himself a master of sources, employing both testaments of Scripture and the Fathers with ease and unerring appositeness. The sermons are a tapestry of quotations which, however, never seem forced. There is abundant illustration out of daily experience, but it is never developed further than is required for immediate application. This technique is a familiar one from St. Thomas's theological writings. Thus, we pray "Thy will be done" in the manner of a sick man who, consulting a doctor, does not take medicine according to his own will (he would be a fool to do so) but in accord with the doctor's will.

These *opuscula* of St. Thomas became source works for much medieval pulpit instruction, which is reason enough to consider them. An additional importance of the threefold catechesis (there is a fourth candidate for inclusion, a *commentariolus de Salutatione Angelica*, but it seems not to have been delivered on this occasion), is that it gives us the saint's mind on what instruction the Christian person needs, and in what order. He himself speaks of the "three things necessary to man for salvation; namely, knowledge of what to believe (*scientia credendorum*), what to wish for (*desiderandorum*), and what to do (*operandorum*). The first is taught in the Creed . . . the second in the Lord's Prayer; the third in the Law. . . ."[72] In other words, the catechesis takes its ordering from the message itself in St. Thomas's view: the act of faith and the object of faith (which is God and the mystery of salvation); the sacraments, dealt with by him under the credal phrase *communionem sanctorum*, which he understands to mean a community of goods in the Church, or holy things shared by Christ the Head with his members;[73] prayer, both of praise and petition, which is most perfectly epitomized by the prayer Christ taught; and the commands of Christ, obedience to which he identified as proof of love for him. The beauty of St. Thomas's treatment of divine love (thirteen and one-half pages in Mandonnet) before he attacks the commandments of the Decalogue individually is striking. One is led to wonder why the *Catechismus Romanus* of 1566 began its treatment with the first commandment and confines to a single sentence its treatment of the twofold law of the Gospel.[74]

In any case, it is an important question whether we have here the clear mind of St. Thomas on the optimum form a catechesis should take or whether it is just what he thought he could accomplish between Septuagesima Sunday and the Tuesday of Holy Week in a given year. About twelve years before, at the request of the archbishop of Palermo, he had written a little treatise on the sacraments.[75] Does his very concise treatment of them here under *sanctorum communionem* prove that he thought that this much sufficed in relation to the rest of his exposition? Or was he merely falling in with medieval practice by commenting on the two prayers from the baptismal liturgy plus the Christian rule of life? In earlier times treatment of the sacraments – at least the three of initiation – came after baptism at the Easter or Pentecost Vigil. Perhaps on such a historical principle St. Thomas felt that a full-scale treatment of them did not properly belong in a lenten framework.

We probably should not suppose that we have in these reported sermons any definitive response to a question of total catechetical theory. What they are is the richest kind of treasury of popular exposition upon which much good pulpit material was written in succeeding centuries.

John Gerson (1363–1420), chancellor of the University of Paris, surely requires mention as we come on to the period when the catechism took shape as a child's book. Even while chancellor he taught catechism (1409–1412). The story is frequently told of his having spent the last years of his life in Lyons despite the death of his sworn enemy John the Fearless and his theoretical freedom to return. Gerson engaged in works of priestly zeal in his last years, among them catechizing the young at the Church of St. Paul and writing the little book *On Drawing the Little Ones to Christ.*[76] Taking as his text the words of Christ about letting the little ones come to him, Gerson considers four matters in the field of teaching: how needful it is to Christ and the Church that the little ones come; types of scandal that can keep them off; the proper zeal that should mark those who lead the little ones to Christ; and a personal *apologia* against his detractors as to why, despite the gap between his conduct and a child's, he nonetheless can bring them to Christ. Gerson addresses himself here to the need for catechetics and the spirit that should mark its practitioners. He is strong for love and condescension in teaching the little ones, and he cannot abide turgid patterns of speech with them. His great fear is of the corruption of unchastity that may overtake them if they progress from youth to age uninstructed. When he comes to name the ways in which the young are led to Christ he lists: "Public preaching. Admonition in private. The disciplining proper to teachers. Finally, and most characteristic of the Christian religion, confession."[77] He is eloquent on the supreme efficacy of this sacrament as formative of Christian character, and he spends considerable time describing how to keep the trust and friendship of children even though, as their confessor, one comes to know their weaknesses and the dark places in their souls.

Gerson in a letter on the reform of theological studies (1400?) asked theological faculties to produce little treatises dealing with the main points of religion, the commandments especially, for the use of simple folk, just as the faculty of medicine had produced a little medicinal summary in a recent time of plague.[78] He did something of the kind himself in his *Opus tripertitum*, a treatise on the commandments, confession, and how to die well.[79] It was published widely and made mandatory reading for many clerics by their bishops (for example, Francis of Luxembourg, bishop of Mans, in 1507). Gerson himself even proposed at the beginning of his book that it be divided up on tablets and posted in places where people gather, "parish churches, schools, hospitals, religious houses." He proposed at the beginning of the second section on confession that a *tabula* be made containing the number and kinds of sins, which the uninstructed penitent could first inspect and then be quizzed on. Following his own suggestion, he then proposed his examination of conscience as a series of direct questions on the seven capital sins. This question-and-answer form underlay the printed *libelli* which penitents employed in the pre-Reformation period to prepare for their annual confession. The priest would quiz them on the chief prayers and points of doctrine before he would hear their sins and absolve them. Gerson's points of consideration for the Christian prince, written for Charles VII, indicates what form such *libelli* might take before dismemberment into sections.[80] Gerson also wrote a small, catechism-like book called *L'ABC des simples gens* not printed in his collected works.

The late fifteenth century witnessed all sorts of "mirrors" to help one live and die well which stressed the virtues, vices, and commandments as aids to confessing properly. The Waldensians worked out a set of instructions in question form, *Interrogacions memors,* which the Bohemian brethren followed in writing their *Kinderfragen.* Luther was acquainted with the latter and relied on it in 1523 for his earliest catechetical writings.[81] In 1526 he employed the Wittenberg translation of it done the previous year in high and low German, *Eyn Bökeschen vor de Leyen unde Kinder.* In 1529 his *Kurze Auslegung der Zehn Gebote* went onto charts; then, the commandments, confession, and the sacraments of baptism and the Eucharist. These formed the first edition of his catechism. In June of that year it appeared in Latin and in German as an *Enchiridion* and was reedited six times by 1542.

Mention of this child's catechism brings us to where we wished to be. Luther's little work is immediately recognizable as late medieval. It proceeds in the order: Ten Commandments, creed, Lord's Prayer, baptism, and Lord's Supper. Subsequent editions contain a treatment in questions and answers of the order ("economy") of salvation, another "systematical connection" of the same, and questions and answers for those who would prepare themselves for the Lord's Supper. "Historical catechisms" of both testaments follow, then a "table of duties" for states in life, prayers, and hymns.

The smaller catechisms of Canisius and Bellarmine are not greatly unlike Luther's editorially. In them and that of the Spaniard Ripalda the pattern for the next four hundred years is set. The two chief prayers, the commandments, and the sacraments provide the framework. Lists of sins, virtues, and vices complement this basic treatment. There is no attempt to derive instruction on the Christian life from the story of salvation as it is contained in the inspired Scriptures. Neither is there any attempt to "teach as Christ did," or "proclaim the good news of salvation" in the manner of the apostolic period. Scripture is used and used extensively but not in a way the patristic period would be familiar with.

In brief, then, the efforts of men like Overberg, Hirscher, Pichler, and the modern giants of the catechetical revival must be seen for what they are: a break clean away from fifteen centuries of pedagogic practice and a return to better, surer ways of teaching Christ, in a way suited to children, which is quite new. *Analysis* of prayers, commandments, sacred practices, had dominated the field. The great contribution of the "new catechetics" has been *synthesis:* the setting into place of each dogma and moral demand in a framework of God's saving action in biblical times made present to us in every age in joyful liturgical celebration.

NOTES

1. See A. Boyer, "Catéchisme," in *Catholicisme, Hier, Aujourd'hui, Demain,* dir. G. Jacquemet, II (Paris: Letouzey et Ané, 1949), 646ff.; C. Hézard, *Histoire du catéchisme* (Paris: Librairie des Catéchismes, 1900); [*Dictionnaire de Théologie Catholique,* ed. A. Vacant, E. Mangenot, E. Amann, 15 vols. (Paris: Letouzey et Ané, 1909-1950); hereafter cited as *DTC*.] E. Mangenot, "Catéchisme," in *DTC*, 2, pp. 1895-1906.

2. G. Bardy, "Catéchèse," in *Catholicisme*, II, 645.

3. [The Ancient Christian Writers series, ed. J. Quasten, W. J. Burghardt, and J. C. Plumpe, 40 vols. (Westminster, MD: Newman Press, 1946-1975); hereafter cited as ACW.] James A. Kleist, trans., *The Didaché* . . ., no. 6 (ACW, 1948), pp. 3-15.

4. H. Leclercq, "Catéchèse," in *Dictionnaire d'Archéologie Chrétienne et de Liturgie* 2 (Paris: Letouzey et Ané, 1925), 2530-2534. See also J.-P. Audet, *La Didachè* (Paris: Gabalda, 1958), pp. 61, 101ff., who argues that a late interpolation in the present text made a prebaptismal catechesis of what had originally been designed as postbaptismal.

5. See J. P. Christopher's instructive note on *katēcheîn* (literally "to echo") as derived from ancient sing-school methods, in his [translation of] St. Augustine, *The First Catechetical Instruction,* no. 2 (ACW, 1946), p. 93, n. 4. The first use of the verb *catechizare* is ascribed to Tertullian, *De corona militis,* 11; *catechismus* to Augustine, *De fide et operibus,* XIII, 9.

6. See D. dePuniet, "Baptême" and "Catéchumenat," in *Dictionnaire Apologetique de La Foi Catholique;* Bardy, loc. cit., and "L'enseignement religieux aux prémiers siècles," *Revue Apologetique* 66 (1938, I): 641-655; 67 (1938, II): 5-18. Cf. also J. A. Jungmann, *Katechetik* (Vienna: Herder Verlag, 1953), pp. 5-12. These references are especially helpful because no attempt is made in this present essay to describe the development of the catechumenate.

7. [J. P. Migne, *Patrologia Graeca,* 161 vols., 1857-1865; hereafter cited as *PG*.] *PG* 12, 780, *In Num. hom.,* 27, 1. Origen (d. 254?) came after Tertullian (d. 230?) who in his *De Baptismo* writes as if to catechumens, in the first extended work on Christian initiation after 1 Peter.

8. "XVI. (1) Those who come forward for the first time to hear the word shall be brought to the teachers before all the people come in.

"(2) And let them be examined as to the reason why they have come forward. And those who bring them shall bear witness for them whether they are able to hear. . . .

"XVII. (1) Let a catechumen be instructed for three years (but if earnest, his reception should come sooner). . . .

"XX. (1) . . . If those who bring them bear witness that they have lived piously, 'honored the widows,' fulfilled every [good work] let them hear the gospel. . . . (3) [and] be exorcised daily. . . .

"XXI. (1) And at the hour when the cock crows they shall first [of all] pray over the water. . . . (4) And they shall baptize the little children first. . . . if they cannot [answer for themselves], let their parents answer or someone from their family." – Gregory Dix, *The Apostolic Tradition of St. Hippolytus of Rome* (London: Society for Promoting Christian Knowledge, 1937), pp. 23, 28, 30ff. Hippolytus also gives the Roman rite of baptism which contains this creed, a combination of trinitarian and christological formulas (the latter developed in the *praefatio* of the eucharistic liturgy): "I believe in God the Father Almighty, and in Jesus Christ the Son of God, who was born of the Virgin Mary by the Holy Spirit, was crucified under Pontius Pilate, died, and was buried. He arose on the third day living from the dead, ascended into heaven, sits on the right hand of the Father; He will come to judge the living and the dead. And in the Holy Spirit and holy Church and resurrection in the flesh."

9. *PG* 8, 251f., I, 1 (9). This work by Clement of Alexandria has been translated into English by Simon P. Wood, as *Christ the Educator* (New York: Fathers of the Church, 1954). See p. 5.

10. A. de la Barre, "Clément d'Alexandrie," in *DTC*, 3, 146. See *PG* 8, 60ff.

11. *PG* 8, 251f., I, 1 (6). Cf. Wood, op. cit., p. 4.

12. Cf. David M. Stanley, "Didachē as a Constitutive Element of the Gospel-Form," *Catholic Biblical Quarterly* 17 (April 1955): 216–228.

13. *PG* 8, 251f., I, 12 (21) f., col. 369. Cf. Wood, op. cit., p. 88.

14. R. Hugh Connolly, *Didascalia Apostolorum*, the Syriac Version Translated and Accompanied by the Verona Latin Fragments (Oxford: Clarendon Press, 1929), chap. 8, p. 80.

15. Thus, there are admonitions to married men, married women, bishops, transgressors who repent, etc. For instance, "Hear then, you bishops, and hear, you laymen: I will judge between ram and ram, and between ewe and ewe; that is, between bishop and bishop and between layman and layman: whether layman loves layman, and whether again the layman loves the bishop and honors and fears him as father and Lord. . . ." Connolly, op. cit., chap. 7, p. 60.

16. Ibid., p. 103.

17. Joseph P. Smith, [trans., *Proof of the Apostolic Preaching*, by St. Irenaeus, no. 16] (ACW, 1952), p. 20 ("Introduction"), translated from an Armenian MS first discovered in 1904. Eusebius refers to the work as (*Lógos*) 'eis tēn epídeixin toû 'apostolikoû kērýgmatos. It is frequently referred to simply as *Epideixis*.

18. Ibid., p. 43.

19. Ibid., p. 51. For a history of the Apostles' Creed, its provenance and general acceptance at Rome, cf. J. N. D. Kelly, *Early Christian Creeds* (London: Longmans, Green & Co., 1950), chap. 13.

20. Smith, op. cit., p. 97.

21. *PG* 33, 331–1128; for the last five given after Easter ("mystagogic"), see F. L. Cross, *St. Cyril of Jerusalem's Lectures on the Christian Sacraments* (London: Society for Promoting Christian Knowledge, 1951). X. Le Bachelet discusses the work in *DTC*, 3, 2533ff. The authenticity of the last five is in some doubt, the credit often going to Cyril's successor, Bishop John.

22. Le Bachelet, op. cit., 2560.

23. Ibid., 2540.

24. Ibid., 2575.

25. *PG* 33, 741. Cat. 12, *De Christo incarnato*.

26. *PG* 45, 9–106. Translated by J. H. Srawley, *The Catechetical Oration of Gregory of Nyssa* (London: Society for Promoting Christian Knowledge, 1917), p. 123.

27. Srawley, op. cit., pp. 33f., chap. 5.

28. Ibid., p. 88, chap. 29.

29. [J. P. Migne, *Patrologia Latina*, 217 vols., 1878–1890; hereafter cited as *PL*.] Thus, for example, the *Hermēneia toû symbólou* or *Interpretation of the Creed* of Gelasius of Caesarea (d. 395); a *libellus*, one of six in the *Libelli instructionis* of Niceta, Bishop of Remesiana (late fourth century), for which see A. E. Burn, *Niceta of Remesiana, His Life and Works* (Cambridge: University Press, 1905); the *Explanatio symboli ad initiandos* (*PL* 17, 1155–1160), probably based on notes from a lecture of Ambrose; and four sermons of Augustine, numbered 212–215, addressed to baptismal candidates as they were first given the creed (*traditio symboli*) and later rehearsed it before the bishop (*redditio*), (*PL* 38, 1058–1076). The information above is given in J. N. D. Kelly, trans. *Rufinus . . . A Commentary on the Apostles' Creed*, no. 20 (ACW, 1955), p. 94, nn. 18–22. Cf. also Kelly's *Early Christian Creeds*, esp. chap. 13.

30. Kelly, *Rufinus*, p. 11.

31. Gerald G. Walsh, trans., *An Explanation of the Creed*, by Niceta of Remesiana (New York: Fathers of the Church, 1949), pp. 43–53. Migne wrongly attributes this and other works to Nicetas of Aquileia, *PL* 52, 865–871, an error corrected by Burn, q.v., pp. 38–54.

32. Walsh, op. cit., p. 45 (4).

33. Kelly, *Rufinus*, pp. 29ff., chap. 2.

34. Ibid., pp. 77f., chap. 40.

35. [*Corpus Scriptum Ecclesiasticorum Latinorum* (Vienna, 1866ff.); hereafter cited as *CSEL*.] "Catholic" appears in St. Cyril's creed (*Cat.* 18, 23), and although implied in Tertullian's question in *De Baptismo* 6 (*CSEL* 20, 206), first appears in a Western creed in Niceta of Remesiana. Cf. Kelly, op. cit., p. 141, n. 238; and Walsh, op. cit., (10), p. 49.

36. Kelly, *Rufinus*, (39), p. 74.

37. Ibid. (18), p. 52.

38. *PL* 16, 391, chap. 2; *CSEL* 73 (1955), 91.

39. *PL* 16, 394, chap. 3.

40. Ibid., 407, chap. 9.

41. Ibid., 392, chap. 3.

42. Christopher, op. cit., p. 5.

43. Ibid., p. 23.

44. Ibid.

45. Christopher, op. cit., p. 67.

46. H. Leclercq, "Catéchèse–Catéchisme–Catéchumène," *Dictionnaire d'Archéologie Chrétienne et de Liturgie*, 2 (Paris: Letouzey et Ané, 1925), 2566f.

47. *PL* 83, 814–826, *De officiis*, 1. 2., chaps. 21–27.

48. *PL* 59, 323–368.

49. *PL* 39, Serm. 6, 6; 168, 3; 237; 267.

50. See *PL* 80, 438, Epist. II.

51. *PL* 87, 13–26, sermon of St. Gall on the occasion of the consecration of John as bishop of Constance.

52. St. Bede wrote to Egbert, bishop of York in 734 (the closing year of Bede's life) detailed instructions as to how the rural areas are to be taught the deeper meaning of the Apostles' Creed and Lord's Prayer by their priests: in Latin for the few who can handle it; otherwise, "*Ipsa sua lingua dicere, ac sedule decantare facito.*" The idea of singing them recurs in the passage; also memorization: "*Memoriae radicitus infigere cures,*" he admonishes (*PG* 94, 659).

53. [J. D. Mansi, *Sacrorum conciliorum nova et amplissima collectio*, 31

vols., 1757–1798; hereafter cited as Mansi.] For example, Cloveshowe under Cuthbert of Canterbury (747), a national council, in which a vernacular "spiritual" exposition of the prayers of "Mass, baptism and other ecclesiastical functions carried on before the people" is required, can. 10 (Mansi [Florence: A. Zatta, 1766] 12, 398); Frankfurt in 794, can. 33 (Mansi 13, 908); Arles (813), can. 19 (Mansi 14, 62), put responsibility on parents and sponsors; Mainz (813) did the same and recommended school attendance, cans. 45, 47 (Mansi 14, 74). To St. Boniface of Mainz are credited canons 25 and 26 of a synod at Leipzig (743) requiring godparents to know creed and pater, "that they may be saved by faith and prayer" (PL 89, 822). Charlemagne was responsible for similar legislation in 802 (PL 97, 247, nn. 14, 15), and also instructed priests to have lists of the greater and lesser sins at hand, to aid their people in avoiding the devil's snares (PL 97, 326). For the emperor's role as catechist supreme, cf. Joseph Lecler, *The Two Sovereignties* (New York: Philosophical Library, 1952), pp. 55f.

54. *PL* 100, 515–566.

55. *PL* 101, 1099–1144.

56. Ibid., 1101.

57. *PL* 101, 613–638.

58. *PL* 99, 197ff.

59. Mansi 23, 693.

60. Ibid., 836f.

61. *PL* 141, 196–204.

62. *PL* 150, 857–866.

63. *PL* 178, 611–632.

64. *PL* 172, 1109–1176. Cf. Y. Lefèvre, *L'Elucidarium et les Lucidaires: Contribution, par l'histoire d'un texte, à l'histoire des croyances religieuses en France en moyen-âge* (Paris: De Bocard, 1954), p. 543.

65. *PL* 34, 1285f.

66. *PL* 186, 1496.

67. *PL* 175, 406–414.

68. St. Thomas Aquinas, "Opusculum 34," *Opuscula Omnia*, coll. P. Mandonnet, IV (Paris: Lethielleux, 1927), 401f.

69. The writer is indebted in this section to James E. Kraus for the full text of his dissertation done at the Athenaeum Angelicum, Rome, under Angelus Walz, OP, "The Catechetical Sermons of St. Thomas Aquinas."

70. Ibid., p. 11.

71. St. Thomas Aquinas, *The Catechetical Instructions*, trans. with a commentary by Joseph B. Collins (New York: J. F. Wagner, 1939), p. 155; *The Three Greatest Prayers*, trans. Laurence Shapcote (Westminster, MD: Newman, 1956), p. 17.

72. Mandonnet, op. cit., "De duobus praeceptis charitatis et decem legis praeceptis," IV, 413.

73. Collins, op, cit., pp. 53–57. Mandonnet, op. cit., IV, 381. The Roman Catechism has the same idea, I, 10, 24, where it speaks of the sacraments as holy chains binding us all to Christ in a union of spirit which is none other than membership in the one holy Church. Cf. *Catechismus ex Decreto Concilii Tridentini ad Parochos . . . Editus* (Rome: Typis Sacrae Congregationis de Propaganda Fide, 1845), p. 66.

74. Ibid., p. 221.

75. Mandonnet, op. cit., *De Ecclesiae Sacramentis*, III, 11–18.

76. Joannis Gersonii, "Tractatus de Parvulis Trahendis ad Christum," *Opera Omnia*, III (Antwerp: Ellies du Pin, 1706), 278–291.

77. Ibid., III, 283.
78. Ibid., I, 124.
79. Ibid., I, 426–450.
80. Ibid., III, 234f.
81. See L. Fendt, "Katechismus," Evangelisches Kirchenlexicon, 18/19 (Göttingen: Vandenhoeck and Ruprecht, 1957), 562f.

Mary Charles Bryce's Catholic University doctoral dissertation, The
Influence of the Catechism of the Third Plenary Council of Baltimore
*(University Microfilms, 1970), brought to light little-known but impor-
tant historical background on a book that was possibly the most
important single influence on the doctrinal understanding of many
generations of U.S. Roman Catholics. In the following succinct essay,
she covers the high points of the controversy generated by the*
Baltimore Catechism. *Further background can be found in her essay
reprinted below as Reading 16, "Religious Education in the Pastoral
Letters and National Meetings of the U.S. Hierarchy," in Section C,
"The Modern Catechetical Movement."*

READING 10

The *Baltimore Catechism*— Origin and Reception

MARY CHARLES BRYCE

A S THE *Baltimore Catechism* moves into its second century in
print, it seems fitting to add a kind of postscript to previous
studies published about that volume – especially in light of the nostalgic
desire, sometimes heard today, to return to the use of that ninety-seven-
page book.

The *Baltimore Catechism* got a cool reception when it came out
in 1885. In spite of endorsement by certain diocesan synods – Cincinnati
accepted it in the synod of 1886, the diocese of Harrisburg in 1892,
synod of Chicago in 1897, Davenport in 1904 – the catechism did not
receive a particularly warm welcome. Despite synodal sanction, the
catechism encountered serious resistance in many classrooms. In fact,
other than the approvals by official diocesan assemblies, there is little

This article by Mary Charles Bryce was originally published under the title "Happy
Birthday Baltimore Catechism" in *Catechist* (April 1972), pp. 6-9, 25. Reprinted by
permission of the publisher, Peter Li, Inc., 2451 East River Road, Dayton, OH 43439.
© Peter Li, Inc.

historical evidence testifying to a favorable reception in those early years.

On the other hand, dissatisfaction with the small book mounted steadily during the first ten years. The ordinary of Cleveland, Bishop Richard Gilmour, was one of the earliest critics. Writing to Archbishop James Gibbons of Baltimore on 11 April 1886, he observed that he probably would be denounced for his unfavorable criticism, but he did not withdraw it. Instead, he added in an offhand manner, "Let it come." What his critical evaluations were is not clear – they are not recorded in the Baltimore archdiocesan archives – but Gilmour must have felt himself a qualified judge. He had written a series of children's textbooks and a *Bible History* (1881) which enjoyed record-breaking popularity for at least fifty years.

The most explicit and bitter critic of the work was the anonymous author of nine articles which appeared between September 1885 and October 1886 in *Pastoral Blatt*, a St. Louis-based monthly written in German. Assailing the work for its pedagogical and theological weaknesses, the critic (or critics) specified in detail examples in each of these two categories. The work was pedagogically unsuitable for children, the writer alleged, because of its incomprehensible language, its small size (children are more comfortable with a larger volume), the disproportionate number of yes–no questions (91 of 421), the stunting of thought processes involved in questions that contain complete answers, and finally, the monotony of the entire text which gave equal treatment to all matters.

More importantly, according to *Blatt*'s critic, the catechism was theologically weak on several scores: the brevity of its treatment of God and the angels, the absence of any consideration of divine providence, only one question about the resurrection – a reference to the day it happened rather than to the significance of the event – and insufficient attention to the Holy Spirit.

As a final point the reviewer explained in scornful terms that the title was not justifiable even in its shortened form (the complete title is *A Catechism of Christian Doctrine, Prepared and Enjoined by Order of the Third Plenary Council of Baltimore*) because the catechism was published before Rome's Congregation of the Propaganda had approved the American council's decrees. Unlike the catechism of Trent, the content of the volume did not emerge from decrees or decisions reached during council sessions. Neither was the final copy circulated to all the bishops for a last review before publication.

The *Blatt* critic's unrelieved negativism leaves one a little skeptical about his qualifications to assess the work. Though agreeing with his assessment in general, one cannot fail to question his total lack of objectivity. The manual surely was not starkly worse than other texts of its day. (An interesting aside is the fact that *Pastoral Blatt*'s editor, the Reverend W. Faerber, published a catechism under his own name in 1897. It fared little better with reviewers than had the Baltimore manual at the pens of Faerber's selected critics.)

Dissatisfaction with the new manual continued to spread. An 1895 article in the *American Ecclesiastical Review* admitted the volume's "many faults." Acknowledging that there was both general and specific disapproval of it, Archbishop Sebastian Messmer of Milwaukee (bishop of Green Bay, 1891–1903; archbishop of Milwaukee, 1903–1930) defended it. He pointed out the need for uniformity in the exposition and wording of Christian doctrine, and he maintained that particular quality was of more immediate importance than correcting any of the catechism's weaknesses. Messmer's defense concurred with statements recorded in the synodal decrees referred to above, namely, that uniformity was a quality of prime importance. The desire for memorized statements in a monochromatic pattern across the United States seemed to supersede doctrinal accuracy or pedagogical know-how.

Nor was discontent with the catechism confined to verbal criticism. It was observable in another form—less direct in style but just as pointed and even more concrete: new catechisms. In that first ten-year period, at least seven new catechisms appeared bearing episcopal approval or *imprimaturs* in the dioceses where they were published or written. The very sanction accorded these newer manuals testifies to the bishops' corroboration of the pervading unhappiness with the Baltimore council's so-called text.

Unhappiness with the manual finally reached the attention of the archbishops in the country. A Paulist priest, Augustine F. Hewitt, writing from New York in 1895, voiced a sentiment held by many. Addressing his letter to Archbishop Gibbons, he observed that he had "never heard anyone express a favorable opinion of our present Catechism, and I hope it is true that the Archbishops will provide for its revision."

Indeed, the archbishops did take up the matter in their meeting of that year. Minutes of the meeting reveal that, because the catechism "in its present form seems unpopular," the archbishops discussed the "advisability or necessity of revising it." They decided to poll the bishops in their respective archdioceses on the matter, questioning them "as to whether the present catechism should be revised or another catechism prepared as a substitute for the one now in use." No consideration of retaining the 1885 manual as it was seemed to have been given.

One year later on the assembly's agenda, it was the first matter discussed. The 1896 minutes read: "From the reports of the various Provinces, it was evident that all the Bishops of the country were in favor of some changes whilst the majority recommended a *revision* of the present catechism." The archbishops resolved that a special committee be formed "to revise the catechism on lines suggested by the bishops of the country."

No mention of the catechism affair appeared in the minutes of the next six annual meetings, but the 1902 minutes disclosed the dilemma that had halted progress. The committee "found themselves unable to offer an adequate remedy first because they knew no existing catechism which they could fully recommend; secondly, even if a proper catechism were prepared, the Board of Archbishops has no authority to order its general use." And finally, rumor was that the Holy See was preparing a catechism for universal use. With a hint of relief, the minutes indicated the hierarchy's hope that Rome's projected manual would provide an answer to this country's catechism problem. It did not. When the catechism sanctioned by Pope Pius X appeared in 1905, it claimed no aspiration to become a universal text despite its early widespread acceptance. Nor did Pius urge its universal use.

Strongly expressed criticisms and general dissatisfaction notwithstanding, the *Baltimore Catechism* gained ever-widening circulation as well as additional authoritative approval in some dioceses. Opposition too became more widespread, and from 1895 onward demands for a better catechism became insistent. When no prospect of a revised or improved national catechism seemed visible, catechists and pastors began to write their own manuals, manuals which responded to needs as their authors recognized them. By 1918, at least 72 new texts had appeared; and by 1941, the year when the revised edition of the *Baltimore Catechism* finally did come out, at least 109 additional volumes had been published; 95 percent of them carried *imprimaturs* or other sanctioning statements by bishops.

Paradoxically, authors of new manuals found themselves motivated by the same zeal that had impelled the Baltimore council fathers to promote the 1885 manual: a zeal first for orthodoxy and secondly for a catechetical presentation that would address itself meaningfully to the very young U.S. Catholic. It was on the latter point that they differed widely.

In what ways were these new catechisms unique, or on what grounds did their writers and users consider them an improvement over the Baltimore manual? First, many of the newer books from as early as 1898 onward were volumes in graded series. This meant that children who received an advanced speller, arithmetic, and reader as they progressed from grade to grade also could obtain a progressively advanced religion text – a volume intentionally written to suit a child's age and mental development. Second, an increasing number of religion texts abandoned the question–answer approach to employ a simple expository or narrative method. One of the earliest writers to produce such a work was the brilliant Irish scholar Rev. Peter C. Yorke of San Francisco. The first volume of his graded, non-question-answer series came out in 1898, and the other four volumes followed in successive years. The books were five hardback, illustrated texts, which enjoyed continuous widespread usage on the West Coast through the 1920s.

A third trend involved format. In an effort to appeal to youthful interest, authors took steps toward making children's catechisms attractive. They used slick paper, larger print, and numerous illustrations.

The compilers and writers of the revised Baltimore manual, unfortunately, chose to ignore these trends. In 1941, the revised version appeared. In its new dress, it was not startlingly different from the original work. Its 144 pages contained 38 lessons with 515 questions–answers. (The original had 421.) Many of these questions–answers retained phrases from the 1885 volume. In contrast to the original, the 1941 manual had been in the formation stage for six years, but as with the original, its principal writers were theologians and not pedagogues. The more ideal collaborative authorship would have been professional theologians, pastors, and educators. Reception of the revised version evidently was not unlike that of its predecessor – rather cool and unenthusiastic.

New series of texts, new individual catechisms, and graded religion books, some with workbooks or other student-involving techniques, continued to move into the mainstream of catechetical materials. A number of these clung to the Baltimore text as a basis. The majority did not. The genuine concern for a good and thorough transmission of Christ's Gospel message stimulated the movement for better religious education instruments, manuals, and aids that would respond to the United States Church's many cultural patterns in a pluralistic society. (It is hard to understand how a single manual could ever serve such a diverse population.)

From time to time, in a sort of undulating cycle, the apparent problem of multiple catechisms has surfaced to plague Church leaders in this country. The only solution that appeared feasible in the past was a common catechism. The *Baltimore Catechism* was the concretized hope of Church leaders in the United States. Like other manuals, it served the Catholic community as well as it could in circumstances very different from those of the 1970s.

Today, with the new *General Catechetical Directory* officially shifting the emphasis away from the manual as a primary source of religious education and recognizing other sources and factors involved in transmitting the Gospel message, religion textbooks are put in a broader perspective. No longer are they required to carry such an immense portion of the responsibility.

This much is constant in the ongoing quest for adequate catechetical materials: The zeal that "our forefathers" knew in Baltimore's Third Plenary Council is not absent today; it merely is expressed and implemented in a greater variety of ways.

It is difficult to introduce the trilogy on the history of the Confraterni-
ty of Christian Doctrine written by Joseph Collins, SS, without wishing
to do an original and lengthy essay on Collins' substantial contribu-
tion to catechesis in the United States over a long career.

In addition to his fourteen books and countless articles on aspects
of catechesis and religious education, his contributions include twenty-
five years as director of the National Center of Religious Education—
CCD. As a colleague of his for nearly two years at the United States
Catholic Conference, I was always impressed with his fidelity to the
catechetical tradition of St. Sulpice, a fidelity carried out with great
openness in a new time and a new culture.

Because he knew more of the intimate details of religious
education–catechesis among Roman Catholics than he could ever set
down on paper, I had intended to ask him to do an oral history of his
own recollections of his career so these details would not be lost. His
sudden death on 23 January 1975 at the age of seventy-seven was a
special loss to us who loved him.

The three articles which follow, written during his very active retire-
ment, were to be chapters in what he hoped would be a final contribu-
tion to our understanding of our own catechetical history in the United
States. Readers will not fail to note the way these essays highlight cer-
tain perennial problems of local catechesis and also the lay character
of the Confraternity program. In addition, national leaders may wish
to consider how recent developments in the national catechetical
organizational structure might be out of joint with our own history.

READING 11

The Beginnings of the CCD
in Europe and Its Modern Revival

JOSEPH B. COLLINS

THE CONFRATERNITY of Christian Doctrine well over four
hundred years old. Under other names, such as Religious

Reprinted from *American Ecclesiastical Review* 168 (1974), pp. 695–706, by permission of The Catholic University of America Press.

Education – CCD, the organization continues to grow, especially with its basic parish-oriented structure, in many parts of the world. Whatever the name under which it operates, the Confraternity is basically a lay organization whose broad task is and has been to provide religious education to all – young and old – who are normally deprived of such formation. Such was the thought of a young priest, Castello de Castellano, in 1536, when he gathered together a small group of men and women in Milan, Italy, to conduct schools of Christian doctrine for children, youth, and unlettered adults. The "Company of Christian Doctrine," as it was first known, was soon working throughout the city of Milan and setting up schools in many towns and villages all over northern Italy.[1]

The great success that the Confraternity enjoyed in Milan from the very outset is largely due to a long tradition of lay religion teachers among the poor and illiterate of the city. The level of religious education, it must be recalled, even among the clergy, was at an all-time low. Schools at which Christian doctrine was then offered were few in number and mainly for the rich.[2] There were, nevertheless, in Milan and in other parts of Italy, scattered groups of zealous lay catechists who volunteered to hold regular schools of religion for the poor and ignorant. Moreover, a number of religious congregations arose whose main purpose was to provide religious instruction for the unlettered. Among them were the Order of Regular Clerics, known as the Barnabites, founded by Saint Anthony Zaccaria in 1530; the Regular Clerics of St. Mayene at Somascha near Turin, founded by Saint Jerome Aemilian in 1532; and the Ursuline Sisters, founded in 1535 by Saint Angela Merici at Brescia, Italy.

This was a time of great spiritual unrest. It was the time of the late renaissance when Italy was in the throes of new ideas and readiness to reject the old. Luther's *Large* and *Small Catechisms* appeared as early as 1529 and succeeded in spreading his teachings beyond the Alps in Italy. The graded catechisms of Saint Peter Canisius for children, youth, and adults appeared in 1555–1559. The so-called counter reformation was well begun with the Jesuits of Saint Ignatius Loyola taking a leading part, particularly in the special work of teaching the poor and lowly the fundamentals of religion, the reason for which the Jesuits were founded.[3]

When Saint Charles Borromeo came to Milan as Cardinal Archbishop in 1565, the Confraternity schools were already well established throughout his vast archdiocese. He had distinguished himself during the closing sessions of the Council of Trent through his learning and leadership. He at once gave his enthusiastic support to the educational program of the Confraternity. A major contribution was a guide which he called *A Constitution and Rules of the Confraternity and School of Christian Doctrine for Use in the Province of Milan.*[4] This work of more than 40,000 words explained the objectives and external structure of the Confraternity together with what Saint Charles looked upon as the most important element in the program—a progressively advanced spiritual and moral formation. It was planned for directors and participants in the Confraternity schools. Offering a solid pedagogy, the book had enormous influence on the CCD of its time, not unlike that which Saint Augustine's treatise *On Teaching the Unlettered* exerted on catechetics throughout its entire history up to the present.

The *Constitution* of the Milan Confraternity prescribed principles and methods which, though familiar to us today, were quite new at the time. There is a citation, for example, from the then recently promulgated decrees of the Council of Trent: "The people of all ages and degrees shall be nourished with solid doctrine in a manner that is in keeping with their capacity to understand and to learn."[5] The *Constitution* also offered practical suggestions that were taken from the authoritative *Catechism of the Council of Trent.* It was produced in 1566 by a special commission headed by Cardinal Borromeo that had been set up by the council itself to bring the decrees of the Fathers into the hands of pastors and teachers.[6] The text pointed out that teachers should adapt their words to the age, background, and mental capacity of the learners; careful attention must be given to individual differences in pupils. The document also recommends that basic doctrinal matters shall be divided on three levels—superior or gifted students, those of medium intelligence, and a final gradation for slow learners.

Classes in the schools of Christian doctrine, according to the *Constitution*, were not permitted to exceed eight or ten participants. Each session was forty-five minutes in length; then followed what was called a *disputa* or quiz-discussion for the same length of time. It consisted of a kind of public debate by the students; since the structure was flexible, students carried on their own discussions. Common prayers led by the pupils brought the session to a close.

In writing the *Constitution* for the Confraternity of Milan, Cardinal Borromeo insisted that teachers be examined by a board before assuming full responsibility in the schools. "Catechists," according to the regulations, "should be kind, understanding, and motivated by the fact that they are sharing in the same ministry that was exercised by Christ and the apostles."[7]

Milan Confraternity

The *Constitution* and other documents emanating from Milan at this time spell out the purpose, objectives, and makeup of the so-called "Company of the Schools" which are not radically different from those expressed in CCD structures since the revival of the CCD. The differences are mainly in matters of detail. The chief purpose of the Confraternity, we are told, is "to organize schools of Christian doctrine conducted by trained teachers, where youth and unlettered men and women may be instructed in the truths of the faith." This work, adds the text, is "maximum divinum," truly divine.

The objectives of the Confraternity at Milan are stated as follows:

> The laws of the Church command pastors to teach Christian doctrine, but because of the press of his work, the pastor alone cannot possibly supply the need of his people in this matter. He must therefore get help from others – both from the clergy and from the laity, especially from those who are enrolled in the Confraternity of Christian Doctrine and are trained to take charge of one or more schools for youth and adults in his parish.[8]

The simple external structure of the Confraternity at Milan a generation earlier was implemented and formalized by Charles Borromeo to reflect the overall direction of a central office. This Confraternity bureau, as it was called, consisted of a supervisor, coordinator, and staff for teaching and for spiritual formation. In each parish the work of the Confraternity was in charge of the local pastor or his assistant and various officers who formed a type of commission made up of teachers, helpers, and fishers or home visitors. There were also disciplinarians and record keepers, librarians, etc.

The documents of the time make clear that the directors and teachers in the CCD schools of Milan were carefully selected and trained before being admitted into the company with a solemn ceremony of profession.

Saint Charles Borromeo had reason to be proud of his record of eighteen years in the personal direction of the Confraternity in his archdiocese. At the time of his death in 1584, more than 40,000 children and adults were enrolled in the schools of the Confraternity; they were conducted by some 3,000 teachers, directors, and officers.[9] Father Guissano, a contemporary of Saint Charles, thus described the results of the Confraternity program during the lifetime of the saint:

> In places where even grownups but a while before could not say either the Our Father or the Hail Mary, now even lisping children can answer with intelligence the truths of our faith, and they teach their parents what they are to believe and practice as real Christians.[10]

CCD in Rome

The Confraternity of Christian Doctrine was brought to Rome in 1560 by a delegation of veteran catechists from Milan, where it had its origin in 1536. The new community was led by Marco de Cusano, a layman, and Father Henry Pietra, who took over the duties of spiritual director. They were given headquarters at one of the churches in the center of the city. Thus, they became the latest of many confraternities that for centuries were found in Rome and engaged in a great variety of activities.[11] There are records in Rome of lay confraternities (from *con-fratria* – brotherhood) that go back to the ninth century. The Confraternity of the Scapular of Mary, one of the many confraternities dedicated to the Mother of God, received papal approval in 1267. These societies continued to attract men and women to follow a rule of prayer and good works, such as teaching religion, while still living at home with their families.

An early report on the Confraternity at Rome states that it is "an organization of the laity, under the direction of the Church, based on the model society in Milan; its principal ministry is to teach the catechism to children and adults on Sundays and holidays."[12] Considering the incredibly long list of holidays and holy days in sixteenth-century Rome, nearly one third of each month was devoted to the catechetical apostolate.[13]

The Confraternity flourished in Rome as it had in Milan, and from all accounts it was desperately needed. Schools were set up all over the city and spread throughout the cities and towns that surrounded the Eternal City. The Roman Confraternity enjoyed considerable prestige since some of the most eminent figures in ecclesiastical and civic life were happy to be numbered among the members. Saint Philip Neri, called "the apostle of Rome," and many members of his spiritual family, including the famed Cardinal Baronio, were tireless workers and teachers for the new society. Saint Robert Bellarmine promoted the work of the Confraternity while he was Bishop of Capua and later wrote for it the celebrated catechism that bears his name. Saint Joseph Calasanctius was a longtime worker in the Confraternity and became its president in 1592. In order to give even greater assistance to the work, he founded a religious congregation popularly known as the Piarists in 1621. So also the Jesuits located in Rome were zealous organizers and teachers in the CCD which they set up in many places in the city, such as prisons, hospitals, homes for the sick and aged, convents, private schools.

After slightly more than a decade in Rome, the Confraternity was formally approved by Saint Pius V in 1571 with the Constitution *Ex debito.* The pope, a vigorous promoter of the reforms of the Council of Trent, praised the work of catechizing, blessed the directors and teachers of the Confraternity, and ordered it to be established all over the world.[14]

Marco de Cusano was ordained a priest in 1585. He proceeded to divide the Confraternity in Rome into two distinct societies owing to its great growth. A new society called the Congregation of Regular Clerics of Christian Doctrine arose from the original lay Confraternity, which continued to remain a lay organization. The clerics occupied a building near the Church of St. Agatha in Trastevere, and the lay members of the confraternity came to the same church from their homes.

In 1607, Pope Paul V elevated the society in Rome into an Archconfraternity with the privilege of affiliating with all other Confraternities of Christian Doctrine in the world. The pontiff granted extensive indulgences and spiritual privileges to the members of the Confraternity everywhere. In the same papal letter of 1607, Paul V moved the center of the Archconfraternity to St. Peter's in Rome. There it functioned until transferred by Benedict XIV to the Church of St. Mary of Tears *(S. Maria del Pianto)* where it still remains as the mother of all the worldwide CCD organizations.[15]

The Archconfraternity of Christian Doctrine in Rome enjoyed its period of greatest success during the final decades of the sixteenth century. Records indicate that some 11,000 children and adults were participants in the schools of the Confraternity at Rome under the direction of more than 500 leaders. It is said that the members of the Archconfraternity represented about one tenth of the total inhabitants of the city.[16]

The rapid growth of the Confraternity in Rome and throughout Italy was not accomplished without difficulties; some of them are quite familiar today. Documents are extant containing pleas from directors and teachers for more qualified helpers in the face of overwhelming numbers of learners seeking entry into the schools. There was also a troublesome tradition emanating from the Middle Ages: Teaching Christian doctrine was a function of priests only; hence lay men and women, the latter especially, must not teach this subject either in a church or outside it. Mindful of this fact, Pope Paul V gave his full approval to lay men and women teaching in the places where the Confraternity schools were held. Another difficulty was the low esteem in which the catechist was generally held by priests and people. Pope Benedict XIV in 1742 and St. Pius X at the turn of the present century tried to dispel this image and at the same time elevate the dignity of the "teacher of the catechism" and "to appreciate his work."[17]

Another source of trouble for the Confraternity during its early years was the charge that insufficient "doctrinal matter" was imparted in the Confraternity schools both in Rome and outside the city. In order to end this controversy, it took the authority of Cardinal Bellarmine. He reported to Pope Clement VIII that the catechism was fully and adequately handled by the teachers in the Confraternity schools.[18]

CCD Outside Italy

The continued development of the Confraternity during the seventeenth and eighteenth centuries may be at least partially discerned from reports, extant in the archives of the Confraternity office in Rome, that emanate from the principal countries of Europe.[19] Here it is noted that the first Sunday schools in the modern sense were set up in Milan and Rome under the Confraternity and furthermore that a number of these schools, for instance that of St. Dorothea in Rome as early as 1597, offered free education both in religion and elementary subjects to poor children and youth – thus anticipating the parish school of modern times.[20]

The gradual growth of the Confraternity outside Italy is seen in such cities as Lyons (1595), Geneva (under Saint Francis de Sales, 1615), Cologne (1640), Barcelona (1660), Vienna (1723). In 1710, for example, more than 271 different Confraternity units were aggregated to the Roman Archconfraternity from most of the European countries.[21] The long history of the Confraternity in Ireland during three centuries of persecution is related in part by Martin Brenan in a university study published in 1934 with the title *The Confraternity of Christian Doctrine in Ireland, 1775-1835.*[22]

Father Brenan's text covers the work of CCD in Ireland during a period of more than a century when all teaching of religion was forbidden by law under penalty of death. "The Confraternity," declared Brenan, "had a great part in preserving the Faith of the Irish people during those penal days." He described the famed "hedge schools" conducted in hidden places by lay leaders of the CCD who were trained in secret by priests. "In every parish," according to the writer, "lay people of both sexes were enrolled with the twofold object of their own sanctification and the religious instruction of their children."[23]

The work of catechizing the poor and unlettered, long the almost exclusive domain of the Confraternity, was gradually taken over in many places during the eighteenth and nineteenth centuries by the local parish or institution, usually under the direction of a religious congregation. Religious education to the extent that it was imparted at all became the responsibility of organizations and agencies other than the

Confraternity with its centralization of direction in diocese or parish. This development points to the decadence of the Confraternity both in Italy and in Europe generally.

Other causes contributed to this condition. There was the decrease in numbers and efficiency of the Confraternity schools due to lack of teachers, to want of training for their work, to neglect of the structure and demands of the Confraternity in places where it had been active, and finally to a failure in zeal and motivation on the part of clergy and parents.[24] There was also the inherent difficulty of providing religious education to people of all ages and degrees of religious illiteracy, particularly in Germany and France during the so-called Age of Enlightenment, when reason not faith determined the content of Christian doctrine.[25]

The Church through papal decree and synodal proclamation strove ceaselessly to support the Confraternity and to promote catechetical formation everywhere. Benedict XIV, for example, promulgated a *Motu proprio* in 1759 that reviewed the excellent work of the Confraternity during the past and urged its re-establishment all over the world. It was a good try but too late!

Modern Revival of the CCD

At the turn of the present century, the Confraternity of Christian Doctrine began to enjoy a new recognition and acceptance through the strong support given it by Pope Saint Pius X (1903–1914). His entire life was devoted to the catechetical ministry.

Joseph Sarto, the future pope and saint, was born in 1835 at Riese, a small village in northern Italy.[26] Educated at the seminary in Padua, he was ordained to the priesthood in 1858. After serving as curate and pastor in his native diocese of Treviso, Father Sarto filled a number of responsible posts, including diocesan chancellor and seminary professor. He was named Bishop of Mantua in 1884. Nine years later in 1893, Bishop Sarto was appointed Cardinal Patriarch of Venice by Pope Leo XIII. Here, as at Mantua and indeed throughout his pastoral life, he gave of his experience and zeal to the establishment and promotion of the Confraternity "in order," he declared, "to remedy the ignorance of divine things and to restore all things in Christ."[27]

CCD Under Saint Pius X

It was, however, on assuming the title of Pope Pius X that what became

a truly worldwide catechetical revival took place. One of the first encyclicals of the new pope was *Acerbo nimis,* "On Teaching Christian
Doctrine," that appeared in 1905.[28] In this important document that
has been called "the Magna Carta of the Confraternity," the writer not
only explained the nature and purpose of the religious education but
also gave practical directions on how it can best be achieved. The encyclical points out that catechetical instruction is not to be taken lightly
by the catechist. "We do not wish to give the impression that the
studied simplicity in giving instruction does not require labor and
meditation – on the contrary it demands both more than any other kind
of teaching." The document continues with the following salutary advice even for today:

> No matter what facility from nature a person may have in ideas and
> language, let him always remember that he will never be able to teach
> Christian doctrine to children or to adults without first giving himself to
> very careful study and preparation. They are mistaken who think that
> because of the inexperience and lack of training of the people, the work
> of teaching religion can be performed in a slipshod manner. On the con-
> trary, the less educated the hearers, the more zeal and diligence must be
> used to adapt the sublime truths to their untrained minds; these truths,
> indeed, far surpass the natural understanding of the people, yet must be
> known by all whether the cultured or the uncultured.[29]

The basic thrust of the encyclical was pastoral. It ordered a total
overhauling of the structures of the parish catechetical ministry. Boys
and girls must be taught on Sundays and holy days for one hour about
the fundamental truths of their faith; the young who have arrived at
the age of seven or thereabouts must be prepared to receive the
sacraments of Penance, the Eucharist, and Confirmation; "adults need
instruction no less than the young," and they shall be given opportunities to learn and discuss the entire field of Christian doctrine over
a period of at least five years. To fulfill these weighty responsibilities,
the encyclical commands the following:

> In every parish the society known as the Confraternity of Christian Doc-
> trine is to be canonically established. Through this Confraternity, the
> pastors, especially in places where there is a scarcity of priests, will have
> lay helpers in the teaching of the catechism, who will take up the work
> of imparting knowledge both from a zeal for the glory of God and in order
> to gain the indulgences granted by the sovereign pontiffs.

The work of the Confraternity is not be confined to elementary education. Classes in religion, according to the document, must be organized
in universities and colleges and "especially for boys and girls in public
high schools from which all religious teaching is banned."[30]

The encyclical *Acerbo nimis,* although written for the universal
Church, had still to be implemented in Rome and throughout Italy

before its full import would be felt worldwide. On 18 May 1905, a month after promulgation of the encyclical, the vicar-general for the diocese of Rome in a letter to the parish priests of the city "earnestly recommended that the Confraternity be established at the first opportunity in every parish according to the wishes of the Holy Father."[31] A Constitution for the Confraternity at Rome, newly revised to meet modern conditions, was approved by the pope later in the same year. "It is the wish of the Supreme Pontiff," he declared, "that all other Confraternities of Christian Doctrine must be joined to it in order to profit by the spiritual advantages that have been granted to it and also to gain unity of direction and purpose as well as of method which contribute so much to the success of this apostolate."[32] The same document reaffirmed that the Church of St. Mary of Tears would continue as it had for centuries to be the international headquarters for the Confraternity of Christian Doctrine.

The solicitude of the Holy See for the revival of the Confraternity is evidenced in a questionnaire sent to all ordinaries in the world on the conditions in their respective dioceses. One of the questions was whether there exist in the diocese certain confraternities and other religious organizations, most particularly those recommended by the Holy See, such as the Confraternity of Christian Doctrine, "which aim to teach children and youth the principles of faith, piety, and moral integrity."[33]

In 1910, Pope Pius wrote an encyclical commemorating the death of Saint Charles Borromeo in which he called attention to the great work of the Archbishop of Milan in teaching religion and in promoting the Confraternity of Christian Doctrine. The pontiff pointed out the dangers to the faith resulting from education devoid of a religious character, and added: "We have written that schools of religion should be established wherever possible and they should be plentifully supplied with teachers commendable for their knowledge and integrity."[34]

The specific provisions in *Acerbo nimis* relating to the Confraternity were later incorporated into the Code of Canon Law, which is one of the last achievements of the saintly pontiff. It was completed during his lifetime and, although promulgated four years after his death in 1914, bears his name. The law pertinent to the Confraternity reads as follows:

> The local ordinaries are to see to it that in every parish there shall be established the Confraternities of the Blessed Sacrament and Christian Doctrine which, when canonically established, are *ipso facto* aggregated to the corresponding Archconfraternities at Rome.[35]

It can now be seen, from the few documents selected from the many that are available, how Saint Pius X deservedly is called "the Pope of the Catechism"—taking the term *catechism* in one of its peculiarly European meanings of religious education in general. From 1903 to 1914, it may be said, the groundwork for a catechetical renewal was laid, and a period of reawakening for the Confraternity of Christian Doctrine was at hand.

Notes

1. Gerardo Franza, *Il Catechismo a Roma e L'Arciconfraternita della Dottrina Cristiana* (Alba: Edizioni Paoline, 1958), p. 40.
2. I. Schuster, *L' Insegnamento catechistico nelle parrocchie dalla storia di Venti Secoli* (Milan: Archivi Arcidiocesani, 1937), p. 11.
3. Franza, *Il Catechismo a Roma*, p. 79.
4. Achille Ratti [Pope Pius XI], ed., *Acta Ecclesiae Mediolanensis*, 4 vols. in folio (Milan: Arcidiocesis Ecclesiae Mediolanensis, 1892), 2: cols. 170-234.
5. Council of Trent, Session 17, 1546, *de reform.*, cap. 2, 4, 7.
6. *The Catechism of the Council of Trent*, popularly known as "the Roman Catechism," was translated from the Latin into a number of the modern languages immediately after publication. The first English version did not appear until late in the seventeenth century. Recommended text for reference is a book translated by Charles E. Callan and James McHugh, *The Catechism of the Council of Trent* (New York: Joseph P. Wagner, 1923).
7. Ratti, *Acta*, 3: col. 701.
8. Ibid., col. 193.
9. Cesare Orsenigo, *Life of St. Charles Borromeo* (St. Louis: B. Herder, 1943), p. 96; Franza, *Il Catechismo a Roma*, p. 161.
10. Orsenigo, *St. Charles Borromeo*, p. 290.
11. Aurelius L. Borkowski, *De Confraternitibus ecclesiasticis* (Washington, DC: Catholic University of America, 1918), p. 16.
12. Franza, *Il Catechismo a Roma*, p. 89.
13. Louis Ponnelle and Louis Bordet, *St. Philip Neri and the Roman Society of His Times*, trans. R. F. Kerr (London: Longmans & Co., 1932), p. 360.
14. *Fontes juris canonici*, I, no. 141, p. 248.
15. Located close to the Tiber, near the island of San Bartolomeo, this venerable church derives its name from the image of the Blessed Virgin Mary which, in 1546, miraculously wept because of a brutal murder committed in the adjacent street. The image was removed to the church which commemorates the prodigy in its name: S. Maria del Pianto. The image has been greatly revered by the people and is covered with precious ornaments. Rebuilt in 1612, the church stands today in a poor neighborhood.
16. Franza, *Il Catechismo a Roma*, p. 102.
17. Benedict XIV, *Etsi minime* (1742), *Fontes juris canonici*, I, 324; Pius X, *Acerbo nimis* (1905), *Acta Sanctae Sedis* 36, 129.
18. Franza, *Il Catechismo a Roma*, p. 97.
19. P. Tommaso Piatti, *L'Arciconfraternita della Dottrina Cristiana* (La Commissione catechistica del Vicariato; printed, Rome: Tipografica Agostiana, 1950), pp. 26–27.

20. Franza, *Il Catechismo a Roma*, p. 87.

21. Ibid., p. 211.

22. Martin Brenan, *The Confraternity of Christian Doctrine in Ireland, 1775-1835* (Dublin: Browne & Nolan, 1934).

23. Ibid., p. 10.

24. A. Mangenot, ed., *Dictionnaire de Theologie Catholique*, vol. 4, s.v. "Catechisme"; Mangenot, *Dictionnaire*, vol. 2: col. 1940.

25. Clarence Elwell, *Influence of the Enlightenment on the Catholic Theory of Religious Education in France: 1750-1850* (Cambridge: Harvard University Press, 1944), p. 240.

26. For information on the life and work of St. Pius X, see *A Symposium on the Life and Work of Pope Pius X* (Washington, DC: Confraternity of Christian Doctrine, 1946); Joseph B. Collins, *Catechetical Documents of Pope Pius X* (Paterson, NJ: St. Anthony Guild Press, 1946), pp. xv-xxi.

27. Angelo Marchesan, *Pio X* (Rome: Desclée, 1910), p. 146.

28. Collins, *Pope Pius X*, pp. 13-27; *Life and Work of Pope Pius X*, pp. 94-118.

29. Collins, *Pope Pius X*, p. 105.

30. Ibid., p. 24.

31. *Acta Sanctae Sedis* 37, 126.

32. Ibid.

33. *Acta Apostolicae Sedis* 2, 357.

34. Ibid.

35. *Code of Canon Law*, canon 711:2; canon 1381.

Religious Education and CCD in the United States: Early Years (1902–1935)

JOSEPH B. COLLINS

THIS PART OF OUR STUDY is intended to serve as an introduction to the history of the Confraternity of Christian Doctrine in this country.[1] To paraphrase a biblical saying about the patriarch Joseph, a generation is arising that knows not the name CCD as the progenitor of the many organizations that are today dedicated to the religious education of Catholic children in public schools and devoted to many and sundry kinds of adult formation. A recent survey administered by the National Center of Religious Education – CCD reports "a definite trend toward use of the term Religious Education (44 percent) rather than Religious Education – CCD (13 percent) or of Confraternity of Christian Doctrine (11 percent) in diocesan office titles."[2] Johannes Hofinger, SJ, a pioneer in the worldwide catechetical movement, notes that in recent years many offices of religious education, especially in Latin America, have changed their official designation to "centers or offices of evangelization and catechesis."[3]

The Confraternity of Christian Doctrine, or CCD as it is popularly referred to, is still a living witness to a vital part of the history of Catholic education in America; for us to reflect on its origin and growth allows for a better understanding of much that is happening in religious education today.

It is significant that the Confraternity of Christian Doctrine was flourishing in Europe before the first settlers landed on the eastern shores of the new world. Unlike its beginnings in Italy, the Confraternity in the United States grew by fits and starts. Its origin in one place sometimes marked the date of its demise in another. A complete history of the CCD in this country has yet to be written either on the national level or on the local level. Guidelines and reports of hundreds of diocesan and parish organizations are available for such a history.

Reprinted from *American Ecclesiastical Review* 169 (1975), pp. 48–67; by permission of The Catholic University of America Press.

The need for the Confraternity of Christian Doctrine was found, first of all, in the unsatisfactory conditions for Catholic education that prevailed in the thirteen colonies. Second, the need was recognized in the grave difficulties that Catholics met after the Revolution while attempting to provide religious training for their children in a new climate of postcolonial pluralism. Thought shall now be given to this twofold but interrelated background for the appearance of the CCD at various times and places later in the 1800s.

Catholic Education in Colonial America

Religious education for and on the part of Catholics was vigorously opposed by the Protestant majority in each of the thirteen colonies. From the first settlement in 1607, at Jamestown, to the War of Independence and even for some years after, Catholics were comparatively few in number. Poor and unlettered for the most part, many of them were indentured laborers or servants, and all of them made up a persecuted, disenfranchised, scattered minority in a hostile, highly sectarian environment. There were not many more than 35,000 Catholics in all the colonies in 1775.[4] "The history of Catholic education in America," declared Neil McCluskey, "like the history of the Church itself, is a story of survival and adaptation. From the first years of the colonial period to the time of Revolution, the American Catholic Church lived in the catacombs. . . . Its faithful were denied their freedom of worship, to take part in civic affairs, and to educate their children."[5]

Such conditions obviously were not conducive to any kind of permanent programs of catechetical instruction. Maryland was no exception. Religious freedom in the "Free State" lasted only from the day of the landing of the colonists under the Catholic Calverts in 1634 up to the "glorious revolution" of 1688, which brought William of Orange to the English throne and reopened for colonial Catholics a severe repression similar to that in the mother country. Each colony had its own church schools based on its own sectarian tradition and ideals. Throughout the colonial period of more than a century and a half, Catholics had only their long-standing traditions of family prayer, the catechism learned and recited in the home, and, where available, the liturgy to preserve the faith of their children.

Whatever formal Catholic education was available in colonial times, especially during the late 1700s, was supplied by the private schools and academies set up and administered at great sacrifice by members of orders such as the Jesuits, Franciscans, and Ursulines, to name but a few.[6] Catholic education, then, during the colonial period was sporadic at best. This was in sharp contrast to the denominational schools that enjoyed full freedom and support. Catholics, accordingly, were concerned that the faith was in jeopardy for their children, since they had no other choice than to attend the sectarian schools.

Education in the colonies was a private matter wholly directed by the churches. It embraced the four *R*'s, including religion, according to the establishment of each colony. After the adoption of the *Constitution* and particularly of the *Bill of Rights* (1791) with its guarantee of religious liberty, the fourth *R* began to disappear from the curricula of the American public schools. The fundamental change in policy in the schools of the new republic lay in the rapid proliferation of sects and denominations which were unhappy with the prevailing dominance of certain Protestant influences in the nation's schools. Secularists in theology and in educational policy, such as Horace Mann, sought in the first quarter of the nineteenth century to make the common school wholly secular. Thus evolved the final state of things. The deliberate policy of separation of church and state, the hands-off policy of the states toward religion in the public schools, coupled with a degree of meddling or even direction in public school affairs by certain sectarian groups, brought on a new sense of danger on the part of the Catholic Church and its representatives. Thus, by force of circumstances, the Revolution became the source of the civil life of the new republic and at the same time an occasion for establishment of the Catholic parochial school system and ultimately of the Confraternity of Christian Doctrine.

John Carroll, SJ, member of a longtime Catholic family in Maryland, was appointed first bishop of "all the states in the united republic" in 1789. In his first letter to the faithful, he wrote: "I have considered that the virtuous and Christian education of youth is the principal object of my pastoral care."[7] Although his entire flock at this time numbered fewer than 35,000, Bishop Carroll led the way in setting up schools and colleges. The following decades witnessed the first waves of Catholic immigrants to arrive on our shores eager for the civil and religious freedom promised by the *Constitution*.

Plenary Councils of Baltimore

The plenary councils of Baltimore exerted a strong influence on the history of American Catholic education during all of the nineteenth century. In general, the catechetical provisions of the councils reflected the many strong encyclicals, decrees, and synodal laws that emanated from Rome during this time.[8] The First Plenary Council of Baltimore was held in 1852. It promulgated for the American Church much of the Tridentine catechetical legislation, such as the obligations of pastors and parents relative to Christian instruction for all classes of the people. It urged erection of parish schools and ordered formal lessons in the catechism for all Catholic youth not found in parish schools.[9]

A more detailed and lengthier plea for all Catholics young and old to receive the benefits of Christian education was made by the Second Plenary Council of Baltimore in 1866. To the mandate for parish schools, the council added a demand that the Confraternity of Christian Doctrine be set up when the mandate could not be fulfilled. The decree is as follows:

> Catholic schools cannot be set up in all parishes because of the difficulties that are present. Since the public schools are the only places where daily education is available, it is all the more urgent to use all possible means to minimize the harm which may come to Catholic pupils. For this reason catechetical instruction and the *schools of Christian doctrine* should be established. Pastors should have the boys and girls meet in their own church on Sundays and holydays and even more often in order to teach them the elements of Christian doctrine with zeal and diligence.
>
> Among the most notable of the restorers and patrons of this Society [Confraternity] was St. Charles Borromeo, Archbishop of Milan, whose labors, counsels, and precepts are worthy of being carefully read by all pastors of souls.[10]

This, the earliest mention of the Confraternity of Christian Doctrine in an American document is couched in terms identical to those used of the Confraternity in its beginnings in Europe. It was variously referred to as "Confraternity," "Company," "Sodality," or "Society." The reference to Saint Charles Borromeo, the great sixteenth-century promoter of the Confraternity, identifies the Confraternity in the decree of the council.[11]

The Third Plenary Council of Baltimore was convoked in 1884, and from the viewpoint of specific legislation surpassed its predecessors. On the need for Catholic schools, for instance, to supply the deficiencies of the common schools, the council declared: "Friends of Christian education do not condemn the State for not imparting religious instruction in our public schools because it is well-known that the State has no competency to teach religion."[12] A brave watchword, "Every Child in a Catholic School," grew out of the council's ordinances on Christian education on every level from first grade to college. It was decreed that a commission be appointed to produce a uniform catechism for the whole country. A result was the Baltimore Catechism which appeared with approval of Cardinal (then Archbishop) James Gibbons in the following year.[13]

The councils of Baltimore served to awaken interest in the plight of Catholic youngsters in the public schools. This would ultimately lead to an understanding of and acceptance of the Confraternity of Christian Doctrine.

Analysis of the extensive catechetical legislation from diocesan synods and provincial and national councils up to the turn of the century in this country indicates a great uniformity in providing for religious instruction for Catholic youth in public schools.[14] Frequently repeated in the documents is the stipulation that pastors shall visit the parochial school on weekdays but must give all possible attention to the public school children in Sunday schools and the school of education (*schola catechesmi*). The First Synod of Fall River, Massachusetts, in 1905, ordered that the Confraternity of Christian Doctrine be set up in conformity with the legislation on the CCD in the encyclical of Saint Pius X, *Acerbo nimis* ("On the Teaching of Christian Doctrine") which was issued that same year.[15] "There was an honest effort," concludes Robert Mulvee, "to provide as adequate a catechetical program as possible for those Catholic students who attended public schools."[16] It can be inferred that this copious legislation was effective. It also prepared for the time when the Confraternity would be organized to take over the Sunday schools and other organized means to offer religious education to Catholics attending public schools.

First Confraternity Units in the United States

It is noteworthy that the councils of Baltimore mandated the establishment of parochial schools in every parish in the country and urged with almost equal fervor that adequate Christian instruction be provided to the great majority of Catholic youngsters who frequented the public schools. The councils offered no guidelines to implement the demand for a total parish religious education program to include, for example, catechist training, parent education, texts, facilities, and organization. The disunity between directive and follow-up has persisted ever since. Formal training of catechists to teach religion in a professional manner did not begin generally until the late 1930s or early 1940s.[17] In other words, the councils pointed the way; the know-how and means were not far distant.

The first canonically erected unit of the Confraternity in the United States was organized in the parish of Our Lady of Good Counsel in New York City in 1902. Like its predecessors at Milan in the sixteenth century, the New York CCD was started by zealous members of the laity. In this case they were participants in a Normal Training School for Catechists held during the winter of 1901-02 at a Catholic Settlement House. The purpose of the course was to prepare religious educators to go into the parishes, first, to teach Christian doctrine to children and adults and, second, to provide needed instruction for out-of-school youth.[18]

During the course of the year 1902, the group asked Archbishop Michael A. Corrigan to recognize the organization as the Confraternity of Christian Doctrine and to petition the Holy See for affiliation to the Archconfraternity of Christian Doctrine in Rome. The rescript that came from Cardinal Respighi is as follows:

> This is to certify that the Confraternity of Christian Doctrine has been canonically established in the Church of Our Lady of Good Counsel at New York, New York, and has been affiliated with the Archconfraternity at Rome. Dated 21 May 1902.[19]

James M. Connolly, pastor of the parish, was appointed director of the local CCD unit, and Saint Charles Borromeo was named its patron. The famed Confraternity set up by the saintly archbishop in Milan is clearly the model for the New York organization. This is amply illustrated in the small manual, dated 1902, produced by the local CCD unit and, incidentally, the first known manual for the CCD in this country. "The following rules," states the preface, "are in substance such as St. Charles Borromeo drew up; they are accommodated to the present day."[20]

The structure of the New York City unit of the CCD was relatively simple. Each local unit functioned under a director, who was usually the pastor, and a parish council consisting of lay men and women. The catechetical work was carried out by teachers and fishers (retaining the nomenclature of Milan). The former were trained in the school for catechists which gave rise to the organization.

Another "first" of the CCD in New York was a diocesan congress which took place in 1909. It purposed "to study the problems that confront the CCD in this city and to devise means toward their solution."[21] Although the question of Christian training for Catholic public school youngsters was discussed at the congress, no decision was reached. The New York CCD, as was the case with its Italian model, was particularly concerned with the religious formation of youth and adults wherever they could be found—in parishes, institutions, homes, etc. As a matter of fact, the original CCD in New York, with its headquarters at Our Lady of Good Counsel, did not extend beyond a small number of parishes.[22] At no time was it diocese-wide in its direction and operation. This may account for its gradual absorption after 1913 into Theta Pi Alpha, an organization initiated under Cardinal John Farley to care for Catholic children and youth attending public schools.

The modern revival of the Confraternity of Christian Doctrine in the Archdiocese of New York took place in 1936, when the CCD was officially established by Cardinal Patrick Hayes; it was also affiliated with the Archconfraternity in Rome.[23] For some time the CCD in New York had been quiescent. This is implied by the new director, John S. Middleton, upon his appointment in 1936, in terming himself "uninformed" as to what the CCD is all about and how he could get it organized in the city.[24]

The Confraternity of Christian Doctrine was set up in the Diocese of Pittsburgh by Bishop Regis Canevin in 1907, as mandated by the encyclical of Pope Pius X entitled *Acerbo nimis,* which was issued in 1905.[25] There was a great need in the diocese for catechetical work of all kinds with the result that the organization spread rapidly in parishes throughout the inner city. Within one year a CCD convention was held; delegates from seventy-five units from local parishes participated. This pioneer organization continued to conduct Sunday schools for children and evening sessions for older persons more or less extensively until a new diocesan office was set up in the early 1930s to direct a diocesewide program of religious education for Catholics outside of the parochial schools.[26]

In the following year, 1908, another step was made in catechetical history when the Missionary Confraternity of Christian Doctrine of the Diocese of Pittsburgh was founded. This truly pioneer organization, initiated by three zealous lay teachers from the CCD already functioning in the city, was planned to provide Christian instruction and even places for celebration of the liturgy among poor, mostly foreign-born Catholics living in the mining districts that lay adjacent to the city. After a meeting in late 1908, Bishop Canevin praised the zealous foresight of the group, approved the entire program, and appointed a director for what he called the Missionary Confraternity of Christian Doctrine for the Diocese of Pittsburgh.[27] It was structurally independent of the CCD which was functioning in the city parishes. Both organizations were dependent upon the diocese for direction and to a large extent for financial support.

In 1907, the CCD in the local city parishes issued, under its direction, a small manual, and some years later a manual was published by the Missionary CCD.[28]

The purpose of the Missionary CCD, according to the manual, was:

> to organize and conduct catechizing schools in mining towns, country places, city districts, in charitable and reform institutions or in any other

place where Catholic children are to be found in need of religious instructions.[29]

A director, appointed by the bishop, supervised the work of the society. There was also a diocesan board, composed of directors of the ten active centers, for control and directives. The local structure of the CCD in Pittsburgh, both in the city organization and in the Missionary CCD in the mining areas, included a director (priest) with teachers, fishers, and contributing or associate members. After ten years of service, a report of the organization in 1919 indicated that there were more than 13,000 children and youths in 153 schools of religion conducted by 500 teachers.[30]

The Missionary CCD of the Diocese of Pittsburgh brought forth in truly pioneer fashion some activities that were to appear much later as part of the activities of local CCD units. Thus, for instance, it was planned to minister to the spiritual needs of Catholics in remote and neglected areas, to lead if possible others into the Catholic Church, and also to promote the spread of Catholic literature. This was to become the formal work of the Apostolate to Non-Catholics in the early forties, later known as the Apostolate of Good Will.[31]

The Confraternity of Christian Doctrine was started in Los Angeles on 11 March 1922. Its establishment by Bishop John J. Cantwell was the outgrowth of a need for the religious instruction of a rapidly growing number of Mexican immigrants who settled in the outskirts of the city.[32] The primary impetus toward founding a CCD was given by Verona Spellmire, a public school teacher and volunteer social worker. She was distressed at the ignorance of Christian doctrine among both the young and old whom she met in the diocesan social work programs. As early as 1919, she had read an article in *Our Sunday Visitor* on the work of the Missionary CCD in Pittsburgh. She learned more about the Confraternity from a friend who had worked with it in that city. All this led ultimately to a meeting with her fellow workers at the office of Catholic Charities on 11 March 1922. The director of the office, Robert E. Lucey (at present retired Archbishop of San Antonio), gave the proposal his full support. He offered to seek authorization from Bishop Cantwell to establish the CCD for catechical work among the Spanish-speaking immigrants of the city. It was granted before the close of the meeting, and at the same time William J. Mullane was appointed the first director of the CCD for the Diocese of Los Angeles.

Similar to the Missionary CCD in Pittsburgh, the Los Angeles CCD was originally set up for the physical as well as spiritual welfare of the poor and unlettered. For the first few years, the Confraternity operated out of local centers, mostly in the immigrant quarters of the city, and in all types of situations, such as living rooms, vacant lots, school buildings, a garage, a movie theater, and a number of rectories.[33] Before the end of its second year, the fledgling CCD could boast of more than 150 members. Mullane announced what amounted to new departure for Confraternity structure: "Eventually the Confraternity will become a parish organization with a central governing body and monthly meetings to which representatives will be sent from the parishes."[34]

The structures, both diocesan and parochial, of the Los Angeles Confraternity were outlined in the new constitution of 1924. They were closely modeled on that of the Missionary CCD of Pittsburgh. On the diocesan level, the director, acting in the name of the bishop, had charge of all matters pertaining to the general welfare of the organization; he was responsible for maintaining uniformity in parishes throughout the diocese. The diocese itself was divided into districts with a chairperson in charge who also was a member of the diocesan executive board, which in turn was made up of the director and the usual officers. The local or parish CCD consisted of the director (i.e., pastor or his assistant) and a representative from the active members who formed the local parish board: teachers, fishers or home visitors, and alternates or substitutes. Other matters, such as transportation, allocation of classes, etc., were taken over by the "helpers."[35]

In addition to the active members, there also were associate members who contributed to the financial support of the work. The Los Angeles CCD continued during the early years to be identified with the welfare agency of the diocese by providing, for instance, clothing and other essentials for the poor Mexican children attending the schools of religion. There were also social clubs for mothers and for boys and girls that offered opportunities for recreation and study of Christian doctrine. The CCD took on the development of Junior Confraternities, in high schools and colleges, which had their own officers and meetings – a forerunner of the CCD Newman Clubs to come a decade later.[36]

The early growth of the CCD in Los Angeles was greatly stimulated by the personal support of Bishop Cantwell. Strong pastoral letters were issued in the fall of 1923 and again in 1924 in which, for example, he stated the case for the CCD as follows:

> I desire to call your attention to the work of the Confraternity of Christian Doctrine. This organization is composed of zealous members of the laity who devote a few hours of their time each week to the religious education of the children not attending Catholic schools. It has already proved of considerable help in many places, but in order to meet the needs adequately a great many more workers are required.[37]

The bishop's call for volunteers increased greatly the number of active members and made the people of the diocese aware of the importance of the Confraternity and its effectiveness. In 1924, Thomas J. O'Dwyer was appointed diocesan director. He promoted a policy of greater independence of parish units with relation to the diocesan office to the extent that the Los Angeles CCD was a kind of federation of local units. Teachers training for religious education continued to take on a new importance as the CCD expanded. A special committee prepared a number of pedagogical aids which in time became very popular both within and outside the diocese. Among them were individual lesson outlines, sets of colored pictures, charts, a life of Christ, and a variety of small and large catechisms. A catechetical library was set up at the central office, and the various centers in parishes were supplied with chalkboards and other visual equipment. Practical catechetics was born here in the hard school of necessity.

The year 1926 marked the appointment of Leroy Callahan as the first full-time diocesan director of the Confraternity and opened up a period of ten years of solid growth both within and outside the city of Los Angeles. Callahan built upon the foundation laid by his predecessors. There were already fifty-two CCD centers in operation when he took charge. His brief (he was ordained only one year) parochial experience before his appointment was devoted to the social and religious welfare of the poor Mexicans to whom he dedicated his great talents.

Under Callahan's guidance the CCD took on an importance and influence that was nationwide, since many of the catechetical publications that he wrote or directed from the central office were discovered and used by religious educators in all parts of the country. His materials were used especially when other materials were not abundant in the field. In 1926, for example, *Model Lessons in a Catechism* by Callahan was designed for untrained teachers. It contained an explanation of each lesson with techniques on how to present it to others. *Religious Project Books* by Alice Vignos of the local CCD office was first published in 1929. It combined pictures and "how-to" methods to illustrate booklets on subjects such as prayer, sacraments, liturgy, etc.[38] Another original contribution to religious education, *A Graded Course of Study* (for elementary grades), was planned by Callahan in 1929 and completed a few years later. It included a precommunion prayer class and study of the Church and Gospels for secondary level students.[39]

These modest and inexpensive undertakings served to remove the catechism from the classroom. Through simple and effective techniques each lesson was made more attractive, religion was applied to daily life, and the way opened for the rich and varied manuals and texts that would come a few decades in the future. In Los Angeles, as in other places that made CCD history, methods in religious education were developed to meet immediate and demanding needs.

In the summer of 1928, Callahan expanded the work of the CCD to include a pilot program of six summer vacation schools. The project was suggested a year earlier by Edwin V. O'Hara, pastor at Eugene, Oregon, and founder-director of the National Catholic Rural Life Conference. (O'Hara organized the first Catholic religious vacation schools in 1921 and made them a vital part of a national program of religious education for children and youths in rural areas all over the country.) In 1929, the religious vacation school program in Los Angeles was extended by the director to include the entire diocese. During that summer, 116 schools were organized; 11,500 children participated under the direction of more than 500 teachers and helpers.

In order to provide greater uniformity and assistance to the CCD planners, Callahan and Spellmire produced a small volume entitled *Handbook of Suggestions on Religious Vacation Schools,* which appeared in 1929. The typical religious vacation school program of four weeks was outlined with a lesson plan for each day based on the Bible, catechism, project work, and also hymns and prayers. For the first time, the religious vacation schools in Los Angeles were incorporated into a formal diocesan CCD program. Here was another first in the history of the CCD in Los Angeles. Approximately ten years later, Bishop O'Hara eulogized Alice Vignos at a memorial Mass in Los Angeles. He said: "She focused attention upon your archdiocese [it became such in 1936] as a pioneer and a leader in the Confraternity work."[40]

Other Dioceses Before 1935

A number of dioceses in addition to New York, Pittsburgh, and Los Angeles had a fairly well-developed Confraternity program before the establishment of the National Center of the CCD at Washington, D.C., in May 1935. After that date the Confraternity expanded all over the country both in depth and in effectiveness. The record of the beginning and growth of the CCD in the following dioceses is in chronological order as far as can be determined. Their contribution relative to CCD history is frequently limited, since the existing data from local records are often inadequate.

The Confraternity of Christian Doctrine was set up in the Archdiocese of Dubuque as early as 1925 by Archbishop Francis J. Beckman, when the program of religious vacation schools was incorporated into the Confraternity. John M. Wolfe, who was superintendent of schools as well as director of the CCD, became interested in the vacation schools in 1922, since they were sponsored by the Catholic Rural Life Conference of which he was a member. Wolfe also contributed to the production of the very influential *Manual for Religious Vacation Schools* published and distributed in the early years by the National Catholic Rural Life Conference.[41]

The Diocese of Monterey-Fresno had an active Confraternity program as early as 1927. (The diocese was divided into separate sees in 1963.) In 1927, Bishop MacGinley directed that the CCD be organized in all parishes and appointed John L. Crowley as director. He built the Confraternity around several groups of sisters and laywomen. Teachers were required to be certified, and religion was taught in formal CCD classes during the school year as well as during the summer. The CCD also conducted laywomen's retreats and engaged in some missionary work. A car equipped with a chapel traveled through fruit camps and mining districts of the diocese; the chaplain gave instructions and prepared old and young for the sacraments.[42]

The Confraternity in Santa Fe was organized on a parish (not diocese-wide) basis in 1927, through the efforts of the Sisters of the Society of Missionary Catechists of Our Lady of Victory whose headquarters are in Huntington, Indiana.[43] About one fourth of the teachers in these early CCD schools were from the public schools. The first catechist training course was opened in 1929, with such special lessons as sewing and how to play the organ. A formal ceremony was held for commissioning lay teachers that was conducted by the spiritual director of the Confraternity in the parish or mission. Much credit is deserved by these pioneer missionaries of the CCD. They worked tirelessly amid hardships over a vast, largely unpeopled territory in order to bring the faith to the poor and unlettered.[44]

The Confraternity was organized in the Diocese of Boise shortly after the coming to the diocese of Bishop Edward J. Kelly on 6 March 1928. It was his first official act. P. J. O'Toole is reliably reported as the first director by (now Bishop of Yakima, Washington) Nicholas E. Walsh, native of the Diocese of Boise.[45]

In 1929, the Confraternity was organized in whole or in part in the Diocese of Leavenworth, Kansas (became Archdiocese of Kansas City, Kansas, in 1947) by Bishop Francis Johannes.[46] An inquiry by the present writer was unsuccessful in obtaining further information on the early years of the CCD in this diocese.

Sioux City, Iowa, was another diocese that formally established the Confraternity in the early 1930s. Bishop Edmund Heelan made the announcement, and Clio J. Ivis was appointed diocesan director. Ivis continued in this capacity for many years.[47]

Edwin V. O'Hara, founder and director of the Catholic Rural Life Bureau at the National Catholic Welfare Conference in Washington, D.C., was appointed Bishop of Great Falls, Montana, in 1930.[48] As a pastor in Eugene, Oregon, he had developed what was to become a nationwide program of religious vacation schools under the auspices of the Rural Life Conference. He was already familiar with the work of the Confraternity and clearly saw its role in the conduct of vacation schools.

The first pastoral of the new bishop in January 1931 canonically established the CCD in every parish in the diocese. Patrick J. Tierney was appointed director. Bishop O'Hara drew up the structure of parish units in a "Suggested Constitution" of the CCD which was closely patterned after that of the Los Angeles Confraternity under Callahan.

The main activity of the CCD in the Diocese of Great Falls was the conduct of religious vacation schools. Shortly thereafter extensive parent-educator and home discussion club programs were inaugurated throughout this vast diocese. CCD schools of religion as well as home correspondence courses were also organized. A special parish activity to reach non-Catholics through distribution of Catholic literature was incorporated as part of the regular Confraternity program.

Stone's unpublished dissertation at the Catholic University (previously cited) states that the Diocese of Sacramento established the Confraternity in 1931. The decree was issued by Bishop Robert J. Armstrong; Stephen Keating was named director for the diocese. These facts are substantiated by a recent communication from Russell Terra, present diocesan director of CCD. However, Keating was not a full-time director. There are many similar instances in the early and even later years of CCD history.[49]

The Confraternity was inaugurated in the Diocese of Toledo by Bishop Karl J. Alter in 1931.[50] Hilary Weger was interested in the Confraternity before it was formally organized in the diocese, and he became its first director. He was a pioneer in religious education and a successful author of textbooks. He died in 1962.[51]

The Diocese of Rochester, New York, was active in the catechetical field in 1919, when a released time program of religious instruction for Catholic students in public schools was inaugurated.[52] In June 1932, Bishop John F. O'Hern appointed J. H. Duffy to be director of a Catholic education office for the diocese. This office led to the development of a fully organized CCD program.[53] The first national catechetical congress of the CCD was held at Rochester at the invitation of Archbishop Edward (later Cardinal) Mooney on 30–31 October 1935.[54]

It is not certain that the Confraternity was organized in the Diocese of Spokane, Washington, in 1932, as Father Stone notes in his dissertation on the early history of the CCD in the United States.[55] Bishop Charles D. White, who was appointed to the See of Spokane in 1926, served as director of the CCD until 1954.[56] He set up an active vacation school program and CCD schools of religion that, according to national center files, were operating in the spring of 1935. Bishop White was host to a regional congress of the Confraternity for the entire northwest held 8–10 October 1935 – an indication of Confraternity experience and readiness in the Diocese of Spokane. Because of his expertise in the work of the CCD, Bishop White was named a member of the Bishops' Committee of the National Center in 1947.

The Confraternity of Christian Doctrine was canonically organized in the Diocese of Helena, Montana, on 1 January 1932, by Bishop George J. Finnigan, CSC. The first diocesan director was not appointed until September 1936. The pastoral letter of Bishop Finnigan setting up the CCD emphasized the regulations of canon law relative to the Confraternity. The work of establishing the CCD in the diocese was carried out with the aid of Miriam Marks who was later to become executive secretary of the National Center of the CCD in Washington, D.C.[57]

Bishop Thomas K. Gorman was appointed the first Bishop of the Diocese of Reno, Nevada, in 1931. He had only thirteen priests to assist him with the work of the diocese. As early as 1932, Bishop Gorman and his chancellor, H. A. Meistekothen, were directing various CCD programs, such as vacation schools and study clubs. In 1934, the Confraternity was officially organized in the diocese with Meistekothen acting as diocesan director.[58]

The first steps in setting up the Confraternity in the Archdiocese of St. Paul were initiated by Archbishop John G. Murray in August 1934. In a pastoral letter he urged that family and group study clubs be organized and modeled on the successful program directed by Bishop O'Hara in the Diocese of Great Falls, Montana.[59]

In the same letter the archbishop issued a directive to all pastors that the Confraternity be established in every parish and that the study club program then operating, as well as vacation schools, be placed under the Confraternity.[60] In the following year, 1935, the CCD was formally established in the diocese by Archbishop Murray with Rudolph G. Bandas, noted catechetical writer, as director – a post he was to hold with distinction for many years. Archbishop Murray became one of three members of the first Episcopal Committee of the CCD in 1934, with Bishop O'Hara as chairman and Archbishop McNicholas of Cincinnati as a third member.[61]

The beginning of the Confraternity in the Diocese of Wichita, Kansas, antedates its canonical establishment in 1934 by Bishop August Schwertner.[62] Early in 1928, Leon A. McNeill, diocesan superintendent of schools, was directed by Bishop Schwertner to initiate a program of religious correspondence courses for children, many of whom attended public schools. The graded courses began to operate late in 1929. With significant extensions that include adults and discussion groups, they continue up to the present time under the able direction of McNeill.[63] The CCD Correspondence Courses, as they are nationally known, have a merited place of honor in the early history of CCD programming in this country.

In the spring of 1931, Bishop Schwertner commissioned McNeill to set up a study club program similar to that promoted by Bishop O'Hara in the Diocese of Great Falls, Montana. Supervision of the work, including selection and distribution of texts, was carried out by the office of Catholic schools. The program was successful from the beginning: forty-three clubs at the end of the first year.

In August 1934, the Confraternity was set up in the Wichita Diocese by the bishop with McNeill as director; the various educational programs were coordinated in one office. Parish units of the CCD were organized systematically with full parish structure according to the "Suggested Constitution" of the CCD: a parish *board* consisting of the usual officers plus chairpersons of the various activities of the parish unit, i.e., teachers, helpers, visitors (fishers), study clubs, parents, and distributors of Catholic literature.[64]

Final Reflection

The early years of the sporadic growth and experimentation in the Confraternity came to an end with the creation of the Episcopal Committee of the CCD in 1934, followed by the establishment of the National Center in May 1935.

The next two decades witnessed the full flowering of the Confraternity on a national scale. This was due mainly to the zeal and organizing genius of Bishop Edwin V. O'Hara. As head of the Diocese of Great Falls and chairman of the episcopal committee, he not only made CCD history but also changed the course of religious education in this country.

NOTES

1. *The Confraternity Comes of Age: A Historical Symposium* (Paterson, NJ: St. Anthony Guild Press, 1956), pp. 1–25.

2. Files of the National Center of Religious Education – CCD, Washington, D.C.

3. Johannes Hofinger, "Evangelizing Catechesis: Basic Principles," *The Living Light* 11 (Fall 1974): 338.

4. Harold A. Beutow, *Of Singular Benefit: The Story of U. S. Catholic Education* (New York: Macmillan, 1970), p. 23.

5. Neil G. McCluskey, *Catholic Education in America: A Documentary History* (New York: Columbia University, 1946), p. 3.

6. Edmund G. Goebel, *A Study of Catholic Secondary Education During the Colonial Period up to the First Plenary Council of Baltimore, 1852* (Washington, DC: Catholic University of America Press, 1936), p. 9.

7. Peter Guilday, ed., *The National Pastorals of the American Hierarchy, 1792-1919* (Washington, DC: National Catholic Welfare Conference [N.C.W.C.] Press, 1923), p. 3.

8. Raymond J. Jansen, *Canonical Provisions for Catechetical Instruction: An Historical Synopsis and Commentary* (Washington, DC: Catholic University of America Press, 1937), pp. 31–34.

9. *Concilium Plenarium Baltimori Habitum Anno 1852* (Baltimore: John Murphy, 1853), pp. 46, 47.

10. *Concilii Plenarii Baltimorensis II, Acta et Decreta* (Baltimore: John Murphy, 1868), p. 69.

11. Cf. Joseph B. Collins, "The Beginnings of the CCD in Europe and Its Modern Revival," December 1974 [also reprinted in this sourcebook as Reading 11].

12. *Concilii Plenarii Baltimorensis III, Acta et Decreta* (Baltimore: John Murphy, 1886), p. 84.

13. *A Catechism of Christian Doctrine,* prepared and enjoined by order of the Third Plenary Council of Baltimore, 6 April 1885, cited by Joseph B. Collins, "Catechetics in the United States and the American Ecclesiastical Review," *The American Ecclesiastical Review,* July 1949, p. 323.

14. Robert E. Mulvee, *The Catechetical Legislation in the Dioceses of New England: An Historico-Juridic Study* (Rome: Pontifical Institute of Both Laws, 1964), p. 65.

15. Ibid., p. 72.

16. Ibid., p. 16.

17. Beutow, *Of Singular Benefit,* pp. 190, 247.

18. M. Tallon, *The Confraternity of Christian Doctrine: First Decade of Achievement in the Archdiocese of New York* (New York: Parish Visitors of Mary Immaculate, 1939), p. 3.

19. Trans. from *The Manual of the Confraternity of Christian Doctrine in the Archdiocese of New York* (New York: M. A. O'Connor, 6 October 1902).

20. Ibid., p. vii.

21. Tallon, *Confraternity of Christian Doctrine,* p. 40.

22. John S. Middleton, "Confraternity Organization in New York," in *Proceedings of the National Catechetical Congress of the Confraternity of Christian Doctrine, New York, 1936* (Paterson, NJ: St. Anthony Guild Press, 1937), p. 121.

23. Ibid., p. 120.

24. Letter of Father Middleton to Miriam Marks, Files of the National Center–CCD.

25. Raymond Prindiville, "The Confraternity of Christian Doctrine," *The American Ecclesiastical Review,* August–September 1932, p. 35.

26. Files of the National Center–CCD.

27. Leo Lanham, *The Missionary Confraternity of Christian Doctrine in the Diocese of Pittsburgh* (Washington, DC: Catholic University of America Press, 1945), p. 29.

28. Cf. *Manual of Confraternity of Christian Doctrine* (Lancaster: Manor Press, 1907); and *Manual of the Missionary Confraternity of Christian Doctrine, Diocese of Pittsburgh* (Pittsburgh, 1923).

29. *Manual of the Missionary Confraternity,* p. 15.

30. Lanham, *Missionary Confraternity in Pittsburgh,* p. 78.

31. "The Apostolate of Good Will," in *The Confraternity Comes of Age* (Paterson, NJ: Confraternity Publications, 1956), p. 259.

32. Dennis J. Burke, "The History of the Confraternity of Christian Doctrine in the Diocese of Los Angeles, 1923-1936" (M.A. diss., Catholic University of America, July 1965), p. 19.

33. Ibid., p. 27.

34. Ibid., p. 29.

35. The diocesan and parochial structures of the Los Angeles CCD and the designations of members according to their activities are derived primarily from the Confraternity structure at Milan in the sixteenth century. The original source of this type of organization is found in the Constitution of the Roman Archconfraternity; the designations were taken over by the organizers of the pioneer Confraternities at New York and Pittsburgh.

36. Rhoda Gardner, "The Growth and Development of the Confraternity of Christian Doctrine in the United States," in *Proceedings of the National Catechetical Congress of the Confraternity of Christian Doctrine, Los Angeles, 1940* (Paterson, NJ: St. Anthony Guild Press, 1941), p. 358.

37. Files of the National Center–CCD.

38. Alice Vignos, "Confraternity Projects Defined," in *Proceedings of the National Catechetical Congress of the Confraternity of Christian Doctrine, Rochester, 1935* (Paterson, NJ: St. Anthony Guild Press, 1936), pp. 148–151.

39. Leroy Callahan, "The Catechism Graded for Children," in *Proceedings of the National Congress, Rochester, 1935,* pp. 78–86.

40. Edwin V. O'Hara, "A Tribute to Alice Vignos, A Pioneer," in *Proceedings of the National Congress, Los Angeles, 1940,* p. 525.

41. Sister M. Margaret King, BVM, Office of Education, Dubuque, Iowa, to Father Joseph B. Collins, July 1974; and *Confraternity Comes of Age,* p. 34.

42. Religious Instruction Report, N.C.W.C., 1931, p. 41; and Prindiville, "Confraternity of Christian Doctrine," pp. 47–49.

43. Blanche Richardson, "Holding Our Missions to the Faith," *The Acolyte,* April 1932, p. 910.

44. Prindiville, "Confraternity of Christian Doctrine," pp. 45–47.

45. Bishop Nicholas E. Walsh to Father Joseph B. Collins, September 1974; and William S. Stone, "The History of the Confraternity of Christian Doctrine in the United States" (M.A. diss., Catholic University of America, 1948), p. 34.

46. Stone, "History of the Confraternity," p. 34.

47. Father Leonard Ziegmann, diocesan director of the CCD, telephone conversation with Father Joseph B. Collins.

48. J. G. Shaw, *Edwin Vincent O'Hara* (New York: Farrar, Straus and Cudahy, 1952), p. 125.

49. Father Russell G. Terra, first full-time director of religious education for the Diocese of Sacramento, to Father Joseph B. Collins, July 1974.

50. Stone, "History of the Confraternity," p. 34.

51. The research of Stone (1948) has been confirmed in a recent letter to this writer by Father John T. Hiltz, present director of religious education for the Diocese of Toledo.

52. Robert F. McNamara, *Diocese of Rochester, 1868-1968* (Rochester, NY: Christopher Press, 1968), pp. 307, 410-412.

53. Father Robert F. McNamara, professor of church history, St. Bernard's Seminary, Rochester, New York, to Father Joseph B. Collins, July 1974.

54. *Proceedings of the National Congress, Rochester, 1935.*

55. Stone, "History of the Confraternity," p. 34.

56. Files of the National Center – CCD.

57. Father John M. Robertson, chancellor of Helena Diocese, to Father Joseph B. Collins, July 1974.

58. Msgr. C. J. Righini, vicar general, Diocese of Reno, to Father Joseph B. Collins, July 1974.

59. John T. Maloney, "A Plan for a Diocesan Office of Catechetics" (M.A. diss., Catholic University of America, 1937), p. 88.

60. Mrs. Frank van Valkenberg, "The Confraternity of Christian Doctrine in St. Paul," *Journal of Religious Instruction*, May 1936, p. 813.

61. Files of the National Center – CCD.

62. Maloney, "Plan for Diocesan Office," p. 91.

63. Files of the National Center – CCD.

64. Seventh Annual Educational Report of the Diocese of Wichita, 1934-35, Files of the National Center – CCD.

Bishop O'Hara and a National CCD

JOSEPH B. COLLINS

THE NAME of Father Edwin V. O'Hara, later bishop and arch-bishop, occurs at every step in the progress of the Confraternity of Christian Doctrine in this country. In a word, the history of the CCD in America is a chronicle of the life of this priest and bishop through more than forty years. The present study will focus on the efforts of Bishop O'Hara to make the Confraternity a truly national organiza-tion.[1]

A CCD director in every diocese, a well-balanced program in every parish, and a flexible structure in schools of religion based upon experience – this was his goal. We will point out that to the accomplish-ment of this task he was seemingly destined from the beginning.

Edwin Vincent O'Hara was born on 6 September 1881 near Lanesboro in the Diocese of Winona, Minnesota.[2] His early education was received in the one-room rural school built by his father on a cor-ner of the family farm. Edwin completed his education at St. Thomas College, St. Paul, and at the nearby St. Paul Seminary where he was ordained to the priesthood for the Archdiocese of Oregon City (later Portland, Oregon) on 10 June 1905. Father O'Hara offered his first Mass in his home parish, and his sermon for that happy occasion centered on the importance of religious instruction for children. He pointed out that his thoughts were drawn from the encyclical "On the Teaching of Christian Doctrine," which Pius X had issued a few weeks earlier on 15 April. "Let the little ones come" was his text, which twenty-five years later was to adorn his episcopal crest.

Father O'Hara's first appointment was as assistant pastor of the cathedral parish in Portland. In addition, he assumed a succession of new offices and responsibilities. Teaching religion to grade school children, giving courses on the New Testament in the high school, and conducting inquiry classes for adults convinced the young priest of the

Reprinted from *American Ecclesiastical Review* 169 (1975), pp. 237–255, by permis-sion of The Catholic University of America Press.

absolute necessity of catechetical training—a preoccupation which signally marked his entire life.

In 1907, Father O'Hara was appointed superintendent of schools for the archdiocese and soon afterward became the first president of the Catholic Educational Association of Oregon. He inaugurated institutes for training teachers in the parochial schools, something new at the time. These attracted religious and lay teachers from all over the northwest.

In the rounds of his many offices and duties, Father O'Hara became acutely aware of the pressing social and economic problems among the youth and working classes of the city. Opportunities for their religious education was ever uppermost in his mind. He was soon to learn what catechists for centuries had understood: that catechesis and social welfare go hand in hand. O'Hara organized a boys' recreation center with a library and a home with educational facilities for working girls. As chairperson of the statewide consumers' league, he was personally responsible for passage of the first compulsory minimum wage legislation in the United States. In 1917, the University of Notre Dame awarded Father O'Hara an honorary doctor of laws degree in recognition of his part in the successful efforts made in Oregon toward social justice and economic reform as clearly expressed in his *A Living Wage by Legislation: The Oregon Experience.*[3]

Catholic Rural Life Bureau

During the First World War, Father O'Hara was a Knights of Columbus chaplain with the American forces in France. On his return to Portland and his school work, he felt keenly the neglect of formal religious instruction for children in rural districts. A solution to the problem, as O'Hara saw it, was intimately related to the social and economic improvement of the living standards of the farming population in America. On 30 June 1920, after a year's study based on a national survey which he undertook, O'Hara read a paper entitled "The Rural Problem in Its Bearing on Catholic Education," at the national convention of the Catholic Educational Association in New York. It was a clarion call for organized action. Rural life must be recognized as vitally important for the nation's welfare; social and economic betterment in rural living must go hand in hand with adequate religious education. He outlined a program of study and action in rural parish work and suggested formation of a national school policy relative to the cultural and religious needs of the rural areas of America.

These basic principles provided the foundation for the Catholic

Rural Life Bureau which was organized as part of the National Catholic Welfare Conference (N.C.W.C.) with headquarters at Washington, D.C.[4] O'Hara was appointed director of the bureau with headquarters at Eugene, Oregon – at that time a small country parish with three missions. He moved to Eugene after resigning from his duties as pastor of the cathedral and superintendent of schools. Among the familiar surroundings of a rural parish which served as a working laboratory for his ideas, O'Hara began to concentrate on the catechetical side of his apostolate: to meet the needs of the thousands of Catholic families who lived on the farms of America. He realized at once that something must be done about the inadequacy of Sunday schools in small country parishes when they were not supported by solid religious training in the home. With this in mind, O'Hara, with the aid of his brother, wrote and distributed correspondence courses on the Bible and on the catechism. They proved to be most satisfactory, and demand for them began to go beyond the parish boundaries. Not long after, in 1920, the work was the total responsibility of the Catholic Rural Life Bureau under the directorship of Monsignor Victor Day of Helena, Montana. The latter reported in April 1923 that the correspondence courses were used in nearly all the dioceses in twenty-seven states and in parts of Western Canada.[5]

Religious Vacation Schools

Religious vacation schools were another project initiated and developed by O'Hara through the Catholic Rural Life Bureau. They were conducted in rural areas for several weeks or more during the summer. In 1921, O'Hara organized vacation schools in each of the three missions forming part of his parish at Eugene, Oregon. Four sisters carried out the program. The classes, held in the church, began at 9:00 A.M. and ended at 2:30 P.M. The curriculum included catechism, Bible history, New Testament study, hymns, and projects. The total enrollment was forty-seven. For those who took part, it was pronounced a success. It marked a new epoch in the history of religious education in this country. While making his plans for these vacation schools, O'Hara recalled the Lutheran Bible schools held near his farm home in Minnesota; he and his brothers and sisters had attended them. Some years earlier, when he was conducting a survey on rural education, he inserted a question about the feasibility of setting up Bible schools for Catholic rural youngsters similar to those conducted by the Lutherans.

Whether these vacation schools in the missions of Lane County, Oregon, could claim to be the first under Catholic auspices in this country is a moot point. Actually there is ample evidence to show that Catholic vacation schools existed in a number of scattered places throughout the country in the early decades of the century but on a more or less temporary basis.[6] Streck carefully concludes:

> It remained for Father O'Hara to provide through the Catholic Rural Life Bureau the impetus necessary to bring about a concerted movement for religious vacation schools in all parts of the country. So rapid was their growth that O'Hara could report in 1923 that vacation schools were operating in more than forty dioceses.[7]

The need to expand the Rural Life Bureau to accommodate a growing membership of pastors, rural life directors, farmers, and other interested laypeople became increasingly urgent. In the summer of 1923, O'Hara called a nationwide meeting of Catholic rural life leaders in St. Louis, and he announced that the Rural Life Bureau was now part of the National Catholic Rural Life Conference. He was elected executive secretary of the new organization; he continued to give its program, especially that of religious education in rural areas, his wholehearted support. A few years later, in 1928, the extensive work entailed in organizing and effectually directing numerous projects by the conference brought about a change of headquarters from Eugene, Oregon, to Washington, D.C. The director moved to Washington and assumed residence and office at the N.C.W.C.

Father O'Hara felt strongly the need for a uniform course in the operation of the nation's religious vacation schools. The directors and teachers in the schools, untrained for the most part, needed complete outlines and full lesson plans for each day's work. As a first step, O'Hara reprinted in *St. Isidore's Plow* (Rural Life Bulletin) a brief outline of such a course that was taken from a Rural Life publication in Wichita, Kansas.[8] He was familiar with the original *Handbook of Suggestions on Religious Vacation Schools* written by Miss Alice Vignos and Father Leroy Callahan at the Los Angeles Confraternity office; O'Hara had addressed the Los Angeles CCD on two occasions. He went on to appoint a committee of experienced educators and leaders in Catholic Rural Life to draw up practical guidelines and a program for religious vacation schools. Among these appointed writers were Monsignors John M. Wolfe, Dubuque, and Felix Pitt, Louisville. Monsignor Leon McNeill, Wichita, became chairman of O'Hara's special working committee, which included Father LeRoy Callahan of Los Angeles and Father Aloysius J. Heeg, SJ.[9]

The Religious Vacation School Manual was published in 1931. Revised editions appeared in 1932 and 1933 as practical teacher guidelines – all under the auspices of the National Catholic Rural Life

Conference.[10] The new *Manual* included a program for the entire four weeks of classes with a lesson plan for each day. One hour of the day was devoted to doctrine, and the remainder of each three-hour session to Bible stories, liturgy, hymns, picture lessons, projects, and handcrafts, in addition to supervised games and plays. "It can be doubted," observed Monsignor Edgar Schmiedler of the Rural Life Bureau in the late 1930s, "that there is a single Catholic text now in use that is based on a greater amount of careful and even painstaking experimental work than this 1933 edition of the *Vacation School Manual*."[11]

During 1929 and 1930, O'Hara directed the numerous activities of the National Catholic Rural Life Conference. He took time out in order to publish a book, *Catholic Evidence Work in the United States*, in accord with a request from the apostolic delegate to the United States, Archbishop Amleto Cicognani. O'Hara made an in-depth survey bearing on the status of apologetics and catechetics in this country. His well-supported conclusion testified to the absolute necessity for a national policy to promote religious education of Catholics who due to no fault of their own are "religiously illiterate."[12] From the third chapter, "Teaching Children," we quote what became literally a rallying cry for the rest of his life.

> At once the largest and most hopeful field for Catholic evidence is provided by the children of Catholic parents. Over two million of them are being cared for in Catholic schools. It is unnecessary to say that the ideal is "every child in a Catholic school." Another two million Catholic children, however, are in the public schools. There are in the United States about 18,000 Catholic parish and mission churches, and about 8,000 Catholic schools. Thus 10,000 groups of Catholic children have no opportunity to attend parish schools. For these the Confraternity of Christian Doctrine organized by parishes and dioceses with a well-rounded program of religious vacation schools and year-round religious instruction is an absolute necessity.[13]

The idea of promoting the Confraternity was not a sudden decision on O'Hara's part. He was familiar with the organization and growth of the Confraternity since he was a young priest during the later years of Pope Pius X. He felt that vacation schools were too important to be confined to rural areas or to be the sole responsibility of the Rural Life Conference. He was convinced that the time had come to expand formal religious education for Catholic children and youth attending public schools, as well as for all Catholic adults and people of goodwill everywhere, in a year-round program sponsored by the Confraternity. To carry out such a program is the only purpose for its existence. These thoughts took form in word and plan during the school year of 1929–1930, while he was teaching a course in pastoral problems at the

Catholic University, and at Notre Dame University during the summer of 1930.

Father O'Hara saw to it that a special place on the program was given to the Confraternity at the 1930 meeting of the Rural Life Conference at Springfield, Illinois. Father Leroy Callahan was invited by O'Hara to address the delegates from all over the United States and Canada. He described how the religious vacation schools were working as an integral part of the diocesan CCD in Los Angeles. It was at this meeting, 26–28 August 1930, that O'Hara attended as Bishop-elect of the Diocese of Great Falls, Montana.[14]

Bishop of Great Falls

The twenty-five years of O'Hara's priestly life were, at the age of forty-eight, already filled with noble achievement: the first state minimum wage legislation; his successful effort to preserve the freedom of the Catholic schools, which resulted in the famous Oregon school decision of the United States Supreme Court; his single-handed initiation of the Catholic Rural Life Bureau which grew into the nationwide Catholic Rural Life Conference; the origin and development of the religious vacation school movement which led directly to the nationwide formation of the Confraternity of Christian Doctrine, to which must be added his extensive writings and addresses, lectures, and conferences.

O'Hara's name was well known throughout the country. For a long time his abilities and his labors had been known and appreciated by the Holy See. He had worked in very close harmony with many of the American bishops, and his reputation as an organizer with vision and prudence was already taken for granted by Catholic and non-Catholic leaders in all walks of life.[15] It was then a surprise to no one that Pope Pius XI made Father O'Hara the second bishop of Great Falls, Montana, a rural diocese whence his experience and zeal would be felt in every part of the country.

Bishop O'Hara was consecrated in the cathedral at Portland, Oregon, on 28 October 1930. The Diocese of Great Falls with its vast expanses of territory, its small but energetic Catholic population widely scattered in small cities, towns, and large farms was an ideal place for the bishop to develop his plans for Catholic rural life and education. At the same time he was able to take a leading role in the dissemination of his plans throughout the country. His ordination as bishop was a major breakthrough for the Confraternity in the United States. It was now possible for the CCD to attain national status and obtain support from the American bishops who ruled the church in individual dioceses and over the nation as a whole.

Before this plan was to mature, Bishop O'Hara was determined to set up the Confraternity in good order in his own diocese. On the very afternoon of his consecration, the new bishop called his priests together and announced that he was giving priority to the establishment of the Confraternity in every parish in the diocese. He planned to affiliate officially the Confraternity with the Archconfraternity of Christian Doctrine in Rome. A pastoral letter, the first, followed soon after with specific directives for an immediate program of vacation schools and ultimately of a year-round school of religion in all parishes and missions. "The Confraternity is no perfunctory organization," he wrote in the pastoral, "but it is an authorized agency for home mission work within the diocese."[16]

The pastoral ordered training courses for lay teachers since, it must be remembered, "the Confraternity is a lay organization both in origin and constitution." The bishop also drew up plans for an extensive adult education program through study clubs. He described it a few years later with some pride in a paper read at the first national catechetical congress of the CCD held at Rochester, New York, in October 1935. He began with a definition of a religious discussion club: "A small group of people who meet weekly, usually in homes for definite periods of the year, under selected leadership, to improve by cooperative study and discussion their mastery of the Catholic religion."[17]

While describing the success of his program, the bishop explained that in the spring of 1931 a total of 65 clubs were formed in the diocese; the number grew to 150 in the following fall. "The subjects studied at these sessions were the place of the parent as educator and the ceremonies of the Mass. . . . In 1933 every parish had a chairman of discussion clubs, and 400 clubs began to study the life of Christ. Several parishes had twenty and some as high as thirty clubs with an average of ten members each. During the past year approximately 700 groups were engaged in the study of the early history of the church with the *Acts of the Apostles* as the text." In conclusion, O'Hara asserted: "The discussion club program of the Confraternity is the most practical means of promoting popular adult religious instruction."[18] The seeds of a nationwide program of religious education for public school youngsters, their parents, and adults in general were already planted and ready to develop through the Catholic Rural Life Conference.

The Conference and the CCD

Shaw notes the continuous and inevitable codevelopment of the Rural

Life movement and the Confraternity of Christian Doctrine under the direction of Bishop O'Hara. "The first activities," he writes, "of the Rural Life Conference, its vacation schools, and the correspondence courses which had involved parents in religious education in the home, drew a straight line of development from the Bureau to the Confraternity. It would be quite proper to say that one grew out of the other."[19]

In 1931, the National Catholic Rural Life Conference held its annual meeting at Wichita, Kansas. There the contacts first made with the Confraternity at Springfield, Illinois, the previous year were more clearly outlined. The first day's program at Wichita centered on rural education with emphasis on religious vacation schools. A number of Rural Life directors were also active leaders in the Confraternity in their dioceses. Three Confraternity experts were assigned to important positions in the program: Father Callahan and Miss Vignos of the Los Angeles Confraternity and Father Paul Campbell from the Pittsburgh Missionary Confraternity.

Two years later, in 1933, under O'Hara's direction, a regional meeting of bishops of the Pacific northwest was held at Portland, Oregon, with the intent to organize the CCD in every parish. At the same time the need for a national office for the Confraternity was discussed. Thought was also given by O'Hara to the use of the Rural Life office at the N.C.W.C. in Washington as temporary national headquarters of the CCD, since much of its work involved religious vacation schools.[20] However, later in the same year, 16–19 October, at the Rural Life Conference convention at Milwaukee, O'Hara announced that consideration was being given to the establishment of a national office for the CCD at the Catholic University of America in Washington, D.C.

Conditions at the Catholic University were congenial to O'Hara's plan. First, he readily obtained permission to use the facilities from the chancellor of the university, Archbishop Michael J. Curley of Baltimore. For the first national director, Bishop O'Hara selected an old friend and fellow professor, Dom Augustine Walsh, OSB. Father Walsh had been asked by the apostolic delegate to assume the chair of apologetics at the university, where he was professor of philosophy. Archbishop Curley, at the request of O'Hara, designated the National Shrine of the Immaculate Conception on the campus of the university as the ecclesiastical center of the CCD for this country.[21]

Through most of 1934, O'Hara was making practical plans to obtain approval of the Confraternity in the United States from the Holy See and to petition the American hierarchy to approve a committee of bishops to be responsible for the development and spread of the CCD throughout the country. To bring the situation into full focus, O'Hara invited directors, bishops, and priests from all parts of the United States, with any interest in the Confraternity, to convene at the annual Rural Life Conference convention at St. Paul, Minnesota. Thus, on 7 November 1934, occurred the historic parting of the mother-daughter relationship of the Rural Life Conference and the CCD. The delegates voted to petition the American bishops at their annual meeting a few days later to appoint an episcopal committee that would direct and coordinate the work of the national center of the Confraternity and at the same time give national scope and authority to the organization in this country.

A highlight of the meeting was the long-awaited message from Archbishop Cicognani at the apostolic delegation in Washington to the delegates at the convention. It concluded as follows:

> The Holy Father has desired to place active participation with the clergy in teaching Christian doctrine under the direction of the bishops as one of the principal ends of Catholic Action. Among such collaborators is the venerable Confraternity of Christian Doctrine. It is my earnest prayer that the Confraternity of Christian Doctrine may meet with every success in extending its important work, and I wish the Confraternity, its members and its students, every blessing.[22]

National Center and Bishops' Committee

The American bishops, at their annual meeting in Washington on 11 November 1934, received the petitions from the Confraternity delegates at the Rural Life meeting in St. Paul. Action was favorable for establishment of a national office for the Confraternity. O'Hara explained that it was to be a clearinghouse and a service for diocesan directors and leaders in parish units, not an executive center giving orders for regimented activity. It would have no jurisdiction over diocesan CCD operation; its chief authority, as O'Hara was wont to say, "is to teach the Word of God with goodwill."

There was some discussion relative to the second petition requesting creation of a supervisory committee of bishops over the Confraternity as a national program. Some bishops opposed another committee; one bishop summed up his feelings by saying that he did not think the Confraternity was "important enough" to justify an additional episcopal committee. This was answered by a simple question from Bishop O'Hara. Referring to the number of Catholic children not in Catholic schools, he asked, "Aren't two million children important?"[23]

On 14 November at the closing session, Cardinal George Mundelein appointed the following as members of the Episcopal Committee of the CCD: Archbishop John T. McNicholas, Cincinnati; Archbishop John G. Murray, St. Paul; and Bishop O'Hara. Later on the same day, the administrative board of the N.C.W.C. at its meeting announced the appointment of Bishop O'Hara as chairman of the committee.[24] "That wonderful November 14," wrote Bishop Matthew Brady, "also witnessed the first brief and significant meeting of the new committee. It was decided to open a national center in Washington, D.C., with Father Augustine Walsh as director and Miss Miriam Marks, who had for some years helped to organize the Confraternity in the dioceses of Oregon, Idaho, and Montana, as secretary."[25] Bishop O'Hara was not one to wait and let things cool!

The National Center of the CCD actually opened on 10 May 1935. During the interval, the Confraternity continued to operate from the office of Father Walsh. An active catechetical unit of the CCD comprised of clerical and lay students was functioning in a number of local institutions and parishes.[26] A formal catechetical day was celebrated annually at the national shrine on the campus, CCD meetings were held periodically at the university, and catechetical lectures and summer courses were conducted in conjunction with catechetics courses in the schools of theology and of religious education at the university.

Bishop O'Hara formed a publications department of the Confraternity, while it was still at the university, to prepare for a functioning national office. "I have been getting certain basic suggestions together," he wrote on 9 February 1935 to Father Walsh, "which I am submitting to all of the bishops prior to their meeting after Easter. I enclose a copy for a suggested constitution of the Confraternity for local parish units and also a plan for organization. I am working on a series of leaflets, including those for discussion clubs, vacation schools, parent-educators, etc., so I can submit to my committee of bishops a rounded program for them to approve."[27]

The financial condition of the central office was critical during these formative years. It was supported mainly through the generosity of Archbishop Murray and a number of private donors, including Father John Forest, OFM, director of St. Anthony's Guild, who at this time began to publish all the materials emanating from the national office without cost.

The 1935 Decree

In his work of publicizing the opening of the national office for the entire country, O'Hara was given substantial assistance on 12 January

1935 by the *Decree on the Better Care and Promotion of Catechetical Instruction* from the Holy See. This document stipulated that the Confraternity of Christian Doctrine shall be set up in every parish before all other organizations. Its principal work was to be carried out by lay men and women and religious of both sexes who are properly trained by the clergy for this most important apostolate.[28]

A translation of this document and its distribution, along with many others emanating from the Holy See, was one of the first tasks of the newly located national center. It "moved" with very little to carry from the university to a temporary office in the N.C.W.C. building at 1312 Massachusetts Avenue NW, Washington, D.C. The labor of preparing the foundation for a nationwide CCD was ended; growth in depth and experience was about to begin. Through the next twenty years (1935–1955), Bishop O'Hara was to be the guide, counselor, and devoted friend to the expanding Confraternity.

Bishop of Kansas City

On 15 April 1939 after nine fruitful years as Bishop of Great Falls, O'Hara was appointed to the Diocese of Kansas City, Missouri. It was a recognition on the part of Pope Pius XII of the bishop's outstanding success as a spiritual leader, able administrator, and national figure in the Confraternity movement. The new field of his labors offered a fertile ground for development of religious education; it contained a large urban population surrounded by rural areas in which entire counties were without a known Catholic family. The new bishop had these and other challenges in mind when, on the day of his installation, he asked his people "to share with me the responsibility for the religious and moral training of all the youth of this great diocese."[29]

Bishop O'Hara set about at once to people the areas having no priests and few Catholics with young missionary pastors. Services were organized in simple, inexpensive, yet artistically designed chapels. To accomplish this, he organized a street preaching campaign during the summer, manned by priests and seminarians whom he trained in his own institute under the Confraternity. In fewer than ten years, more than 150 buildings, including churches, chapels, schools, and two colleges, were built to care for the rapidly growing city and surrounding country.[30]

At the close of his first decade of service as shepherd in Kansas City, O'Hara was given a singular tribute of honor and affection from his Protestant and Jewish fellow Kansas Citians in recognition of his unique record of collaboration and good fellowship with citizens of all persuasions. A contemporary issue of *Time* magazine pictured the bishop with two prominent non-Catholic officials busily engaged in "burying the hatchet." It was at this time (1948) that the section of the Confraternity formerly called the Apostolate to Non-Catholics in the *Parish Manual of the CCD* now became the Apostolate of Good Will in all official literature from the national office. The ecumenical movement of today, sparked by Vatican II, displays the same basic pattern as that originally devised by O'Hara and his apostles of good-will at Kansas City, and, indeed, years earlier in the CCD at Great Falls, Montana. This typical activity of the Confraternity in the United States is characteristically American; it is not found in CCD structures in Europe.

The Cause of Pope Pius X

Even before his first private audience as a young priest in 1910 with Pope Pius X, Bishop O'Hara was attracted to the saintly pontiff, never tiring of extolling his vital part in reviving the CCD in modern times. Immediately after the war in 1945, he organized a crusade of prayer for the beatification and eventual canonization of Pius X. A million or more prayer cards for this cause were distributed. In the same year a number of writers interested in Pius X were invited by O'Hara to collaborate on *A Symposium on the Life and Work of Pope Pius X.*[31] This volume contributed to the national interest in the "pope of the catechism," as he was called.

In 1948, Bishop O'Hara accompanied a large pilgrimage to the tomb of Pius X and was highly praised by Pope Pius XII for his work in promoting the cause, as well as for his great leadership of the CCD in America. O'Hara read a paper on the CCD and Pius X at an International Congress of Religious Instruction in Rome, in October 1950. In 1951, he personally led a pilgrimage to Rome for the beatification of the pontiff; and again, in 1954, he was present with a large group sponsored by the U.S. Confraternity at the canonization ceremony at St. Peter's. The pope who had done so much for the CCD during his lifetime is today honored by the Confraternity as its latest and greatest patron saint.

The official correspondence and commendatory letters from the Holy See and from the pope's representative in this country to O'Hara as head of the Bishops' Committee of the CCD would fill a good-sized volume. They reflect the warm confidence and approval that mark all his relations with Rome. The most authoritative statements ever issued from the church at Rome on the efficacy of catechetical instruction, as well as on the necessity of the Confraternity, are recorded during his lifetime.[36] The friendly solicitude of the Holy See was also evidenced in 1954, when Pope Pius XII nominated him as archbishop *ad personam.* The title in this case was not attached to a city, as is customary, but to the *person* of the new archbishop for reasons of personal worth and esteem. The decree of nomination was signed by the papal secretary of state, Cardinal Giovanni Montini, who is the present reigning Pope Paul VI. Cardinal Samuel Stritch, in his sermon at the elevation of the archbishop, declared:

> We could say many things in congratulation, but we say it all in these words – under the inspiration of St. Pius X, he has been and is the great catechist of the Church in the United States.[33]

Golden Jubilee—1955

In October 1955, Archbishop O'Hara celebrated the golden anniversary of his ordination as a priest and silver jubilee as bishop. He combined the two events with that of the seventy-fifth year of the founding of the Diocese of Kansas City. It was another occasion for messages of felicitation and praise from all over this country, Europe, and Latin America, where he did so much to promote inter-American goodwill. An autographed letter of good wishes came from his good friend Pope Pius XII with whom O'Hara had corresponded and worked many times over the years. Archbishop Cicognani, apostolic delegate to the United States, in his message declared: "Your catechetical work has been vast, widely beneficial and magnificent."

Nowhere does the archbishop's catechetical insight appear more clearly than in the message to the CCD delegates which he was to give at the national congress of the CCD held at Buffalo, New York, on 26–30 September 1956. It was not delivered because of his untimely death more than two weeks earlier. His words, to be spoken significantly to the Lay Committee of the CCD, are in part as follows:

> You have been assembled by the power-creating Falls of Niagara on an historic occasion for the CCD and for your catechetical apostolate. This is the Tenth National Catechetical Congress held in the United States to promote the lay apostolate sponsored by St. Pius X. As lay apostles of the catechism you must become conscious of the high dignity of your calling. There is a tendency to belittle catechetical instruction as something of an inferior function. You should read and re-read the estimate of St. Pius X of the catechist in his great encyclical "On the Teaching of Christian Doctrine."[34]

The archbishop went on to a refreshingly broad concept of the subject matter of catechetical instruction as it was discussed at that time:

> The subject matter of the catechist is scripture and tradition, Bible and catechism. It involves theology and the liturgy, history of the Church, lives of the saints, Christian art, the spirit of the Christian home; the encyclicals of the popes, and all Christian literature. Behold the materials and the tools which you must use in your profession as catechists!

The catechism must distinguish carefully, declared the archbishop, between the function of *proclaiming* the message of Christ and *explaining* it. The warm, soul-stirring revelation of the story of God's love in the salvation of humanity must precede and prepare for reception of the truth for daily living. Then followed an early reference to what was called "kerygmatic catechetics."

> *Kerygmatic* theology gets its name from the Greek word for "herald." John the Baptist was a herald who proclaimed the coming of God's kingdom, the necessity of penance for sin, the coming of the redeemer. Christ came proclaiming the kingdom of God, the mercy of God. The catechist must learn to be a herald of the mysteries of faith.

Thus did the archbishop in his final message to his beloved Confraternity workers not only keep himself abreast of the latest modern catechetics but also make a vitally decisive distinction between the proclamation of God's goodness, of Christ's redemptive love (kerygmatic content), and the explanation (teaching skill and method) of the lessons which must be learned and made part of Christian living.

Last Days—a Tribute

Archbishop O'Hara saw the Confraternity grow from a few scattered seeds to a full-grown tree under whose shade many kinds of religious education on all levels flourished and bore fruit. He rejoiced in the latter days of his life when he realized that the national status of the Confraternity was assured and especially when he saw it spread widely on the grassroots level. Well could he repeat with Robert Browning: "This is the last for which the first was made."

The archbishop's life was a veritable flurry of activities. In his diocese he attended to a myriad of details great and small, like Saint Paul with the care of all the churches. On the national scene he was ever planning, making decisions, spreading his influence in person, by letter, and through his subordinates. Yet throughout it all, he managed to keep the even tenor of his way; never did he appear excited or tense. He had a way of doing things without fuss or feathers. He

won people over to his ideas by simply explaining the logic and value
of his purpose. For those who disagreed with him or chose to do little
or nothing, he had the greatest charity and understanding. The key
to this imperturbable equanimity was the deep spiritual foundation of
his life. His daily religious exercises contributed to the attainment of
a serene and calm exterior with a fervent love of God and his Church
which burned in his heart and dynamized all his work.

His was the spirit of the crusader. Only he could send out to friends,
on the forty-fourth anniversary of his ordination and the nineteenth
of his commission as a bishop, a card with a line drawing of a bishop,
staff in hand, a fiery cross emblazoned on his chasuble, seated on a
rock in a position of wearied repose. And above the picture the sadly
thoughtful words of a knight of old: "I'll lay me down and bleed awhile,
Then rise to fight again." The right-hand corner of the card bore the
Confraternity seal: *Deus est.* On a flowing cincture was his motto: "Let
the little ones come."

It was fitting that the archbishop's last days were expended in the
cause of the liturgy, which he loved and to which he gave an essential
place in teaching religion. As president of the North American
Liturgical Conference, he was on his way, at the invitation of the
American hierarchy, to read a paper on "The Restored Holy Week in
the United States" at the International Congress of Pastoral Liturgy
at Assisi when he was stricken on 11 September 1956, in Milan. The
doctors said it was a coronary occlusion. He had been a priest fifty-
one years, a bishop twenty-six years, and was in his seventy-fifth year.

Archbishop Edward Howard of Portland, Oregon, a classmate of
Archbishop O'Hara and his consecrator as Bishop of Great Falls, paid
the ultimate compliment in his eulogy at the funeral:

> "Devotion to every good" would seem to summarize the life of Archbishop
> O'Hara. It is difficult to think of any phase of the Church's mission in
> which he was not interested and active. Ranking above all of his interests
> was, of course, the religious instruction of children. In this country the
> terms Confraternity and Archbishop O'Hara are almost synonymous.

Today, the earthly remains of Archbishop O'Hara lie, at his own
request, in a bare little crypt beneath the chapel of the Benedictine
Sisters of Perpetual Adoration in Kansas City, Missouri. The chapel
is dedicated to St. Pius X.

NOTES

1. "Although some parishes and a few dioceses had organized some aspects
of the Confraternity prior to 1930 (when Father O'Hara became Bishop of Great

Falls, Montana), it was the tireless and dedicated effort of Bishop Edwin V. O'Hara who aroused the Catholics of the country to a national program of organization." Raymond A. Lucker, *Aims of Religious Education in the Early Church in the American Catechetical Movement* (Ph.D. diss., University of St. Thomas, Rome, 1966) (Rome: Catholic Book Agency, 1966), p. 178.

2. J. G. Shaw, *Edwin Vincent O'Hara: American Prelate* (New York: Farrar, Straus and Cudahy, 1957), p. 2.

3. Joseph B. Collins, "Archbishop Edwin V. O'Hara: A Biographical Survey," in *The Confraternity Comes of Age* (Paterson, NJ: Confraternity Publications, 1956), p. 8.

4. Files of the National Center of Religious Education–CCD, Washington, D.C.

5. Philip Witte, *Twenty-five Years of Crusading: A History of the National Catholic Rural Life Conference* (Des Moines: National Catholic Rural Life Conference, 1948), p. 187.

6. Leo J. Streck, "A Study of the Curriculum of Religious Vacation Schools" (M.A. diss., Catholic University of America, 1938), p. 6.

7. Witte, *Years of Crusading*, p. 183.

8. Monsignor Leon McNeill to Father Joseph B. Collins, June 1966.

9. Witte, *Years of Crusading*, p. 186.

10. See also Leon McNeill, "The Religious Vacation School and the Revised Manual," in *Proceedings of the National Catechetical Congress of the Confraternity of Christian Doctrine, Rochester, 1935* (Paterson, NJ: St. Anthony Guild Press, 1936), pp. 136–143.

11. Edgar Schmiedler cited in *Proceedings of the National Congress, Rochester, 1935*, p. 138.

12. Edwin V. O'Hara, *Catholic Evidence Work in the United States* (Huntington, IN: Our Sunday Visitor Press, n.d.).

13. Ibid., p. 89.

14. Shaw, *Edwin Vincent O'Hara*, p. 123.

15. Collins, *Archbishop Edwin V. O'Hara*, p. 14.

16. Shaw, *Edwin Vincent O'Hara*, p. 128.

17. *Proceedings of the National Congress, Rochester, 1935*, p. 44.

18. Ibid., p. 49.

19. Shaw, *Edwin Vincent O'Hara*, p. 121.

20. Letter to Bishop O'Hara from Father Edgar Schmiedler, O'Hara's successor as director of the Rural Life Bureau and Conference, in Witte, *Years of Crusading*, p. 91.

21. Files of the National Center–CCD; *Code of Canon Law*, canon 717:1–2.

22. Files of the National Center–CCD.

23. Shaw, *Edwin Vincent O'Hara*, p. 146.

24. Files of the National Center–CCD.

25. Matthew F. Brady, "The Episcopal Committee of the Confraternity of Christian Doctrine," in *Confraternity Comes of Age*, p. 109.

26. The present writer organized and directed this unit under Father Walsh; Joseph B. Collins, "The CCD at the Catholic University," in *Proceedings of Group Meetings and Official Statements on the CCD. Wartime Volume, 1941–1944* (Washington, DC: Confraternity of Christian Doctrine, 1946), pp. 33–36.

27. Files of the National Center–CCD.

28. "Provido sane consilio," *Acta Apostolicae Sedis* 27, 152.

29. National Catholic Welfare Conference (N.C.W.C.) News Service, 10 June 1939.

30. "A Decade of Building in the Diocese of Kansas City" (leaflet). Files of the National Center—CCD.

31. *A Symposium on the Life and Work of Pope Pius X* (Paterson, NJ: St. Anthony Guild Press, 1946).

32. Cf. volumes (total of eleven) of *Proceedings* of the national CCD congresses that were held from 1935 (Rochester, New York) to 1956 (Buffalo, New York), including *Wartime Volume, 1941–1944.*

33. Shaw, *Edwin Vincent O'Hara,* p. 254.

34. Edwin V. O'Hara, "The Apostolate of the Lay Committee on the National Center of the Confraternity of Christian Doctrine," in *Proceedings of the Tenth National Congress of the Confraternity of Christian Doctrine, Buffalo, 1956* (Washington, DC: Confraternity of Christian Doctrine, 1958), pp. 17, 22–23.

Jungmann and the Kerygmatic Theology Controversy

In order to appreciate fully Jungmann's contribution to the modern catechetical renewal, one must properly situate him in the context in which he lived, with its problems which he sought to address. A good bit of Jungmann's work was done in the 1930s, when a cadre of European theologians was struggling to break theology out of a scholastic or neoscholastic straitjacket. Theology seemed to them locked in a sort of eternal now, where nothing changed, where the formulations of Thomas had forever set the categories of theological discourse.

These theologians—Adam, de Lubac, Daniélou, Congar, Rahner, and others less well known—saw, as did Jungmann, the almost hopelessly disjunctive character of the ordinary Christian's understanding of what the seminal issues of Christian faith actually were.[1] For the Catholic masses, fish on Friday was potentially more important than concern for the poor. The understanding of many persons was a mishmash that could best be accepted in teeth-gritted faith. The situation of theology, especially as it was taught in the seminaries, was also deplorable.[2] This was a time when persons seeking Christian understanding found more insight in Abbot Marmion than in Garrigou-Lagrange but had to defend their preference as a taste for spiritual reading instead of for the complexities of theology.[3] Eventually, many came to realize that Marmion met their needs because his theology was better.

Within this context, Jungmann's work can be best understood when one remembers his two chief concerns: history and pastoral theology. As a historian, Jungmann was working along the lines of the theologians mentioned above, and of their forebears, who had been quietly working for a century to reclaim the full Christian tradition.[4] *They were willing to undertake the patient research into origins that preceded Trent and Chalcedon and Nicea. As a result of these studies, which gradually had an enormous cumulative force, theology was moving out of nonhistorical orthodoxy, in which scholasticism had thrived, and was recovering its deeper roots. All the fixities of the scholastic vision and its neoscholastic revision could not withstand the pressures of historical investigation.*

To forget that Jungmann was a historian is to forget one half of his life concern; to forget he was a pastoral theologian is to forget the other half.[5] Throughout all his written works one finds that his vision never strays far from the needs of the ordinary person trying to live faith intelligently.[6] Basically, Jungmann had a special respect, very much on a par with Rahner's, for the intelligence and intuitive sense of ordinary persons. He was convinced that the faith of Christians did not have to be perceived as opaque and complicated. In The Good News Yesterday and Today, which is generally seen as the work that launched the modern catechetical renewal, Jungmann argued for a cohesive and unified presentation of the Christian mystery that could reclaim the intelligibility it possessed in the beginning. I suggest that in this work there is something classic, in the sense that it strikes a chord in any person privy to the nonunified, nonintegrated understandings of many adult Christians today.

Jungmann suggested that theology (meaning, of course, the scholastic theology of his day) was not suitable fare for nourishing the faith of ordinary people and that it should be replaced with the kerygma, that is, with lucid presentations of the core of Christian faith.[7] He saw that the core itself should be the person of Jesus, in whom God's long-hidden secret was whispered. Because of his familiarity with the preaching of the Fathers, Jungmann sought to incorporate into his catechetical program their method of liberally using the New Testament to interpret the Old Testament and their preference for a narratio of God's saving design for humanity. Jungmann stressed the value of a historical and narrative approach to catechesis rather than an abstract, philosophical one.

Resulting partly from Jungmann's book The Good News Yesterday and Today, a considerable controversy arose when some set out two different theologies — one a "kerygmatic" theology, intended for ordinary people not trained as theologians, the other a theology of the schools, meant for professional theologians. This solution came from a conviction that scholastic theology was both immovable and *unsuitable for the nourishment of the people. As Jungmann points out in his essay "Kerygmatic Theology," Reading 14 (Part 2), many soon realized that what was needed was not two theologies but rather one theology imbued with a historical sense and unified in the person of Jesus.*

I have always found Jungmann's position to be remarkably close to that of Rahner in a number of essays written to clarify the links among various theological topics. In some sense, this effort has been Rahner's lifelong project, culminating in his unified foundational study of the Christian understanding, Foundations of Christian Theology.[8] *Unfortunately, Jungmann lacked the astute epistemology of Rahner, which permitted him to distinguish levels of reflection.*

I suggest that Jungmann's "Theology and Kerygmatic Teaching," Reading 15, be read in conjunction with Rahner's essay "The Prospects for Dogmatic Theology," not in this sourcebook, where Rahner makes the following comment so much in the spirit of Jungmann:

> . . . *the strictest theology, that most passionately devoted to reality alone and ever on the alert for new questions, the most scientific theology, is itself in the long run, the most kerygmatic. The fact that our textbooks [of theology] are little alive, serve proclamation and witness so little, is not due to their superabundance of . . . theology but because they offer so little of it, precisely because as relics of the past they are unable even to preserve the past in its purity.*[9]

To be appreciated properly, then, Jungmann's contribution needs to be viewed in its relationship and similarity to the pastoral concerns of theologians like Rahner.

It does not appear proper to view Jungmann's work as a Roman Catholic variety of a trend in Protestant theology of his day: neo-orthodoxy.[10] *To attempt a critique of Jungmann's thought as some sort of Roman Catholic first cousin to neoorthodoxy might be tempting due to certain superficial similarities between the Roman Catholic doctrinal reformulations of the 1900s and the Barthian approach in Protestant thought. However, such a lumping of Jungmann with the neoorthodox school, even as "closet" neoorthodox, is improper and can only lead to a misrepresentation of Jungmann's work. The term* neoorthodoxy *is in danger of becoming a code word to describe the disregarding of human experience in the name of doctrinal purity. Such a use of the term is not faithful to Barth's thought, and it is seriously misused in describing Jungmann's.*[11] *The angle from which best to understand Jungmann's thought is not neoorthodoxy but rather the angle of liturgical renewal, the renewal of the way Christians worship in public and in common.*

A second caveat with regard to Jungmann's thought: His catechetical theory is to be found in his own writings rather than interpreted through those who worked to popularize the catechetical renewal in the United States in the early 1960s. To suggest that Jungmann's program was that of a "kerygmatic renewal," and to mean by the term a one-sided emphasis on "pure" dogma, is to lift "kerygmatic" out of its context in Jungmann and make it refer to something quite different from what Jungmann intended.[12] *For him, kerygmatic renewal was a synonym for catechetical renewal or, even better, pastoral renewal. Similarly, to suggest that Jungmann's concern was not anthropocentric is improper and incorrect. His program was one of wholistic catechesis, aimed at unifying the lived faith of Christians. Again, Jungmann's writings themselves are the proper testimony to my assertions here.*

My hope is that those willing to explore the origins of the modern catechetical renewal will come to understand the special contribution, based on wide-ranging scholarship, of Josef Jungmann.

NOTES

1. One finds concern for unifying theology and making it more coherent in the writings of all these theologians. For some examples, see Henri de Lubac, *Catholicism* (New York: New American Library, 1964), esp. pp. ix–xiv and pp. 166–180 [*Catholicism* was first published in 1937]; Karl Rahner, *Hearers of the Word* (New York: Herder and Herder, 1969), esp. pp. 18–19 [the 1st ed. of this work appeared in 1941].

2. See Rahner's essay "The Prospects for Dogmatic Theology," where he calls for a radical reexamination of the seminary curriculum and comments on the "kerygmatic theology" controversy. Some of Rahner's concerns here echo Jungmann's, and I suspect the essay was originally written during the 1930s. It is the first essay of the collection, and Rahner in his preface both notes that the pieces were "disinterred" from periodicals and lists a number of uncollected essays, the bulk of which were written in the 1930s. See Karl Rahner, "The Prospects for Dogmatic Theology," *Theological Investigations*, vol. 1 (Baltimore: Helicon Press, 1961), pp. 1–18.

3. "Everything else to do with the mysteries of Christ's life is no longer to be found in dogmatic theology but only in the literature of edification." Ibid., p. 11.

4. See esp., Josef A. Jungmann's works: *The Mass of the Roman Rite* (New York: Benziger Bros., 1951); idem, *The Early Liturgy to the Time of Gregory the Great* (Notre Dame, IN: University of Notre Dame Press, 1959); idem, *Pastoral Liturgy* (New York: Herder and Herder, 1962).

5. Mary Collins has noted the way Jungmann looked to the pastoral practice of the liturgy for clues to the theological stance it represented. Here, in a special way, Jungmann's two interests of history and pastoral concern come together. See Mary Collins, "Critical Questions for Liturgical Theology," *Worship* 53, no. 4 (July 1979): 302–317.

6. See, for example, Jungmann's essays in part 3 of *Pastoral Liturgy,* all grouped under the heading, "The Fundamentals of Liturgy and Kerygma," pp. 323–416.

7. In *The Good News Yesterday and Today* (New York: Sadlier, 1962), Jungmann makes clear that he does not see catechesis as a one-dimensional matter. He explicitly states that catechesis alone and preaching alone are not sufficient for the program he is advocating.

> This growth [in faith] cannot be furthered by the means of preaching and catechizing alone, as experience shows. At times fruitful understanding has not been the outcome of will-controlled thought processes. In any event, the Church's life, particularly as found in well-ordered *divine worship* [Jungmann's italics], is admirably suited to bring about a true understanding of the Christian message. This is particularly true of ordinary people [pp. 81–82].
>
> As the success of education is only in a very limited way the fruit of the carefully planned work of the teacher and much more the result of the many and varied influences of environment, so too one should not expect an easy familiarity with the central doctrines of faith to grow out of skillful teaching alone. Lived, but above all prayed, dogma will prove to be the best school; and so far as prayer is concerned, the prayer of the Church—the liturgy—takes first place.
>
> Liturgical prayer, as the divine worship of an assembled community, is oriented to the expression of what is communal and objective—even in its prayer of petition. . . . Hence liturgical prayer possesses a powerful educative influence and thus is of great pastoral signficance [p. 114].

8. Karl Rahner, *Foundations of Christian Faith* (New York: Seabury Press, 1978). The following comments on Rahner's book make use of terminology that hearkens back to the scientific-pastoral theology dispute sparked by Jungmann's *The Good News.*

> The theological education of candidates for the ministry has long been a concern of Karl Rahner. As early as 1954, he called for a revamping of the traditional German academic program. Its heavily "scientific" emphasis and its division into an ever-increasing number of disciplines, each with its own distinct methodology, had rotted theological education of its unity and made it inappropriate as a preparation for pastoral office.
>
> As a way forward, Rahner suggested the adaptation by theology of a distinction made in the faculties of law and medicine between a *Grundkurs* (basic course) and more advanced courses for specialists. The *Grundkurs* would be frankly pastoral in orientation. It would eschew much of the traditional scientific paraphernalia *while concentrating on a deepening of the students' existential grasp on the central core of the Gospel message.* [Italics added.] The personal integration of theology and piety and the task of preaching in a contemporary context were to be the main concerns of the new course. [Daniel Donovan, "Rahner's 'Grundkurs': Frankly Pastoral," *The Ecumenist* 16, no. 5 (July-August 1978): 65.]

9. Rahner, "Prospects," p. 7.

10. Padraic O'Hare seems to make this claim in his attempt to critique

the origins of the Roman Catholic catechetical renewal, as if it were of the same foundations as the neoorthodox shift in Protestantism. See Padraic O'Hare, "Religious Education: Neo-Orthodox Influence and Empirical Shift," *Religious Education* 73, no. 6 (November-December 1978): 627–639.

Boardman Kathan makes the same claim when he suggests "that the Catholic catechetical movement of Jungmann, Hofinger, and the Lumen Vitae group, with its emphasis on kerygma, grace, proclamation of the Word, might be regarded as a counterpart of the Protestant movement of theological recovery which has been labeled neo-orthodoxy." Boardman Kathan, "Introduction" to *Pioneers of Religious Education: Festschrift for Herman C. Wornom*, Special issue of *Religious Education* 73, no. 5S (September-October 1978): S4.

11. Possibly the chief similarity between Jungmann's theology and Barth's is that they were both offering what Metz calls "corrective theology." See Johann Metz, *Faith in History and Society* (New York: Seabury Press, 1980), p. 13, n. 15.

12. I find this tendency in: Mary Boys, *Biblical Interpretation in Religious Education: A Study of the Kerygmatic Era* (Birmingham: Religious Education Press, 1980).

READING 14 (Part 1)

The Kerygma in the History of the Pastoral Activity of the Church

JOSEF A. JUNGMANN

B Y THE WORD *kerygma*, "message," we mean the Christian teaching insofar as it is intended to be proclaimed, that is, to be realized through pastoral care as the basis of Christian life.[1] Kerygma is thus to be distinguished from Christian doctrine insofar as Christian doctrine is illuminated in all aspects by theology and presented as a logically coordinated system of knowledge.[2] While the growth and the continuous development of individual theological concepts, especially of the dogmas themselves, have long been the object of thorough researches and are made use of in the history of

Reprinted from Appendix II of *Handing on the Faith*, by Josef Jungmann (New York: Herder and Herder, 1962), pp. 387–397, by permission of The Crossroad Publishing Company.

dogma, the history of kerygma and its different elements has up until now attracted little attention.

We shall attempt to give only a brief historical outline of the kerygmatic point of view, confining it to what is of importance for a knowledge of the present position of the problem, especially for catechetics. But it is hoped that even such a brief outline might induce some readers to take up seriously one or other of the particular questions that are raised.

The preaching of the apostles was in the first place a witness to the resurrection of the Lord, of an event which had publicly revealed that Jesus of Nazareth truly was the Messiah and that he redeemed the world through his death on the cross. The Gospels enlarge upon this theme retrospectively by showing the miraculous power and divine origin of him who rose from the dead. They also tell of the time in between when the Holy Spirit is poured out upon those who believe in Christ and have been gathered as his Church through Baptism.[3] Christ as the one who brought redemption is thus clearly at the center of the preaching.

This remained the practice throughout Christian antiquity, as is demonstrated by the sermons of the early teachers and the pictorial language of early Christian art.

There was a certain preference in the early centuries for the Old Testament to be used with the new in preaching the faith; it was also commented upon in long homilies, although these were less concerned with the literal meaning of Deuteronomy or of the Psalms, as with some mysterious evidence of the central mysteries in the New Testament.[4] In Adam was seen the type of the new Adam, Christ; and in Eve, who was created from Adam's side, the Virgin Mary or Holy Mother Church. The saving wood of the ark of Noë was the wood of the cross, and in the eight people who were saved was discerned a reference to the eighth day, the day of Christ's resurrection and of the new creation. Even the Book of Leviticus, which hardly contains material applicable to the New Testament, served Origen as a quarry for images seemingly foreshadowing the new Law. Aaron and his sons represent Christ and the apostles; the Jewish laws of purification and ritual are seen to be fulfilled in a new manner in Christ and in the moral law which he propounded. The four spirits, in the vision of Ezechiel (Ezech. 1:5 et seq.), are regarded by Irenaeus and by many later authors as symbols of Christ; the human face points to his incarnation, the figure of a bull to his sacrificial calling, the lion to the victory of his resurrection, the eagle to his ascension into heaven.[5] We are familiar with the pictorial representation

of Old Testament scenes found in the catacombs. They were misunderstood only until it was realized that they represent allusions
to the redemption accomplished in the New Testament. Isaac, Jonas,
and the three young men in the fiery furnace represent the death
and the resurrection of Christ and of those who die and rise with him
in Baptism.

The message of salvation preached by the early Church found
its first systematic summary in the Apostles' Creed. In it, as well
as in its kindred formulas, the message of Christ is unfolded more
fully; at the same time, the Trinitarian structure of the faith is emphasized. In the realm of prayer there were the divine praises or dox-
ologies for which a basic outline gradually became evident in the third
century. "Glory be to the Father through Jesus Christ in the Holy
Spirit," or, placing the divinity of Christ in the foreground: "Glory
be to the Father through the Son in the Holy Ghost."[6]

At this point were felt the first signs of the threat by heresy to
the kerygma. Arianism, which menaced the Church from the fourth
to the sixth century, denied the equality of natures between Father
and Son and, hence, Christ's divinity. To justify their teaching, the
Arians used to point to the manner in which the Church prayed, addressing the Father through the Son, the Son being thereby subordinated to the Father. The defenders of the faith replied that such
references to the Son applied only to his humanity, to Christ Jesus
the mediator. But this answer made no impact and failed to prevent
confusion among the faithful. Thus it happened that in many parts
of the Church, in the East as well as in Spain and Gaul, where the
Arian Germanic tribes were particularly powerful, the words
"through Christ" in prayers, and the idea of the God-Man as the
special mediator in the language of theology, were allowed to recede
into the background, even though there was no intention of denying
or weakening this truth.

There was all the more emphasis, however, on the divinity of
Christ and the divine majesty and general dignity of the Lord. The
most effective form of preaching the faith is the celebration of a feast.
Besides the feast of Easter, followed by fifty days of celebration
which for centuries and throughout Christendom was the only feast
of the Church, there now appeared a second festal cycle, Christmas
and Epiphany. Both existed before the Arian heresy but at that time
experienced a rapid development. Hitherto the work of redemption
accomplished by the passion and death of Christ had been celebrated;
in the Christmas cycle the incarnation of the Son of God became the
object of special adoration. Besides his work, the person of the Savior
was also specially honored. The conception and birth of the

Redeemer, and thus the Virgin Mother Mary, assumed particular importance. The great Marian feasts which in the meantime had arisen in the East were adopted by the West after the sixth century: Mary's birth, Annunciation, Purification, and Assumption.

It is due to the narrowness of mind in humanity that what undoubtedly was enrichment and clarification in one respect proved a loss in another. The early Middle Ages saw the rise of the German tribes which soon assumed a leading role in the Church. They were people without any higher culture, and the missionaries active among them had to content themselves with giving the most elementary religious instruction. On the other hand the age of the great Fathers of the Church had ended. Participation in the liturgical feasts became the chief means of imparting religious education. A certain vulgarism in the average preaching of faith, and in religious notions, was thus inevitable. Moreover, the new peoples having come into the Church from Arianism were animated all the more by hatred of the *perfidia Ariana*.[7] This was especially true of the West Gothic Church in Spain which, soon after the conversion of the people to the Catholic faith in 589, experienced a "golden age" – the only Doctor of the Church in the seventh century was Isidore of Seville, a Spaniard – and thus became a model for the rest of the Western Church. The culture of the eighth and ninth centuries was based upon these foundations. The *fides Trinitatis* became the leading concept of the Creed. Trinitarian formulas were used at the beginning of documents and of any pious work. Adoration of the most holy Trinity became the central theme of Christian worship. Prefaces for Sunday Mass, which until then had referred to the redemption, resurrection, sanctification of the faithful, admission through Christ to God's glory, were replaced by the Preface of the Trinity. The divinity of Christ was emphasized so much that in the preaching of the Gospel the notions of God and Christ were often interchanged. A collection of model catecheses from the Carolingian period which have been ascribed to St. Boniface are phrased in various places in such a manner that it would almost appear as if God was born of the Virgin Mary, who endured insults and outrages, blows and a scourging, and died on the cross for us.[8] Expressions such as "God's body" for the body of Christ, "the martyrdom of God" for the sufferings of Christ, remained for a very long time current in medieval sermons.

It is clear that these expressions are thoroughly orthodox, since they contain but the *communicatio idiomatum*. It is still the same dogmatic structure which confronts us, but it is another aspect, another side of that structure, which was then preferred in everyday instructions and in practical devotions. Only rarely was there reference to the transfigured Christ, who lives and reigns with the Father, who is the head of the Church. And, logically, it was equally rare to hear that the Church is the Body of Christ and that Christians are incorporated into it at Baptism, thus bearing the divine life within themselves.[9] Prayers of that time which have been preserved refer much more frequently to humankind's personal misery and sinfulness than to its grace and redemption. Apologists from the ninth to the eleventh centuries provide ample evidence. Liturgical prayers, too, unless they originated in earlier times, were by preference addressed to Christ himself or to the blessed Trinity. Intercessions made by the Mother of God and the saints grew in esteem and importance. The Eucharist became the object of supreme adoration; indeed, at the turn of the twelfth century we can find traces of a veritable eucharistic movement spreading throughout Christendom. But it was not the closeness of Christ which the faithful sought in a more intimate participation in the Mass and Communion but rather remoteness from him, an attitude of adoration toward the holy Persons but made from afar. The deposit of faith was less a well-rounded whole than so many individual doctrines, incidents from the childhood and the passion of Christ, liturgical devotions with their climax in the sacraments, and among popular customs a growing emphasis on indulgences and the veneration of numerous saints. Moral instruction, including the popular enumerations, dominated the teaching of the faith.[10] Knowledge of the faith, an understanding of its content, was reduced to a minimum in the average instructions and indeed could be so reduced because and insofar as the practice of the faith made up for it.

On the other hand the clarifications of scholastic theology at the height of the Middle Ages have contributed much toward greater emphasis being given again to the essentials of the faith in popular instructions. The *devotio moderna* and, to some extent, even German mysticism had already applied themselves to the task of acquainting the laity with the results of that labor. At this point the revolution of Luther and of the reformers occurred which sought to simplify Christian teaching and practice by a single violent stroke, an undertaking in which they sacrificed some essential doctrines of the Christian tradition. As far as the threatened doctrines were concerned, the Council of Trent clarified these with authority and provided in the *Catechismus Romanus*, which it ordered to be drawn up, as well as in later catechisms, a firm example of orthodoxy. It happened also, in this development, that the protection required against strong heretical movements tended to influence also the structure of the defended faith insofar as the doctrines attacked had to be specially accented. Catholic teaching thus came to be dominated by matters such as the hierarchical structure of the Church, the *opus operatum* in the sacraments, the Real Presence, the value of good works. In addition, the knowledge increasingly gained from the then revived researches of theologians had to be integrated into the religious instructions. It thus came about that as particular doctrines were made known with greater precision the understanding of the whole hardly increased. The facts of the history of redemption were grasped by the intellect but not related sufficiently to the sanctifying powers in the Church and in the sacraments, nor were they seen as a whole.

Integration in the faith and in the life of the Christian community still provided a sufficient substitute for a more thoughtful understanding of the faith and of its inner cohesion. On the other hand, the new religious revival reinforced endeavors which aimed at a Christianity more consciously understood and realized. This was the object of the retreats recommended by St. Ignatius and their popularization through missions preached to the faithful.[11] This was the object also of the movement originated in France in Saint Sulpice, which made the mystery of the Incarnation of the Son of God the focal point of its devotion.[12] And it was also the object of the growth in veneration of the Sacred Heart of Jesus by which, in symbolic language such as was then easily understood, the notion of a just God was supplemented by reference to the redemptive love of the God-Man.[13]

But there were attempts once more, in the age of enlightenment, at injecting, by violent means, unity into the concept of the world — this time by rationalist elimination of the mysteries of faith in favor of a purely natural world order for which the work of the Redeemer and the sacraments of the Church had no more than moral significance. The practice of an age secure in the faith which had emphasized the objective validity of the sacraments was opposed by a subjectivism which appeared to recognize the achievements of the natural man and woman alone.[14]

Even though the age of enlightenment in its pretentious form was but a short interlude in the intellectual currents of the modern world, the temptation of an enlightened, rationalist, if not materialist, outlook is still increasing among the masses under the impact of the triumphs of modern science and technology. The pastoral work of the Church had increasingly to meet the intellectual curiosity of modern men and women in new forms of teaching the faith which promoted understanding and comprehension and allowed the notes of the "good news" to ring again from among the multitude of doctrines.

Some nineteenth-century efforts to restore especially the Kingdom of God to its central place (prompted by, among others, the German Catholic writer J. B. Hirscher) were at first unsuccessful because it was difficult to draw clear lines of demarcation between the preaching of the faith and scholarly theology.[15] The manner of presenting the faith remained unchanged in that century. On the basis of the findings of theology, it was sought, above all, to propound clear single concepts and to build with these as comprehensive a knowledge of the faith as possible.

A new attitude sprang from the developments which gave birth to the liturgical movement. There was an increasing appreciation for history and tradition in the nineteenth century: Christian antiquity, the monuments of the catacombs, the writings of the Fathers, and the liturgical sacramental life of the early Church were rediscovered. A first fruit was the gradual return to a fuller understanding of the Church.[16] Decisive steps were taken under St. Pius X, which resulted in a return to the fuller sacramental life of ancient ecclesiastical tradition. It came suddenly to be recognized that the life of the Church can be renewed only by gathering the faithful around the altar and by their direct participation in the Mass. Thus arose the liturgical movement. At first it was only a few who recognized in it the outline of a simple but deep Christian faith, a liberating return to the great truths of faith. A new source of inspiration besides the liturgy was sacred Scripture. But it was soon recognized that this renewal of religious life in the Church must not be dissipated in partisan movements which in some special way might be added to already existing pastoral methods and aids. Rather, the whole of pastoral work ought to be based on some large and uniform program. A kind of faith such as is illuminated in the Roman liturgy as heir to Christian antiquity ought to be unfolded with equal and greater clarity in the actual teaching of the faith. Sermon and catechesis, religious art and the organization of services ought to strive jointly to promote a consciousness of the faith upon which the liturgical and sacramental life may be based and from which a joyful Christian faith can arise. This will be possible only when out of the many accretions of the centuries the one single message, the kerygma of the early Church, is once again allowed to emerge. To accomplish this, Christ must be restored to the center of the faith.[17] The restoration of the kerygma to its full power and clarity is, therefore, a principal task of modern pastoral work.

NOTES

1. Kerygma originally referred to the preaching of the Gospel to non-Christians; cf. the historical research undertaken by A. Rétif, "Qu'estce que le kérygme?" *Nouvelle Revue théologique* 71 (1949): 910–922; idem, *Foi au Christ et mission d'après les Actes des Apôtres* (Paris: Editions du Cerf, 1953), pp. 11ff.; Kr. Stendahl, "Kerygma und Kerygmatisch," *Theologische Literaturzeitung* 77 (1952): 715–720. Rétif makes a distinction between kerygma on the one hand and catechesis and didascalics on the other. Whereas kerygma announced the Kingdom of God which came in the Person of Christ and seeks primarily to bring all to the true faith, catechesis (or διδαχή) offered an elementary, and chiefly also moral, introduction to the doctrines of Christianity themselves; didascalics (διδασκαλία), frequently mentioned in pastoral letters, is a more advanced form of instructions using both argumentation and sacred Scripture. Rétif admits, however, that the terminology in the New Testament is fluid. In any case the Greek Fathers used the word, κήρυγμα, in a broader sense, e.g., Basilius, *De Spiritu Sancto*, c. 27 (Migne, *Patrologica Graeca*, vol. 32, cols. 185ff., with annotation no. 64). We, too, would distinguish kerygma from catechesis, insofar as by the former we mean the essential content. Our understanding of the term "Christian kerygma" is also closer to the original in the sense that the message of salvation, which came in the Person of Christ, must today be preached anew in a de-Christianized world.

2. See above [Josef A. Jungmann, *Handing on the Faith* (New York: Herder and Herder, 1962)], p. 96.

3. H. Schürmann, "Aufbau und Struktur der neutestamentlichen Verkündigung," in *Paderborner Schriften zur Pädagogik und Katechese*, 2 (Paderborn, W. Ger., 1949).

4. Consult also: the works of J. Daniélou, esp. *Sacramentum futuri* (Paris, 1950); idem *The Bible and the Liturgy* (Notre Dame, IN: University of Notre Dame Press, 1956).

5. Karl Künstle, *Ikonographie der christlichen Kunst*, vol. I (Freiburg: Herder, 1928), pp. 611f.; O. Casel, "Älteste christliche Kunst und Christusmysterium," *Jahrbuch für Liturgiewissenschaft* 12 (1934): 1–86.

6. Josef A. Jungmann, *Die Stellung Christi im liturgischen Gebet* (Münster, 1925), pp. 131ff.

7. Josef A. Jungmann, "Die Abwehr des germanischen Arianismus und der Umbruch der religiosen Kultur im frühen Mittelalter," *Zeitschrift für katholische Theologie* 69 (1947): 36–99, esp. pp. 61f.

8. Jungmann, "Die Abwehr," pp. 78f. Also *Ps.-Bonifatius, Sermones* (Migne, *Patrologia Latina*, vol. 89, cols. 843–872).

9. Jungmann, "Die Abwehr," p. 94.

10. As above [Jungmann, *Handing on the Faith*], p. 15.

11. Z. J. Maher, *Under the Seal of the Fisherman* (Los Altos, CA: Jesuit House of Retreats, 1948); Hugo Rahner, *The Spirituality of St. Ignatius Loyola*, trans. F. J. Smith (Westminster, MD: Newman, 1953).

12. Pierre Pourrat, *Father Olier*, trans. W. S. Reilly (Baltimore: Voice Publ. Co., 1932).

13. L. Verheylezoon, *Devotion to the Sacred Heart* (Westminster, MD: Newman, 1955); J. Galot, *The Heart of Christ*, trans. John Chapin (Westminster, MD; Newman, 1955); J. Stierli, *Heart of the Saviour* (New York: Herder and Herder, 1958).

14. F. X. Arnold, *Grundsätzliches und Geschichtliches zur Theologie der Seelsorge*, Untersuchungen zur Theologie der Seelsorge, 2 (Freiburg: Herder, 1949), pp. 58ff. and pp. 88ff.

15. F. X. Arnold, *Dienst am Glauben*, Untersuchungen zur Theologie der Seelsorge, 1 (Freiburg: Herder, 1948), esp. pp. 31ff.

16. O. Rousseau (Benedictines of Westminster Priory), *The Progress of the Liturgy* (Westminster, MD: Newman, 1951), in which a decisive chapter in the prehistory of the liturgical movement is entitled: "German Ecclesiology in the Nineteenth Century," pp. 51–68. The chapter deals chiefly with the work of Möhler and the Tübingen School.

17. Th. Kampmann, "Die Gegenwartsgestalt der Kirche und die christliche Erziehung," in *Paderborner Schriften zur Pädagogik und Katechetik*, 3 (Paderborn, W. Ger., 1951), p. 19: "Within that period of Church History of which we are contemporaries, no other happening has as great significance as the liturgico-kerygmatical, the sacramental-biblical revival." Compare this with the synoptic review of H. Elfers, "Verkündigung heute," *Die Kirche in der Welt* 4 (1951): 9–16, 185–190, 329–338; 5 (1952): 15–18.

Kerygmatic Theology

JOSEF A. JUNGMANN

W HENEVER THE RENEWAL of the content of the Christian message is mentioned nowadays, phrases such as "theology of the 'message' " and "kerygmatic theology" are used. What is meant by them?

As we have shown in various places in this book [*Handing on the Faith*],[1] the efforts to bring about such a renewal do not imply a special kind of theology but a clear and effective presentation of Christ's message itself. The message has to be defined apart from theology and in its own right. No other claim was intended by the present author in his 1936 book,[2] or in the treatises on the subject which followed.[3] In subsequent contributions to this subject, however, the opinion was advanced that the "message" should be differentiated from theology proper, remaining much closer to the original presentation of the "good news" in the Bible and in the writings of the Fathers, and that a special theology for the use of pastors was required, a theology of the message.[4] This last thesis, especially, has been the subject of lively discussions in many journals and reviews, at first in German-speaking countries[5] and later elsewhere.[6] The thesis has now been rejected almost universally.[7] While admitting the urgency of the matter as seen by the kerygmaticists, most critics regarded as unnecessary a special theology of the "message"; this task had to be solved, they held, by the theologians themselves. But it was also generally recognized that the traditional school theology could not cope with it and that it had become too far removed from the urgent pastoral problems.

The "school theology" referred to was not, of course, the kind of research that deals with various theological problems in a historical or speculative manner without regard for any practical considera-

Reprinted from Appendix III of *Handing on the Faith*, by Josef Jungmann (New York: Herder and Herder, 1962), pp. 398–405, by permission of The Crossroad Publishing Company.

tions. What was meant was the summarizing systematic presentation, the doctrine as it is usually propounded in lectures, in manuals
of theology, especially in dogmatics. It has been said of it that it
should be more closely linked to live issues (Schröteler), that it should
be more conscious of its charismatic character, in virtue of which
it is "speaking from the Spirit of God" (Stolz), that the faith alone
should be "unfolded into fuller and deeper knowledge" in theology
(Beumer), that the truths of revelation must be seen as truths of
salvation, in short, that theology should be a theology of salvation.[8]
The German theologian Michael Schmaus, in his *Katholische
Dogmatik*,[9] has shown – even before the controversy began – how
this problem should be met. Theology, says Schmaus, must free itself
of its lack of life by entering into history, into the history of salvation: "the historical Christ, who died, rose again and was
transfigured."[10] Schmaus, therefore, demands a christocentric point
of view also for scientific theology; Christ is part of his definition
of theology, the proper subject of which is not "God in himself"[11]
but God "insofar as he has revealed himself in Christ and has preserved this revelation of himself in the Church and throughout
time."[12]

If theology is understood in this sense, then the aims implied
in a "theology of the message" have actually been realized in their
essentials, and such a specialized theology could be dispensed with
altogether. Is there any reason why we should continue to speak of
a "theology of the message"? We can justify its use if by it we mean
all those theoretical discussions and practical efforts which serve to
make manifest and to unfold the kerygma and which should lead to
a renewal of the content of the message in sermon, catechesis, and
in the forms of worship. In that case it would be better to use the
term *kerygmatics*, in which catechetics and homiletics would be
contained.

Many studies on this subject have been published, for instance,
researches on the rules governing religious language and on the
changes which these have undergone in different ages and
cultures.[13] Individual religious concepts, such as salvation, grace,
mystery, the Kingdom of God, heaven, etc., do not, of course, appear in the origins of our faith in the form of pure concepts; they
contain symbolical elements which necessarily have been taken from
the surrounding cultures. Although we reject a "demythologizing"[14]
of the New Testament, which in Protestant theology has been
demanded by Rudolf Bultmann, a realization is, nevertheless, required of the part played by imagination and time. The assessment
of their significance is a task for exegesis, which should be followed

up by a study of the symbols borrowed from Patristic times and the Middle Ages: This study can be of immediate value for a transmission of the message through the elucidation of our own religious terminology and through judgment on present studies.[15]

More important, however, than this analysis of individual terms and concepts with reference to cultural factors, should be the historical study of the principal themes of the Christian message with reference to the continuous task of effectively presenting to humankind "the good news." This inquiry would be concerned with questions about the themes which in particular instances had been given prominence in the transmission of the message and why this was done in so many different ways.[16] The history of Christian feasts can, to a certain extent, provide the clues.[17] It is evidently not mere chance that the resurrection was, in Christian antiquity, considered to be the sum total of all the benefits of redemption,[18] since Easter was the sole feast celebrated in the Church, or that in that era many books were written on *De resurrectione*. Furthermore, it is not accidental that the cross of Christ was seen and symbolically represented as a transfigured paschal cross and as the beginning of salvation rather than as an object lesson in redemptive sufferings. It is also significant for the early Byzantine Church that Marian themes predominated in sermons, since it had instituted and developed the older feasts of our Lady in answer to the christological controversies. One would also have to inquire into the basic changes in the propagation of the Christian message. What radical transformations, have, for example, occurred in the paschal sermon?[19] How much was the concept of the Church or of the Communion of Saints changed under the influence of intellectual currents in the catechisms?[20] We might inquire into the different views of the Eucharist that have been held through the centuries and how deeply these determined the forms of the Mass. To bring out the fullness which the Christian message attained at some stage, or to realize the decay from which we perhaps are still suffering today, is to perform a service of greater value for the kerygmatic renewal.

Much has already been done in this connection in Christian archeology and indeed in internal Church history. We need but recall the researches of Franz Josef Dölger on the images which the early Christian Church developed for Christ (*sol salutis, sol institiae, Ichthus*) or for Baptism (*sphragis*). These researches have been continued in his school, and important contributions have been made to them by, among others, Hugo Rahner.[21] In France Jean Daniélou has published detailed studies on the role of typology in Christian antiquity and, in particular, on the use of the Old Testament in the presentation of the redemption in the New Testament.[22] Some marginal subjects, such as Christian iconography or the history of devotion[23] and not least the history of literature, can add much to the history of the proclamation of the Christian message. Studies on the history of the content of catechesis and sermons are today in process of preparation.[24]

Finally, the notion of a theology of the message, in the wider sense of the term, ought to include also the practical efforts which aim at presenting the message of salvation as a whole, or in parts, in all its richness and not merely as an object of pure scholarship. It is possible to connect theology proper with the concrete propagation of the message in catechesis and sermon. There have been some attempts, for instance, at presenting theology books for the laity or popular catechisms. It is the task of the official catechisms to achieve in a comprehensive form the true ideal of spreading the Christian message.

NOTES

1. As above [Josef A. Jungmann, *Handing on the Faith* (New York: Herder and Herder, 1962)], pp. 36, 96, 137, etc.

2. Josef A. Jungmann, *Die Frohbotschaft und unsere Glaubensverkündigung* (Regensburg: Pustet, 1936).

3. F. Lakner, "Das Zentralobjekt der Theologie," *Zeitschrift für katholische Theologie* 62 (1938): 1–36; idem, "Theorie einer Verkündigungstheologie," in *Theologie der Zeit*, vol. 3 (Vienna, 1939), pp. 1–63; J. B. Lotz, "Wissenschaft und Verkündigung," *Zeitschrift für katholische Theologie* 62 (1938): 465–501; Hugo Rahner, *Eine Theologie der Verkündigung*, 2nd ed., Freiburg: Herder, 1939); F. Dander, *Christus alles und in allen. Gedanken zum Aufbau einer Seelsorgedogmatik* (Innsbruck: Rauch, 1939).

4. Consult especially the works of F. Lakner and J. B. Lotz in note 3 above.

5. A survey on the discussion is offered in the first part of the book of E. Kappler, *Die Verkündigungstheologie*, Studia Friburgensia, 2 (Fribourg, 1949), pp. 7–110: "Darstellung des kerygmatischen Schrifttums"; Kappler's own position in the rest of the book (pp. 113–262) cannot be considered to advance the discussion, since he often misunderstands basic thoughts (for example, the distinction between *verum* and *bonum* as being the respective views of theology and of kerygmatics – as if when preaching the message, by emphasizing truth as truth of salvation and as a goal to be attained, we attribute to the will a role that should be played by the intellect) and finally because he fails to see the problem as such. For since a deepening of the life of faith is necessarily conditioned by a more intensive assent to eternal truth, it is self-evident "that a proclamation of the faith developed in the content of faith is not capable *eo*

ipso of increasing proportionately its exercise" (pp. 245f. and p. 194); cf. also the critical observations work by W. Croce, *Zeitschrift für katholische Theologie* 72 (1950): 121f.; and M. Nicoláu, *Revista española de Teología* 12 (1952): 44f.

6. Consult G. B. Guzzetti, "Saggio bibliografico sulla teologia della predicazione," *La Scuola cattolica* 78 (Milan, 1950), pp. 350–356. This bibliography is a part of a special number that was dedicated to the kerygmatic problem. Among those works mentioned, a special place must be accorded to the historical survey done by G. B. Guzzetti, "La controversia sulla teologia della predicazione" (pp. 260–282), as well as the penetrating study of G. Corti, "Alla radice della controversia kerigmatica" (pp. 283–301): the facts of salvation are recommended as the starting point also for theology; cf. also the fine piece of work by C. Colombo, "Teologia e evangelizzazione" (pp. 302–324), and others. He refers to kindred thoughts in the development of M. J. Scheeben and E. Mersch.

7. Worthy of consideration is the judgment of B. Poschmann in *Théol. Revue* 39 (1940): 122, who thinks it useful if the repetition of dogmatics, such as is often customary at the end of theological studies in seminaries, could be given in the way proposed by kerygmatic theology.

8. More precise passages, cf. Kappler, *Die Verkündigungstheologie*, pp. 22–28.

9. *Katholische Dogmatik*, 3rd/4th ed., 5 vols. (Munich: Hueber Verlag, 1948–1953).

10. M. Schmaus, "Brauchen wir eine Theologie der Verkündigung?," in *Die Seelsorge*, vol. 16 (Hildesheim, 1938), pp. 1–12; idem, "Ein Wort zur Verkündigungstheologie," *Theologie und Glaube* 33 (1941): 312–322, esp. pp. 318f.

11. The majority of theologians declare that "the subject" of theology is *Deus sub ratione Deitatis*, cf. M. J. Congar, "Théologie," in *Dictionnaire de Théologie Catholique* 15 (1946): 341–352, esp. pp. 456f. This concept is connected with the continued use of the Platonic and Aristotelian concept of science, according to which science can deal only with the general and contingent, not with concrete facts. Compare Lakner, "Theorie einer Verkündigungstheologie," p. 15; and Schmaus, "Ein Wort," pp. 319f. See also C. Journet, *The Wisdom of Faith*, trans. R. F. Smith (Westminster, MD: Newman, 1951), pp. 76–77, 86–88.

12. M. Schmaus, op. cit., vol. 1 (3/4) (1948), pp. 26f.; compare this with vol. 2 (3/4) (1949), pp. ixf. (preface to the first edition). Consult J. C. Murray, "Towards a Theology for the Layman," *Theological Studies* 5 (1944): 43–75, 340–376, who, without directly attacking the current concept of the subject matter of theology, proposes *Christus totus*, especially for those theological courses which laypeople who study at various colleges must take in order to prepare themselves for Catholic Action (pp. 359ff.).

13. A work of this kind is P. Bolkovac, *Seelsorge und Sprache* (Nuremberg, 1946).

14. O. Cullmann, "Rudolf Bultmann's Concept of Myth and the New Testament," *Theology Digest* 4 (1956): 140–145.

15. As above (Jungmann, *Handing on the Faith*], p. 244.

16. On the importance of historical studies which are able "to show us faulty developments, to make us understand better the present situation and so indicate the way to be taken in the future," cf. H. Elfers, "Verkündigung heute," *Die Kirche in der Welt* 5 (1952): 17.

17. As a very modest attempt in this direction, consult the work of the

author, Josef A. Jungmann, *Liturgical Worship* (New York: F. Pustet, 1941), pp. 30-46 ["Das Christusgeheimnis im Kirchenjahr," in *Gewordene Liturgie* (Innsbruck: Rauch, 1941), pp. 295-321].

18. See above [Jungmann, *Handing on the Faith*], p. 381.

19. Br. Dreher, "Die Osterpredigt," in *Untersuchungen zur Theologie der Seelsorge*, 3 (Freiburg: Herder, 1951).

20. Consult above [Jungmann, *Handing on the Faith*], pp. 145ff. and p. 383; and also C. E. Elwell, *The Influence of the Enlightenment on the Catholic Theory of Religious Education in France, 1750-1850* (Cambridge: Harvard University Press, 1944), esp. pp. 203-228.

21. Hugo Rahner, *Griechische Mythen in christlicher Deutung* (Zurich, 1945). Of the many treatises in the *Zeitschrift für katholische Theologie*, we cite particularly *Mysterium lunae* (1939-1940); *Antenna Crucis* (1941-1943; 1953).

22. J. Daniélou, *Bible et Liturgie*, Lex Orandi, 11 (Paris: Editions du Cerf, 1951); trans. as *The Bible and the Liturgy* (Notre Dame, IN: University of Notre Dame Press, 1956).

23. Especially important is P. Pourrat, *Christian Spirituality*, trans. W. H. Mitchell and S. P. Jacques, 3 vols. (New York: P. J. Kenedy, 1922-1928), vol. 4 (1954) (in various editions).

24. Here we must place those famous studies from which we have quoted frequently in the course of this book [*Handing on the Faith*]: *Untersuchungen zur Theologie der Seelsorge*, edited by F. X. Arnold. There is a history of catechesis according to various subjects, but from a Protestant standpoint (Baptism, Confession, Last Supper, Confirmation) contained in the first volume of G. v. Zezschwitz, *System der christlich-kirchlichen Katechetik*, 2 vols. (Leipzig, 1864-1872). A partial treatment of the history of catechetics is contained in G. H. Gerberding, *The Lutheran Catechist* (Philadelphia: Lutheran Publication Society, 1910), pp. 45-88. For a thorough study of catechisms, consult J. Hofinger, *Geschichte des Katechismus* in *Österreich von Canisius bis zur Gegenwart. Mit besonderer Berücksichtigung der gleichzeitigen gesamtdeutschen Katechismusgeschichte* (Innsbruck, 1937), pp. 129-212; using the Austrian catechism of 1777, he has thrown much light on the changes which the treatment of the content of the more important doctrines has undergone.

Theology and Kerygmatic Teaching

JOSEF A. JUNGMANN

WHEN WE NOW CONSIDER what were the symptoms preceding the de-Christianization of the masses, we lament their frightful ignorance in matters of religion. This lament gives some cause for surprise at least in respect of those countries in which religious teaching is obligatory in schools. For in these countries each pupil receives for a period of eight years or more a wide religious instruction which gives more theology than the average priest received in the Middle Ages. Moreover, it is upon religious instruction that modern catechesis has concentrated its effort.

However, this frequent and general lament is not unfounded. Either our catechetical methods have not been adapted to the children's capacities, or our reproaches do not mean what they say. Probably there is some truth in both suppositions.[1]

It is not really ignorance of the basic points of Christian doctrine that we regret. Most people know all the sacraments; they know about the person of Christ, as well as about our Lady, Peter and Paul, Adam and Eve, and a good many others. They know enough about the commandments of God and of the Church.

But what is lacking among the faithful is a sense of unity, seeing it all as a whole, an understanding of the wonderful message of divine grace. All they retain of Christian doctrine is a string of dogmas and moral precepts, threats and promises, customs and rites, tasks and duties imposed on unfortunate Catholics, whilst the non-Catholic gets off free. They are averse to believing in and acting up to their beliefs, a reluctance which, in an atmosphere of unbelief and materialism, soon leads to disaster for the individual Catholic.

That is how most of us look at the present state of religious ignorance, and that is what we have to face up to. Both our teaching and our catechisms are too much in the nature of theological treatises.

The function of science is to dissect, examine, and describe the component elements. It is the same with theology. The first heresies forced theologians to be scientific, when a point of doctrine was

Reprinted from *Lumen Vitae* 5 (1950), pp. 258–263. Reproduced by courtesy of *Lumen Vitae.* Copyright *Lumen Vitae* 1950.

wrongly interpreted or a mystery brought down to the level of a natural truth quite accessible to human intelligence. Therefore, that point of doctrine or that mystery (e.g., the relationship between the Father and the Son, the two natures in Christ, grace and liberty) was subjected to examination, defined, defended against false interpretations by new definitions, and saved from misunderstanding by fresh distinctions being made. As a result, new concepts arose, useful for a more complete understanding of the truth.

Later the scholastics exploited the patristic inheritance; they systematically explored the frontiers of science and faith in order to reestablish the harmony between the two. The contribution of the scholastics is indispensable in our days when human reason, self-satisfied and critical, is asserting itself. Thus, Catholic theology presents a complete, logically built structure, a clear system which, even when it does not convert an opponent, reveals its inestimable value by giving to the priest, the messenger of the faith, such a psychological certainty that he fears no objection that might be raised nor any philosophy invented by humankind.

This scientific work implies an outward activity, a defense of the frontiers; it casts its light, not so much on the essentials of Christian doctrine, on the fundamental points of redemption, as on the obscure and difficult questions, e.g., reconciling the unity and the trinity in God, the action of the divine will upon human will, the powers of the Church, the mode of operation of the sacraments, casuistry. Our redemption in Christ, our possession by him in virtue of Baptism, and, consequently, the obligation upon us to imitate him, all these things are no doubt dealt with—but only cursorily, as though evident; rapidly, as immaterial to and lost in a mass of more difficult questions.

Of course, there has always been a difference between a catechism and a theological textbook.

The catechism is more simple, the questions are set out in a traditional order, and the answers are given without proof. But the form and arrangement smack of the dogma course. The catechism begins with a definition of faith, then the sources of revelation; it creates the impression that Christianity is a set of theses pertaining to an advanced science, to which one must assent by faith; there is no suggestion that it is a renewal of humanity which affects us profoundly. The Church is represented as a visible society and is defended against any attempt at "spiritualizing" it by proofs which were elaborated at the time of the Reformation. Its fundamental structure, the community of those who are sanctified in Christ, is not brought out. The doctrine of grace begins with a crystal-clear definition and the distinction between actual and sanctifying grace, and it is presented as an enigmatic condition of God's favor, a wonderful character that must be in our actions if they are to be pleasing to God. We do not take into account that this isolation of the concept of grace is justified in a scientific treatise but not in a course of religious instruction. There is, then, some reason for the reproach that we are still speaking the language of the thirteenth century, or that of the centuries of controversy to which we owe our theological treatises.

Because of heresies, a clear line of demarcation was imperative, even in popular instruction. That explains why, since the middle of the sixteenth century, our textbooks have followed the analytic method. Today, when Christians have to face not heresy but indifference, they need to be aware of what they possess, to rejoice in their riches, to see the whole plan of salvation and begin to shape their lives accordingly. Doubtless, in the science of theology, Christian doctrine is seen as one whole; but it is a logical whole, a kind of well-guarded fortress. For preaching purposes we should rather present the vision of a vast panorama. The Catholic should not get the impression of being obliged to adhere to a multitude of individual points of doctrine (between which the theologian alone knows the logical connection). He or she should immediately perceive the grandiose plan of God who, in Christ, wishes to draw all people to him. This plan should make all the rest intelligible – intelligible not in the way of a logical argument but as a teleological whole (having, of course, its own logical cohesion).

The object of theological study is, to use the current formula, *Deus sub ratione Deitatis*. But pastoral theology does not attempt to cover every point of doctrine within the limits of human knowledge. It points to a goal and the way to that goal; it preaches Christian doctrine as the aim of our aspirations and efforts; it shows where lies the treasure for which humanity should sell all in order to possess it, the wonderful way of salvation, the invitation of God to his great banquet. We should group the Christian truths round a central fact from which they receive their light. As someone has well said, they should be presented not as links in a chain but like the spokes of a wheel: Seen from the center, they are like rays issuing from a source of light.

This center can only be Christ, our Lord. The best way to come to a knowledge of him is to follow the unfolding of the story of our salvation. The method advised and outlined by St. Augustine to the deacon Deogratias, in his *De catechizandis rudibus,* consists in gathering from the Old Testament the divine preparations for the coming of the Savior and in explaining his appearance in the New Testament and his work until the founding of the Church. The *Katholische*

Religionsbüchlein of the Viennese, Wilhelm Pichler, deserves mention as a guide in this method. It has been in use in Austria for thirty years in the teaching of small children and has been translated into more than a score of languages.

The basic plan, as described above, should predominate even in the detailed statement or explanation. All the parts must be joined together to make one single whole. Beginning with some bits of fundamental theology and then going on to a philosophical explanation of God and his attributes is not as valuable as taking the Christian life as your starting point. This latter method was adopted by many authors in the sixteenth century, e.g., Contarini, who begins with: "What is a Christian?" The French catechism of 1947 has adopted it; the title of its first lesson is "The Catholic." We have to deal with baptized children who are already in the Kingdom of God and through us are to be made conscious of what they are and what then must remain. From this point of view our religious teaching of children is comparable to the religious initiations given to the newly baptized in the earliest days of Christianity.

The teaching about God will thus contain the elements of a rational proof of his existence, as answer to the question: "How can we come to the knowledge of God?"; and this will be developed and underlined by extracts from the Old and New Testaments, especially our Lord's words concerning his Heavenly Father.

Christology should not be merely a recital of facts: the Incarnation, passion, and resurrection. We should insist on their redemptive significance, thus bringing in the doctrine of grace. Christ, the second Adam, has come into the world to raise up a new man and woman; by his sufferings and death he has opened up to us the way to resurrection and eternal life.

It is important that the Church should appear as the fruit and continuation of his work. Our Lord Jesus Christ teaches through the Church; that explains its infallibility. As high-priest, he works sacerdotally through his human instruments; that explains the power and efficacy of their word. When the Church promulgates commandments and precepts, it is the crook of the Good Shepherd, guiding the faithful.

Grace and the sacraments must be taken out of their isolation and thus avoid the mistake of being taken for "things." They should not be put immediately after the moral section because that makes them appear simply as helps for the keeping of the commandments; they should follow immediately the lessons on Christ and the Church, as indicated in the creed. For, here again, as children of God we are made like to Christ, the Son of God made man; by grace we share gratuitously in his privileges; we have entered by him and through him into the house of the Father. More precise definitions may find their place in the context, but the front of the picture must be taken up with this presentation of the whole plan, which the child must never forget.

The teaching of Christian doctrine will then have once more the accent of good news, the invitation to the Kingdom of God. The response will be a joyful echo in the hearts of the children and above all in youth. The latter are less tractable to a series of propositions to which one must adhere under penalty of damnation, less disposed to practice a religion and morality which appear to them to be nothing but a set of promises, devotions, and duties which one is bound to accept willy-nilly.

These foundations once laid will allow moral teaching in a new spirit. Morality will be seen as our behavior, in response to a call from God.[2]

The foregoing considerations show that kerygmatic teaching requires more than a very clear exposition of doctrinal truths and more than their application to life (rather in the manner of a technical school where they give lots of practical exercises). The doctrine itself must be transformed by its incorporation into the whole of the good news and adapted to its nature.

We do not, however, intend to set up a new theology against dogmatic theology. The discussion which was started some ten years ago in many German and a few foreign reviews on the need for a kerygmatic theology has been sidetracked far away from the real question. The main point is not that of an independent theology but that of the special rules for preaching in the light of theology.

The realization of this fundamental problem is nowadays growing without too many discussions, in larger circles, and finds its place in religious and homiletic publications; already the new method inspires some religious textbooks.[3] This is a matter for rejoicing.

NOTES

1. We must add that religious instruction limited to childhood only achieves incomplete results. See article by G. Delcuve, ["Le probleme de la formation religieuse dans le monde moderne,"] *Lumen Vitae* 4 (1949): 217. The same problem arises for high schools.

2. See J. Hofinger, "In What Order Should Religious Truths Be Presented?" *Lumen Vitae* 2 (1947): 719–746. See also Hofinger's "Our Message," *Lumen Vitae* 5 (1950): 264–280.

3. See F. X. Arnold, "Revival in Dogmatic Preaching and Catechetics," *Lumen Vitae* 3 (1948): 488–518, esp. p. 503.

In some ways, Mary Charles Bryce's survey of the concern for catechesis found in the pastoral letters of the U.S. bishops is a companion piece to Joseph Collins' trilogy on the history of the Confraternity of Christian Doctrine, as well as to her own historical essay on the Baltimore Catechism. In this survey, Sister Bryce shows how concern with leading children and adults to a deeper, better-informed faith has been a continuing preoccupation of our pastoral leaders from the beginning. However, she does not ignore some of the important gaps found in the matters the bishops paid attention to. Both aspects of this history are instructive for us today as we decide on policies for shaping our future.

READING 16

Religious Education in the Pastoral Letters and National Meetings of the U.S. Hierarchy

MARY CHARLES BRYCE

THE SIGNIFICANCE of recent statements on religious education by the U.S. bishops can be fully appreciated only when they are compared to their previous pronouncements.

The pastoral letter *To Teach as Jesus Did*, which appeared at the end of 1972, addresses the matter of the Church's educational mission and how that mission is interpreted in this country. The document *Basic Teachings of Catholic Religious Education*, issued early in 1973, has a more limited focus. It deals with the "content" of religious education. Though both are likely to have far-reaching and long-lasting effects on the Church here, it is not the purpose of this article to do a critique of the documents themselves. The immediate ancestry of each of the two statements is explained elsewhere in this issue. The objective of the present study is to situate the two in the broader context of episcopal interest in catechesis[1] as expressed in previous pastorals

Reprinted from *The Living Light* 10 (1973), pp. 249–263. © 1973 National Conference of Catholic Bishops. Used by permission.

and in the bishops' resolute concern to maintain orthodoxy in the teaching of doctrine.

Pastoral Letters Under Scrutiny

In the one hundred-eighty-one years between 1792 when Bishop John Carroll wrote the first pastoral and 1973 when the National Conference of Catholic Bishops issued the latest, the United States hierarchy has published one hundred and two pastoral letters. They run from two paragraphs totaling eleven lines to many thousands of words.[2] Some are brief statements of positions issued during a given crisis; others are lengthy writings more exhortatory and pastoral in tone. Some address a single issue; some cover a variety of topics. All exhibit the hierarchy's recognition of its pastoral responsibility for and to the faithful. *To Teach as Jesus Did,* however, is the only one given over entirely to religious education. All previous statements were embedded in treatises on other topics.

Writing prior to the flowering of the parochial schools, Bishop John Carroll expressed his apostolic interests and priorities in his only pastoral in 1792. A kind of "state of the union message," the letter treated the importance of education, training young men for the priesthood, the urgency of caring for the poor, building and repainting church buildings, attendance at Sunday Mass, support of the Church, and devotion to the Mother of God, in that order. Though he specified the importance of schools, Carroll's educational concerns centered on a broader view of religious instruction. "I have considered the virtuous and Christian instruction of youth as a principal object of pastoral solicitude," he wrote. In warm, encouraging tones he reminded parents and pastors of the serious responsibility of religious instruction and of walking in "the observance of all Christian duties."[3] He told them that in doing so they not only rendered an acceptable service to God but also labored for "the preservation and increase of true religion, for the benefit of our common country, whose welfare depends on the morals of its citizens. . . ."[4]

Three catechetical themes emerged in that first pastoral, themes that laced through and surfaced in those later pastorals which in some way treated of the educational ministry: (1) the responsibility and obligation of parents in the matter of religious instruction of their offspring, (2) an almost exclusive concentration on the religious instruction of children, and (3) instilling of Christian morals as a dominant purpose and value in religious education.

Parental Responsibility

Although it is sometimes held that the current enthusiasm for parents as the principal educators of their children is an innovative theory, the United States bishops have been publicly advocating this since 1792. In at least nineteen of the letters dating from Carroll's day to the present, parents were explicitly urged to recognize and exercise their rights as religious educators. In the 1829 "Pastoral to the Laity," the bishops addressed mothers and fathers directly: "Dearly beloved . . . God has made you the guardians of those children to lead them to his service on earth." And again, "Attend to the education of your child, teaching him first to seek the kingdom of God and His justice."[5]

The bishops told parents: "Begin with them in their earliest childhood, whilst the mind is yet pure and docile and their baptismal innocence uncontaminated." Then when school age demands, "placing them at school, seek for those teachers who will cultivate the seed which you have sown."[6] Admitting that they may need some assistance, the bishops later recommended that parents "fortify their faith by reading those explanations and compilations which are calculated to strengthen themselves and to enable them to instruct their children."[7] That was in the pastoral of 1833. One hundred years later when parish schools were far more numerous than they had been a century earlier, the bishops stressed anew that "parents are in a true sense the vicars of God in the education of their children."[8] It was an echo of their favorite theme. Even the growing numbers of parish schools did not alter the lyrics. *To Teach as Jesus Did* continues it in our day. Parents, today's bishops wrote, are still the primary educators particularly in the matter of religious education.[9]

Child-centered, School-centered

Reviewing the frequent reminders to parents already hints at the second of the Carroll themes, i.e., focus on children's religious instruction. Addressing the clergy in 1829 the bishops "affectionately" reminded pastors of one of their duties, "solicitude for the instructions of youth." "If the great truths of religion be not deeply inculcated upon the youthful mind," they insisted, "your discourses will be scarcely intelligible to those who will have been left untaught."[10] Four years later they pointed out that "the education of the rising generation is, beloved brethren, a subject of first importance."[11] Echoing and reechoing Carroll's concern for childhood instructions, the bishops solidified the presumption that catechesis is meant for the young and the very young.

The prevailing characteristic of this child-centered programming was its school-centeredness. From the time of the First Provincial Council in 1829 to the present day, exhortations addressed to parents and clergy alike specified the school as the principal locus for religious instruction. The thirty-fourth decree of that first of seven provincial councils in Baltimore initiated legislation on Catholic parochial schools.[12] The majority of subsequent pastorals that touched on religious instruction presumed a classroom setting. "Religion teaching and religious training should form part of every school system of education," noted the 1866 letter.[13] And in 1933, addressing the "Present Crisis" of the depression years, the prelates called for a strengthening of courses in religion and urged teachers (particularly priests) to "make religion the most attractive of all subjects taught."[14] Parents were commended for requiring excellence in their Catholic schools in the 1949 pastoral entitled "The Christian Family."[15] Their insistent demands included "schools in which the best standards of instruction and training are integrated in the teaching of religion."[16] According to their "spiritual leaders, the Bishops," United States Catholics knew in 1967 "that the positive training of their children in the fundamentals of religion was a training which cannot be soundly imparted elsewhere than in schools dedicated to the purpose."[17] Two pastorals even described the school as modeled on the family hearth. "The home is the first school," observed the 1948 letter.[18] The next year's letter maintained that "It [the home] is [the child's] constant school."[19]

Although the bishops stressed the home, they recognized the de facto situation that most formal education takes place in schools. They, like most Roman Catholics, seem to share the expectations that all Americans have of the educational system. It appears to be an American syndrome to look to the schools for remedies (and subtly blame them) for the ills of society. (In an era when highway deaths mounted, driving lessons were introduced into the curriculum. When sexual permissiveness and aberrations increased, classes in sex education came in. The most recent example is the effort made by schools to counter the drug culture.) Even Catholic leaders at times lapse into the Socratic position that holds, consciously or unconsciously, that knowledge is virtue.

Sometimes the bishops directed their remarks to the role of religion in general education. Writing after the close of World War I, they cautioned the nation's rulers: "Let them seriously consider whether it be the part of political wisdom to exclude from the ordinance of the State and from a public instruction the teaching of the Gospel."[20] In their 1953 address to the nation on the importance of Christian faith, they warned that "when education tries to thrive in a moral and religious vacuum it degenerates into a dead and deadening juxtaposition of facts."[21]

With few exceptions the pastorals made only broad references to religious instruction, but the occasional exceptions when they became specific were significant. In the 1919 letter the bishops urged parents, teachers, and pastors to instruct properly those in their charge concerning "the origin, nature and the value of the Holy Sacrifice, the meaning of the sacred rites with which it is offered and the order of the liturgy as it advances from season to season."[22] Forty-seven years later a similar reminder appeared. The spiritual purpose of "Advent will again come into its own," observed the 1966 pastoral, if in all Christian homes, churches, and schools "liturgical observances are practiced with fresh fervor." Therefore, "we urge instruction based upon it."[23]

It was only in the late sixties that the hierarchy gave explicit attention to adult religious education. Earlier allusions to it were embedded in passages on preaching, reading the Scriptures, and advice on coping with critical national or social ills. For example, the 1931 letter, "Economic Crisis," closed with this admonition: Catholic organizations should "study the social teaching of the Church so as to help prepare Catholics to take their full part in this great task of our time."[24]

Twice in 1966 the bishops pointed up the need for adult education. In "Penitential Observance" they recommended "spiritual studies, beginning with the Scriptures . . . ," and in "Race Relations and Poverty," acknowledged that "adult education is also a great necessity."[25] Two years later they projected more concrete hopes: "We also hope to see established centers of education in family life . . . together with collegiate or adult education programs," they wrote in the 1968 pastoral, a letter affirming the encyclical *Humanae vitae.*[26] In two more recent pastorals the chief shepherds included the continuing education of the clergy among their considerations.[27]

Moral Education

The third theme which had surfaced in Carroll's time is stressed in the hierarchy's pastoral writings in our day. That theme is the exhortation to moral excellence and its role in the "educational ministry." Morality, in the religious context, is in the realm of response. Conscious of God's beneficent goodness, a person endeavors to direct his or her life according to principles found in Christ's life and the Gospel. That this is a part of catechesis has been brought out in the *General Catechetical Directory:* "Catechesis must include not only those things which are to be believed, but also those things which are to be done" (no. 30). Reminders of the importance of Christian moral teaching in the episcopal letters showed up most often, though not exclusively, in the context of schools and general education. Formal education tended to hold the spotlight. The purpose of our Catholic schools, the bishops stated in their Depression-era letter of 1933, was "to fit men for life in eternity as well as in time." More explicitly this meant:

> . . . to teach men to think rightly and to live rightly; to instill sound principles in our youth, principles not only of civic righteousness, but of Catholic faith and morality. . . .[28]

"Without religious education, moral education is impossible," the prelates maintained in 1952. Cautioning the nation against a kind of moral bankruptcy they contended that the state must uphold that standard of morality "which flows necessarily from belief in God and in God's law."[29] Reason alone, the bishops insisted, was insufficient. "Man needs not merely the truths which reason can discover. . . ." On the contrary, they explained:

> Only the life of Christian faith can guarantee to man in his present state the moral life; and the Christian life is lived in its entirety only through the Church.[30]

From 1950 on the pastorals alluded to and pointed up the importance of moral education with ever-greater frequency.[31]

The Pastorals in Retrospect

The pastoral letters clearly exhibit the bishops' enduring concern for good catechesis. They manifest a clear consistency of purpose in repeated admonitions to the clergy and laity alike to provide and promote the best in religious education for the faithful. The fact that the "faithful" in this case was almost exclusively interpreted as "children," and that catechesis was heavily school-centered, can only be fully appreciated when placed against the backdrop of the periods in which they were written. As such, the pastorals indeed reflect emphases, viewpoints, and priorities of their day. Although the strengths and weaknesses of the documents can be fully grasped only in the circumstances of their own eras, certain significant elements seem to have particular relevance for the serious-minded, pastorally oriented leaders of today. A study of the vocabulary is revealing. Dozens of allusions to "religious instruction" appeared in the letters, thus highlighting a concern for content and indoctrination. A form of the term *catechesis* occurred only four times: Parents were reminded in 1833 to "have their children catechized,"[32] and the 1970 letter insisted that "catechetical preparation" should precede marriage.[33] *Catechism* first appeared in the 1854 letter in a statement illustrating the written and unwritten deposit of divine truth. The apostles, the pastoral noted, had no *catechism* "such as our children now learn." The 1964 letter reminded parents whose children were not attending Catholic schools that they "must see that their children attend catechism classes."[34] Only twice was the New Testament message described in kerygmatic terms. "How beautiful . . . [is he] who brings *good tidings*," exclaimed the 1843 letter. One hundred-twenty-four years later, in the 1967 letter, the Gospel was called the "Good News."[35]

Inasmuch as the majority of the pastorals were written after 1919,[36] certain other points come to mind. For instance, in view of the fact that the catechetical renewal was well underway by the third decade of this century, it is surprising to find no evidence of its existence and development until 1964. The pastoral of that year acknowledged the contribution which the scriptural, catechetical, and liturgical renewals had made toward enabling people to take a more understanding part in Christian life,[37] yet none of the catechetical principles promulgated by these movements came to the fore. The role of the believing community in catechesis was not touched on until the pastoral "The Church in Our Day" appeared in 1967.[38] Then it was only hinted at. The didactic quality of the liturgy received no recognition in the letters. Study the liturgy, yes, but "allow the experience of the Mysteries to inform you" was nowhere to be found.

One lacuna is outstanding, one that transcends the particular eras that the respective letters represent. Its absence somehow demands an explanation. The value and imperativeness of religious education is repeatedly stressed, but the very heart of religious education, its nature and substance, is at best implied or alluded to. It was not until 1972 – one hundred eighty years after Carroll's letter – that the bishops addressed themselves to catechesis as a whole, its scope, purpose, and ideals. To understand the full significance of *To Teach*, it is necessary to note that for the first time the bishops have given over an entire pastoral letter to catechetics or religious education. Their subsequent publication *Basic Teachings of Catholic Religious Education* not only complements the 1972 pastoral, by "determining the content of faith instruction,"[39] but also maintains the bishops' traditional concern for doctrine.

Other Manifestations of Episcopal Interest

While the letters portray a certain collective picture of episcopal concern for catechesis, they do not tell the entire story. Throughout the Church's history in this country, bishops have exercised their pastoral ministry of catechizing in several ways. Action in this realm was expressed mostly by writing or commissioning the writing of catechisms, but some bishops actually gave instructions as a regular practice. Carroll wrote a catechism in 1793.[40] One of his successors, Ambrose Maréchal, sanctioned the writing of another in 1826.[41] John Cheverus, Boston's first bishop, translated Claude Fleury's *Catéchisme Historique* for his diocese between 1810 and 1813.[42] John England, bishop of Charleston, not only compiled a catechism in 1821 but also engaged in catechizing. "I conversed with some persons who sought explanations and in the evening baptized three black adults and blessed two couples," he wrote in his diary on 13 February 1821. On 7 June of that same year he recorded that he "saw and continued the instructions of three catechumens, also saw another woman who became a catechumen, heard confessions and saw and conversed with some of the children."[43]

Moved by its persuasive bishop, Frank P. Kenrick, the second Diocesan Synod of Philadelphia formally adopted Ireland's Butler Catechism for the English-speaking Catholics and the 1836 version of Peter Canisius' German catechism, known as the "Augsburg Catechism," for his German-speaking flock of Philadelphia.[44] The catechism of Bishop Jean Baptiste David, written in 1825, was such a popular manual that it was still being used in the Bardstown–Louisville area as late as 1934.[45] Augustin Verot, the bishop first of Georgia and later of Florida, who made himself internationally known in his vigorous debate on the universal catechism issue at Vatican Council I, wrote a twenty-eight-page catechism in 1869.[46] Both David's and Verot's catechisms had a decided influence on the catechism promulgated after the Third Plenary Council of Baltimore.[47]

Even during the period when the Baltimore Catechism dominated the scene, individual bishops continued their activity in catechetical publications. With few exceptions – Bishop Sebastian Byrne's translation of Pius X's manuals is an outstanding example here[48] – they no longer directly produced texts, but they seemed to have no hesitancy about approving them. Bishop Patrick W. Riordan of San Francisco approved the innovative five-book graded series by Peter C. Yorke in the diocese of San Francisco in 1900,[49] just as Samuel A. Stritch, archbishop of Milwaukee, did in 1931 for the Edward A. Fitzpatrick *Highway to Heaven* series.[50]

Recorded episcopal concern for religious education is found in a third source. A review of the published minutes from the hierarchy's annual meetings revealed persistent regard for the "vexing matter of the catechism" as the fathers of the 1829 Provincial Council had described it. And indeed it was the "catechism," not catechesis as such, which consistently held the bishops' attention. Dissatisfaction with the Baltimore manual found its way into the archbishops' meetings of 1895, 1896, and 1902. Debate centered on whether to sponsor a revision of the 1885 catechism or to launch the composition of a new one. An element of relief seems to emerge from between the lines of the 1902 minutes after the archbishops learned that "it was rumored that the Holy See thought of ordering the preparation of a catechism for universal use." The prelates voted to discontinue their consideration of the matter until the intention of the Holy See was determined.[51] Minutes of subsequent archiepiscopal meetings disclosed no further discussion on the question.

By 1930 the scene had shifted to Washington. The setting was different, so were the individual participants, but the problem was unchanged as the quest for an ideal catechism took the floor again. At that meeting the newly published Italian catechism of Pietro Cardinal Gasparri was proposed.[52] Recommending that one or two items in the manual be adapted in order to relate to American users more meaningfully, the motion was made and carried that no action be taken until an agreement be reached with Gasparri on the matter. According to the 1931 minutes, Gasparri accepted the proposed adaptations, but the minutes recorded no decision to promulgate the catechism on a nationwide basis.[53]

Almost every year after 1934, when an episcopal committee for revising the Baltimore Catechism was named, until the beginning of Vatican Council II, discussion about catechisms came to the fore. In 1936 Bishop Edwin O'Hara reported that several hundred catechisms had been prepared in recent years, indicating dissatisfaction with the Baltimore manual. In a rather detailed presentation he reported the findings of an extensive study of attacks on the catechism. Critiques had been tallied and fell generally into three categories, he said. Those categories were: "(1) Theological inaccuracies; (2) Difficulty in its language for children; (3) Questionable approval by ecclesiastical authorities."[54] Meanwhile, he continued, the revision work continued, and special working committees were busy on the project.

Archbishop John T. McNicholas of Cincinnati made a progress report on the revision during the 1939 meeting. He stated that thirty-five

bishops had made suggestions with regard to changes and several appointed theologians to assist in the revision. 501 questions appeared with answers in the new Catechism; 2 appendices, giving pertinent documents and a thorough alphabetical index.[55]

Even after the finally published revision of Catechism No. 3 in 1948, the catechism frequently held the spotlight at annual meetings. Bishop Matthew Brady reported in 1957 that the Baltimore Catechism was being continuously updated to conform to changes coming from Rome. He provided such illustrations as Pius XII's encyclical *Mystici corporis*, his defining of the dogma of Mary's Assumption, plus legislation concerning the new eucharistic fast, and the 1955 decree of the Sacred Congregation of Rites on the matter of fasting and abstinence.[56]

Meanwhile, another candidate came to the fore as a nominee to be this country's national catechism. According to the 1956 minutes, a then-new German manual was recommended. The minutes read: "The bishops of Germany have approved a Catechism for the uniform instruction of youth 10 to 13 years of age." It was moved and seconded "that any action regarding the preparation of a suitable Catechism to replace the Baltimore text be postponed until we see the translation of the German Catechism."[57]

A new endeavor to compose a national catechism was introduced in this country by the Bishops' Committee of the Confraternity of Christian Doctrine in its 1963 meeting. The move was formally approved by the hierarchy as a whole at its national meeting on 11 November 1964.[58] During the next four years, the proposed catechism shifted in design and purpose to become a projected sourcebook. Those four years were filled with multiple meetings of the episcopal committee and their many consultants examining the pros and cons of numerous recommendations and possible options. From these there emerged, according to Joseph Collins, "a decided preference for a narrative, biblical-liturgical type text, one that would be used only as a sourcebook — not a textbook — for writers, teachers, pastors, and priests engaged in the field of catechetics."[59] The fact is that neither the sourcebook nor catechism materialized because of the work that had already begun to develop in a somewhat different direction.

Vatican II set the tone for a new era in catechesis when the council fathers bypassed the issue of a universal catechism and recommended that directories be composed "with respect to the catechetical instruction of the Christian people."[60] That recommendation and the subsequent action which proved their determined intent to follow through with an international directory halted the United States movement. The project was suspended in anticipation of the promised *General Catechetical Directory*, which appeared in June 1971.

Conclusions

What became clear in this study of the bishops' pastorals is the hierarchy's constant concern for orthodoxy of doctrine. This was further confirmed by a survey of their individual activities in writing or sponsoring catechisms and corporate decisions in annual meetings. In their promulgated letters, they exhorted, reminded, entreated, and occasionally rebuked; but the constancy of their message did not waver: The truths of religion (Christianity) were to be delivered.

Actions of their annual gatherings complemented the epistle messages. Just as their pastorals concentrated primarily on the school, their discussions at the annual meetings focused on the catechism. It seems that the prelates viewed that manual as a syllabus which enunciated the corpus of fundamental doctrine, and as such the catechism can be seen as a direct ancestor of the recent *Basic Teachings of Catholic Religious Education.*

An analysis of their decisions and actions makes two points clear: (1) The bishops' steadfastness of purpose notwithstanding, they were not wedded to a single manual; (2) nor was the Baltimore Catechism ever so fixed that it precluded change. In numerous discussions at their annual meetings, the hierarchy displayed a lack of unanimity in support of the Baltimore Catechism. From time to time they considered adopting other manuals on a national scale. Some even wrote their own manuals, while others sponsored or sanctioned the writing of catechisms in their particular dioceses. On the second point, the bishops insisted on clarifications and emendations to certain catechism questions as Vatican pronouncements were made, thus manifesting an openness to doctrinal development.

The recent publications *To Teach* and *Basic Teachings* are natural outgrowths of what appears to be the constant preoccupation of the American hierarchy. *To Teach* expands the notion of catechesis by providing a broader concept of religious education and explicating the scope, forms, and purpose of catechizing. In *Basic Teachings* one recognizes the resolute concern for fundamental doctrinal content. Although a didactic prose style has replaced the terse question-answer form of the older catechisms, the fundamental principle is the same, a zeal for orthodox doctrinal content in religion texts. While the pastoral *To Teach* continues to recognize the parochial school as the most effective locus for catechesis, it does recognize that catechetical activity is broadly pastoral in objectives and, as the *General Catechetical Directory* emphasizes, must involve and have the support of the entire Christian community.

NOTES

1. The term *catechesis* (and its derivatives) was used interchangeably with *religious education* in *To Teach as Jesus Did* (Pastoral Letter, 1972). It occurred only four times in *Basic Teachings of Catholic Religious Education* (1973). Berard L. Marthaler refines the distinction between the two terms. In a brief but careful treatment he suggests "with some hesitation that religious education is primarily an academic enterprise," while catechesis in modern usage "includes the kerygma, preparation for the sacraments as well as more advanced instructions to nourish and sustain a living faith in the community and its individual members." *Catechetics in Context* (Huntington, IN: Our Sunday Visitor, 1973), p. 35.

2. The succinct statement, "Birth Control Laws" (20 November 1970), opposing federal involvement in population control, is the shortest. The "Pastoral Letter, 1919," touching on national and international problems in the aftermath of World War I, is the most lengthy.

3. "Bishop Carroll's Pastoral Letter (1792)," in Hugh J. Nolan, *Pastoral Letters of the American Hierarchy, 1792-1970* (Huntington, IN: Our Sunday Visitor, 1971), p. 6. Unless otherwise indicated subsequent references to the pastoral letters will be made to this volume.

4. Nolan, p. 7.

5. Nolan, p. 24.

6. Nolan, p. 25.

7. Nolan, pp. 55-56.

8. Nolan, p. 296.

9. *To Teach as Jesus Did*, pars. 25, 52-59.

10. Nolan, pp. 45-46.

11. Nolan, p. 56.

12. *Concilia Provincialia, Baltimori (1829-1840)* (Baltimore: John Murphy, 1842), p. 78.

13. Nolan, p. 158.

14. Nolan, p. 310.

15. Nolan, pp. 416-420.

16. Nolan, p. 410.

17. Nolan, p. 489.

18. Nolan, p. 410.

19. Nolan, p. 417.

20. Nolan, p. 239.

21. Nolan, p. 480.

22. Nolan, p. 219.

23. Nolan, p. 609. See also an early statement in the 1952 letter which points to the concern that "the teachings of Jesus Christ, . . . will bless and sanctify our country." No specific teachings were indicated, however. See p. 459.

24. Nolan, p. 290.

25. Nolan, p. 609. Pertinent here is a remark found in the minutes of the bishops' meeting of 1961. In the context of a floor discussion on confirmation the point was made that "religious instruction is not to stop at any age." ("Minutes, 1961," in *Minutes of the Annual Meetings of the Bishops of the United States, 1955-1962*, p. 45.)

26. Nolan, p. 688.

27. Nolan, p. 718; *The Program of Priestly Formation* (Washington, DC: National Conference of Catholic Bishops, 1971), pp. 20, 120–121.

28. Nolan, p. 291.

29. Nolan, pp. 463–464.

30. Nolan, p. 466.

31. Further exhortations to morality and moral education may be found in Nolan, pp. 10, 221, 376, 377, 419, 453, 456, 457, 463, 480, 498, 501, 513, 537, 585, 683, 684; *Program of Priestly Formation*, p. 7 (65, 66, 67); *To Teach as Jesus Did,* p. 3 (no. 111); *Basic Teachings,* pp. 18–20 (nos. 17–19).

32. Nolan, p. 56.

33. Nolan, p. 143.

34. Nolan, pp. 165; 423.

35. Nolan, pp. 112; 648.

36. No pastorals appeared between the letter following the Third Plenary Council, 1884, and that of the "Bishops Program of Social Reconstruction" promulgated 12 February 1919. "No single reason explains this long interval," Nolan wrote. The archbishops had met annually from 1890 on, but because they considered these meetings to have no canonical status, they issued no pastorals. Impelled by the need to bring order out of the prevailing chaos caused by World War I, they sanctioned the publication of their plans for reconstruction in 1919. Thereafter, too, they decided to meet annually. The first of these renewed gatherings was held in September 1919. Subsequent to that meeting, the second pastoral of that year, the long "Pastoral Letter, 1919" appeared. See Nolan, pp. 189–190, 212–261.

37. Nolan, p. 593.

38. Nolan, pp. 633–634.

39. *Basic Teachings,* p. 1.

40. No copy of this catechism is known to the present writer. John D. Gilmary Shea maintained that the "Carroll Catechism" was in direct line with catechisms long used in England, which, in turn, were offshoots from the Bellarmine stock. Cf. John Gilmary Shea, *The Catholic Church in the United States,* III (New York: John G. Shea, 1890), pp. 95–96.

41. *A Short Catechism* (Baltimore: Fielding Lucas, Jr., n.d.). This small volume contains sixty-three pages and bears the following sanction on the title page: "Published with the Approbation of the Most Rev. Archbishop Maréchal."

42. *Fleury's Short Historical Catechism Revised by the Rt. Rev. Bishop Cheverus* (Baltimore: Lucas Brothers, n.d.). Raymond O'Brien wrote that this work was completed and approved in 1810, the year it appeared. Héloise Songe maintained that it came out in 1813. See Raymond O'Brien, "History of Our English Catechism," *Ecclesiastical Review* 91 (1934): 590. Alice Héloise Songe, "Bibliographical Survey of Catholic Textbooks Published in the United States from 1764 through 1865" (M.A. thesis, Catholic University of America, 1956), p. 42.

43. *Diary of Rt. Rev. John England, First Bishop of Charleston,* in the Charleston Diocesan Archives, Charleston, South Carolina. No copy of the original catechism was available to the present writer. However, a revised edition, dated 1873, is in the possession of the Generalate and Motherhouse of the Sisters of Charity of Our Lady of Mercy in Charleston. The present writer possesses a duplicated copy of that 1873 work. A selection from the original

catechism may be found in Sebastian G. Messmer's *The Works of the Rt. Rev. John England,* vol. 4 (Cleveland: Arthur H. Clark Co., 1908), p. 159. *of Bardstown* (Bardstown, KY: N. Wickliffe and S. Bailey, 1825). The Catholic University Library has two copies of this original manual.

46. Augustin Verot, *Catechism of Christian Doctrine* (Baltimore: Murphy, 1869). The writer possesses one of the original Verot manuals.

47. A textual comparison made by the present author revealed that of the 421 questions with answers in the original Baltimore manual, 239 were identical to those in David's catechism and 180 to those in Verot's. See Mary Charles Bryce, *The Influence of the Catechism of the Third Plenary Council of Baltimore on Widely Used Elementary Religion Text Books from Its Composition in 1885 to Its 1941 Revision* (Ann Arbor: University Microfilms, 1970), p. 113.

48. *Christian Doctrine,* prescribed by Pope Pius X, trans. by Thomas Sebastian Byrne (New York: F. Pustet, 1906).

49. Peter C. Yorke, *Text-Books of Religion* (San Francisco: Text Book Publishing Co., 1900).

50. Edward A. Fitzpatrick, ed., *Highway to Heaven* series (Milwaukee: Bruce, 1931).

51. Baltimore Archdiocesan Archives 94-B-1; 94-S-3; 100-D-4.

52. *Catechismus Catholicus* (Rome: Typis polyglottis Vaticanis, 1931). See Pietro Cardinal Gasparri, *The Catholic Catechism,* trans. Hugh Pope (New York: P. J. Kenedy & Sons, 1932). Gasparri was better known as the principal figure in the codification of Canon Law under Benedict XV.

53. "Minutes, 1931," in *Minutes of the Annual Meetings of the Bishops of the United States, 1919–1935,* pp. 22–23.

54. "Minutes, 1936," in *Minutes of the Annual Meetings . . . 1936–1946,* p. 29.

55. "Minutes, 1939," p. 22. For a fuller treatment of the revision of the Baltimore Catechism see Francis J. Connell, "Catechism Revision," in *Confraternity Comes of Age* (Paterson, NJ: Confraternity Publications, 1956), pp. 188–199.

56. "Minutes, 1957," in *Minutes of the Annual Meetings . . . 1955–1962,* p. 38.

57. "Minutes, 1956," Ibid., p. 48.

58. "Minutes, 1964," in *Minutes of the Annual Meetings . . . 1963–1965,* p. 83.

59. Joseph B. Collins, "Some Guidelines for a New American Catechism," in *Catechetics for the Future,* ed. Alois Müller (New York: Herder and Herder, 1970), p. 104.

60. "Decree on the Bishops' Pastoral Office in the Church," no. 44.

The drive for uniformity is still with us in a time of dizzying pluralism. Michael Donnellan's incisive summary of his doctoral research into a hundred-year quest for global uniformity in catechetical matters delineates some important issues to be considered in dealing with catechesis for particular cultures. His essay is also especially valuable for providing background needed to understand the way Vatican Council II dealt with catechetical matters and how the council's decisions led to the General Catechetical Directory. *On this last matter, this essay complements the one following, dealing with the genesis of the* General Catechetical Directory.

READING 17

Bishops and Uniformity in Religious Education: Vatican I to Vatican II

MICHAEL DONNELLAN

POPE JOHN XXIII once described the catechism as "the constant preoccupation of the Church," and he quoted approvingly, to that effect, from the almost forgotten decree of the First Vatican Council on the catechism.[1] That decree assumes fresh significance when contrasted with the *General Catechetical Directory* published a century later. These two documents represent the parameters of the uniform mold that stamped Catholic religious education during the past one hundred years. Where the 1870 decree opened the door to an official policy of uniformity, the 1971 directory officially endorsed a policy of cultural diversity.[2]

Both documents also tell something about the relationship between the episcopate and catechesis, a topic that so far has attracted little commentary in theological journals.[3] In an attempt to throw some

Reprinted from *The Living Light* 10 (1973), pp. 237–248. © 1973 National Conference of Catholic Bishops. Used by permission.

light on that relationship, three factors must be considered: first, the nature of the catechism; second, the interaction between bishop and catechism; and third, the movement for a uniform catechism launched at Vatican Council I and its undoing at Vatican II.

Nature of the Catechism

The demise of the catechism must surely be a major landmark of change within Roman Catholicism, change that was ushered in by the Second Vatican Council. For almost four centuries it had been the exclusive and universal instrument of religious education to such an extent that the participants at Vatican II, bishops and experts, were themselves the products of a catechism education. By shaping the intelligibility of the Christian message for so many Catholics for so long a time, the catechism ultimately was better known than the Bible and more influential than any official Church document.[4] The durability of the catechism was symbolic of the Church's own self-image as an unchanging society. While there was a wide diversity of catechisms there was but a single literary genre embracing all of them, the main characteristics of which were: (1) its kerygmatic function, (2) systematic intent, (3) apologetic style, (4) didactic framework, and (5) linguistic rigidity.

1) The function of the catechism was to articulate Christian belief in propositional statements. These statements represented a particular understanding of the *kerygma* or core expression of the Gospel. The catechism was one of several instructional models that evolved over the centuries to prepare people for baptism and provide an elementary understanding of the Church's teaching for those already baptized. The catechumenate was an earlier model welding biblical typology and liturgical celebration into an intensive learning experience for small communities. Centuries later the catechism took over as the medium of mass instruction. Since its appearance coincided with the development of printing, teaching the Christian message inevitably became oriented toward the printed text.

2) The authors of catechisms attempted to draw up as systematic an explanation of Christian belief as possible, which summarized the whole of Catholic teaching. Although the authors were systematic in presentation, they did not differentiate the hierarchy of truths. Equal stress, therefore, was frequently given to dogma, discipline, and theological opinion in the learning process.

3) Since the catechism was born amid the polemics of the Reformation, its style was heavily apologetic, emphasizing a defense of con-

tested teaching. This apologetic temper was sustained down the years, first by controversy during the Enlightenment period, then by the unfortunate scare mentality that prevailed during the Modernist crisis.

4) The catechism was designed around the question and answer format, which was suitable for a time of general illiteracy. This didactic framework of the book was identical throughout the Church, with some few exceptions. The material covered, somewhat uniformly, four areas: creed, code, cult, and church. With the growth of universal education, religion became part of the regular school curriculum, and more detailed catechisms proliferated.

5) The formulation of questions and answers remained largely unchanged over the centuries. A majority of catechisms can be traced to the same parent stock of the counter-Reformation period. Phraseology was often identical or varied little from one book to the next. Updating the catechism, especially after Vatican I, usually meant little more than altering the number of formulas to be memorized.

Bishop and Catechism

As catechisms became entrenched on the pastoral scene, there was a corresponding involvement on the part of bishops, a number of whom wrote manuals of their own. It would be a mistake, however, to anchor the role of the bishop in religious education to the arrival of printed religion texts. When the catechumenate was in its heyday the most prominent leaders in catechesis were bishops, such as Cyril of Jerusalem, Ambrose of Milan, and Augustine of Hippo.[5] Even minimal acquaintance with the writings of this early period suggests that the success of the catechumenate was due primarily to the bishop's personal involvement. According to the Fathers, the duties of a bishop included the ministry of catechesis, which was essential for the building up of the Church.

No bleaker period marks the history of religious education than that which unfolded after the decline of the catechumenate in the sixth century. From then on one would be hard put to pinpoint bishops of any stature in the teaching of religion until the Tridentine reform some ten centuries later. During that long interim it was the theologians and the universities that filled the vacuum and provided the leadership in catechetical renewal.[6] John Gerson, for example, chancellor of the University of Paris in the fifteenth century, typifies that trend combining both the theory and practice of religious instruction to a unique degree. Not surprisingly, therefore, when the Council of Trent launched its *aggiornamento*, it was the theologians who became the catechism makers, with one notable exception, the archbishop of Milan, Charles Borromeo.

In the years after Trent, bishops became prominent once again in catechesis to the point that in some dioceses the appointment of a new bishop signaled the compilation of a new catechism. When the next ecumenical council, Vatican I, was convened, the catechism was placed on the agenda at the suggestion of a Spanish archbishop, Juan Ignacio Moreno of Valladolid.[7] As matters turned out, the only pastoral concern aired and voted on by the bishops at the council was that of the catechism. Because the issue of infallibility loomed so large at Vatican I, the pastoral issue has received short shrift from both theologians and historians writing about the council.

Catechism at Vatican I

To the bishops in 1870, there was much at stake in the brief *schema* on the catechism which they debated at length. This *schema* entitled "The Compilation and Adoption of a Single Short Catechism for the Universal Church" came up for discussion in February that year. Ostensibly the document dealt with eliminating the troublesome multiplicity of elementary catechisms and substituting a single religion text which was to be obligatory for the entire Church. From the first day of debate, however, polarization of opinion set in, as the underlying issue surfaced of bishops' rights vis-à-vis Roman centralization.[8]

Bishops opposing the proposal for a uniform catechism took issue with the obligatory clause. Archbishop Felix Dupanloup of Orleans, France, for example, who spoke from a wide background in religious education, saw the impracticality and inadequacy of imposing a single religion text in a multicultural society.[9] (He himself had written several major works on the teaching of religion.) Dupanloup, among others, also underscored the threat such a venture posed to the right of bishops to edit their own catechisms. Contrary to original planning, the issue became a divisive one, and as debate wore on, the problem centered more on the relationship of bishops to the Holy See than on the improvement of religious education. Thus, another opponent of the proposal, Archbishop Haynald of Hungary, aroused the assembly to cries of indignation when he declared: "To catechize the people is one of the great duties and rights of a bishop; if a catechism is dictated to us, our sermons will be dictated next."[10]

Six days of a debate without humor but not without rancor ended

in a stalemate, and the *schema* was sent back for revision. After reviewing the forty-one speeches that had been made and examining many
written amendments, the commission in charge of the project rewrote
the *schema* but made only minor alterations. This precipitated two further days of speeches and still another twenty amendments before a
vote on the decree was taken on 4 May 1870. When the results were
tallied, they read: 491 in favor, 56 against, and 44 qualified approval
(*placet juxta modum*).[11] While the mood of the council was definitely
for uniformity, nonetheless, the vote showed that one fifth of the fathers
remained either opposed or dissatisfied with the project.

In retrospect, the involvement of the worldwide assembly of
bishops in 1870 with the issue of religious education was in itself a
unique event. The debate demonstrated not merely that catechesis was
really their precinct, but it also provided several bishops with the only
forum during the entire council to raise urgent pastoral problems. Unfortunately, the search for consensus protracted the debate, which from
the start was hampered by faulty parliamentary procedures, and the
real pastoral problems became obscured. "A single faith, a single
catechism" had been the slogan of those advocating reform, but that
was a facile solution to the complex problems disturbing so many
bishops. A majority, nonetheless, motivated by different pressures,
coalesced in favor of uniformity. Some, equating unity with uniformity, believed that rejection of the proposal would weaken the already
threatened unity of the Church. Besides, such an action could be interpreted as disrespectful to Pope Pius IX, in whose name the decree was
presented. Others, faced with profound social changes taking place all
around, especially the problems created by massive migration, clung
to uniformity of instruction as a panacea. Fear of state influence and
regulation of religious education in some dioceses was another pressure,
and there was already some ominous precedent for this. Another factor, not to be discounted, was the clash of different theological approaches with the catechism as the battleground, a pattern that was
to recur after Vatican II. Overshadowing all of these concerns was the
question whether the council should or should not define papal infallibility, and divided opinion on this had repercussions on all other issues.
Ultimately, the council produced a groundswell in favor of cen-
tralism in the Church, but only a minority of bishops were far-seeing
and forceful enough to caution against it. Their position was vindicated
a century later when the movement for collegiality was launched at
Vatican II. Their viewpoint was also reflected in the *General
Catechetical Directory* of 1971 which explicitly recognizes pluralism as
an accepted dimension of human life today. Bishops who a hundred

years earlier had voiced their criticism of an imposed uniformity did so out of an awareness that cultural diversity was already a fact of life in the nineteenth century. Men like Dupanloup, who had shown personal leadership in religious education, were perceptive enough to note that diversity in the long run enriches Christian unity.

Before its final adjournment, Vatican I held eighty-nine general meetings, and ten of those were given over to the proposal for a single catechism. Were it not for the complete suspension of the council on the outbreak of the Franco-Prussian War, that proposal would have been promulgated in solemn session. Instead, it became part of the unfinished business of Vatican I, business that another generation of canonists would try but fail to complete and still another ecumenical council would be called upon to reconsider.

After Vatican I

Two abortive attempts were made subsequently to implement the controversial decree of Vatican I. The first paralleled the codification of canon law begun under Pius X and completed under Benedict XV. What was envisaged was a master manual, something more radical than the bishops, in 1870, had in mind. Literally, the project called for a codification of all Christian doctrine, a text on which every other catechism was to be modeled, even down to uniformity of wording. A priest from the diocese of Columbus, Ohio, Roderick MacEachen, was given charge of the project.[12] When Rome postponed the idea MacEachen returned to the United States in 1919 and became a lecturer in catechetics at Catholic University. A second attempt was made by Cardinal Peter Gasparri, one of the chief architects of the new code of canon law, when there were grounds for believing that Pius XI might reconvene Vatican I. Gasparri's efforts were thwarted, and he brought out a catechism under his own name in 1930.[13] All of this might be a mere footnote to the history of Vatican I were it not for the fact that the idea of a master manual was revived in 1959 and again in 1967, anticipating the *General Catechetical Directory*.

Perhaps the most far-reaching effects of these attempts at uniformity was that primary responsibility for religious education passed from bishops to bureaucracy. Laws were enacted, new structures were created, documents were issued, guidelines proposed, and, in general, bishops held accountable to Rome for implementing its directives. In one sense the goal of uniformity in the decree of Vatican I was within reach, not as originally intended, but indirectly by means of a centra-

lized organization. The leadership role assumed by Roman Congregations may have been necessitated in the complex changing world of
the twentieth century. On balance, however, the advantages of cen-
tralized control were offset by a diminishing of the episcopal role. It
too became bureaucratized. As Bishop Christopher Butler of
Westminster, England, aptly put it: "The paperwork is fantastic.
Theologically a bishop is not supposed to be a business executive, yet
that is what he has to be."[14] In religious education the bishop's function was all too easily reduced to a canonical rather than catechetical
context. There were some few exceptions of bishops who gave leadership to religious educators. In the United States, Archbishop Edwin
V. O'Hara of Kansas City will long be remembered for his tremendous
zeal in building up the Confraternity of Christian Doctrine. It was the
CCD that eventually became the vehicle through which creative renewal
in catechesis was transplanted from Europe to America. Pope John's
decision to hold another ecumenical council gave that renewal momentum even though the initial suggestions for the council's agenda belie
that fact.

Catechesis at Vatican II

An examination of the preparatory documentation for Vatican II
reveals a somewhat disillusioning welter of suggestions favoring uniformity in catechesis.[15] A few bishops, attuned to the movements for
renewal then already under way in the Church, made recommendations
that showed they had read the signs of the times. Yet twenty-two
specific requests were put forward for a single catechism for the entire
Church, and many other recommendations implicitly favored such a
religion text. To crown it all there was a curial recommendation for
a master text, or codification of basic teachings,[16] which in fact was
a throwback to the MacEachen project of 1918. Nor did the proposals
from the Catholic universities mirror any great sensitivity to updating
Catholic religious education, except for some pastoral observations from
Rome's Gregorian University.

In the light of later developments, perhaps the most insightful
recommendation turned out to be that of Bishop Pierre-Marie Lacointe
of Beauvais in France. He advocated that instead of a universal
catechism, as Vatican I had projected, it would be much more beneficial
to the Church to have what he termed a "Directorium," catechetical
guidelines adapted to different age groups.[17] Viewed against the
prevailing outlook, Lacointe's suggestion makes him appear as one of
the few prophets of the new Jerusalem amid so many prophets of doom.

Lacointe sent his suggestion, as did most other bishops, to the preparatory commission in 1959. Some twelve years later the "Directorium" became a reality.

When the council opened on 11 October 1962, the agenda included a *schema* on "The Care of Souls." One chapter of this document dealt with catechesis, which chapter in turn was a composite of three separate *schemata* drawn up earlier. The much-touted proposal for a uniform catechism was now officially abandoned, and in its stead the new *schema* advocated a set of guidelines or a "directory" to serve as a basis for various national directories. The bishops never got around to discussing this. The topic failed to get out of committee because of the myriad redrafting of council documents. Ultimately, the chapter on catechesis was whittled down to a recommendation in the final document on the Office of Bishops which called for the preparation of a Catechetical Directory (*Christus Dominus*, 44). Not until the first synod of bishops gathered in Rome in 1967 was this recommendation back in the public arena once again.[18]

Vatican II, however, had highlighted the responsibility of bishops in preaching and teaching in several of its major documents. For example, "The Bishop should be first and foremost a herald of the faith, leading new disciples to Christ" (*Ad gentes*, 20).

"In exercising their duty of teaching, they should announce the gospel of Christ to men, a task which is eminent among the chief duties of bishops" (*Christus Dominus*, 12; also *De Ecclesia*, 25).

"It devolves on sacred bishops, *who have the apostolic teaching,* to give the faithful entrusted to them suitable instruction in the right use of the divine books, especially the New Testament and above all the Gospels . . ." (*Dei verbum*, 25).

In preparation for the synod another attempt was made to rehabilitate the hopeless goal of a uniform catechism. A report, drawn up in Rome, advocated a moratorium on new catechisms and compilation of a model text to which all future catechisms should conform.[19] The point was made that, since the Council of Trent had come up with its catechism for pastors and Vatican I with its decree on a single catechism, Vatican II should have generated a similar project. The report, having made a case for the catechism, then proposed that it be executed by the forthcoming synod. This document must be interpreted against the background of the widespread controversy which was then raging over the so-called Dutch Catechism, a new catechetical handbook for adults. Fortunately, Cardinal Jean Villot chose rather to address himself to the question of the directory or guidelines when he spoke to the synod on the topic. This directory, he affirmed, was to be a sign of collegiality and would not usurp the compilation of directories by the various conferences of bishops. Since the project was destined for use by bishops' conferences as they saw fit, the role of the curial Congregation in its composition shifted from that of legislator to counselor.[20] That shift of emphasis closed one chapter in the history of Catholic religious education. Mercifully, the specter of uniformity had been finally exorcized from the landscape of catechetics.

Conclusions

What do we learn about the relationship between bishops and catechesis from a survey of one hundred years spanning the Vatican I decree and the post–Vatican II directory? A recapitulation and comparison of both endeavors can be summarized thus:

Projected Catechism, Vatican I	*Post–Vatican II Directory*
First recommended by a bishop in the preparatory stage	First recommended by a bishop in the preparatory stage
The issue was debated in the council itself	The issue was debated in a council commission
Intended for elementary instruction of children and illiterates	Intended for national bishops' conferences
Uniform and obligatory for the whole Church	A general document addressed to bishops only; advisory, not legislative
Based on existing catechisms, especially that of Robert Bellarmine	Based mainly on Vatican II documents
Initiated by Rome and to be composed by Roman theologians	Initiated by Rome but with collaboration of the bishops
To be written in Latin, with approved translations, but never realized	Published with approved translations from the Latin after four years of preparation

Vatican II, it is claimed, reinterpreted Vatican I on a number of points, and the concern over catechesis exemplifies how the later council did in fact alter the policy of the previous council. Opposition to the decree on uniformity at Vatican I was allied to a legitimate fear that such an undertaking would weaken the rights of individual bishops. Vatican II, in developing the concept of collegiality, enhanced the role of bishops. This development influenced the editing of the subsequent *General Catechetical Directory* so that it was designed in consultation with episcopal conferences, was not imposed but sent to them for approval, and was executed as a service document for their benefit. Three general conclusions arising from this change of official posture are relevant for the future of catechesis.

First, the bishop, not the catechism, is a bond of unity in the Church.[21] That unity will be hampered, if the lesson of the past is any indication, by the imposition of uniformity. There must be room for diversity, a recognition that there is more than one way of preaching the good news, more than one language in which to give thanks. That means developing models of instruction that cater to the diversity of subcultures within the same culture. Bishops must see to it that religious education is brought within reach of all ages and all groups. It is a concern for the entire community not just school children.

Second, the bishop's unifying role in the religious education community suggests that he be bridge-builder where there is polarization. Regrettably, the catechism, after Vatican II, became a battleground once again leading to a loss of vision, a hardening of hearts, and an embarrassment for educators. Unity has been weakened in the course of catechetical controversy, and it will not be restored by enunciating the old simplicities. It will take bishops with foresight, courage, and concern for religious education to build the necessary bridges (*Christus Dominus*, 13).

Third, Vatican II gave birth to new structures capable of maintaining the balance between unity and diversity, something that had befuddled the bishops at Vatican I.[22] These structures enable a new generation of bishops to become more directly involved in religious education. (1) At the international level there is the Synod of Bishops which, as already noted, tackled the project of the catechetical directory at its first meeting in 1967. For its next and fourth meeting in 1974, the synod will take up the topic of evangelization, a topic which touches intimately the broad spectrum of contemporary catechesis. (2) At the national or regional level there is the conference of bishops which is equipped to cope with the religious education needs of its own people better than any legislative action from Rome. Thus, according to the prudential judgment of the Dutch hierarchy who commissioned it, the 1966 Dutch Catechism was an effective tool for postconciliar education of adult Catholics in Holland. (3) At the local level there are diocesan and parish councils which, depending on selection and freedom of action, can make or break religious education programs. Likewise, the availability of full-time and professionally trained personnel can raise the educational level of the local community. When that grassroots organization has episcopal backing, a diocese can generate concern, inventiveness, and competence.[23]

To sum up, then, democratization of the Church after Vatican II set in motion a gradual shift from centralization toward collegiality, from subordination to subsidiarity for the local church, from uniformity to unity as a goal of catechesis. That development had its genesis in Vatican I, and all credit to the bishops who made it possible. The dilemma of Vatican I, however, concerning the rights and responsibilities of bishops in religious education has not been fully resolved. Catechisms, directories, and programs produced by conferences of bishops still must get prior review and approval from Rome, according to the *General Catechetical Directory* (no. 134). If individual bishops, prior to Vatican I, were free to edit their catechisms without such prior approval, then an entire national conference of bishops should be no less free in a similar endeavor today. Although the 1971 directory brought to an end a pointless search for uniformity, it can be faulted for not imbibing more fully the spirit of collegiality.

One hopes it will not take as long to clarify this aspect of the relationship between bishops and catechesis as it did to remedy the shortcomings of Vatican I on this very issue.

NOTES

1. In an address given in St. Peter's Basilica, Rome, 22 February 1962. See *Acta Apostolicae Sedis* 54 (1962): 170–171.

2. A detailed bibliography on the issues discussed here is given in the present writer's doctoral study, *A Rationale for a Universal Catechism, Vatican I to Vatican II* (Ann Arbor: Microfilms, 1972).

3. One of the few significant contributions on this topic is Archbishop Denis Hurley, "The Bishop's Role in the Catechetical Renewal," in *Teaching All Nations,* ed. Johannes Hofinger (New York: Herder and Herder, 1961), pp. 341–356. Mention should be made also of the contribution by a member of the Canadian hierarchy to catechetical literature: Bishop Gerald Emmet Carter, *Modern Challenge to Religious Education* (New York: Sadlier, 1961).

4. Thus a former apostolic delegate to the United States, Archbishop (later Cardinal) Cicognani, summed up the esteem that the catechism evoked when he said, "No human book can compare with the catechism in certitude or in power. It transforms tender children into sure theologians. . . . The catechism is a fortress against atheism and a bulwark for the freedom and the life of man." Sermon to the delegates at the CCD Congress in Chicago, 1951. See *The Confraternity Comes of Age* (Paterson, NJ: Confraternity Publications, 1956).

5. Cf. W. Burghardt, "Catechetics in the Early Church," *The Living Light* 1 (1964): 110–118.

6. Cf. J. A. Jungmann, "Religious Education in Late Medieval Times," in *Shaping the Christian Message*, ed. Gerard S. Sloyan (New York: Macmillan, 1958), pp. 38–62.

7. [J. D. Mansi, *Sacrorum conciliorum nova et amplissima collectio;* hereafter cited as Mansi.] See Mansi, vol. 49:160, 219.

8. Published documentation of the Vatican I debate can be found in the Mansi collection, vols. 49–51 (Paris: 1923–1927), although some material is still not available outside of the Vatican archives.

9. Mansi, vol. 50:718–724.

10. Mansi, vol. 50:849.

11. Mansi, vol. 51:501–512.

12. This is confirmed from documentation in the archives of the diocese of Columbus, Ohio. See also Roderick MacEachen, "The Unification of Catechetical Instruction," *Ecclesiastical Review* 58 (1918): 249–258.

13. Cardinal Peter Gasparri, *The Catholic Catechism,* trans. Hugh Pope (New York: P. J. Kenedy & Sons, 1932). It was adopted as an official catechism by the bishops of Mexico but met with little success there.

14. See "The Future of the Episcopate," *Herder Correspondence* 5 (1968): 358.

15. The relevant preparatory documents of Vatican II are included in the *Acta et Documenta* (Vatican City Press), esp. series 1, vols. 2–4.

16. Referred to as the *Catechismus Fons,* see *Acta et Documenta* III (1960): 156.

17. *Acta et Documenta,* I, vol. 11, app. 11, 482.

18. For a historical overview of the fate of the *schemata* on catechetics at Vatican II see the introduction to Berard Marthaler's *Catechetics in Context: Notes and Commentary on the General Catechetical Directory* (Huntington, IN: Our Sunday Visitor, 1972), pp. xvi–xxi.

19. A copy of this report, an eighteen-page document in Latin, was made available to the present writer during the course of his research in Rome.

20. The document was published by the Sacred Congregation for the Clergy and the official English translation approved by that Congregation. *General Catechetical Directory* (Washington, DC: United States Catholic Conference, 1971).

21. Cf. Edward Schillebeeckx, *The Unifying Role of the Bishop, Concilium,* vol. 71 (New York: Herder and Herder, 1972).

22. Cf. "The Synod of Bishops," *Herder Correspondence* 6 (1969): 355–384.

23. Two examples of creativeness and professionalism in official diocesan religious education materials are the *Green Bay Plan* (Curriculum Plan and Lesson Plans), Diocesan Department of Education, Green Bay, Wisconsin, and the *Programs and Resources* documents from the archdiocese of Baltimore (1971).

As Michael Donnellan made clear in the previous essay, the fuller scenario of Vatican Council II's treatment of catechetical matters involves issues that had been lingering in the wings for many decades before they came to center stage for collegial examination. Fully cognizant of Donnellan's study and with the skill of the trained historian, Berard Marthaler presents his research on the precise sequence of events at Vatican II which led to the publication in 1971 of the General Catechetical Directory. *In an almost decisive way, concern for uniformity eventually came to be seen as a lesser value when compared with concern for cultural diversity and theological pluralism.*

Marthaler's essay highlights catechesis as a key concern of the bishops in their pastoral role. Sometimes in the past the role of the bishop vis-à-vis catechesis has been caricatured as one of monitoring doctrinal uniformity and purity. At Vatican II and in the General Catechetical Directory, *however, that role is set out as a key aspect of the "care of souls," a much broader matter with a more person-centered focus.*

Marthaler also shows how there emerged from the slow progress of insight at Vatican II and in the GCD *a conviction that catechetical activity has its own special character "shaped by factors other than the inner logic of a doctrinal synthesis."*

Finally, readers have in this essay a fine example of a "hermeneutics of documents" in practice. Marthaler painstakingly uncovers the step-by-step processes that led to a document easily misunderstood when not seen in its origins and slow evolution. This essay could be combined with Avery Dulles' "The Hermeneutics of Dogmatic Statements" (The Survival of Dogma) *as a way of showing students of catechesis the need for historical background as a first step to full understanding of official documents.*

READING 18

The Genesis and Genius of the *General Catechetical Directory*

BERARD MARTHALER

THE *Directorium Catechisticum Generale* published in Rome in the summer of 1971 is the brainchild of the late bishop of Beauvais,

Reprinted from *Catechetics in Context,* by Berard Marthaler, pp. xvi–xxx. © 1973 by Our Sunday Visitor, Inc., Huntington, Indiana. All rights reserved.

the Most Rev. Pierre-Marie Lacointe. Though he lived to see his proposal adopted by the Second Vatican Council, he died in 1965 before it began to take shape. The directory developed gradually through three stages:

I. The initial stage corresponds to the period of the "antepreparatory" and preparatory phases of Vatican II when the idea of a directory was first broached.

II. The second stage coincides with the council itself (October 1962 – December 1965). It was the time during which the proposal was refined and approved.

III. The final stage, when the project was implemented, took place in the postconciliar period. The genesis of the document is worth careful study because it goes a long way to explain the genius of the directory, that is, its shape and purpose.

I

Of all the bishops, religious superiors, and representatives of Catholic universities who sent in proposals for the agenda of Vatican II, only Bishop Lacointe formally recommended a directory. He correctly anticipated that others would urge the resumption of a project left unfinished at the end of the First Vatican Council, namely, the redaction of a universal catechism for children.[1] The bishop of Beauvais argued that a single catechism for the whole Church was not possible or, at least, not proper: Literal uniformity is inconceivable. Much better and more useful in his opinion would be directives for a plurality of catecheses for different classes of children and adults.[2]

In the period 1961–62, three preparatory commissions drafted schemas treating some aspects of catechesis.[3] Though there were commission members who continued to favor a universal catechism, the idea of a directory began to take hold.

The Preparatory Commission for the Eastern Churches drafted a series of schemas, one of which was "The Catechism and Catechetical Education." It argued that the growing diversity in the world makes it ever more necessary to ensure uniform teaching and learning about Christian doctrine. The commission urged a kind of "compendium" which it described as a single catechism for the universal Church. As might be expected the Eastern churches recommended that the catechism, backed by the authority of an ecumenical council, give due respect to the Oriental rites. The schema is very brief, filling about two and a half printed pages.[4]

Meanwhile, the preparatory commission *de disciplina cleri et populi*

Christiani received a mandate from the Central Preparatory Commission — that is, the steering committee — (1) to draw up plans for a new catechism containing the principal elements of the sacred liturgy and church history, as well as social doctrine, and (2) to give a new impetus to catechesis for adults.[5] In response, the commission *de disciplina* drafted a schema consisting of a preamble and three chapters: I, *De catechismo et de libris catechistis* ("The Catechism and Catechetical Books"); II, *De institutionis catecheticae organizatione* ("The Organization of Catechetical Education"); III, *De methodo institutionis catecheticae trahendae* ("The Method to Be Used in Catechetical Education"). The printed text fills fourteen pages.[6]

In the course of its work the commission adopted the position that a single catechism for the universal Church was not feasible *(non expedire)* because conditions differ greatly from country to country and individual to individual. On the other hand, it opposed a proliferation of catechisms which would permit each diocese to have its own. Instead, it proposed a common directory for the universal Church. The directory would establish "rules and general norms, which would have to be observed in compiling individual catechisms." It would be concerned with the goals of catechesis, the principal tenets of doctrine, and the wording of formulas. It would leave the application of the general norms in specific situations to the episcopal conferences.[7]

The third group to make a report on catechesis was the Preparatory Commission for the Sacraments which drafted an eight-page schema, "Preparation for Marriage." The commission pointed out that the Church insists on catechetical instruction for an adult receiving baptism or confirmation. *A pari*, it argues there should be a catechesis for Christians planning marriage; it should include an examination about Christian doctrine.[8]

Since three commissions had treated different aspects of catechesis, the central commission which coordinated the work of all the committees remanded the schemas to the subcommission which dealt with "mixed matters." The subcommission decided in the summer of 1962 to incorporate everything on catechetics in a new schema *De cura animarum* ("The Care of Souls"). The first part of the new schema dealt with the pastoral office of bishops; the other part took up specific issues of pastoral care. The earlier schema drawn up by the preparatory commission *de disciplina cleri et populi Christiani* was reworked and incorporated into this second part as chapter 1. Besides the introduction, it consisted of twenty-seven articles (135–161) and almost three pages of notes. Incorporated in the text proper is a recommendation for prenuptial instruction (art. 157) and, in the notes, an animadversion about the Oriental rites (n. 4).[9]

This schema too was explicit in its preference for a directory over a universal catechism.[10] In terms of the development of the *General Catechetical Directory*, it represents an advance over the previous texts in two important ways: First, this version of *De cura animarum* introduces the notion that episcopal conferences should produce their own catechetical directories (art. 161) in addition to the "common catechetical directory" for the whole church (art. 136); second, it furnishes in a footnote the first description of what a catechetical directory should include:

> (1) There shall be a presentation of the formulas of the fundamental truths of faith and moral teaching as well as those prayer formulas which it is proper for all to memorize in their entirety. (2) There shall be determined the norms to be observed in compiling individual catechisms – (norms) pertaining to the goal to be pursued in catechesis and the principal articles of doctrine that are to be expounded. (3) There shall be related for the faithful of the Latin rite – and vice versa for the faithful of the Oriental rites – respective notions concerning the hierarchy, liturgy, ecclesiastical traditions of each of the Oriental rites so that mutual knowledge of East and West be better advanced and the unity of the Church shine forth in variety, and its variety in unity.[11]

II

The Second Vatican Council formally convened on 11 October 1962, but during and between sessions the work of the commissions continued, perhaps even more intensely than before. The schema *De cura animarum* was reworked and shortened. The 1963 version consisted of sixty articles distributed in five chapters and seven appendices. The fifth chapter dealt with catechesis.[12]

Chapter five reduced the general considerations on catechesis to eight articles (53–60), the last of which prescribed a directory "which would treat the fundamental principles of catechesis and formation of the Christian people, the organization of catechetical education and the production of appropriate texts." A footnote says, "The schema of this directory is added in an appendix" – the important "Appendix Seven."[13]

Much of the original schema prepared by the commission *de disciplina cleri* survived successive editing and rewriting. It is recognizable as the chief source for the thirty-nine articles of Appendix Seven. The appendix was proposed as the model for the projected directory. Article 17 repeats the injunction that "in each Episcopal Conference a directory for catechesis be produced according to the norms contained in this common directory." The outline of the common directory which appeared in a footnote in the previous redaction is now incorporated into the body of the text (art. 18) and made applicable to the particular directories as well. Furthermore, an important change is introduced into the first sentence:

> a) There shall be a presentation of the formulas of the fundamental truths of faith and moral teaching *in the same or almost the same words used to express them over the centuries.* . . . [14]

A pair of footnotes explains precisely what is intended. Formulas of this kind refer to:

> a) The principal mysteries of faith, namely: (1) the unity and trinity of God, (2) the incarnation, passion, death, and resurrection of our Lord Jesus Christ. Likewise to the creation and origin and also the end of man; revelation; the church; sanctifying grace; the seven Sacraments; Mary, the Virgin Mother of God. The formulas ought to be retained intact in compiling catechisms even though they may accommodate the explanation of the formulas to the particular disposition of the persons to whom they are directed.
> b) The decalogue and the precepts of the Church; the seven corporal works of mercy and the seven spiritual works of mercy; the theological and cardinal virtues; the seven gifts of the Holy Spirit; the seven capital sins. [15]

Another note specifies the prayers to be committed to memory:

> The Sign of the Cross. The Our Father, that is, the Lord's Prayer. The Hail Mary, that is, the Angelic Salutation. The Creed, that is, the Symbolum of the Apostles. Salve Regina. Confiteor. The Angelus. Acts of faith, hope, charity, and sorrow or contrition. [16]

Repeating the caution against a proliferation of catechisms (art. 21), the appendix adds:

> Bishops in their national conferences shall see to it that, according to the norms enunciated in their own catechetical directory, a single or common catechism be produced for the whole country or at least for one or another region of the country if the special circumstances of places and persons require it (art. 22).

Meanwhile, another schema, "The Bishops and Diocesan Government," came up for discussion at the second session of the council in November 1963.[17] After a debate highlighted by dramatic encounters, this schema was sent back to committee. In the spring of 1964, an entirely new schema came to life, "The Pastoral Office of Bishops," which in fact resulted from mating the schema on bishops and diocesan governments with the schema on the care of souls. During the course of the year, it was amended and modified, and the main lines of the decree *Christus Dominus* were set.[18] Article 44 of the decree, something of a catchall, presented a general mandate prescribing the revision of the Code of Canon Law, general directories for pastoral care, and a general directory treating "the catechetical education of the Christian people, and should deal with fundamental principles of such education, its organization, and the composition of books on the subject."[19] A footnote stated that, in compiling these directories, the guidelines (*directoria*) in Appendix Seven of the earlier draft on pastoral care must be kept uppermost in mind.[20]

The definitive text of *Christus Dominus*, promulgated on 28 October 1965, retains the *mandatum generale* in article 44 unchanged but deletes the footnote reference to Appendix Seven. The only mention of what had gone before is in the text itself: "In the preparation of these directories, too, special attention is to be given to the views which have been expressed by individual commissions and Fathers of the Council."

III

After the council, it fell to the Sacred Congregation for the Clergy to implement the mandate of the decree on the pastoral office of bishops in the Church. Archbishop Pietro Palazzini, the secretary of the Congregation, has published a detailed account of the directory's postconciliar history based on archival material.[21] Using the different drafts as benchmarks, we can trace the final stage in the genesis of the directory through three phases of unequal length.

From June 1966 to August 1967, the work consisted largely in setting up working committees and the development of a design for the directory. In the preliminary phase the project was carried forward by specialists residing in Rome, experts from the universities and other ecclesiastical faculties, and the catechetical arm of the Sacred Congregation for the Clergy. They drew up a rough draft of the directory. Meanwhile, a commission of theologians working from February through May 1967 outlined points for the contents of catechesis.

The second phase began with the report of Cardinal Villot, then prefect of the Congregation, to the synod of bishops in October 1967. This is the period of broad consultation with the episcopal conferences and internationally recognized experts. Villot asked that each episcopal conference, sometime before Easter 1968, send in "a written memorandum of what it feels the *General Catechetical Directory* should include, and especially as it touches upon the matter or content of catechesis."[22]

After the synod, in January 1968, Cardinal Villot sent the presidents of the episcopal conferences a list of twelve questions. He asked that each conference respond "giving particular consideration to problems of greater importance and also adding others which seem to you to be timely." The main thrust of the directory can already be seen in the twelve issues raised by the Sacred Congregation for the Clergy:

1) Function and importance of catechesis.

2) What fundamental principles relating to the nature and purpose of catechesis should be known?

3) What is the base for the close connection of catechesis with proclaiming the Gospel, with pastoral liturgy, and with the total life of the Church?

4) What must be said of the matter of catechesis and of the inner unity which should exist between the doctrine to be taught and the life of faith and charity which must be nourished (general principles)?

5) What particular events and what tests in salvation history might be considered essential?

6) What about the various kinds of catechesis and methods more closely adapted to modern conditions and also the need of continued investigation?

7) Consider those who have the duty to catechize and also those who engage in its promotion and supervision, without omitting the responsibility of the entire ecclesial community.

8) How can preparation that is spiritual, doctrinal, and practical be carried out for those who perform the work of catechists?

9) As for those who are to be catechized—what about their psychological and sociological situation in today's conditions?

10) The especial importance of Christian education for adults.

11) (What would be) the general outline of the structural organization for catechetical instruction?

12) A carefully worked out list of books pertaining to catechetics.

The list was not intended to be exhaustive, for a postscript was added: "Everything of whatsoever kind besides the above that seems to be useful and timely can be of use in preparing the General Directory." Also important for an understanding of the sources of the directory is a statement in Cardinal Villot's letter: "Investigations, studies, as well as the outlines of already published directories can be of great service in making up the General Directory."[23]

In May 1968, an international commission of experts assembled in Rome to plan the directory on the basis of suggestions and recommendations sent in by the episcopal conferences in response to the twelve questions. They were: Bishop Anthyme Bayala of Upper Volta (Africa); Bishop Benitez of Villarrica, Paraguay; Canon Joseph Bournique, Paris; Rt. Rev. Msgr. Aldo Del Monte, Italy; Rev. Robert Gaudet, Canada; Rev. Ladislas Czonka, Hungary; Rt. Rev. Msgr. Russell Neighbor, United States; Rev. Klemens Tilmann, Germany; and Rev. A. Zenner, Germany. Each member of the commission was given a specific assignment.[24] Their work was submitted to a plenary meeting of the Sacred Congregation for the Clergy in October 1968. Though the Congregation directed some revisions, it approved the criteria and the schema in general. Another commission took up the task of reworking the text.

In April 1969, this tentative draft was forwarded to the episcopal conferences for their reactions to the directory as a whole and to each of its parts. Though the overwhelming majority of the conferences — twenty-three of twenty-seven responding — were on the whole favorable,[25] their recommendations led to extensive changes in some sections. The modified draft was submitted to a special theological commission (January to June 1970).

At this point, the text was sent for review to the Sacred Congregation for the Doctrine of Faith which subsequently (November) suggested a "mixed commission" to polish (*perfezionare*) the text of the directory in conformity with the observations made by the consultors and cardinals of the dicastery. The mixed commission — a "joint committee" of six, three representatives of the Sacred Congregation for the Doctrine of Faith and three of the Sacred Congregation for the Clergy — carried the work into 1971.

It was during this last phase that the question of an appendix to the directory was first broached. After the second consultation with the episcopal conferences in 1968, an addendum *de puerorum confessione et communione* had been drawn up by a special commission. In June 1970, it was sent to the conferences for their views. Subsequently, the text of the addendum was reworked on the basis of the replies sent in by the conferences of bishops.

The Sacred Congregation for the Doctrine of Faith approved the final text of the directory on 24 February 1971. In March, the Secretariat of State authorized publication dated Easter Sunday, 11 April 1971. Two months later when printed copies were available, Cardinal Wright, prefect of the Sacred Congregation for the Clergy, introduced the *General Catechetical Directory* to the public at a news conference on 17 June.[26]

The published text of the *General Catechetical Directory*, when compared with the draft circulated among the episcopal conferences in 1969, displays many similarities and some distinctive characteristics.[27] Both are divided into six parts. In the first two parts, the similarities outshine the differences: minor editorial changes in part one and some reordering of paragraphs and additions in chapter 2 of part two, notably the phrase "maturity of faith" in paragraphs 21–30. Part four represents an abridgment and thorough overhaul of chapter 1 of part five in the 1969 version. The statement of principles found in the earlier edition has fallen by the way, and the paragraph on experience (74) is introduced. Except for the concluding paragraphs (96–97), part five in the *GCD* corresponds closely to chapter 3 of part four in the 1969 draft. Besides the addendum, which is new, the most significant changes are found in parts three and six.

The 1969 version of part three had four chapters: (1) "Subject Matter of Catechesis and Its Christocentric Nature," (2) "Essential Elements of the Christian Message for a Full Introduction into the Mystery of Faith," (3) "Anthropological Implications in Catechesis," (4) "The Sources of Catechesis." The first two chapters, written from a strongly christocentric point of view, presented a synthesis of Catholic doctrine. They neatly integrated a catechetical dimension with the synthesis and could easily be read as an archetype for all catechesis. Part three in the published edition has little in common with its predecessor. It states explicitly that the *GCD* does not attempt "to show a suitable way for ordering the truths of faith according to an organic plan in a kind of synthesis which could take just account of their objective hierarchy . . ." (36). This is the task of theology and not catechesis as such.

The distinction between an objective order of importance and "the hierarchy of truths to be observed in catechesis" (43) accounts for much of the change in spirit and style. While the directory acknowledges that some truths have priority over others, it is not possible to deduce from this alone "an order which must be followed in the exposition of content" (46). In other words, catechetical activity is shaped by factors other than the inner logic of a doctrinal synthesis. According to circumstances, "it is right to begin with God and proceed to Christ, or to do the reverse; similarly, it is permissible to begin with man and proceed to God, or to do the reverse; and so on" (ibid.). Thus, the *General Catechetical Directory* does not attempt to draw up a doctrinal synthesis, nor to predetermine the best way to order the contents of catechesis. Given the directory's emphatic insistence on adaptation to each socioeconomic and psychological condition, it is difficult to see how the authors of part three could have taken any other tack.

While part six is not entirely new, it has been substantially altered. The two most noticeable changes concern formation of catechists and the relationship of the episcopal conferences to the Apostolic See. The directory itself symbolizes the move away from the chimera of a universal catechism. It takes another step away from book-centered catechesis by twice stating that the role of catechists is more important than texts, methods, and organization (71, 108). As a result, the directory in its final form goes into some detail about the structures and importance of catechetical formation (108–115).

Though the second change is peripheral (or, at least, extrinsic) to catechesis itself, the relationship of individual bishops and episcopal conferences to the Holy See raises a series of theoretical and practical questions.[28] Vatican II is explicit in stating that bishops have primary responsibility for the ministry of the word, which extends to teaching the faithful and seeing to it that appropriate catechetical training is provided for their collaborators (*Christus Dominus*, 12, 14). Their pastoral activity is carried out in unity with the Roman pontiff (ibid. 13). Certain passages in the *General Catechetical Directory*, however, have evoked a discussion about the competence and prerogatives of the episcopal conferences. The 1969 version of the directory, sent to the conferences for their reactions and recommendations, did not mention that national directories, catechisms, and "programs for preaching the word of God produced by the Conferences of Bishops" be submitted to the Apostolic See for review and approval (cf. 117, 118, 119, 134). (The Sacred Congregation for the Clergy is sensitive to the practical problems that a literal observance of this requirement entails. Is it possible for a central office, no matter how well staffed, to examine in detail – for that is what approval would imply – all the material of these kinds produced in the Catholic world?)

Since the directory is the handiwork of uncounted contributors working alone and in committees, it is impossible to know the sources for all the material that was fed into it. Some are obvious. As expected, the documents of Vatican II are the most frequently cited. Next in prominence are the papal encyclicals and allocutions of Pope Paul VI. The spirit, orientation, and much of the content was also shaped by (or, if not shaped by, at least has a great affinity with) the catechetical directories commissioned by the national hierarchies of France and Italy and by the six International Catechetical Study Weeks held between 1959 and 1968. One is reminded of Cardinal Villot's instruction, quoted above, that "investigations, studies, as well as outlines of already published directories can be of great service in making up the General Directory."

La Directoire de Pastoral Catéchétique for use in the dioceses of France appeared in 1964. It was cited several times in the 1969 version, and its influence appears most direct in part five of the *General Catechetical Directory*, "Catechesis According to Age Levels."[29] The similarity between the *GCD* and the *Documento di base* issued by the Italian hierarchy in 1970 is even greater. Throughout the *GCD*, many phrases echo the Italian work, especially in parts two, three, and five (the *Documento di base* is also dependent on the French directory). The similarities are explainable by the fact that Rt. Rev. Msgr. Aldo Del Monte, a principal architect of the Italian directory, was also a member of the original commission of international experts which designed the *General Catechetical Directory*. Moreover, the Catechetical Office in the Sacred Congregation for the Clergy had access to the working papers drawn up by the Italian team.[30]

Less explicit but not less significant is the influence of the six International Catechetical Study Weeks in shaping the *General Catechetical Directory*. At least four (Bayala, Benitez, Bournique, and Tilmann) of the 1968 committee of experts participated in one or more of these seminars. The first international study week, organized by Johannes Hofinger, was held at Nijmegen (1959). It examined the relationship of the liturgy to catechetical activity. Eichstätt (1960), a landmark in the history of modern catechetics, gave the kerygmatic approach a new impetus, outlined principles for a renewal of catechesis, and called for careful planning. It offered a blueprint for the renewal of catechesis, echoes of which resound throughout the *GCD*. Bangkok (1962) introduced the notion of "pre-evangelization." It talked of "preparing the ground" and "using a language with which men are familiar." The study weeks at Katigondo (1964) and Manila (1967) refined the ideas of the previous conferences and together with them furnish much of the vocabulary found in part two. Their emphasis on evangelization, conversion, faith, salvation history, adaptation, and the "anthropological" approach forms the heart of pastoral catechesis.[31]

Cardinal Villot, then prefect of the Sacred Congregation for the Clergy, attended and twice addressed the International Catechetical Study Week at Medellín (Colombia) in August 1968. The assembly passed a formal resolution asking that "the conclusions reached by the delegates of the International Study Week at Medellín be utilized in discussions and deliberations" leading to the *General Catechetical Directory*. The delegates also drew Cardinal Villot's attention to the need for a pluralistic approach to catechesis.[32] That Medellín is the principal source for part one of the *GCD* is obvious to all who are familiar with the work of that conference. Thus, it was more than a historical curiosity and a matter of courtesy when Canon Bournique, addressing the International Catechetical Congress in Rome, praised "the meetings organized by Father Hofinger." He singled out Eichstätt, Bangkok, Katigondo, Manila, and Medellín, "all of which have played a decisive role." Bournique's words carry weight for he seems to have been involved with the directory from its inception to its completion.[33]

In summary, the history of the *GCD* from the time it was first suggested by the bishop of Beauvais in the late fifties to its publication in 1971 accounts for and highlights several of the main features stressed in the foreword to the directory itself:

1) It grew out of the decrees of Vatican II on the pastoral office of the bishops and is "chiefly intended for bishops, Conferences of Bishops, and in general all who under their leadership and direction have responsibility in the catechetical field."

2) As it now stands, the directory is in large part the product of consultation and collaboration with episcopal conferences around the world. It draws from contemporary studies and the thought of recognized experts, albeit mostly European, in the catechetical field.

3) The intent of the directory is "to provide the basic principles of pastoral theology" and not pedagogical theory. Its stress on pastoral action puts the *GCD* very much in the mainstream of the modern catechetical movement.

4) From the very beginning, the chief concern of many involved with the project was the "contents" of catechesis, including doctrinal and prayer formulas.

5) It is a *directory* presenting guidelines for the production of national and regional directories and indirectly for catechisms and other catechetical materials.

These last two points need emphasis lest there be some misapprehension about the purpose and design of the directory. It is concerned chiefly with the ministry of the word, focusing more on pastoral action than on principles of education. It is an example of a fairly new genre of ecclesiastical writings. The directory represents a studied effort to give an orientation–direction–to catechetical theory and procedures.[34] At the conclusion of the International Catechetical Congress in Rome, 20–25 September 1971, Archbishop James Knox of Melbourne, a member of the Sacred Congregation for the Clergy, read a statement which was subsequently included in the formal conclusions of the congress:

> The Delegates of the Congress are appreciative of the spirit and intention in which the *Directorium Catechisticum Generale* has been published. As Cardinal Wright declared to the press: "The basic purpose of the Directory is to provide an orientation for religious formation, rather than to establish binding rules."

It contains updated orientational guidelines rather than prescriptions. The Directory will serve as a basic document meant to be adapted to local cultural and pastoral situations of each country under the guidance of the local Episcopal Conference in consultation with the Holy See.[35]

If on the one hand, the *GCD* does not have, and was not intended to have, the imperative tone of legislation; on the other, it is not and was not intended to be a new kind of catechism. G. Caprile makes the point that the architects of the directory faced the issue of content squarely and resolved it by excluding any formulas which in some way might have misled readers to take it for a modified version of a universal catechism.[36] One member of the early catechetical subcommittee preparing for Vatican II has recently made public some recommendations he proposed in July 1961. The publication of the *GCD*, he is pleased to note, means acceptance of a basic distinction that he advocated: Catechetical formulas are one thing; a catechism — that is, content and a catechism text for students — is another; something else again is a directory which ought to include all aspects, cultural as well as organizational, of catechesis.[37] While the *General Catechetical Directory* encompasses many socio-cultural and administrative aspects of catechesis, the foreword makes it clear that not all parts "are of the same importance." It is different in scope and purpose from a *catechism*, however the term is understood.

In the interval between the official publication date in April and the actual dissemination of the directory in June 1971, the Latin text was printed and copies sent to the bishops of the world. An Italian translation by the Catechetical Center of the Salesians in Turin is advertised in the same issue of *L'Osservatore Romano* in which Cardinal Wright's press conference is reported. Almost immediately the Sacred Congregation for the Clergy delegated the United States Catholic Conference (USCC) to translate the directory into English. In two months' time, the staff of the National Center for Religious Education — CCD had readied an English translation. Uncorrected galley proofs were available by mid-September both to the USCC delegates to the International Catechetical Congress in Rome and to the Sacred Congregation for the Clergy. At some point, the Congregation had second thoughts about the USCC translation and engaged its own translators. (One can only guess the reason that the Congregation rejected the first translation: errors in the galley sheets? the literary style?) Finally, in early December 1971, the United States Catholic Conference issued the directory with the following rubric on the title page: "This is the only English translation of the *Directorium Catechisticum Generale* approved by the Sacred Congregation for the Clergy." A measure of the interest in the directory in North America is the fact that seventy-five-thousand copies of the authorized English translation were distributed in the first year.

NOTES

1. A doctoral dissertation by Michael T. Donnellan narrates the history of this abortive project, *Rationale for a Universal Catechism, Vatican I to Vatican II* (Ann Arbor: Microfilms, 1972).

A compendium of the suggestions prepared for Vatican II appears in *Acta et documenta Concilio Oecumenico Vaticano II apparendo*, series I, Appendix Voluminis II (*Analyticus conspectus consiliorum et votorum quae ab episcopis et praelatis data sunt:* Pars 2) (Typis Polyglottis Vaticanis, 1960), pp. 480–486.

2. "Potiusquam catechismum universalem edere, utilius ducitur 'Directorium' quoddam parere, in quo sint consilia apta ad diversa genera hominum et puerorum catechizanda." Ibid., p. 482. Shortly before plans for Vatican II were announced, the French hierarchy in 1957 commissioned a *Directoire de la Pastorale Catéchétique* for use in the dioceses of France. Cf. *Documentation catéchistique*, n. 47 (1960), p. 56.

3. V. Carbone, "Gli schemi preparatori del Concilio Ecumenico Vaticano II," *Monitor Ecclesiasticus* 96 (1971): 3–38. This article lists the schemas of all twelve preparatory commissions and secretariats and describes what action, if any, was finally taken on them.

4. *Schema decreti de catechismo et catechetica institutione propositum a Commissione de Ecclesiis Orientalibus* (Typis Polyglottis Vaticanis, 1962), p. 6.

5. *Quaestiones commissionibus praeparatoriis Concilii Oecumenici Vaticani II positae* (Typis Polyglottis Vaticanis, 1960), p. 12.

6. *Schema decreti de catechetica populi Christiani institutione* (Typis Polyglottis Vaticanis, 1962).

7. Ibid., pp. 4, 5.

8. *Schema decreti de praeparatione ad matrimonium* (Typis Polyglottis Vaticanis, 1962), pp. 6–8.

9. *Schema decreti de cura animarum*, in *Schemata constitutionum et decretorum ex quibus argumenta in Concilio disceptanda seligentur*, series III (Typis Polyglottis Vaticanis, 1962), pp. 95–180.

10. Ibid., p. 159, n. 1.

11. Ibid., pp. 159–160, n. 4.

12. *Schema decreti de cura animarum* (Typis Polyglottis Vaticanis, 1963), pp. 113–123.

13. Ibid., p. 36, n. 5.

14. Ibid., p. 117.

15. Ibid., pp. 122–123, n. 6.

16. Ibid., p. 123, n. 7.

17. *Schema decreti de episcopis ac de Dioceseon regimine*, in *Schemata constitutionum et decretorum*, series III, pp. 69–70.

18. *Schema decreti de pastorali episcoporum munere in ecclesia.* Textus emendatus et relationes (Typis Polyglottis Vaticanis, 1964).

19. ". . . in quo agatur de fundamentalibus ejudem institutionis prin-

cipiis et ordinatione deque elaboratione librorum ad rem pertinentium . . ."
(pp. 89-90). My translation is more literal if less literary than that of J. Gallagher
in the standard English version used elsewhere in these pages. Cf. *The
Documents of Vatican II*, ed. W. Abbot, trans. J. Gallagher (New York, 1966),
pp. 428-429.

20. Ibid., p. 91, n. 5.

21. "Percata a S. Congregatione pro Clericis in catechetica," in *Atti del Congresso Catechistico Internazionale* (Rome, 20-25 September 1971) (Rome:
Editrice Studium, 1972), pp. 147-212. The section most germane to the directory is subtitled "Dall'idea di un catechismo unico al Direttorio Catechistico
generale" (pp. 187-212). Monsignor Palazzini read an extract from this last section at the International Catechetical Congress in Rome, 23 September 1971,
which can be found in *International Catechetical Congress: Selected Documentation*, ed. Wm. J. Tobin (Washington, DC: United States Catholic Conference,
1972), pp. 86-90. The English version is an abridgment of the Italian and differs from the latter on some minor points.

22. *Communicatio em.mo card. Iohanus Villot Sacrae Congregationis Con-
cillii Praefectus* (Typis Polyglottis Vaticanis, 1967). At the beginning of 1968
the name of the congregation was changed to "pro Clericis."

23. A typescript copy of Cardinal Villot's letter to Archbishop Dearden,
then president of the National Conference of Catholic Bishops in the United
States, is on file in the National Center of Religious Education – CCD. It is dated
8 January 1968.

The same questions were sent out to the "Young Churches" over the
signature of Cardinal Agagianian, prefect of the Congregation for the Propagation of the Faith. Cf. D. S. Amalorpavadass, in *The Medellin Papers*, eds. J.
Hofinger and T. J. Sheridan (Manila: East Asian Pastoral Institute, 1969), p. 93.

24. A memorandum prepared for his staff by Monsignor Neighbor, director of the National Center of Religious Education – CCD, lists in addition to
the above the names of Rev. Ladislas Czonka of Hungary and Msgr. Sergio
Goretti who represented the Sacred Congregation for the Clergy. Father Gaudet
died before he was able to contribute to the work of the commission.

According to the memorandum, Monsignor Neighbor's assignment was to
"present the four sources of catechesis mentioned in the Vatican Documents,
i.e., Scripture, Tradition, Liturgy and Life in the Church in a unified
way. . . . The Holy See requests each member of the commission to employ
the services of experts in their own countries to assist in the preparation of
this document." The material prepared by the U.S. team of experts appeared
as "The Sources of Catechesis and Their Use," *The Living Light* 6 (Summer
1969): 6-34.

25. Palazzini reports that, of the four conferences which opposed the draft,
three rendered a judgment "assai critico" and one, "del tutto negativo," *Atti del
Congresso*, p. 211, n. 193.

26. Cf. *L'Osservatore Romano*, 18 June 1971.

27. *The General Catechetical Directory: An Outline for Examination by
Bishops' Conferences* (Rome: Sacred Congregation for the Clergy, 1969). The
mimeograph text covers 151 typewritten pages, double-spaced.

28. Cf. G. Duperray, "Le ministere de la parole comme action pastorale,"
Catéchèse, supplement numero 45 (October 1971): 212-216.

29. The text of *Le Directoire de Pastorale Catéchétique à l'usage des
dioceses de France* appears in *Catéchèse* 14 (January 1964): 1-81.

30. The full title of the Italian document is *Il rinnovamento della catechesi: Documento di base* (Rome: Edizioni Pastorali Italiane, 1971). Since it is a foundational statement, it is generally referred to by the more descriptive subtitle. Cf. my article, "The Renewal of Catechesis in Italy," *Religious Education* 65 (September-October 1971): 357–363.

31. Luis Erdozain has surveyed the contributions made by these study weeks in a very useful article, "The Evolution of Catechetics," *Lumen Vitae* 25 (1970): 1–31 [also reprinted in this sourcebook as Reading 8]. He gives a good introductory bibliography.

32. Cf. *Medellin Papers*, p. 209.

33. Cf. *Atti del Congresso*, p. 142; *International Catechetical Congress: Selected Documentation*, p. 78.

34. Religious orders have long had "directories," distinct from their Rule and Constitutions, which describe procedures and practices within the community, e.g., chapter procedures, ascetical practices. They have neither the authority nor the obligatory character of constitutions (cf. *Dictionnaire de Doit Canonique*, 4:1271). Despite the fact that the label was originally suggested by a Frenchman, George Duperray writes: "La dénomination est peut-être mal choisie. Le mot 'Orientations' aurait peut-être mieux convenu et, certainement, moins prêté à équivoque." *Catéchèse*, p. 206, n. (14).

Besides the national directories mentioned above, there are two other modern precedents for the *General Catechetical Directory (GCD)*. Previously, the Sacred Congregation for the Clergy published the *Directorium generale pro Ministro Pastorale quoad "Turismum,"* *Acta Apostolicae Sedis* [hereafter cited as *AAS*] 61 (1969): 361–384. (It was translated into English as *General Directory of the Pastoral of Tourism*.) Like the *GCD* it was authorized by *Christus Dominus*, art. 44, and appeared in an early draft as "Appendix prima" in the 1963 version of *De cura animarum* (cf. note 10 above). The Secretariat for Unity has recently issued a Directory for Ecumenism: *Directorium ad ea quae a Concilio Vaticano Secundo de re oecumenica promulgata sunt exsequenda.* Pars prima, *AAS* 59 (1967): 574–592; Pars altera, *AAS* 62 (1970): 705–724.

35. Cf. *International Catechetical Congress: Selected Documentation*, p. 134. An Italian translation of Archbishop Knox's statement, though not attributed to him, appears among the conclusions of the congress in *Atti del Congresso*, pp. 497–498. An account of Cardinal Wright's remarks to the press appeared in the *National Catholic Register*, 10 October 1971.

When work on the *GCD* was just getting underway, the participants at the Medellin Study Week petitioned Cardinal Villot "that the International Directory when completed be presented to the National Hierarchy of each country *not* as a normative document, but that it be promulgated in such a way that it leaves the national hierarchies free to exercise that flexibility of approach and expression so clearly indicated by the exigencies of this moment in history." *Medellin Papers*, p. 209.

36. Cf. *Civiltà Cattolica* (n. 2906), 17 July 1971, p. 170. Cardinal Wright made much the same point in his news conference, cf. *L'Osservatore Romano*, 18 June 1971.

37. "Sia nel direttorio universale che nel formulario mi sembra che sarebbe utile precisare i termini, per non perpetuare la confusione durata fino ad ora: altro e il 'formulario della catechesi' altro è il 'Catechismo' (contenuto) e il 'Catechismo testo' degli alunni, e diverso è il *'direttorio'* che deve includere tutti gli aspetti sia culturali che organizzativi della Catechesi." *La rivista del*

catechismo 8 (July-August 1971): 272. The editorial note claiming authorship and explaining the nature of the document is signed "G. B. B.," presumably Giam Battista Belloli, the editor of the review.

Those wishing to know more of the background of the United States' National Catechetical Directory *will find in the following article by* Mary Charles Bryce *a valuable contextualizing essay that points to key source material. In addition, her own critique of the directory is helpful, as is her listing of the best of the critiques that had appeared up to the time of her essay.*

READING 19

Sharing the Light of Faith: Catechetical Threshold for the U.S. Church

MARY CHARLES BRYCE

IN 1979, the United States Catholic Church published its catechetical directory *Sharing the Light of Faith.** The 182-page volume terminated nearly six years of actual work, 1973–1979. The measure of its worth cannot be determined, however, by either the number of its pages or the time and money it required for composition, editing, and publication. Because of the extensive consultation which involved countless men and women from almost every diocese in cooperation with their bishops, the American Catholic community can rightfully claim the document as its own.

It is "Catholic" in that *Sharing the Light of Faith* is in the mainstream of the modern catechetical movement. Though it cites only official church documents (papal encyclicals, the declarations of Vatican Council II, episcopal letters, etc.), the influence of Eichstätt, Katigondo, Medellín, and the writings of pioneers in the field, both European and American, is obviously there. *Sharing the Light of Faith* is distinctively "American" in that it addresses the catechetical needs of the church in the United States in concrete terms, adapting the best catechetical theory to existing situations. It presents a comprehensive

Reprinted from *Lumen Vitae* 34 (1979), pp. 393–407. Reproduced by courtesy of *Lumen Vitae.* Copyright *Lumen Vitae* 1979.

view of American Catholic life unlike any other official statement. It is basically a self-portrait, with warts and all.

It may be true that once one affirms the positive value of pluralism and adaptation it is no longer possible to speak of an international catechetical movement. On the other hand, catechists the world over face many of the same kinds of problems and struggle with basically the same task, namely, helping to make the faith of the Christian community become "living, conscious, and active" (*Christus Dominus*, no. 14). These pages are written on the assumption that catechists in other countries can find much in *Sharing the Light of Faith* that is of interest and perhaps of use in their own work.

This article reviews the directory in three parts, thus providing an overview of both the context and contents of the work. The first part will describe how the directory developed. This indeed may be the most significant aspect of the directory itself. A survey of the contents, chapter by chapter, comprises the second part. Part three will present a brief critique, noting the assets of the volume as well as some of its more glaring shortcomings.

I. Development and Consultation

Realistically, the enterprise had been an eight-year process dating from 1971. Unknown to thousands of participants attending the CCD congress in Miami, Florida, in October of that year, ten to twelve persons gathered informally to brainstorm the possibilities and ways of developing a catechetical directory for the church in this pluralistic, multifaceted nation.[1] A number of the people in the assembled group had taken part in the International Catechetical Congress held in Rome the preceding month (20–25 September 1971). The newly published *Directorium Catechisticum Generale* had dominated conversations and addresses during that six-day meeting. The significance of the *General Catechetical Directory* for the church in the United States had not eluded the American delegates to the congress.

One of the people present in both Rome and Miami was William E. McManus, then auxiliary bishop of Chicago, now ordinary in Fort Wayne, Indiana. At the time, Bishop McManus chaired the Committee on Education for the United States Catholic Conference (USCC).

According to the accounts of several who were present at the unreported Miami gathering, Bishop McManus led the informal discussion. At one point Carl Pfeiffer, then a member of the USCC, cited an article written by Berard L. Marthaler, OFM Conv., of the Catholic University of America. That article had described the *Documento di base* published the year before by the Italian Episcopal Conference.[2] It was not so much the document as the consultation process that interested Pfeiffer. Marthaler, who was also present in Miami, summarized the efforts to involve both experts and practitioners in the production of the *Documento di base.* The Miami thinkers observed that, indeed, "the process could be as important as the product."

Subsequently, the Administrative Board of the United States Catholic Conference asked Bishop McManus to have his committee, the Bishops' Committee on Education, work up a plan for the development of a national directory and report back to the board.[3]

In February 1972, the committee made its report in the form of a thirteen-page proposal to the board.[4] That same proposal was presented to the general assembly of bishops on 11 April 1972 at their spring meeting in Atlanta, Georgia. After considerable discussion and one amendment, which increased the directory's working committee to twelve, "four of whom would be bishops,"[5] the proposal was approved.

The development of the directory is public record as described by Wilfrid H. Paradis and others.[6] It is sufficient here to provide a chronology of progress from the time of the bishops commissioning the directory to the date of its publication.

In April 1972, the bishops' Committee of Policy and Review was named. Seven bishops formed that committee. In February 1973, the search for a project director began. Wilfrid H. Paradis, priest of the diocese of Manchester, New Hampshire, was selected on 2 June 1973. On 4 September 1973, Sister Mariella Frye, a Mission Helper of the Sacred Heart, was named associate director.

The twelve-person directory committee was named in October 1973. This committee, working under the Committee of Policy and Review, was charged with decision-making authority in all aspects. It worked in tandem, too, with the project director, Paradis, and associate director, Frye. The bishops endorsed the principle of consultation and broad representation on the directory, "but they left no doubt from the beginning it would be their document."[7] The directory committee held the first of a long series of meetings on 7–9 December 1973.

The six months from 1 October 1973 through 31 March 1974 marked the initial public consultation.[8] That consultation was based on the preliminary outline in a 58-page booklet entitled *Toward a National Catechetical Directory.* That booklet drew 17,412 responses from 113 dioceses (83 percent of all the dioceses). The second consultation based on the first draft of the proposed directory began on 1 January 1975 and ended on April 30 of that same year. A total of 76,342 recommendations were received in response to that draft. On the first day of January 1977, the third consultation began. Ninety percent of the dioceses responded by the time that consultation on the second draft closed on 15 March 1977.[9] Late that summer the third draft was mailed to all the bishops prior to their scheduled November meeting in Washington, D.C.

On 17 November 1977, the plenary assembly of United States bishops approved the directory as amended. The tally was 216 to 12 in favor of the project. Early in 1978, the amended draft (the fourth edition of the directory) was sent to the Sacred Congregation for the Clergy for approval. Approval of the directory was given in a letter dated 30 October 1978 and addressed to Archbishop John R. Quinn, chairman of the National Conference of Catholic Bishops in the United States.

Archbishop Maximino, who signed the letter, commented that the Sacred Congregation for the Clergy found the directory to be "outstanding for its ecclesial spirit, its clarity of expression . . . its solid argument and flexibility."[10] In general, the *Congregatio pro clericis* called for the reworking of three points: (1) regarding revelation; (2) on the matter of catechesis for the sacrament of reconciliation; (3) clarification on the specific nature of priesthood.[11] After the draft was reworked incorporating these latest recommendations, it was sent to the printer and appeared in bound form in March 1979.

II. The Directory: Survey of Contents

Eleven chapters in addition to a preface, conclusion, appendices, and index are enclosed in the directory's ivory-colored binding. Throughout the volume, paragraphs or subject-area sections are consecutively numbered. This lends itself to easy references and cross-references. An overview of each chapter may assist one to recognize the comprehensive corpus of the directory as a whole.

The preface is key to understanding the directory, describing as it does the rationale, the intended users, and the historical background of catechesis in the United States. This opening section sets down three principles which underlie the bishops' promulgation of the document: "the bishops' desire for dialogue: within the Catholic community; between the Catholic church and other Christian churches, as well as with representatives of other religions; and between the church and the human family" (no. 4). A subtle reference to the several Protestant and Jewish groups consulted on the first and second drafts is contained in that statement.

1. Some cultural and religious characteristics affecting catechesis in the United States. The unique and complex factors which both characterize and confront the church in the United States are delineated in this beginning chapter. "The picture presented here and elsewhere . . . is a sober one" with its reminders of advances made in science and technology, alongside the dangers of the arms race and threats to once stable elements in life. The catechist is called upon to "take the negative as well as the positive aspects . . . into account" (no. 29).

2. The catechetical ministry of the Church. In an address to catechists on 1 March, Archbishop Jean Jadot, apostolic delegate to the United States, used the directory as source and guide for his remarks. In the context of that address he observed that chapter 2, which, he said, "I am using at this point may, in time, be considered the greatest contribution of the . . . Directory. The principal reason for this judgment . . . is the rich description that is given of catechesis, its purposes and goals."[12]

In several ways, that eight-page section, along with the preface and chapter 1, forms a basis to understanding the document as a whole. Chapter 2 places catechesis in the context of the ecclesial reality – the believing, inquiring, worshiping, committed faithful. Jadot's term "rich description" is more than apt, for the chapter seems to make a conscious effort to avoid *defining* catechesis. Instead, catechesis is *described* in the phenomenological sense to depict what is a broad and open-ended presentation. Marthaler expressed it well when he wrote that "the *NCD* presented a comprehensive picture of everything that falls within the category of catechetical activity."[13] Every other chapter in the document has cross references to chapter 2.

3. Revelation, faith, and catechesis. This chapter relies on kerygmatic theology's view of faith as response to the Gospel message. Evidence of committee controversy and compromise is transparent in these six pages as the text makes a distinction between *revelation* – "that divine public revelation which closed at the end of the apostolic age" – and *manifestation* – "by which God continues to make himself known and shares himself with human beings through his presence in the Church and the world" (no. 50). Catechists are exhorted to draw upon all sources (signs): biblical, liturgical, ecclesial, and natural (no. 60). The matter of revelation is not confined to this chapter but courses through the volume.

4. The Church and catechesis. Chapter 4 reflects the spirit and thrust of Vatican II with its scriptural images, people of God, Body of Christ, Kingdom, servants, and pilgrims. The special attention to the Church in dialogue (nos. 75–81) emphasizes the ecumenical spirit that the directory espouses. The Church is visible, according to *Shar-*

ing the Light of Faith, in its communal beauty signified by its "unity, holiness, catholicity, and apostolicity" (no. 81).

5. **Principal elements of the Christian message.** Here the fundamental elements of the Christian message are highlighted: the mystery of the "One God; creation, Jesus Christ; the Holy Spirit; the Church; the sacraments; the life of grace; the moral life; Mary and the saints; and death, judgment, and eternity" (no. 82). This chapter reflects the strong influence of the U.S. bishops' document *Basic Teachings of Catholic Religious Education,* promulgated in January 1973. That work is modified in this chapter, however (especially in nos. 101–105), as one discerns the influence of two other writings: *Sexual Ethics,* promulgated by the Sacred Congregation for the Doctrine of the Faith,[14] and *To Live in Christ Jesus,* issued by the United States National Conference of Catholic Bishops in 1976.[15]

6. **Catechesis for a worshiping community.** Because of the centrality of the Eucharist and other sacraments to Christian life, chapter 6 is of particular significance to catechesis. This is the second longest chapter in the work (eighteen pages)[16] and treats comprehensively the interrelationship of catechesis and liturgy, in the context of the believing, worshiping, witnessing Christian community. It takes special note of Vatican II's revised rites of the sacraments and cites the new *Rite of Christian Initiation of Adults* as model and norm (nos. 115, 227) for liturgical and catechetical practice. Chapter 6 is essential for catechesis in a pastoral setting.

7. **Catechesis for social ministry.** This is one of the outstanding chapters in the volume. It emphasizes the fact that the Church's teaching on social justice is as valid as its teaching of doctrine. Chapter 7 seems to echo the tenets promulgated by Pope Paul VI and the Second General Assembly of the Synod of Bishops in the statement *Justice in the World.*[17] Three themes dominate the section: (1) social justice *per se,* which "helps us evaluate our responsibility for the kind of society we . . . support and share in"; (2) the social consequences of sin – "sin is expressed in some of the structures of human communities . . . responsibility for correcting a situation of 'social sin' rests upon all who participate in the society in question"; (3) the relationship of justice and charity – "justice reaches its fulfillment in charity . . . charity excuses from none of the demands of justice; it calls one to go beyond justice and engage in sacrificial service of others in imitation of Christ . . ." (no. 165).

8. **Catechesis toward maturity of faith.** Chapter 7 is a detailed approach to the principle of adaptation which the *General Catechetical Directory* insisted upon. It considers the relationship between faith-life and human development, how people grow in their ability to perceive

and respond to God's revelation; formation of conscience; catechesis and sexuality; catechesis for those with special needs and factors which are characteristic of the faith-life in the United States (no. 172).

The value of experience is treated extensively in this chapter. "Experiential learning which can be considered a form of inductive methodology gives rise to concern and questions, hopes and anxieties . . . which increase one's desire to penetrate more deeply into life's meaning" (no. 176d). This chapter may be considered by some to be the most helpful because of its guidance in setting up teacher training programs and evaluation criteria.

9. Catechetical personnel. The very title provides, as do others in the work, the clue to the subject of this chapter. It projects the ideal personal qualifications for the catechist and addresses the distinctive roles of "parents, teachers, principals in Catholic schools, parish catechists, coordinators or directors . . . those who work in . . . catechetical offices; deacons, priests, and bishops. All are catechists with distinctive roles" (no. 204).

This chapter carries the theme promulgated in the previous one with the insistence that all Christians – including catechists – from the least to the last need to grow in faith and understanding. One means, though not the sole one, is formal study, including "studies in theology, scripture, liturgy, psychology, educational theory, and administration, as well as practical experience with children and adults" (no. 214). More specifically, it is "imperative that priests continue their education after ordination. This can be done to some degree through reading, participating in discussions, and attending lectures. . . . This is particularly important because of the rapid changes in society and in many fields of knowledge" (no. 217).

10. Organization for catechesis. "Appropriate structures can help ensure opportunities for the entire Christian community to grow in faith" (no. 220). These are ancillary but nonetheless important dimensions for the community's growth in Christian life. Effective planning, responsible administrators, goal setting and accountability, and evaluation and research are some of the emphases insisted upon here. Parish and diocesan structures come in for serious scrutiny; campus ministry and characteristics of particular situations such as military personnel are cited. "At all levels high priority must be given to providing structures within and through which the total catechesis of God's people can be accomplished" (no. 248).

11. Catechetical resources. This final chapter is a call to recognize the sources and resources at one's disposal for catechesis in our present day. The Church has availed itself of cultural expressions through the ages. Music, poetry, dance, drama, mosaics, sculpture, architecture, and stained glass have sometimes been primary catechetical tools. They are still effective today, but they share this ancillary role with television, films, filmstrips, slides, tapes, and photography.

Sharing the Light of Faith insists on catechists' learning "how to take media into account as a crucial part of the cultural background and experience of those being catechized" (no. 261).

Conclusion. In summary, the directory states that this volume exists to foster hope and confidence in the work of catechizing. It is directed principally toward those consciously engaged in the catechetical ministry. The authors close with the statement that, "in the spirit of the brightening dawn of Easter, we seek to lead people and to be led, ever more fully into the light." That is what Sharing the Light of Faith is all about.

III. Critical Assessment

Outstanding characteristics of the directory are those particular features and strengths which make it unique and point up its appropriateness for the church in this country. They fall into five categories: (1) the role of the total community in catechesis, (2) delineation of four major tasks of catechesis, (3) a particular emphasis on social justice as a responsibility of catechesis, (4) adult catechesis as normative and in keeping with the lifelong nature of catechesis, and (5) the ecumenical dimension of catechesis.

1. Role of the ecclesial community in catechesis. The *General Catechetical Directory* had already insisted on the indispensable role of the community of believers.[18] One finds that same insistence in the new *Rite of Christian Initiation of Adults*[19] and echoed specifically in the 1977 synod.[20] In effect, the directory reiterates that insistence and puts it in the context of the multicultural, pluralistic setting of the United States. *Sharing the Light of Faith* states that "all members of the community of believers are called to share in this ministry [. . . no. 204], sharing goals and values [no. 209], insights [no. 245], common visions [no. 133]," etc. In short, catechesis is a collaborative mission in which every member of the Church is involved, whether consciously or not.

Realizing that, one soon discerns a not-so-surprising socialization theory threading through the volume.[21] Growth in faith and understanding, formation of Christian thought and practices occur in dialogue and in mutual relationships, in sacramental experiences, in exchanges of reflection on individual understandings and insights, as well as in concentrated personal or collective study. All of this takes place in a community setting with a conscious acknowledgment of personal freedom and the gratuitous gift of faith.

2. **Delineation of four major tasks of catechesis.** One of the most welcome innovations of the directory is its identifying distinctive tasks of catechesis. These go along with the "rich description" in chapter 2, as Jadot observed, and return the concept of catechesis to that which the early Church held, as exemplified in Peter's second letter, in the *Didache*, in Cyril of Jerusalem's catechesis, and those of Ambrose, Chrysostom, Augustine, and Theodore of Mopsuestia. The four major tasks of catechesis, according to *Sharing the Light of Faith*, are these: (1) to proclaim Christ's message, (2) to participate in efforts to develop and maintain the Christian community, (3) to lead people to worship and prayer, and (4) to motivate them to serve others.[22] These represent an incorporation and development of the U.S. bishops' earlier document *To Teach as Jesus Did* (1972), with its emphasis on *didache, koinonia,* and *diakonia.*[23] More significantly, this delineation of tasks broadens the scope of catechesis from the almost exclusive cognitive confinement associated with it from the sixteenth century down to the early twentieth century. Once more chapter 2 comes into focus for its descriptive approach that is complemented by the fourfold task charging catechesis not only with the responsibility of intellectualizing formation of Christian truth and doctrine but also with the challenge of incorporating Christian principles, tenets, and values into everyday living.

3. **The role of social justice in a catechetical context.** The remarkable thing about this feature is its multiform uniqueness: (1) Stirred, no doubt, by the 1971 synod and especially by the experiences of the Third World, the inclusion of social ministry is nevertheless decidedly identifiable by tone and illustration with life in the United States; and, (2) furthermore, it manifests a carefully drawn out relationship of charity, faith, and justice.

Although concentrated particularly in chapter 7, "Catechesis for Social Ministry," themes of social justice course through the entire volume. Those themes echo such principles as the dignity of the human person (no. 156), the Church's responsibility for the promotion of justice (no. 160), and the role of catechesis in awakening and fostering a critical sense (no. 170). *Sharing the Light of Faith* calls for generosity (no. 96) and illustrates the relationship of charity to justice: "Justice is the foundation of charity" (no. 165c) — not only out of their excess are Christians called to generosity but also out of the needs of others (no. 105b). "The good and faithful servant acts out of concern and love" (no. 66). "It is essential that catechesis concerning justice, mercy, and peace be part of the catechetical process" (no. 170).

4. Adult catechesis: normative and lifelong. In a nation where a Catholic school system has flourished and catechesis has been identified with children's learning, emphasis on adult catechesis is almost an anomaly and causes surprise in some circles. When placed in the context of an aging population with its increased emphasis on adult education in terms of second careers, special interest areas, and the like, one is forced to rethink the unexpected emphasis which both the *GCD* (no. 20) and *Sharing the Light of Faith* (nos. 182–188) place on catechesis as a lifelong process with special focus on adults.

The ideal of a living faith is growth, increase, and maturity. Vatican II declared that the purpose of catechesis is to assist every person's faith to become "living, conscious, and active."[24] Considering these and other factors, it is logical to acknowledge the continuous demand for catechesis and to admit the normative character of adult catechesis.[25]

The guidelines which *Sharing the Light of Faith* delineates (no. 185) are supported by scholarly studies of human development in the history of adult learning movements, the witness role of the ecclesial community, and the spirit of inquiry characteristic of thinking adults. "The primary reason for adult catechesis," the directory notes, "is to help adults themselves grow to maturity of faith as members of the Church and society" (no. 40).

5. The ecumenical dimension of catechesis. The United States is marked by a great diversity of culture, national origins, religious adherence, racial distinctions, and life experiences. In the light of that, there can be little wonder that ecumenism is upheld and included in the directory. "Religious pluralism of the United States offers an important opportunity to advance ecumenism," the document observes (no. 75). Its inclusion is consistent with themes of respect for the human person (no. 170), for religious freedom (nos. 58, 80, 101, etc.), social justice (nos. 14, 76, 160), and the quest for unity (nos. 73, 80, 95).

Sharing the Light of Faith gives particular attention to Eastern Catholic churches who are in communion with Rome. Those churches, which trace their origins to the apostolic churches in Constantinople, Alexandria, Antioch, and Jerusalem, are "usually organized according to the major traditions: Byzantine, Antiochene, Chaldean, Armenian, and Alexandrian. Those with established hierarchies in the United States are the Ukrainians, Ruthenians, and Melkites, all of the Byzantine tradition, and the Maronites of the Antiochene tradition. Those without their own hierarchies here include the Romanians, Russians, Byelorussians, Italo-Albanians, and Italo-Greeks of the Byzantine tradition and the Armenians, Syrians, Chaldeans, and Malankarese" (no. 15).

Special efforts were made to interest and inform all Catholics about the "rich diversity found within Catholic unity" (no. 3). To assure the inclusion of their contributions, representatives from Eastern traditions were involved. Miss Mary Balouny is a Melchite Rite Catholic and a member of the directory committee from the beginning. Bishop Basil Losten joined the Committee of Policy and Review shortly after the project got underway. Monsignor Seely Beggiani, rector of the Maronite Seminary in Washington, D.C., and Rev. John Zeyack of the Byzantine Eparchy of Passaic, New Jersey, collaborated continuously with the directory committee once the initial projects got organized.

The volume directs special attention to Christianity's relationship to the Jewish people (no. 77). *Sharing the Light of Faith* urges scholarly cooperation with Jews to promote "mutual understanding of Christian and Jewish traditions . . ." (no. 77).

Acknowledging that "almost all religions strive to answer the restless searching of the human heart" (no. 79), the directory further encourages ecumenical dialogue with Moslems (no. 78), Hindus, Buddhists, and others. The aim of ecumenical activity is growth in mutual understanding, but *Sharing the Light of Faith* cautions against fostering religious indifferentism (no. 80).[26]

Shortcomings in the directory. *Sharing the Light of Faith* is not without its weaknesses. It is, after all, a human document. Notable shortcomings are: (1) the failure to incorporate references to the catechumenate for children as found in the new *Rite of Christian Initiation of Adults*;[27] (2) sidestepping a decisive stand in pastoral practice for the sacrament of confirmation; (3) the absence of attention to catechesis on peace in this strife-torn era in human history; (4) a vagueness in terms of catechesis for social justice: despite the emphasis accorded to social ministry, the complexity of issues seems too often to dull or obscure specific catechetical approaches; and (5) omission of the Beatitudes: references are made to them in three places (nos. 100, 105, 176) but, unlike the Ten Commandments, they are *not* presented as a model in the volume.

Less significant details also surface on the negative side. These include glaring lacunae in the index: There is no entry for "salvation history" which is the key to the document's presentation of doctrine. Absent too are references to "sharing," which is part of the volume's title, and occurs numerous times in the text. Similarly, references to "purpose," "tasks," so often stressed throughout the work, are missing from that valuable cross-referencing section.

The text itself is irregular. At times the tone is clearly juridical and authoritative but in other places more inviting, narrative, and inductive. Some of the passages seem to emerge from theology manuals while in other cases the language is more biblical and appealing. The fact that the work was composed by a committee explains both its strengths and its weaknesses. In the main, the volume appears to represent numerous compromises usually characteristic of committee projects.

Conclusion. In summary, the assets of the document outweigh its shortcomings. *Sharing the Light of Faith* will undoubtedly have a decided impact on the revitalizing of Christian inquiry and catechesis for the present and immediate future. In a sense, it is a "present" word, indicating where the U.S. church stands at this period in its life vis-à-vis its pastoral ministry as a whole.[28] Plans call for a revision in five years.

In one sense, the directory's crowning honor is that it exists, that it has come to be in 1979, fourteen years after the last session of Vatican II. That is remarkable in itself—that a church so widely diversified and scattered could produce this document is indeed notable.

This is a document of the U.S. bishops. They have been involved in its origin, its composition, its editing, and its final publication. It bears the marks of the plurality, multiplicity, yet unity of that episcopal body and the people the bishops represent and lead. *Sharing the Light of Faith* brings the church in the United States to a new threshold, not only in terms of catechetics but also in terms of its own self-awareness as an identifiable witness to Christian presence in today's world.

NOTES

* *Sharing the Light of Faith: The National Catechetical Directory* (Washington, DC: United States Catholic Conference, 1979).

1. Actually, that was not the first time such a project had been entertained. In November 1963 the Bishops' Committee of the Confraternity of Christian Doctrine had begun considering the composition of a text to replace the Baltimore Catechism (1885; 1941). As their study of that project progressed over the next several years, they came to the conclusion, in September 1966, that a "sourcebook," guidelines for teachers and others, would be preferable. The idea was not implemented, and interest waned. The project was finally abandoned. See "National Catechism Project," in CCD Files, United States Catholic Conference (USCC).

2. "The Renewal of Catechesis in Italy," *Religious Education* 66 (September-October 1976): 357–363 (an American interdenominational journal).

3. Minutes of Administrative Board, USCC, 13 November 1971, Washington, D.C.

4. See "Proposed Plan," Education Document I, p. 10, in *National Catechetical Directory*, Documentation Files [hereafter cited as *NCD* Files].

5. Minutes of Twelfth General Meeting, USCC, 11–13 April 1972, Atlanta, Georgia.

6. Once the project got underway, Wilfrid H. Paradis, project director,

kept a careful account of the directory's progress. Both he and Mariella Frye kept the public informed through periodical writings. See Wilfrid H. Paradis, "The National Catechetical Directory: A Progress Report," *The Living Light* 11 (1974): 416–433; idem, "Update on the National Catechetical Directory," *The Living Light* 12 (1975): 412–421; idem, "Sharing the Light of Faith: An Overview," *The Catechist* 11 (May 1978): 16f. See Mariella Frye, "The Catechetical Directory: A Progress Report," *Our Sunday Visitor* 63 (15 September 1974): 1; idem, "The National Catechetical Directory: Major Issues and Concerns in the Field," *The Living Light* 11 (1974): 434–444. See also: Patricia Feistritzer, "The National Catechetical Directory: A Challenging Process," *Momentum* 4 (4 December 1973): 28–32; A. Buchholz, "A Critique of the National Catechetical Directory," *Homiletic and Pastoral Review* 75 (June 1975): 49–53.

7. Berard L. Marthaler, "Commentary," manuscript copy, p. 4.

8. Consultation of the faithful has always been an ideal and a practice in the Church but not always easily accomplished. The German Catechism, *Der Katechismus der Bistümer Deutschlands* (1955), appeared in final form after review copies had been widely disseminated to the faithful, clergy, and bishops in that country. Subjected to "public criticism," it resulted in an astonishing twelve thousand recommendations and as many changes. See Joseph A. Jungmann, "The New German Catechism," *Lumen Vitae* 10 (1956): 573–586. See also *Lexikon der Pastoral Theologie,* vol. 5, pp. 242–243.

9. The periodical *The New Catholic World* had issued a special number devoted to analyses of the second draft. Each of the eleven chapters was critiqued by a specialist in the topic-area of the respective chapters. See *New Catholic World* 220 (March-April 1977).

10. See letter, 30 October 1978, p. 1, *NCD* Files.

11. Ibid., p. 2.

12. The address was given in its entirety in *Origins* 8 (15 March 1979): 612ff. The setting for the talk was the annual "Sun-belt Conference," in North Carolina.

13. See Berard L. Marthaler, "Defining While Not Defining: The Paradox of the National Directory," *PACE* 9 (1978–1979): Community–G.

14. This document is dated 29 November 1975 and found in *Acta Apostolicae Sedis* 68 (1976): 77–96.

15. Published by the National Conference of Catholic Bishops, Washington, D.C., 1976.

16. Chapter 8, with twenty pages, is the longest chapter in the work.

17. *Acta Apostolicae Sedis* 63 (1971): 923–942.

18. *General Catechetical Directory;* see foreword, and nos. 13, 21, 35, and others.

19. See the *Rite of Christian Initiation of Adults (RCIA)* (English translation) (Washington, DC: USCC, 1974), nos. 41, 105, 135, 168.

20. In the "Thirty-four Points," the synod fathers insisted that catechesis is dependent on the faith experience of the Church. See 24 and 31: "Catechesis is an ecclesial task." *L'Osservatore Romano* (English-language edition), 27 October 1977.

21. "Human beings are social by nature. This means that family, state, and society are natural contexts for human life. They are essential for personal development, including the religious dimension." *Sharing,* no. 158. See also Vatican Council II, *Gaudium et spes* (7 December 1965), no. 42.

22. See *Sharing,* esp. nos. 213, 227, 228.

23. The 1973 outline, *Toward a National Catechetical Directory*, on which the first consultation was based, relied heavily on the bishops' work *To Teach as Jesus Did* (Pastoral Letter, 1972).

24. Vatican Council II, *Christus Dominus* (28 October 1965), no. 14.

25. See *GCD*, no. 20; *Synod '77*, 15 of "Thirty-four Points"; *RCIA* in toto.

26. The synod also insisted on the ecumenical dimension of catechesis. It strongly stressed "right to religious liberty" (see no. 6 in "Thirty-four Points") and that catechesis must have a "solid ecumenical dimension" while avoiding "religious indifferentism and false irenicism" (no. 5 of "Thirty-four Points").

27. This failure is in contradiction of the directory's own citation of the new rite as normative for sacramental catechesis. See *Sharing*, nos. 115, 227. See *RCIA*, nos. 360–369.

28. The fact that two studies based on the directory are already published and a third is in the making attests to its importance. The study by Ann Marie Mongoven, *Signs of Catechesis* (New York: Paulist Press, 1979), is an overview of the *NCD* with special emphasis on the signs (sources). Thomas F. Sullivan's *Discussion Guide to Sharing the Light of Faith* (Washington, DC: National Catholic Education Association, 1979) is designed to familiarize users with the principal teachings of the document. Berard L. Marthaler, OFM Conv., has been commissioned to write an "official" commentary on the directory. At this writing that work has not yet been published. Because of Marthaler's position as consultant to the directory committee, his commentary promises to be extremely informative. [Later published as Berard L. Marthaler, *Sharing the Light of Faith: An Official Commentary* (Washington, DC: USCC, 1981)]. See also Gabriel Moran, "The National Catechetical Directory," *National Catholic Reporter* 15 (1 June 1979): 18.

Anyone who has tried to write a summary of developments during several decades knows the difficulties of such an undertaking. To be successful, such an overview must tie together seemingly disparate strands. Berard Marthaler's newly revised essay on the modern catechetical movement among Roman Catholics is a well-crafted, tightly woven account that will be appreciated by those searching for a panoramic view of the catechetical movement in the twentieth century.

READING 20

The Modern Catechetical Movement in Roman Catholicism: Issues and Personalities

BERARD MARTHALER

THE WORK OF RENEWAL in religious education among Roman Catholics has been underway since the turn of the century. It is in part a response to a felt need among many leaders for a more effective catechesis and in part a result of socio-economic and theological developments which conspired to bring about radical changes in the Church. Behind (or more properly, in front of) it all were individuals who interpreted these needs and focused the developments. The history of the modern catechetical movement is largely a story of farsighted people.

The parochial school and church-related college did much to shape religious education among Roman Catholics in contemporary America, but the greatest impact was made by the catechetical movement. It cut across traditional institutional structures, caused the demise of many old assumptions which passed for absolutes, and gave birth to

Reprinted, with changes, from the September–October 1978 Special Edition issue of the journal *Religious Education*, pp. S77–S91, by permission of the publisher, The Religious Education Association, 409 Prospect Street, New Haven, CT 06510. Membership or subscription available for $25.00 per year.

a new spirit and vision. Catechesis is pastoral in intent and means. The catechetical movement set out to nurture the faith of individuals and communities so that, in the words of Vatican Council II, it becomes "living, conscious, and active."[1]

Up to the present the modern catechetical movement has evolved through three more or less distinct phases. The first began with a quest to find a more effective method than the one then in use and gradually evolved into the second phase, which was more concerned with content than method. And most recently, the third phase sees catechetics broadening its ken to include a variety of educational ministries and instructional strategies.

I

The initial efforts at reform in Catholic religious education took place in the years before World War I. They began in German-speaking countries with a desire to find a more effective method than the question-answer approach of the traditional catechism lesson. The "Munich Method" was the result. It represented a conscious effort to adapt the educational psychology of Johann Friedrich Herbart (1776–1841) as interpreted by Tuiskon Ziller (1817–1882) to catechetical instruction.

The Munich Method consisted of three well-defined steps – presentation, explanation, and application – which corresponded to the steps in the learning process identified by neo-Herbartians, viz., perception, understanding, and practice. It purported to address each of the learner's "faculties": the senses and imagination in the presentation, the intellect in the explanation, the will and emotions in application. Thus, the lesson began with the presentation of a story, usually from the Bible, followed by an explanation of the doctrinal or moral truth it illustrated, and culminating with an application to everyday life.[2]

Joseph J. Baierl of St. Bernard's Seminary, Rochester, N.Y., introduced the method in the United States in a series of explanatory texts for teachers, *The Creed Explained* (1919). It was popularized through the efforts of Anthony Fuerst (1904–1975) of St. Mary's Seminary, Cleveland, and Rudolph G. Bandas (1896–1965) of St. Paul Seminary in Minnesota. Though Bandas later became critical of the direction of the modern catechetics, his early work, *Catechetical Methods* (1929), had far-reaching effects on the way the catechism came to be taught in the United States.

The Munich Method underwent several adaptations and modifications in the United States, but it never won universal acceptance. It was criticized because it fostered passive learning and because it focused on stories rather than life experiences. Moreover, it reaped the criticisms directed against Herbartian pedagogy itself, which had peaked in this country even before the Munich Method was introduced. One by-product of the method, generally credited to Herbartian pedagogy, which endures in modern catechesis is the ubiquitous lesson plan.

Probably no one did more to point up the inadequacies of the catechism than Francis H. Drinkwater (b. 1884) of Birmingham, England. For almost fifty years Canon Drinkwater edited a small monthly, *The Sower,* designed to improve methods of religious instruction. He used its pages in season and out of season to criticize the catechism. In the first place, it was never intended for children; in the second, its language was too filled with definitions and abstractions (for which he blamed theologians); and, he felt, it exacerbated the divisions among Christians because it nurtured a race of Catholics

> ... who would not explain their faith even to their friends; whose idea of defending the church would be to throw brickbats at non-Catholic lecturers and hecklers, cheerfully regardless of the embarrassment so caused to other Catholics.[3]

These early attempts to find more effective methods for catechesis point up two characteristics dominant in the twentieth-century renewal in Christian education among Roman Catholics. First, it signaled a reaction against the spirit of the Counter-Reformation and the inadequacies of the traditional teaching of religion based primarily if not solely on the catechism. Second, it showed a degree of openness to the insights and discoveries of educational psychology and represented an attempt to introduce learning theory in catechesis.

II

Another tendency characteristic of modern catechetics emerged as the movement evolved into a second phase, namely, a renewed interest in the Church of the apostolic and patristic era.

From one point of view, the second phase in the modern catechetical movement represented a disenchantment with "method" and a desire for more "content." From another point of view, it represented the convergence of the catechetical with the liturgical and kerygmatic movements in Roman Catholic circles. The common concern in all three movements (later legitimated by the Second Vatican Council) was to return to Christ as the center of the Christian life and message and to deemphasize, even purge, the accretions of time which had gathered like barnacles on the bark of Peter. More is required of Christian education than the handing on of shopworn formulas, tired customs, and trite devotions.

It is an exaggeration to claim as is sometimes done that the modern catechetical movement represents "a restoration, not an innovation."[4] Though fascinated with the structures and practices of the ancient Church, the movement could not remain satisfied with copying the past. The fascination with the early Church was born not out of antiquarian interests but out of a desire to recapture something of its vitality and spirit. One result, for example, was to bring back into common par-lance – at least, among professionals – the word *catechesis* and its cognates, catechetical, catechist, catechumen, etc. In an effort to pro-vide theological underpinnings for their position, the movement's leaders emphasized the Church's *pastoral* mission rather than its educa-tional ministry, which they associated with schooling and all the academic structures and paraphernalia it implies. They preferred to speak of catechesis rather than religious education. As they described it, catechesis is the process whereby an individual is initiated into and instructed in the life and thought of the Church. Catechesis speaks not merely to the mind but to the whole person. Catechesis is education *in* the faith, not merely instruction *about* the faith.

New leaders emerged in almost every country, but the name that dominates the second phase of the modern catechetical revival is Josef Jungmann (1889-1975). Though he is best known for his contribution to liturgical studies, Jungmann began his scholarly career with a doc-toral dissertation on the catechetical and kerygmatic formulations of the doctrine of grace in the first three centuries. In 1936 he published *Die Frohbotschaft und unsere Glaubensverkündigung,* which caused an immediate sensation.[5] Jungmann put more emphasis on the need for a religious understanding of the Christian message than on orthodox interpretation of certain doctrines and proper teaching methods. The kerygma is "good news" which should be welcomed, not looked upon as imposing a fabric of joyless obligations. Jungmann's recommenda-tions had consequences for every aspect of Church life. Leaders in the catechetical movement saw him as an ally, but he met opposition from the establishment who (rightly) suspected he was undermining the status quo. He personified the common concerns of the liturgical, catechetical, and kerygmatic movements in the years immediately preceding and subsequent to World War II. It was only with Vatican II that he saw his early work vindicated.

The close alliance which began in those years between the liturgical and catechetical movements continues to be a hallmark of American catechesis. Virgil Michel (1890–1938) – a monk of St. John's Abbey, Collegeville, Minnesota, who is credited with spearheading the liturgical revival in this country – sensed the need for sound catechesis if the vitality of the Mass and sacraments were to be restored. Many of the Americans who took the lead in modern catechetics, Jane Marie Murray, Bishop Edwin O'Hara, Mary Perkins Ryan, Gerard S. Sloyan, and Mary Charles Bryce to name only a few, were also active in the National Liturgical Conference and allied activities. *Orate Fratres* (now *Worship*) in the beginning concentrated almost as much on catechesis as it did on liturgy.

The kerygmatic movement among Roman Catholics dates from the 1930s in German-speaking lands. It was popularized in North America in the 1950s principally through the writings of Jungmann and the lectures of Johannes Hofinger who was then associated with the East Asian Pastoral Institute in Manila. The manner of presenting the Gospel message in New Testament times – the proclamation of the Good News and the call for repentance and conversion – gave spirit and substance to the movement. The leaders defined catechesis in terms of the ministry of the word, seeing it as closely connected with evangelization.

The German tendency to focus almost exclusively on the Scriptures for both method and content was challenged on two fronts. In French-speaking countries, the value of Jean Piaget's findings for religious education was recognized in the 1950s.[6] Developmental psychology made an early impact on theory and practice in France and Belgium.

The French school of catechetics popularized still another theme in the 1950s and 1960s: "maturity of faith."[7] It was a logical outcome of the developmental approach. Pierre-André Liégé and Joseph Colomb, among others, cited Scripture and Tradition to show that faith cannot be reduced to a static reality like a deposit in a bank vault which one preserves by secrecy and surveillance. Moreover, the profession of faith is not a moment in one's life, isolated from the context of everyday living, but a complex, dynamic force. French authors argued the need for catechesis to relate faith to the process of growth and maturation of individuals and groups if men and women are to become truly adult Christians.

Whereas the catechetical movement in many places got its inspiration and direction from gifted individuals who emerged in positions of leadership, in Belgium the movement was institutionalized. In 1946 the Cathechetical Documentary Center, a resource library sponsored by the Jesuits in Louvain, moved to Brussels and became *Lumen Vitae,*

International Institute of Pastoral Catechetics. Under the able direction of George Delcuve (1908–1976), assisted by Marcel van Caster and Andre Godin, the center sponsored workshops and a training program for catechists from all over the world and published a quarterly by the same name. The international character of *Lumen Vitae*, both the institute and the periodical, needs to be emphasized because it was from there that many of the ideas underlying modern catechetics were disseminated throughout the Catholic world. Delcuve and his colleagues popularized a highly structured approach to catechesis called "pedagogy of signs." Ideally, every catechetical program weaves together Bible, doctrine, liturgy, and Christian witness in such a way as to present the Christian message as an organic whole. In the wake of Vatican II greater emphasis was put on "signs of the times" so that the catechetical themes came to be grouped under four modified headings: biblical signs; liturgical signs; ecclesial signs, that is, creedal symbols and witness of the church community; and natural signs, which include signs of the times.[8]

A reaction against the kerygmatic approach came from the emerging nations. Just as developmental psychology made evident the need to adapt to the age of the learner, missionaries and catechists in Africa and Asia found it necessary to adapt the Christian message to different linguistic and cultural patterns. Simple proclamation of the Good News is not enough; it must be interpreted. The word of God, yes, but incarnate in the words of humanity. In the decade 1959–1968, Johannes Hofinger helped organize six International Catechetical Study Weeks. The first of these seminars met at Nijmegen (1959); it examined the place of the liturgy in catechetical activities. The theme was taken up again the following year at Eichstätt. The Eichstätt Study Week is a landmark in the history of modern catechetics: It brought the kerygmatic approach and the "pedagogy of signs" together and outlined principles for a renewal of catechesis and the liturgy which were implemented in the main at Vatican II. Bangkok (1962) popularized the notion of "pre-evangelization," for which Alfonso M. Nebreda was the herald in the United States. The seminars at Katigondo (1964) and Manila (1967) developed and refined the ideas of the previous conferences. A synthesis of the work done at these later study weeks furnishes an outline of the themes which have come to define pastoral catechesis: evangelization, conversion, faith, salvation history, cultural adaptation, and the "anthropological" approach.

The sixth International Catechetical Study Week was held at Medellin (1968). Its importance for contemporary catechetics is due to several factors. Medellin challenged catechesis to come to grips with the political and socio-economic order which shapes the religious attitudes of communities as well as individuals. Picking up a theme from Vatican II, it asserted that there can be no lasting renewal in catechesis unless there is reform in the Church and in society at large and that one of the tasks of catechesis is to work for that reform. The conferees at Medellin made another contribution by asking that their deliberations, especially a resolution accepting pluralism as a positive value in catechetical activity, be recognized in the *General Catechetical Directory* which was then being written. The existence as well as much of the content of part 1 of the directory is traceable to Medellin.[9]

In the United States there also was a reaction against the kerygmatic approach. Gabriel Moran charged that "salvation history" was in danger of becoming a system as rigid as the scholasticism it was seeking to replace in catechetical texts. He criticized Jungmann for leaving little room for individuals to reflect on their own experience and for failing to relate salvation history to the personal history of those being catechized. As a Christian Brother, Moran brought practical insights gained from a good deal of teaching experience to the discussion; as the author of several works on revelation, he situated the discussion on the nature and goals of catechesis in the context of theology and education. In his earlier writings Moran addressed the means and contents of revelation with an eye to improving catechesis in the Catholic community. Among Catholics, Moran was one of the first to lament an overemphasis on child-centered catechesis to the neglect of adult needs. In his later works—those which date from after his *Design for Religion* (1970)—he is critical of catechetics as being too concerned with Church and institutional issues and not enough concerned with broader educational and societal issues. In the decade after the publication of his two works *Theology of Revelation* and *Catechesis of Revelation* (1966), Brother Moran had unrivalled influence on catechesis in the United States. It was due to him more than anyone else that American Catholics looked less to European "experts" and more to their own experience and instincts for theoretical and practical guidance. Even when people disagreed with him, they acknowledged Gabriel Moran's insights and his acumen in defining issues.[10]

III

Someone has said that religious education is an arctic sea where the icebergs float in pairs. This is the image that comes to mind when one reviews the work of the International Catechetical Study Weeks. They tried to chart a course between method and content, between anthropology and theology, between personal and institutional goals, between religious and socio-political realities. The task, always difficult, appeared in a new light in the 1960s and 1970s. The polarities came to be seen as twin peaks of the same glacier rather than separate ice floes.

At the same time, other dichotomies which have neatly compartmentalized human experience are being blurred if not dissolved. While Catholic theologians continue to admit a certain duality, they now deny the sharp dualism which made antipodes of matter and spirit, body and soul, nature and supernature, the secular and sacred, immanence and transcendence. It is in this context that the third phase of modern catechetics evolved. It is an era of ecumenism in which Catholics and Protestants are searching to find out what they hold in common as well as what divides them. The realities of the Third World force Christians to take other religious traditions seriously. Change has come to be seen as a positive force for good, and the future has become a factor in planning for the present. People are interested in their historical roots once more.

Just as the proclamation of the word was the dominant characteristic of the second phase of the modern catechetical movement, the interpretation of experience is the distingishing feature of the third phase. Piet Schoonenberg, the Dutch theologian whose impact on modern catechetics is not fully appreciated, wrote in 1970: "From a mere approach to the message, experience has become the theme itself of catechesis. Catechesis has become the interpretation of experience. It has to clarify experience, that is, it has to articulate and enlighten the experience and existence of those for whom the message is intended."[11]

If North Americans have made a distinctive contribution to modern catechetics (and I would argue that we have), it is in this area of experiential catechesis. Experience is a theme which runs through the educational literature of the United States like a haunting melody; some contend it is simply another aspect of American pragmatism. Despite a certain abhorrence among Roman Catholics for John Dewey's philosophy of education earlier in the century, his influence in contemporary catechetics is as unmistakable as it is pervasive. The European theorists did not clearly explicate (and perhaps did not recognize) the fact that the catechetical forms and structures of the early Church which they wanted to restore were almost entirely experiential. Early Christians had a number of prayer formulas but few doctrinal statements other than biblical formulas and the creeds. Indeed, the medium was the message: The values and style of life to which the

Christian community gave witness was its strongest attraction. One came to know the significance of baptism and the Eucharist by experiencing them.

Probably no technological advance, including the modern electronic media, exercised greater influence on Christian education than the printing press. Up through the fifteenth century, catechesis for all its deficiencies was oral and experiential. Its success or failure clearly depended on parents, teacher, catechist, social environment, and cultural patterns. With the printing press came standardization – stereotyped formulas and verbal expressions as touchstones of doctrinal orthodoxy. Everyone, including Catholics, imitated Luther's catechisms, and the printed page became the focal point of religious education. As Canon Drinkwater never tired of pointing out, little more was expected of catechists than to hear the recitation of the lessons. The standardized questions and answers made dialogue all but impossible. "Orthophony" (thought by many to be the same as orthodoxy) covered a multitude of sins.

The so-called Baltimore Catechism approved by the U.S. bishops in 1884 also served as a syllabus for the catechesis of children. It was the basis for graded textbooks which resembled conventional American study guides and workbooks more than traditional catechisms. With the advent of multimedia presentations and other kinds of educational hardware, as well as inductive learning methods, the nature and function of textbooks changed. In the 1930s Jane Marie Murray, OP, (b. 1896), and a group of her Dominican sisters from near Grand Rapids, Michigan, undertook a series of religion texts, *The Christ Life Series,* for the elementary grades.[12] It was distinctive in that it represented a first attempt in this country to design textbooks with the avowed purpose of bringing children to take an active part in the liturgical life of the Church. The series, moreover, put a premium on the experience of the learner.

The important contributions of women to the modern catechetical movement surface most dramatically in the development of religion texts and related catechetical materials. By combining practical experience with sound learning theory, they have exercised an immeasurable influence in transforming the vision and spirit of catechesis at the grass roots. Maria de la Cruz Aymes, HHS, born in Mexico City, learned of the kerygmatic approach from Johannes Hofinger and about the need for something better than the traditional catechism from the children she taught after World War II in New York's Spanish Harlem and in Hunter's Point in the San Francisco Bay area.[13] In the 1950s, she initiated the *On Our Way* series which became the prototype of today's religion texts in Catholic schools. It is a complete "program":

Besides artful books for the children's use, it includes pedagogical and theological background, notes for parents, lesson plans, and guides for teachers.

The *On Our Way* series was originally designed, unlike most texts then in circulation, for instruction in nonschool programs usually under the banner of the CCD (Confraternity of Christian Doctrine). The ground had been prepared for the acceptance of Sister de la Cruz's work by what is seen in retrospect as a truly pioneering venture by Rosalia Walsh. Sister Walsh, whose community, the Mission Helpers of the Sacred Heart, worked mostly among blacks and in rural areas, published *The Adaptive Way* (1949-51), a set of manuals for training religion teachers of children in the CCD and similar nonschool programs. She introduced fresh and imaginative methods which relied a great deal on experiential approaches. These innovative texts, intended originally for the CCD, soon had a major impact on school materials, with teachers adapting their methods and contents for use in more formal classroom settings. Publishers incorporated them so that for a variety of commerical, pastoral, and educational reasons religion texts designed for the Catholic market, including *On Our Way* (known in its later editions as *The New Life Series*), now frequently appear in two versions, one for the parochial school and one for the CCD and similar programs.

Hand in hand with the evolution of new educational techniques and catechetical materials came a change in the role of the teacher. Teacher-catechists, professional and volunteer, became ever more central to the learning-teaching process. They require a variety of skills and in-depth knowledge to carry on their work. Before most were aware of the changes coming over the Church, Gerard S. Sloyan recognized the needs of catechists and set out to meet them. A priest of the diocese of Trenton, N.J., he was appointed head of the Department of Religious Education at the Catholic University of America in 1957. The department had been organized in 1931, but despite the driving concern of its sometime head, William H. Russell (1895-1953),[14] to make Catholic religious education more christocentric, Catholic University's graduate program reflected the preoccupation of the 1930s with method. Sloyan, however, influenced by Drinkwater, the kerygmatic and liturgical movements, and later by *Lumen Vitae,* sensed the inadequacies of catechesis were due more to content and attitude than method and techniques.

In 1958 Sloyan edited a series of essays, mostly by European authors, under the title *Shaping the Christian Message.* This small work provided the underlying philosophy for the revitalization of the graduate program at the Catholic University in the early sixties. The course offerings of those years (and to some extent still) can readily be grouped around the "four signs": Bible, doctrine, liturgy, and Christian witness. Marquette University, Fordham, Loyola (Chicago), and other Catholic institutions of higher learning soon joined in the effort, offering a variety of summer workshops, teacher training seminars, and graduate degree programs. Despite the fact that graduate programs in Christian education and catechetics under Catholic auspices grew up apart from the seminary curriculum, they tend generally to give greater importance to theological formation than educational practice.[15]

Notwithstanding the contention that many of the models now being developed in Christian education represent an effort to restore and rejuvenate traditional ways, they also represent a reaction against some of the more recent but well entrenched structures. Some changes have been dictated by economic and social conditions beyond the control of parishes and dioceses. Other developments, however, have been in reaction against the lifeless rigidity of the printed texts with their stereotyped formulas and schools with their overly organized structures. Marshall McLuhan pointed out the limitations of the "Gutenberg Galaxy," and progressive educators have advocated ungraded classes, programmed learning, and community education among other innovative models. It is in this context, therefore, that the models currently popular among Roman Catholic catechists must be measured. Weekend retreats for teenagers, encounter groups for married couples, cassette lecture series, and educational television are just a few.

One does not have to question the successes of the schools to observe that the aura which Americans have bestowed on them has misled many Christians into thinking the school is the natural habitat of religious education. In the boom years immediately after World War II, it was common for Catholic parishes to build the school before the church. Many still measure religious education programs against the yardstick of school structures: classroom furnishings, the number of hours in formal course work, the mastery of textbook material, etc. Others, however, have reacted negatively to the school model. The two reasons most often cited for disenchantment with religious education programs in the school are: (1) Schools emphasize the cognitive elements of religion, and (2) as long as the school model holds sway, adult religious education will never be given the priority it deserves.

One alternative is the baptismal catechumenate, which the 1977 Synod of Bishops held up as the "model of all catechesis."[16] In 1972 the Vatican promulgated the *Rite of Christian Initiation of Adults* which authorized a modified and modernized version of the ancient catechumenate. To some extent it is an outgrowth of the efforts in the early phase of the liturgical and catechetical movements to restore old forms and recapture the vitality of the early Church. It is also an outgrowth of a new emphasis (aided and abetted by several other official church documents) to give greater priority to adult catechesis. The rites of the adult catechumenate are designed to confront the nominal or would-be Christian with a choice of lifestyles. Each step in the initiation process is seen to have special significance. More than mere ritual is involved (if indeed it is ever proper to speak of "mere" ritual). It is another example of how sacramental catechesis is viewed less and less in purely didactic terms and is seen more and more in terms of experience.

The *Rite of Christian Initiation of Adults* like other revised rites promulgated since Vatican II signals another change in modern catechetics. There is a growing emphasis on the role of the community in catechesis. Ultimately, it is the Church community by its lifestyle, purpose, and spirit which evangelizes, catechizes, and provides the context in which all grow to maturity in Christ. It is not to deny the intrinsic worth of participation in the liturgy and ritual, and the performance of acts of service, to point out that active fellowship in the Christian community also has an educational value. The new rites recognize what the pioneers in church renewal always claimed, namely, that full, active, and intelligent participation in the liturgy presumes sound catechesis. And on the other hand, the liturgy is what gives catechesis life and substance. This is a common principle which ancient and modern catechetics share.

The modern catechetical movement prepared the ground for many of the Church reforms mandated by the Second Vatican Council. In turn the council legitimated the movement. The *General Catechetical Directory,* commissioned by Vatican II, defined catechesis as a form of the ministry of the word. Shortly after its publication in 1971, an International Catechetical Congress convened in Rome to examine the scope of the document and to recommend ways of implementing it. The delegates soon recognized that, thanks to Father Hofinger's study weeks, *Lumen Vitae,* catechetical and pastoral centers in Europe and the Third World, graduate programs in the United States, etc., they spoke with a single voice. The congress reaffirmed pluralism as a positive value and the need for adaptation at the local level. Overall, it viewed catechesis as a pastoral activity whose task is to nurture a living, conscious, and active faith.[17]

Two events in 1977 brought the modern catechetical movement into even greater prominence: the completion of a national catechetical directory and the Synod of Bishops which met in Rome to examine

"Catechesis in Our Time." The *General Catechetical Directory* had laid down broad principles governing the contents of catechesis and the training of catechists; it also called for a series of national and regional directories to provide practical guidelines for individual countries and cultural blocs. The National Conference of Catholic Bishops, at its fall meeting in Washington, D.C., put the finishing touches on the American directory, titled *Sharing the Light of Faith.* It was the culmination of a process begun in the spring of 1972 when the hierarchy approved a comprehensive plan to develop a directory for the United States. The project was entrusted to the able leadership of Wilfrid Paradis, a priest of Manchester, New Hampshire, and a broadly representative working committee. They initiated the most extensive consultation ever undertaken in the American church. By design, the consultation process was intended not only to provide input for the national directory but also to educate Catholics to the nature and possibilities of catechesis in the contemporary world.[18]

If *Sharing the Light of Faith* climaxes the chapter in the history of American catechetics recounted in these pages, the 1977 Synod of Bishops marks the beginning of another. Its theme, "Catechesis in Our Time," followed logically on "Evangelization in the Modern World," the topic of the 1974 synod. The working papers prepared for the synod reiterated the fundamental principles of the catechetical movement, emphasizing that catechesis is an aspect of the ministry of the word and the task of the entire Christian community, not simply the responsibility of a few. At the end of their deliberations the bishops issued a "Message to the People of God" in which they acknowledge that "the vitality and strength of the entire catechetical activity of the Church is clearly felt almost everywhere" (par. 1).[19] It credited the catechetical movement for its contribution to renewal in the Christian community as a whole but was not content to rest with past success. The synod pointed out the complexities of catechesis itself and the problems it faces in today's world. The "Message to the People of God" ended on a note of optimism, however, saying "the future belongs to believers, whose hope will not deceive them (Rom. 5:5)" (par. 17). It was in this spirit that the modern catechetical movement was born and in this spirit will continue to thrive.

NOTES

1. Vatican Council II, "Decreee on the Pastoral Office of Bishops" (*Christus Dominus*), no. 14. Cf. W. Abbott, ed., *The Documents of Vatican II* (New York: American Press, 1966), p. 406.

2. H. W. Offele, *Geschichte und Grundanliegen der sogenannten Mün-*

chener katechetischen Method (Munich: Deutscher Katechetenverein, 1961). Joseph A. Jungmann, *Handing on the Faith: A Manual of Catechetics*, trans. and ed. A. N. Fuerst (New York: Herder and Herder, 1959), pp. 174–221. R. G. Bandas, *Catechetical Methods* (New York: J. F. Wagner, 1929), p. 176–210.

3. F. H. Drinkwater, *Educational Essays* (London: Burns Oates, 1951), p. 408. See also D. Doyle, "F. H. Drinkwater on the Use and Abuse of Catechisms," *The Living Light* 18 (Winter 1981): 345–355.

4. R. A. Lucker, *The Aims of Religious Education in the Early Church and in the American Catechetical Movement* (Rome: Catholic Book Agency, 1966).

5. Joseph A. Jungmann's *Die Frobotschaft und unsere Glaubensverkündigung* at the urging of the Holy Office was withdrawn from the market and thus appeared in English only many years later in an abridged version as *The Good News Yesterday and Today* (New York: Sadlier, 1962). By that time the main lines of Jungmann's thought were already known in the United States through his other writings (principally, *Handing on the Faith*, cited above) and the lectures of visiting German scholars. Cf. Johannes Hofinger, "J. A. Jungmann (1889–1975): In Memoriam," *The Living Light* 13 (Fall 1976): 350–359. See also J. Goldbrunner, "Catechetical Method as Handmaid of Kerygma," *Worship* 35 (March 1961): 198–209.

6. Cf. George Delcuve, "The Catechetical Movement in France," *Lumen Vitae* 12 (1957): 671–702.

7. Cf. C. Gobert, "Vers la maturité spirituelle," *Christus* 2 (1955): 67–81. A. Brien, "La foi adulte," *Etudes* 293 (April 1957): 1–21. Pierre-André Liégé, *Consider Christian Maturity* (Chicago: Priory Press, 1965).

8. T. M. Kalita, "The Four Sources Revisited," *The Living Light* 11 (Winter 1974): 509–514. Cf. my *Catechetics in Context* (Huntington, IN: Our Sunday Visitor, 1973), pp. 69–70. J. Pelissier, "The International Centre, 'Lumen Vitae'," *Lumen Vitae* 15 (1960): 217–230. See also K. Barker, *Religious Education, Catechesis, and Freedom* (Birmingham: Religious Education Press, 1981), p. 68, n. 97.

9. Cf. L. Erdozain, "The Evolution of Catechetics," *Lumen Vitae* 25 (1970): 7–31. J. Hofinger and T. J. Sheridan, eds., *The Medellin Papers* (Manila: East Asian Pastoral Institute, 1969), p. 209.

10. Barker, *Religious Education, Catechesis, and Freedom*, pp. 76–78, 128–159, 181–183.

11. "Revelation and Experience," *Lumen Vitae* 25 (1970): 552.

12. Cf. L. M. Lazie, "Jane Marie Murray," *The Living Light* 12 (Summer 1975): 270–275.

13. Wm. J. Reedy, "Maria de la Cruz Aymes," *The Living Light* 12 (Summer 1975): 293–297.

14. A chronicle of the developments in the department can be found in a Ph.D. dissertation, Rosemary Rodgers, *The Changing Concept of College Theology: A Case Study* (Ann Arbor: University Microfilms, 1973). Though Sister Rodgers is mostly concerned with the undergraduate program, issues concerning orientation, personnel, and administration are inextricably woven into her chronicle. Cf. also Lucker, *Aims of Religious Education in the Early Church*, pp. 171–176.

15. The program at Notre Dame University, under the direction of James Michael Lee, consciously pursued another direction than the graduate programs mentioned above. Lee emphasized the instruction-teaching dimension of religious

education, cf. J. M. Lee, *The Shape of Religious Instruction* (Dayton: Pflaum, 1971).

16. "Message to the People of God," *Origins* (10 November 1977): 325.

17. *Atti del Congresso Catechistico Internazionale* (Rome: Editrice Studium, 1972). Wm. J. Tobin, ed., *International Catechetical Congress: Selected Documentation* (Washington, DC: United States Catholic Conference, 1972).

18. Cf. B. L. Marthaler, *Sharing the Light of Faith: An Official Commentary* (Washington, DC: United States Catholic Conference, 1981), pp. 4-8.

19. "Message to the People of God," p. 323. For further information on the 1977 synod, cf. *The Living Light* 13 (Fall 1976): 328-348; 14 (Fall 1977): 425-455; 15 (Spring 1978), entire issue.

Few persons in the United States have made a contribution to the catechetical scene as complex and difficult to assess as Gabriel Moran, currently professor of religious education at New York University. In 1966, the publication of his Catholic University doctoral dissertation in two volumes, Theology of Revelation *and* Catechesis of Revelation, *popularized the catechetical renewal at the same time it severely critiqued some of its errors. By means of these two books, his thought influenced catechesis worldwide.*

Since that time, his provocative reflections on religious education have made him something of a gadfly, ever challenging presuppositions and taken-for-granted procedures. The scope of Moran's thinking deserves and even demands special study all by itself.

In the following piece, Moran appends, almost a dozen years later, a critical reflection to one of his "gadfly" essays that caused a furor when it first appeared in Commonweal *(18 December 1970) under the title "Catechetics, R.I.P." For this sourcebook, Moran has heavily edited his original text, and interested readers will find his deletions as illuminating as his own introductory commentary.*

As editor of the sourcebook, I am indebted to Gabriel Moran for his contribution in the original essay and his commentary on it.

READING 21

Catechetics in Context ... Later Reflections

GABRIEL MORAN

I AM GLAD TO HAVE the opportunity to contribute a new introduction to this essay written eleven years ago. The essay was transitional for me, as it indicates a move from my concern with catechetics to a concern in which catechetics is one part of the story. I was also urging a transition for the church in my claim that the

---

This reading is an updated and expanded version of an earlier article by Gabriel Moran, "Catechetics, R.I.P.," which appeared in *Commonweal*, 18 December 1970, pp. 299–302.

catechetical movement had gone about as far as it could and that what was needed now was other reforms of church structure and church language.

A decade later my main argument still seems to me to be valid. I think that the church is indeed in a transition, but I now realize that the transition may last decades rather than years. A catechetical *movement* did reach a kind of conclusion with the national dissemination of theories, practices, roles, and curricula that had been developing in Europe since the 1940s. The *National Catechetical Directory* is testimony that the catechetical movement succeeded in penetrating all of the country's dioceses so that most Catholics have been affected by it and many Catholics can speak a catechetical language.

In the first part of this article I was trying to turn the reader's attention to the context of the catechetical movement. I probably moved too aggressively against the word *catechetics*. Worst of all was the title ("Catechetics, R.I.P."), a slick phrase that the editor put on the article and one that I would not have approved had I been asked. The article (or the title) made me *persona non grata* in many dioceses of the United States. Obviously, I cannot put all the blame on the journal's editor who changed my title ("Religious Education: The Next Phase"). Presumably some people read more than the title and were still offended by the article. Authors cannot hope to provoke thinking without offending a few people. However, on the assumption that I offended many people I should not have, I would like to comment on the two main points of this article: (1) language, catechetical and otherwise, and (2) church patterns of involvement in education.

1) What I was trying to say about the limitations of catechetical language has become clearer to me in the intervening decade. Catechetics is one case of a larger question that concerns both the Catholic church's relation to other churches and the Christian churches' relation to the nonchurch world. Catechetics is not only a church language but a Catholic church language. Despite occasional references to it by Protestant educators, the dialect remains a foreign one to Protestant denominations. That fact does not invalidate catechetics. On the contrary, catechetics is alive in Roman Catholicism because of the strong sacramental tradition which this church has had. The renewed interest in the catechumenate is evidence of the meaning and the vitality of catechetics. A functioning language has to be a specific language. Catechetical language is alive insofar as it has specificity, concreteness, and reference to Catholic practices.

There is a problem, however, which Christians – especially Christian educators – must face today. We all speak at least two languages:

the internal language of our religious tradition and the language of our contemporary secular society. The two languages are not entirely separate; words have moved in both directions. One definition of an educator might be that he or she works at the intersection of languages.

When the two languages are closely related and are sometimes in conflict there is an inevitable tendency to make one the judge of the other. A further step is to make one language a subset of the other. In the case of Christian and secular languages, one could plausibly argue for either of the two arrangements: (a) The church language speaks of realities greater than any secular language can; Christians simply announce that what they have is the final judge of human reasoning and empirical realities; or (b) everyone acknowledges that the church is today spoken of as one institution among many in society; church language seems to consist of words that are within a contemporary language such as American English. I would argue that a religious educator should resist both tendencies and be aware that there are two languages which are sometimes parallel, sometimes overlapping, and possibly converging toward a reality beyond words.

An example may clarify this position. I recently gave a talk to an ecumenical organization that asked me to speak on the education of adults. I developed the thesis that we need a more adequate meaning of adulthood than the one which dominates our culture. A reactor to the talk said I was dealing with the wrong issue: Adulthood is not enough; we ought to educate for a congregation in mission to the kingdom of God. My response was that he was not offering a different objective but was speaking a different language. We had agreed on one thing, namely, the inadequacy of the meaning of "adult." Two strategies are then possible: (a) declare that being adult is not enough and offer a church formulated objective; (b) resist the secular reduction of the word *adult* by using materials drawn from Christian (and perhaps other religious) sources.

I have no objection to people using a language that is biblical, theological, and catechetical when the occasion is appropriate. The liturgical event is the most obvious occasion. However, religious education must include stepping outside of that language or at least building a bridge to the language of the nonchurch world. This issue is at work in the problem of the church's adult education programs. People may not be able to recognize their religious questioning in a theological-catechetical language, however elegant and self-consistent such language may be. They need a religious educator who can straddle two languages.

2) On the suggestion I made for church educational patterns, there

is less to be said. I admitted that my proposal was an extreme one
so as to cause a jolt. I proposed in this article that the *teaching* (as
distinct from other educational influences) of religion should be separate
from church sponsorship of education. There are two parts to that proposal, the first referring to Christian involvement in educational settings outside the church, the second referring to changes in the Catholic
school.

The last decade has seen movement on both parts of the proposal.
The teaching of religion outside of religiously affiliated institutions has
continued to grow. Unfortunately, the growth has been painfully slow,
with most of the progress confined to the private and state universities.
The unavailability of religion courses outside the university remains
a shocking deficiency in this culture. The teaching of religion in public
schools, adult education centers, nursing homes, prisons, and anywhere
else that is possible seems to me a vocation worthy of a Christian
religious educator.

The news is better on the side of the Catholic school. The problem
I referred to in the article of talking always of percentages of Catholic
children is largely past. The schools have diversified and now justify
themselves on other grounds than the percentage of Catholic children
they reach. In a sense "the Catholic school" has passed into "Catholic
schools." Some of them have a faculty, student body, and objectives
not unlike those of schools of the 1940s. However, others serve society in more ways than by turning out Catholic citizens. Especially in
urban settings some Catholic schools are doing effective and admirable
work for the whole community. Within any Catholic school the study
of religion should be available but on a basis clearly distinct from an
organization inducting its members. I find that many Catholic school
teachers immediately understand my reference to two languages. They
cannot assume an agreed upon Catholic church language while they
work in (one kind of) a Catholic school.

The parish director of religious education is an embodiment of the
tension between catechetics and (secular) education. The DRE is often
taken to be a representative of the church and therefore one who ad-
vocates the doctrines and practices of Christianity. The DRE needs
to use critical thinking that creates distance (but not too much) from
the church that supports the DRE. As a group, the DREs are the most
aware of living with two different languages, both of which must be
preserved. The diverse Catholic schools and the parish director of
religious education have a rough economic road ahead. They need all
the encouragement they can get. I would hope that my distinguishing
a catechetical language and its noncatechetical context is of some help.

During the past decade I have worked in a great many settings, both church and nonchurch, to test the validity of what I wrote in this article. I am more convinced than ever that religious education must find a home in specific church terms and also in places where church language is inappropriate. I have no wish to attack people who speak a catechetical language, but I do object to their assuming that there is no other way to engage in religious education. In recent years I have worked in a doctoral program of religious education at New York University. Some church people cannot believe it when I tell them that we have about forty courses in religious education, none of which is on the Bible, theology, or ministry. I do not claim that such a program is superior to a church program, nor am I asking any catechetical personnel to join me. I would suggest, however, that the existence of such religious education outside of church language might give occasional pause to people who work in catechetics. Perhaps there are possibilities for the church and its educational work that cannot be stated in current church language.

[Following is the Commonweal *article by Gabriel Moran, newly revised by the author.]*

The emergence of the word *catechetics* in American Catholic literature of the late 1950s signified the entrance onto our shores of new theological and educational ideas. Insofar as American Catholicism could profit from new ideas coming from anywhere, the "catechetical movement" can still be applauded as a success. Looking back on that movement, however, one can see grave inadequacies in both its theology and its educational theory. The theology was a powerful but narrow neoorthodoxy which preserved biblical categories from contamination by contemporary ideas. The time-lag in American Catholicism's acquaintance with modern biblical study made it ripe for a theology which was going out of favor in many other places. The educational framework was even more severely limited. It seemed to suppose a priest in a pulpit talking to little children or at least to adults being treated like little children. When the educational theory was any better, one could suspect that it was because American Catholics were getting John Dewey via French and German translations.

The word *catechetics* has remained a European import which never really took hold in this country. Certainly, American Protestants could never make any sense out of the word, a fact which should have given pause to American Catholics. Nonetheless, for a time in the 1960s catechetics struggled to come into its own as a discipline. With only a few exceptions (for example, Gerard Sloyan or Bernard Cooke), the new field did not draw the support of the best minds in the American Catholic church. The university world wanted no part of it. As a result, catechetics remained a parish-school-CCD project, and it was left to the seminary to make catechetics into a respectable field of learning.

The catechetics course, left over from some bygone day in the seminary curriculum, seemed to be stirring to life like some long-sleeping giant. Then a funny thing happened to catechetics on the way to becoming a discipline: It disappeared. There is something very peculiar about a field which disappears as it improves. The attempt to build religion departments in Catholic schools has not succeeded because the courses and the teachers keep disappearing. When religion courses are improved they gradually come to look like something other than religion. Likewise, the more that religion teachers are prepared, the less they generally seem interested in teaching a religion course in school.

What has happened is fairly easy to see in retrospect. Catechetics was created from a peculiar kind of theology and a primitive form of education. Some people tried to improve the theology, and other people worked at the educational side. However, the improvement of theology and education did not improve catechetics; it blew the field apart. What had been good theologically was reabsorbed into theology; what was good educationally is being assimilated into general education. No one's theories killed catechetics; it collapsed of its own weight.

Where do we stand today after the demise of catechetics? We are certainly not worse off than we were ten years ago. However, a feeling of having been duped may make it seem that way. Catholics on both the left and the right today complain about what has happened in the catechetical movement. The right-wingers have been marshaling their forces around this issue during the last two or three years. They appear ready to make their all-out stand on this ground to save the church. I sympathize with their nostalgic search, and I respect their clarity of purpose and their dedication to means. It remains true, nonetheless, that the right-wing adversaries of catechetics have no workable alternatives. Their proposed solutions are more inadequate than the programs which they can so easily criticize. They waste their energies searching out heresy at a time when that problem has been swallowed by the much larger question of the existence of any Christianity at all. Their aim to extirpate heresy by direct means is incompatible with the educative process. As a result, they are not addressing the problems that affect our world. It is not a matter of faddishness, selling out, or weak-kneed conformism, as they would put it in their vocabulary. It is a question of dealing with the religious and educational scene that now exists, whether or not one approves of it.

The fringe of liberal critics has even less reason for a belligerent attitude toward catechetics. They apparently had assumed that a few catechetical experts would fix up the school curriculum and that the church would make comfortable progress. They may now be a bit peeved that it has not gone very smoothly. Perhaps their children still do not like the religion course in the local school. Things may even seem to have gotten more confused than ever before. At such a point there is always the temptation to look for a scapegoat. What the critic should really be asking is why he or she has not been in the game all along. The critic hoped that someone else's theories were all that was needed. Let the beleaguered teacher in the Catholic school or CCD apply the theories. What time has revealed is the need for a more radical restructuring of institutions that would demand involvement of every Christian.

It is only after the walls have come tumbling down that there can appear the really enormous problem of religion in education and education in religion. What should one call the study of the interrelation of religion and education? Logically, it should no doubt be called "religious education." However, that term carries a burden of historical connotations almost as heavy as the word *catechetics*. *Religious education,* a term which preceded and then accompanied catechetics, was preempted by one group of Christians doing one set of things to one age-level of people. Insofar as *religious education* is a bland and general term, it could conceivably be saved from its ecclesiocentric bias. Whether the term is worth the effort to save is questionable. In any case, it is likely that the term will have to die in its older meaning before it can be reborn to a new significance.

One can applaud the current attempts to establish religious education departments that prepare educators with a major in religion. At the same time, people in these ventures seem unaware of the historic problem that they are tackling. If religious education is to be a genuine field of study, not a cover for indoctrination, it must be born from a combination of sound religion and good education. Such a combination would be more threatening to the Christian church than anything produced by the catechetical movement. Anyone who sets out to educate in the field of religion has to put Scripture, liturgy, and Christian theology into a broader context that does not afford Christianity a normative role. I think that this step should be taken and must be taken. I am simply raising a forewarning to churches and church-related schools that they should not take this step unaware of the implications and then complain later than the investment has been a failure. Church institutions should not be too pretentious about what they are doing in religious studies departments or religious education schools until they have gotten a credible distance from an ecclesiastically introverted position.

For the first time in its history, Christianity is facing an ecumenical era which will demand a religious understanding worked out in the context of a single world history. As Mircea Eliade has recently pointed out, this historical moment of confrontation with the world's religious scene is a painful and even humiliating one for the Western church. The religious movement at work in the 1970s is liable to have an effect opposite of the religious movement of the 1950s that brought people back to church. The religious attitude of the coming generation was aptly put in the title of a recent article by a university chaplain: "Never on Sunday." Whether this fact is more an indication of the naive anti-institutionalism of the new generation or of the corrupt rigidity of the old church might be debated. In either case, the existence of anything called church is going to be in question for the near future.

By an ecumenical era, therefore, I do not mean one in which Catholics and Protestants are going to drink tea together. An ecumenical era is one in which any organized religion will have difficulty getting a hearing in a world which is doing its religious thing elsewhere. In such a world, no religious group can expect to have members because they were born into its tradition. Any organized religious group will have to be constantly devising means to make its position intelligible to all intelligent and responsible adults. Education thus becomes a central concern of all the members at all times rather than a peripheral task of a few experts who train children.

The job of moving out into the broader educational scene might seem overwhelming for any religious body. People who have lived in Sunday schools are hardly ready to take on the Ivy League. Somewhat surprisingly, however, there is help coming from the opposite direction. People who are interested simply in education are coming upon many questions which, either from cowardliness or piety, had been relegated to the churches. It is becoming increasingly difficult to sidestep these sticky issues. Questions of irrational force, human value, inner spirit, disintegrating community, and mystical symbolism cannot be avoided much longer in anyone's education.

Those of us who are still interested enough in a Christian church to believe that it is worth reforming should be looking to these larger religious and educational needs of our society. Because the church seems to be engaged in serving the religious and educational needs of another era, its credibility is hurt even when it seems to be successful. In the religious sphere, it directs nearly all its attention to people between the ages of six and seventeen. That period of life is one when a strongly religious atmosphere and an explicitly Christian teaching should be kept to a low key. In an ecumenical era we need almost the reverse of what we have, that is, we need a religious environment before the age of six and the availability of Christian theology after age seventeen.

Educationally, the Catholic church is still trying to reach the greatest number of people it can. This objective is also self-defeating. It was perhaps a mistake of Catholic school critics to emphasize that Catholic schools were reaching only 50, 40, or 30 percent of Catholic children. Possibly the extension of the system to that large a percentage was a major part of the problem. In any case, the most crucial question is not one of percentage at all. The question is why the church is now in the business of schools. To accept percentages of Catholic children as the basis of discussion is to think in terms of the church's educational service in the past. The church got into the school business to preserve itself and to serve the religious and educational needs of a future generation of church members.

Nearly everyone admits that the situation has changed drastically, but few people seem willing to draw the educational conclusions. The church's educational contribution in the ecumenical era should be to raise the educational level of the whole community by whatever means and to whatever degree is possible. No one could fault the church for not solving the whole educational problem – so long as the church is facing in the right direction. What is specifically an educational contribution should be made without regard to whether the recipients are Christians or not. Some efforts are being made in this direction, but often the people engaged in them are not entirely clear about the nature of their involvement. Neither church sponsors nor church school teachers have been unambiguously clear about being in the educational field without a vested interest.

No matter what is done, educational ventures which have "official" church sponsorship are sure to be suspect for the present. To counteract this tendency I would go so far as to make this drastic suggestion: Wherever there is official church sponsorship of education, the teaching of religion should be avoided. Admittedly, this is to bend over backward to avoid the charge of ulterior motives. Such a maneuver should not always be necessary, but it is needed at this moment for a church trying to establish itself at the entrance to an ecumenical era. The proposal may be hopelessly naive in supposing that any human institution could be that selfless, but it is a challenge which might test the church's claim to serve the needs of all God's creation. Sometimes, individuals and institutions have only a choice between high heroism and painful death.

Christians, like everyone else, should not be prevented from teaching their own religious tradition. I am proposing, however, that this teaching should be in a context clearly distinguishable from an official party line. The individual can be unambiguously a member of a church group, but the titles, clothes, books, architecture, etc., must indicate an autonomy of thought and responsibility. Religious questions, including the existence of a Christian church, should be explored in adult education centers, in secular universities, in private community ventures, on television, and in dozens of other places. One cannot deny the tenuousness of these structures for education in religion, but that cannot be the decisive issue here. If the future belongs to this framework it becomes necessary for many of us to get into such projects and to improve the structure. The success, as well as the failures, of some small attempts might lead the way toward a larger shift of resources.

I am aware of the magnitude of the change I am proposing. It is assumed that individual Christians can unofficially engage in education but that an official church exists for education in the religious area. I am claiming that the reverse is true. It makes sense for an official church to back educational projects, but religions ought to be taught in an atmosphere free of any church structure. If such a reversal were to occur it would be a near miracle. It would also cause conflict that would threaten the life of the church. It would also show that the church clearly had a life that is worth threatening.

PART TWO
Issues

*In his overview of the modern catechetical movement, Reading 18,
Berard Marthaler notes: "If North Americans have made a distinctive
contribution to modern catechetics . . . it is in this area of experiential
catechesis." The matter continues to be of key significance. In the following essay, the catechist and theologian Piet Schoonenberg delineates
the relationship between experience and revelation, while emphasizing
the folly of splitting one from the other.*

READING 22

Revelation and Experience

PIET SCHOONENBERG

E XPRESSIONS SUCH AS "revelation," "Word of God," and "God
speaks" are becoming increasingly more difficult to use. In our
time they seem to indicate something superfluous, even foreign. In fact,
the formal questions may be asked: What is the significance of God's
speech? Why does God speak? But also their content has become prob-
lematic: What do we mean by God's kingdom, grace, and salvation?
One could answer that Christ has always been a sign of contradiction
and a scandal, that it would be a bad sign if this were no longer the
case. Today unfortunately Christ and God are no longer experienced

Reprinted from *Lumen Vitae* 25 (1970), pp. 551–560. Reproduced by courtesy of *Lumen
Vitae.* Copyright *Lumen Vitae* 1970. Translated by John Van Den Hengel, SCJ,
Nijmegen.

as a scandal. They, or more accurately their names, are simply mean-ingless to many. Instead of being absurd, the Christian message has become empty of meaning.

It is possible to seek to understand this situation from the per-spective of today's secularization.[1] The attitude of contemporary catechesis to the process of secularization can be positive since secular-ization has Christian roots and since it is a challenge to comprehend better the Christian message. But it would be much too optimistic to think that we have already found a language suited to the proclama-tion of this message. Moreover, the question is being raised with ever greater frequency: Where are modern men and women, particularly our young people, to be reached? Is it in the family? in the schools? in the churches? Furthermore, it is no secret that, in their search for reflec-tion, meditation, and religion, our youth are bypassing Christianity in favor of the religions and psycho-techniques of the East, witness the popularity of Zen Buddhism.

In this situation it is not surprising that today catechesis wishes to begin at the opposite end, namely, with the experience of those for whom the catechesis is intended. Pedagogically and didactically this has always been necessary. Of what value is a message whose words have no relationship to the experience of the listener? For that reason catechists have always tried, more or less successfully, to relate the content of the message to the experience of the young—for it was to them that in the past the message was addressed primarily. Until recently, the well-known Munich Method provided the pattern by which the distance between the message—or doctrine—and experience was bridged. Since then some remarkable and, in my view, essential changes have taken place in catechesis. From a mere approach to the message, experience has become the theme itself of catechesis. Catechesis has become the interpretation of experience. It has to clarify existence, that is, it has to articulate and enlighten the experience and existence of those for whom the message was intended. Thus, in 1964, the Higher Catechetical Institute of Nijmegen stated in its *Fundamentals and Pro-grams of a New Catechesis:* "By catechesis we mean: throwing light on the whole of human existence as God's salvific action by witness-ing to the mystery of Christ through the word, for the purpose of awakening and fostering the faith and prompting man to live truly in accord with that faith."[2] In another book published by this same in-stitute, the same position—spiced with polemics against indoctrination, biblicism, and the dualism of nature-grace—is maintained.[3] In the above definition there is mention of "the word," which attests to the mystery of Christ; but the term *proclamation* is lacking. Proclamation, however, is the theme of the preliminary report of the final session of the Dutch Pastoral Council.[4] Here, the emphasis was placed on a different aspect. Existence, experience, and their interpretation are indicated by the words "present truth." But the main emphasis is placed upon the proclamation and its inner tension between "possessed truth" and "promised truth." The conception of catechesis as interpretation of experience and existence by means of biblical pericopes is, it seems, presented in its most radical form in *Fundamentalkatechetik* by Hubert Halbfas.[5]

Meanwhile, two things seem certain. First, the conception of catechesis as an interpretation of experience or as an illumination of existence assumed for itself an important position in the sixties. Second, the question must now be raised: How is this interpretation related to proclamation? What is the place of interpretation and what is the place of the message? These questions summarize the theme of this meeting, which can be stated in the form of an alternative: catechesis of interpretation or catechesis of proclamation? What follows is a theological reflection upon this alternative. My immediate response is that it appears to me as a false alternative at least when restricted to interpretation of the experience of the listener or of modern humanity. This experience must not only be articulated but also completed. On the other hand, the message (revelation) which is proclaimed is also an experience, namely, the experience of the Christ-event. In this way, revelation or the Word of God on the one hand and experience or existence on the other hand point to one another. In this article I will deal first with revelation and then with experience.

I. Revelation

1) **God speaks.** Revelation is also called the Word of God. The latter expression can also be reflected upon philosophically, which could be very fruitful in this theological exposition. Let us ask ourselves what it means to say "the Word of God." How can we imagine that "God speaks"? We certainly may not picture it as if God emits sounds or as if he acts as a partner in a conversation. God does not act according to the norms of innerworldly causes, as if he would replace them. He does not take the place of a human speaker. God is the unlimited causality, the source of every innerworldly causality. He makes the action and speech of each to be their own. It may be a beautiful thought that God, making his voice resound from heaven, informs us about something. That something of the sort could happen literally, that God could create sound waves so that human words could be heard, can

perhaps not be denied. But the sense of this escapes me. Rather, God's Word and speech will mean that God speaks through human beings. Of course, this does not mean that he speaks through us as the organist expresses himself or herself through an organ. That would be another form of shortchanging humanity. The speech will be divine to the extent that it is also fully human speech, inasmuch as God takes hold of a human being, allowing him or her to experience his salvation and his presence so that humankind will express this presence and salvation and thereby God. God's Word cannot be thought of in any other way than as an experience of God in human words. It presupposes that the Word of God implies necessarily and essentially human experience.

This philosophical consideration is confirmed by the Bible inasmuch as it presents the Word of God most frequently as proceeding from the mouths of humans, particularly of the prophets. Although there also are other representations of the Word of God, it may be proposed as the voice of God coming to humankind. Thus, for instance, God speaks to Moses and Elijah; Isaiah and Ezechiel perceive God's Word in their vocational visions; a voice from heaven resounds for Jesus at the Jordan and for the apostles on the mountain of the transfiguration. However, when the prophets repeatedly add "thus speaks Yahweh" or "it is the Lord Yahweh who speaks," it ought not to be interpreted as a word spoken previously by God. Since they have been sent by Yahweh, and continue to be sent, and since, according to the Semitic mentality, the envoy of someone is that person's alter ego, i.e., the extension of oneself, the expression "thus speaks Yahweh" means that he is speaking at the moment through the mouth and the experience of the prophets.

2) **Different theologies in the Old and in the New Testament.** In the reflections above we have touched upon two views of divine speech in the Bible. Today, it is generally acknowledged that both in the Old and in the New Testaments we find different views of the same salvific event. This gives rise to different theologies. For our purpose it is important to pay attention in the Old Testament to the distinction between prophetic and apocalyptic theology.[6] The prophets interpret God's salvific activity in the history in which they find themselves. They see this history as being ever open to both sides: Through human sins it can lead to disaster, but on the other hand God's offer remains, and when the people accept it God will guide this history to a future of salvation. The apocalyptic authors are the heirs of these prophetic promises. They have expanded these to extend over the whole cosmos and over the whole of history, even beyond the boundaries of death. They have presented this, however, within a definite framework. In this

framework history is predestined and determined by God with the chastisement of the evil and the salvation of the elect. This takes place in a totally different, posthistorical world, which follows an earthly history of sadness and afflictions and occurs in a future era separated from the present evil era by a catastrophe of worldly proportions. Apocalyptism is thus a prophetism composed according to the melody of a divine predestination and of a dualism of the present and a future era.

It is well known that apocalyptism also plays an important role in the New Testament. It has even been called the first Christian theology. Its influence has never totally disappeared from Christian theology. Witness to this are the controversies of the sixteenth and seventeenth centuries concerning predestination and our present distaste for a dualistic world-view and for "paying a down payment" on heaven. Apocalyptism in the New Testament is not limited to the Book of Revelation or to such apocalyptic passages as Mark, chapter 13, and parallels. Its influence is also present as an indispensable part of the preaching of Jesus concerning the kingdom of God and in the preaching of the apostles concerning the resurrection and glorification of Jesus.

On the other hand, from the beginning of the proclamation of Jesus we discover another view, another theology, side by side with the apocalyptic view. For Jesus, the final reign of God of the apocalyptics is already present. It takes place when through the Spirit of God demons are driven out. It is promised to the poor; it sets its requirements. Even now it is a future being realized. In this we discover a theology that comes close to that of the prophets. This neotestamentary theological point of view can be characterized with the words *gospel, message,* and *happy tidings* so dear to Mark and Paul. While the apocalyptic theology gives an overall view from the opened heavens, the theology of the gospel states what happens here on earth through God and calls upon us to take part in it.

In the Old and New Testaments we find, therefore, a plurality of theologies. In other words, the one revelation is articulated in different theologies. However, this formula does not do sufficient justice to the situation. It says that the content of the one revelation is articulated in different ways, while the formal event is rendered by the one concept "revelation." What we have stated above about apocalyptism, prophetism, and gospel-theology ought, however, to bring us a step further. The event indicated by revelation has obtained its name from only one of these theologies, namely, from the apocalyptic. *Revelation* is the usual translation of *apokalypsis,* which literally means *disclosure.*

Revelation is thus presented as a disclosure of a secret or a mystery hidden in God.[7] This mystery is usually disclosed by an angel (angelus interpres) to a seer, who in symbolic visions sees the history of the world and the final state. A totally different sound comes from the theology inspired by the prophets and the gospel. Here God is active in an event upon earth, in our history, which is experienced and proclaimed in faith. The stage of apocalyptism is usually heaven, where earthly history is read out of a heavenly book of divine prescience. The stage of the other theology is our earth. Apocalyptic theology presents itself as a transmission of visions and oral communications; the other theology bears witness directly of a personal experience.

3) **Revelation as event and experience.** A philosophical reflection and especially the Scriptures have led us to the insight that revelation means more than a word of God resounding from the heavens, more than an unveiling of secrets or decisions hidden in God and in heaven by means of visions and oral communications. Another concept of revelation is that of a proclamation of a factual and experienced salvific event. That which in common language we call "revelation" is presented either as apocalypsis or as evangelion. Because of our philosophical reflection we evaluate the first concept as more symbolic or metaphorical and the second as more realistic. The concept of "evangelion" is closer to the earthly reality and – and this must be insisted upon – to the God in earthly reality. "Evangelion" presupposes directly the *experience* of God in earthly reality, in our history. The evangelist gives witness to that which he has heard, seen, and touched in the incarnate Word (1 John 1:1–3). In a community which lives from this experience, apocalyptism does have its place since it gives evidence to the hope grown through this experience, but it does not express directly the experience at the base of it. Because of its symbolic language, it remains foreign to experience, just as in the case of the dogmas which use a more metaphysical language.

Thus, the event of revelation, as it is presented in the Bible, has bearing upon experience. The question remains, however, of which experience are we speaking? In the line of the Dutch *Fundamentals and Programs of a New Catechesis*, it is also possible to speak of the clarification of human existence as a salvific activity of God. But then the question becomes even more pressing. Of which human existence are we speaking? Is it the "total" human existence of which the *Fundamentals and Programs of a New Catechesis* speaks? That is not excluded. I should say that this is not to be excluded. Total human existence according to the Bible is to be interpreted as God's salvific activity since the God of Jesus wills to be the Father of all. He does not leave us without evidence of himself in the good things he does for us (Acts 14:17), and he is not far from any of us (Acts 17:27). Of this general salvific presence of God and of this possible general experience of God, I will yet have an opportunity to speak. First, I wish to manifest that the biblical message refers primarily to a certain experience, to a *particular* area of the general salvific history.

An initial phase of it is already found in the Old Testament from which, for example, the spring and harvest festivals, namely, the feast of the unleavened bread and Pentecost, received their interpretation more and more along the lines of the events of the Exodus and of the Sinai. These became normative for the experience of Israel, the guarantee for the present and future salvific activity of God. As a result even Deutero-Isaiah, who admonishes his fellow Israelites not to look back any longer upon God's earlier works (Isa. 43:18f.), cannot but look upon His present activity as a new exodus.

In the New Testament there is an expectation of the final activity of God on the last day. God is active in his Spirit, who is his gift par excellence. Yet, all this is concentrated around the one fundamental event: the Christ-event, the ministry, the death, and the glorification of Jesus. It is important in this context that the Son of Man desired in the end is no other than Jesus, that the day of Yahweh has become the day of Christ, and that he is invoked in the "Maranatha" as the teacher on earth. Even more important is the fact that the great experience of the early community, the experience of the Spirit, is always connected with Jesus. The Spirit gives witness to him. It leads to the confession that Jesus is Lord (1 Cor. 12:3). He makes believers, through his various gifts, members of the same body, which is the body of Christ, that is, Christ himself. He is the Spirit of Christ and vice versa: "The Lord is the Spirit" (2 Cor. 3:17). Also, the Lord is ever-present, but this Lord is not any divine being but the historical Jesus, "the Jesus, whom you have crucified" (Acts 2:36). In this way an ever-present experience of salvation receives interpretation. But fundamental and primary is the proclamation of a particular salvific event that has taken place in Jesus. Without this event the present experience of salvation of Christians not only could not be articulated but also would have no foundation. It could not exist. Christian existence is communicated only after human existence is addressed by the proclamation and saved through faith in this preaching.[8] I would like to develop this further from the point of view of experience.

II. Experience

1) **Catechesis of interpretation.** It has been pointed out already

that in today's catechesis the experience of the listener is not only the point of departure for the proclamation but also the theme of catechesis. I have already indicated my agreement with this development. Now, however, something must be said about the dual character of this experience. On the one hand, it is already Christian so that this catechesis must be an interpretation of this experience. On the other hand, this experience is also a quest for a "something more," for a "vis-à-vis" peculiar to the history of salvation and the person of Christ.

The experience of the listener, who as an active listener is also a partner, is the theme of catechesis and applies of course to both Christian adults and youth who in any way by means of education come into contact with Christianity. In fact, it is valid for many more in our society, including those who in no way wish to be called Christian any longer. I do not intend to call each human being an anonymous Christian because this type of terminology seems empty to me. In this context, the statement of Dorothee Sölle that "church is also outside the church"[9] seems much more pertinent. There is a certain church of action which does not coincide with the church of doctrine and sacraments.[10] Better yet, there is a Christian and biblical inspiration which has pervaded our society, which does not mean automatically that all the good in our society is derived from a Christian or biblical inspiration. All this should be interpreted in catechesis with modesty and without undue appropriation. The Christian origin can in many instances be shown as well as their agreement with the gospel. In this way, according to the words of the Dutch *Fundamentals and Programs of a New Catechesis,* an interpretation of human existence as salvific history is accomplished. When in honesty and in poverty of spirit we regard present events, we can observe with gratitude that there are many facets of today's life that can be understood as concurring with the gospel and as a fruit of the Spirit. This is visible especially in the ceaseless protest against injustice. Also, the call for a macroethics, the ethics of structures, should be seen as truly evangelical. Christianity of our time is called upon to discover also in structures the area of activity of the Spirit, just as some time ago we discovered, and to a large extent must still discover, the body as such an area. All this can be said in justification of a "catechesis of interpretation."

2) **Catechesis of proclamation.** However, this type of catechesis should not have the final or the only word. Youth, but also adults, the marginal Christians and the committed Christians, all are in need of salvation, in need of Christ. The experience of our time not only is Christian but also must be converted and saved. In any case, it can ever continue to grow more Christian. The catechesis of interpretation may

not eject the catechesis of proclamation. Wherever this occurs it usually has two sources. First, there is the fear to fall once again into a type of preaching that fails to accord with experience. The fear exists that a catechesis making use of a biblical terminology remains just as unviable as the previous, more dogmatic, catechesis. Second, the talk of a "something more" or a "vis-à-vis" is interpreted as belonging to another age or to a different supernatural level of reality.[11] Limiting myself to the second theological objection, I must add that a split-level or a two-storied theology is only one, and deficient at that, reconstruction of the gracious character of God's gifts. If God is a God not only up there but first of all a God ahead of us, then grace is not a second level but a given future. It is thus both a critique and a promise.

However solid an evangelical ground the critique of structures may have, it must itself be subject to the critique of the gospel. If, for example, the church would refrain from preaching the conversion of the hearts of men beside the evangelical betterment of structures, it is in danger of exchanging one ideology for another. In the final analysis, our preaching should never cease to criticize the established church, but it must equally beware of institutionalizing the critique. It can achieve this because it is a promise, a promise of God's kingdom, which constantly transcends that which has already been accomplished. It is always a new future, until as the ultimate future it transcends even the boundaries of death.

NOTES

1. This was the theme of a meeting of the European Coordinating and Research Team for Catechesis held in the week of Pentecost 1968 in Madrid. The following presentation was given in the week of Pentecost 1970 at a meeting of the same European team in Vogelenzang, The Netherlands.

2. Higher Institute of Catechetics of Nijmegen (Holland), *Fundamentals and Programs of a New Catechesis* (Pittsburgh: Duquesne University Press, 1966), pp. 86f.

3. Ernst Thuring, *Houding en verhouding. Gedachten over hedendaagse katechese* ('s Hertogenbosch: L. C. G. Malmberg, 1969).

4. *Ontwerp-rapport "Vragen rond de verkondiging,"* "De Horstink" (Amersfoort, 1969).

5. Hubert Halbfas, *Fundamentalkatechetik* (Düsseldorf: Patmos-Verlag, 1968).

6. This has been pointed out by Jürgen Moltmann in *Theology of Hope* (London: SCM Press, 1967), pp. 124–138.

7. "Mysterion" is derived from apocalyptism and not from the mystery religions.

8. Since, as we saw, revelation includes experience, we are properly not concerned here with a tension between revelation and experience, but with a tension within the experience of salvation itself. It is a tension between a particular experience of Christ and a general experience of salvation. This tension can be observed also within revelation and the history of salvation. Then it is a matter of the relationship of the general to the particular revelation of Christ, as well as of the general history of salvation to the Christ-event.

9. Dorothee Sölle, "Kirche ist auch ausserhalb der Kirche," in *Kölner Vorträge zur Kirchenreform* (Wuppertal: Jugenddienst-Verlag, 1965), pp. 5–16.

10. This is perhaps a better version of the older doctrine of the "soul" and "body" of the church.

11. Thuring, *Houding en verhouding,* pp. 134–137.

One cannot probe very deeply into recent catechetical theory without coming to recognize the key role played by the French Dominican, Piere-André Liégé. Again and again in seminal writings on catechesis, one finds references to his work.

The following piece, written before Vatican Council II, is a classic statement of catechetical theory which, because of its succinct style, deserves careful reading and reflection. Liégé's treatment of evangelization and his distinguishing it from catechesis is particularly important. One finds clear echoes of Liégé's thought in Pope Paul VI's apostolic exhortation on evangelization, Evangelii nuntiandi, *echoes which suggest that Liégé himself may have written one of the earlier drafts of that important document.*

Several of Liégé's concerns in this piece, particularly his stress on adult faith, can be found highlighted in the General Catechetical Directory.

READING 23

The Ministry of the Word: From Kerygma to Catechesis

PIERE-ANDRÉ LIÉGÉ

A N A PRIORI PRINCIPLE of the ministry of transmitting the Word in the Church will inspire these pages: *This ministry must*

Reprinted from *Lumen Vitae* 17 (1962), pp. 21–36. Reproduced by courtesy of *Lumen Vitae.* Copyright *Lumen Vitae* 1962.

reproduce, as far as possible, the very forms in which God revealed himself. Insistence is usually laid, quite rightly, on the faithfulness of the Church's testimony to Revelation. Less care seems to be taken over fidelity to the means used by God. The Church is prophetical; that is, God continues to reveal his Word in her and through her, in continuity with the history of Revelation.

Before justifying theologically the classic distinction between the two principal periods of the prophetical ministry of the Church — kerygma and catechesis — we must first consider a few fundamental elements of a theology of the mystery of God's Word. Then we will be able to see the continuity in the Church's ministry of the Word. From this reflection on the Church's prophetical ministry, the distinction we intend to explain will emerge. Such is the plan of what the reader will find here.

I. The Mystery of God's Word

1) **The Word, an act of God.** Theological reflection on God's Word, as outlined in the second part of Isaias, St. John, and St. Paul, leads to the assertion that God's Word is fundamentally a *revealing act of God.*

a. Dominating all the manifestations of the Word immanent to history, summing them up, there is one act by which God decided to become present to history for his own glory. This is what St. Paul will call the preexistence of the mystery hidden in God even before the creation (Eph. 1). When we say that the formal motive of faith is God himself making himself known, we mean that by grace the believer finds himself or herself placed in communion with the transcendent act of the Word of God, by means of the historical manifestations of this Word. Thus, only the Word *of* God will be such in the fullest sense, not merely words *about* God authenticated by him.

b. This act of the Word engages the entire personality of the living God in his intention of Revelation. According to the realism of the term *Dabar,* it is God himself coming forward to be present in history, to make it question him. Our anthropological distinctions between the heart, the mind, and action cannot be applied to the act of God's Word without depriving him of totality. That is why God's Word is both noetic and dynamic, revealing awareness and creating principle: love, light, power, and judgment. The classic definition of Revelation — "locutio Dei ad homines per modum magisterii" — shows clearly the poverty with which the idea of God's Word has sometimes been clad. Isaias expresses it much better: "As the rain and the snow come down from heaven and return no more thither, but soak the earth and water it, and make it to spring and give seed to the sower and bread to the eater, so shall my word be, which shall go forth from my mouth. It shall not return to me void, but it shall do whatsoever I please, and shall prosper in the things for which I sent it" (Isa. 55:10–12).

c. That is why the act of God's Word will reveal both the plan of God's glory and the personality of the living God—God at the heart of his will's plan and of his action in human history, becoming thus sacred history and his Kingdom. With the same intensity with which the divine plan is revealed will the countenance of God be revealed.

2) **Manifestations of God's Word.** The transcendent act of the Word is only accessible to us through its immanence in the various historical manifestations which constitute revealed history.

a. God's Word, entire and perfect in its divine source, has made use of many and progressive interventions in the course of time, unified, however, by his revealing intention.

b. The manifestations of God's Word take the form of events and conscious contact: *God speaks by acting; he acts in speaking.* He expresses himself as a person using concrete communion, not confining himself to the mediation of explicit ideas. He unveils himself to the historical consciousness of a community and by means of events, of which the content of actual Revelation is what the prophets were charged to deliver.

c. Revelation progresses in the measure that the act of God's Word is more involved in the divine manifestations, making clear the meaning of sacred history. For being God's Word, however, each manifestation does not imply fresh affirmation and more explicit contact. God speaks, even when he repeats himself!

3) **Jesus Christ, plenitude of God's Word.** It is through and in Jesus Christ that the full act of God's Word identifies itself in sacred history. God's revealing interventions in the Old Testament did not equal the revealing intention itself. The prophets were not identified either with the holy events or with the Holy Spirit who inspired them. In the revealing event of Christ the manifestation of God's Word attains its plenitude, summing up and surpassing all the prophetical revelations of the Old Testament. The prologue to the Epistle to the Hebrews declares as much: "God, who at sundry times and in diverse

manners, spoke in times past to the fathers by the prophets, last of all in these days, has spoken to us by his Son, whom he has appointed heir of all things, by whom also he made the world" (Heb. 1:1-3).

Jesus Christ, plenitude of God's Word: What do we mean more precisely?

a. By his preaching and works, Jesus Christ brought to an end the prophetical signs of God's appearance in history. The synoptic Gospels show him taking up, to explain their full and universal significance, all the manifestations of God to the Jewish people and proclaiming the imminence of God's definitive coming. "The time is accomplished," said he, "and the Kingdom of God is at hand. Repent and believe the Gospel" (Mark 1:15).

b. By his resurrection, Jesus Christ manifested fully and definitely the intention of God's glory. By this event, God's Word showed human history its final destination and showed the divine power which would set it en route for eternal life. As in the Old Testament, God manifested himself in an event teaming with Revelation. It was a personal event, concerning Christ himself, the divine meaning of which he proclaimed. No wonder that Paul placed Christ's resurrection at the heart of kerygma and that he wrote to the Colossians: "I am made a minister according to the dispensation of God, which is given me toward you, that I may fulfill the Word of God, the mystery which has been hidden from ages and generations, but now is manifested to his saints, to whom God would make known the riches of the glory of this mystery among the gentiles, which is Christ, in you the hope of glory" (Col. 1:25-28). To the elders at Ephesus, also, he said: "I have not spared to declare unto you all the counsel of God" (Acts 20:27).

c. God's Word, which is Jesus Christ in his paschal humanity, has a universal bearing, the beginning of accomplishment in humanity. It calls for expansion, not to be surpassed nor a fuller revelation in history. Pentecost is included in this event, Word of Jesus Christ. The eternal Gospel (Rev. 14:6) will proclaim this accomplishment, and the blessed will sing "the canticle of Moses, the servant of God, and the canticle of the Lamb" (Rev. 15:3).

d. Finally, in Jesus Christ, through his manifestations of glory, his person, his works, his words, his pasch, God revealed, as far as human minds can receive it on earth, the mystery of God in himself. He is the Word, substantial and no longer intermediary prophet, eternal witness of God's plan and of the Godhead. As St. John puts it: "He that comes from above, is above all. He that is of the earth, of the earth he is, and of the earth speaks. He that comes from heaven is above all, and what he has seen and heard he testifies . . . he that has received his testimony has set to his seal that God is true. For he whom God has sent speaks the words of God, for God does not give the Spirit by measure" (John 3:31–35).

That Jesus Christ is the Logos, there is the radical principle of the identity of his historical manifestation with the plenary act of God's Word.

That he is judge of the living and dead, constituted by the Father, there is the consequence of this personal identification with God's Word which, present in history, judges it while calling it and casting it forward.

II. The Prophetical Ministry of the Church

1) **God's Word in the Church.** If Jesus Christ is the plenitude of God's Word, God has nothing other to reveal to his Church than what he has manifested in Jesus Christ. Revelation has been closed since the apostolic age, the Apostles being the last of the prophets in the strictest sense of the word; it fell to them to bring out the full meaning of God's Word of the coming of Christ, in the light of Our Lord's own words and the charism of the Holy Spirit at Pentecost. Just as the words of prophecy made one with the deeds of the prophets in the Old Testament, Christ's Word continued by the Apostles makes one with the event of the resurrection.

God still speaks in and through the apostolic Church. *Revelation has become Tradition.* That is to say, the Holy Spirit makes God's Word actual in the period of the Church's existence by preserving the memory, living, accurate, and active, of all that Christ is in his personal mystery and his communication to men. Living Tradition constitutes a continued prophetism in the Church—not only an objective memory and magisterium but also the entire presence and power of God's Word, realized fully in Jesus Christ and extension of salvation in humanity.

God's revealing act, then, continues to express itself adequately in the event Jesus Christ. But what are the expressions of this event in the daily life of the Church and in the world? Maintaining the full significance of the term *Word* which we have seen, it can be said that *everything which expresses the presence of God in Jesus Christ within the Church is the derived Word of God:* proclamation of the message, signs of grace, celebration of sacraments, reading of Scripture. The whole Church is God's Word, having nothing else to express than what Jesus Christ is for her and what he does in her.

2) **The ministry of the Word.** "We will give ourselves continually to prayer and to the *ministry of the Word*" (Acts 6:4).

If it is right to see every Church ministry as an expression of God's Word in Jesus Christ, it is also permitted to mean by the ministry of the Word what the Apostles meant in the Acts, the expression of the *proclaimed Word.* Let us not forget, however, that, understood in this sense, the ministry is placed in a context of signs, without which it would be too noetic and purely verbal. It is in this sense that we are going to speak of the ministry of the Word in the Church: the Church's preaching, in continuity with the transcendent act of God's Word, which gives it authority and power in grace, according to the plenitude of historical revelation given in Jesus Christ. As St. Paul asserts: "Faith then comes by hearing, and hearing by the Word of Christ" (Rom. 10:17), and again: "The Word is nigh thee, even in thy mouth and in thy heart. This is the Word of faith which we preach. For if thou confess with thy mouth the Lord Jesus, and believe in thy heart that God has raised him up from the dead thou shalt be saved. For with the heart we believe unto justice, but with the mouth confession is made unto salvation" (Rom. 10:8–11).

3) **An acting Word.** What has been said allows us to allot its true place to the mystery of the Word in the Mass of Church action. One would lessen it by reducing its efficacy to being merely occasional; on occasions when the Word is proclaimed, God will act for humanity's salvation. The only function of the Word, then, would be to evoke Jesus Christ and his significance in grace. No, it is in the message, human in form, of prophetical testimony that God makes the interior testimony of the Holy Spirit reside, in continuity with the transcendent act of the Word. That is why the word of the Church declares and realizes truth, salvation, reconciliation, resurrection in Jesus Christ. It is a noetic and dynamic word in the message composed in human terms. Otherwise, the prophetical ministry would be reduced to a professorship in religion. "The Word of the Lord increased and multiplied," we read (Acts 12:24). And St. Paul again writes: "It (the proclaimed Gospel) is the power of God unto salvation to everyone that believes" (Rom. 1:16). "In Christ Jesus, by the Gospel, I have begotten you" (1 Cor. 4:15).

We seem not to have retained the same conviction of the power of the Word in the Holy Spirit which the Apostles had but to reserve this efficacy to the sacraments exclusively. A typical example of this is François Mauriac's answer to the question: "What do you expect from the priest?" His answer: "Dare I admit that I am mistaken enough to expect nothing? I only ask him to give me God, not to talk to me about Him. I do not underestimate the ministry of the Word, but you asked for my personal demands. To my mind, a priest's best preaching is his own life. A good priest has nothing to tell me. I look at him, and that is enough. The liturgy is enough, too, it is silent preaching. The religious order that preaches best is the Benedictine Order, because they do not climb into the pulpit, but make us live the drama of the Mass, and make us grasp the sublime daily action. How will I understand Kierkegaard who writes that God is Some One we speak to, and not Some One we talk about! How I pity Protestants whose worship is only words! The holy liturgy – the only preaching that appeals to me and convinces me . . ."

To remain among the literary appreciations, Bernanos was nearer the mark when he made the curate of Torcy say to a fellow priest: "Teaching, my little man, is no joke! I am not talking of those who carry it off too easily; you will see quite enough of them as life goes on, you will soon know them, and the consoling truths they utter. Truth delivers first, and consoles afterwards. Besides, we have no right to call it consolation. Why not condolence? The Word of God! It is a red-hot iron. And you who teach want to take it up with tongs for fear of burning yourself, why don't you grasp it with both hands? . . ."

St. Paul says the last word when writing to the Thessalonians: "We give thanks to God without ceasing because that when you had received of us the Word of the hearing of God, you received it not as the word of men, but (as it is indeed) the Word of God who works in you who have believed" (1 Thess. 2:13). The Apostle was in a position, after the incident at Lystra (Acts 14:8–19), to distinguish between persuasive discourses and the wisdom of God's Word.

III. Kerygma and Catechesis

The exercise of the Church's ministry of the Word in the earliest days of the Church makes a clear enough distinction between the function of evangelization and those of catechesis ("kerygma" and "didachè"). In his great doctrinal epistles St. Paul gives catechesis to those whom he has already converted by the Gospel. The author of the Epistle to the Hebrews distinguishes between "the *first elements* of the words of God" and "the *doctrine* of justice," or "the *word of the beginning* of Christ" and "things *more perfect*" (Heb. 5:12–14; 6:1–3). In the fourth century the historian Eusebius mentions the same distinctions, speaking of the preachers of the Gospel of the first centuries. "To those who had heard nothing of the Word of faith, they went eagerly to speak and transmit the Gospel, the book of divine teaching. They *laid the foundations* among stranger peoples, then appointed pastors and left to them the care of those whom they had brought to believe . . ." (H.E., III, 37).

It is this distinction which we must now found theologically, that is, starting from what God's Word is, from its transcendent act to its immanence in the heart of the believer, passing through its historical manifestations in the history of salvation. The act of the ministry of the Word has its place between the act of God's Word announcing the mystery of Christ and the act of faith by which the believer gives glory to the Word of the Lord (Acts 13:48). It is in relation to these two terms that the mediation of the Church will assign the norms of its exercise and special pedagogy. First, let us examine the term *act of faith*, in order to come back to the term *Word of God* later.

1) **The dialectic periods of faith.** Modern theology and pastoral have rightly insisted on the dogmatic character of faith, on the objectivity of its contents and the orthodoxy of its assertions. This is a necessary reaction against subjectivism of religious feeling and philosophies of religion. It is evident, nevertheless, that this reaction, often somewhat unilateral, sometimes resulted in separating our basic catechesis on the faith and biblical Tradition, older in itself than the modern opposition of subjective and objective. In biblical Tradition the faith first appears as a *conversion*.

It is nonetheless evident, and probably for the same reasons, that basic catechesis on the faith is somewhat separated from its pastoral sources in a Christian situation where there is little question of conversion. The person who becomes a believer is first of all one who *converts his or her heart* and whole life to the living God, whose coming he or she has recognized, whose call he has heard, and whose Word he has received. To be a believer is to imitate those champions who are praised in chapter 11 of the Epistle to the Hebrews, of whom Abraham is the father, as St. Paul says (Rom. 4:17).

a. The faith, then, is first presented as an act of *conversion*. Does that mean that there will be no belief and adherence to a settled Revelation, at least in the newborn stages? We must be careful not to confuse opposition and distinction, in this case, to oppose two types of faith, one of which will be the meeting between persons, the other, simply accepting as true.

On God's side, the Word which calls to faith is necessarily revelation: "I am the living God, I will give you life if you accept to expect glory from me alone, and acknowledge your Lord Jesus Christ." On the believer's side, changing life and deciding to welcome God, which is conversion (*melanoia*), imply of necessity a fixed recognition of the identity and intention of the God who has called him or her: "I surrender my life into your hands because you are the Lord of life. You shall rule my life and I will work for your glory." Concretely, conversion is fixed upon the identity and significance of Christ. This recognition of Christ by the believer will find itself caught up in a free act of complete donation, of one person to another, much richer than a mere accepting as true the divine teaching concerning Christ. This is the beginning of the life of faith for one passing from unbelief to the Christian faith.

b. Faith must ripen. It will pass from the stage of conversion to *communion.* It is just the same as in human meetings when the first encounter only gives a global and indistinct intuition of the person met, intuition which will develop into deeper and deeper intimacy, into a sort of divination with the beloved and union with His life.

To one who has been converted to God in Christ, it is given to enter gradually into all the aspects of Christ's mystery into which he or she has been introduced. It is not so much a religious science as a knowledge of concrete communion, giving realism to all the elements which translate into human terms the riches of God's Word in the Tradition of the Church, the continuation of Pentecost.

c. If we chose for our heading *dialectic* periods of the faith, it was to point out that from conversion to communion there is more than mere chronology in the life of faith, more than passing from what the Council of Orange called *initium fidei* to *augmentum fidei* (cf. Denzinger, 178).

Chronology changes into a really organic structure of faith. It is like an extension of conversion to communion and back again. Conversion develops into communion but on condition that communion is ceaselessly animated by fuller conversion. In return, what finds itself intensified in the faith of communion was already included in the global act of conversion, which had nothing of an act without doctrine, in spite of certain appearances. Conversion surpasses itself in communion, but there is no faith of communion which has not first been and continues to be faith of conversion. It is like a crypt which runs the whole length of the nave and not like a porch which is left behind when entering the nave.

There are not two kinds of faith nor two successive stages of faith— stage of conversion, stage of doctrinal belief—but two dialectic elements of Christian faith, one living reality. The postcommunion for the Sunday before the Epiphany seems to illustrate this analysis: "Enlighten, O Lord, thy people, and inflame their hearts with the splendor of thy grace so that they may ceaselessly recognize their Savior (faith of conversion?) and their desires may be fulfilled" (faith of communion?).

2) **Dialectic periods of God's Word.** Faith ever refers us back to God's Word, its basis. We said above that God's Word is indissociably dynamic and noetic.

Were there only question of accepting beliefs, God's Word could be reduced to a Word that teaches. If there is question of stirring up continual conversion and introducing conscious communion, we can see the correspondence which must exist between the act of the divine Word and the believer's act of faith in all its fullness.

That is why one could, with a delicate sense of shades, since we mean dialectic extension and not opposition, compare the periods of faith and the fundamental attributes of the act of God's Word. This would lead us to say:

a. that it is *chiefly the dynamic aspect of God's Word which stirs faith as conversion*, bringing forward humanity's life, the divine assault, judgment. As the Epistle to the Hebrews expresses it: "Keener than a two-edged sword, it separates even soul and spirit, joints and marrow, it discerns the intentions and thoughts of the heart" (Heb. 4:12) — not that the noetic attribute of the act of the Word is absent or inactive.

b. that it is *chiefly the noetic aspect of God's Word which nourishes the faith as communion:* enlightenment, wisdom. According to the wish of St. Paul to the Ephesians: "May the God of Our Lord Jesus Christ, the Father of glory, give you a spirit of wisdom to reveal and make you understand . . ." (Eph. 1:17) — without outdating the converting action of God's Word.

3) **Dialectic periods of the prophetical ministry in the Church.** If the act of prophetical ministry must model itself on the revealing act of God, cause of the act of faith, we see at once that certain consequences impose themselves on this ministry:

a. *The primordial function of the ministry of the Word in the Church will be to stir up the faith of conversion, basis of all life of faith, without ever being able to suppose it completely acquired,* even from baptism for a child born into the Church by this sacrament.

Baptism is the sacrament of faith. In the case of baptism of infants, the Church receives them as participating members of a community adult in faith, capable of taking charge of these neophytes to lead them to the adult age of faith, when they can ratify personally their public profession of faith — conversion to Christ — and the obligations of a holy life which result from it. If it takes about twenty years to form an adult socially and psychologically, why should it take less – outside exceptional cases – to reach the adult Christian state? Baptismal ratification continues, then, for some twenty years until the child, born prematurely into the Church, by the maturity of his or her conversion has come up with the convert baptized as an adult, thus becoming a fully responsible baptized soul. Now, it is by evangelization, the exact meaning of which we will define later, continued right through adolescence that the infant members of a baptized community will be brought up to the full exercise of their membership of the same community – for the Church is a community of adults. This does not mean that an adolescent cannot have already set out on the path of Christian conversion but that this conversion only acquires its dynamism and stability after passing through the first experiences of human existence. *Adherence to beliefs is not enough, although it must always determine and express conversion better, in the personal ratification of the baptismal promises.*

b. In its doctrinal function, the ministry of preaching must always have missionary energy so as to sustain and deepen conversion, to assist the interior strengthening of belief. This applies specially to Lenten preaching and missions in the home country.

c. It will be sterile to pass on the details of belief before having at least roused conversion; we know the danger of confusing faith with a mere formal orthodoxy; but it would be infidelity to the Word to neglect deepening the faith of communion inaugurated at conversion.

From our foregoing reflections, two types of prophetical ministry in the Church prove themselves necessary:

A primordial word (call it: missionary preaching, kerygma, evangelization).

Subsequent preaching (call it: doctrinal preaching, catechesis) in which several forms should be distinguished. St. Thomas Aquinas, for example, distinguishes four kinds of ministry of the Word; the first is evangelization (*conversiva ad fidem*); the second is catechesis – catechism preparatory for sacramental practice; the third regards spiritual life (*de conversatione christianae vitae*); the fourth concerns the deepening of the more profound mysteries of faith (*Summa Theologica*, IIIa, 71, 4, ad 3m). It seems essential to us, as our preceding analyses suggest, to stress the two basic accents of the prophetical ministry. Even if the practical exercise of this ministry unites the two, which is quite normal, it is useful to consider them separately, especially concerning kerygma.

It remains, therefore, to examine the two essential functions of the ministry of the Word – evangelization and catechesis.

4) **Evangelization.** Properly speaking this is: *the first impact with the Good News of God's coming in Christ to found his Kingdom in the power of the Holy Spirit to rouse personal conversion and lead to entrance into the Church by baptism.* The dynamic Word, usually accompanied by signs: God has come; he comes today; he will come to judge the world; but the judgment is already taking place because of the Gospel.

In the New Testament, the verb *to evangelize*, used in an active sense, means "to proclaim the event of the Good News of Jesus Christ" (Cf. Luke 9:6; 20:1; Acts 14:7; Rom. 15:20; 1 Cor. 1:17; 9:16). It is the first mission received by the Apostles: "Go, teach the Gospel to every creature" (Mark 16:15).

The *Gospel* is the absolutely Good News which comes from God and concerns his Kingdom among humankind, expression of the plan of his love (Mark 1:14; Rom. 1:1; 15:16; 2 Cor. 11:7; 1 Thess. 2:8-9; 1 Pet. 4:17). It is a Gospel of peace (Eph. 6:15), of salvation (Eph. 1:13), of grace (Acts 20:24).

Christ proclaimed *the Gospel of the Kingdom of God* (Mark 1:15).

After Pentecost, the Apostles proclaimed the *Gospel of the reign of Christ,* made king by his resurrection, and definitely fulfilling the preceding promises of the Kingdom. As St. Paul says: "*My Gospel, the message of Jesus Christ, the Revelation of the mystery which was kept secret from eternity, which now is made manifest . . .*" (Rom. 16:25).

After the period of historical evangelization will come the *eternal Gospel* proclaiming, with the end of history, the Good News of the Kingdom and the judgment in glory (Rev. 14:6).

He who announces the Gospel is compared to the heralds (*kerux*) of felicitous royal proclamations in the ancient civilizations, for the Gospel must be proclaimed publicly and universally.

The kerygmatical Word, then (from *kerygma*, the contents of a proclamation entrusted to a herald), does not go into the details of the *credo*, not through doctrinal minimalism but because the Revelation is globally and dynamically contained in the proclamation of Jesus Christ, as within a personal synthesis. It certainly intends to make souls attentive to God revealing himself in Christ – but by causing a break in former existence and a passionate attachment, a decision for life. Looked at from close range, nothing is as doctrinal as kerygma – but under the form of a *message.*

Under the occasional manner of testimony rendered to Christ by the dedication of daily life, or in the more determined manner of a missionary announcement, we have found the specific place of the ministry of the missionary word in the Church of today as in the Church of the first centuries. This is not the place to examine its demands; it has sufficed to give the character of its principles.

5) **Catechesis.** We are not going to consider the different types of catechesis but to reflect on the whole ministry of the Word which deepens the primordial work of evangelization. Catechesis exposes the totality of contents in Revelation – Tradition in the unity of the Christian mystery. We mention a few of the essential laws of this transmission of the Word.

a. **Catechesis flows from the Gospel.** The Gospel is taken here in its meaning defined above: announcement of the Good News of the coming of the reign of God in Christ, made king of humankind by his death and resurrection. It is the contents of the apostolic proclamation (or *kerygma*), to which man has been enabled to convert his whole life. All Revelation is a development of the dynamic message; all catechesis is a continuation of evangelization. There is no growth in faith without previous conversion which remains active.

Two conclusions can be drawn from this:

All catechesis should be christocentric. It is by Jesus Christ that God manifested and still manifests his glory in history. If conversion means to recognize Christ's exact identity, Christ becomes the subject of attribution of the whole revealed mystery. Whatever aspect of this mystery is studied, there will always be question of Christ, plenitude of God's Word.

All catechesis must bring man back to the initial act of his conversion, act which, in one way, he never gets beyond. In the measure that conversion has not been chronologically distinct from catechesis, as for baptized infants, catechesis will always have a dialectic period of evangelization, without which it would be mere religious instruction.

b. **Catechesis must unify the different aspects of the Christian mystery and preserve the organic balance of Revelation.** This results from the kerygmatical origin of the Christian *credo*. Living faith first feeds on synthesis. Catechesis which did not continually bring out the unity of Christianism as one organic whole flowing from one kernel and being resumed in it, would not bring to birth in people's hearts the reality of the Christian mystery. It would stop at committing to memory a collection of articles of faith. Development of the different aspects of the mystery should be made according to the *concrete logic of revelation*, not according to an a priori logic or personal system but according to the logic of the events of salvation, through which God proved his will to save and his presence in history. God's wisdom inscribed itself through events; sacred history is, therefore, the bearer of a divine intention which unifies it and manifests the analogy of faith.

Does that mean that one plan imposes itself on all Christian catechesis? No, of course not. But it seems to me that both personal choice and adaptation to individuals should arrange to follow this development:

• *Jesus Christ, the revealer of God's plan and mystery* — proclamation of the Kingdom by the coming of the king.

• *Jesus Christ, the personal realization of God's plan* — pasch of the triumphant Christ.

• *Jesus Christ, perfecting his kingship, in the Church* — the Spirit and the Church, extension of Christ's pasch until his parousia.

Each aspect of the Christian mystery must be given the importance belonging to it from its proximity to the center of Revelation. This means, *first of all*, the avoidance of pseudospeculative fantasies, empty of religious sap, and subtle developments on points where God's Word is reticent. It *also* means resisting the want of balance which subjective spirituality, peripheric devotions, and theological variance of opinion fatally introduce into presentation of the faith. While the official magisterium protects the deposit of faith against unorthodox deviations, the catechesis of ordinary magisterium must be careful not to stress unduly the latest dogma defined or elucidated as the most important. The faith of the Church on one aspect of the Christian mystery is usually expressed in several dogmatic or disciplinary regulations which must be taken together and not isolated. Every council has a limited aim according to the contestations which have rendered it necessary. Catechesis could not be chiefly antiheretical, although it must meet the needs and problems of the modern mentality.

Within the contents of the faith, different plans could be arranged; some aspects of the mystery are the already positive anticipation of the glorious life of intimacy with Christ; others are less susceptible of interiorization, such as the dogmas concerning the significance of evil; others again form the object of adherence to the will of Christ for the historical period of the Kingdom, everything touching sacrament or salvation, except the sacred humanity of Our Savior and the communion of saints. The two last plans obviously draw their light from the first, which dictates an order of catechesis on the Church, for example, in which the reality of the Holy Spirit completely dominates the reality of the Church's institution.

c. **Catechesis creates a Christian community.** It is addressed to a people, not to a collection of individuals, a people destined to become more and more such as their faith increases. Catechesis for one person treats him or her as a member of a people.

The duty of catechesis, therefore, is clear; it must bring out the ecclesial nature of the whole Christian mystery. As Christ is the center, the Kingdom is present everywhere. This is not one particular aspect which can be taken among others but an aspect which must influence all the others.

d. **Christian catechesis is indissociably dogmatic, moral, and liturgical.** This is so because it is the same living Christ in whom we believe, who, in immediate dependence of faith, gives a new meaning to the whole life of the believer and calls for new behavior from him or her. It is the living Christ, too, who comes sacramentally to consecrate with his presence human situations, to make them a definite part of the mystery.

Here, the catechist's task will be to bring out the aspects of the Christian mystery by their *significance* as much as and more than by their explanation. The significance concerns the whole person and affects one's behavior as much as one's convictions, while the explanation chiefly appeals to intelligence. This will lead to proposing vital and personal analogies, taken from human experience, rather than purely conceptual ones in order to penetrate Christ's mystery. God's behavior through Christ reveals human experience in itself and dictates its laws, while thoughtful human experience can discover in faith the meaning of the mystery of love. This gives back to anthropomorphisms a place given them by the Bible but often denied by learned theology. For human pietists and intellectuals, wishing to be pure, often become abstract, while concrete spirituality is lived by the whole person.

In practice, catechesis naturally has doctrinal, moral, or sacramental emphasis. To prevent emphasis becoming separation, catechetical thought must bring out the unity of faith in Christ and of the moral and cultural acts involved in it.

e. **In its expression, catechesis must retain traditional Christian language, while creating a modern Christian vocabulary.** A certain vocabulary is the inheritance of Judeo-Christian tradition. We know the importance of language for creating a community and transmitting a spiritual tradition. When this has, besides, the guarantee of biblical inspiration, we realize that Christian catechesis must pass it on as a living heritage. More than of dogmatic formulas, we are thinking of Revelation's grand expressions: *Kingdom, Life, Glory, Grace, Parousia, Testimony, World, Mission, Mystery,* etc., which must fix Christian attention. But a needed complement to this effort is the creation of modern equivalents which will convey God's Word clearly to the mentality and sensibility of today.

We said, at the outset, that the whole ministry of the Word in the Church should be faithful not only to the contents of Revelation but also to the forms of pedagogy used by God in manifesting himself in the history of salvation. The distinction, in unity, of the two functions of evangelization and catechesis in the ministry of the Word, is one of the most important applications of this principle. We only hope we have proved it in a sufficiently convincing manner.

The problem of evangelizing such "Christians" is one that confronts the Church in its current mission. "The first task in the Church's mission . . . is evangelization . . . in all places where the Gospel has not yet been announced, a matter to be decided on sociological grounds as well as on geographical ones."[5] Evangelization must be undertaken within "Christian" societies among those "Christians" who have never been converted.

The second important feature of Liégé's article was its insistence that the community of believers must itself be a sign of the truth of the Gospel. These communities must themselves be a lived proclamation, by means of a quality of life that both astonishes and attracts. Liégé insisted that the Church be the "human community where one does the truth," and not simply speaks it.[6]

> The manifestation of God's Word takes the form of events and conscious contact: God speaks by acting; he acts in speaking. He expresses himself as a Person, using concrete communion, not confining Himself to the mediation of explicit ideas. He unveils Himself to the historical consciousness of a community, by means of events, of which the content of actual revelation the prophets were charged to deliver. . . . Everything which expresses the presence of God in Jesus Christ within the Church is the derived Word of God. . . . The whole Church is God's word, having nothing else to express than what Jesus Christ is for her and what he does in her.[7]

The Church's prophetic ministry cannot be reduced to a professorship of religion or a purely verbal mission. Liégé's emphasis on this point broadens the understanding of the work of evangelization from that of verbal proclamation to that of a presence in the world that includes but goes beyond verbal proclamation.

Pre-evangelization is the term popularized by Nebreda but invented by Liégé for the work of providing a climate of truth and fidelity to conscience, within which the Gospel can be credible.[8] The Church must address itself to remedying inhuman conditions of everyday life that may so oppress people that they are unable to recognize the call of the Gospel. In short, "the work of pre-evangelization is inseparable from a collective combat to transform social structures."[9]

Liégé's seminal piece contains two procedural recommendations for the work of evangelization, which have become standard in modern catechetical theory. First, the work of evangelization must be free of artifice and any sort of deception. Liégé rejects as "dishonest propaganda" any sort of indoctrination that might violate freedom of conscience. Second, the work of evangelization must be adapted to the human group being addressed. The Gospel is quite the opposite of an esoteric message; each person, each mentality is capable of receiving the Good

News. Such, Liégé suggests, would seem to be the significance of the miracle of tongues at the first Pentecost proclamation. The adaptation demanded by evangelization involves more than the adaptation of language. "There is in this matter more than a question of language. There is rather a question of human experience, of one's sensibility, of mentality." It is a work "accomplished only by a creative effort to translate the eternal Christ in a language which makes him truly present in this time and in this place."[10]

The International Catechetical Study Weeks

Such are the main lines of Liégé's ideas, which, though expressed in 1954, have been repeated, nuanced, and amplified since that time, especially in the international catechetical study weeks, beginning with the Bangkok study week in 1962. At Bangkok were made certain careful distinctions about the stages of catechesis that had been appropriately passed over at Eichstätt in 1960, when attention was focused on the kerygma itself.[11] Eichstätt's deliberations were on a more fundamental level than those of Bangkok, which attempted to apply the principles elucidated at Eichstätt to more specific problems of the missions. As a result, the Bangkok study week focused on three different stages of mission catechesis: pre-evangelization, evangelization, and catechesis proper. Especially through the presence of Alfonso Nebreda, Liégé's former student, many of the key ideas of Liégé's 1954 analysis were elaborated in great detail. Particular stress was put on the principle of adaptation.

> The guiding principle of pre-evangelization is anthropocentrical, because we start with the man as he is. The way must be prepared in order that a person be able to understand the message not as a mere presentation of words which make sense to us, but as a challenge by words which make sense to him. This follows from the very essence of the message, which demands that we speak to and not at a man.
>
> Positive apologetics proceeds from a true understanding and appreciation of whatever is good and acceptable in a man's culture. It consists in taking due consideration of the man with whom we speak, and in removing the personal concrete obstacles which prevent his ready acceptance of the kerygma.[12]

Fidelity to the Gospel message must include fidelity to the men and women who are expected to hear the message and, therefore, must become the word of God in the words of *these* people.

By 1964 and the Katigondo study week, the categories of Bangkok (pre-evangelization, evangelization, and catechesis proper) had become standard ones in catechetical circles and were consistently used to clarify the work of catechesis. The Katigondo week centered its attention on the recently approved Constitution on the Liturgy and on the adaptation of liturgical rites to African cultures.[13] Stress was put on understanding the religious attitude of the African together with his or her psychological and cultural traits so that the imposition of Western catechetical and liturgical forms in Africa could be brought to an end.[14] Similarly, the Manila International Catechetical Study Week of 1967 used the Bangkok-Liégé categories to achieve its goal of rethinking the purpose of the mission apostolate in the light of the broader outlook of the Second Vatican Council, especially its work of liturgical reform.[15] Concern with evangelization accounts for the special attention given at the Manila week to the authentic religious values present in non-Christian religions. As at Katigondo, the principle of adaptation was highlighted, this time in the report of the Indian catechist D. S. Amalorpavadass.[16] In summary, one might say that Katigondo and Manila represent a consolidation of catechetical insights from Eichstätt and Bangkok, as well as a close study of the implications of Vatican II. There were, however, no dramatic developments on the question of evangelization.

Catechetical reflection on the work of evangelization reached a high in 1968 at the Sixth International Study Week on Catechetics, held in Medellín, Colombia. The work of that week can be best appreciated in the light of the special context in which it was undertaken.

> ... the Sixth International Catechetical Study Week was held in a continent boiling with unrest and in an atmosphere of near revolution that called forth the most outspoken declarations about the position of the Church and of catechetics. ... Modern catechetics benefitted from this attack on its relevance and came well through its baptism of fire.[17]

Out of this situation important new ground was broken in understanding the work of evangelization, particularly on two key issues: the importance of the catechetical context and of concern for liberation-development.

The catechetical leaders at Medellín recognized that a credible proclamation of the Gospel must be radically historicized by being addressed to the concrete human situation of a particular people at a time in history. Further, the Church and humankind must meet within the total human situation, by entering and becoming a living presence with that situation.

> Contemporary catechesis, in agreement with a more adequate theology of revelation, recognizes in the historical situations and in the authentic human aspirations, the first sign to which we must be attentive in order to discover the plan of God for the men of today. Such situations, therefore, are an indispensable part of the content of catechesis. The progressive

discovery of the total sense and definitive orientation of such aspirations and tensions, verified at each moment of the historical process, is an essential task of the prophetic mission of the Church.

To grasp the total significance of these human realities it will be necessary to live fully with the men of our time. Thus, these human realities will be progressively and seriously interpreted in our own time within their present context in the light of the living experiences of the people of Israel, of the man Christ, and of the sacramental ecclesial community where the Spirit of the Risen Christ is alive and continues to operate. Thus, a clearer understanding of man will help toward a deepening of the Christian message, and this deepening in its turn will promote a better understanding of man.[18]

Such a task demands the use of the best tools of modern social science in order to come to an accurate understanding of the multidimensioned human context.

The task further demands that the Church enter the social situation on the side of human development. The work of evangelization demands that one not reduce the Gospel to words or to mere modifications of language. The Gospel must rather be announced by visible signs acceptable to modern humanity, especially the sign of a life committed to human liberation, development, and unity.

A joint pastoral effort demands also the frank and definitive acceptance of the process of social change. Whatever the situation, those responsible must strive to meet them, knowing that these situations are in evolution, that one of the tasks of catechesis consists in helping that evolution and giving it some meaning. The forms of evolution can be very different from gradual up to violently revolutionary. In every case it is imperative that we make not only a diagnosis but an effort of imagination in order to foresee and promote new forms of existence animated by the Gospel.[19]

Such a statement is a good illustration of the distance catechetical theory had traversed in the eight years since Eichstätt, where preoccupation had been with the theological components of the message to be proclaimed. In less than a decade catechetical consciousness had been raised and broadened considerably on the question of evangelization.

To be sure, it would be a mistake to credit these developments to the catechetical community alone. The conclusions of Medellín owe much to the deliberations of Vatican II, as well as to two encyclicals of Pope Paul, *Ecclesiam suam* of 1964 and *Populorum progressio* of 1967. Among the documents of the Second Vatican Council, in particular, one finds different principles affecting evangelization set forth with a clarity and directness that rivals and even goes beyond many of the statements of the previous catechetical weeks. It may be that catechetical theorists must return to the council documents for their best justification of the current directions of the catechetical movement, as well as for some of the most lucid statements of these principles.

Among the documents that might be most profitably studied are *Lumen Gentium*, for its stress on the Church as the actualization of the Gospel (no. 1); *Gaudium et Spes*, for its confidence in the presence of grace in all men (no. 41), its affirmation of freedom of conscience (no. 58), its stress on respect for local cultures (no. 62), and its insistence on the witness value of the Church's own integral life (no. 21); and *Dei Verbum*, for its treatment of revelation as event first and then word (no. 4). A brilliant treatise on evangelization is found in *Ad Gentes* (the "Decree on the Church's Missionary Activity"). Among points it strongly emphasizes are the need for the witness of the community (nos. 6, 11, 12), for radical adaptation to various cultures (nos. 15, 18, 20–22), and for the Church to lead the struggle for human liberation as part of its work of evangelization (no. 12). *Ad Gentes* firmly rejects all attempts at deception (no. 13).

Such thinking was a matter of record in 1968. What Medellín did was to apply an entire range of thinking in the Church to the specific work of evangelization in such a way that Medellín's conclusions were a step beyond the original insights. The *General Catechetical Directory* further continues this dialectic.

In the directory the word *evangelization* occurs in fewer than a dozen different paragraphs. The entire directory, however, deals with the theme in its broad sense. In addition, Part 1 of the directory reads like a summary of the many insights regarding evangelization that had come to the fore since Liége's astute analysis: the need for new forms of expression of the message (no. 2), the importance of fostering and entering the struggle for human progress and its attendant liberation of the human person (no. 4), the function of the ministry of the word in searching out the values hidden in various human cultures (no. 5), and an insistence that evangelization consists of more than "merely eliminating ignorance of the doctrine which must be taught" (no. 9).

The themes of adaptation and of human development occur as running stitches in the total fabric of the directory. Catechesis is to be geared to different age levels and different cultural milieus.[20] The Church is not addressing her message of joy to some abstracted, disembodied "humanity" but to particular persons in their full historicity. Neither is her message simply a series of abstracted verbal formulas. Her very life, her communion in the Spirit of Jesus must be the core of her message to the world.

> The chief of these signs is the Church itself. Hence it is clear how necessary it is that the ecclesial community, according to the mind of the Church and under the guidance of the bishops, remove or correct things that mar

the appearance of the Church and constitute an obstacle for men to embrace the faith.

Catechists, therefore, have the duty not only to impart catechesis directly, but also to offer their help in making the ecclesial community come alive, so that it will be able to give a witness that is authentically Christian [General Catechetical Directory, no. 35].

The directory, then, as well as the entire catechetical renewal of the preceding two decades which it embodies, provides a useful context in which the theme of evangelization of the 1974 bishops' synod can be viewed. In addition, the study document used in preparation for the synod is best appreciated when situated in relation to the light shed on the question of evangelization by catechists within the preceding twenty years. This document, *The Evangelization of the Modern World*, is more a series of questions on the dilemmas still facing the work of evangelization than any sort of position paper. The study document evidently wishes to initiate dialogue among the bishops on the broad question of evangelization. It may be possible to detect, however, a single dominant question underlying all others in this nineteen-page document. The question is: How is it possible for the Roman Catholic Church to be a more credible sign of the Gospel in a period of rapid social change?

In this new form the world is taking on, Christ who suffered and rose again must be present as the principle of eternal life, to which we are all called, as the meaning of history, and as the model of the new man. In other words he must be present as the foundation of man's entire hope.

This salvific presence of Christ is realized through the medium of the Church: God wills all men to be saved in the unity of the People of God and through the ministry of this People. The Church's mediation is accomplished evangelization [*The Evangelization of the Modern World*, no. 1].

Such a way of introducing the evangelization dilemma suggested that the synod would approach its theme out of a broad framework, i.e., that of presence and witness. Because such a direction sees the Church itself as the evangelical sign and event, it puts evangelization in much broader perspective than one of simple verbal proclamation.

One can only hope that, in the continuing examination of this important theme, the reflections of catechetical thinkers will continue to be of service to the Church.

NOTES

1. Alfonso M. Nebreda, "Fundamental Catechesis," in *The Medellin Papers*, ed. J. Hofinger and T. Sheridan (Manila: East Asian Pastoral Institute, 1969), pp. 26–54. The precise reference to Liégé's article is on p. 44.

2. Piere-André Liégé, "Evangélisation," in *Catholicisme, Hier, Aujourd'hui, Demain*, vol. 4 (Paris: Letouzey et Ané, 1954), cols. 755-764. Liégé is best known in the United States for his small work *Consider Christian Maturity* (Chicago: Priory Press, 1965), a translation of *Adultes dans le Christ*. Liégé began his teaching career at Le Saulchoir and in 1951 became professor of pastoral catechetics at the Institutes Catholiques in Paris and Lille.

3. A biographical note in one of Nebreda's *Lumen Vitae* articles gives the following information: "It gives us special pleasure to publish the report by Father Nebreda, who represented *Lumen Vitae* at the Bangkok Session. Having completed his theological studies in Japan, Father Nebreda followed the courses at 'Lumen Vitae' International Institute for Catechetical and Pastoral Formation from 1959-1960. He also studied under Father Liégé at the Paris Institute for Catechetical Pastoral." See Alfonso Nebreda, "East Asian Study Week on Mission Catechetics," *Lumen Vitae* 17 (1962): 717. [This article by Nebreda is also reprinted in this sourcebook, without the biographical note, as Reading 3.]

4. Alfonso Nebreda, *Kerygma in Crisis?* (Chicago: Loyola University Press, 1965).

5. P.-A. Liégé, "Evangélisation," 757.

6. Ibid., 761.

7. Piere-André Liégé, "The Ministry of the Word: From Kerygma to Catechesis," *Lumen Vitae* 17 (1962): 22-23. This passage is included here because it summarizes the sense of whole sections of the earlier article in *Catholicisme*.

8. P.-A. Liégé, "Evangélisation," 761. See also Luis Erdozain's account of the genesis of the term *pre-evangelization* in "The Evolution of Catechetics," *Lumen Vitae* 25 (1970): 16-17. [This article by Erdozain is also reprinted in this sourcebook as Reading 8.] The term is open to considerable misunderstanding, as Gabriel Moran noted in *Catechesis of Revelation* (New York: Herder and Herder, 1966), pp. 136-138. At any rate, pre-evangelization is being used less today than previously and, then, only when carefully defined.

9. P.-A. Liégé, "Evangélisation," 761.

10. Ibid., 760.

11. Erdozain, "The Evolution of Catechetics," p. 15.

12. Nebreda, "East Asian Study Week," pp. 724-725.

13. See "Final Resolutions, Pan-African Catechetical Study Week," *Teaching All Nations* 1 (1964): 521-523 [also reprinted in this sourcebook as Reading 4].

14. The best expression of this stress on adaptation at Katigondo is found in X. Seumois, "How to Adapt Modern Catechesis to Africa Today," *Teaching All Nations* 1 (1964): 418-433.

15. Material related to the Manila study week can be found in *Teaching All Nations* 3, no. 4 (1966); and *Teaching All Nations* 4, nos. 1, 2, 3 (1967).

16. D. S. Amalorpavadass, "Workshop on Recent Developments in Catechetics," *Teaching All Nations* 4 (1967): 377-380.

17. Terrence Sheridan, "The Occasion," in *The Medellin Papers*, pp. 11-12.

18. "General Conclusions of the International Study Week," in *The Medellin Papers*, p. 217. [This article is also reprinted in this sourcebook as Reading 6.]

19. Ibid., pp. 215–216.

20. Cf. *General Catechetical Directory* (Washington, DC: United States Catholic Conference, 1971), nos. 8, 34. See also part 5, "Catechesis According to Age Levels."

Those who attended the International Catechetical Congress in Rome in 1971 remember that one of the most stirring addresses was D. S. Amalorpavadass' presentation on catechetical theory. A model of clarity, this address, "Catechesis as a Pastoral Task of the Church," has in a brief period become a catechetical classic, especially for the way it delineates the relationship of catechesis to the other ministries of the Church.

READING 25

Catechesis as a Pastoral Task of the Church

D. S. AMALORPAVADASS

I. Nature and Place of Catechesis in the Overall Pastoral Mission of the Church

Taken up in the tension between the first and second coming of the Lord, between his Pasch and Parousia, the Church, the community of Christ's disciples, has to fulfill her eschatological mission by announcing the kingdom of God and gathering humankind from the four winds like a harvest for God. She is on earth the germ and initial stage of God's kingdom and is an all-embracing sacrament of salvation to all

Reprinted from *Lumen Vitae* 27 (1972), pp. 259–280. Reproduced by courtesy of *Lumen Vitae.* Copyright *Lumen Vitae* 1972. This article was the keynote address of Fr. D. S. Amalorpavadass at the International Congress on Catechetics, Rome, 20–25 September 1971.

humankind (*Lumen gentium*, no. 48). The one action she has to do before the Lord returns is to proclaim the Christ-event, the Pasch of the Lord. The one function she has to fulfill is to be the primary and fundamental sacrament of salvation. This saving mission of hers is triple: prophetic, liturgical, and directive. She fulfills this triple mission by a threefold pastoral ministry: the ministry of the Word through the mediation of proclamation, the ministry of worship through the mediation of celebration, and the ministry of guidance through the mediation of organization and education of the Christian community in charity and maturity for witness and service. These three functions are but three aspects or elements of a single mission, and hence they call for and complete one another.

The prophetical mission of the Church consists in proclaiming the mystery of salvation to the whole world and in inviting men and women to respond to God's call and welcome the salvation offered. She fulfills this mission by the ministry of the Word: the latter is an ecclesial action, a pastoral function, and a privileged expression of living Tradition by which God's Word is transmitted in various ways and forms in order to raise, awaken, and nourish faith. It renders God's Word actual and relevant for the time and place and categories of audience by the mediation of a truly human word. It includes different functions of the Church: (a) the infallible magisterium of the Church, as the guardian and transmitter of the deposit of faith, (b) the role of theology as a reflection on faith and Christian experience or as a systematic treatment and scientific investigation of the truths of faith, and (c) the pastoral ministry of the Word by evangelization, catechesis, and homily.

This proclamation of the Word is a fundamental ministry or task of the Church as Jesus himself has shown it by his example: "He went round the whole of Galilee teaching in their Synagogues, proclaiming the Good News of the kingdom and curing all kinds of diseases and sickness among the people" (Matt. 4:23; cf. Mark 13:13). After the example of the master, the Apostles did the same, "We shall devote ourselves to prayer and to the service of the Word" (Acts 6:4).

The Church, the community of believers, is constituted precisely by the proclamation of the Word. From the seed of the Word only particular churches are founded all over the world and grow. Men and women are reborn, so to say, through the Word of God (1 Pet. 1:23) and joined to the Church. The Church itself, once constituted, lives and is nourished by the Word of God as much as by the Eucharistic Bread (Acts 2:42).

Without the ministry of the Word everything degenerates: liturgy into magic and ritualism, the law into legalism and juridicism, institutions into institutionalism, and pastors into administrative bosses. A constant prophetic effort is called for to set right this deviation and degeneration. The prophetic mission of the Church is often misunderstood and underestimated, and there is the tendency to attach oneself to the law and the rites. The role of priests of the Old Testament and pagan religions is mostly cultic, but in the New Testament the accent is laid, as by St. Paul, on the prophetic. What is sacerdotal in Christianity is subordinated to what is prophetic (Rom. 15:15). The ritual or cultic activity exists precisely because there is first of all a Gospel to proclaim. A liturgy of the Eucharist could exist precisely because there is a liturgy of the Word. The liturgy of the Eucharist has no meaning or consistence without the liturgy of the Word, just as sacrifice is meaningless without a covenant.

This ministry of the Word prepares for and leads to liturgy; liturgy itself contains a service of the word, a proclamation, and serves as the best catechesis. Both the ministry of the Word and the ministry of worship call for and lead to the ministry of guidance for an effective witnessing and humble service of charity in the world.

The ministry of the Word comprises two distinct and dialectical periods with specific forms, contents, and ends: they are *evangelization* and *catechesis*.

Evangelization is a primary and fundamental ministry of the Word; the two constitutive elements of it are kerygma and sign. Kerygma is the oral and verbal announcement or the heralding of the Gospel of Jesus Christ by unfolding the creative and dynamic potentialities of God's Word. But this must be accompanied and testified by signs (whether physical or moral miracles, or the unique sign of the Resurrection of Christ, or the universal and infallible sign of fraternal charity and humble service). It is addressed to the non-Christians or nonconverts in view of calling them to faith and conversion. The announcement of the Word is, therefore, made in a global, dynamic, and interpellating manner.

Catechesis is a second or subsequent ministry of the Word. It also transmits God's Word, but it is done in an enlightening and educative way. It is addressed only to Christians or converts or those who have made the first act of faith as a response to evangelization. It is done in view of awakening, nourishing, and educating their faith and of deepening and completing their initial conversion.

Between these two ministries of the Word, there is a capital event, namely, initial conversion and first act of faith.

II. Aim and Tasks of Catechesis

The end of catechesis is the education of the faith of the converts or the baptized. Catechesis aims at awakening, nourishing, and developing the faith, while renewing, deepening, and perfecting the initial conversion, making it ever more personal and actual. This faith, born of baptism, needs the Word of God to nourish and develop itself; the seed of faith has to grow from the infant stage to the full maturity of an adult and responsible Christian. It is the function of catechesis to foster this growth of faith and to develop the life of God's children.

The life of faith which the baptized are expected to lead requires an education of faith which is the task of catechesis. For this catechesis must take into account the whole of a person's life, secular and religious, and make regular references to the actual living conditions of the charges, which include not only the social, economic, and political facts but also cultic and religious realities and groups. It must evoke the life situations of the catechized and their fundamental aspirations which find expression and seek fulfillment in the current trends and events of the given society at a given period of history. Life, whole and entire, in its concrete setting should be enlightened and led by faith. Catechesis should therefore shed light on all the data, problems, and situations of personal and family life, of social and professional milieus, so that these may be seen, understood, judged, and finally lived by the Christians in accordance with the Word of Christ, the Gospel, and in full logical concord with one's original commitment to Christ. Thus, they will bear witness to Christ in their milieus and professions, consecrate the world to the creator, and have the lordship of Christ universally recognized.

This lifelong education of faith implies first and foremost a gradual but total transformation of men and women into Christ. This transformation is achieved both in the sacramental life and in the round-the-clock life of faith to which catechesis gives an initiation and formation.

Here are *some of the implications* of an education of faith and the aspects of transformation of life: It should give a new world view, set up a different hierarchy of values, cause a change of attitudes, form the whole person, educate his or her liberty, guide him or her toward Christian maturity, integrate the person in the church-community, and lead that person to commit himself or herself to the tasks of society and integral development of humanity. This education of faith will result in a new morality, a moral life growing from the very faith of conversion and commitment, a paschal life, a life of one dead and risen with Christ, a life in the spirit of the Risen Lord, a life of charity which is the fulfillment of the whole law. The life of faith is ultimately a participation in the trinitarian life; hence, it will put the charges in a living contact and intimate fellowship with the Father, through the Son, in the Spirit. This fellowship is fostered by a life of prayer which will have as its climax the full, active, intelligent, and fruitful participation in the sacred liturgy. This experience will create in the believers an untold urge to bear witness to Christ, to put themselves at the service of humanity in a spirit of humility and charity. This they will do both individually and as members of the ecclesial community.

III. The Process of Catechesis or Catechetical Pedagogy

This topic often awakens in many an expectation for practical guidelines with regard to the education in faith since, as a matter of fact, catechesis is linked in the minds of many with methods and techniques, devices and recipes. This expectation is quite legitimate and understandable, given the notion of catechesis we have inherited and the pressing problems we encounter in our pastoral ministry.

So we should state clearly at the very outset that, first of all, catechesis is more than method and techniques; it is a pedagogy, *a religious pedagogy*; second, method and pedagogy are not one and the same, though people usually mix them up in ordinary conversation; and third, catechetical pedagogy is not the mere adoption or the application of general profane pedagogy to religious education; there is something known as the *originality of catechetical pedagogy*. This originality springs from the special end and objective of catechesis as well as from the very nature, dynamics, and procedure of divine revelation, faith, and the mission of the Church. Now we shall cover the topic under three headings.

A. Theological and Anthropological Basis of a Catechetical Pedagogy Worth the Name

Catechetical pedagogy is based, on the one hand, on theology and all its sources (Scripture, liturgy, living Tradition, and magisterium and Christian witnessing) and, on the other, on all the human (behavioral) sciences, notably anthropology.

The process of the education of faith is to be patterned on the very process of revelation and faith and on that of the triple dynamism of personality development, group life, and humankind's historical adventure. It is therefore necessary to gather the salient points of these subjects in order to develop a catechetical pedagogy properly so called or to assure an education of faith worth the name. The movement and stages, the elements and aspects of a religious pedagogy are all based on the right understanding of God's revelation to humanity and humanity's response to God, the mission of the Church in the world, and the ministry of the Word, especially catechesis.

1) **Revelation.** *Inadequate notion of revelation.* The notion of revelation which we have inherited from our catechesis and sometimes from our theological studies is mostly notional and abstract, overessentialist and objectivist, exclusively of the past and static, impersonal and individualistic.

We understood *revelation* rather as the manifestation of doctrines beyond humanity's understanding or as the articles of faith about God, the world, and humanity's salvation, done in an impersonal way, in a distant past, dropped, so to say, from heaven outside the context of history with no reference to the community of men and women, etc. *Faith,* the answer of humankind to God, would be just accepting what God reveals by giving an assent of the intellect to the truths, not on any intrinsic evidence or relevance to one's life but on the authority of God who attests, who can neither deceive nor be deceived. Against this background, *catechesis* or *preaching* meant handing on the revealed doctrines, the emphasis being on *what* we have to communicate or on *teaching* the truths. This led to the composition and use of notional and moralistic catechisms during the last three or four centuries. These proposed the Christian message as a complete system of religious truths to be believed, moral duties to be fulfilled, and ritualistic practices of worship to be observed. Catechesis came to be assimilated to secular subjects, with a classroom setting, syllabus, and textbooks, and followed the process of academic teaching, with the catechist becoming a religion teacher. In short, catechesis became subject matter to be taught and learnt, meant only for children and in a school setting. All this explains the present state of catechesis with which we are not pleased and which we want to renew.

Adequate notion of revelation. Revelation properly understood is concrete and relevant, historical and existential, actual and dynamic, personalist and social.

It is *personalist,* that is, concerned first and foremost *with persons* and not things; what is revealed is not something but somebody. Before making known something, namely, the plan of salvation for humankind, God reveals someone, i.e., himself. The action is personal from subject to subject. Likewise, it is not revealed in the air but to persons, to a people. In this understanding, humanity is not a distant and passive recipient of something nor an object which undergoes an impact but the person directly and actively involved in an event that takes place here and now; the person is part of the process and is within the process that is going on; he or she is one engaged personally with his or her whole being in a living encounter with another.

Revelation is therefore an *interpersonal relationship* between God and an individual. The invisible God unveils the mystery of his person and manifests himself to a person. The living God enters into a person-to-person relationship with that person, the divine "I" calling to the human "Thou." The distant, transcendent, and all-holy God takes the initiative, breaks the silence of eternity, bridges the gulf, comes closer to men and women, lives among sinful humans, and becomes immanent to their life and history. He opens a dialogue with men and women and, out of the abundance of His love, speaks to them as friends – as he did with Abraham, Moses, David, and the Apostles – and invites them to fellowship with himself in view of a communion of thought and love with the three Persons, the Father, the Son, and the Holy Spirit (cf. *Dei verbum,* no. 1). Revelation is thus both personalized and personalizing.

Now this self-manifestation of God takes place *through a self-communication,* through God's gift of self to men and women. He gives himself to them to be received by them. In the very act of the total gift of self takes place the manifestation of the mystery of God's self and his intimate life and all that it implies, namely, his eternal designs for humanity's salvation in Jesus Christ (Eph. 1:3–12).

This communication is *social and communitarian;* it is addressed to a people and not merely to individuals. God relates himself to persons in communication and communion, not simply as individuals and isolated units, shut out from each other, but as belonging to a collectivity, to a people, as members of a living community so that the interpersonal relationship between God and humanity can be the source and climax of the interpersonal relationship among men and women, with one another, so that the human community in which revelation takes place may gradually be built up and transformed into a community of faith and love, of witnessing and service, which in short is none other than a community of salvation. Thus, revelation also gathers and builds up a commmunity.

All this takes place gradually, in the course of *history;* so revelation is also *historical.* Humanity being what it is, namely, subject to conditions of time and space, revelation too is subject to a process and progress, hence, to duration and stages.

It was first announced to our fathers and mothers through the prophets, then promulgated by Christ, and finally preached by the

Apostles on Christ's order to every creature. "After speaking to us in many places and varied ways through the prophets, God, last of all in these days has spoken to us by his Son" (Heb. 1:1–2). What we must emphasize is that revelation takes place concretely and actually in the very events and trends of human history, in the midst of the life-experience and situations of a living community of men and women. Thus, humanity stands at no time outside the process of revelation but always within it.

Now, in this encounter of God and in this witnessing of his self-manifestation, there is a dramatic element; humanity experiences the eruption of the living God in its existence; it is totally shaken and broken to pieces, so to say, in its thoughts, views, aims, and values. Meeting the living God and coming into personal contact with the Holy One is a shattering experience, as testified to by the narratives of the vocation of the prophets and theophanies to Israel. The self-manifestation and communication of God to humanity is not a smooth unveiling of his mystery as gnosticism would understand, but it is accompanied by a judgment on the world and history, on men and women and their actions, and thereby constitutes a call to conversion, with a certain degree of urgency. In this sense, revelation realizes not only the history of salvation but also a history of judgment.

2) **Faith, response to revelation.** If God's Word is revelation, humanity's word is faith. If the initiative belongs to God, the response is humanity's. Therefore, God's Word invites humanity's word, God's openness calls for humankind's openness, God's action interpellates humanity's reaction, God's self-gift expects a human self-gift. Therefore, revelation calls for *faith.* Faith is a personal and vital encounter with the living God, a total acceptance of the revealing and giving Person by a loving surrender of one's whole being, and an unreserved commitment to live for him and to order one's life according to his Word. All this should result in the sealing of a covenant and the realization of a fellowship in love. Therefore, our interpersonal relationship is one of dialogue, covenant, and fellowship. It is not merely an intellectual assent to revealed truths. Christianity is not a philosophy, an ideology, or a religious system. It is, above all, a Person and a life, an acceptance of a Person and a living relation with him. Hence, the education of faith does not consist in imparting a religious knowledge or in giving religious instruction – unless knowledge is taken in the deep biblical sense of knowing a person concretely in an existential and vital context of dynamic interpersonal relationship – but in initiating and educating one to a life of personal and community relationship with the Father through the Son in the Spirit and with one another in the

world of today. Therefore, humanity's response or reaction to God's revelation, as explained above, will be essentially attention and being open to God, expectation and listening, openness and acceptance, and reciprocal self-gift in a total surrender and dedication of oneself. This is what we call faith. Faith is not, as hitherto understood and taught, a *mere* intellectual assent to doctrinal propositions revealed in a remote past by a distant and unknown being called God (outside the context of an actual interpersonal relationship, outside a living process, outside the context of history and society, without any involvement on the part of humanity).

3) **Signs of revelation.** Our interpersonal relationship with God and others is established and fostered through signs; they are the media of communication. Signs are the expression of ourselves, of our whole body. Now, the signs of intercommunication between God and humanity—through revelation and faith—are words and deeds. Since the relationship is a dialogue between God and humanity, it calls for the Word of God and the word of humanity. Now, the Word must be understood in the broad sense, not only oral expressions but also gestures and actions called deeds. Hence, the Vatican Dogmatic Constitution on Divine Revelation says: "The plan of revelation is realized by deeds and words having an inner unity . . . the deeds wrought by God in the history of salvation manifest and confirm the teachings and realities signified by the words, while the words proclaim the deeds and clarify the mystery contained in them" (*Dei verbum*, no. 2). Both the word and the deed constitute the total language of communication.

4) **Jesus Christ, the greatest sign of revelation: Word and deed.** Jesus Christ is the greatest sign and the supreme medium of revelation.

The meeting point between God's revelation and human faith, between God's Word and humanity's word, or rather the very encounter of God and humanity is the Word Incarnate, the God-Man. He is not merely the Word of God but the very deed of God. He is not a medium of revelation but revelation itself. To see Christ is to see God, to meet Christ is to meet God, to hear Christ is to hear the Word of God. To be united with him is to be in communion with God. Similarly, he is not merely a sign of humanity's response to God but the very response of humanity, the perfect "Amen" of humankind to the Father.

Finally, He is not merely a recipient of God's self-gift but the very self-gift of God. In Him, not only God gives himself to humanity but humankind gives itself to God. In Jesus, God is revealed and recognized, shown and seen, announced and heard, offered and responded to, given and received; God's mystery is unveiled and penetrated. He is the total, ultimate, and definite revelation of God, as well as the complete and perfect response of humanity. In Jesus Christ, we have the perfect dialogue, the model interpersonal relationship, and the deepest fellowship between God and humankind; He is, in one word, "the Sacrament of man's encounter with God." Therefore, there could be nothing more and nothing new outside Jesus Christ; there can be no further revelation as such. It amounts to saying that there is no salvation and revelation outside Jesus Christ, whether people lived contemporaneous to, before, or after his human existence. Today as yesterday and always it is Jesus Christ who reveals God and saves us. It is in this sense revelation is said to be closed with the Apostles and the early Church.

5) **Ongoing revelation.** Now, this definitive and total revelation of God in Jesus Christ should be made available to the successive generations to the end of times by the Apostles and the Church. The interpersonal relationship between God and humankind and with one another in Jesus Christ should be experienced by everyone. This is done through the inspired books (Scripture), the Church's teaching (magisterium), her cult (liturgy), her life of charity and service (witnessing), and her preaching (evangelization, catechesis). If so, we can go a little further and say that, in a certain sense, this revelation and faith in Israel (Old Testament), in Jesus Christ and in the Church (New Testament), is not merely something of the past but also *of the present.* Though the Christ-event has taken place "once and for all" at a definite moment of history; still, as far as we are concerned, the revelation of God in Jesus Christ is an ongoing process, is an ever-present happening in which each one of us has to be involved and to which each one of us has to respond and react. It is an ongoing process of growing and widening interpersonal relationship. For the Christ of yesterday is the same today and forever. The Spirit that he communicated through his Resurrection is present everywhere, especially in the Church transcending time and space.

If God continues to reveal himself to us here and now, how are we to recognize, discern, and interpret it?

As we have mentioned above, revelation, which is a mystery of interpersonal relationship between God and humanity and among individuals, cannot be perceived, recognized, understood, or realized except through the medium of signs.

What were the signs by which the people of the past recognized divine revelation and interpreted it? In the Old Testament, God was revealing himself by intervening in human history and getting involved in the history of Israel in particular. He was revealing himself and humanity itself to humans from within and through the events of history and the life-experiences of the people. These were so many signs of God's revelation or the God-human interpersonal relationship. As ordinary people could not interpret these signs of the times and recognize God's presence and action in those events and experiences, the prophets interpreted them for the people and enabled them to discover their meaning. They could do so because on the one hand they themselves lived those events and situations in full solidarity with their fellows and on the other hand they were men and messengers of God, the bearers and heralds of his Word.

Now, what are the signs of the present revelation of God to us? How can we know that God reveals to us today? How can we enter into a personal relationship and fellowship with him? Through the Word of God as found in the Bible, the preaching and teaching of the Church, her liturgy and sacraments, and her life-testimony over the centuries and in today's society. To this can be added what Vatican Council II calls:

- "the many voices of our age" which the people of God should hear, distinguish, interpret, and judge in the light of the divine Word (*Gaudium et spes*, no. 44).
- "the signs of the times" which the Church has the duty of scrutinizing and interpreting in the light of the Gospel, in order to respond to the perennial questions which men and women ask, in a language intelligible to each generation (*Gaudium et spes*, no. 4).
- "the events, needs, and desires" in which the people of God should decipher authentic signs of God's presence and purpose (*Gaudium et spes*, no. 11).

6) **Relevance and interpretation of the signs: anthropology.** But these signs are no signs for us if they do not mean anything for us, if they are not relevant to our life, if they are not related to our human existence. "God's revelation would have no meaning for us if it was not also revelation of the meaning of human existence. We can indeed read God's revelation in the signs to the precise extent of our capacity to read in them also the revelation of the meaning of human existence."[1] The signs will enable us to discern and interpret the revelation only if they are basically related to our human experience.

Why is it so? How is it that relevance is linked with human existence and meaningfulness with our life? The answer is anthropology. From the beginning, humanity has been, as willed by God, the lord and priest of the whole of creation—"having all things under his feet, and crowned with glory and honor" (Ps. 8). As such humans have been conscious of themselves and of their mastery over everything, and they have been understanding everything else starting from themselves. But today with greater mastery of nature, the world, and space, with scientific discoveries and technological advance, humanity has really become the center and summit of the universe and humans are conscious of it. Therefore, the radically new phenomenon of today is the fuller discovery of humanity by itself; for the first time in history humanity is fully conscious of itself and is fascinated by itself. The discovery of oneself is the greatest of all discoveries. Every other discovery is related to and determined by the discovery of oneself. Therefore, "according to the almost unanimous opinion of believers and unbelievers alike, all things on earth should be related to man as their center and crown" (*Gaudium et spes*, no. 12). Hence, the pivotal point of the Church, the missionary, and the catechist is "man himself whole and entire."

Humans are not static beings or mere essences; they are in existence and constantly in movement. They are taken up by a triple dynamism in view of a triple becoming: (a) the vital dynamism of personality development, (b) the dynamism of intense group life, and (c) the dynamism of humankind's historical adventure.

The vital dynamism of *personality* is constituted precisely by human experience consisting of basic yearnings and values, major problems and tensions, relations and situations, through which humans realize their becoming and grow into persons.

The *role of groups* is great and their importance is daily growing. Humanity gets sensitized, recognizes and discovers itself, articulates its feelings and aspirations through groups. It finds there support and stimulus; it grows and develops. It realizes its basic aspirations and gets educated in social life through the experience of group life. The group is more and more appealing as it becomes ever more relevant and enriching of persons; it gives a sense of movement and progress, growth and fulfillment.

Finally, humans are embarked on an *adventure of history* as individuals and groups, as men and women, as young and old, as people and nations. In this venture they are awakened to their tasks and responsibilities and want to play their roles in the historical "becoming." Tending toward a total consummation under the dynamic impulse of creation, they engage their whole being, assess their vital and prime needs, marshal their energies, pool their resources, become conscious of the possibilities, and make efforts to work out a better life and to achieve full liberation to prepare an ever brighter future. This, they know, can only be achieved by transforming the world and, in the process of it, transforming themselves; integral development of the whole person and every person. Thus conceived, humankind's historical adventure is essentially its "becoming." Therefore, a catechist or a preacher should feel solidarity with humanity's adventure of history, have a sense of history, enter into its movement, and be aware of the dynamic realities of human evolution.

Now, the relevance of anything is determined by its deep connection with this triple dynamism of life in which humanity is taken up. It is within that realm and with reference to it that humanity understands anything as meaningful, reacts to it positively and engages its whole person. Therefore, human experience is the medium by which God's Word is addressed to humans, and human experience is the milieu in which it is received by them.

7) **Dialectics between the past and the present.** Against this background the narration in stereotyped formulas of past events and the life-experiences of bygone generations as found in the salvation history will be irrelevant to the concerns of today's men and women and therefore will not constitute the sign of today's revelation unless these narratives can enlighten and give meaning to the signs of our times, namely, to the events and trends of contemporary history and our life-experience today. It is not sufficient to explain or repeat the message of the Bible in an abstract and impersonal way, without any vital connection with our present existence. It is the relevant interpretation of present happenings that will give value and credibility to the signs of past revelation.[2]

So the message of salvation – which is given through the sign of the events of the history of Israel, through Jesus Christ (in his human existence, in his ministry, in his Gospel, especially in the paschal mystery, in the sending of the Spirit), in the living Tradition of the Church, in its authentic magisterium, in its Christian worship and experience in the world – has to be reinterpreted and reformulated today in such a way that it may become as a fresh word, a warm word, a word for today, a word for humankind, a meaningful human word of today, a word related to the thought and life of our contemporaries.

In other words, today's life-situations and human problems have to be enlightened and interpreted by similar human life-situations lived in the past revelation, namely, in the history of salvation, in the sense that revelation takes place not merely through the spoken word or the written word but also and chiefly through the medium and milieu of human experience. Thus, revelation takes place for us here and now through the reinterpretation of the Word of God for our life-situations today in the language of our contemporaries.

"The Gospel message, to which the Church gives witness in the world, cannot be articulated without taking seriously the bearing of the world on this message. Therefore, the work of theology is to be carried on in the light of both the Gospel message and society, i.e., the contribution of various cultures, their sciences, arts, literature, and religions." Again, "Christianity must recognize that the philosophies and humanisms of our cultural environment contain indispensable elements for Christian proclamation and theology" (Brussels Theological Congress, nos. 3, 8).

On the other hand, *the signs of the present revelation, namely, what constitute our actual experience, will have no basis or meaning or raison d'être* unless they are closely linked with those of the past revelations in a dialectical relationship (the dialectics between past and present), in the sense that the signs of today's revelation have to be discerned and enlightened, interpreted and understood, by the signs and words of the past revelation (otherwise, we will fall into individualism, subjectivism, indirect rationalism, and modernism). The danger today, therefore, is to hold on to one reality but neglect the other, instead of maintaining clear bipolarity and a perpetual tension between both.

But both the past and present revelations have their unity and consistence, value and reliability, in Jesus Christ through whom alone the Father reveals himself and his designs for us, whether in the past, or in the present, or in the future.[3]

8) **God's revelation and the Church's mission.** If divine revelation and faith are not primarily and essentially the communication and reception of truths but rather a living knowledge of persons and dynamic and meaningful relationship in a life-context of forging a friendship, sealing a covenant, and growing into fellowship with God and with one another, then the mission of the Church consists in being the sign and instrument of this interpersonal relationship and fellowship.

As *Lumen gentium* states, "By her very relationship with Christ, the Church is a kind of Sacrament or sign of intimate union with God, and of the unity of humankind. She is also an instrument for the achievement of such union and unity" (no. 1).

The mission of the Church is, in short, communion or salvation of humanity. Mission today is, therefore, the means of revelation; for what is revealed is already mission fulfilled. The gradual unfolding of God's plan and the progressive realization of it go together. And this unfolding and fulfillment take place within a believing community and through the instrumentality and mediation of a faith-community which we call the Church.

That is why *Ad gentes* can state: "The mission of the Church is nothing else and nothing less than the epiphany or manifestation of

God's plan of salvation and its fulfillment in the world and in the course of world history" (no. 9).

It is through the preaching of the Church which has received the mission to make disciples of all nations that revelation is made *living and actual*. Hence, the mission of the Church is the same as the end and object of revelation, namely, *communion between God and humankind in Jesus Christ*. The Church in Christ makes possible and continues divine revelation for all humanity through time and space.

9) **Revelation and catechesis.** Catechesis is a form and period of the ministry of the Word by which the mission of the Church is revealed and fulfilled. That is to say, the revelation-faith process takes place and is continued also through catechesis; in and through catechesis is realized the mystery of God's self-communication and people's response in their mutual encounter and interpersonal fellowship.

Therefore, all the elements that we gather up from a reflection on the theology of revelation, faith, and mission of the Church as well as on anthropology should be applied to catechesis. Any pedagogy of faith which takes them into account and makes possible, during catechesis, the process of revelation to a group of men and women here and now will be a genuine and adequate catechetical pedagogy.[4]

B. Characteristics of Religious Pedagogy

1) Viewed thus, pedagogy is *much more than a juxtaposition of the subject* (humanity to be catechized) *and the message* (the Word of God to be proclaimed) *by the use of techniques and methods*. Pedagogy is chiefly determined, as we emphasized above, by the specific end. For it is one thing to know the message of salvation and the person to whom it is addressed, it is quite another that this passage reaches that person, provokes a response, brings about a genuine interpersonal relationship with God and others, and thus transforms the person's life. The specific aim of catechesis as the living and personal encounter of the catechized with God, their total surrender to him, and their gradual initiation into the mystery of God through Christ along with fellow men and women cannot be simply realized by a juxtaposition of the subject and object to be taught. *It consists in the dynamics or the dynamic procedure in which the catechized are guided from within, with due respect for their freedom, to interpret their life, to discover God, and to establish a genuine interpersonal relationship with God and others, through the Word proclaimed, in a vital context of relevance and transformation, leading to communion with God in prayer and in service to fellow men and women and society at large.*

proach, the environmental approach, the incarnational approach), from mere acceptance to creativity.

Obvious Conclusions

In the spiritual itinerary or in the long period of education of faith, we have to note that:

1) We are concerned with two major ministries, two forms and periods of the Word, evangelization (precatechesis) and catechesis. What distinguishes them is the capital event of faith and conversion. Catechesis has for its aim the education of faith and deepening of conversion. Unless and until there is initial conversion to the person of Jesus Christ and first act of faith, we cannot start catechesis, and it is useless to catechize those who are not converted or who do not believe. In catechesis, we do proclaim the Word, but the form of proclamation that most of our people need, especially the youth, first and foremost, is not catechesis but evangelization: a creative, dynamic, global, and interpellating Word, for the first result we expect is faith and conversion.

2) Not only the majority of non-Christians who want to join the Church but also a good number of the faithful, youth and adults, do not have the faith that we speak of. Our whole pastorate at present supposes faith too easily and too quickly. It takes too much for granted that our Christians are believers. Our pastoral ministry, far from being an education of faith, is sometimes only a ritualization of their lives. Sacramentalization is no doubt useful and necessary and so cannot be abandoned, but before that the proclamation of the Word is absolutely indispensable: The Gospel must be announced. There can be no education of faith without the announcement of the Word. Any renewal of parish or pastorate supposes that we give primacy to the Word, that we go back to the Word of God; otherwise, paganism, superstition, and magic, and jurisdicism will develop under Christian labels and coverings.

3) The Word that we proclaim in evangelization or catechesis will not be meaningful and appear relevant to modern people in the technological society *unless* it appears as a human word, a word that concerns men and women, that joins in their preoccupation, that deepens the yearning, that meets them in their life-situations, that starts from and recognizes their problems and difficulties, that appeals to their highest values and fulfills their deepest aspirations. In short,

the God's Word that we want to proclaim should become a genuine and meaningful human word. Jesus Christ, the Word of God, should first of all be a word of humanity to become a Word of God. It is by revealing human to human that Jesus Christ will reveal God to humanity and enable it to respond to God in faith. Here is precisely a service of interpretation to be rendered by catechesis and by the catechist.

4) *The catechist* can no longer catechize by lecturing to his or her audience from outside in an uncommitted way. He or she has to be within and hence must belong to a human group. The catechist has to be in full solidarity with his or her group and live all the events and aspects of life, including tensions and conflicts, in a committed way. One has first of all to interpret and discover for oneself the designs of God in one's life, environment, and community; only then can one share with others from within what one has discovered by observation and involvement, by listening to God's Word and meditating on it. Without this personal meditation, assimilation, interiorization, and discovery, without a personal relationship with God and the consequent conversion and transformation, a catechist cannnot fulfill his or her prophetic function. Therefore, a catechist is best defined as a pedagogue or a guru, as one who has experienced God by means of a genuine interpersonal relationship and fellowship and guides others to the same experience by a personal testimony of word and deed. In that, the catechist himself or herself becomes the very sign of the actual revelation and plays the role of the prophet by interpreting the significance and guiding his or her charges to respond to it in faith in the community of the Church, the replica of the communion with the Father, the Son, and the Holy Spirit.

NOTES

1. H. Bouillard, *The Logic of Faith* [New York: Sheed and Ward, 1967], pp. 21–23.
2. The two hundred theologians gathered in Brussels in September 1970 in the World Congress of Theology on the Future of the Church have emphasized this point in their concluding guidelines or statements: "The great christological confessions and definitions of the past have a lasting significance for the Church of today. But they cannot be interpreted without taking into account their historical context. Nor can they be simply repeated in a stereotyped manner. To speak to men of different ages and cultures, the Christian message must find really new formulations" (no. 6).
3. One conclusion of the International Study Week on Catechetics held in Medellin in August 1968 is very pertinent here: "Contemporary catechesis,

year," especially during lenten and paschal seasons. It can also be compared to the very life and the paschal mystery of Jesus Christ.

Ad gentes says (nos. 13–14): "By the working of the divine grace, the new convert sets out on a spiritual journey. . . . He journeys from the old man to the new one perfected in Christ . . . this transition should be gradually developed during the time of the catechumenate. . . . The catechumenate is not a mere expounding of doctrine and precepts, but a training period for a whole Christian life. It is an apprenticeship of appropriate length during which disciples are formed to Christ. Therefore, catechumens should be properly instructed in the mystery of salvation and in the practice of Gospel morality; they should be introduced into the life of faith, liturgy, and love which God's people lives."

In short, the whole catechumenate can be called a process of Christian initiation or a long education in faith. The various stages of this education or initiation or journey should be marked, and we should not pass on to the next stage till the previous stage is well done. The stages are: (1) the stage of precatechumenal community, (2) the stage of catechumenal community, (3) the stage of baptismal community, (4) the stage of neophytal community, and (5) the stage of eucharistic community.

This image of the spiritual journey and the various stages which mark it, together with the corresponding ministries of the Church, are well expressed in the definition of the catechumenate given by Coudreau which we have slightly modified.

The catechumenate is the Church in the totality of her members (priests, religious, lay people) and the totality of her action (Word, sacrament, and witness) which makes herself present to the catechumens, welcomes them, makes them ascend the steps of the porch and pass through the baptistry, introduces them into the Church (the community), and leads them up to the sanctuary (the mystery) in order to send them back to the world as witnesses and servants (mission).

Now, most Christians are baptized as children, and on account of it we take for granted their faith and conversion. As a matter of fact, and that often enough, they have neither an initial conversion nor a living faith. This is so due to the fact that they did not pass through the catechumenate nor had they an education of faith and formation in the ambience of a faith-community through catechesis. Thus, suddenly, they find themselves as full-fledged members and mature Christians of the eucharistic community. In this supposition we simply administer the sacraments. In reality what they need is not sacramentalization but evangelization; an education of faith and the process of adult conversion must be assured before and during the ministry of any sacrament. In short, though they are already baptized, we must somehow see to it that they pass through the various stages which precede the stage of eucharistic community and that the corresponding ministry of the Church during those stages be available to them, namely, evangelization, precatechesis, process of faith and adult conversion, catechesis, mystagogy, and education in charity and maturity for witness and service.

2) **Education of faith through humanity's life span: from childhood to adulthood passing through adolescence.** The education of faith or catechesis should take into account this long period of formation, mark the stages and work out different pedagogies suited to each age group and life-situation. Otherwise, there will be repetitions resulting in boredom and disgust; otherwise, there will be irrelevance. The Word of God will become meaningless, and it will not be heard and understood. It will not help them to meet God, discover his revealed designs, and respond to him according to his will in each particular situation. This brings us to work out specialized pedagogy for each group — *childhood:* 1-6 years, 6-9 years, 9-12 years; *adolescence:* 12-14 years, 15-18 years, 18-21 years; *adulthood.*

It is not for us now to enter into the details of each specialized pedagogy meant for the different age-groups, but we must recall and emphasize that each age-group requires a specialized pedagogy.

3) **The stages of the movement in an act of catechesis.** The dynamic concept of pedagogy described above and the interpersonal relationship involved make it obvious that there is a movement within every catechesis. The rhythm of this movement, the stages, and their duration may vary from age-group to age-group, but what is common to every catechesis is that there is a certain procedure with definite steps. They are:

- Evocation of a human experience, reflection on it, and interpretation of its significance at the human level to the point of exhausting it.
- Interpretation of its fuller meaning and ultimate fulfillment in the light of God's Word proclaimed.
- With the discovery of the relevance of the Word to life, reviewing and living the human experience in full consonance with faith.

This calls for a radical changeover from the formula of explanation of doctrine and application to life to the formula of the interpretation of the signs of life and discovery of God's designs for us today.

This is a change from the deductive to the inductive method, from the doctrinal approach to the experiential approach (the human ap-

2) *Now this education of faith implies education of freedom.* In this process we are in contact with two persons, between two freedoms, and face to face with two mysteries, the mystery of God who reveals and the mystery of the human being who responds to this revelation — both in the mystery of Jesus Christ. We are between two freedoms, God's freedom to take the initiative and offer a covenant of fellowship and the human freedom to respond to him, to accept the offer of covenant and thereby attain human destiny, the desire which is deeply embedded in the self. Anyone who is involved in this process should be extremely delicate. *The role of the catechist is not, first of all, to teach this and that but to be attentive to what takes place, to create an atmosphere in which people may discern God's presence, to foster proper dispositions so that one may respond positively and freely to God's action,* to help people to read the signs of revelation in their lives, to guide them along the way to the discovery of God, and finally, when they have discovered and met each other, to foster their relationships and deepen their fellowship. Here, we cannot force or dictate a response, we cannot formulate or impose a stereotyped answer to be given to God, we cannot accelerate the rhythm or speed in order to bring about this encounter. For it is an interplay of two freedoms; nay more, God deals with each one in a unique way. The one who wants to guide must be attentive, must listen, and must follow the rhythm and direction of the learners' movement.

3) *Such a religious pedagogy cannot but be a process, a gradual one, and a continuous one, since faith is not a mere intellectual knowledge of truth about God and the world but the discovery of persons and since revelation and faith are themselves a lifelong process.* If every person is a mystery, especially God, and if this mystery is unveiled only gradually, humans also can have access to it and penetrate it only gradually. Hence, a progressive revelation of God's mystery implies a gradual discovery of it by men and women. Consequently, one's initiation into it by the help of religious pedagogy can take place only gradually. No one can say, "I know God," once that person has learnt by heart the creed, the doctrinal summary of Christian belief. What we do not know of God is more than what we know of him. What we know of God is more dissimilar than similar to what we do not know. There is no room for any self-complacency. There is no wonder that mystics and Hindu philosophers speak so often in a negative theological terminology: "God is not this," "God is not that."

4) The whole of life and all of human history — past, present, and future — can be and are *a milieu and sign of revelation.* They have to be interpreted by God's Word, and the discovery is from within one's

life, group, community, milieu, and the world. We have therefore to be attentive to everything and to be in expectation of seeing God and discovering his designs.

5) If revelation-faith is thus a full lifetime process and a daylong affair, catechesis must extend to every minute, every event, and every aspect of life, to every age-group, nay, to the whole span of one's life. *Catechesis acquires thereby a universal dimension.* Catechesis can never be stopped under the pretext that we know enough or that it is a mere repetition. God reveals himself continuously, and therefore people must be ready to respond to him continuously in faith.

6) *The interpretation of the signs of life has to be done* not by individuals, in isolation, however charismatic they may be, but *by the entire community,* pooling together and recognizing the various charisms *in the total context of the community's experience,* not only today's experience but also the faith experience of bygone generations and that of the coming generations.

C. The Process and Procedure of Catechesis

The religious pedagogy or the education of faith is best described as a *long spiritual journey in quest of the living God* and the gradual discovery of him, resulting in an ever more intimate and ever deeper communion in Jesus Christ. This spiritual journey is marked by *several stages.* This can be considered with reference to three goals:

- Christian initiation of adult converts from the state of unbelief to the state of living faith as full-fledged Christians through a restored adult catechumenate.
- Education of faith of children born to Christian parents from childhood up to the state of mature adult Christians, through a catechesis of various age-groups and social and professional milieus or, inversely, starting with adult catechesis and thereby realizing the education of faith of children and youth.
- The stages of the movement or procedure in any catechesis.

1) **Christian initiation of adult converts.** Catechumenate is the best example of the various needs and situations of a humanity in quest of God and the corresponding ministry of the Church offered in successive stages to meet those needs and to guide humanity on its journey through successive life-situations. The journey of a catechumen is comparable to the journey of Israel from Egypt up to the Promised Land or to the life of the Church lived mystically every year in the "liturgical

in agreement with a more adequate theology of revelation, recognizes in the historical situation, in authentic human aspirations, the first signs to which we must be attentive in order to discover the plan of God for the men of today. Such situations therefore are an indispensable part of the content of catechesis. The progressive discovery of the total sense and definitive orientation of such aspirations and tensions, verified at each moment of the historical process, is an essential task of the prophetic mission of the Church.

"To grasp the total significance of these human realities it will be necessary to live fully with men of our time. Thus these human realities will be progressively and seriously interpreted in their own time in the light of the living experiences of the people of Israel, of the man Christ and of the sacramental ecclesial community where the Spirit of the risen Christ is alive and continues to operate" (*Teaching All Nations* 5, no. 4 [1968]: 517–518).

4. *Catechesis* can be defined, therefore, as the ministry of the Church by which "a human group is enabled to interpret its life-situations, live it, and express it in the light of God's Word" (Jacques Audinet, *Teaching All Nations* 5, no. 4 [1968]: 427).

Or, as "the prophetic ministry of the ecclesial community that, through the light of the gospel and the guidance of the Spirit:
1) recognizes within man and his environment
2) the initial signs of the ongoing saving action of God
3) and by gradually unfolding their total meaning and significance through Christian witnessing, the testimony of the Scriptures, and the teaching of the Magisterium
4) leads men to freely acknowledge Jesus 'who by the Revelation of the Father and His love
5) fully reveals man to man himself and makes his supreme calling clear.' "
Jose M. Calle, "Catechesis for the Seventies," *Teaching All Nations* 7, no. 3 (1970): 239.

*The following article by a Protestant, Christian-education leader sets
forth the various ways the Bible tends to be used in Christian education, primarily by Protestant denominations. Iris Cully astutely points
out the difficulties connected with each of the three approaches she
describes. Roman Catholic readers will note the similarity of Cully's
own recommendations to certain of the concerns of catechesis.*

READING 26

Problems of Bible Instruction in American Catechetical Literature

IRIS V. CULLY

I. The Relationship Between the Bible and the Christian Way of Life

The Bible has been the basic instructional material within United States
Protestantism since the rise of the Sunday school early in the nineteenth century. The Bible has never been taught in order that the story

Reprinted from *Catechetics for the Future*, Concilium, ed. Alois Muller, vol. 53, pp.
128–139. Copyright © 1970 by The Crossroad Publishing Company. Used by
permission.

the direction of the Sunday morning curriculum materials now in process of development.

IV. Third Solution: Experience-centered

The basis for this kind of curriculum is the affirmation that the Christian faith is to be lived now, in particular personal and corporate situations. The Bible is a "resource" in the sense that it is the "lore" of the people of God, our story, and we need to know it in order to realize our roots. The Bible is also the human story. It presents the human situation (sin), points to God's redeeming work in Israel and through Christ, and gives evidence of his constant renewing power by the action of the Holy Spirit. The Bible is a living word as we hear God speak through its words, but a careful selection has to be made of the words appropriate for our time.

The United Church of Christ has the nearest approximation to such an experienced-centered curriculum. The purpose is that the learners shall understand and see themselves in relation to other people, to the created world, to the church community, and to God. This is basically a psychological orientation. Biblical stories are chosen to enable the pupil to identify. Biblical passages are chosen which affirm God's presence or in which the prophets or apostles comment on situations in a way which would be pertinent for today. The wonder of humanity's place in God's creation is captured through some of the psalms. The earliest use of a full-scale biblical course is a study of the Gospel of Mark in grade 7 (age twelve). Further units on biblical material follow for the adolescent and adult levels.

This is an "existential" use of the Bible. The traditionalist would assert that the learner would never get the full picture of the biblical story, see its basic meaning, or grasp its essential unity. It could also be asserted that the criterion of choice would leave important areas of biblical material unnoticed, would overemphasize some themes and ignore others. Proponents of the theory reply that only in this way can one motivate people to read the Bible, and that biblical history arouses only antiquarian interest. The methodology is to explore the meaning of a biblical story or passage primarily as it might speak in a contemporary context. The child would be encouraged to draw a modern parallel to a biblical story or to illustrate it in a modern setting. The United Church curriculum has a reading book for ten-year-olds on biblical archaeology. The framework is the visit of an American family to the "dig" at which the father is working. The ancient is made immediate and becomes a possible area for study because it represents a situation in which a contemporary family finds itself. The thrust of the discussion of a biblical passage would be less exegetical (What was the writer saying?) than expository (What can this say for us?).

The Episcopal Church's curriculum, popularly known as "The Seabury Series," centers on life issues. Whereas three strands are intertwined in the teacher's planning (life situation, Bible, and the life of the Christian community), each course of study develops around a need of the learner. The nine-year-old, concerned about the rules of the game, needs to see the relationship of law and grace. The study book tells the biblical story from creation to covenant in the setting of a family who read and discuss it together in the light of their own lives. The seven-year-old, alert to the world of science, learns about humanity's place in God's world. Every teacher's manual contains resources for developing units of study, including one section outlining biblical materials that might be pertinent and giving suggestions for their use. Mark's Gospel is the basic biblical material for grade 6; it is suggested that the class spend the first few weeks reading and discussing the material (attractively printed in a special reading book) and then use it whenever it has bearing for situational units developed in the course of the year.

The basic method is discussion in small groups, but the meaning of the material is also explored through drawing and writing, role-playing, and the use of puppets. This curriculum is used in a framework that emphasizes the worshiping community, and in many parishes the family have attended morning worship together before separating into classes. Biblical materials from the liturgy play a part in the learning situation.

V. Implications

The question of the use of biblical material in a curriculum is never a matter of the quantity of biblical stories or passages used nor even of the proportion of biblical to nonbiblical material. The focus is on the goal to be achieved. Those who affirm the Bible to be the basic textbook for religious learning believe that Christians must be well acquainted with the main outlines. The goal is to convince them of the persistence of God's purpose in the face of humanity's varying responses as the basis for the assurance of God's continuing work in his world and through his people. The purpose also is to help them, through precept and example, to continue this witness in their own lives.

In experience-centered curricula, the goal sought is the strengthening and encouraging of the learner through the word of grace spoken

the topics and basic biblical passage for each Sunday in a six-year cycle. Old and New Testament materials may be alternated, but a whole
book is studied in sequence, and the basic writings are included in the
cycle. The session outlines, interpretation, and methodology are left
to the curriculum developers. The larger denominations continue this
as a service to congregations who cling to the long familiar outline for
biblical study but develop such lessons only for young people and
adults. The independent publishers frequently try to avoid the
theological implications of the Bible by using a moralistic and pietistic
approach and interpreting the Bible as God's law for living. Stories of
biblical people become examples for godly living. Understood in this
way, any story can be used, even with young children; the overriding
aim prevents the writer from being troubled by his distortions of the
original meanings.

The basic methodology is to begin by reading the biblical text, retell
it in story form, ask questions to fix the content in mind, illustrate
with a parallel situation from personal experience, then ask how the
biblical story gives the answer for life. The basic method is that of question and answer (there is usually a "correct" answer), and the learner
may be asked to provide simple illustrations.

The biblically based approach is rational. There is an assumption
that, when one knows what the Bible says, one will be moved to act
accordingly. This may work for people with a deep religious orientation but depends for its success on the learner's and teacher's acceptance of fundamental propositions.

III. Second Solution: The Combination Approach

Curriculum developers in some denominations believe that a contex-
tual approach should be used but realize that they must write a curriculum acceptable to congregations which define religious education
in terms of learning the Bible. These may start with experience-centered
goals and unit outlines, but the development is in terms of biblical
material.

The American Baptist Convention, together with the Disciples of
Christ, has just completed the first year of a projected new curriculum.
It is based on an elaborate series of objectives developed by sixteen
denominations working cooperatively through the National Council of
Churches.[2] The three-year cycle themes are: (1) knowing the living
God, (2) responding to God's call to live in Christ, and (3) being the
community of Christian love. The place of the Bible is indicated by the
principle of the "crossing-point": "the intersection of the learner's per-

sisting life concerns with the dynamic of the gospel."[3] This is based on an extensive list of Scripture references related to each theme. Most units of study begin with a life situation, but in each year there will be one completely biblical study. In grades 1–2 this material is taken from the life and teachings of Jesus; in grades 3–4 it is "experiencing Advent–Christmas" (and a later Easter unit); in grades 5–6, a semester of Bible study and a similar course at the secondary school level. One of the three basic adult study courses is biblical.

The Presbyterian Church in the United States (with the Moravian Church and the Reformed Church of America) has developed a curriculum with a two-year cycle alternating the themes of the Bible and the Christian life. The biblical theme is described in an adult study book entitled *The Mighty Acts of God,*[4] and there are biblical story books for use at various age levels. The purpose is to ground the learner in the biblical story as *anamnesis,* or remembered history. Other reading books and teaching units are based on the experience of the learner; the Church is the basis of a third approach. The methods for carrying out this purpose include storytelling, informal dramatizations, the use of visual aids, and discussions which ask what the story says and what it is saying for us. This is loosely referred to as an "existential" approach to biblical study.

The Lutheran Church in America, in a curriculum completed a few years ago, also tries to balance the elements of biblical material and life experience. The learning theory indicates that development should be from information to understanding, to changed attitudes, and to action. But such changes are difficult to evaluate, and in the written materials the understanding of biblical material becomes a strong component in both subject matter and methods.

The United Methodist Church's curriculum (which is required reading in the largest single Protestant denomination in the United States) must be placed in this category. Methodist theology has usually been liberal with a strongly moral accent and emphasis on personal life witness. The Bible in Methodist teaching tends toward both moral command and moral example. It reflects a theology of grace with Pelagian overtones. A number of rural churches cling to a biblical curriculum. Although the membership in suburban churches is larger, denominational leaders have been loath to alienate the loyal rural constituencies, despite their own educational and theological training which urges them in the direction of an experience-centered curriculum. Some recent materials for use with young people at weekend conferences give leaders freedom to build on a wealth of perceptive materials in which the Bible speaks incisively to contemporary situations. This may herald might be memorized but has primarily been used as a guide to the Christian life. It was presumed that Christians could be known by how they acted and that the Bible could tell them how to act. Few Protestant groups today hold to so simple a view, but a basic question faces educators whenever they develop a new curriculum: In what way does the Bible point to Christian living? Two possible approaches emerge. If one reads the Bible, will one find the answers? That is, does the Holy Spirit guide primarily through this source? Or does one begin the study with life itself and ask how the Bible speaks? These are popularly referred to as the "biblical" or the "experience–centered" approaches to religious learning.

"Christian living" needs also to be defined. To what exent is it personal or corporate? Will devout Christians improve social conditions through the personal integrity of their lives, or does the social setting of a community affect the possibilities for the growth of faith? Parents, aware of their own lack of biblical knowledge, and clergy, disturbed by the inability of congregations to respond to biblical allusions, emphasize the need for ways to teach biblical content, especially to the young. Professional educators frequently insist that there is little motivation for learning the content of the Bible unless this can be shown to have some meaning for the learner's life. No one expects a definitive solution to this problem. In a "free market" those responsible for education in a particular parish would make the choice which seemed to them most appropriate. But Protestant curricula are subsidized by individual denominations. Various pressures, including promotional materials, leadership training programs, and specific units of study closely tied to the work and worship forms of a denomination, encourage the use of an official curriculum.

Three solutions are represented in current curriculum development. Naturally enough, these begin with the Bible, begin with life experience, or attempt to combine both.

II. First Solution: Begin with the Bible

The thesis is that a knowledge and understanding of the essentials of biblical history are necessary for the learner to know how to live as a Christian in his or her personal life and as a member of society. Becoming aware of how God made himself known through the history of his people, Christians will see themselves in this line of succession and know that they also must cultivate a life of faithful obedience.

The primary example of such a curriculum is one which the Presbyterian Church in the United States is about to put into circulation. Teaching goals are stated operationally in terms of the development of five abilities, one of which is "the ability to interpret the Bible intelligently." The American psychologist-educator Jerome S. Bruner has stated the principle that "any idea or problem or body of knowledge can be presented in a form simple enough so that any particular learner can understand it in a recognizable form."[1] The Swiss psychologist Jean Piaget has described stages in cognitive development from concrete operational to abstract operational. A core curriculum is developed for learners between the ages of six and fifteen (in American terms from grades 1 through 10). In the concrete operational stage children are introduced to stories about biblical people (grades 1–2); they then study four key periods in the biblical experience: Exodus–Covenant, kingdom, life of Christ, and the formation of the Church (grades 3–4); they conclude with a two-year survey of biblical history (grades 5–6). Assuming a basic knowledge of content, the curriculum moves into the abstract-operational stage of development by stressing the meaning of the material. Interpretative skills are learned in grades 7–9, where the structure of the Bible, its authority, and its interpretative method are studied. The interpretation in practice follows (grades 9–10): worship, ethics, theologizing. After this intensive grounding, young people and adults are encouraged to continue their studies in available elective courses.

This approach is grounded in Calvinist theology expressed in contemporary forms of orthodoxy. Highly respectful of biblical scholarship, the proponents of this method want Christians to know what the Bible says and means before they try to choose from among its writings what they think will apply to life. The methodology for conveying a content-centered curriculum is based on a pupil workbook whose readings point constantly to the biblical text itself and have the kinds of exercises (quiz, sentence-completion) which will teach the learner how to read the text accurately. The emphasis in later workbooks is on learning how to interpret. Every classroom has a basic library consisting of biblical dictionaries, encyclopedias, wordbooks, and concordances to assist in these learning tasks. Charts, maps, and time-lines help the pupil to grasp the geographical and chronological background. Filmstrips, records, and films make the information more vivid.

Another type of biblical curriculum continues the nineteenth-century Sunday school method in modified form. A uniform lesson series outline is prepared by the National Council of the Churches of Christ; it is widely used by independent curriculum publishers who are patronized by churches rejecting the less completely biblical materials of their main-line denominational educators. The outlines simply specify

to him or her in the experiences of biblical people. The teacher points
back to the biblical record. Some would say that it is less threatening
to see oneself in a person who lived long ago (as Jacob and Esau) than
to be called upon to face ugly feelings against one's own brother.[5] It
could also be easier to stay in the historical mood and avoid the immediate situation. On the other hand, the experience-based curriculum
lends itself to a nonreligious ethicalism on the part of teachers who
lack a theological and biblical training. Unfortunately, this is an inadequacy of many teachers in Protestant Sunday church schools where
the system of voluntary, nonprofessional teachers is a principle staunch-
ly defended as an expression of both witness and service. Such teaching
ranges from simple lessons in morality to an intellectual discussion of
ethics, but it would not be a teaching of the Christian faith unless it
had a biblical foundation. A completely biblical teaching can be an
escape from real problems. A completely life-centered teaching escapes
being secular only when the teacher brings to it a deep knowledge and
understanding of the Bible.

One problem, even in an experience-centered curriculum, is to introduce an emphasis on social concern comparable to that of personal
development. The Bible is a book about a people who did not have the
intensely individual outlook on life that characterizes the modern
Western world. Yet we have managed to translate it into such terms.
The corporate responsibility of families in Israel and of the whole people of Israel before God should enable us to bring biblical insights to
bear more tellingly on the responsibility of Christian families, of the
Church, and of so-called Christian peoples for the deep-seated problems
of humanity. No curriculum shows evidence of sensing this parallel.
We read about the disappearance of the ten tribes, the return from ex-
ile of Judah, and the scattering of the Church from Jerusalem but are
not led to draw implications for ourselves.

A persistently asked question is whether the modern person can
identify with biblical people by drawing on these psychological and
sociological parallels. Are the sonorous phrases of the translation in
the way? Are the traditional pictures which come to mind a stumbling
block? Do we need line drawings, cartoons, abstract art, and multimedia
presentations where the biblical and the contemporary overlap? Cor-
ita Kent's word-pictures bring startling immediacy when she parallels
advertising slogans with well-worn biblical verses. Drama has been used
as a method for involving the learner, but this requires more effort than
the Sunday school can provide if the learner is to identify in a profound
way with a biblical person. Films can do this when Christians are willing to become involved in the kind of secular interpretation to be found

in Pasolini's *The Gospel According to St. Matthew.* Some religious people found that film offensive, but so did some who first participated in the story. An adult group could understand the compelling power of the crucified Christ over men and women more by reading Pär Lagerkvist's *Barabbas* than by studying a prepared textbook on the life of Christ. The professional artist can evoke the kind of deep emotional response which leads to confrontation and to commitment.

The problem of teaching the Bible to secular Christians is the problem of inducing those who do not read the Bible to do so. No device has had this effect. Church people are politely respectful of the subject, and they feel strongly that, if children were taught the contents of the Bible, they would grow into biblically knowledgeable adults. The result is that adolescents think of the Bible as a children's book. The question is not squarely faced because many denominational officials still hold to the illusion that the insistence in the hinterlands upon having biblical materials, and the sales by nondenominational publishers of biblical curricula, indicate a widespread need. They do not. This protest comes from people with a residual biblical tradition. The crucial problem in American Protestantism is how to hold within the institutional church the increasingly well-educated, middle-class and working-class members whose very education and daily life incline them toward secularity and even scepticism.

A study of the Bible as the book of the acts of God, or as the drama of redemption, will not provide the answer. Americans are nonhistorical, glorying in the present. Moreover, biblical scholars have become aware that this particular way of affirming the unity of the Bible has ignored the Writings, has not sufficiently incorporated the prophetic tradition, and has omitted the Revelation, which is posthistorical. Since curriculum development requires years from the planning stage to printed material, correction of this point of view will require time.

Protestant educators have yet to realize that the largest number of Bible hearers sit in the congregation on a Sunday morning. Much as we avoid facing it, this is the total exposure of most Protestants to the Bible. We would prefer the picture of the family Bible, of a daily devotional use of the Bible, or of parents reading Bible stories to their children. This simply does not happen; the long-cherished affirmation of Protestantism as based on a biblically literate people does not exist today. The liturgy could become a base for a biblical curriculum. Some awareness of this is to be found in the present cooperative efforts at developing a two- or three-year lectionary cycle for Sunday readings. The stress on exegetical preaching in the recent past has been a well-placed effort to bring biblical words to bear on contemporary life. A few parishes have developed small groups meeting weekly to study a lectionary passage. The increase of vernacular renderings of the Scriptures is an attempt to get away from the numbing effect of the too familiar. Making the most of this weekly exposure to the Scriptures may be the most effective source for bringing its word to adults. Generations of children have attended Protestant Sunday schools and grown up without any mature understanding of the Bible. Each twenty years a new curriculum promises to do an improved job, but nothing changes. The problem does not lie in the choice of material or of methods. It lies in the secular orientation of American Protestants who find that they can live effectively without the Bible. Until or unless they find otherwise, they will continue to espouse its use – for children.

VI. Other Fields of Discussion

This discussion has outlined developments in the United States. A similar account could be given of Canada; both the United Church of Canada and the Anglicans are using experience-oriented curricula. In England, the agreed syllabi which formed the bases for religious learning in the school were strongly biblical. These have been under attack by Ronald Goldman, principal of Didsbury College of Education, Manchester, whose research has indicated that they seem to produce more confusion than light. His co-workers are developing experience-centered courses of study.

The discussion could have been paralleled by references to recent developments in American Catholic curricula, most of which are now biblically oriented within the framework of a liturgical and sacramental understanding. The Bible is apparent as holy history in the *Come to the Father* series (Paulist Press), an import from Canada, and in *The Christian Inheritance* series. The life-experience approach is more effectively presented in several Catholic curricula than in any Protestant series. Such Catholic series include *Time for Living* (Herder and Herder); *Life, Love, Joy,* developed by the National Center of the Confraternity of Christian Doctrine (Silver Burdett, publishers); and Argus Communications' multimedia presentations for youth and adults. Protestant parishes are among their most eager users.

The Bible comes to us as the written record of the word of God, and – for people who like to read – this is a useful form of communication. The McLuhan thesis of a new tribalism should make us reflect that the Bible began as an oral tradition. The story needs to be heard: to be told by person to person, to be witnessed to in personal and community experience, and to be celebrated in the liturgy. The next attempts at curriculum rewriting may have to take seriously such kinds of response to the Bible.

NOTES

1. Jerome S. Bruner, *Toward a Theory of Instruction* (Cambridge, MA: Belknap Press of Harvard University, 1964), p. 44.
2. *The Church's Educational Ministry: A Curriculum Plan* (St. Louis: Bethany Press, 1965), the work of the Cooperative Curriculum Project.
3. Joseph D. Ban, *Education for Change* (Valley Forge, PA: Judson Press, 1968), explaining the bases for the curriculum, pp. 10, 59f.
4. Arnold B. Rhodes, *The Mighty Acts of God* (Richmond, VA: CLC Press, 1964).
5. Cf. Iris V. Cully, *Imparting the Word: The Bible in Christian Education* (Philadelphia: Westminster Press, 1962), chap. 7, p. 106.

CURRICULAR MATERIALS NOTED

Choose Life. Chicago: Argus Communications, 1968 ff.
Christian Faith and Action. Philadelphia: Board of Christian Education, United Presbyterian Church, 1970.
Christian Faith and Work Plan. Valley Forge: American Baptist Convention, Judson Graded Series, 1969.
The Christian Inheritance. St. Paul: North Central Publishing (distributed by Liturgical Press, Collegeville, MN), 1968 ff.
The Church's Teaching Series. New York: Seabury Press, 1955 ff.
Come to the Father. Glen Rock, NJ: Paulist Press, 1966 ff.
Covenant Life Curriculum. Richmond: Covenant Life Press, 1964 ff.
Sunday Church School Series. Philadelphia: Lutheran Church of America, Lutheran Church Press, 1964 ff.
Time for Living. New York: Herder and Herder, 1968 ff.
United Church Curriculum. Philadelphia: United Church Press, 1962 ff.
Wesley Series. Nashville: United Methodist Church, the Graded Press, 1967 ff.

*In "Faith, Theology, and Belief," Richard McBrien makes distinctions
of special importance to catechetical practitioners. Those wishing more
background on these matters may want to read the section on religious
language in John Macquarrie's* Principles of Christian Theology; *"The
Hermeneutics of Dogmatic Statements," in Avery Dulles'* The Survival
of Dogma; *or the oft-cited chapter, "Faith," in Wilfred Cantwell Smith's*
The Meaning and End of Religion.

READING 27

Faith, Theology, and Belief

RICHARD P. McBRIEN

I HAVE BEEN CONVINCED for some time that the source of
many, if not most, of the troubles in the Catholic Church today
is our stubborn failure to discern the differences among faith, theology,
and belief.

Many Catholics who should know better (even a cardinal or two
may come readily to mind) continue to insist that faith and belief are
somehow independent of theology. They assure nervous audiences of
parents that the job of the religious educator is not to teach the views
of modern theologians but to teach the faith, indeed "to teach as Jesus
did" (the title of one of the American bishops' recent catechetical
documents).

Reprinted from *Commonweal* 101 (15 November 1974), pp. 134–137, by permission
of Commonweal Publishing Co., Inc.

I could cite actual statements and identify the speakers, but that would serve no useful purpose. We are now long past the time when such purveyors of gross theological distortions have to be exposed. They are known, and competent religious educators do not take them seriously any longer.

In the meantime, however, many innocent bystanders remain confused. They wonder if there is any point or purpose to being and remaining a Christian. The shadow of a question mark hovers ominously over everything in sight.

In this essay I propose a way out of the problem. It is a matter of clarifying fundamental concepts and the interrelationships which exist among them. My thesis may be summarized in this fashion: Faith. is not theology is not belief.

1) **Faith is not theology.** Faith is a way of perceiving reality. The person of faith "sees" more than meets the eye. Faith apprehends the "beyond in our midst" (Bonhoeffer), the "other dimension" (Dupré), the ultimacy of secular experience (Gilkey), the Ground of being (Tillich). It is a judgment of faith that reality is more than the sum of persons, places, things, and events which constitute both history and the cosmos. The person of faith discerns those "signals of transcendence" (Berger) intermingled with the sights and sounds, the sensations and the smells of ordinary, everyday human experience. Faith is a stance, a posture, a fundamental attitude. Faith infers the reality of God from reality itself. But like all inferences, the evidence is circumstantial.

But inference is, after all, something to go on. It is not sheerly arbitrary. If a man wakes up in the morning and finds the ground covered with fresh snow, he has every right to infer that snow fell during the night, even though he never actually saw a flake of it descend. The analogy cannot be applied precisely to our presumed experience of God, but the analogy is applicable in some measure nonetheless. We infer that reality is ultimately gracious and provident in our own experience of gracious and provident people. We infer that the world is rooted in love by reason of our own experience of love. We infer that the transcendent God is real in our own experience of the transcendent virtues of loyalty, generosity, compassion, justice, honesty, truthfulness, sensitivity, gentleness, and love.

Faith involves a risk-taking. We did not need Kierkegaard to tell us that, but we sometimes talk and act as if there were no risk at all. Infallibility stands at the ready. In this view, religious people – especially Catholics – are supposedly more certain than others of the reality of God and of the divine plan of salvation. The more one thinks and speaks of God, so it seems to be assumed, the more certain one becomes of the object of those thoughts and words. That's not true, of course, and the great Christian mystics should have impressed the contrary lesson upon us by now. The closer we approach toward God, the more deafening the silence. The more intensive the quest, the more elusive the goal.

Faith is that precognitive, prereflective, prescientific perception of God in the midst of life. But unalloyed faith doesn't exist. Nowhere can we discover and isolate "pure faith." Pure faith exists only in the mind, as a logical construct. Real faith, on the other hand, exists always and only in a cognitive (more or less), reflective (more or less), scientific state. Every thought about the meaning of faith is precisely that: a thought about the meaning of faith. Every word of interpretation designed to articulate and illuminate the meaning and implications of faith is, again, precisely that: a word of interpretation, not faith itself. When Catholic public figures warn the rank and file against the contamination of "the faith" by "theology," they simply don't know what they are talking about.

Faith is not theology, to be sure, but neither does faith exist apart from, or independent of, theology. Theology comes into play at that very moment when the person of faith becomes intellectually conscious of that faith. From the very beginning faith exists in a theologically interpreted state. Indeed, it is a redundancy to put it that way: "theologically interpreted." For the interpretation of one's faith is theology itself.

Theology is, as St. Anselm of Canterbury defined it nine centuries ago, "faith seeking understanding." Theology is that process by which we bring our presumed perception of God to the level of expression. Theology is the verbalizing, in a more or less systematic manner, of the experience of God within human experience.

Theology may emerge in the form of a painting, a piece of music, a dance, a cathedral, a bodily posture, or, in its most recognizable form, in spoken and written words. These forms, of course, never do complete justice to the perception which they hope to express. Not all theology is good theology. We can ineptly translate our experience into language, or we can have a thoroughly distorted or even false experience of God in the first place, which no form, however cleverly constructed, can ever redeem.

When all is said and done, religious educators, bishops, preachers, and the Church at large do not transmit "the faith." They transmit particular interpretations or understandings of faith. In direct words: They transmit theologies.

It is entirely beside the point to warn religious educators against teaching theology instead of handing on the faith. The faith exists always and only in some theological form. The question before the Church today and forever is not *whether* the faith shall be transmitted according to some theological interpretation but rather *which* theological interpretation is best suited to the task at a particular moment in time.

What is so offensive about appeals to "the faith" over against the "private views" of theologians is that *a particular theology* is subtly being cloaked in the aura of faith itself. Consequently, an attack upon that theology is automatically perceived as an attack upon the faith (as an attack upon the character and performance of the U.S. president was once conveniently perceived as an attack upon the office and institution of the presidency). What some cardinal of the Roman Catholic Church learned in his theology courses (or catechism classes) in the 1920s or 1930s or what he himself may have taught as a professor of theology in the 1930s or 1940s may be useful or not in making sense of such Pauline texts as, "God was in Christ reconciling the world to himself" (2 Cor. 5:19), but that theology remains only that: a theology, a specific, time-conditioned, culturally conditioned interpretation of the vast expanse of human history and, in particular, of that crucial segment of human history wherein the Christ-event comes clearly into view and focus.

And so we reach the supreme contradiction of the piece: "The faith" which must not be confined and corrupted by *any* theology can only be understood in terms of *one* theology, in this instance the scholastic theology popular in Catholic seminaries just prior to Vatican Council II.

2) **Theology is not belief.** If theology is faith brought to the level of self-consciousness, then belief is theology in a kind of snapshot or frozen state. Theology is a *process;* belief is one of its several *products.* Other products include sacred Scripture (this is exceedingly important to remember lest one mistakenly conclude that theology is reflection on the biblical message; it is entirely the other way round: the biblical message is itself a product of theological reflection), doctrines (beliefs elevated to the level of official approbation), dogmas (doctrines that carry the highest level of official approbation, the denial of which normally separates one from the community of faith), liturgies (*lex orandi, lex credendi* – the perception of God in ritualized form), artistic works (churches, statues, paintings, music, dance, and so forth).

In stop-action language: Theology follows faith, and belief follows theology. But this is said only for purposes of distinguishing among the three elements. As we have already seen, faith and theology do not really exist apart from one another, whereas belief and theology can and do exist apart. The theologian can express all sorts of judgments about the reality of God as he or she presumably experiences God, without at the same time resorting to formulas or propositions which have received an official (doctrine) or quasi-official status (catechism, religion textbook, etc.) within the community of faith.

And that has been yet another serious distortion of the meaning of theology and of its relationship to belief and/or doctrine. Many, especially in the Roman Catholic tradition, have assumed that theology is essentially the study of Church teachings. Indeed, Catholic seminary courses were for many years labeled simply "Dogma." The task of the theologian, in this view, is to analyze, explain, and defend what is already "on the books" (in Denzinger and in modern papal documents). With that kind of understanding of theology abroad in the Catholic Church throughout most of this century, it is hardly surprising that the dissident posture of some contemporary Catholic theologians should have shocked and infuriated so many of their brothers and sisters in the Church. But theologians are not commissioned to be the Church's (or the pope's) press secretaries. They are more nearly her pundits.

3) **Faith is not belief.** There are many beliefs but only one faith. There are many Christian beliefs but only one Christian faith. Faith is a way of perceiving God in human experience. Christian faith is a way of perceiving God in Jesus Christ as the key and focal point of all human experience.

Over the centuries of Christian history there have been literally thousands of beliefs held and transmitted at one time or another, i.e., interpretations of faith which significant segments of the Christian community found useful for expressing and articulating their own perception of God in Christ. Some of these beliefs endured the test of time (e.g., the great christological dogmas), while others have been consigned to the intellectual rummage room (e.g., the "two swords" theory of papal authority). What has been true in Christian history is true in the contemporary Christian community. Hundreds of different beliefs vie with one another for a kind of momentary or long-term dominance. Some of these beliefs are grounded solidly in the history of the Church (e.g., belief in the Real Presence of Christ in the Eucharist), while others have very short and tender roots indeed (e.g., belief in the pope as an absolute, infallible monarch).

The sorting-out process is never finished. We are faced constantly with the problem of evaluating and reevaluating our beliefs in the light of our ongoing experience and our fundamental (theological) interpretations of that experience, and these in turn are judged against that instinct of faith which somehow gives the whole Church its inner coherence and its radical identity and continuity. It is at the point of the "somehow" in the preceding sentence that our rich poetry about the Holy Spirit inserts itself.

At key historical moments in that sorting-out process, representative leaders of the whole Church may be compelled to assemble in solemn ecumenical council (the broader the representation, the more ecumenical the council) to confront an issue of belief that threatens the very unity of the Church. Their task is not to draw the circle so tightly that many will fall beyond its limits but to draw it as generously as conscience allows so that as many as possible might continue to stand together within it. Nothing in this essay is intended to be prejudicial to the important, irreplaceable function of what we Catholics call the official magisterium, but neither does this essay support the ultramontane mentality which still prevails in certain vocal sectors of the American Catholic community and even among some of its pastoral leaders. For papal and/or episcopal pronouncements are no less conditioned than the biblical message itself. And if we have adjusted ourselves at long last to the *critical* reading of sacred Scripture, then it is certainly time that we similarly abjured our galloping fundamentalism in the use and abuse of ecclesiastical documents and doctrines. It is never enough to know what a conciliar text *said*. What did the text *mean* in its original formulation? And what can the text *mean* for us *today?*

4) **Unity in diversity.** Diversity and pluralism is a fact of life in the Church today. It was a fact of life in the Church of yesterday, in biblical and postbiblical times alike. And it will remain a fact of life in the Church until the very end of history. So long as we find ourselves in these peculiarly human circumstances where no one can claim to have seen God (John 1:18), we shall proceed in a groping, tentative, provisional, and halting manner: trusting our perceptions as far as we can, articulating our convictions as modestly as we can, formulating our beliefs as fairly as we can, and respecting those with different theologies and different beliefs as conscientiously as we can.

But we cannot conclude that diversity and pluralism, on the one hand, and unifying theological principles, on the other, are forever mutually exclusive. We Christians may differ in the way we express our perception of God and formulate those expressions consensually, but we are one in the conviction that the God of our theology and of our belief is a real, living God.

We Christians may differ in the way we express our perception of God in Jesus Christ and in the way we formulate those perceptions officially, but we are one in the conviction that the God of our theology and of our belief is truly present in Jesus of Nazareth to the extent that it can be said of Jesus alone that he is indeed the Lord of history (Phil. 2:5–11).

We Christians, and particularly we Catholic Christians, may differ in the way we express our perception of God in the community of faith called the Church and we may differ, too, in the way we dogmatize that perception of God in the Church, but we are one in the conviction that there is indeed more to the Church than meets the eye, that God is present there in such wise that we can call it the Body of Christ, the Temple of the Holy Spirit, the People of God of the New Covenant.

And finally, we Christians, and particularly we Catholic Christians, may differ in the way we express our perception of God in those ritual signs and symbols we call sacraments and we may differ in the way we precisely formulate our apprehension of God in those sacred rites, but we are one in the conviction that the God of our theology and of our belief is truly present within and under these signs which serve as climactic points of encounter between God and ourselves.

The struggle to believe is not necessarily made any easier by the mere enumeration of these abiding elements of Christian faith. Nevertheless, they might provide a tangible and meaningful context within which we can make sense of, and apply, three key principles which the Second Vatican Council bequeathed to us: (1) Not all beliefs are of equal importance. "In Catholic teaching there exists an order or 'hierarchy' of truths, since they vary in their relationship to the foundation of Christian faith" ("Decree on Ecumenism," no. 11). (2) There are very few beliefs indeed which one must accept in order to remain in good standing within the Christian community. "In order to restore communion and unity or preserve them, one must 'impose no burden beyond what is indispensable' (Acts 15:28)" ("Decree on Ecumenism," no. 18). (3) One cannot question the integrity of those with whom one chooses to disagree on matters of theology and/or belief. "Let there be unity in what is necessary, freedom in what is unsettled, and charity in any case" ("Pastoral Constitution on the Church in the Modern World," no. 92).

The relationship between catechesis and religious education continues to be a problem, especially for persons educating within church structures. While all seem to agree that catechesis and religious education are not the same and should not be confused, not all agree on the relative merits of each category. The following article explores, particularly from a catechetical angle, some ways that catechesis and religious education can enrich each other.

READING 28

Catechesis: An Enriching Category for Religious Education

MICHAEL WARREN

THE UNDERLYING CONVICTION of this essay is that the time has now come for a more deliberate convergence of catechetical and religious education theory.[1] In a real way, the convergence reached a milestone at a convention of the Association of Professors and Researchers in Religious Education (APRRE) some years ago, during a sharing of religious educational and catechetical perspec-

Reprinted from the March–April 1981 issue of the journal *Religious Education*, pp. 115–127, by permission of the publisher, The Religious Education Association, 409 Prospect Street, New Haven, CT 06510. Membership or subscription available for $25.00 per year.

tives by Charles Melchert and John Westerhoff.[2] During the years preceding the Melchert-Westerhoff exchange, the APRRE was attended by an increasing number of persons viewing Christian education and religious education from differing perspectives. They listened to papers and transposed one another's categories quietly and respectfully without ever fully speaking to one another's standpoints as standpoints the way Westerhoff and Melchert did in 1976. The process had not enabled them to speak to those issues previously.

By *convergence* I am not suggesting a blurring of the sharp lines of focus that set off one perspective from another, or a striving for some new hybrid entity utilizing the best features of each. For the present, *convergence* will mean a taking seriously of one another's perspectives as differing but complementary and a recognition that each has its own special genius by which the other can be enriched. Time might prove the effort to speak from one perspective to another has been wasted because it was not successful or even not worth the effort. My own prediction, however, is that our understanding of religious education will be enriched and even changed by greater attention to catechesis, the same way catechesis has been and continues to be challenged by religious education theory.

My own part in fostering what I choose to term a convergence will lie in pointing out key features of catechesis that could well be taken more note of by those who name themselves as religious educators and/or Christian educators. I do not expect us to develop a common language. The attempt would be undesirable because the two perspectives are needed as complementary and the two languages are needed to describe subtly different ways of looking at similar phenomena. My hope is that we may all become more comfortable with one another's perspectives, better able to cross over into one another's professional space, and better equipped to develop a certain bilingual fluency enabling us to appreciate the subtleties of one another's ideas. Basic to any proper hermeneutic is the matter of knowing well one's own frame of reference and its accompanying biases. Attending to these complementary languages may aid some in better seeing where they stand.

I propose two ground-rule convictions to guide the discussion. The first is that both catechesis and religious education will profit by avoiding exaggerated claims for themselves. Each can admit a checkered history of some successes and failures. In fact, hidden in many of the successes are the seeds of what turned out to be serious misjudgments needing later careful correction. Examples from religious education might include the professionalization of religious education in North America during this century, a development that gave status to the practitioners but which was never quite welcomed by the religious educatees.[3] Likewise, the broad and intelligent vision of George Albert Coe was unfortunately tied to a naively optimistic hope for the progressive betterment of humankind, a hope in process of being discredited even as his books were appearing.[4] From the catechetical side, Josef Jungmann's overall program for the renewal of the Christian self-understanding of adult Catholics eventually was seen as an "in-house" proclamation of meanings cut off from the wider world of reality.[5]

Both religious education and catechesis have in fact been struggling forward in the face of intense critiques from within and a mixed historical legacy. Each at the present time is in the midst of a critical examination of its history and of its present and future goals. Being in touch with this ferment may help us be more open to critical questions from another perspective.

A second ground-rule conviction is that our theory is incomplete. No matter how well we may speak of it or how much we may want to create a future guided by it, at the local level it does not exist with anything like the purity of our mind's-eye vision. What we say we are is not quite what we are; our practice does not measure up to our theory. This admission will be important for my own presentation of features of catechesis able to enrich religious education, since this presentation will have a clear theoretical edge. Catechesis is both gifted with and afflicted by a body of official Roman Catholic documents outlining what it is to be and out of which a theoretician must carefully select the most significant features. My presentation will highlight features of catechesis that need to be stressed in the future, if catechesis is to fulfill its own promise, but which are not immediately evident in much local practice.[6]

The aspects of catechesis I wish to set forth are five: the catechetical tradition as a tradition, plus four features of catechesis — its being a work of the community, its framework of pastoral ministry, its celebrative mode, and its occasional character.

The special value of the catechetical tradition can be found in its historical roots and in the worldwide character of its modern development. Both features are made accessible through a catechetical language which emerges from the historical roots of the tradition.

In dealing with the catechetical tradition, I wish to affirm at the outset that, as with so many other aspects of Christian history, there is a special sense in which persons with a catechetical perspective have only in fairly recent times self-consciously appropriated that tradition. This is especially true in the United States, where what began at

Catholic University in the 1950s as studies in the "history of religious education" gradually evolved into even deeper probings of a catechetical tradition. These studies gradually led to a deliberate use of catechetical language as the language fostered by the tradition.[7]

Ironically, to date, one of the most comprehensive histories of the catechetical tradition done in English over the past half century is the one written by Presbyterian Lewis Sherrill.[8] At this juncture someone will point out that what Sherrill referred to in the title of his book as "Christian education" I am choosing to call catechesis. Though I welcome such a reminder I am trying here to affirm a tradition common to Christians before the sixteenth century, fidelity to which will involve a greater sensitivity to the language of catechesis. Almost in counterpoint to its title, the text of Sherrill's book shows he knew well the language and the tradition of catechesis.

Sherrill himself points out the dangers of ignoring any part of that history in order to claim a tiny but less embarrassing part of it. He names two specific temptations to distortion.

> The first can see little good before the Reformation until the stream has been re-ascended to its fountain source, with the frequent consequence that men of this view are essentially unrooted in history. The second can see little except perversion in the Protestant stream and would draw inspiration from the relatively undivided church as it existed before 1517, with the consequent temptation to repeat the characteristic mistakes which unfitted the medieval church to be a house of the spirit to those whom Christianity had helped to set free.[9]

These words can be a reminder to us that the common tradition of Protestants and Catholics is to be found in the full fifteen hundred years that preceded the great Renaissance reform. An understanding of catechetical principles and of catechetical language should open this period to all Christians interested in claiming their common tradition.

Catechesis, then, seeks to stand squarely within a long tradition and to stand there aware of all the hermeneutical tasks demanded by such a standpoint. There is a sense in which catechetical theory is more phenomenological than some religious education theory, because it deals with the phenomenon of the tradition and is concerned with the actual ways groups of Christians have strived to embody faith and to invite new members to stand with them within the circle of faith. If a danger to catechesis is to stand so much within a specific tradition that it is possible to forget the wider world beyond the community, the danger to some religious education theory could be one of taking a stance so theoretical as to be almost Gnostic.

Another feature of the catechetical tradition is its worldwide character. The modern catechetical movement has as its landmarks a series of international meetings to which leaders throughout the world could come to share perspectives and raise consciousness.[10] Whatever the liabilities of the 1977 Roman synod dealing with catechesis – and there were several – the great value of that sharing was its surfacing of common worldwide issues affecting the way persons grow into Christian faith in various social contexts.[11]

A special but not fully recognized liability of the religious education movement in North America has been its geographical and chronological localization. Chronologically, it has been bounded at its narrowest by the 1903 founding of the Religious Education Association and at its widest by the founding of the United States republic or the federation of Canadian provinces. Geographically, it has tended to be bounded by the Rio Grande River, the Arctic Slope, and the hidden language boundaries in between. Ironically, religious education theory, which prides itself on looking beyond the ecclesiastical, can itself be broadened by catechesis which looks further back in history and far beyond North America.

To back up my position here, I invite a casual survey of the content and interests of North American religious educators as reflected in the pages of *Religious Education* over the past thirty years. The matters treated and the manner of their treatment do not in general reflect an international interest or a long historical view. On the other hand, an examination of the English-language edition of *Lumen Vitae*, since its start in 1950, or of the U.S. catechetical periodical *The Living Light* will suggest more international connections. While recognizing the positive value of the periodical *Religious Education*'s interests in a specific North American situation, I presume that today more and more religious educators on this continent are striving for a broader, international perspective. Catechetical literature and the international catechetical movement offer that perspective.

The first and most central of the four features of catechesis that is significant for religious educators and Christian educators is its community centeredness. Of all aspects of catechesis, this is the one most directive of its total activity. The *General Catechetical Directory*, a charter of guiding norms for catechesis published in Rome in 1971, describes catechesis as follows:

> Within the scope of pastoral activity, catechesis is the term to be used for that form of ecclesial action which leads both communities and individual members of the faithful to maturity of faith.
> With the aid of catechesis, communities of Christians acquire for themselves a more profound living knowledge of God ... [and] build themselves up by striving to make their faith mature and enlightened,

and to share this mature faith with men [and women] who desire to possess it (no. 21).[12]

This passage locates the context of catechesis in the community and names the chief agent of catechesis as the same community. Within this principle lie the seeds of a revolution in how local churches think of the process of fostering a maturing faith and in how they actually do it.[13] Catechesis is not to be a peripheral activity engaged in by those too young to resist. It is rather a multiform activity, the chief agent of which is the community itself.[14]

If the community is the prime agent of catechesis, there is a sense in which the community is also the prime embodiment of the message in its own life. At some level the community is the message. Once the community's life becomes central, several related matters achieve special importance. One of these is the relation of a faith community with local culture. Over the past twenty years, catechetical literature shows much more intense reflection on this question than does the literature of religious education.[15]

The community embodies the Christian way, but it embodies it in the forms and language of its own local culture. The two words used somewhat interchangeably for this process are *enculturation* and *indigenization*. Basically, they suggest that the local community is to be a native community by which the Christian message will be expressed with the originality and genius of that local life.[16] From this angle, catechesis is as much concerned with the struggle of individuals and communities to speak their own word as it is to foster prepackaged understandings.

Perhaps this perspective finds a classic statement in the following excerpt from one of the speeches given in 1968 at the International Catechetical Congress in Medellin, Colombia.

> When the language of our catechesis finds again the very originality of the Incarnation, it will be at the same time human and divine, interior and transcendent. . . . This perspective runs a risk of upsetting a little our concept of education, of programs, and also of the very structure of what we call catechesis. Indeed we will discover again the Bible, the liturgy, the dogmatic language. But we will not pay attention to their content in itself alone but to the way in which what they express is related to the experience and the image which this group has of itself. . . . This is what has made up what is best in the history of the Church: a new image of man confronting our tradition and expressing it anew for the present time. . . . Christianity invents itself anew. In this way catechesis becomes the place where the Christian group creates the experience of faith and invents a new language to express it.[17]

Of course, catechesis is aware, as are we all, that culture itself must be critiqued and judged by the gospel. Critical reflection is the other side of indigenization. Persons unfamiliar with the recent history of catechetical theory are generally unaware how closely related are catechesis and the fostering of critical consciousness, especially in the Third World countries.[18] Catechesis for critical reflection has been going on among those who have never heard of the critical theory of Habermas. A recent statement of the Roman Catholic bishops of Peru put the matter this way:

> The Gospel authentically preached to an oppressed man [or woman] achieves necessarily a conscientizing function, that is, it helps him to perceive his personhood and his dignity as a son of God, the situation of spoliation and injustice in which he lives, with all its economic, social, and political implications, and then to act against them.[19]

In the face of these principles it will not do any longer to caricature catechesis as an oppressive message imposed on persons from outside.[20] The socialization theme in catechesis arises not from a desire to impose understanding on persons in ways they cannot resist but out of fidelity to its communal nature and out of recognition that faith is not "transmitted" in teacher-student interactions but within a community concerned with living Jesus' way.

A second key feature of catechesis is the special conceptual framework within which it is set. Though I know of no one who would deny that catechesis is educational, its framework is not that of education but rather that of pastoral ministry. Catechesis places its activity unabashedly within the community of persons struggling to go deeper in reflecting on reality in the light of Jesus-faith. Thus, catechesis is distinct while at the same time closely related to all the other ministries: to the ministry of healing, to ministries of counsel and education, and to ministries of play and worship.[21]

Some may say that catechesis is by my own admission too tightly "churchy." I say instead that its relationship to other ministries makes catechesis wholistic and open to a wide range of human needs that surface in this world of ours, many of them quite unchurchy. Whereas education has been struggling to distinguish its deliberative and intentional aspects from those more everyday personal or social experiences that are educational almost by accident, catechesis has been extending its focus to the multiple ways meanings take root in a person and to the connection between a ministry of meanings (called the ministry of the word) and a variety of other ministries undertaken by ecclesial groups.

Seeing catechesis or Christian education within the basic category of pastoral ministry does not deny them their very real educative character, though it does choose to see the educative dimensions of these activities as subservient to their ministerial dimensions. Catechesis' understanding of itself in this regard is explicit and coherent. I myself judge that in the United States many have overstated the possibilities of education as the cure-all for multiple ills. Thus, alcoholism, illegal and dangerous driving habits, and economic imbalances are subjected to the therapy of education. The churches have aped society's stance in this matter and in its related tendency to see the greatest hope in the tight institutionalization of education we call schooling.

The churches have their own genius, their own distinctive wisdom, and this vision should be affirmed as part of our identity. It is unnecessary and inadvisable to abandon our category of pastoral ministry for one of education. The better approach is to hold fast to our understanding of the ministry of meanings as part of pastoral ministry and then consciously to cross over into the field of education with its specialized concepts and language. Working from this end, we may well enrich education; working from the other end, as we have in the past, I am not sure we have enriched education, though I am inclined to see that we have very much confused pastoral ministry.[22]

Catechesis is activity in a celebrative mode. This is the third feature of catechesis I wish to highlight. Catechesis most properly fits into the context of worship, as can be seen in its original place as part of the gradual and ritual walking step by step into the center of the community's life, a process we know as the catechumenate. The focus of catechesis, in its most perfect moments, was not the classroom but the chapel.[23] The goal of catechesis was not so much understandings as it was activity directed by those understandings, especially the activities of prayerful worship and care for the outcasts.

Although the ritual, celebrative aspect of catechesis had been suppressed for centuries, it was never totally lost.[24] Today, that character of catechesis can, I think, enrich our understanding of religious education and Christian education.[25] Robert W. Lynn and Elliott Wright have pointed out that, when Christian education became equipped with all the professionalism of progressive education, it began not to prosper but to decline. One of the components of the old-time Sunday school overlooked by the professionals with their valuable specialized training was this very celebrative character, to which the Sunday school paid special attention.[26]

Today, those engaged in ministry to young people are coming to see that it is almost impossible for churches to succeed with out-of-school educational programs for young people unless these programs have a strong celebrative dimension. It is the celebrative component that allows all participants to be human together on an equal footing because worship–like play–functions most properly out of statuslessness and out of what humans have in common rather than out of higher-and-lower roles. Educational theorist Dwayne Huebner told recently of his disillusion with the possibilities of secular education and of his renewed hope in church education as education offering the possibility of equality rather than of manipulation. "In the chapel all are equal": was the way he put it.[27] Indeed, the chapel is where catechesis finds its fulfillment.

A final and key feature of catechesis is its occasional but lifelong character. I realize that, as practiced in many places, catechesis functions in a way quite the opposite of this character. The usual formula for catechesis and for Christian education, also, is one that makes it continuous and terminal. It begins about age seven and continues, fall semester and spring semester, with possible vacation schools thrown in, until these captive audiences reach an age when they can shout, "Enough." At that point, often immediately after confirmation, catechesis and/or Christian education is terminated.

Catechesis, however, is meant to be occasional, with the prime occasion being the early intense period of preparation for Easter and its accompanying baptism of a new group of initiates. Catechesis is occasional in other senses as well. Faith questions erupt in the lives of individuals and communities in unplanned ways, especially during periods of transition, and those questions must be dealt with as they arise. This occasional character of catechesis makes most sense when tied to its lifelong character. In any person's biography, transitions are lifelong, and crises that call for systematic kinds of learning erupt more or less regularly. Through catechesis the community attends to these seasons of a person's life throughout his or her lifetime. Indeed, it is the lifelong character of catechesis that allows us not to try to do too much on any single occasion, not to try each time to recapitulate every understanding.[28]

The occasional but lifelong character of catechesis offers a reminder to religious education about the sort of goals it should set for itself, especially in dealing with adults. Although both secular and religious adult educators have recognized the importance of lifelong education and short-term programs, catechesis realizes that theory in particular programs. Catechesis also offers religious education and Christian education a reminder of the gradual character of human growth and of the patience needed to deal with it.

At the beginning of this essay I stated my conviction that we need the two complementary perspectives of religious education and catechesis. Now, I would like to state briefly some ways religious education theory enriches and some ways it challenges catechetical theory. However, in explaining how catechesis is enriched by religious education, I do not wish to give the impression that catechists are on one side of an ideological fence and religious educators on the other. The fact of the matter, especially in the United States, is that leading catechetical theorists are knowledgeable and, in some instances, outstanding religious education theorists. Our better catechetical thinkers move with trained self-consciousness from one theoretical framework to another. They elaborate the principles of catechesis fully warned, by sound understandings of both education and religion, against possible distortions. With this clarification in mind, then, what are the ways religious education enriches catechesis?

1) Religious education reminds catechesis that religion is a wider phenomenon than Christian faith. Religious education as an umbrella term is capable of covering persons who approach education and religion from myriad perspectives. Catechesis could not provide such a forum because it is not broad enough. One can see this benefit made concrete in the exchanges at this APRRE meeting and in the meetings of the Religious Education Association.

2) Religious education provides catechists with a complementary body of theory that explores the conjunction of religion and education. This body of theory provides catechesis with many challenges to its own presuppositions. These healthy doses of "ideological suspicion" are needed for any disciplined inquiry to make progress in clarifying its fundamental principles and procedures.

3) Religious education's concern for the study of religion as a humanistic discipline, open to inquiry in public education even at very early ages, is of special importance to catechists.[29] Appreciation of the human encounter with transcendence in its multiple forms can be as important as an appreciation of literature and the other arts in helping us lay hold of the wisdom of our human past.

Catechesis is further enriched by specific challenges to give a better account of itself and to clarify its principles. One of the most persistent of these challenges is the accusation that catechesis is undertaken in an atmosphere of unfreedom. For example, the very fact that catechetical thinkers find in socialization theory a helpful social science model to explain the comprehensive nature of catechesis makes it all the more suspect to those who see in the very concept of socialization overtones of manipulation. Letty Russell of Yale took this very tack recently when she wrote:

> Education and theology as academic disciplines are not always associated with liberation. Education is often viewed as a process of enculturation

or socialization into a particular culture. And, just as often, theology is viewed as analysis of the origins and teachings of a religious community. In this perspective the disciplines contribute to maintaining the *status quo* in society, continuing the oppression of those already at a disadvantage because of racism, sexism, and classism.[30]

This view seems to suspect that religious socialization is a kind of shell game put over on those young enough to be duped and, as such, is counter to liberation.

Those doing religious education from a catechetical angle have to take seriously and answer this accusation and others like it.[31] Indeed, in many places what is called catechesis (and in some places, what is called "Christian education") is manipulation, especially of those too young to resist. Yet catechists must also ask, paraphrasing an oft-cited question posed by George A. Coe, who is actually changing the world.[32] Change, at least in Third World countries, seems to be coming from basic communities of faith in Christ, gathered together in that kind of critical reflection on their human situation in the light of the gospel that must be called ongoing catechetical reflection.[33]

Another question catechetics must face is the difference between formal catechesis, a process I could describe as instruction-in-the-context-of-ritual, and informal catechesis, which would include a range of activities that could all be called "catechetical." This is an issue secular educators and religious educators alike are grappling with,[34] and I judge that the same kind of clarification they are struggling toward is also needed in catechesis.

The purpose of this essay has been to encourage some professional crossing over into one another's theoretical frames of reference, in order to enrich an expanding body of religious education theory. As theorists we are raising important questions for one another, challenging each other to go deeper in probing our presuppositions and taking another look at exactly where we stand. The challenge can at times be frustrating, but its value, one can hope, will be enduring. Our hope is similar to that suggested by Clifford Geertz in the following passage:

> ... the French anthropologist, Levi-Strauss, remarks that scientific explanation does not consist, as we have been led to imagine, in the reduction of the complex to the simple. Rather, it consists, he says, in a substitution of a complexity more intelligible for one which is less. So far as the study of man is concerned, one may go even further, I think, and argue that explanation often consists of substituting complex pictures for simple ones while striving somehow to retain the persuasive clarity that went with the simple ones. . . .
>
> Scientific advancement commonly consists in a progressive complication of what once seemed a beautifully simple set of notions but now seems an unbearably simplistic one. It is after this sort of disenchantment occurs that intelligibility, and thus explanatory power, comes to rest on the

possibility of substituting the involved but comprehensible for the involved but incomprehensible. . . . Whitehead once offered to the natural sciences the maxim: "Seek simplicity and distrust it"; to the social sciences he might well have offered: "Seek complexity and order it."[35]

NOTES

1. The past ten years have seen a shift among U.S. Roman Catholics toward a more consciously catechetical language and toward a more nuanced use of the language of religious education. Currently, there is some controversy over which language is the more appropriate. The issue is not an exclusively Roman Catholic one, though its full significance among all the Christian denominations may not become clear for some time. For a treatment of some issues in the matter see Kieran Scott, "Communicative Competence and Religious Education," *Lumen Vitae* 35, no. 1 (1980): 75–96.

2. These papers were later published. See Charles F. Melchert, "What Is Religious Education?" and John H. Westerhoff, "A Call to Catechesis," *The Living Light* 14, no. 3 (1977): 339–352 and 354–358.

3. See "Old-Time School *vs.* New-Time School," chap. 5 in Robert W. Lynn and Elliott Wright, *The Big Little School* (New York: Harper & Row, 1971), pp. 77–99. (This book is now also available as a "2nd ed. rev. and enlarged," *The Big Little School: 200 Years of the Sunday School* [Birmingham: Religious Education Press, 1980]. All later citations are, however, to the first edition.)

4. See George Albert Coe, *Social Theory of Religious Education* (New York: Charles Scribner's Sons, 1917). Compare Coe's vision with "The American Idea of Progress," in Russell B. Nye, *This Almost Chosen People* (Lansing: University of Michigan Press, 1966), pp. 1–42.

5. See Mary C. Boys, *"Heilgeschichte" as a Hermeneutical Principle in Religious Education* (Ann Arbor: University Microfilms, 1979).

6. Dr. Dwayne Huebner of Columbia Teachers' College noted the gap between theory and practice at a recent conference on religious education:

> This conference is a manifestation of the social division of labor and points to our problems of historical responsibility and continuity. The papers were prepared and responded to by members of the academic community. The audience, in large measure, were practitioners of religious education. The latter came to listen and to raise questions of the academics, perhaps to interpret their language. The trend that started at the turn of the century is now institutionalized into roles and social hierarchies. Groups of experts, usually university faculty, are frequently drawn together to attempt the reformulation of religious education, which means to produce more useful language with which a variety of people might talk about religious education and to establish the linguistic boundaries and definitions of the field. What do we know about how the practitioners of religious education speak about their work and their experiences, or how the students speak about their experiences? The division of labor, constructed and reinforced over the past several decades, means that those who partake of religious education infrequently participate in the construction or criticism of the public language of religious education. They await the pronouncements of the specialists. Furthermore, the specialists infrequently attempt to describe how language is used by the practitioners, or to

describe the work of the practitioner. This neglect is common to education in more secular domains as well.
See Dwayne Huebner, "The Language of Education," in *Tradition and Transformation in Religious Education*, ed. Padraic O'Hare (Birmingham: Religious Education Press, 1979), p. 93.

7. This evolution can be found in a survey of titles of doctoral dissertations done within the Department of Religion and Religious Education over a twenty-year period, as well as in a comparison of the use of language by Gerard Sloyan, the department's chairperson in the late 1950s and early 1960s, and by Berard Marthaler, its present chair.

8. Lewis Sherrill, *The Rise of Christian Education* (New York: Macmillan, 1944). It is notable that Sherrill's fellow Presbyterian C. Ellis Nelson has written one of the best statements by a U.S. thinker on catechetical principles, which, however, is cast in the language of Christian education. See C. Ellis Nelson, *Where Faith Begins* (Atlanta: John Knox Press, 1967).

9. Sherrill, *Rise of Christian Education*, pp. 284–285.

10. For an overview of these catechetical meetings, see Luis Erdozain, "The Evolution of Catechetics," *Lumen Vitae* 25, no. 1 (1970): 9–31. [Also reprinted in this sourcebook as Reading 8.]

11. Some of these issues are surveyed in Michael Warren, "A Third World Focus," *Religious Education* 74, no. 5 (1979): 496–502.

12. The best text of the *General Catechetical Directory* for study purposes is Berard L. Marthaler, *Catechetics in Context: Notes and Commentary on the General Catechetical Directory* (Huntington, IN: Our Sunday Visitor Press, 1973).

13. Nelson's *Where Faith Begins* and John H. Westerhoff's *Will Our Children Have Faith?* (New York: Seabury Press, 1976) are examples of a search for a community-based revolution in fostering faith.

14. Secular education has also been struggling with the relationship of the community to the educational environments and institutions meant to serve the community. See, for example, Lawrence A. Cremin, *Public Education* (New York: Basic Books, 1976), esp. pp. 21–29.
Over the past several years a number of critiques have appeared of the way the educational needs of adolescents are met in U.S. society and of their eventual impact on the relationship between young people and local communities. See: James J. Coleman, ed., *Youth: Transition to Adulthood* (Chicago: University of Chicago Press, 1974); John H. Martin, ed., *The Education of Adolescents* (Washington, DC: U.S. Government Printing Office, 1976); Joseph F. Kett, *Rites of Passage* (New York: Basic Books, 1977), esp. chaps. 7–9, pp. 173–272; Gisela Konopka, *Young Girls: A Portrait of Adolescence* (Englewood Cliffs, NJ: Prentice-Hall, 1976), esp. chaps. 6–7, pp. 112–136. See also the important essays by Michael Apple and Dwayne Huebner in *Curriculum Theorizing*, ed. Wm. Pinar (San Francisco: McCutchan, 1975).

15. In the United States, of all those dealing with religious education or catechesis, the greatest contribution on this matter has been made by the well-read Gabriel Moran through his wide-ranging and astute critiques of contemporary culture.

16. There is an important issue here, and one that Gabriel Moran misjudges in his essay "Two Languages of Religious Education," *The Living Light* 14, no. 1 (1977): 7–15, when he says:

The ecclesiastical language of religious education is governed by the relation of theology (including the Christian Scriptures) to catechesis/Christian education. Nothing is allowed into the "content" of catechesis/Christian education unless approved by theology [p. 8].

Catechetics cannot dialogue with theology because theology controls the language [p. 10].

The life of the community, not some oppressive "theological" content, is what determines the form catechesis takes. But then theology itself as an inquiry is formed by the experience of struggling to be Christian in a particular context. For an important statement on this matter, see Aloysius Pieris, "Towards an Asian Theology of Liberation: Some Religio-Cultural Guidelines," *East Asian Pastoral Review* 16, no. 1 (1979): 206–230. See also D. S. Amalorpavadass, "Theology of Evangelization in the Indian Context," in *Service and Salvation: Nagpur Theological Conference on Evangelization*, ed. J. Pathrapankal (Bangalore: Theological Publications in India, 1973), pp. 19–39.

17. Jacques Audinet, "Catechetical Renewal in the Present Situation," in *The Medellin Papers*, ed. J. Hofinger and T. Sheridan (Manila: East Asian Pastoral Institute, 1969), pp. 66–67.

18. For some sources on this matter, see Warren, "A Third World Focus." Note also the concern with the need to critique the social conditions of those being catechized found in the formal conclusions of the Medellin catechetical meeting. One of these principles is stated as follows:

> A joint pastoral effort demands also the frank and definitive acceptance of the process of social change. Whatever the situations those responsible must strive to meet them, knowing that these situations are in evolution, that one of the tasks of catechesis consists in helping that evolution and giving it meaning. The forms of evolution can be very different, from gradual up to violently revolutionary. In every case it is imperative that we make not only a diagnosis but an effort of imagination in order to foresee and promote new forms of existence animated by the Gospel [*Medellin Papers*, pp. 215–216].

Joseph Komonchak has noted well the little-known fact of the influence of the 1968 catechetical meeting in Medellin on the later bishops' meeting there. The International Catechetical Congress met in Medellin in August 1968, just prior to the famous meeting of Latin American bishops. It was the catechists who enunciated some of the key principles of liberation later taken up and affirmed by the bishops. See Joseph A. Komonchak, "Christ's Church in Today's World: Medellin, Puebla, and the United States," *The Living Light* 17, no. 2 (1980): 108–120.

19. Cited by Bishop Dammert, "Justice and Catechesis," an intervention made at the 1977 Roman synod on catechesis, *Teaching All Nations* 15, no. 1 (1978): 42.

20. See the treatment of catechesis in Scott, "Communicative Competence," pp. 82–83.

21. See "The Catechetical Ministry of the Church," chap. 2 of *Sharing the Light of Faith: National Catechetical Directory for Catholics in the United States* (Washington, DC: United States Catholic Conference, 1979), pp. 18–25. Another statement of the relationship among these ministries is D. S. Amalorpavadass, "Nature, Purpose, and Process of Catechesis Within the Pastoral Activity of the Church," in *International Catechetical Congress: Selected*

Documentation, ed. William Tobin (Washington, DC: United States Catholic Conference, 1972), pp. 39–59.

22. For a more extended treatment of this matter, see M. Warren, "A Framework for Catholic Education," in *Emerging Issues in Religious Education,* ed. Gloria Durka and Joanmarie Smith (New York: Paulist Press, 1976), pp. 99–113.

23. For source material, see Hugh M. Riley, *Christian Initiation* (Washington, DC: Consortium Press, 1974).

24. See, for example, the emphasis on worship, prayer, the singing of hymns, and other forms of celebration found throughout Dupanloup's classic *The Ministry of Catechizing,* written in 1868. The final section of personal recollections of childhood catechesis is quite instructive from this point of view. See Bishop Felix Dupanloup, *The Ministry of Catechizing* (London: Griffith Farran Okeden and Welsh, 1890), esp. pp. 539–612.

25. Wilfred Cantwell Smith stresses the need to understand the full range of the human expressions of faith, without stopping short at its conceptual expressions only.

> Faith can be expressed—more historically: faith has been expressed, observably—in words, both prose and poetry; in patterns of deeds, both ritual and morality; in art, in institutions, in law, in community, in character, and in still many other ways.

Catechetics, as a body of theory, attempts to attend to this wide band of faith-expressivity. See Wilfred Cantwell Smith, *The Meaning and End of Religion* (New York: Harper & Row, 1978), pp. 170–192, esp. p. 171.

26. Lynn and Wright's *Big Little School* (pp. 98–99) ends with the following passage:

> In spite of all the negative evaluations of sophisticated culture, the Sunday school may add up to an education alternative more humane than public or private institutions which have responded to industrial society's insatiable desire for more technologists and bureaucrats. Restless students have hardly asked for the tutelage of little misses doing their duty on Sunday, but they are often searching for something akin to what the Sunday school offers. They want to know what life does, or might, mean. At its best, the Sunday school has tried to illuminate Protestantism's answers to these questions. Knowing the road from Damascus to Jerusalem prior to entering the chaotic maze of modern ideologies may prepare a mind to deal with the traumas which threaten each person today. The possibility is worth contemplating.
>
> Not so long ago in the modern technological age Willie Morris, the editor-in-chief of *Harper's* magazine, went to a Methodist Sunday school in the deep South. He recalls that: ". . . our teacher told us stories about the Bible, or helped us make religious posters, or led us in singing: Jesus loves me! this I know. . . . Later as we grew older there would be more sophisticated Sunday school sessions, when we would sit in small circles and talk about religion and how we could get the children who had not showed up that Sunday more interested in it. We would hold hands and pray, and whisper the benediction, and dream up projects to make our class the most active in the whole church and how best to help out the preacher in his many duties. We would read Bible verses and discuss their hidden meaning."

That is how it was around 1870, too. It may not be that way in the year 2000, and yet the big little school may still be around. The technological whizzes, seminary professors, liberal intellectuals, and religious faddists have little idea how slowly minds change in that still forceful, white middle-class Protestant culture which largely shaped the United States. Politicians and Madison Avenue [advertisers] know better and make use of the continuities. Those Protestant goals of prosperity and future blessedness – and sometimes purity – long ago became the aims of Americans of all races and religions. As long as any evangelicals remain, they will be ardently striving to put purity back in the center of the pattern for reconciliation worked out by Lyman Beecher. The chances are fairly good that the method for the task will be a Sunday school.

27. These remarks by Dwayne Huebner were made in private conversation.

28. For concrete application of these ideas to young people, see M. Warren, "Youth Catechesis in the 80's," *Origins* 9, no. 44 (10 April 1980): 690–697.

29. For a good theoretical overview of religion study at even very early ages in state-run schools, see Michael Grimmitt, *What Can I Do in R. E.? A Guide to New Approaches* (Great Wakering, Essex: Mayhew-McCrimmon, 1973). For a full curriculum outline, see Birmingham District Council Education Committee, *Living Together: A Teacher's Handbook of Suggestions for Religious Education* (Birmingham, England, 1975).

30. Letty Russell, "Education as Exodus," a paper delivered at the regional Association of Professors and Researchers in Religious Education (APRRE) meeting, Princeton Theological Seminary (April 1980), p. 3. In the middle of the cited passage, Russell includes a footnote reference to the introductory paragraphs of Berard L. Marthaler, "Socialization as a Model for Catechetics," in *Foundations of Religious Education*, ed. Padraic O'Hare (New York: Paulist Press, 1978), pp. 64–92.

31. A recent doctoral study done at Catholic University explores the many facets of the question of freedom in religious education and catechetical theory. The study's conclusions regarding the potential of communities for safeguarding freedom are worth noting. See Kenneth R. Barker, "The Issue of Human Freedom in Selected Contemporary Catechetical Theorists" (Ph.D. diss., Catholic University of America, 1980).

32. The much-quoted question of Coe: "Shall the primary purpose of Christian Education be to hand on a religion or to create a new world?" is found in George Albert Coe, *What Is Christian Education?* (New York: Charles Scribner's Sons, 1929), p. 29.

33. A good statement of the possibilities of such communal reflection for liberation is the World Council of Churches statement, "Toward a Church in Solidarity with the Poor," *East Asian Pastoral Review* 27, no. 2 (1980): 157–171.

34. This is one of the issues dealt with by Lawrence Cremin in *Public Education*, already cited. For a religious education effort in the same direction, see Melchert, "What Is Religious Education?" esp. pp. 339–342.

35. Clifford Geertz, "The Impact of the Concept of Culture on the Concept of Man," in *New Views on the Nature of Man*, ed. John R. Platt (Chicago: University of Chicago Press, 1965), pp. 93–94; also in Clifford Geertz, *The Interpretation of Cultures* (New York: Harper & Row, Harper Colophon Books, 1973), pp. 33–34.

*At present, the moral education debate continues without letup. Radical
critiques of Lawrence Kohlberg appear at the same time that Kohlberg
continues to clarify his own research. The following is presented here
for the valuable way it comprehensively reviews moral education, for
its useful noting of background readings, and for its examination of
the relationship between moral education and religious education.*

READING 29

Moral Education in a Christian Context

CATHERINE DOOLEY

IN RECENT YEARS social scientists of very different back-
grounds have written extensively on the subject of moral education. Religious educators have also shown renewed interest in the topic.
In fact, their interest seems to have been stimulated by the work done
in the area of moral development by Piaget and Kohlberg. In these
pages, therefore, I propose to examine the meaning of moral education, some of its theoretical perspectives, and particularly its place in
religious education: In what ways are moral education and religious
education related? Are there ways in which religious education can
positively contribute to moral development?

Reprinted from *The Living Light* 12 (1975), pp. 510–525. © 1975 National Conference
of Catholic Bishops. Used by permission.

What Is Moral Education?

At the beginning of John Wilson's book *Introduction to Moral Education,* he states that moral education is a "name for nothing clear."[1] As one begins to survey the literature, one has a feeling that he may be right. The words *moral development* are words defined by different people in different ways, and moral behavior and development are determined by the interaction of a great number of factors. Norman Williams distinguishes between the two main uses of the word *moral.* When statements are made such as, "He is a moral man," *moral* is being used in an evaluative sense. This usage implies judgment. The second use of the word may be called the descriptive use, "having to do with right and wrong," e.g., when we say, "This is a moral problem." For Williams, moral education is evaluative, referring to processes which aim at making the child moral as opposed to immoral. Moral development is descriptive, referring to the way in which a child's approach to right and wrong varies as he or she matures. However, Williams points out that one meaning cannot be studied except in relation to the other.

> Clearly, we cannot study how a child becomes moral without looking at the totality of his approaches to right and wrong. We cannot relate a descriptive developmental study to any practical measures of moral education without knowing which aims we would evaluate as moral ones.[2]

Douglas Graham states that the word *moral* has three main uses. It may refer to "resistance to temptation," to the control of behavior by reference to internalized standards without any genuine understanding of the reason for their acceptance, or to behavior which is carried out in reference to rules or principles which are rationally accepted because the reasons for accepting them are understood and felt to be legitimate. Graham goes on to state that the third meaning of *moral* is frequently regarded as the only proper use because, to be capable of a high level of morality, one must have sufficient intellectual capacity to understand the nature of moral rules and the capacity to analyze dilemmas in terms of these principles. On the other hand, he says it could be argued that *morality* in the first two senses may be a prerequisite for the development of *morality* in the third sense.[3]

Norman Bull broadly describes the process of moral education as the socialization of the child, shaping him or her into a conforming member of society. Bull defines *morality* as "the term used to describe living together in human society." For him, morality implies both conformity to prevailing social morality and also pursuit of the good life — "and that is by no means necessarily the same as following the accepted moral code."[4]

Lawrence Kohlberg is perhaps the most definite on how he views moral education. "Moral education involves the stimulation of the child's natural development through universal stages."[5] Kohlberg's thesis is that the stage-developmental theory stimulates the child's moral judgment to the next stage of development and stimulates the child's ability to act consistently in accordance with his or her own moral judgment. Kohlberg's aim would be to see that the person develops to an autonomous level of moral development whereby he or she would act in accord with universal principles.

In this essay, moral education will refer to the direct and indirect interventions which affect the child's capacity to think both about issues of right and wrong and about behavior and values. Moral education includes more factors than cognitive reasoning although this is a basic factor. The ultimate aim of moral education would be to raise the level of moral judgment and consequent actions in such a way that judgment and behavior are based as much as possible upon general moral principles that can be applied to new and changing circumstances.

Theoretical Perspectives on Moral Education

Historically, there have been a number of approaches to the question of moral education. Those to be briefly considered here are the social-group approach, conscience formation, the maturationist or psycho-analytic, the learning-theory or behaviorist school, and the cognitive developmental.[6]

Social-group Approach

In this theory moral behavior is treated as a function of social control or control by others. Basically, the social-group approach is a sociological theory but has strong psychological implications. The theory is applicable to all societies because all persons identify with one reference group or another. Contemporary examples of highly operative social-group theory are the Israeli kibbutz and the ashrams of the followers of Indian gurus, in which group norms are the strongest motivation for the individual's actions. In this perspective the object of study is not the individual but two or more persons in relationship. The individual is defined by his or her position in the group. Behavior is controlled by forces and pressures active in the group. Even though the individual members of a group may change, the groups retain their identity because the individual's sense of affiliation with a group is often distinct from and more important than a relationship to particular members. Two of the basic concepts in this theory are *norm* and *role*.

Derek Wright defines a *norm* as a way of feeling, thinking, behaving, or believing which is relatively uniform among the members of a group and which becomes a force or pressure upon each member of the group by virtue of the fact that the rest expect him or her to behave in a certain way. Norms are related to the group's purpose, and their positive function is to facilitate the achievement of group goals.

The term *role* refers to the norms associated with a particular position in a group. It is the set of expectations that members have about how a particular individual will behave and about the functions of that person within the group. Specific roles carry their own sets of special obligations. A person's moral behavior often may be greatly affected by his or her social role. A common example is the behavior change that takes place when a couple becomes parents concerned about raising children.

A number of elements makes up the process of social influence. Some of the major ones are: social facilitation – the presence of others intensifies motivation; effect dependency – self-esteem is dependent upon others' approval and acceptance; information dependency – when uncertain what to do, the person turns to others for information; and identity confusion – the person is temporarily confused or has lost a sense of himself or herself as a separate person. These aspects present ways in which individuals may differ from each other. Perhaps the most important fact is that sometimes individuals, after evaluating the group norms, take a stand against group pressures because the norms are inadequate and contradict personal moral judgment. Another variable to be considered is that often the standards operative for an individual are not those of the reference group to which he or she belongs but, rather, of a group to which the individual wishes to belong. Nevertheless, in social-group theory, independent moral behavior is seen as conformity to *some* reference group. It is difficult to refute this approach because it is always possible to formulate some reference group for the individual. However, it would seem that research, beginning with the studies of Hartshorne and May,[7] would put more emphasis on the immediate social context, the specific situation, as being the determining factor in morality. Morality that is determined by a reference group loses its power when the individual is removed from the group's influence or when there is no possibility of being detected if one should defect from the group standards. Many people show moral restraint even when the possibility of being seen by others is not present. This process of inner motivation and self-control has traditionally been termed conscience.

Conscience Formation

Paul Tillich quotes Richard Rothe as stating that "the word *conscience* should be excluded from all scientific treatment of ethics since its connotations are so manifold and contradictory that the term cannot be saved for a useful definition."[8] Not only is the term unclear but also its history is confused. However, since conscience is one of the chief vehicles for moral education in the Roman Catholic Church, it is necessary to include it in a discussion of moral education in a Christian context.

The history of conscience, in spite of the varied interpretations it has produced, shows some definite trends.

Early in the biblical era the reality of conscience appears as extrinsic, objective, and collective. Theophany gives way finally to human prophets who speak in the name of God. The prophets, the conscience of Israel, stress interior dispositions and begin to mention individual responsibility. "Repent and be converted from your idols; turn yourselves away from all your abomination" (Exod. 14:6). The prophets look forward to the day "when I will place my law within them and write it upon their hearts" (Jer. 31:33). For the prophets, conscience is not the voice of man but the voice of God who speaks to men and women.

In the New Testament, St. Paul is the first to use the idea of conscience. "He describes conscience as a judge of past activity, a norm for future action, the habitual quality of a person's Christianity, and even as the Christian ego or personality. Conscience points out to the Christian what he or she should do in the particular circumstances of his or her life." [9]

Paul Tillich states:

> . . . in the New Testament, conscience has a primarily ethical meaning and only indirectly does it have religious significance. The acceptance of the gospels is not a demand of the conscience. Conscience does not give laws, but it accuses and condemns him who has not fulfilled the law. Consequently, it is not considered to be a special quality of Christians, but an element of human nature generally.[10]

St. Paul's emphasis on the internal and subjective dispositions of humanity introduces into Christian thought the idea of conscience as the director of human activity. The Fathers of the Church explicitly make the last step in the interiorization of conscience: Conscience becomes the voice of the human person and only mediately and indirectly the voice of God. The scholastics objectified conscience and studied it from a philosophical viewpoint: Was conscience a faculty, a habit, or an act? The Thomistic school distinguished conscience: the judgment of the practical reason (*conscientia*) about a particular act from the power of judgment situated in the inmost part of the soul (*synteresis*). St. Bonaventure placed more emphasis on the will: the subjective voice of reason was open to God through the mediation of law. Gradually, conscience came to be treated in the moral theology manuals from an extrinsic, legalistic, and impersonal point of view. The authority of the Church increasingly took the place of conscience. It was the Church that decided, more and more obviously and explicitly, upon what was good and evil and what was meritorious or sinful. Regard for conscience was pushed into the background, becoming oppressive and sin-oriented. In line with the theological renewal taking place today, which goes back to the primitive sources of Scripture and the Fathers of the Church, conscience is again being considered in the light of relationship and covenant—the responsibility of the Christian before the call of God.

Catholic theologians generally adopt St. Thomas' distinction of *synteresis* (the power of conscience situated in the inmost part of the soul) and *conscientia* (the judgment of the practical reason). *Synteresis* has two aspects: an almost intuitive knowledge of the good and a tendency to express the good in action. Under the twofold influence of *synteresis*, conscience then is the concrete judgment of the practical reason about the loving or unloving quality of an action.

Outside theology, philosophers, psychologists, and sociologists all define conscience from within their own frameworks. Freud equates "the special institution in the mind," as he calls the ego ideal, with conscience. The ego ideal represents a kind of idea or fantasy of a perfect self as against the imperfect self which is the object of criticism. The main source of the criticism which is the basis for the formation of the ego ideal is the parents, although they are reinforced by all those who influence the child. The ego ideal is positive, rooted in love rather than fear. It grows and develops consciously as the child builds up his or her ego ideals. Freud failed to differentiate this positive and creative aspect of the moral self from the negative superego, and little is known of the genesis and nature of the ego ideal. The superego is the negative aspect serving two functions: It both represses insupportable desires and experiences and carries the guilt resulting from identifications in early childhood, aggressions which had to be directed inward, and heteronomous precepts that have become interiorized. Identification, guilt, and the avoidance of guilt are the determining forces in a child's moral growth.

Behaviorists would say that conscience is a conditioned reflex, built up in childhood by punishments following upon offenses. Fear of punishment motivates moral learning. Since emotional conditioning is the vital factor, what is called conscience is a system of generalized conditioned anxiety responses.

For structural developmental theorists, conscience would mean a developed interior morality. Piaget says that this comes about from reciprocity and cooperation.

What is the origin of conscience? The traditional view held that a child was born with a conscience. This tradition, bound up with the doctrine of original sin and the "age of reason," imputed sin and guilt to the child's innate immaturity and egocentricity. Studies since 1900 propose that the child is not born with a built-in "faculty" of conscience. Conscience develops as the result of socialization, as part of normal growth. Norman Bull suggests that there are natural processes which develop a sense of moral obligation in the child.[11] First, the child imitates the actions of those closest to him or her, normally parents. Then, through the subconscious process of suggestion, he or she absorbs feelings and mental attitudes. Through the process of identification, the child incorporates personal characteristics; the child impersonates them. Finally, the impersonated characteristics become his or her own, forming an inner ego ideal, the child's picture of himself or herself as he or she should be. Bull says that this ego ideal is the moral self, the source of the universal sense of moral obligation. But the ego ideal is in conflict with the ego, and this produces a unique self-consciousness: "the self-criticism that we call conscience; and the self-control that we call will." Thus, external controls give way to informal controls. Convention gives way to conviction.

Kohlberg's studies support a developmental point of view and maintain that moral judgment cannot be explained as simply internalization of cultural rules through verbal learning, reinforcement, or identification. Relating his work to the earlier findings of Hartshorne and May, he points to a "view of overt adolescent moral conduct as a product of the development of broad social cognitive capacities and values rather than of a superego or of introjection of parental standards." He concludes:

> The develoment of a morality of identification with authority is dependent upon "natural" social role-taking and the development of concepts of reciprocity, justice, and group welfare in the years from four to twelve.[12]

Kohlberg concludes that the major consistencies in moral conduct represent decision-making capacities rather than fixed behavior traits. Kohlberg's studies indicate that there is a natural sense of justice intuitively known by the child that develops through a long series of transformations that are called stages. The theory of moral stages means that the thinking of the child is qualitatively different from the adult's thinking: It is not just a difference in degree of knowledge or sophistication. These stages follow an invariant sequence and each later stage is a cognitively and morally more adequate stage. Each stage comes closer to finding an intrinsic and universal basis for value. Because moral internalization is closely related to cognitive development of moral concepts, Kohlberg takes exception to "theorists who have assumed that the basic features of adult conscience have developed by early childhood, between five and eight years of age." Moral judgment data indicate that anything clearly like "conscience" develops relatively late.[13]

In the light of both theological considerations of conscience and psychology, how does a child develop conscience? In the broadest sense, conscience develops through the influence of all the morally significant impressions drawn from the human environment together with one's life experience. For example, important factors in conscience development would be the cultural and familial environment, which offers specific values for assimilation; the process of education, which includes principles that would provide more immediate sources of conscience judgments; and the practice of virtue, prayer, openness to the spirit. Specific attention would need to be given to the stimulation of decision-making abilities and role-taking capacities at the child's level of development in order that conscience might function in terms of autonomy. If conscience develops as part of normal growth, then the growth patterns of children must be used as a basis for this education. This means that the internalization of parental values – acting as prepersonal censorship and control – is necessary and meaningful for the young child. But the child must be gradually empowered to replace immature concepts of morality by more mature concepts as the child moves through stages of moral growth. This is necessary so that conscience does not remain predetermined by childhood experiences. These experiences must constantly be realigned in accord with the situation in which one finds oneself and with the adult values to which one commits oneself. This presumes then that conscience formation is not completed by adolescence but is a lifelong process in which the autonomous adult ego chooses the values, norms, and standards by which the person will live. Conscience becomes a dynamic concept and, although related to the unconscious values of superego, it is a practical judgment toward defining and directing one's life in accord with the fundamental option. For the Christian, conscience is more than moral evolution or moral knowledge, it is the faculty for ultimate commitment.

Learning-theory or Behaviorist Approach

The behaviorist school would include psychologists such as Watson,

Pavlov, Thorndike, Eysenck, and B. F. Skinner. Learning theory defines morality in terms of specific acts and avoidances which are learned on the basis of rewards and punishments. Moral behavior and values are acquired by the same kind of processes by which any other behavior is learned. The typical procedure is to use direct or vicarious reinforcement with little or no accompanying rationale, to elicit behaviors in the laboratory which are "good" in terms of some culturally shared standard of conduct. In this theory, the person is the product of the environment, and it is the relationship between the behavior and the environment that forms the self. Learning or behavior change is quantitative or incremental and can take place during a person's whole life. The environment is carefully constructed to reinforce or to discourage behavior. One of the difficulties of learning theory seems to be that it is not clear how far reinforcement responses may be generalized and thus how far they may be applied in situations differing from those in which they were learned. The more rapidly environmental factors change, the less appropriate any generalized habits which have been formed are likely to be. The concept of morality which comes from this theory is adaptive or functional. Essentially, it produces an external morality in which the child's behavior is hedonistic. That morality is defined by whatever behaviors are rewarded or punished by authority or have stimulus or conceptual elements in common.

Maturationist or Psychoanalytic Approach

This theory would provide a biological model for moral develoment and would include the Freudian family of theorists. In this approach the person is not as passive as in the behaviorist model. The focus is more on the affective side of development, and the person incorporates new modes of behavior as physical maturation takes place. The motivation for change is an instinctual drive. A major factor is the introjection of values, i.e., the process of taking over unthinkingly values given by parents and other authority figures.

Briefly, and at the risk of oversimplifying, the basic components of the personality for Freud are the *id,* the *ego,* and the *superego.*[14] The id constitutes the central core of the personality and is the inner source of psychological energy. According to Freud, the id is the source of all our instincts and drives. The ego is that aspect of the personality which makes it possible to adjust to reality. Its main function is to carry out the wishes of the id and to delay or control behavior so that the fullest gratification is achieved. The superego is the policing agent. It controls the drives and reflexes of the id. If it fails to do so, it produces guilt in accord with the internalized prohibitions of conscience. The superego also facilitates behavior which is in agreement with its ego ideals and helps the individual to experience pleasure. The superego begins to develop in childhood through interaction of the child and parents. When a child is punished, he or she gradually learns to internalize these inhibitions, and this control becomes that part of the superego known as conscience. The *ego ideal* function of the superego is to hold before the ego those positive values that parents and/or society judge worthwhile. The ego ideal is what the ego aspires to become. In both its functions, the superego represents the voice of society and particularly the voice of parents within one's own personality.

These two functions of the superego are acquired by identification. This is the mechanism used to explain how children develop qualities and behavior patterns similar to those of their parents and other significant adults. An identification means an emotional or feeling identification — an actual feeling as if you were that person. The images of the other form a differentiated structure which represent not what the child thinks himself or herself to be but what that child thinks he or she would like to become. Though the parents form the primary content of the ego ideal, subsequent attachments also contribute to its formation, leaving a sediment in the form of values and goals.

The research methods are in a therapeutic context, based on clinical experience and are furthered by longitudinal studies. The concepts of this theory are not closely related logically to one another in such a way that the theory constitutes a single integrated whole. Freud's own ideas shifted considerably in the course of his writings and were again revised by his followers. The ideas are generally difficult to test empirically by the usual methods of scientific investigation. Because the theory is very broad, it has more of an indirect influence on research in moral development. This theory has suggested general kinds of questions such as the nature of the relationship between children and their parents, especially in the earlier years of life. Psychoanalytic theory has tended to overemphasize the negative, restrictive aspects of moral control and of guilt as a basis of morality, but it has been important in drawing attention to the fact that persons are often unable to make moral judgments because of emotional disorders. Perhaps the concept of "identification" has been overemphasized, but it has pointed out the importance of empathy or the ability to take on another person's view.

Cognitive Developmentalist Approach

This school includes the thought of Piaget, Elkind, and Kohlberg, among others. In this approach the emphasis is placed upon the cognitive, although Piaget has insisted on the association of cognition with action. The person is self-activating, assimilating experience and accommodating it by reorganizing his or her own system of meaning. The child moves through qualitatively different stages that are invariant, hierarchically ordered, and cognitive. The developmental process goes forward on the disequilibrium generated by the interaction between the child and the environment. The research methods used are interviews. The content of the interview is separated from the form or structure which determines the level of moral reasoning. The methods of research are closely associated with empirical data, and the theory has generally an internal consistency.

Moral development in this approach requires not merely responsiveness to experience and training or internalization of given values but also an active organizing process by which the individual can work out his or her own moral guidelines in the light of universal principles. A primary task of this theory, according to Kohlberg, should be to establish genuine developmental dimensions of moral judgment in the sense of types of judgment which increase at each stage.

The psychoanalytic theory and the behaviorist theory are basically hedonistic. However, all of these theories have some aspects that are important for moral development. Some degree of conditioning of certain basic patterns of moral behavior in the early life of the child is necessary. The power of identification is strong and is a prerequisite for the ability to empathize and to develop a concept of self; socialization develops the capacity to understand one's own rights and obligations and those of others. Modeling is the factor that gives credibility to words. There are many aspects to moral development, and there should be many approaches.

What Is the Relationship of Moral Education to Religious Education?

Some years ago, from the Roman Catholic perspective at least, this would have been a nonquestion because, in the minds of Catholic educators, the terms were synonymous. The reasoning went something like this: Religion creates a code of moral standards, and it provides the motivation for people to obey that code. This viewpoint has traditionally been reinforced by the teachings of moral theologians through the ages.

Underlying the belief that religion creates morals is a debased image of God, that of a divine being with the characteristics of an awesome judge who, because he created and sustains human life, is also the author of a moral code that must be obeyed. God is made out to be the authority figure, par excellence, although he is sometimes seen as kindly enough. The research from psychology suggests that such a God-image is internalized by young children as they generalize and interpret through limited experience the authority that their parents and other adults have over them. This image of God is often reinforced by the type of education children receive. The concept weakens, if it does not destroy, human morality because a person's moral life turns into obedience motivated by rewards and punishments. Thus, to live by a set of moral standards with an authoritarian God to reinforce them is to avoid the necessity of making a personal moral decision in particular circumstances.

This perception of God is contrary to the teachings and person of Jesus, who taught men and women principles by which to live in relationship to the Father and who, by his own example at times, went beyond the law. The basis of the life of Jesus was his relationship to the Father manifested in his love for others. Ronald Goldman, in writing of the aims of religious education, says that to use religion directly as a means of teaching moral values is to start the wrong way around. "We start with the nature of the world we live in, the nature of human life, the nature of God, and what kind of a relationship he has with us. The center of this is the fact of love." Goldman adds that there is *a* Christian ethic, which is the law of love, but there is no system of ethics laying down specific commands for each situation or human problem we encounter. This is why Christianity is so difficult. "It offers a moral freedom of which many are afraid, and from which they will retreat into authoritarian moral negatives." Goldman's conclusion is that moral specifics are by-products of religious faith. All the moral implications of Christian love can be and often are accepted by humanists. What is different for Christians is the ultimate source of their authority for loving and the moral power that should flow from their belief in God.[15] James Gustafson affirms this: "Believing (in a strong sense) certain things about God does, should, and ought to affect what I have called moral selfhood, and the moral actions of persons."[16] Gustafson, using 1 John 4, shows the relationship of religion and morality and indicates how a moral imperative to love is inferred from a religious belief, from a statement of Revelation. But the relationship is one of fundamental option. There are moral dispositions and attitudes which religious persons ought to have if their actions are to be consistent with their beliefs. Religious moral training is not confined to authoritative rules of conduct and to sanctions of punishment and reward in heaven. It can and it ought to, like other moral nurture, aid in developing autonomous, morally responsible persons.

Although religion and morality are separate areas, I think it can be shown that they are complementary. Just as approaches to moral education are varied, so too religious education is defined in different but complementary ways. The term has been commonly used in this country to describe the instructional practice of imparting the truths of the faith. *Religious education,* however, is a broad term covering the entire gamut of study about religion. It may include studying the religious themes in literature, history of religions, and comparative religions; or it may have confessional overtones. Catechesis, on the other hand, always involves the whole person and is directed toward commitment. The primary content of the religious learning experience is faith. When the scriptural meaning of faith is examined, we see that it is expressed in terms of relationship, a response to God's call. Therefore, the aim of catechesis is to initiate and educate one to a life of personal community relationship with the father, through the son in the spirit, and with one another in the world today. Relationships are developed and strengthened in community; community is the primary environment in which religious learning takes place. Growth in faith is a constant search for ways to respond. Effective religious education demands that students be personally and actively involved in this search, which is the learning process. A student has to decide for himself or herself, and choices always involve risks. But in this series of choices, there is the process of change. This is the process of faith because the biblical understanding of faith is that it brings about a transformation, a "new heart." The act of faith necessarily involves a conversion of the one making it. At some time Christians must internalize and affirm their faith by their way of life. The educational role of the faith community is to foster growth, to help individuals to come to conversion, to develop persons becoming "fully mature with the fullness of Christ himself" (Eph. 4:13).

When one compares the characteristics of religious education and moral education, they seem to have many common qualities. They both arise out of the experience of self-consciousness and are subject to the process of maturation. Both involve a searing quality that is first experienced within the self and then in the community. Maturation in both areas depends upon experience. The main experiential determinants of moral development seem to be the amount and variety of social experience, the opportunity to take a number of roles and to encounter other perspectives. The goal in both is maturity. The major emphasis in catechesis is belief in God and the nature of our relationship with him. The conviction that God is, that he is love, and that this is all of a piece with the whole of life does not preclude the value of moral theory. But the exploration of this belief, acting within its assumptions, and observing adults who are also searching, who show respect for students as persons, and who can communicate a loving relationship is a more realistic way of moral education than direct moral exhortation made within a religious context. The actual experience of a lived Christianity is the only way in which the Christian life becomes credible. So, too, it is only in the experience of a just community institution that a sense of justice will be developed in the young.

Moral development theory has an important religious function. It helps to clarify the doctrine of person—how a human person grows, changes, and becomes. The concept of humanity influences our concept of God and vice versa. And most importantly, moral development theory sets up a dialogue and puts the hard question to the religious educator—does your doctrine free a person to develop his or her full human capacities?

And then there are the questions that take us beyond the limits of ethics, beyond the framework of rational and scientific terms. "Why be just?" presupposes the question, "Why live?" Kohlberg states that "ultimate moral maturity requires a mature solution to the question of the meaning of life. This in turn is hardly a moral question: it is an ontological or a religious one."[17] Kohlberg characterizes his metaphorical "Stage 7" by saying that contemplative experiences of nonegoistic or nondualistic variety are involved. Although these experiences are expressed in theistic terms, they need not be. The essential is the sense of being a part of the whole of life and the adoption of a cosmic, as opposed to a universal humanistic (Stage 6), perspective. From my viewpoint, experiences involving metaethical questions are essentially religious in dimension, in that they are breakthrough revelations which are accepted in faith. There is no way to avoid the commitments which underlie our choices. The function of religious education is to assist others to locate the symbolic sources of their final commitment and to go beyond justice to the ultimate principle of love. Paul Tillich describes the relationship between justice and love in this way:

> Love does not do more than justice demands but love is the ultimate principle of justice. Love reunites; justice preserves what is to be united. It is the form through which love performs its work. Justice in its ultimate meaning is creative justice, and creative justice is the form of reuniting love.[18]

Religious education and moral education have distinctly different rationales to be recognized and appreciated. Moral education, particularly Kohlberg's schema, has challenged religious education in the area of methodology. We again have to take a long, hard look at the developmental levels of children and adults to see if there is a developmental correlation between the learner and the content. Kohlberg's methodology is forcing us to be more open-ended in our presentation of content, to approach it more inductively, to see the value of conflict, and to see the necessity of integration with other areas of the curriculum, but, above all, with the child's own experience and life. The theory should stimulate us to become more aware of the influences that shape existing moral attitudes and structures. Perhaps the greatest service has been to underline the fact that religion and morality are not the same thing. This should cause us to redefine our aims and goals.

Religious education can motivate morality. The ultimate principle in Christianity is the great commandment. Where morality would be inspired by the motivation of love, it would be powerfully reinforced. The need of men and women to search for meaning and purpose in life can be enlightened by religious truth which can provide a frame of reference through which all of life can be related, experienced, and interpreted. It would seem that every moral issue is ultimately a religious issue, since it involves persons and therefore a concept of the nature of persons. Christianity is founded upon love for God, and therefore for others, and the claims of love upon each person.

There must be a clear distinction between religious education and morality; and the motivation, of one by the other, must also be understood.

NOTES

1. John Wilson, Norman Williams, and Barry Sugarman, *Introduction to Moral Education* (Baltimore: Penguin Books, 1967), p. 11.

2. Norman Williams and Sheila Williams, *The Moral Development of Children* (London: Macmillan, 1970), p. 11.

3. Douglas Graham, *Moral Learning and Development* (New York: John Wiley and Sons, 1972), pp. 10–11.

4. Norman Bull, *Moral Education* (Beverly Hills: Sage Publications, 1969), p. 117.

5. Lawrence Kohlberg, "Moral Development and Moral Education," in *Psychology and Educational Practice*, ed. G. Lesser (Chicago: Scott Foresman, 1971), p. 429.

6. This typology is taken from Derek Wright, *The Psychology of Moral Behavior* (Baltimore: Penguin Books, 1971), pp. 24–50.

7. Hugh Hartshorne and Mark May, *Studies in Deceit, Book 1,* Studies in the Nature of Character, vol. 1 (New York: Macmillan, 1928).

8. Paul Tillich, "A Conscience Above Moralism," in *Conscience*, ed. C. Ellis Nelson (New York: Newman Press, 1973), p. 46.

9. Charles Curran, "The Christian Conscience Today," in *Conscience*, pp. 132–133.

10. Tillich, "A Conscience Above Moralism," p. 49.

11. Bull, *Moral Education,* p. 54.

12. Lawrence Kohlberg, "Moral Development and Identification," in *The 62nd Yearbook of the National Society for the Study of Education,* Part 1: Child Psychology (Chicago: University of Chicago Press, 1963), p. 323.

13. Lawrence Kohlberg, "Development of Moral Character and Ideology," in *Review of Child Development Research,* ed. M. L. Hoffman and L. W. Hoffman (New York: Russell Sage Foundation, 1964), p. 314.

14. Sigmund Freud, *An Outline of Psychoanalysis* (New York: Norton, 1949), p. 121.

15. Ronald Goldman, *Readiness for Religion* (New York: Seabury Press, 1965), pp. 60–61.

16. James Gustafson, "Education for Moral Responsibility," in *Moral Education: Five Lectures,* by James Gustafson et al., with an intro. by Nancy and Theodore Sizer (Cambridge: Harvard University Press, 1970), p. 24.

17. Lawrence Kohlberg, "Continuities in Childhood and Adult Moral Development – Revisited," in *Collected Papers on Moral Development and Moral Education* (Cambridge: Center for Moral Development, 1973), p. 55.

18. Paul Tillich, *Love, Power, and Justice* (New York: Oxford University Press, 1954), p. 71.

For most persons today, the term indoctrination *has a pejorative connotation, suggesting activity that ultimately does not respect human freedom. In the following article, Jewish educator Barry Chazan's careful analysis of the term challenges us to rethink our understanding of indoctrination and to reexamine the shape of a nonindoctrinating religious education.*

READING 30

"Indoctrination" and Religious Education

BARRY CHAZAN

RELIGIOUS EDUCATION has the dubious distinction of being a priori associated with the concept "indoctrination." Indeed, religious education (along with moral and political education) is usually cited as *the* classic and paradigmatic case of indoctrinating activity. Sometimes, this association is simply presented as an explanation of the nature of the process of religious education; in many instances, however, this association has become a vehicle of an emotive polemic against the religious education enterprise.

Reprinted from the July–August 1972 issue of the journal *Religious Education*, pp. 243–252, by permission of the publisher, The Religious Education Association, 409 Prospect Street, New Haven, CT 06510. Membership or subscription available for $25.00 per year.

The subject of this paper is the relationship between indoctrination and religious education. Our discussion will center on the following two questions: (1) What is indoctrination? (2) Is religious education *the* paradigmatic case of indoctrination?

Indoctrination as a Term of Disapproval

The most immediate and striking sense of *indoctrination* is as a term of disapproval.[1] That is, *indoctrination* first and foremost refers to certain sorts of activities of the educational sphere which are disapproved of, regarded as undesirable, or rejected. *Indoctrination* is usually contrasted with such positive value terms as *education, teaching,* or *instruction.*[2] Even theoreticians and educators who regard indoctrination as an indispensable and legitimate aspect of education, nevertheless, consider it a "necessary evil," and they urge restrained and minimal use of it as an aspect of normal education.[3] In short, the initial and predominant thrust of indoctrination is its negative emotive meaning.

As a result of its negative emotive thrust, one tendency in the understanding of indoctrination is simply to regard it as any sort of unfavorable or undesirable activity of the educational sphere, i.e., as the antithesis of education. What is regarded as undesirable or unfavorable is, of course, dependent on one's particular ideological stance and conception of education. Thus, for some, the teaching of Marx is indoctrination; for others, the teaching of Jefferson. Indeed, depending upon one's ideology, indoctrination may run the gamut from the statements of Chairman Mao to the exhortations of Amos of Tekoa. Consequently, according to such a conception, religious education is or is not indoctrination depending upon one's sympathy or disdain for the religious sphere and the religious way of life.

While both convenient and popular, such an approach to the explication of indoctrination is incomplete. It is surely true that there is *an* emotive aspect to and impact of this term, and it is important to emphasize that this concept is a term of disapproval. However, this conclusion should in no way negate the equally important fact that the term *indoctrination* also has a descriptive and denotative sense, i.e., that it also refers to an activity or phenomenon which can be analyzed and described. In this sense, the emotive meaning of the term is simply a reaction to and/or evaluation of some describable and analyzable activity or phenomenon. The fact of the emotive meaning of the term in no way negates the existence of its descriptive sense, and it should not come in its stead. We may indeed start from the premise that indoctrination is an undesirable activity. The consequent task is to discover the nature of this undesirable activity, to see why it is regarded as undesirable, and to see whether such an activity is equivalent to religious education.

Three Conceptions of "Indoctrination"

Analyses of indoctrination in the literature of contemporary philosophy and philosophy of education have proceeded by attempting to isolate *the* characteristic (or group of characteristics) which distinguishes this activity from such approved activities as education or teaching. The search for such a distinguishing characteristic has frequently focused on one (or more) of the following three criteria: method, content, aim.

The Method Argument. According to the method argument (represented by Atkinson, Moore, and, perhaps, Green),[4] *indoctrination* refers to the transmission of contents to the young via undesirable or distasteful *methods*. Such methods are characterized by the fact that they are aimed at guaranteeing a student's acceptance of beliefs and/or ability to defend such beliefs; however, they do so by excluding alternative beliefs or by presenting them in such a way as to guarantee their rejection. That is, indoctrinating methods "stack the deck"—they ensure acceptance of certain beliefs by loading the argument. Procedures often associated with indoctrination include: stilted, incomplete, or one-sided arguments; deliberate falsification or suppression of evidence; charisma; repetition; management of facts; drilling. In some cases, force (rubber truncheons, dark rooms) is also associated with indoctrination. All of these procedures are indoctrinating according to this school in that they enable the presentation and imposition of carefully tailored arguments aimed at guaranteeing the acceptance of certain desired beliefs, i.e., they are methods which juggle facts and arguments so as to ensure the acceptance of desired conclusions. The claim of this school, then, is that it is the use of such illegitimate methods which characterizes the indoctrinating activity.

The Content Argument. The second conception of "indoctrination" (best represented by Wilson and Gregory and Woods)[5] regards the *content* being taught rather than the methods being used as the defining feature of indoctrination. That is, indoctrination is a question of *what* one teaches, rather than how. Proponents of this school denote two essential characteristics of the contents of indoctrination. First, such contents are uncertain and/or speculative beliefs, in the sense that there is not enough evidence for their validity so that any sane and sensible person when presented with the relevant evidence would hold such beliefs. That is, the contents of indoctrination are beliefs for which there is no convincing or publicly acceptable evidence: "The salient characteristic of doctrines is the fact that they are not known to be true or false."[6]

The second characteristic of indoctrinating contents is that they are integrated bodies or systems of beliefs about the most basic and ultimate issues of human existence. Indoctrination is not simply a question of inculcating the belief that Schweppes is tastier than Coca-Cola but rather of inculcating beliefs in God, Socialism, the Good. In short, the contents of indoctrination have to do with people's most basic beliefs, world-views, or "philosophies of life." The three spheres regarded as the paradigmatic cases of indoctrination by the content school are religious, political, and moral education. According to this school, these three spheres represent the prime examples of the transmission of comprehensive ideologies or belief systems which are not known to be true or false and whose verification is speculative.

The Intention Argument. The third position on the nature of indoctrination (best represented by Hare and White)[7] claims that the defining characteristic of this concept is neither unique methods nor contents but rather the *intention* underlying the activity. According to this contention, *indoctrination* refers to the desire to implant unshakably beliefs in others, i.e., to the concern with having the young accept their beliefs from their elders in a nonquestioning, noncritical manner: "Indoctrination begins when we are trying to stop the growth in our children of the capacity to think for themselves."[8]

The objective of education is to bring students to the point where they ultimately think and decide for themselves; the objective of indoctrination is forever to avoid such a realization and instead to train the student to be thought for by others. The true indoctrinator, then, is distinguished by his or her illiberal and authoritarian intention.

Despite their obvious differences, there are two features which all three conceptions of "indoctrination" have in common. First, they all regard indoctrination as a distasteful activity. In the case of the content and intention schools, indoctrination is to be avoided at *all* costs; in the case of the methods argument, as much as possible. Second, all three schools regard religious, political, and moral education as the paradigmatic examples of indoctrination. The method school claims that religious education is indoctrination because of the way religious educators teach; the content school equates religious education with indoctrination because of what is taught; and the intention school sees the aim of the religious educator as equivalent to that of the indoctrinator. Thus, while the rationale differs, the conclusion of these three schools vis-à-vis the equation of indoctrination with religious education is the same.

Critique of the Three Positions

Each of the three positions just discussed has a flaw which prevents it from fully and accurately defining the concept in question.

The Method Argument. The method argument claims that there are methods unique to indoctrination which thereby constitute its defining element. The flaw of this argument is the fact that the so-called unique methods of indoctrination are not unique at all but are, in fact, frequently employed in and characteristic of other sorts of activities. For example, one method frequently presented as a prominent example of indoctrinating activity are procedures which circumvent a student's reasoning. Yet several of the very procedures employed and legitimized in teaching and education are precisely of this nature. For example, in certain aspects of swimming or language instruction the essential focus is not the student's ability to reason or his or her rational assent but rather ability to internalize and perform certain skills. In much of affective education, the focus is at least equally if not exclusively on the students' ability to develop positive feelings and attitudes, over and above their ability to understand rationally. Hence, the utilization of procedures which in themselves are not always aimed at a student's cognitive powers is not an adequate criterion of indoctrination for there are several spheres of life and education not regarded as indoctrination in which such procedures are used and legitimized.

Thus, nonrational procedures are not always unique to indoctrination. Similarly, the partial or selective appeal to reasons is also not a priori exclusive to indoctrination but may also appear in such legitimate activities as teaching and education. For example, the third grade teacher engaged in moral education who does not cite Hare's theory of universalizability of moral principles, or Moore's theory of the indefinability of good is not indoctrinating by the mere fact that he or she is selective in the choice of contents. Rather, we would be more likely to regard him or her as *teaching* or *educating* in terms of the developmental potential of children of that age. Similarly, the high school history teacher who uses one textbook rather than another or who explains an event in terms of a particular historiographic conception is also not necessarily indoctrinating, although he or she too is being selective. The fact of selectivity or appeal to certain reasons is not in itself the distinguishing criterion between indoctrination and education. Even the distortion of facts need not necessarily be indoctrination. For example, the teacher who claims that New York is the largest city in the world, on the basis of reference to a 1948 almanac, is not an indoctrinator but a poorly or inadequately prepared teacher.

Thus, we have seen that many of the so-called unique methods of indoctrination are also to be found in education. Similarly, certain other so-called methods of indoctrination, while not equivalent to education, are characteristic of other types of persuasion dissimilar from indoctrination. That is, not only are the so-called methods of indoctrination sometimes characteristic of *educational* activities, but also they are characteristic of other types of persuasion clearly distinguishable from indoctrination.[9] For example, the continuous application of electric shock to a person's body, or the constant presentation of a steak dinner, upon receipt of certain responses (methods sometimes associated with indoctrination) are not indoctrination but conditioning. In such instances, one attempts to gain control over the way a person talks, behaves, and perhaps even feels. There is, however, no guarantee that the subject's thinking has been affected (unless, of course, one argues that *thinking* is to be defined in exclusively behavioral or verbal terms). The conditioned person has, in a certain sense, been trained to say certain things or to act in certain ways, although that person may not necessarily believe in or agree with what he or she has said or done. As John Wilson indicates, a conditioned person may well say: "I have an irresistible feeling of repulsion about doing X, though I know it is perfectly all right to do it."[10] That is, conditioning does not necessarily affect one's thinking or beliefs, whereas indoctrination does.

Similarly, force does not necessarily affect one's beliefs or thinking. A person forced to affirm fascism under threat of a gun is not necessarily regarded as believing in fascism. It is clearly recognized in both popular and legal thought that such decisions made under duress do not necessarily reflect a conscious choice by a person (indeed, one of the standard ways of attempting to avoid prosecution is to claim that one was forced or was "simply obeying orders"). The police chief who places a suspect in a dark room and beats him or her for a confession is not an indoctrinator but rather, a beast. Conditioning and force are not equivalent to indoctrination since the latter activity is not simply a question of mouthing words and behaving in certain ways. Instead, the indoctrinated person is one who maintains certain ideas, attitudes, and practices and who is capable of presenting a rationale and justification for these beliefs. In short, the indoctrinated person is expected to act just like a rational person, except that this rationality has been carefully planned from the outset.

The method argument fails, then, since it does not provide us with a criterion which truly distinguishes indoctrination from other activities. The so-called methods of indoctrination are either also characteristic of teaching and education or of such other sorts of persuasion as conditioning and force. Method, then, is not a sufficiently satisfactory criterion for the concept "indoctrination."

The Content Argument. The content school claims that *indoctrination* is defined by the selection and transmission of nonverifiable belief systems, the sterling examples of which are morality, religion, and politics. The objections to indoctrination, according to this school, are twofold: (1) Its contents are not known to be definitely true; (2) it involves arbitrary selection of certain contents at the expense of others.

The first problem with the content argument is its notion of verification. This school assumes that there exists one fixed set of rational and objective criteria for the verification of all phenomena. Such criteria are implied in the phrases: "the sane and sensible person," "rational beliefs," or "the rationality of the contents."[11] It is, however, simplistic to assume one set of fixed and certain rules of verification even within such specific spheres as science and mathematics, let alone for all spheres of human discourse and meaning. Indeed, contemporary philosophers of science and epistemologists have gone to great lengths to show that the principles of verification in the sciences themselves are constructs and substantive structures which the scientist creates and/or accepts.[12] Further, such constructs are not fixed but rather are dynamic in nature and constantly subject to revision.

Indeed, the criterion of rationality is ultimately an amorphous and undefined phenomenon. Does rationality refer to some metaphysical order, to some universal human structure, to agreed-upon rules and principles? Beyond excluding certain clearly unacceptable criteria of verification (e.g., arbitrary will, authority per se, raw feelings) and beyond emphasizing the necessity of reference to reasons, the term *rationality* means very little. Thus, for example, Wilson's notion of "sane and sensible people" as the criterion of rationality is not a very helpful concept. For it is not at all clear who is, or what determines, a sane and sensible person. In certain cases, such a person is so defined by one local culture in a way which directly contradicts the assumptions of another or competing culture. Thus, the sane and sensible person of the "silent majority"—or even the sane and sensible liberal—is regarded as a reject by the sane and sensible radical. Further, sane and sensible people often disagree; what happens to verification in such cases? Finally, sane and sensible people have been known to do things regarded as insane and insensible by others, by history, and even by themselves. In many cases, the notion of "sane and sensible people" simply degenerates into the concept of majority rule, which is indeed an uncomfortable criterion of verification.

A more likely conception of verification than that implied by the content school is the position that there exist criteria of verification *relevant to a certain sphere*, in terms of which some beliefs can be said to be more certain than others. Thus, for example, in terms of scientific criteria of testing or observation, certain scientific theories may be regarded as more valid than others. Such an argument would be legitimate; it is, however, far different from the claim that *scientific* principles of testing or observation are a priori more valid than *moral* principles of justice or *religious* principles of faith. The "facts" of science can clearly be said to be more certain than the fallacies or falsehoods of science, i.e., certain facts *are* more certain *in terms of the substantive structure and syntax of science.* However, this does not mean that the truths of science can be said to be a priori more certain than the truths of religion, morality, and politics. Religion, morality, and politics also have their "facts" which are rooted in and verified by certain assumptions and principles. Thus, it is, in fact, inaccurate to speak of the nonverifiable nature of such spheres. At the most, one can question the validity of the criteria of verification of the religious, moral, or political spheres; this, however, is a claim far different from that of the content school.

In short, then, the content school has mistaken the clearly evident fact that religion, morality, and politics are different from science and mathematics to mean that the latter are verifiable whereas the former are not. What is, in fact, the case is that the latter are verifiable in ways *different* from the former. Politics, religion, and morality are clearly verifiable, albeit within their respective realms of discourse.

The second claim of the content school, vis-à-vis the selectivity of contents in indoctrinating activities, reflects a naiveté concerning the nature of education. The simple fact, not taken into consideration by this argument, is that *all* education is selection. Since teachers, students, and school systems reflect and are limited by certain histories, neighborhoods, cultures, and value systems and since there will always be more to learn than there is time, education will always imply selection. The most liberal teacher (in physics, chemistry, and algebra, as well as in religion, morality, and politics) uses certain texts rather than others, and even journals of philosophy of education and religious education accept certain papers while rejecting others. Thus, the notion of nonselective education is either unreal (as manifested in certain aspects of progressive education or the new educational romanticism) or even evil. Thus, to argue that selectivity is a criterion of indoctrination is, in fact, to establish the very same criterion for indoctrination and education. The content school is indeed correct in arguing that certain sorts of contents, i.e., comprehensive belief systems, are related to indoctrination. However, as we shall shortly see, such contents *in themselves* are not the only or singular criterion of the concept "indoctrination." Thus, while adding to our understanding of the concept "indoctrination," the content school does not ultimately present us with a comprehensive enough conception of the term.

The Intention Argument. The intention argument rejects both method and content as the defining criteria of *indoctrination* and argues instead that *indoctrination* is defined by aim or intention. If one's intention is to implant contents in such a way that they will be unshakably accepted, without free, critical, and rational reflection, then this is an indoctrinating activity. If, however, one's intention is to equip a student ultimately to be able to accept or reject ideas on the basis of his or her own rational and autonomous judgment, then this is an educative activity. According to this conception, it is not contents or methods in themselves which determine indoctrination but rather one's intention or objective vis-à-vis contents and methods. Thus, one could conceivably teach communism, Judaism, or Puritan morality or one could even force a child to remove its head from a lit oven without such activities being necessarily equivalent to indoctrination.

There are two problems with this conception. First, if intention is taken in too simplistic a sense, then this position emerges as naively liberal. For it is obvious that there are certain aspects of education which are not aimed at, or even open to, the child's rational or autonomous judgment. Traffic laws, language, and eating habits are but a few of the areas in which the rational and autonomous assent of the child may be a desideratum although it is not an imperative for justification of the educational activity. We would regard teaching a child to cross the street when there is a green light and/or cautiously as good education, whether the child approves of or even fully understands the action or not. That is, certain aspects of education dealing with the transmission of behaviors, habits, and values which are indispensable to the child or society's very ability to function (e.g. reading, writing, language, traffic laws) are not conditional on a student's rational assent. In addition to being naive, the overly liberal goal may even be antiliberal. In order to attain the objective of rational and autonomous judgment, the educator may sometimes have to pursue seemingly nonliberal, proximate goals and activities. Once again, it may seem very illiberal to remove a child's head from a lit oven without his assent, but this may be the only possible option available to the educator interested in the fact that the child remain alive so that he or she might someday be able to think and choose for himself or herself. Similarly, it may seem extremely liberal and nonindoctrinating to create a structureless, curriculumless, teacherless school; however, such procedures may ultimately be the epitome of illiberalism in that they may restrict rather than expand the child's experiences, expose him or her solely to the whims of the peer group, and deny him or her the opportunity to attain those skills which are ultimately indispensable to autonomous and rational judgment.[13]

The second problem with the intention school is that it does not take seriously enough the important distinction of the content school vis-à-vis different forms of educational subjects or contents. The intention school would have us believe that the liberal intention is *the* criterion of education in all cases, whereas an authoritarian intention is the criterion of indoctrination in *all* cases. What is more accurately the case is that the intention to impose contents on students is only indoctrination in those spheres where student agreement or acceptance is an a priori and minimal criterion. That is, the intention to indoctrinate can only take place in potentially indoctrinational spheres, i.e., vis-à-vis contents which encompass comprehensive belief systems and which ultimately rest on an individual's acceptance or rejection. Thus, the intention school weakens its relatively strong argument by too easily disregarding the content school's claim vis-à-vis the distinctiveness of the indoctrinating content.

There is, however, an obvious strength in the intention argument which makes it the soundest of these three attempts to locate the distinguishing criterion of indoctrination. It is undoubtedly true that an indoctrinator is ultimately one who wishes to impose his or her beliefs on others or who wants others automatically to accept these beliefs. It is his or her purpose which characterizes such a person as an indoctrinator, and it is this purpose which makes indoctrination a "bad" activity. For the assumption (of some elements of modern society) is that a person should ultimately be allowed to choose, decide, and act upon values and beliefs which the person himself or herself accepts. Preparation for such a state is regarded as the approved activity education, and impediments to such a state are regarded as the disapproved activity indoctrination.

Indoctrination

Our analysis and critique of these three attempts to define *indoctrina-*

tion enable us to see more clearly the problems involved in the issue, as well as enabling us to propose a more exact notion of the concept. The general problem with all three schools, aside from the specific critiques discussed in the last section, is their too rigid adherence to the method-content-intention distinction. They all err, or more accurately, they all give partial conceptions as a result of their attempts to establish one of the three criteria of method, content, or intention as *the* defining characteristic of indoctrination. The truth is that indoctrination must be approached as an activity which encompasses certain types of intentions, contents, and methods *as a whole*. The search for *the one* distinguishing characteristic of indoctrination, while appealing because of its potential simplicity, is ultimately misleading and imprecise.

However, when taken together, these three schools do set the frame for an accurate delineation of indoctrination. Thus, indoctrination *is* defined by certain spheres of human existence or knowledge, i.e., by a certain content area. The nature of this sphere is comprehensive belief systems which must be accepted or rejected by a thinking and freely choosing individual. Indoctrination, then, is in part delineated by spheres of life in which contents only become valid, acceptable, or even "true" when accepted or rejected by a thinking and choosing agent.[14] Thus, such activities as the forceful removal of children's heads from ovens, teaching swimming, or language instruction cannot be indoctrination, not because of their methods but because of the spheres of life in which they occur (e.g., because of their contents). In short, then, indoctrination can only take place in spheres, content areas, or situations where a student's rational, autonomous acceptance is indispensable.

However, indoctrination is not simply defined by a certain sphere of contents; it also refers to the transmission of – or concern with – certain kinds of contents *for certain purposes*. That is, indoctrination involves the *intention* to transmit contents which ultimately require rational acceptance by a student *in a way which thwarts or represses such rational acceptance*. Indoctrination, then, is clearly an issue of authoritarian intention, albeit vis-à-vis certain types of contents. This constellation of content and intention obviously has a direct connection with certain sorts of methods. If one wants a student to accept his or her beliefs in an unquestioning manner, then certain types of methods, e.g., charisma, distorted reasoning, selective presentation of material, will be especially relevant. It is undoubtedly true that certain kinds of methods are usually associated with indoctrination since certain kinds of methods flow from and are especially effective for the objective of thwarting the reasoning and autonomy of students. While certain sorts of methods do not in themselves define indoctrination, they are reflective of indoctrinating contents and intentions.

Thus, it is possible to characterize *indoctrination* as the attempt authoritatively and unquestionably to impose on others beliefs and belief systems whose acceptance really should be rooted in the agent's own free and rational acceptance. Such a definition solves several problems. First, it explains the very blatant fact that certain contents — e.g., religion, morality, politics — are almost always associated with indoctrination. Such a (potential) association is logically legitimate, since these content areas are the prime examples of comprehensive belief systems which demand free and rational affirmation or rejection by an agent. Such contents are legitimately associated with indoctrination, albeit in a *formal and potential* sense, just as mothers are associated with babies. Second, this definition explains why certain methods are frequently associated with indoctrination, without establishing method as the sole criterion of the concept. Experience has shown that certain methods are indeed associated with indoctrination, not, however, as the defining criterion but rather because they have proven themselves to be effective means of attaining indoctrinational objectives. Third, this definition explains why certain objectives, e.g., critical or rational thinking, are usually presented as the antithesis of indoctrination — not because critical thinking is good education in *all* spheres but because it is so in *some very crucial* spheres of education and life. In this context, this definition explains why we can have indoctrination in only certain spheres or content areas, whereas in other spheres, even when the activity looks very much like indoctrination, indoctrination is (logically) impossible. Finally, this definition explains why religious, moral, and political education are usually regarded as the paradigmatic cases of indoctrination. For these three educational spheres automatically fulfill *one* of the logical requirements of indoctrination, i.e., the content dimension. Thus, religious, moral, and political education *are* potential examples of indoctrinating activity, not, however, because their contents are arbitrary, speculative, or false but because these are three prominent examples of the transmission of comprehensive belief systems whose verification and operability depend upon a student's rational and autonomous acceptance.

Is Religious Education the Paradigmatic Case of Indoctrination?

Our discussion of the nature of indoctrination clearly implies that there is a connection between religious (and political and moral) education and indoctrination, in that the former activity is more likely or potentially able to turn into indoctrination than other educational activities. The crucial question at this point is whether the fact that indoctrination and religious education are or are likely to be *associated* means that they are *the same thing*, whether the fact that religious education *may* be indoctrination means that it *must* be.

The answer to this question is provided by reference to the redefinition of *indoctrination* suggested in the last section. There we proposed three criteria for indoctrination: contents of a certain sort, i.e., comprehensive belief systems; the intention to implant unshakably such contents; and the use of methods efficient for realization of such an objective. The question, then, is whether religious education fulfills these three criteria.

In terms of the first logical criterion, it is clear that religious education may indeed be consistent with indoctrination, since the subject of both activities is indeed comprehensive belief systems. However, this is but one criterion of indoctrination. The second and third criteria of indoctrination—the intention unshakably to implant certain beliefs via appropriate methods—need not at all logically apply to religious education. While it is surely a historical and sociological fact that in many cases religious education has implied such an intention and methods, it is by no means true that such need be the case or that such is the logical nature of religious education. For in fact, there surely are examples—or it is easily possible to conceive—of a religious education which does not involve the imposition of beliefs in an arbitrary manner but rather is concerned with the best possible presentation of these contents in order to enable a student eventually to make an intelligible and free decision vis-à-vis his or her religious beliefs and commitments. That is, the logical nature of religious education in no way entails the indoctrinating intention or methods. Thus, in the formal sense, it would be incorrect to a priori regard religious education as the paradigmatic case of indoctrination.

The crucial point in this discussion is the manner in which to treat the question, "Is religious education the paradigmatic case of indoctrination?" If such a question is understood as referring to the history of religious education, or to the nature of contemporary religious educational practice, then the answer is clearly affirmative. However, if the question is taken in its purely logical sense (*is* meaning "entails" or "need entail") then the answer is clearly negative. Religious education is related to indoctrination in the same way that women are related to babies and men to killing; there surely is a potential link between the two, but one does not automatically entail the other.

Toward a Nonindoctrinating Religious Education

If this conclusion is correct, then the next step in such a discussion of religious education would be the explication of the nature of a nonindoctrinating religious education. We shall not engage in such an exercise here beyond indicating that: (1) we regard such an education as eminently feasible, (2) it would deal with that corpus of ideas, beliefs, and behaviors central to and derived from any specific religion, and (3) it would be concerned both with transmission and justification of the heritage, as well as with preparation of the young for an eventual free and reasoned decision vis-à-vis acceptance or rejection of such a heritage. The full explication of a nonindoctrinating religious education would depend upon the elucidation of these points and their translation into operative educational principles and practices.[15]

Our argument in this paper has not at all attempted to deny many of the historical or contemporary facts about religious education as indoctrination. Instead, we have claimed that a careful analysis of the concept reveals much inaccuracy in the way we talk about and engage in religious education. Our suggestion has been that a more careful analysis of the concept "indoctrination" implies that religious education can exist in a nonindoctrinating fashion. However, an analysis of an educational concept can only take us up to this point; the next step is in the realm of educational value decisions. Logically, religious education can be nonindoctrinating, but ultimately, language is only a tool for expressing our meaning and preferences. The ultimate question, then, is whether one regards nonindoctrinating religious education or religious indoctrination as the desirable and worthwhile activity. At this point, the analytic philosopher has finished his or her task and (as a philosopher) has no more to say.

NOTES

1. The meaning of and theoretical assumptions underlying the notion of "terms of disapproval" are best elucidated by: C. L. Stevenson, *Ethics and Language* (New Haven, CT: Yale University Press, 1944); and idem, *Facts and Value* (New Haven, CT: Yale University Press, 1963).

2. For discussions of the concept *education* as an evaluative term, see: Israel Scheffler, *The Language of Education* (Springfield, IL: Charles C. Thomas, 1960), pp. 11–35; and Jonas Solits, *An Introduction to the Analysis of Educational Concepts* (Reading, MA: Addison-Wesley, 1968), pp. 2–7.

3. See, for example, the cautious affirmations of indoctrination as a legitimate educational activity by: Willis Moore, "Indoctrination as a Normative Conception," *Studies in Philosophy and Education* 4 (Summer 1966); and Thomas Green, "A Topology of the Teaching Concept," *Studies in Philosophy and Education* 3 (Winter 1964–1965): 284–319.

4. See: R. F. Atkinson, "Instruction and Indoctrination" in *Philosophical Analysis and Education*, ed. R. Archambault (London: Routledge and Kegan Paul, 1965), pp. 171–183; Moore, "Indoctrination as a Normative Conception"; Green, "A Topology of the Teaching Concept."

5. John Wilson, "Education and Indoctrination," in *Aims in Education*, ed. T. H. B. Hollins (Manchester: Manchester University Press, 1968), pp. 24–46; also, John Wilson, "Comments on Flew's 'What Is Indoctrination?'" *Studies in Philosophy and Education* 4 (1966): 390–395; I. M. Gregory and R. G. Woods, "Indoctrination," in The Philosophy of Education Society of Great Britain, *Proceedings of the Annual Conference*, vol. 4 (January 1970), pp. 77–104.

6. Gregory and Woods, "Indoctrination," p. 81.

7. R. M. Hare, "Adolescents into Adults," in *Aims in Education*, pp. 47–70; J. P. White, "Indoctrination," in *The Concept of Education*, ed. R. S. Peters (London: Routledge and Kegan Paul, 1967), pp. 177–191; see also J. P. White, "Indoctrination: Reply to I. M. Gregory and R. G. Woods," in The Philosophy of Education Society of Great Britain, *Proceedings of the Annual Conference*, vol. 4 (January 1970), pp. 107–120.

8. Hare, "Adolescents into Adults," p. 52.

9. See the following discussion of different types of persuasion: J. A. A. Brown, *Types of Persuasion* (London: Penguin Books, 1963).

10. John Wilson, Norman Williams, and Barry Sugarman, *Introduction to Moral Education* (London: Penguin Books, 1967), p. 169.

11. Wilson, "Education and Indoctrination," pp. 28, 34.

12. See, for example: Stephen Toulmin, *The Philosophy of Science* (New York: Harper & Row, 1963); Richard Rudner, *Philosophy of Social Science* (Englewood Cliffs, NJ: Prentice-Hall, 1966); Robert Borger and Frank Cioffi, eds., *Explanation in the Behavioral Sciences* (Cambridge: Cambridge University Press, 1970).

13. See: R. S. Peters, *Ethics and Education* (London: George Allen and Unwin, 1966); and John Dewey, *Experience and Education* (New York: Collier Books, 1938).

14. The claim here is not that all such contents are subjective or relative. Rather, our argument is that there are certain content areas in which teaching is only completed (and in which contents may be said to be verified) when the agent has freely and intelligently accepted or rejected the contents.

15. See the following discussion of "open-ended religion" for *some* similar perspectives: Edwin C. Cox, *Changing Aims in Religious Education* (London: Routledge and Kegan Paul, 1966).

Some Protestant educators are finding in the categories of catechesis elements helpful for describing what they themselves seek to do in Christian education. No Protestant leader has explored this matter as carefully as has John Westerhoff, professor of Christian education at Duke University. As the following essay was written expressly for this sourcebook, the editor owes Dr. Westerhoff special thanks for this "last word."

READING 31

Catechetics: An Anglican Perspective

JOHN H. WESTERHOFF III

THE FACT THAT there is some question today about what constitutes the educational ministry of the church needs no documentation. Once clear commitments, understandings, and ways have given way to confusion. We lack a comprehensive theory and practice adequate to our times. I contend that Christians—Roman Catholic, Orthodox, and Protestant—need to put aside their separate historic understandings and ways of educational ministry and together shape a renewed and reformed understanding of catechetics as a dimension of practical theology. The limited aim of this essay is to stimulate this process by presenting a very broad outline of one possible understanding from my own limited Anglican perspective. In no way is it intended to suggest an end to discussion. However, if it is successful, it will aid persons with very different understandings to talk with each other.

Anglican, Roman Catholic, Protestant, and Orthodox Christians all seek to discover the processes by which persons are best initiated into the Christian community and its baptismal faith and the processes by which persons throughout their lifetimes are best helped to live into their baptisms by making the faith of the church conscious, living, and active in their lives.

In this shared effort, the Anglican communion has traditionally sought to be fully catholic and fully protestant. It has affirmed, therefore, catholic substance and its rightful concern for the communal nature of the Christian faith, for the conserving of the church's tradition, and for the initiation and formation of persons into this community and its tradition. It also has affirmed protestant principle and its rightful concern for the personal nature of the Christian faith, for a necessary prophetic judgment on and the church's understanding of its tradition, and for the transformation of the church and a reinterpretation of its tradition through the liberating processes of education.

Historically, therefore, Roman Catholics and Protestants have developed significantly different understandings and ways of educational ministry. As each group has faced critically the results of its own labors, each has become attracted to those of the other. At times, it seems as if we pass each other in the night. For example, some Roman Catholics have chosen to avoid the language of catechetics and chosen that of Christian religious education, while some Protestants have turned from Christian education to Christian nurture (catechesis). Others have acknowledged the importance of religious education and catechetics but chosen to keep them separated. This essay intends reconciliation and unity.

While the language of catechetics has been ignored by many Protestants and associated with the ecclesiastical establishment's conservative efforts at doctrinal indoctrination by some Roman Catholics, catechetics still provides, I believe, the best conceptual framework for understanding the church's essential and foundational concern for the formation and transformation of Christian character, conscience, and conduct.

Insofar as the language of catechetics is archaic, it provides a sense of continuity with the past in a day when our efforts are shallow because we are singularly enamored of the new and have fallen in love with the educational mind-set of our individualistic, relativistic, post-Enlightenment age. Insofar as it represents understandings and ways which have been able to adjust to changing situations and needs throughout history (see John Westerhoff and O. C. Edwards, *A Faithful Church: Issues in the History of Catechism* [New York: Morehouse-Barlow, 1981]), it provides us with a framework for developing a faithful ministry for our own day. More important, perhaps, in an ecumenical era it is good to have a word whose use goes back to a time when the church was united.

Once theology was thought to comprise three levels of reflection and discourse: Fundamental theology reflected on the Christian tradition as it is expressed in the established creedal formulations of the universal church and in the Word of God as conveyed in the holy Scriptures; constructive theology reflected on the church's tradition in the light of a particular historical, social, and cultural setting so as to illumine the dimensions of modern experience and communal life; and practical theology reflected on what it means to live as a believer in Jesus Christ and a member of his church in our day. As such, practical theology comprised five interrelated dimensions: liturgical, ascetical, moral, pastoral, and catechetical. Regrettably, at some point in modern history the liturgical among some became preaching; among others, technique; and among still others, an aspect of church history. The ascetical (spirituality) was either ignored or became technique; the moral was subsumed under systematic or constructive theology; the pastoral became counseling and typically was modeled after secular psychology; and the catechetical became religious education and was modeled after secular pedagogy. Thus, within the theological encyclopedia, ministerial studies became estranged from the theoretical concerns of Scripture, church history, theology, and ethics and focused on the how-to of institutional life. Worst, ministerial studies became devoid of theological foundations as well as of spiritual (ascetical) and moral dimensions. Until we can reestablish the discipline of practical theology, with catechetics as one dimension of this integrated multidimensional enterprise, the church will be devoid of an adequate means for being a responsible community of Christian faith.

To illustrate this understanding of catechesis as one dimension of practical theology, it might be helpful to explore the nature of liturgical catechesis. Liturgics (the activity of God's people) refers to both our cultic life of symbols, myth, and ritual and our daily life of signs, concepts, and reflective actions. Catechesis has the responsibility of helping persons and community to reflect on their daily lives and thereby prepare for meaningful cultic life and to reflect on cultic life and prepare for responsible daily life. Catechesis refers also to the catechetical elements within the rites (for example, the catechumenal process within the rite of Christian initiation) and rituals of the church (for example, the service of the Word within the Holy Eucharist and the act of spiritual direction or guidance within the rite of reconciliation). Further, catechesis serves to introduce persons to the rites and rituals of the church so that they might more fully participate in them. So it is that catechesis plays a specific though integrated role of reflection on experience and action within every aspect of personal and communal life: the liturgical, ascetical, moral, and pastoral. Thus, while catechetics and liturgics are distinguishable, they cannot be separated. To be concerned about one is to be concerned about the other.

Within the framework of practical theology, catechetics addresses the content of these aims: to transmit, sustain, and deepen a Christian perception and understanding of life and our lives; to aid persons in community to live in a conscious, responsible relationship with the Holy Trinity; and to enable persons to acknowledge and actualize their human potential for personal and corporate redeemed life. As such, catechetics addresses the process content of the Christian faith. It attempts to answer three "how" questions: How is Christian faith— understood as perception—acquired, enhanced, and enlivened; how is divine revelation, understood as relational experience of God, made known; and how is our vocation, understood as perfected personal and communal life, realized?

Catechesis addresses the nature and character of the interactive, dialectical processes of enculturation and acculturation. It attends to the processes by which persons mature in the faith of the church and grow in their baptism within an intentional community of Christian faith which shares a common memory, vision, authority, and rituals. Such a community is more like a nurturing, caring family than a task-oriented, goal-oriented institution. To catechize is to participate with others in a shared lifelong pilgrimage of daily conversions and nurture within a story-formed visionary community, that is, ever to be shaped by the Gospel tradition within a community by continually moving from experience to reflection to action. To be a catechumen is to be a pilgrim; to be a catechist is to be a copilgrim, that is, a compassionate companion and guide, journeying with other pilgrims in a community which shares the threefold authority of Scripture, tradition, and reason. Thus, catechetics and catechesis address the ends and means of believing, being, and behaving in community. Understood best as a communal interactive process, *catechesis* can be defined as deliberate, systematic, and sustained interpersonal, helping relationships of acknowledged value which aid persons within a faith community to know God, live in relationship to God, and act with God in the world.

Catechesis implies intentional, responsible, faithful activities (it is not accidental); it implies lifelong sustained efforts (it is not only for children); it implies the necessity of open, mutually helpful, interpersonal relationships and interactions between persons in a community (it is not indoctrination); it implies concern for the political, the social, and the economic as well as every aspect of church life (it is not limited to one aspect of life or the church's ministry); it implies the presence of something we can only call "wholeness," that is, it involves the entire person, the totality of his or her life, and it affects all of that person's relationships—with God, self, neighbor, and the natural world.

Catechesis aims to provide persons with a communal context for living into their baptism, that is, an environment for experiencing the ever-converting and nurturing presence of Christ as they, day-by-day, in community, gather in the Lord's name to be confronted by God's Word, respond to the gift of faith, pray for the world and church, share God's peace, present the offerings and oblations of their lives and labors, make thanksgiving for God's grace, break bread and share the gifts of God and are thereby nourished to love and serve the Lord. Catechesis aims to provide persons with a context for falling in love with Christ and thereby having their eyes and ears opened to perceive and hence experience personally the Gospel of God's kingdom; it further aims to provide a context for persons to live in a growing and developing relationship with Christ that they might be a sign of God's kingdom come; and last, it aims to provide a context for persons to reflect and act with Christ on behalf of God's kingdom coming.

Catechesis in the Church

The church is the family of God, a visible, historical, human community called to convert and nurture people in the Gospel tradition so that they might live under its merciful judgment and inspiration to the end that God's will is done and God's reign acknowledged. The church is the body of Christ, a hidden, prophetic creature of God's spirit, an instrument of God's transforming power, and a witness to God's continuing revelation in history.

It is one church, a paradox to the mind: sinful, yet holy; immanent yet transcendent; divided yet one; continuously in need of reform, yet the bearer of God's transforming eternal Word; a human institution and a holy community; a disparate assembly of baptized sinners living, sometimes unconsciously, by grace, yet also an intentional, obedient, steadfast, faithful company of converted, visible saints; a mystery even to itself, but aware, in often incomprehensible ways, that it has a mission in the world and a ministry both to those who by birth or decision find themselves, not entirely by choice, within that family which bears the name Christian and to all people.

The church's mission, like Christ's, is to live in and for the Gospel, to witness to and to be a sign of God's reign, that is, to become what it already is, only more so, the incarnate body of Christ, infused by the Holy Spirit and living in relationship with the Father.

The church is a pilgrim community of memory and vision. The vocation of the church is to hear God speak, to see God act, and to witness in word and deed to these experiences. Christianity from the beginning has been essentially a missionary community to which the Gospel has been committed. The responsibility of being a living sign of and witness to that Gospel is the vocation of every Christian. Christians, as ambassadors of Christ and the Gospel, are to be of service to all people so that individual and corporate life might be more truly human and enriching.

Catechesis implies, therefore, the need for (1) a knowledge and understanding of the church's living tradition, including its ethical norms and the reflective, cognitive abilities to use that tradition in responsible moral decision-making; (2) a deepened authentic piety or character—unifying attitudes, affections, sensibilities, motivations, commitments, and values into an exemplary style of communal life; and (3) a clear vision of God's will for individual and corporate human life with concomitant skills for its realization. Thereby, the activities of believing, being, and behaving are united in the lives of persons who in community have a relationship to Christ and a commitment to the Gospel.

Catechesis is a ministry of the Word in which the faith is proclaimed and interpreted in verbal and nonverbal ways for the formation and transformation of persons who are to be understood as communal beings rather than individuals in their lifelong quest to live in a love relationship with God and neighbor. It is a ministry of the Word in which persons are both converted and initiated into the communal life of the church as well as nurtured and nourished in its particular and peculiar perceptions, understandings, and ways of life. Catechesis occurs within a community of faith where persons strive to be Christian together. Catechesis aims to enable the faith community to live under the judgment and inspiration of the Gospel to the end that God's will is done and God's community comes. It unites all deliberate, systematic, and sustained efforts to discover the will of God, to evaluate the community's interior and exterior life, and to equip and stimulate the community for greater faithfulness.

Catechesis, best understood as intentional socialization or, better, "enculturation" and "education," includes every aspect of the church's life intended to incorporate persons into the life of an ever-changing (reforming), tradition-bearing (catholic) community of Christian faith. As such it is concerned for both continuity (conserving an authoritative tradition) and change (making a prophetic judgment on its understanding of that tradition). It is a process intended to both recall and reconstruct the church's tradition so that it might become conscious and active in the lives of maturing persons in community. It is the process by which persons learn to know, internalize, and apply the Christian revelation in daily individual and corporate life. As such, catechesis aims to enable the faithful to meet the twofold responsibility which Christian faith asks of them: community with God and neighbor. Catechesis, therefore, is a life's work shared by all those who are called to participate in the mission and ministry of the Christian church. It values the interaction of faithful souls in community, striving to be faithful in-but-not-of-the-world. The fundamental question which catechesis asks is this: What is it to be Christian together in community and in the world? To answer this question is to understand the means by which we become Christian within a community of faith. Catechesis, therefore, intends to help us understand the implications of Christian faith for life and our lives, to evaluate critically every aspect of our individual and corporate understandings and ways, and to become equipped and inspired for faithful activity in church and society.

Importantly, catechesis acknowledges that we are enculturated or socialized within a community of memory and vision. Baptism incorporates us into a family with a story, a living tradition. This adoption into the church creates a change intrinsic to the self. We are historical beings, implicitly and explicitly influenced and formed by the communities in which we live and grow. Catechesis acknowledges this influence and challenges the community to be morally responsible for both the ways in which it aids persons to live in community and for the ways by which it influences the lives of others. While catechesis affirms that persons are both determined and free, the products of nurture and the agents of nurture, it makes it incumbent upon the community of faith to accept responsibility for disciplined, intentional, and faithful life together.

It would be useful if we abandoned the original, no longer accepted, understanding of socialization as a process which focuses on the transmitter of culture and describes the recipient as a passive participant in a unidirectional model of cultural transmission. We could then adopt the more recently, generally accepted, understanding which focuses on the recipient and describes the recipient as an active participant in an interactive model of cultural transmission which encourages continuous, gradual adaptation and change.

I have a suspicion that the differentiation some have drawn between socialization and education in terms of process is inadequate. Perhaps the real difference lies in our understanding of the learner.

Might the language of education perceive the learner as an individual who associates with others and forms institutions, and might the language of socialization perceive the learner as a communal being whose identity and growth can only be understood in terms of life in a community which shares a common memory, vision, authority, rituals, and family-like life together?

When we ask the questions – what is the content we are going to make available, and what are we going to do with it? – are we not asking if it is possible to be a Christian and believe whatever one wishes or interpret the community's tradition in any way one pleases? Is not the answer to both, "No"? We live in a wasteland of relativity where individuals believe they can write their own creeds and interpret Scripture any way they like. Catholicism's concern for an ordered authority may lead to tyranny, but Protestantism's concern for freedom will only lead to anarchy, a far greater danger to community.

Vincent of Lerins wrote, "We must hold what has been believed everywhere, always and by all." The creeds are at once the criteria and the norms for believing and behaving. A Christian teacher is not free to teach or encourage private opinions but only to propagate and defend "the faith that was delivered to the Saints." The "modern mind" stands under the judgment of the *kerygma*. We are to bend our thoughts to the mental habits of the apostolic message, for "repentance" means a "change of mind."

The Bible is the community's sacred book. St. Hilery wrote, "Scripture is not in the hearing, but in the understanding." The book and the church cannot be separated, and the apostolic message of the creeds provides us with a principle of interpretation so that Scripture might be adequately and rightly understood. For St. Irenaeus the reading of Scripture must be guided by that "rule of faith" (i.e., that profession of belief every catechumen recites before baptism). Our freedom is in obedience. There is a body of apostolic tradition into which Christians are to be formed, and there is a limit set by the authority of the community beyond which one is not free to interpret.

There are those who contend that an emphasis on communal authority and socialization as formation in the community's tradition is too conserving. Perhaps they forget that the *kerygma* of the community, as found in the apostolic confessions and the Gospels, can in and of itself provide both the stimulant and means by which continual reform is possible without losing continuity with the past.

Catechesis, Culture, and Transformation

Catechesis, understood as the process of enculturation, has been misunderstood as a singularly conservative process aimed at the shaping of another's life by a tyrannical authority. Catechesis, however, is a process that importantly aims at avoiding the relativistic, existential educational processes which easily fall prey to anarchical freedom. Catechesis understood as a community activity has been misunderstood as unconcerned for persons. Catechesis, however, does aim to avoid the trap of individualism so prevalent in our culture. Catechesis properly aims at leading persons to radical reorientations in their perceptions, experiences, and lives. It witnesses to the Lordship of Christ, to the good news of God's new possibility, and to the Gospel's prophetic protest against all false religiousness so that the church will not lose its soul. It could lose its soul by becoming an institution of cultural continuity maintaining the status quo rather than an institution of cultural change living in and for God's kingdom. Catechesis seeks to provide the means by which the church might continually transform its life and the lives of its people into a body of committed believers, willing to give anything and everything to the cause of historically mediating God's reconciling love in the world.

Christian faith does run counter to many ordinary understandings and ways of life. It is hardly possible for anything less than a converted, disciplined body to be the historical agent of God's work in the world. Conversions are a necessary aspect of every developing, mature Christian's faith. The church can no longer surrender to the illusion that child nurture, in and of itself, can or will rekindle the fire of Christian faith either in persons or in the church. We have expected too much of nurture. We can nurture persons into institutional religion but not into mature Christian faith. The Christian faith by its very nature demands transformations. We do not gradually educate persons by stages to be Christian. To be Christian is to be baptized into the community of the faithful, but to be a mature Christian is to be continually converted and nurtured in the Gospel tradition within a living community of Christian faith.

Authentic Christian life is personal and social life lived on behalf of God's reign in the political, social, and economic world. One cannot be nurtured into such life – not in this world. Every culture (and institution, including the church) strives to socialize persons to live in harmony with life as it is. The culture calls upon its religious institutions to bless the status quo, and it calls upon religion's educational institutions to nurture persons into an acceptance of life as it is.

But God calls his/her people to be signs of Shalom, the vanguard of God's kingdom, a community of cultural change. To live in the conviction that such countercultural life is our Christian vocation in-but-not-of-the-world necessitates conversions as well as nurture.

Who but the converted can adequately nurture? And who but the nurtured can be adequately prepared for the radical nature of transformed life? Without the witness of Word-in-deed, which is evangelization, conversions cannot occur. Without assimilation, the converted cannot be adequately nurtured to bear witness in the world; without conversions and nurture, the church will have difficulty being the Church of Jesus Christ, the bearer of the Gospel in the world. Evangelization and assimilation both must be acknowledged as aspects of a faithful catechesis.

Catechesis focuses, therefore, on spiritual formation and the growth of persons and on the spiritual transformation and change of persons within a community of faith. Catechesis proclaims and explains the Gospel so that faith might be made conscious, living, and active. Catechesis as intentional enculturation is, therefore, a pastoral ministry producing continual change and assimilation, reform, and growth. Thus, catechetics, as one important dimension of practical theology, seeks to integrate liturgical, ascetical, moral, and pastoral aspects of the church's life with the church's authoritative tradition.

As I come to a close in this brief essay, I am aware of how much more needs to be said and how many questions and concerns remain. All I can hope is that these reflections will stimulate and provide some grounds for an ecumenical discussion. Only from that conversion will any of us discover a comprehensive theory and practice faithful to the Gospel and our times. And all I can do is express my gratitude for the opportunity to contribute an Anglican perspective on this essential task.

APPENDIX

READING 32

Apostolic Exhortation *Evangelii Nuntiandi* of His Holiness Pope Paul VI to the Episcopate, to the Clergy, and to All the Faithful of the Entire World December 8, 1975

On Evangelization in the Modern World

POPE PAUL VI

Venerable Brothers
and Dear Sons and Daughters:
Health and the Apostolic Blessing

Introduction

Special commitment
to evangelization

1. There is no doubt that the effort to proclaim the Gospel to the people of today, who are buoyed up by hope but at the same time often oppressed by fear and distress, is a service rendered to the Christian community and also to the whole of humanity.

For this reason the duty of confirming the brethren – a duty which with the office of being the Successor of Peter[1] we have received from the Lord, and which is for us a "daily preoccupation,"[2] a program of life and action, and a fundamental commitment of our Pontificate – seems to us all the more noble and necessary when it is a matter of encouraging our brethren in their mission as evangelizers, in order that, in this time of uncertainty and confusion, they may accomplish this task with ever increasing love, zeal and joy.

Reprinted from *Evangelii Nuntiandi* (1975); 1975 Publications Office, United States Catholic Conference, Washington, D.C. Used with permission.

On the occasion
of three events

2. This is precisely what we wish to do here, at the end of this Holy Year during which the Church, "striving to proclaim the Gospel to all people,"[3] has had the single aim of fulfilling her duty of being the messenger of the Good News of Jesus Christ – the Good News proclaimed through two fundamental commands: "Put on the new self"[4] and "Be reconciled to God."[5]

We wish to do so on this tenth anniversary of the closing of the Second Vatican Council, the objectives of which are definitively summed up in this single one: to make the Church of the twentieth century ever better fitted for proclaiming the Gospel to the people of the twentieth century.

We wish to do so one year after the Third General Assembly of the Synod of Bishops, which, as is well known, was devoted to evangelization; and we do so all the more willingly because it has been asked of us by the Synod Fathers themselves. In fact, at the end of that memorable Assembly, the Fathers decided to remit to the Pastor of the universal Church, with great trust and simplicity, the fruits of all their labors, stating that they awaited from him a fresh forward impulse, capable of creating, within a Church still more firmly rooted in the undying power and strength of Pentecost, a new period of evangelization.[6]

Theme frequently emphasized
in the course of our Pontificate

3. We have stressed the importance of this theme of evangelization on many occasions, well before the Synod took place. On 22 June 1973 we said to the Sacred College of Cardinals: "The conditions of the society in which we live oblige all of us therefore to revise methods, to seek by every means to study how we can bring the Christian message to modern man. For it is only in the Christian message that modern man can find the answer to his questions and energy for his commitment of human solidarity."[7] And we added that in order to give a valid answer to the demands of the Council which call for our attention, it is absolutely necessary for us to take into account a heritage of faith that the Church has the duty of preserving in its untouchable purity, and of presenting it to the people of our time, in a way that is as understandable and persuasive as possible.

In the line
of the 1974 Synod

4. This fidelity both to a message whose servants we are and to the people to whom we must transmit it living and intact is the central axis of evangelization. It poses three burning questions, which the 1974 Synod kept constantly in mind:

• In our day, what has happened to that hidden energy of the Good News, which is able to have a powerful effect on man's conscience?

• To what extent and in what way is that evangelical force capable of really transforming the people of this century?

• What methods should be followed in order that the power of the Gospel may have its effect?

Basically, these inquiries make explicit the fundamental question that the Church is asking herself today and which may be expressed in the following terms: after the Council and thanks to the Council, which was a time given her by God, at this turning point of history, does the Church or does she not find herself better equipped to proclaim the Gospel and to put it into people's hearts with conviction, freedom of spirit and effectiveness?

Invitation to meditation

5. We can all see the urgency of giving a loyal, humble and courageous answer to this question, and of acting accordingly.

In our "anxiety for all the Churches,"[8] we would like to help our Brethren and sons and daughters to reply to these inquiries. Our words come from the wealth of the Synod and are meant to be a meditation on evangelization. May they succeed in inviting the whole People of God assembled in the Church to make the same meditation; and may they give a fresh impulse to everyone, especially those "who are assiduous in preaching and teaching,"[9] so that each one of them may follow "a straight course in the message of the truth,"[10] and may work as a preacher of the Gospel and acquit himself perfectly of his ministry.

Such an exhortation seems to us to be of capital importance, for the presentation of the Gospel message is not an optional contribution for the Church. It is the duty incumbent on her by the command of the Lord Jesus, so that people can believe and be saved. This message is indeed necessary. It is unique. It cannot be replaced. It does not permit either indifference, syncretism or accommodation. It is a question of people's salvation. It is the beauty of the Revelation that it represents. It brings with it a wisdom that is not of this world. It is able to stir up by itself faith – faith that rests on the power of God.[11] It is truth. It merits having the apostle consecrate to it all his time and all his energies, and to sacrifice for it, if necessary, his own life.

I
From Christ the Evangelizer to the Evangelizing Church

Witness and mission of Jesus

6. The witness that the Lord gives of himself and that Saint Luke gathered together in his Gospel – "I must proclaim the Good News of the kingdom of God"[12] – without doubt has enormous consequences, for it sums up the whole mission of Jesus: "That is what I was sent to do."[13] These words take on their full significance if one links them with the previous verses, in which Christ has just applied to himself the words of the Prophet Isaiah: "The Spirit of the Lord has been given to me, for he has anointed me. He has sent me to bring the good news to the poor."[14]

Going from town to town, preaching to the poorest – and frequently the most receptive – the joyful news of the fulfillment of the promises and of the Covenant offered by God is the mission for which Jesus declares that he is sent by the Father. And all the aspects of his mystery – the Incarnation itself, his miracles, his teaching, the gathering together of the disciples, the sending out of the Twelve, the Cross and the Resurrection, the permanence of his presence in the midst of his own – were components of his evangelizing activity.

Jesus, the first Evangelizer

7. During the Synod, the Bishops very frequently referred to this truth: Jesus himself, the Good News of God,[15] was the very first and the greatest evangelizer; he was so through and through: to perfection and to the point of the sacrifice of his earthly life.

To evangelize: what meaning did this imperative have for Christ? It is certainly not easy to express in a complete synthesis the meaning, the content and the modes of evangelization as Jesus conceived it and put it into practice. In any case the attempt to make such a synthesis will never end. Let it suffice for us to recall a few essential aspects.

Proclamation of the Kingdom of God

8. As an evangelizer, Christ first of all proclaims a kingdom, the Kingdom of God; and this is so important that, by comparison, everything else becomes "the rest," which is "given in addition."[16] Only the Kingdom therefore is absolute, and it makes everything else relative. The Lord will delight in describing in many ways the happiness of belonging to this Kingdom (a paradoxical happiness which is made up of things that the world rejects),[17] the demands of the Kingdom and its Magna Charta,[18] the heralds of the Kingdom,[19] its mysteries,[20] its children,[21] the vigilance and fidelity demanded of whoever awaits its definitive coming.[22]

Proclamation of liberating salvation

9. As the kernel and center of his Good News, Christ proclaims salvation, this great gift of God which is liberation from everything that oppresses man but which is above all liberation from sin and the Evil One, in the joy of knowing God and being known by him, of seeing him, and of being given over to him. All of this is begun during the life of Christ and definitively accomplished by his death and Resurrection. But it must be patiently carried on during the course of history, in order to be realized fully on the day of the final coming of Christ, whose date is known to no one except the Father.[23]

At the price of crucifying effort

10. This Kingdom and this salvation, which are the key words of Jesus Christ's evangelization, are available to every human being as grace and mercy, and yet at the same time each individual must gain them by force—they belong to the violent, says the Lord,[24] through toil and suffering, through a life lived according to the Gospel, through abnegation and the Cross, through the spirit of the beatitudes. But above all each individual gains them through a total interior renewal

which the Gospel calls *metanoia;* it is a radical conversion, a profound change of mind and heart.[25]

Tireless preaching

11. Christ accomplished this proclamation of the Kingdom of God through the untiring preaching of a word which, it will be said, has no equal elsewhere: "Here is a teaching that is new, and with authority behind it."[26] "And he won the approval of all, and they were astonished by the gracious words that came from his lips."[27] "There has never been anybody who has spoken like him."[28] His words reveal the secret of God, his plan and his promise, and thereby change the heart of man and his destiny.

With evangelical signs

12. But Christ also carries out this proclamation by innumerable signs, which amaze the crowds and at the same time draw them to him in order to see him, listen to him and allow themselves to be transformed by him: the sick are cured, water is changed into wine, bread is multiplied, the dead come back to life. And among all these signs there is the one to which he attaches great importance: the humble and the poor are evangelized, become his disciples and gather together "in his name" in the great community of those who believe in him. For this Jesus who declared, "I must preach the Good News of the Kingdom of God,"[29] is the same Jesus of whom John the Evangelist said that he had come and was to die "to gather together in unity the scattered children of God."[30] Thus he accomplishes his revelation, completing it and confirming it by the entire revelation that he makes of himself, by words and deeds, by signs and miracles, and more especially by his death, by his Resurrection and by the sending of the Spirit of Truth.[31]

For an evangelized
and evangelizing community

13. Those who sincerely accept the Good News, through the power of this acceptance and of shared faith, therefore gather together in Jesus' name in order to seek together the Kingdom, build it up and live it. They make up a community which is in its turn evangelizing. The command to the Twelve to go out and proclaim the Good News is also valid for all Christians, though in a different way. It is precisely for this reason that Peter calls Christians "a people set apart to sing

the praises of God,"[32] those marvellous things that each one was able to hear in his own language.[33] Moreover, the Good News of the Kingdom which is coming and which has begun is meant for all people of all times. Those who have received the Good News and who have been gathered by it into the community of salvation can and must communicate and spread it.

Evangelization: vocation proper to the Church

14. The Church knows this. She has a vivid awareness of the fact that the Saviour's words, "I must proclaim the Good News of the kingdom of God,"[34] apply in all truth to herself. She willingly adds with Saint Paul: "Not that I boast of preaching the gospel, since it is a duty that has been laid on me; I should be punished if I did not preach it!"[35] It is with joy and consolation that at the end of the great Assembly of 1974 we heard these illuminating words: "We wish to confirm once more that the task of evangelizing all people constitutes the essential mission of the Church."[36] It is a task and mission which the vast and profound changes of present-day society make all the more urgent. Evangelizing is in fact the grace and vocation proper to the Church, her deepest identity. She exists in order to evangelize, that is to say in order to preach and teach, to be the channel of the gift of grace, to reconcile sinners with God, and to perpetuate Christ's sacrifice in the Mass, which is the memorial of his death and glorious Resurrection.

Reciprocal links between the Church and evangelization

15. Anyone who re-reads in the New Testament the origins of the Church, follows her history step by step and watches her live and act, sees that she is linked to evangelization in her most intimate being:

• The Church is born of the evangelizing activity of Jesus and the Twelve. She is the normal, desired, most immediate and most visible fruit of this activity: "Go, therefore, make disciples of all the nations."[37] Now, "they accepted what he said and were baptized. That very day about three thousand were added to their number. . . . Day by day the Lord added to their community those destined to be saved."[38]

• Having been born consequently out of being sent, the Church in her turn is sent by Jesus. The Church remains in the world when

the Lord of glory returns to the Father. She remains as a sign –
simultaneously obscure and luminous – of a new presence of Jesus, of
his departure and of his permanent presence. She prolongs and continues him. And it is above all his mission and his condition of being
an evangelizer that she is called upon to continue.[39] For the Christian
community is never closed in upon itself. The intimate life of this
community – the life of listening to the Word and the Apostles' teaching,
charity lived in a fraternal way, the sharing of bread[40] – this intimate
life only acquires its full meaning when it becomes a witness, when it
evokes admiration and conversion, and when it becomes the preaching
and proclamation of the Good News. Thus it is the whole Church that
receives the mission to evangelize, and the work of each individual
member is important for the whole.

• The Church is an evangelizer, but she begins by being evangelized herself. She is the community of believers, the community of hope
lived and communicated, the community of brotherly love; and she
needs to listen unceasingly to what she must believe, to her reasons
for hoping, to the new commandment of love. She is the People of God
immersed in the world, and often tempted by idols, and she always
needs to hear the proclamation of the "mighty works of God"[41] which
converted her to the Lord; she always needs to be called together afresh
by him and reunited. In brief, this means that she has a constant need
of being evangelized, if she wishes to retain freshness, vigor and
strength in order to proclaim the Gospel. The Second Vatican Council
recalled[42] and the 1974 Synod vigorously took up again this theme of
the Church which is evangelized by constant conversion and renewal,
in order to evangelize the world with credibility.

• The Church is the depositary of the Good News to be proclaimed.
The promises of the New Alliance in Jesus Christ, the teaching of the
Lord and the Apostles, the Word of life, the sources of grace and of
God's loving kindness, the path of salvation – all these things have been
entrusted to her. It is the content of the Gospel, and therefore of
evangelization, that she preserves as a precious living heritage, not in
order to keep it hidden but to communicate it.

• Having been sent and evangelized, the Church herself sends out
evangelizers. She puts on their lips the saving Word, she explains to
them the message of which she herself is the depositary, she gives them
the mandate which she herself has received, and she sends them out
to preach. To preach not their own selves or their personal ideas,[43] but
a Gospel of which neither she nor they are the absolute masters and
owners, to dispose of it as they wish, but a Gospel of which they are
the ministers, in order to pass it on with complete fidelity.

The Church,
inseparable from Christ

16. There is thus a profound link between Christ, the Church and evangelization. During the period of the Church that we are living in, it is she who has the task of evangelizing. This mandate is not accomplished without her, and still less against her.

It is certainly fitting to recall this fact at a moment like the present one when it happens that not without sorrow we can hear people – whom we wish to believe are well-intentioned but who are certainly misguided in their attitude – continually claiming to love Christ but without the Church, to listen to Christ but not the Church, to belong to Christ but outside the Church. The absurdity of this dichotomy is clearly evident in this phrase of the Gospel: "Anyone who rejects you rejects me."[44] And how can one wish to love Christ without loving the Church, if the finest witness to Christ is that of Saint Paul: "Christ loved the Church and sacrificed himself for her"?[45]

II
What is Evangelization?

Complexity
of evangelizing action

17. In the Church's evangelizing activity there are of course certain elements and aspects to be specially insisted on. Some of them are so important that there will be a tendency simply to identify them with evangelization. Thus it has been possible to define evangelization in terms of proclaiming Christ to those who do not know him, of preaching, of catechesis, of conferring Baptism and the other Sacraments.

Any partial and fragmentary definition which attempts to render the reality of evangelization in all its richness, complexity and dynamism does so only at the risk of impoverishing it and even of distorting it. It is impossible to grasp the concept of evangelization unless one tries to keep in view all its essential elements.

These elements were strongly emphasized at the last Synod, and are still the subject of frequent study, as a result of the Synod's work. We rejoice in the fact that these elements basically follow the lines of those transmitted to us by the Second Vatican Council, especially in *Lumen Gentium, Gaudium et Spes* and *Ad Gentes.*

Renewal of Humanity

18. For the Church, evangelizing means bringing the Good News into all the strata of humanity, and through its influence transforming humanity from within and making it new: "Now I am making the whole of creation new."[46] But there is no new humanity if there are not first of all new persons renewed by Baptism[47] and by lives lived according to the Gospel.[48] The purpose of evangelization is therefore precisely this interior change, and if it had to be expressed in one sentence the best way of stating it would be to say that the Church evangelizes when she seeks to convert,[49] solely through the divine power of the Message she proclaims, both the personal and collective consciences of people, the activities in which they engage, and the lives and concrete milieux which are theirs.

And of the strata of humanity

19. Strata of humanity which are transformed: for the Church it is a question not only of preaching the Gospel in ever wider geographic areas or to ever greater numbers of people, but also of affecting and as it were upsetting, through the power of the Gospel, mankind's criteria of judgment, determining values, points of interest, lines of thought, sources of inspiration and models of life, which are in contrast with the Word of God and the plan of salvation.

Evangelization of cultures

20. All this could be expressed in the following words: what matters is to evangelize man's culture and cultures (not in a purely decorative way as it were by applying a thin veneer, but in a vital way, in depth and right to their very roots), in the wide and rich sense which these terms have in *Gaudium et Spes*,[50] always taking the person as one's starting point and always coming back to the relationships of people among themselves and with God.

The Gospel, and therefore evangelization, are certainly not identical with culture, and they are independent in regard to all cultures. Nevertheless, the Kingdom which the Gospel proclaims is lived by men who are profoundly linked to a culture, and the building up of the Kingdom cannot avoid borrowing the elements of human culture or cultures. Though independent of cultures, the Gospel and evangelization are not necessarily incompatible with them; rather they are capable of permeating them all without becoming subject to any one of them.

The split between the Gospel and culture is without a doubt the drama of our time, just as it was of other times. Therefore every effort must be made to ensure a full evangelization of culture, or more correctly of cultures. They have to be regenerated by an encounter with the Gospel. But this encounter will not take place if the Gospel is not proclaimed.

Primary importance of witness of life

21. Above all the Gospel must be proclaimed by witness. Take a Christian or a handful of Christians who, in the midst of their own community, show their capacity for understanding and acceptance, their sharing of life and destiny with other people, their solidarity with the efforts of all for whatever is noble and good. Let us suppose that, in addition, they radiate in an altogether simple and unaffected way their faith in values that go beyond current values, and their hope in something that is not seen and that one would not dare to imagine. Through this wordless witness these Christians stir up irresistible questions in the hearts of those who see how they live: Why are they like this? Why do they live in this way? What or who is it that inspires them? Why are they in our midst? Such a witness is already a silent proclamation of the Good News and a very powerful and effective one. Here we have an initial act of evangelization. The above questions will perhaps be the first that many non-Christians will ask, whether they are people to whom Christ has never been proclaimed, or baptized people who do not practice, or people who live as nominal Christians but according to principles that are in no way Christian, or people who are seeking, and not without suffering, something or someone whom they sense but cannot name. Other questions will arise, deeper and more demanding ones, questions evoked by this witness which involves presence, sharing, solidarity, and which is an essential element, and generally the first one, in evangelization.[51]

All Christians are called to this witness, and in this way they can be real evangelizers. We are thinking especially of the responsibility incumbent on immigrants in the country that receives them.

Need of explicit proclamation

22. Nevertheless this always remains insufficient, because even the

finest witness will prove ineffective in the long run if it is not explained, justified – what Peter called always having "your answer ready for people who ask you the reason for the hope that you all have"[52] – and made explicit by a clear and unequivocal proclamation of the Lord Jesus. The Good News proclaimed by the witness of life sooner or later has to be proclaimed by the word of life. There is no true evangelization if the name, the teaching, the life, the promises, the Kingdom and the mystery of Jesus of Nazareth, the Son of God are not proclaimed. The history of the Church, from the discourse of Peter on the morning of Pentecost onwards, has been intermingled and identified with the history of this proclamation. At every new phase of human history, the Church, constantly gripped by the desire to evangelize, has but one preoccupation: whom to send to proclaim the mystery of Jesus? In what way is this mystery to be proclaimed? How can one ensure that it will resound and reach all those who should hear it? This proclamation – kerygma, preaching or catechesis – occupies such an important place in evangelization that it has often become synonymous with it; and yet it is only one aspect of evangelization.

For a vital
and community acceptance

23. In fact the proclamation only reaches full development when it is listened to, accepted and assimilated, and when it arouses a genuine adherence in the one who has thus received it. An adherence to the truths which the Lord in his mercy has revealed; still more, an adherence to a program of life – a life henceforth transformed – which he proposes. In a word, adherence to the Kingdom, that is to say the "new world," to the new state of things, to the new manner of being, of living, of living in community, which the Gospel inaugurates. Such an adherence, which cannot remain abstract and unincarnated, reveals itself concretely by a visible entry into a community of believers. Thus those whose life has been transformed enter a community which is itself a sign of transformation, a sign of newness of life: it is the Church, the visible sacrament of salvation.[53] But entry into the ecclesial community will in its turn be expressed through many other signs which prolong and unfold the sign of the Church. In the dynamism of evangelization, a person who accepts the Church as the Word which saves[54] normally translates it into the following sacramental acts: adherence to the Church, and acceptance of the Sacraments, which manifest and support this adherence through the grace which they confer.

Involving a
new apostolate

24. Finally: the person who has been evangelized goes on to evangelize others. Here lies the test of truth, the touchstone of evangelization: it is unthinkable that a person should accept the Word and give himself to the Kingdom without becoming a person who bears witness to it and proclaims it in his turn.

To complete these considerations on the meaning of evangelization, a final observation must be made, one which we consider will help to clarify the reflections that follow.

Evangelization, as we have said, is a complex process made up of varied elements: the renewal of humanity, witness, explicit proclamation, inner adherence, entry into the community, acceptance of signs, apostolic initiative. These elements may appear to be contradictory, indeed mutually exclusive. In fact they are complementary and mutually enriching. Each one must always be seen in relationship with the others. The value of the last Synod was to have constantly invited us to relate these elements rather than to place them in opposition one to the other, in order to reach a full understanding of the Church's evangelizing activity.

It is this global vision which we now wish to outline, by examining the content of evangelization and the methods of evangelizing and by clarifying to whom the Gospel message is addressed and who today is responsible for it.

III
The Content of Evangelization

Essential content
and secondary elements

25. In the message which the Church proclaims there are certainly many secondary elements. Their presentation depends greatly on changing circumstances. They themselves also change. But there is the essential content, the living substance, which cannot be modified or ignored without seriously diluting the nature of evangelization itself.

Witness given
to the Father's love

26. It is not superfluous to recall the following points: to evangelize

is first of all to bear witness, in a simple and direct way, to God revealed by Jesus Christ, in the Holy Spirit; to bear witness that in his Son God has loved the world – that in his Incarnate Word he has given being to all things and has called men to eternal life. Perhaps this attestation of God will be for many people the unknown God[55] whom they adore without giving him a name, or whom they seek by a secret call of the heart when they experience the emptiness of all idols. But it is fully evangelizing in manifesting the fact that for man the Creator is not an anonymous and remote power; he is the Father: ". . . that we should be called children of God; and so we are."[56] And thus we are one another's brothers and sisters in God.

At the center of the message: salvation in Jesus Christ

27. Evangelization will also always contain – as the foundation, center and at the same time summit of its dynamism – a clear proclamation that, in Jesus Christ, the Son of God made man, who died and rose from the dead, salvation is offered to all men, as a gift of God's grace and mercy.[57] And not an immanent salvation, meeting material or even spiritual needs, restricted to the framework of temporal existence and completely identified with temporal desires, hopes, affairs and struggles, but a salvation which exceeds all these limits in order to reach fulfillment in a communion with the one and only divine Absolute: a transcendent and eschatological salvation, which indeed has its beginning in this life but which is fulfilled in eternity.

Under the sign of hope

28. Consequently evangelization cannot but include the prophetic proclamation of a hereafter, man's profound and definitive calling, in both continuity and discontinuity with the present situation: beyond time and history, beyond the transient reality of this world, and beyond the things of this world, of which a hidden dimension will one day be revealed – beyond man himself, whose true destiny is not restricted to his temporal aspect but will be revealed in the future life.[58] Evangelization therefore also includes the preaching of hope in the promises made by God in the new Covenant in Jesus Christ, the preaching of God's love for us and of our love for God; the preaching of brotherly love for all men – the capacity of giving and forgiving, of self-denial, of helping one's brother and sister – which, springing from the love of God, is the kernel of the Gospel; the preaching of the mystery of evil and of the active search for good. The preaching likewise – and

this is always urgent—of the search for God himself through prayer which is principally that of adoration and thanksgiving, but also through communion with the visible sign of the encounter with God which is the Church of Jesus Christ; and this communion in its turn is expressed by the application of those other signs of Christ living and acting in the Church which are the Sacraments. To live the Sacraments in this way, bringing their celebration to a true fullness, is not, as some would claim, to impede or to accept a distortion of evangelization: it is rather to complete it. For in its totality, evangelization—over and above the preaching of a message—consists in the implantation of the Church, which does not exist without the driving force which is the sacramental life culminating in the Eucharist.[59]

Message touching life as a whole

29. But evangelization would not be complete if it did not take account of the unceasing interplay of the Gospel and of man's concrete life, both personal and social. This is why evangelization involves an explicit message, adapted to the different situations constantly being realized, about the rights and duties of every human being, about family life without which personal growth and development is hardly possible,[60] about life in society, about international life, peace, justice and development—a message especially energetic today about liberation.

A message of liberation

30. It is well known in what terms numerous Bishops from all the continents spoke of this at the last Synod, especially the Bishops from the Third World, with a pastoral accent resonant with the voice of the millions of sons and daughters of the Church who make up those peoples. Peoples, as we know, engaged with all their energy in the effort and struggle to overcome everything which condemns them to remain on the margin of life: famine, chronic disease, illiteracy, poverty, injustices in international relations and especially in commercial exchanges, situations of economic and cultural neo-colonialism sometimes as cruel as the old political colonialism. The Church, as the Bishops repeated, has the duty to proclaim the liberation of millions of human beings, many of whom are her own children—the duty of assisting the

birth of this liberation, of giving witness to it, of ensuring that it is complete. That is not foreign to evangelization.

Necessarily linked
to human advancement

31. Between evangelization and human advancement—development and liberation—there are in fact profound links. These include links of an anthropological order, because the man who is to be evangelized is not an abstract being but is subject to social and economic questions. They also include links in the theological order, since one cannot dissociate the plan of creation from the plan of Redemption. The latter plan touches the very concrete situations of injustice to be combatted and of justice to be restored. They include links of the eminently evangelical order, which is that of charity: how in fact can one proclaim the new commandment without promoting in justice and in peace the true, authentic advancement of man? We ourself have taken care to point this out, by recalling that it is impossible to accept "that in evangelization one could or should ignore the importance of the problems so much discussed today, concerning justice, liberation, development and peace in the world. This would be to forget the lesson which comes to us from the Gospel concerning love of our neighbor who is suffering and in need."[61]

The same voices which during the Synod touched on this burning theme with zeal, intelligence and courage have, to our great joy, furnished the enlightening principles for a proper understanding of the importance and profound meaning of liberation, such as it was proclaimed and achieved by Jesus of Nazareth and such as it is preached by the Church.

Without reduction
or ambiguity

•32. We must not ignore the fact that many, even generous Christians who are sensitive to the dramatic questions involved in the problem of liberation, in their wish to commit the Church to the liberation effort are frequently tempted to reduce her mission to the dimensions of a simply temporal project. They would reduce her aims to a man-centered goal; the salvation of which she is the messenger would be reduced to material well-being. Her activity, forgetful of all spiritual and religious preoccupation, would become initiatives of the political or social order. But if this were so, the Church would lose her fundamental meaning. Her message of liberation would no longer have any originality and would easily be open to monopolization and manipulation by ideological systems and political parties. She would have no more authority to proclaim freedom as in the name of God. This is why we have wished to emphasize, in the same address at the opening of the Synod, "the need to restate clearly the specifically religious finality of evangelization. This latter would lose its reason for existence if it were to diverge from the religious axis that guides it: the Kingdom of God, before anything else, in its fully theological meaning. . . ."[62]

Evangelical liberation

33. With regard to the liberation which evangelization proclaims and strives to put into practice one should rather say this:

• it cannot be contained in the simple and restricted dimension of economics, politics, social or cultural life; it must envisage the whole man, in all his aspects, right up to and including his openness to the absolute, even the divine Absolute;

• it is therefore attached to a certain concept of man, to a view of man which it can never sacrifice to the needs of any strategy, practice or short-term efficiency.

Centered on the Kingdom of God

34. Hence, when preaching liberation and associating herself with those who are working and suffering for it, the Church is certainly not willing to restrict her mission only to the religious field and dissociate herself from man's temporal problems. Nevertheless she reaffirms the primacy of her spiritual vocation and refuses to replace the proclamation of the Kingdom by the proclamation of forms of human liberation; she even states that her contribution to liberation is incomplete if she neglects to proclaim salvation in Jesus Christ.

On an evangelical concept of man

35. The Church links human liberation and salvation in Jesus Christ, but she never identifies them, because she knows through revelation, historical experience and the reflection of faith that not every notion of liberation is necessarily consistent and compatible with an evangelical vision of man, of things and of events; she knows too that in order that God's Kingdom should come it is not enough to establish liberation and to create well-being and development.

And what is more, the Church has the firm conviction that all temporal liberation, all political liberation – even if it endeavors to find its justification in such or such a page of the Old or New Testament, even if it claims for its ideological postulates and its norms of action theological data and conclusions, even if it pretends to be today's theology – carries within itself the germ of its own negation and fails to reach the ideal that it proposes for itself, whenever its profound motives are not those of justice in charity, whenever its zeal lacks a truly spiritual dimension and whenever its final goal is not salvation and happiness in God.

Involving
a necessary conversion

36. The Church considers it to be undoubtedly important to build up structures which are more human, more just, more respectful of the rights of the person and less oppressive and less enslaving, but she is conscious that the best structures and the most idealized systems soon become inhuman if the inhuman inclinations of the human heart are not made wholesome, if those who live in these structures or who rule them do not undergo a conversion of heart and of outlook.

Excluding violence

37. The Church cannot accept violence, especially the force of arms – which is uncontrollable once it is let loose – and indiscriminate death as the path to liberation, because she knows that violence always provokes violence and irresistibly engenders new forms of oppression and enslavement which are often harder to bear than those from which they claimed to bring freedom. We said this clearly during our journey in Colombia: "We exhort you not to place your trust in violence and revolution: that is contrary to the Christian spirit, and it can also delay instead of advancing that social uplifting to which you lawfully aspire."[63] "We must say and reaffirm that violence is not in accord with the Gospel, that it is not Christian; and that sudden or violent changes of structures would be deceitful, ineffective of themselves, and certainly not in conformity with the dignity of the people"[64]

Specific contribution
of the Church

38. Having said this, we rejoice that the Church is becoming ever more conscious of the proper manner and strictly evangelical means

that she possesses in order to collaborate in the liberaton of many. And what is she doing? She is trying more and more to encourage large numbers of Christians to devote themselves to the liberation of men. She is providing these Christian "liberators" with the inspiration of faith, the motivation of fraternal love, a social teaching which the true Christian cannot ignore and which he must make the foundation of his wisdom and of his experience in order to translate it concretely into forms of action, participation and commitment. All this must characterize the spirit of a committed Christian, without confusion with tactical attitudes or with the service of a political system. The Church strives always to insert the Christian struggle for liberation into the universal plan of salvation which she herself proclaims.

What we have just recalled comes out more than once in the Synod debates. In fact we devoted to this theme a few clarifying words in our address to the Fathers at the end of the Assembly.[65]

It is to be hoped that all these considerations will help to remove the ambiguity which the word "liberation" very often takes on in ideologies, political systems or groups. The liberation which evangelization proclaims and prepares is the one which Christ himself announced and gave to man by his sacrifice.

Religious liberty

39. The necessity of ensuring fundamental human rights cannot be separated from this just liberation which is bound up with evangelization and which endeavors to secure structures safeguarding human freedoms. Among these fundamental human rights, religious liberty occupies a place of primary importance. We recently spoke of the relevance of this matter, emphasizing "how many Christians still today, because they are Christians, because they are Catholics, live oppressed by systematic persecution! The drama of fidelity to Christ and of the freedom of religion continues, even if it is disguised by categorical declarations in favor of the rights of the person and of life in society!"[66]

IV
The Methods of Evangelization

Search
for suitable means

40. The obvious importance of the content of evangelization must not overshadow the importance of the ways and means.

This question of "how to evangelize" is permanently relevant, because the methods of evangelizing vary according to the different circumstances of time, place and culture, and because they thereby present a certain challenge to our capacity for discovery and adaptation.

On us particularly, the pastors of the Church, rests the responsibility for reshaping with boldness and wisdom, but in complete fidelity to the content of evangelization, the means that are most suitable and effective for communicating the Gospel message to the men and women of our times.

Let it suffice, in this meditation, to mention a number of methods which, for one reason or another, have a fundamental importance.

The witness of life

41. Without repeating everything that we have already mentioned, it is appropriate first of all to emphasize the following point: for the Church, the first means of evangelization is the witness of an authentically Christian life, given over to God in a communion that nothing should destroy and at the same time given to one's neighbor with limitless zeal. As we said recently to a group of lay people, "Modern man listens more willingly to witnesses than to teachers, and if he does listen to teachers, it is because they are witnesses."[67] Saint Peter expressed this well when he held up the example of a reverent and chaste life that wins over even without a word those who refuse to obey the word.[68] It is therefore primarily by her conduct and by her life that the Church will evangelize the world, in other words, by her living witness of fidelity to the Lord Jesus – the witness of poverty and detachment, of freedom in the face of the powers of this world, in short, the witness of sanctity.

A living preaching

42. Secondly, it is not superfluous to emphasize the importance and necessity of preaching. "And how are they to believe in him of whom they have never heard? And how are they to hear without a preacher? . . . So faith comes from what is heard and what is heard comes by the preaching of Christ."[69] This law once laid down by the Apostle Paul maintains its full force today.

Preaching, the verbal proclamation of a message, is indeed always indispensable. We are well aware that modern man is sated by talk; he is obviously often tired of listening and, what is worse, impervious to words. We are also aware that many psychologists and sociologists express the view that modern man has passed beyond the civilization of the word, which is now ineffective and useless, and that today he lives in the civilization of the image. These facts should certainly impel us to employ, for the purpose of transmitting the Gospel message, the modern means which this civilization has produced. Very positive efforts have in fact already been made in this sphere. We cannot but praise them and encourage their further development. The fatigue produced these days by so much empty talk and the relevance of many other forms of communication must not however diminish the permanent power of the word, or cause a loss of confidence in it. The word remains ever relevant, especially when it is the bearer of the power of God.[70] This is why Saint Paul's axiom, "Faith comes from what is heard,"[71] also retains its relevance: it is the Word that is heard which leads to belief.

Liturgy
of the Word

43. This evangelizing preaching takes on many forms, and zeal will inspire the reshaping of them almost indefinitely. In fact there are innumerable events in life and human situations which offer the opportunity for a discreet but incisive statement of what the Lord has to say in this or that particular circumstance. It suffices to have true spiritual sensitivity for reading God's message in events. But at a time when the liturgy renewed by the Council has given greatly increased value to the Liturgy of the Word, it would be a mistake not to see in the homily an important and very adaptable instrument of evangelization. Of course it is necessary to know and put to good use the exigencies and the possibilities of the homily, so that it can acquire all its pastoral effectiveness. But above all it is necessary to be convinced of this and to devote oneself to it with love. This preaching, inserted in a unique way into the Eucharistic celebration, from which it receives special force and vigor, certainly has a particular role in evangelization, to the extent that it expresses the profound faith of the sacred minister and is impregnated with love. The faithful assembled as a Paschal Church, celebrating the feast of the Lord present in their midst, expect much from this preaching, and will greatly benefit from it provided that it is simple, clear, direct, well-adapted, profoundly dependent on Gospel teaching and faithful to the Magisterium, animated by a balanced apostolic ardor coming from its own characteristic nature, full of hope, fostering belief, and productive of peace and unity. Many

parochial or other communities live and are held together thanks to the Sunday homily, when it possesses these qualities.

Let us add that, thanks to the same liturgical renewal, the Eucharistic celebration is not the only appropriate moment for the homily. The homily has a place and must not be neglected in the celebration of all the Sacraments, at paraliturgies, and in assemblies of the faithful. It will always be a privileged occasion for communicating the Word of the Lord.

Catechetics

44. A means of evangelization that must not be neglected is that of catechetical instruction. The intelligence, especially that of children and young people, needs to learn through systematic religious instruction the fundamental teachings, the living content of the truth which God has wished to convey to us and which the Church has sought to express in an ever richer fashion during the course of her long history. No one will deny that this instruction must be given to form patterns of Christian living and not to remain only notional. Truly the effort for evangelization will profit greatly – at the level of catechetical instruction given at church, in the schools, where this is possible, and in every case in Christian homes – if those giving catechetical instruction have suitable texts, updated with wisdom and competence, under the authority of the Bishops. The methods must be adapted to the age, culture and aptitude of the persons concerned; they must seek always to fix in the memory, intelligence and heart the essential truths that must impregnate all of life. It is necessary above all to prepare good instructors – parochial catechists, teachers, parents – who are desirous of perfecting themselves in this superior art, which is indispensable and requires religious instruction. Moreover, without neglecting in any way the training of children, one sees that present conditions render ever more urgent catechetical instruction, under the form of the catechumenate, for innumerable young people and adults who, touched by grace, discover little by little the face of Christ and feel the need of giving themselves to him.

Utilization
of the mass media

45. Our century is characterized by the mass media or means of social communication, and the first proclamation, catechesis or the further deepening of faith cannot do without these means, as we have already emphasized.

When they are put at the service of the Gospel, they are capable of increasing almost indefinitely the area in which the Word of God is heard; they enable the Good News to reach millions of people. The Church would feel guilty before the Lord if she did not utilize these powerful means that human skill is daily rendering more perfect. It is through them that she proclaims "from the housetops"[72] the message of which she is the depository. In them she finds a modern and effective version of the pulpit. Thanks to them she succeeds in speaking to the multitudes.

Nevertheless the use of the means of social communication for evangelization presents a challenge: through them the evangelical message should reach vast numbers of people, but with the capacity of piercing the conscience of each individual, of implanting itself in his heart as though he were the only person being addressed, with all his most individual and personal qualities, and evoke an entirely personal adherence and commitment.

Indispensable personal contact

46. For this reason, side-by-side with the collective proclamation of the Gospel, the other form of transmission, the person-to-person one, remains valid and important. The Lord often used it (for example with Nicodemus, Zacchaeus, the Samaritan woman, Simon the Pharisee), and so did the Apostles. In the long run, is there any other way of handing on the Gospel than by transmitting to another person one's personal experience of faith? It must not happen that the pressing need to proclaim the Good News to the multitudes should cause us to forget this form of proclamation whereby an individual's personal conscience is reached and touched by an entirely unique word that he receives from someone else. We can never sufficiently praise those priests who through the Sacrament of Penance or through pastoral dialogue show their readiness to guide people in the ways of the Gospel, to support them in their efforts, to raise them up if they have fallen, and always to assist them with discernment and availability.

Role of the Sacraments

47. Yet, one can never sufficiently stress the fact that evangelization does not consist only of the preaching and teaching of a doctrine. For evangelization must touch life: the natural life to which it gives

a new meaning, thanks to the evangelical perspectives that it reveals; and the supernatural life, which is not the negation but the purification and elevation of the natural life.

This supernatural life finds its living expression in the seven Sacraments and in the admirable radiation of grace and holiness which they possess.

Evangelization thus exercises its full capacity when it achieves the most intimate relationship, or better still a permanent and unbroken intercommunication, between the Word and the Sacraments. In a certain sense it is a mistake to make a contrast between evangelization and sacramentalization, as is sometimes done. It is indeed true that a certain way of administering the Sacraments, without the solid support of catechesis regarding these same Sacraments and a global catechesis, could end up by depriving them of their effectiveness to a great extent. The role of evangelization is precisely to educate people in the faith in such a way as to lead each individual Christian to live the Sacraments as true Sacraments of faith — and not to receive them passively or to undergo them.

Popular piety

48. Here we touch upon an aspect of evangelization which cannot leave us insensitive. We wish to speak about what today is often called popular religiosity.

One finds among the people particular expressions of the search for God and for faith, both in the regions where the Church has been established for centuries and where she is in the course of becoming established. These expressions were for a long time regarded as less pure and were sometimes despised, but today they are almost everywhere being rediscovered. During the last Synod the Bishops studied their significance with remarkable pastoral realism and zeal.

Popular religiosity of course certainly has its limits. It is often subject to penetration by many distortions of religion and even superstitions. It frequently remains at the level of forms of worship not involving a true acceptance by faith. It can even lead to the creation of sects and endanger the true ecclesial community.

But if it is well oriented, above all by a pedagogy of evangelization, it is rich in values. It manifests a thirst for God which only the simple and poor can know. It makes people capable of generosity and sacrifice even to the point of heroism, when it is a question of manifesting belief. It involves an acute awareness of profound attributes of God: fatherhood, providence, loving and constant presence. It engenders interior attitudes rarely observed to the same degree elsewhere: patience, the sense of the Cross in daily life, detachment, openness to others, devotion. By reason of these aspects, we readily call it "popular piety," that is, religion of the people, rather than religiosity.

Pastoral charity must dictate to all those whom the Lord has placed as leaders of the ecclesial communities the proper attitude in regard to this reality, which is at the same time so rich and so vulnerable. Above all one must be sensitive to it, know how to perceive its interior dimensions and undeniable values, be ready to help it to overcome its risks of deviation. When it is well oriented, this popular religiosity can be more and more for multitudes of our people a true encounter with God in Jesus Christ.

V
The Beneficiaries of Evangelization

Addressed to everyone

49. Jesus' last words in Saint Mark's Gospel confer on the evangelization which the Lord entrusts to his Apostles a limitless universality: "Go out to the whole world; proclaim the Good News to all creation."[73]

The Twelve and the first generation of Christians understood well the lesson of this text and other similar ones; they made them into a program of action. Even persecution, by scattering the Apostles, helped to spread the Word and to establish the Church in ever more distant regions. The admission of Paul to the rank of the Apostles and his charism as the preacher to the pagans (the non-Jews) of Jesus' Coming underlined this universality still more.

Despite all the obstacles

50. In the course of twenty centuries of history, the generations of Christians have periodically faced various obstacles to this universal mission. On the one hand, on the part of the evangelizers themselves, there has been the temptation for various reasons to narrow down the field of their missionary activity. On the other hand, there has been the often humanly insurmountable resistance of the people being addressed by the evangelizer. Furthermore, we must note with sadness

that the evangelizing work of the Church is strongly opposed, if not prevented, by certain public powers. Even in our own day it happens that preachers of God's Word are deprived of their rights, persecuted, threatened or eliminated solely for preaching Jesus Christ and his Gospel. But we are confident that despite these painful trials the activity of these apostles will never meet final failure in any part of the world.

Despite such adversities the Church constantly renews her deepest inspiration, that which comes to her directly from the Lord: To the whole world! To all creation! Right to the ends of the earth! She did this once more at the last Synod, as an appeal not to imprison the proclamation of the Gospel by limiting it to one sector of mankind or to one class of people or to a single type of civilization. Some examples are revealing.

First proclamation
to those who are far off

51. To reveal Jesus Christ and his Gospel to those who do not know them has been, ever since the morning of Pentecost, the fundamental program which the Church has taken on as received from her Founder. The whole of the New Testament, and in a special way the Acts of the Apostles, bears witness to a privileged and in a sense exemplary moment of this missionary effort which will subsequently leave its mark on the whole history of the Church.

She carries out this first proclamation of Jesus Christ by a complex and diversified activity which is sometimes termed "pre-evangelization" but which is already evangelization in a true sense, although at its initial and still incomplete stage. An almost indefinite range of means can be used for this purpose: explicit preaching, of course, but also art, the scientific approach, philosophical research and legitimate recourse to the sentiments of the human heart.

Renewed proclamation
to a dechristianized world

52. This first proclamation is addressed especially to those who have never heard the Good News of Jesus, or to children. But, as a result of the frequent situations of dechristianization in our day, it also proves equally necessary for innumerable people who have been baptized but who live quite outside Christian life, for simple people who have a certain faith but an imperfect knowledge of the foundations of that faith, for intellectuals who feel the need to know Jesus Christ in

a light different from the instruction they received as children, and for many others.

Non-Christian religions

53. This first proclamation is also addressed to the immense sections of mankind who practice non-Christian religions. The Church respects and esteems these non-Christian religions because they are the living expression of the soul of vast groups of people. They carry within them the echo of thousands of years of searching for God, a quest which is incomplete but often made with great sincerity and righteousness of heart. They possess an impressive patrimony of deeply religious texts. They have taught generations of people how to pray. They are all impregnated with innumerable "seeds of the Word"[74] and can constitute a true "preparation for the Gospel,"[75] to quote a felicitous term used by the Second Vatican Council and borrowed from Eusebius of Caesarea.

Such a situation certainly raises complex and delicate questions that must be studied in the light of Christian Tradition and the Church's Magisterium, in order to offer to the missionaries of today and of tomorrow new horizons in their contacts with non-Christian religions. We wish to point out, above all today, that neither respect and esteem for these religions nor the complexity of the questions raised is an invitation to the Church to withhold from these non-Christians the proclamation of Jesus Christ. On the contrary the Church holds that these multitudes have the right to know the riches of the mystery of Christ[76] – riches in which we believe that the whole of humanity can find, in unsuspected fullness, everything that it is gropingly searching for concerning God, man and his destiny, life and death, and truth. Even in the face of natural religious expressions most worthy of esteem, the Church finds support in the fact that the religion of Jesus, which she proclaims through evangelization, objectively places man in relation with the plan of God, with his living presence and with his action; she thus causes an encounter with the mystery of divine paternity that bends over towards humanity. In other words, our religion effectively establishes with God an authentic and living relationship which the other religions do not succeed in doing, even though they have, as it were, their arms stretched out towards heaven.

This is why the Church keeps her missionary spirit alive, and even wishes to intensify it in the moment of history in which we are living.

She feels responsible before entire peoples. She has no rest so long as she has not done her best to proclaim the Good News of Jesus the Saviour. She is always preparing new generations of apostles. Let us state this fact with joy at a time when there are not lacking those who think and even say that ardor and the apostolic spirit are exhausted, and that the time of the missions is now past. The Synod has replied that the missionary proclamation never ceases and that the Church will always be striving for the fulfillment of this proclamation.

Support for the faith
of believers

54. Nevertheless the Church does not feel dispensed from paying unflagging attention also to those who have received the faith and who have been in contact with the Gospel often for generations. Thus she seeks to deepen, consolidate, nourish and make ever more mature the faith of those who are already called the faithful or believers, in order that they may be so still more.

This faith is nearly always today exposed to secularism, even to militant atheism. It is a faith exposed to trials and threats, and even more, a faith besieged and actively opposed. It runs the risk of perishing from suffocation or starvation if it is not fed and sustained each day. To evangelize must therefore very often be to give this necessary food and sustenance to the faith of believers, especially through a catechesis full of Gospel vitality and in a language suited to people and circumstances.

The Church also has a lively solicitude for the Christians who are not in full communion with her. While preparing with them the unity willed by Christ, and precisely in order to realize unity in truth, she has the consciousness that she would be gravely lacking in her duty if she did not give witness before them of the fullness of the revelation whose deposit she guards.

Non-believers

55. Also significant is the preoccupation of the last Synod in regard to two spheres which are very different from one another but which at the same time are very close by reason of the challenge which they make to evangelization, each in its own way.

The first sphere is the one which can be called the increase of unbelief in the modern world. The Synod endeavored to describe this modern world: how many currents of thought, values and counter-values, latent aspirations or seeds of destruction, old convictions which disappear and new convictions which arise are covered by this generic name!

From the spiritual point of view, the modern world seems to be for ever immersed in what a modern author has termed "the drama of atheistic humanism."[77]

On the one hand one is forced to note in the very heart of this contemporary world the phenomenon which is becoming almost its most striking characteristic: secularism. We are not speaking of secularization, which is the effort, in itself just and legitimate and in no way incompatible with faith or religion, to discover in creation, in each thing or each happening in the universe, the laws which regulate them with a certain autonomy, but with the inner conviction that the Creator has placed these laws there. The last Council has in this sense affirmed the legitimate autonomy of culture and particularly of the sciences.[78] Here we are thinking of a true secularism: a concept of the world according to which the latter is self-explanatory, without any need for recourse to God, who thus becomes superfluous and an encumbrance. This sort of secularism, in order to recognize the power of man, therefore ends up by doing without God and even by denying him.

New forms of atheism seem to flow from it: a man-centered atheism, no longer abstract and metaphysical but pragmatic, systematic and militant. Hand in hand with this atheistic secularism, we are daily faced, under the most diverse forms, with a consumer society, the pursuit of pleasure set up as the supreme value, a desire for power and domination, and discrimination of every kind: the inhuman tendencies of this "humanism."

In this same modern world, on the other hand, and this is a paradox, one cannot deny the existence of real stepping-stones to Christianity, and of evangelical values at least in the form of a sense of emptiness or nostalgia. It would not be an exaggeration to say that there exists a powerful and tragic appeal to be evangelized.

The non-practicing

56. The second sphere is that of those who do not practice. Today there is a very large number of baptized people who for the most part have not formally renounced their Baptism but who are entirely indifferent to it and not living in accordance with it. The phenomenon of the non-practicing is a very ancient one in the history of Christianity; it is the result of a natural weakness, a profound inconsistency which we unfortunately bear deep within us. Today however it shows certain new characteristics. It is often the result of the uprooting typical

of our time. It also springs from the fact that Christians live in close proximity with nonbelievers and constantly experience the effects of unbelief. Furthermore, the non-practicing Christians of today, more so than those of previous periods, seek to explain and justify their position in the name of an interior religion, of personal independence or authenticity.

Thus we have atheists and unbelievers on the one side and those who do not practice on the other, and both groups put up a considerable resistance to evangelization. The resistance of the former takes the form of a certain refusal and an inability to grasp the new order of things, the new meaning of the world, of life and of history; such is not possible if one does not start from a divine absolute. The resistance of the second group takes the form of inertia and the slightly hostile attitude of the person who feels that he is one of the family, who claims to know it all and to have tried it all and who no longer believes it.

Atheistic secularism and the absence of religious practice are found among adults and among the young, among the leaders of society and among the ordinary people, at all levels of education, and in both the old Churches and the young ones. The Church's evangelizing action cannot ignore these two worlds, nor must it come to a standstill when faced with them; it must constantly seek the proper means and language for presenting, or re-presenting, to them God's revelation and faith in Jesus Christ.

Proclamation to the multitudes

57. Like Christ during the time of his preaching, like the Twelve on the morning of Pentecost, the Church too sees before her an immense multitude of people who need the Gospel and have a right to it, for God "wants everyone to be saved and reach full knowledge of the truth."[79]

The Church is deeply aware of her duty to preach salvation to all. Knowing that the Gospel message is not reserved to a small group of the initiated, the privileged or the elect but is destined for everyone, she shares Christ's anguish at the sight of the wandering and exhausted crowds "like sheep without a shepherd" and she often repeats his words: "I feel sorry for all these people."[80] But the Church is also conscious of the fact that, if the preaching of the Gospel is to be effective, she must address her message to the heart of the multitudes, to communities of the faithful whose action can and must reach others.

Ecclesial
communautes de base

58. The last Synod devoted considerable attention to these "small communities," or *communautés de base*, because they· are often talked about in the Church today. What are they, and why should they be the special beneficiaries of evangelization and at the same time evangelizers themselves?

According to the various statements heard in the Synod, such communities flourish more or less throughout the Church. They differ greatly among themselves, both within the same region and even more so from one region to another.

In some regions they appear and develop, almost without exception, within the Church, having solidarity with her life, being nourished by her teaching and united with her pastors. In these cases, they spring from the need to live the Church's life more intensely, or from the desire and quest for a more human dimension such as larger ecclesial communities can only offer with difficulty, especially in the big modern cities which lend themselves both to life in the mass and to anonymity. Such communities can quite simply be in their own way an extension on the spiritual and religious level – worship, deepening of faith, fraternal charity, prayer, contact with pastors – of the small sociological community such as the village, etc. Or again their aim may be to bring together, for the purpose of listening to and meditating on the Word, for the Sacraments and the bond of the agape, groups of people who are linked by age, culture, civil state or social situation: married couples, young people, professional people, etc., people who already happen to be united in the struggle for justice, brotherly aid to the poor, human advancement. In still other cases they bring Christians together in places where the shortage of priests does not favor the normal life of a parish community. This is all presupposed within communities constituted by the Church, especially individual Churches and parishes.

In other regions, on the other hand, *communautés de base* come together in a spirit of bitter criticism of the Church, which they are quick to stigmatize as "institutional" and to which they set themselves up in opposition as charismatic communities, free from structures and inspired only by the Gospel. Thus their obvious characteristic is an attitude of fault-finding and of rejection with regard to the Church's outward manifestations: her hierarchy, her signs. They are radically opposed to the Church. By following these lines their main inspiration very quickly becomes ideological, and it rarely happens that they do not quickly fall victim to some political option or current of thought, and then to a system, even a party, with all the attendant risks of becoming its instrument.

The difference is already notable: the communities which by their spirit of opposition cut themselves off from the Church, and whose unity they wound, can well be called *communautés de base*, but in this case it is a strictly sociological name. They could not, without a misuse of terms, be called ecclesial *communautés de base*, even if, while being hostile to the hierarchy, they claim to remain within the unity of the Church. This name belongs to the other groups, those which come together within the Church in order to unite themselves to the Church and to cause the Church to grow.

These latter communities will be a place of evangelization, for the benefit of the bigger communities, especially the individual Churches. And, as we said at the end of the last Synod, they will be a hope for the universal Church to the extent:

• that they seek their nourishment in the Word of God and do not allow themselves to be ensnared by political polarization or fashionable ideologies, which are ready to exploit their immense human potential;

• that they avoid the ever present temptation of systematic protest and a hypercritical attitude, under the pretext of authenticity and a spirit of collaboration;

• that they remain firmly attached to the local Church in which they are inserted, and to the universal Church, thus avoiding the very real danger of becoming isolated within themselves, then of believing themselves to be the only authentic Church of Christ, and hence of condemning the other ecclesial communities;

• that they maintain a sincere communion with the pastors whom the Lord gives to his Church, and with the Magisterium which the Spirit of Christ has entrusted to these pastors;

• that they never look on themselves as the sole beneficiaries or sole agents of evangelization – or even the only depositaries of the Gospel – but, being aware that the Church is much more vast and diversified, accept the fact that this Church becomes incarnate in other ways than through themselves;

• that they constantly grow in missionary consciousness, fervor, commitment and zeal;

• that they show themselves to be universal in all things and never sectarian.

On these conditions, which are certainly demanding but also up-lifting, the ecclesial *communautés de base* will correspond to their most fundamental vocation: as hearers of the Gospel which is proclaimed to them and privileged beneficiaries of evangelization, they will soon become proclaimers of the Gospel themselves.

VI
The Workers for Evangelization

The Church:
missionary in her entirety

59. If people proclaim in the world the Gospel of salvation, they do so by the command of, in the name of and with the grace of Christ the Saviour. "They will never have a preacher unless one is sent,"[81] wrote he who was without doubt one of the greatest evangelizers. No one can do it without having been sent.

But who then has the mission of evangelizing?

The Second Vatican Council gave a clear reply to this question: it is upon the Church that "there rests, by divine mandate, the duty of going out into the whole world and preaching the gospel to every creature."[82] And in another text: ". . . the whole Church is missionary, and the work of evangelization is a basic duty of the People of God."[83]

We have already mentioned this intimate connection between the Church and evangelization. While the Church is proclaiming the Kingdom of God and building it up, she is establishing herself in the midst of the world as the sign and instrument of this Kingdom which is and which is to come. The Council repeats the following expression of Saint Augustine on the missionary activity of the Twelve: "They preached the word of truth and brought forth Churches."[84]

An ecclesial act

60. The observation that the Church has been sent out and given a mandate to evangelize the world should awaken in us two convictions.

The first is this: evangelization is for no one an individual and isolated act; it is one that is deeply ecclesial. When the most obscure preacher, catechist or pastor in the most distant land preaches the Gospel, gathers his little community together or administers a Sacrament, even alone, he is carrying out an ecclesial act, and his action is certainly attached to the evangelizing activity of the whole Church by institutional relationships, but also by profound invisible links in the order of grace. This presupposes that he acts not in virtue of a mission which he attributes to himself or by a personal inspiration, but in union with the mission of the Church and in her name.

From this flows the second conviction: if each individual evangelizes in the name of the Church, who herself does so by virtue of a mandate from the Lord, no evangelizer is the absolute master of his evangelizing action, with a discretionary power to carry it out in accordance with individualistic criteria and perspectives; he acts in communion with the Church and her pastors.

We have remarked that the Church is entirely and completely evangelizing. This means that, in the whole world and in each part of the world where she is present, the Church feels responsible for the task of spreading the Gospel.

The perspective
of the universal Church

61. Brothers and sons and daughters, at this stage of our reflection, we wish to pause with you at a question which is particularly important at the present time. In the celebration of the liturgy, in their witness before judges and executioners and in their apologetical texts, the first Christians readily expressed their deep faith in the Church by describing her as being spread throughout the universe. They were fully conscious of belonging to a large community which neither space nor time can limit: "From the just Abel right to the last of the elect,"[85] "indeed to the ends of the earth,"[86] "to the end of time."[87]

This is how the Lord wanted his Church to be: universal, a great tree whose branches shelter the birds of the air,[88] a net which catches fish of every kind[89] or which Peter drew in filled with one hundred and fifty-three big fish,[90] a flock which a single shepherd pastures.[91] A universal Church without boundaries or frontiers except, alas, those of the heart and mind of sinful man.

The perspective
of the individual Church

62. Nevertheless this universal Church is in practice incarnate in the individual Churches made up of such or such an actual part of mankind, speaking such and such a language, heirs of a cultural patrimony, of a vision of the world, of an historical past, of a particular human substratum. Receptivity to the wealth of the individual Church corresponds to a special sensitivity of modern man.

Let us be very careful not to conceive of the universal Church as the sum, or, if one can say so, the more or less anomalous federation of essentially different individual Churches. In the mind of the Lord the Church is universal by vocation and mission, but when she puts down her roots in a variety of cultural, social and human terrains, she takes on different external expressions and appearances in each part of the world.

Thus each individual Church that would voluntarily cut itself off from the universal Church would lose its relationship to God's plan and would be impoverished in its ecclesial dimension. But, at the same time, a Church *toto orbe diffusa* would become an abstraction if she did not take body and life precisely through the individual Churches. Only continual attention to these two poles of the Church will enable us to perceive the richness of this relationship between the universal Church and the individual Churches.

Adaptation and fidelity in expression

63. The individual Churches, intimately built up not only of people but also of aspirations, of riches and limitations, of ways of praying, of loving, of looking at life and the world which distinguish this or that human gathering, have the task of assimilating the essence of the Gospel message and of transposing it, without the slightest betrayal of its essential truth, into the language that these particular people understand, then of proclaiming it in this language.

The transposition has to be done with the discernment, seriousness, respect and competence which the matter calls for in the field of liturgical expression,[92] and in the areas of catechesis, theological formulation, secondary ecclesial structures, and ministries. And the word "language" should be understood here less in the semantic or literary sense than in the sense which one may call anthropological and cultural.

The question is undoubtedly a delicate one. Evangelization loses much of its force and effectiveness if it does not take into consideration the actual people to whom it is addressed, if it does not use their language, their signs and symbols, if it does not answer the questions they ask, and if it does not have an impact on their concrete life. But on the other hand evangelization risks losing its power and disappearing altogether if one empties or adulterates its content under the pretext of translating it; if, in other words, one sacrifices this reality and destroys the unity without which there is no universality, out of a wish to adapt a universal reality to a local situation. Now, only a Church which preserves the awareness of her universality and shows that she is in fact universal is capable of having a message which can be heard by all, regardless of regional frontiers.

Legitimate attention to individual Churches cannot fail to enrich the Church. Such attention is indispensable and urgent. It responds to the very deep aspirations of peoples and human communities to find their own identity ever more clearly.

Openness
to the universal Church

64. But this enrichment requires that the individual Churches should keep their profound openness towards the universal Church. It is quite remarkable, moreover, that the most simple Christians, the ones who are most faithful to the Gospel and most open to the true meaning of the Church, have a completely spontaneous sensitivity to this universal dimension. They instinctively and very strongly feel the need for it, they easily recognize themselves in such a dimension. They feel with it and suffer very deeply within themselves when, in the name of theories which they do not understand, they are forced to accept a Church deprived of this universality, a regionalist Church, with no horizon.

As history in fact shows, whenever an individual Church has cut itself off from the universal Church and from its living and visible center – sometimes with the best of intentions, with theological, sociological, political or pastoral arguments, or even in the desire for a certain freedom of movement or action – it has escaped only with great difficulty (if indeed it has escaped) from two equally serious dangers. The first danger is that of a withering isolationism, and then, before long, of a crumbling away, with each of its cells breaking away from it just as it itself has broken away from the central nucleus. The second danger is that of losing its freedom when, being cut off from the center and from the other Churches which gave it strength and energy, it finds itself all alone and a prey to the most varied forces of enslavery and exploitation.

The more an individual Church is attached to the universal Church by solid bonds of communion, in charity and loyalty, in receptiveness to the Magisterium of Peter, in the unity of the *lex orandi* which is also the *lex credendi*, in the desire for unity with all the other Churches which make up the whole – the more such a Church will be capable of translating the treasure of faith into the legitimate variety of expressions of the profession of faith, of prayer and worship, of Christian life and conduct and of the spiritual influence on the people among which it dwells. The more will it also be truly evangelizing, that is to say capable of drawing upon the universal patrimony in order to enable its own people to profit from it, and capable too of communicating to the universal Church the experience and the life of this people, for the benefit of all.

The unchangeable deposit of faith

65. It was precisely in this sense that at the end of the last Synod we spoke clear words full of paternal affection, insisting on the role of Peter's Successor as a visible, living and dynamic principle of the unity between the Churches and thus of the universality of the one Church.[93] We also insisted on the grave responsibility incumbent upon us, but which we share with our Brothers in the Episcopate, of preserving unaltered the content of the Catholic faith which the Lord entrusted to the Apostles. While being translated into all expressions, this content must be neither impaired nor mutilated. While being clothed with the outward forms proper to each people, and made explicit by theological expression which takes account of differing cultural, social and even racial milieux, it must remain the content of the Catholic faith just exactly as the ecclesial Magisterium has received it and transmits it.

Differing tasks

66. The whole Church therefore is called upon to evangelize, and yet within her we have different evangelizing tasks to accomplish. This diversity of services in the unity of the same mission makes up the richness and beauty of evangelization. We shall briefly recall these tasks.

First, we would point out in the pages of the Gospel the insistence with which the Lord entrusts to the Apostles the task of proclaiming the Word. He chose them,[94] trained them during several years of intimate company,[95] constituted[96] and sent them out[97] as authorized witnesses and teachers of the message of salvation. And the Twelve in their turn sent out their successors who, in the apostolic line, continue to preach the Good News.

The Successor of Peter

67. The Successor of Peter is thus, by the will of Christ, entrusted

with the pre-eminent ministry of teaching the revealed truth. The New Testament often shows Peter "filled with the Holy Spirit" speaking in the name of all.[98] It is precisely for this reason that Saint Leo the Great describes him as he who has merited the primacy of the apostolate.[99] This is also why the voice of the Church shows the Pope "at the highest point – *in apice, in specula* – of the apostolate."[100] The Second Vatican Council wished to reaffirm this when it declared that "Christ's mandate to preach the Gospel to every creature (cf. Mk 16:15) primarily and immediately concerns the Bishops with Peter and under Peter."[101]

The full, supreme and universal power[102] which Christ gives to his Vicar for the pastoral government of his Church is thus specially exercised by the Pope in the activity of preaching and causing to be preached the Good News of salvation.

Bishops and priests

68. In union with the Successor of Peter, the Bishops, who are successors of the Apostles, receive through the power of their episcopal ordination the authority to teach the revealed truth in the Church. They are teachers of the faith.

Associated with the Bishops in the ministry of evangelization and responsible by a special title are those who through priestly ordination "act in the person of Christ."[103] They are eduators of the People of God in the faith and preachers, while at the same time being ministers of the Eucharist and of the other Sacraments.

We pastors are therefore invited to take note of this duty, more than any other members of the Church. What identifies our priestly service, gives a profound unity to the thousand and one tasks which claim our attention day by day and throughout our lives, and confers a distinct character on our activities, is this aim, ever present in all our action: to proclaim the Gospel of God.[104]

A mark of our identity which no doubts ought to encroach upon and no objection eclipse is this: as pastors, we have been chosen by the mercy of the Supreme Pastor,[105] in spite of our inadequacy, to proclaim with authority the Word of God, to assemble the scattered People of God, to feed this People with the signs of the action of Christ which are the Sacraments, to set this People on the road to salvation, to maintain it in that unity of which we are, at different levels, active and living instruments, and unceasingly to keep this community gathered around Christ faithful to its deepest vocation. And when we do all these things, within our human limits and by the grace of God, it is a work of evangelization that we are carrying out. This includes ourself as Pastor of the universal Church, our Brother Bishops at the head of the individual Churches, priests and deacons united with their Bishops and whose assistants they are, by a communion which has its source in the Sacrament of Orders and in the charity of the Church.

Religious

69. Religious, for their part, find in their consecrated life a privileged means of effective evangelization. At the deepest level of their being they are caught up in the dynamism of the Church's life, which is thirsty for the divine Absolute and called to holiness. It is to this holiness that they bear witness. They embody the Church in her desire to give herself completely to the radical demands of the beatitudes. By their lives they are a sign of total availability to God, the Church and the brethren.

As such they have a special importance in the context of the witness which, as we have said, is of prime importance in evangelization. At the same time as being a challenge to the world and to the Church herself, this silent witness of poverty and abnegation, of purity and sincerity, of self-sacrifice in obedience, can become an eloquent witness capable of touching also non-Christians who have good will and are sensitive to certain values.

In this perspective one perceives the role played in evangelization by religious men and women consecrated to prayer, silence, penance and sacrifice. Other religious, in great numbers, give themselves directly to the proclamation of Christ. Their missionary activity depends clearly on the hierarchy and must be coordinated with the pastoral plan which the latter adopts. But who does not see the immense contribution that these religious have brought and continue to bring to evangelization? Thanks to their consecration, they are eminently willing and free to leave everything and to go and proclaim the Gospel even to the ends of the earth. They are enterprising and their apostolate is often marked by an originality, by a genius that demands admiration. They are generous: often they are found at the outposts of the mission, and they take the greatest of risks for their health and their very lives. Truly the Church owes them much.

The laity

70. Lay people, whose particular vocation places them in the midst

of the world and in charge of the most varied temporal tasks, must for this very reason exercise a very special form of evangelization.

Their primary and immediate task is not to establish and develop the ecclesial community – this is the specific role of the pastors – but to put to use every Christian and evangelical possibility latent but already present and active in the affairs of the world. Their own field of evangelizing activity is the vast and complicated world of politics, society and economics, but also the world of culture, of the sciences and the arts, of international life, of the mass media. It also includes other realities which are open to evangelization, such as human love, the family, the education of children and adolescents, professional work, suffering. The more Gospel-inspired lay people there are engaged in these realities, clearly involved in them, competent to promote them and conscious that they must exercise to the full their Christian powers which are often buried and suffocated, the more these realities will be at the service of the Kingdom of God and therefore of salvation in Jesus Christ, without in any way losing or sacrificing their human content but rather pointing to a transcendent dimension which is often disregarded.

The family

71. One cannot fail to stress the evangelizing action of the family in the evangelizing apostolate of the laity.

At different moments in the Church's history and also in the Second Vatican Council, the family has well deserved the beautiful name of "domestic Church."[106] This means that there should be found in every Christian family the various aspects of the entire Church. Furthermore, the family, like the Church, ought to be a place where the Gospel is transmitted and from which the Gospel radiates.

In a family which is conscious of this mission, all the members evangelize and are evangelized. The parents not only communicate the Gospel to their children, but from their children they can themselves receive the same Gospel as deeply lived by them.

And such a family becomes the evangelizer of many other families, and of the neighborhood of which it forms part. Families resulting from a mixed marriage also have the duty of proclaiming Christ to the children in the fullness of the consequences of a common Baptism; they have moreover the difficult task of becoming builders of unity.

Young people

72. Circumstances invite us to make special mention of the young.

Their increasing number and growing presence in society and likewise the problems assailing them should awaken in everyone the desire to offer them with zeal and intelligence the Gospel ideal as something to be known and lived. And on the other hand, young people who are well trained in faith and prayer must become more and more the apostles of youth. The Church counts greatly on their contribution, and we ourselves have often manifested our full confidence in them.

Diversified ministries

73. Hence the active presence of the laity in the temporal realities takes on all its importance. One cannot, however, neglect or forget the other dimension: the laity can also feel themselves called, or be called, to work with their pastors in the service of the ecclesial community, for its growth and life, by exercising a great variety of ministries according to the grace and charisms which the Lord is pleased to give them.

We cannot but experience a great inner joy when we see so many pastors, religious and lay people, fired with their mission to evangelize, seeking ever more suitable ways of proclaiming the Gospel effectively. We encourage the openness which the Church is showing today in this direction and with this solicitude. It is an openness to meditation first of all, and then to ecclesial ministries capable of renewing and strengthening the evangelizing vigor of the Church.

It is certain that, side-by-side with the ordained ministries, whereby certain people are appointed pastors and consecrate themselves in a special way to the service of the community, the Church recognizes the place of non-ordained ministries which are able to offer a particular service to the Church.

A glance at the origins of the Church is very illuminating, and gives the benefit of an early experience in the matter of ministries. It was an experience which was all the more valuable in that it enabled the Church to consolidate herself and to grow and spread. Attention to the sources however has to be complemented by attention to the present needs of mankind and of the Church. To drink at these ever inspiring sources without sacrificing anything of their values, and at the same time to know how to adapt oneself to the demands and needs of today—these are the criteria which will make it possible to seek wisely and to discover the ministries which the Church needs and which many of her members will gladly embrace for the sake of ensuring greater vitality in the ecclesial community. These ministries will have a real pastoral value to the extent that they are established with absolute respect for unity and adhering to the directives of the pastors, who are the ones who are responsible for the Church's unity and the builders thereof.

These ministries, apparently new but closely tied up with the Church's living experience down the centuries – such as catechists, directors of prayer and chant, Christians devoted to the service of God's Word or to assisting their brethren in need, the heads of small communities, or other persons charged with the responsibility of apostolic movements – these ministries are valuable for the establishment, life, and growth of the Church, and for her capacity to influence her surroundings and to reach those who are remote from her. We owe also our special esteem to all the laypeople who accept to consecrate a part of their time, their energies, and sometimes their entire lives, to the service of the missions.

A serious preparation is needed for all workers for evangelization. Such preparation is all the more necessary for those who devote themselves to the ministry of the Word. Being animated by the conviction, ceaselessly deepened, of the greatness and riches of the Word of God, those who have the mission of transmitting it must give the maximum attention to the dignity, precision and adaptation of their language. Everyone knows that the art of speaking takes on today a very great importance. How would preachers and catechists be able to neglect this?

We earnestly desire that in each individual Church the Bishops should be vigilant concerning the adequate formation of all the ministers of the Word. This serious preparation will increase in them the indispensable assurance and also the enthusiasm to proclaim today Jesus Christ.

VII
The Spirit of Evangelization

Pressing appeal

74. We would not wish to end this encounter with our beloved Brethren and sons and daughters without a pressing appeal concerning the interior attitudes which must animate those who work for evangelization.

In the name of the Lord Jesus Christ, and in the name of the Apostles Peter and Paul, we wish to exhort all those who, thanks to the charisms of the Holy Spirit and to the mandate of the Church, are true evangelizers, to be worthy of this vocation, to exercise it without the reticence of doubt or fear, and not to neglect the conditions that will make this evangelization not only possible but also active and fruitful. These, among many others, are the fundamental conditions which we consider it important to emphasize.

Under the action of the Holy Spirit

75. Evangelization will never be possible without the action of the Holy Spirit. The Spirit descends on Jesus of Nazareth at the moment of his baptism when the voice of the Father – "This is my beloved Son with whom I am well pleased"[107] – manifests in an external way the election of Jesus and his mission. Jesus is "led by the Spirit" to experience in the desert the decisive combat and the supreme test before beginning this mission.[108] It is "in the power of the Spirit"[109] that he returns to Galilee and begins his preaching at Nazareth, applying to himself the passage of Isaiah: "The Spirit of the Lord is upon me." And he proclaims: "Today this Scripture has been fulfilled."[110] To the disciples whom he was about to send forth he says, breathing on them: "Receive the Holy Spirit."[111]

In fact, it is only after the coming of the Holy Spirit on the day of Pentecost that the Apostles depart to all the ends of the earth in order to begin the great work of the Church's evangelization. Peter explains this event as the fulfillment of the prophecy of Joel: "I will pour out my Spirit."[112] Peter is filled with the Holy Spirit so that he can speak to the people about Jesus, the Son of God.[113] Paul too is filled with the Holy Spirit[114] before dedicating himself to his apostolic ministry, as is Stephen when he is chosen for the ministry of service and later on for the witness of blood.[115] The Spirit, who causes Peter, Paul and the Twelve to speak, and who inspires the words that they are to utter, also comes down "on those who heard the word."[116]

It is in the "consolation of the Holy Spirit" that the Church increases.[117] The Holy Spirit is the soul of the Church. It is he who explains to the faithful the deep meaning of the teaching of Jesus and of his mystery. It is the Holy Spirit who, today just as at the beginning of the Church, acts in every evangelizer who allows himself to be possessed and led by him. The Holy Spirit places on his lips the words which he could not find by himself, and at the same time the Holy Spirit predisposes the soul of the hearer to be open and receptive to the Good News and to the Kingdom being proclaimed.

Techniques of evangelization are good, but even the most advanced ones could not replace the gentle action of the Spirit. The most perfect preparation of the evangelizer has no effect without the Holy Spirit. Without the Holy Spirit the most convincing dialectic has no power over the heart of man. Without him the most highly developed schemas resting on a sociological or psychological basis are quickly seen to be quite valueless.

We live in the Church at a privileged moment of the Spirit. Everywhere people are trying to know him better, as the Scripture reveals him. They are happy to place themselves under his inspiration. They are gathering about him; they want to let themselves be led by him. Now if the Spirit of God has a pre-eminent place in the whole life of the Church, it is in her evangelizing mission that he is most active. It is not by chance that the great inauguration of evangelization took place on the morning of Pentecost, under the inspiration of the Spirit.

It must be said that the Holy Spirit is the principal agent of evangelization: it is he who impels each individual to proclaim the Gospel, and it is he who in the depths of consciences causes the word of salvation to be accepted and understood.[118] But it can equally be said that he is the goal of evangelization: he alone stirs up the new creation, the new humanity of which evangelization is to be the result, with that unity in variety which evangelization wishes to achieve within the Christian community. Through the Holy Spirit the Gospel penetrates to the heart of the world, for it is he who causes people to discern the signs of the times – signs willed by God – which evangelization reveals and puts to use within history.

The Bishops' Synod of 1974, which insisted strongly on the place of the Holy Spirit in evangelization, also expressed the desire that pastors and theologians – and we would also say the faithful marked by the seal of the Spirit by Baptism – should study more thoroughly the nature and manner of the Holy Spirit's action in evangelization today. This is our desire too, and we exhort all evangelizers, whoever they may be, to pray without ceasing to the Holy Spirit with faith and fervor and to let themselves prudently be guided by him as the decisive inspirer of their plans, their initiatives and their evangelizing activity.

Authentic witnesses of life

76. Let us now consider the very persons of the evangelizers.

It is often said nowadays that the present century thirsts for authenticity. Especially in regard to young people it is said that they have a horror of the artificial or false and that they are searching above all for truth and honesty.

These "signs of the times" should find us vigilant. Either tacitly or aloud – but always forcefully – we are being asked: Do you really believe what you are proclaiming? Do you live what you believe? Do you really preach what you live? The witness of life has become more than ever an essential condition for real effectiveness in preaching. Precisely because of this we are, to a certain extent, responsible for the progress of the Gospel that we proclaim.

"What is the state of the Church ten years after the Council?" we asked at the beginning of this meditation. Is she firmly established in the midst of the world and yet free and independent enough to call for the world's attention? Does she testify to solidarity with people and at the same time to the divine Absolute? Is she more ardent in contemplation and adoration and more zealous in missionary, charitable and liberating action? Is she ever more committed to the effort to search for the restoration of the complete unity of Christians, a unity that makes more effective the common witness, "so that the world may believe"?[119] We are all responsible for the answers that could be given to these questions.

We therefore address our exhortation to our brethren in the Episcopate, placed by the Holy Spirit to govern the Church.[120] We exhort the priests and deacons, the Bishops' collaborators in assembling the People of God and in animating spiritually the local communities. We exhort the religious, witnesses of a Church called to holiness and hence themselves invited to a life that bears testimony to the beatitudes of the Gospel. We exhort the laity: Christian families, youth, adults, all those who exercise a trade or profession, leaders, without forgetting the poor who are often rich in faith and hope – all lay people who are conscious of their evangelizing role in the service of their Church or in the midst of society and the world. We say to all of them: our evangelizing zeal must spring from true holiness of life, and, as the Second Vatican Council suggests, preaching must in its turn make the preacher grow in holiness, which is nourished by prayer and above all by love for the Eucharist.[121]

The world which, paradoxically, despite innumerable signs of the denial of God, is nevertheless searching for him in unexpected ways and painfully experiencing the need of him – the world is calling for evangelizers to speak to it of a God whom the evangelists themselves should know and be familiar with as if they could see the invisible.[122] The world calls for and expects from us simplicity of life, the spirit of prayer, charity towards all, especially towards the lowly and the poor, obedience and humility, detachment and self-sacrifice. Without this mark of holiness, our word will have difficulty in touching the heart of modern man. It risks being vain and sterile.

The search
for unity

77. The power of evangelization will find itself considerably diminished if those who proclaim the Gospel are divided among themselves in all sorts of ways. Is this not perhaps one of the great sicknesses of evangelization today? Indeed, if the Gospel that we proclaim is seen to be rent by doctrinal disputes, ideological polarizations or mutual condemnations among Christians, at the mercy of the latter's differing views on Christ and the Church and even because of their different concepts of society and human institutions, how can those to whom we address our preaching fail to be disturbed, disoriented, even scandalized?

The Lord's spiritual testament tells us that unity among his followers is not only the proof that we are his but also the proof that he is sent by the Father. It is the test of the credibility of Christians and of Christ himself. As evangelizers, we must offer Christ's faithful not the image of people divided and separated by unedifying quarrels, but the image of people who are mature in faith and capable of finding a meeting-point beyond the real tensions, thanks to a shared, sincere and disinterested search for truth. Yes, the destiny of evangelization is certainly bound up with the witness of unity given by the Church. This is a source of responsibility and also of comfort.

At this point we wish to emphasize the sign of unity among all Christians as the way and instrument of evangelization. The division among Christians is a serious reality which impedes the very work of Christ. The Second Vatican Council states clearly and emphatically that this division "damages the most holy cause of preaching the Gospel to all men, and it impedes many from embracing the faith."[123] For this reason, in proclaiming the Holy Year we considered it necessary to recall to all the faithful of the Catholic world that "before all men can be brought together and restored to the grace of God our Father, communion must be re-established between those who by faith have acknowledged and accepted Jesus Christ as the Lord of mercy who sets men free and unites them in the Spirit of love and truth."[124]

And it is with a strong feeling of Christian hope that we look to the efforts being made in the Christian world for this restoration of the full unity willed by Christ. Saint Paul assures us that "hope does not disappoint us."[125] While we still work to obtain full unity from the Lord, we wish to see prayer intensified. Moreover we make our own the desire of the Fathers of the Third General Assembly of the Synod of Bishops, for a collaboration marked by greater commitment with the Christian brethren with whom we are not yet united in perfect unity, taking as a basis the foundation of Baptism and the patrimony of faith which is common to us. By doing this we can already give a greater common witness to Christ before the world in the very work of evangelization. Christ's command urges us to do this; the duty of preaching and of giving witness to the Gospel requires this.

Servants of the truth

78. The Gospel entrusted to us is also the word of truth. A truth which liberates[126] and which alone gives peace of heart is what people are looking for when we proclaim the Good News to them. The truth about God, about man and his mysterious destiny, about the world; the difficult truth that we seek in the Word of God and of which, we repeat, we are neither the masters nor the owners, but the depositaries, the heralds and the servants.

Every evangelizer is expected to have a reverence for truth, especially since the truth that he studies and communicates is none other than revealed truth and hence, more than any other, a sharing in the first truth which is God himself. The preacher of the Gospel will therefore be a person who even at the price of personal renunciation and suffering always seeks the truth that he must transmit to others. He never betrays or hides the truth out of a desire to please men, in order to astonish or to shock, nor for the sake of originality or a desire to make an impression. He does not refuse truth. He does not obscure revealed truth by being too idle to search for it, or for the sake of his own comfort, or out of fear. He does not neglect to study it. He serves it generously, without making it serve him.

We are the pastors of the faithful people, and our pastoral service impels us to preserve, defend, and to communicate the truth regardless of the sacrifices that this involves. So many eminent and holy pastors have left us the example of this love of truth. In many cases it was an heroic love. The God of truth expects us to be the vigilant defenders and devoted preachers of truth.

Men of learning – whether you be theologians, exegetes or historians – the work of evangelization needs your tireless work of research, and also care and tact in transmitting the truth to which your studies lead you but which is always greater than the heart of men, being the very truth of God.

Parents and teachers, your task – and the many conflicts of the present day do not make it an easy one – is to help your children and your students to discover truth, including religious and spiritual truth.

Animated by love

79. The work of evangelization presupposes in the evangelizer an ever increasing love for those whom he is evangelizing. That model evangelizer, the Apostle Paul, wrote these words to the Thessalonians, and they are a program for us all: "With such yearning love we chose to impart to you not only the gospel of God but our very selves, so dear had you become to us."[127] What is this love? It is much more than that of a teacher; it is the love of a father; and again, it is the love of a mother.[128] It is this love that the Lord expects from every preacher of the Gospel, from every builder of the Church. A sign of love will be the concern to give the truth and to bring people into unity. Another sign of love will be a devotion to the proclamation of Jesus Christ, without reservation or turning back. Let us add some other signs of this love.

The first is respect for the religious and spiritual situation of those being evangelized. Respect for their tempo and pace; no one has the right to force them excessively. Respect for their conscience and convictions, which are not to be treated in a harsh manner.

Another sign of this love is concern not to wound the other person, especially if he or she is weak in faith,[129] with statements that may be clear for those who are already initiated but which for the faithful can be a source of bewilderment and scandal, like a wound in the soul.

Yet another sign of love will be the effort to transmit to Christians, not doubts and uncertainties born of an erudition poorly assimilated, but certainties that are solid because they are anchored in the Word of God. The faithful need these certainties for their Christian life; they have a right to them, as children of God who abandon themselves entirely into his arms and to the exigencies of love.

With the fervor of the Saints

80. Our appeal here is inspired by the fervor of the greatest preachers and evangelizers, whose lives were devoted to the apostolate.

Among these we are glad to point out those whom we have proposed to the veneration of the faithful during the course of the Holy Year. They have known how to overcome many obstacles to evangelization.

Such obstacles are also present today, and we shall limit ourself to mentioning the lack of fervor. It is all the more serious because it comes from within. It is manifested in fatigue, disenchantment, compromise, lack of interest and above all lack of joy and hope. We exhort all those who have the task of evangelizing, by whatever title and at whatever level, always to nourish spiritual fervor.[130]

This fervor demands first of all that we should know how to put aside the excuses which would impede evangelization. The most insidious of these excuses are certainly the ones which people claim to find support for in such and such a teaching of the Council.

Thus one too frequently hears it said, in various terms, that to impose a truth, be it that of the Gospel, or to impose a way, be it that of salvation, cannot but be a violation of religious liberty. Besides, it is added, why proclaim the Gospel when the whole world is saved by uprightness of heart? We know likewise that the world and history are filled with "seeds of the Word"; is it not therefore an illusion to claim to bring the Gospel where it already exists in the seeds that the Lord himself has sown?

Anyone who takes the trouble to study in the Council's documents the questions upon which these excuses draw too superficially will find quite a different view.

It would certainly be an error to impose something on the consciences of our brethren. But to propose to their consciences the truth of the Gospel and salvation in Jesus Christ, with complete clarity and with a total respect for the free options which it presents—"without coercion, or dishonorable or unworthy pressure"[131]—far from being an attack on religious liberty is fully to respect that liberty, which is offered the choice of a way that even nonbelievers consider noble and uplifting. Is it then a crime against others' freedom to proclaim with joy a Good News which one has come to know through the Lord's mercy?[132] And why should only falsehood and error, debasement and pornography have the right to be put before people and often unfortunately imposed on them by the destructive propaganda of the mass media, by the tolerance of legislation, the timidity of the good and the impudence of the wicked? The respectful presentation of Christ and his Kingdom is more than the evangelizer's right; it is his duty. It is likewise the right of his fellowmen to receive from him the proclamation of the Good News of salvation. God can accomplish this salvation in whomsoever he wishes by ways which he alone knows.[133] And yet, if his Son came, it was precisely in order to reveal to us, by his word and by his life, the ordinary paths of salvation. And he has commanded us to transmit this revelation to others with his own authority. It would be useful if every Christian and every evangelizer were to pray about the following thought: men can gain salvation also in other ways, by God's mercy, even though we do not preach the Gospel to them; but as for us, can we gain salvation if, through negligence or fear or shame — what Saint Paul called "blushing for the Gospel"[134] — or as a result of false ideas, we fail to preach it? For that would be to betray the call of God, who wishes the seed to bear fruit through the voice of the ministers of the Gospel; and it will depend on us whether this grows into trees and produces its full fruit.

Let us therefore preserve our fervor of spirit. Let us preserve the delightful and comforting joy of evangelizing, even when it is in tears that we must sow. May it mean for us — as it did for John the Baptist, for Peter and Paul, for the other Apostles and for a multitude of splendid evangelizers all through the Church's history — an interior enthusiasm that nobody and nothing can quench. May it be the great joy of our consecrated lives. And may the world of our time, which is searching, sometimes with anguish, sometimes with hope, be enabled to receive the Good News not from evangelizers who are dejected, discouraged, impatient or anxious, but from ministers of the Gospel whose lives glow with fervor, who have first received the joy of Christ, and who are willing to risk their lives so that the Kingdom may be proclaimed and the Church established in the midst of the world.

Conclusion

Heritage
of the Holy Year

81. This then, Brothers and sons and daughters, is our heartfelt plea. It echoes the voice of our Brethren assembled for the Third General Assembly of the Synod of Bishops. This is the task we have wished to give you at the close of a Holy Year which has enabled us to see better than ever the needs and the appeals of a multitude of brethren, both Christians and non-Christians, who await from the Church the Word of salvation.

May the light of the Holy Year, which has shone in the local Churches and in Rome for millions of consciences reconciled with God, continue to shine in the same way after the Jubilee through a program of pastoral action with evangelization as its basic feature, for these years which mark the eve of a new century, the eve also of the third millennium of Christianity.

Mary,
Star of evangelization

82. This is the desire that we rejoice to entrust to the hands and the heart of the Immaculate Blessed Virgin Mary, on this day which is especially consecrated to her and which is also the tenth anniversary of the close of the Second Vatican Council. On the morning of Pentecost she watched over with her prayer the beginning of evangelization prompted by the Holy Spirit: may she be the Star of the evangelization ever renewed which the Church, docile to her Lord's command, must promote and accomplish, especially in these times which are difficult but full of hope!

In the name of Christ we bless you, your communities, your families, all those who are dear to you, in the words which Paul addressed to the Philippians: "I give thanks to my God every time I think of you—which is constantly, in every prayer I utter—rejoicing, as I plead on your behalf, at the way you have all continually helped to promote the gospel . . . I hold all of you dear—you who . . . are sharers of my gracious lot . . . to defend the solid grounds on which the gospel rests. God himself can testify how much I long for each of you with the affection of Christ Jesus!"[135]

Given in Rome, at Saint Peter's, on the Solemnity of the Immaculate Conception of the Blessed Virgin Mary, December 8, 1975, the thirteenth year of our Pontificate.

NOTES

1. Cf. Lk 22:32.
2. 2 Cor 11:28.
3. Cf. Second Vatican Ecumenical Council, Decree on the Church's Missionary Activity *Ad Gentes*, 1: *AAS* 58 (1966), p. 947.
4. Cf. Eph 4:24, 2:15; Col 3:10; Gal 3:27; Rom 13:14; 2 Cor 5:17.
5. 2 Cor 5:20.
6. Cf. Paul VI, Address for the closing of the Third General Assembly of the Synod of Bishops (October 26, 1974): *AAS* 66 (1974), pp. 634–635; 637.
7. Paul VI, Address to the College of Cardinals (June 22, 1973): *AAS* 65 (1973), p. 383.
8. 2 Cor 11:28.
9. 1 Tim 5:17.
10. 2 Tim 2:15.

11. Cf. 1 Cor 2:5.
12. Lk 4:43.
13. Ibid.
14. Lk 4:18; cf. Is 61:1.
15. Cf. Mk 1:1; Rom 1:1-3.
16. Cf. Mt 6:33.
17. Cf. Mt 5:3-12.
18. Cf. Mt 5-7.
19. Cf. Mt 10.
20. Cf. Mt 13.
21. Cf. Mt 18.
22. Cf. Mt 24-25.
23. Cf. Mt 24:36; Acts 1:7; 1 Thess 5:1-2.
24. Cf. Mt 11:12; Lk 16:16.
25. Cf. Mt 4:17.
26. Mk 1:27.
27. Lk 4:22.
28. Jn 7:46.
29. Lk 4:43.
30. Jn 11:52.

31. Cf. Second Vatican Ecumenical Council, Dogmatic Constitution on Divine Revelation *Dei Verbum*, 4: *AAS* 58 (1966), pp. 818-819.
32. 1 Pt 2:9.
33. Cf. Acts 2:11.
34. Lk 4:43.
35. 1 Cor 9:16.
36. "Declaration of the Synod Fathers," 4: *L'Osservatore Romano* (October 27, 1974), p. 6.
37. Mt 28:19.
38. Acts 2:41, 47.
39. Cf. Second Vatican Ecumenical Council, Dogmatic Constitution on the Church *Lumen Gentium*, 8: *AAS* 57 (1965), p. 11; Decree on the Church's Missionary Activity *Ad Gentes*, 5: *AAS* 58 (1966), pp. 951-952.
40. Cf. Acts 2:42-46; 4:32-35; 5:12-16.
41. Cf. Acts 2:11; 1 Pt 2:9.
42. Cf. Decree on the Church's Missionary Activity *Ad Gentes*, 5, 11-12: *AAS* 58 (1966), pp. 951-952, 959-961.
43. Cf. 2 Cor 4:5; Saint Augustine, *Sermo XLVI, De Pastoribus: CCL XLI*, pp. 529-530.
44. Lk 10:16; cf. Saint Cyprian, *De Unitate Ecclesiae*, 14: *PL* 4, 527; Saint Augustine, *Enarrat.* 88, *Sermo*, 2, 14: *PL* 37, 1140; Saint John Chrysostom, *Hom. de capto Eutropio*, 6: *PG* 52, 402.
45. Eph 5:25.
46. Rev 21:5, cf. 2 Cor 5:17; Gal 6:15.
47. Cf. Rom 6:4.
48. Cf. Eph 4:23-24; Col 3:9-10.
49. Cf. Rom 1:16; 1 Cor 1:18, 2:4.
50. Cf. 53: *AAS* 58 (1966), p. 1075.
51. Cf. Tertullian *Apologeticum*, 39: *CCL*, I, pp. 150-153; Minucius Felix, *Octavius* 9 and 31: *CSLP*, Turin 1963 [second edition], pp. 11-13, 47-48.
52. 1 Pt 3:15.

53. Cf. Second Vatican Ecumenical Council, Dogmatic Constitution on the Church *Lumen Gentium*, 1, 9, 48: *AAS* 57 (1965), pp. 5, 12–14, 53–54; Pastoral Constitution on the Church in the Modern World *Gaudium et Spes*, 42, 45: *AAS* 58 (1966), pp. 1060–1061, 1065–1066; Decree on the Church's Missionary Activity *Ad Gentes*, 1, 5: *AAS* 58 (1966), pp. 947, 951–952.

54. Cf. Rom 1:16; 1 Cor 1:18.

55. Cf. Acts 17:22–23.

56. 1 Jn 3:1; cf. Rom 8:14–17.

57. Cf. Eph 2:8; Rom 1:16. Cf. Sacred Congregation for the Doctrine of the Faith, *Declaratio ad fidem tuendam in mysteria Incarnationis et SS. Trinitatis e quibusdam recentibus erroribus* (February 21, 1972): *AAS* 64 (1972), pp. 237–241.

58. Cf. 1 Jn 3:2; Rom 8:29; Phil 3:20–21. Cf. Second Vatican Ecumenical Council, Dogmatic Constitution on the Church *Lumen Gentium*, 48–51: *AAS* 57 (1965), pp. 53–58.

59. Cf. Sacred Congregation for the Doctrine of the Faith, *Declaratio circa Catholicam Doctrinam de Ecclesia contra non-nullos errores hodiernos tuendam* (June 24, 1973): *AAS* 65 (1973), pp. 396–408.

60. Cf. Second Vatican Ecumenical Council, Pastoral Constitution on the Church in the Modern World *Gaudium et Spes*, 47–52: *AAS* 58 (1966), pp. 1067–1074; Paul VI, Encyclical Letter *Humanae Vitae: AAS* 60 (1968), pp. 481–503.

61. Paul VI, Address for the opening of the Third General Assembly of the Synod of Bishops (September 27, 1974): *AAS* 66 (1974), p. 562.

62. Ibid.

63. Paul VI, Address to the *Campesinos* of Colombia (August 23, 1968): *AAS* 60 (1968), p. 623.

64. Paul VI, Address for the "Day of Development" at Bogotá (August 23, 1968): *AAS* 60 (1968), p. 627; cf. Saint Augustine, *Epistola* 229, 2: *PL* 33, 1020.

65. Paul VI, Address for the closing of the Third General Assembly of the Synod of Bishops (October 26, 1974): *AAS* 66 (1974), p. 637.

66. Address given on October 15, 1975: *L'Osservatore Romano* (October 17, 1975).

67. Pope Paul VI, Address to the Members of the *Consilium de Laicis* (October 2, 1974): *AAS* 66 (1974), p. 568.

68. Cf. 1 Pt 3:1.

69. Rom 10:14, 17.

70. Cf. 1 Cor 2:1–5.

71. Rom 10:17.

72. Cf. Mt 10:27; Lk 12:3.

73. Mk 16:15.

74. Cf. Saint Justin, *I Apol.* 46, 1–4: *PG* 6, *II Apol.* 7 (8) 1–4; 10, 1–3; 13, 3–4; *Florilegium Patristicum* II, Bonn 1911 [second edition], pp. 81, 125, 129, 133; Clement of Alexandria, *Stromata* I, 19, 91; 94: *S. Ch.* pp. 117–118; 119–120; Second Vatican Ecumenical Council, Decree on the Church's Missionary Activity *Ad Gentes*, 11: *AAS* 58 (1966), p. 960; cf. Dogmatic Constitution on the Church *Lumen Gentium*, 17: *AAS* 57 (1965), p. 21.

75. Eusebius of Caesarea, *Praeparatio Evangelica* I, 1: *PG* 21, 26–28; cf. Second Vatican Ecumenical Council, Dogmatic Constitution on the Church *Lumen Gentium*, 16: *AAS* 57 (1965), p. 20.

76. Cf. Eph 3:8.
77. Cf. Henri de Lubac, *Le drame de l'humanisme athée*, ed. Spes, Paris, 1945.
78. Cf. Pastoral Constitution on the Church in the Modern World *Gaudium et Spes*, 59: *AAS* 58 (1966), p. 1080.
79. 1 Tim 2:4.
80. Mt 9:36; 15:32.
81. Rom 10:15.
82. Declaration on Religious Liberty *Dignitatis Humanae*, 13: *AAS* 58 (1966), p. 939; cf. Dogmatic Constitution on the Church *Lumen Gentium*, 5: *AAS* 57 (1965), pp. 7-8; Decree on the Church's Missionary Activity *Ad Gentes*, 1: *AAS* 58 (1966), p. 947.
83. Decree on the Church's Missionary Activity *Ad Gentes*, 35: *AAS* 58 (1966), p. 983.
84. Saint Augustine, *Enarratio in Ps 44:23 CCL* XXXVIII, p. 510; cf. Decree on the Church's Missionary Activity *Ad Gentes*, 1: *AAS* 58 (1966), p. 947.
85. Saint Gregory the Great, *Homil. in Evangelia* 19, 1: *PL* 76, 1154.
86. Acta 1:8; cf. *Didache* 9, 1; Funk, *Patres Apostolici*, 1, 22.
87. Mt 28:20.
88. Cf. Mt 13:32.
89. Cf. Mt 13:47.
90. Cf. Jn 21:11.
91. Cf. Jn 10:1-16.
92. Cf. Second Vatican Ecumenical Council, Constitution on the Sacred Liturgy *Sacrosanctum Concilium*, 37-38: *AAS* 56 (1964), p. 110; cf. also the liturgical books and other documents subsequently issued by the Holy See for the putting into practice of the liturgical reform desired by the same Council.
93. Paul VI, Address for the closing of the Third General Assembly of the Synod of Bishops (October 26, 1974): *AAS* 66 (1974), p. 636.
94. Cf. Jn 15:16; Mk 3:13-19; Lk 6:13-16.
95. Cf. Acts 1:21-22.
96. Cf. Mk 3:14.
97. Cf. Mk 3:14-15; Lk 9:2.
98. Acts 4:8; cf. 2:14; 3:12.
99. Cf. St Leo the Great, *Sermo* 69, 3; *Sermo* 70, 1-3; *Sermo* 94, 3; *Sermo* 95, 2: *S.C.* 200, pp. 50-52; 58-66; 258-260; 268.
100. Cf. First Ecumenical Council of Lyons, Constitution *Ad apostolicae dignitatis: Conciliorum Oecumenicorum Decreta*, ed. *Istituto per le Scienze Religiose*, Bologna 1973 [third edition], p. 278; Ecumenical Council of Vienne, Constitution *Ad providam Christi*, ed. cit., p. 343; Fifth Lateran Ecumenical Council, Constitution *In apostolici culminis*, ed. cit., p. 608; Constitution *Postquam ad universalis*, ed. cit., p. 609; Constitution *Supernae dispositionis*, ed. cit., p. 614; Constitution *Divina disponente clementia*, ed. cit., p. 638.
101. Decree on the Church's Missionary Activity *Ad Gentes*, 38: *AAS* 58 (1966), p. 985.
102. Cf. Second Vatican Ecumenical Council, Dogmatic Constitution on the Church *Lumen Gentium*, 22: *AAS* 57 (1965), p. 26.
103. Cf. Second Vatican Ecumenical Council, Dogmatic Constitution on the Church *Lumen Gentium*, 10, 37: *AAS* 57 (1965), pp. 14, 43; Decree on the Church's Missionary Activity *Ad Gentes*, 39: *AAS* 58 (1966), p. 986; Decree on the Ministry and Life of Priests *Presbyterorum Ordinis*, 2, 12, 13: *AAS* 58 (1966), pp. 992, 1010, 1011.

104. Cf. 1 Thess 2:9.

105. Cf. 1 Pt 5:4.

106. Dogmatic Constitution on the Church *Lumen Gentium*, 11: *AAS* 57 (1965), p. 16; Decree on the Apostolate of the Laity *Apostolicam Actuositatem*, 11: *AAS* 58 (1966), p. 848; Saint John Chrysostom, *In Genesim Serm.* VI, 2; VII, 1: *PG* 54, 607–68.

107. Mt 3:17.

108. Mt 4:1.

109. Lk 4:14.

110. Lk 4:18, 21; cf. Is 61:1.

111. Jn 20:22.

112. Acts 2:17.

113. Cf. Acts 4:8.

114. Cf. Acts 9:17.

115. Cf. Acts 6:5, 10; 7:55.

116. Acts 10:44.

117. Acts 9:31.

118. Cf. Second Vatican Ecumenical Council, Decree on the Church's Missionary Activity *Ad Gentes*, 4: *AAS* 58 (1966), pp. 950–951.

119. Jn 17:21.

120. Cf. Acts 20:28.

121. Cf. Decree on the Ministry and Life of Priests *Presbyterorum Ordinis*, 13: *AAS* 58 (1966), p. 1011.

122. Cf. Heb. 11:27.

123. Decree on the Church's Missionary Activity *Ad Gentes*, 6: *AAS* 58 (1966), pp. 954–955; cf. Decree on Ecumenism *Unitatis Redintegratio*, 1: *AAS* 57 (1965), pp. 90–91.

124. Bull *Apostolorum Limina*, VII: *AAS* 66 (1974), p. 305.

125. Rom 5:5.

126. Cf. Jn 8:32.

127. 1 Thess 2:8; cf. Phil 1:8.

128. Cf. 1 Thess 2:7–11; 1 Cor 4:15; Gal 4:19.

129. Cf. 1 Cor 8:9–13; Rom 14:15.

130. Cf. Rom 12:11.

131. Cf. Second Vatican Ecumenical Council, Declaration on Religious Liberty *Dignitatis Humanae*, 4: *AAS* 58 (1966), p. 933.

132. Cf. Ibid., 9–14: loc. cit., pp. 935–940.

133. Cf. Second Vatican Ecumenical Council, Decree on the Church's Missionary Activity *Ad Gentes*, 7: *AAS* 58 (1966), p. 955.

134. Cf. Rom 1:16.

135. Phil 1:3–4, 7–8.